# The German and the Austrian Navies / *Die Deutsche und die Österreichische Marine*: Volume One *(Band Nummer 1)*

(in English and German / auf Englisch und Deutsch)

By Marc E. Nonnenkamp / von Marc E. Nonnenkamp

First bilingual printing in English and German.

Printed in the United States of America by Marc E. Nonnenkamp through CreateSpace (paperback) and through Amazon Kindle (as an e-book).

ISBN-13: 978-1456573027

ISBN-10: 1456573020

**Dedication:** Dedicated to the memory of the 155,000 German and Austrian sailors who perished in Two World Wars – may God grant their descendants the grace never to be called upon to make a similar sacrifice.

*Den 155,000 gefallenen deutschen und österreichischen Seemänner des Ersten und Zweiten Weltkrieges gewidmet*

**Acknowledgements:** I wish to thank Captain (CA) George J. Albert, Jr. (Army Field Historian of the California Center for Military History in Eureka) for his official endorsement of this literary work. Many thanks as well for endorsements, contributions and corrections by Hermann Landmeyer (Marineortungsschule MOS, Militärschule Bremerhaven of the Federal German Navy), by Mario Wegmann (Marinefliegergeschwader 3 "Graf Zeppelin" Nordholz – Naval Air Wing of the Federal German Navy), by the Deutscher Marinebund E.V. on Facebook.com (the German Naval League of Kiel, Germany – founded in 1891 by Kaiser Wilhelm II and Grand Admiral Alfred von Tirpitz), by Mr. Alexander Traiber of www.kuk-kriegsmarine.at (the "Friends of Historical Ships" Society of Vienna, Austria) and by Mr. Michael Emmerich of www.german-navy.de, a historical website which has received more than 18 million visitors to date.

**Cover Illustration:** Imperial German Small Cruiser "S.M.S. Leipzig" (1906) – courtesy of Captain (CA) George J. Albert, Jr., Army Field Historian of the California Center for Military History (shown flying the Standard of Kaiser Wilhelm II – mit Kaiserflagge)

**Endorsement by Captain George J. Albert, Jr.**

1 July 2009

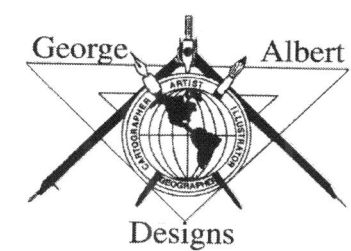

Designs

Captain (CA) George J. Albert Jr.
Army Field Historian
California Center for Military History
1517 E Street
Eureka, CA 95501

This letter is an endorsement for Marc E. Nonnenkamp's book, which is a "catalogue" of named vessels (as opposed to those which merely had "pennant" numbers) in the German, West German, East German, Austro-Hungarian, Austrian, and Austro-Venetian Navies. The "slant" of the book is highly sympathetic to the old Habsburg Monarchy of the First German (Holy Roman) and Austro-Hungarian Empires. This book fills an existing gap in the history of the world's navies, and the illustrations on the author's website are exceptional. I look forward to receiving a copy of this interesting work when it is published.

Respectfully,
/s/
Captain George J. Albert Jr.
Army Field Historian

## List of Illustrations

## Table of Contents (numbered by Chapter and Subject)

Note: the Roman numeral numbering system for categories of vessels within the chapters comes from the author's website at www.theborromeofamily.com (the site includes an extensive gallery of illustrations for the vessels as well)

## Chapter 1 (Kapitel Eins): The History of the German and the Austrian Navies ("Die Geschichte der Deutschen sowie der Österreichischen Marine")

*Ich interessiere mich sehr für die Geschichte der Deutschen sowie der Österreichischen Marine. Zum Beispiel, ich habe eine persönliche Sammlung von 333 Bildern von deutschen sowie österreichischen Schiffen und Seefahrzeugen, die zwischen 1354 bis 2010 getauft wurden. Zwischen 1924 bis 1936 diente mein Großvater Wilhelm Johannes Nonnenkamp (1903-1972) zuerst als Matrose und dann als Unteroffizier bei der deutschen Reichsmarine und bei der deutschen Kriegsmarine. Danach war mein Großvater beim deutschen Zoll, bis er 1963 in den Ruhestand ging. Deutschland und Österreich haben eine reiche Seefahrt-und Marine-Geschichte. Seit dem Jahre 983 (d.h. vor 1,028 Jahren) hat Deutschland eine Admiralität. Heute hat ebenfalls die Bundesrepublik Deutschland eine "Deutsche Marine." Die Tradition der Österreichischen Marine ist heute noch aktiv und zwar in der "Kriegsmarine" Kroatiens. Es gibt heute noch 1,5 Millionen Personen, die in Kroatien deutschsprachig (zweisprachig Kroatisch und Deutsch) sind. Davor war Kroatien ein ganz treues Teil des Österreich-Ungarischen Reiches, genau so wie die Tschechei (d.h. Böhmen, Mähren, das Sudetenland und Oberschlesien), die Slowakei (mit Zips), Weißruthenien, Slowenien (Krain sowie Küstenland), Ungarn, Siebenbürgen, Galizien, Lodomerien, Wojwodina (Banat), Slavonien, Dalmatien, Bosnien-Herzegowina, Cattaro, Liechtenstein, Görz und natürlich auch Südtirol. Seit der friedlichen deutschen Wiedervereinigung im Jahre 1990 heißt die Marine die "Deutsche Marine." Von 1956 bis 1990 war es Marine die "Bundesmarine" in Westdeutschland (Bundesrepublik) und die "Volksmarine" in Ostdeutschland (die ehemalige DDR). Zwischen 1945 und 1956 gab es im Westen einen "Deutschen Minenräumdienst." Im dritten Reich war es die "Kriegsmarine" (1935-1945); vorher die "Reichsmarine" (1922-1935). Die preußisch-deutsche "Kaiserliche Marine" hatten wir von 1871 bis 1922, und die preußisch-deutsche "Norddeutsche Bundesmarine" hatten wir von 1867 bis 1871. Die brandenburgisch-preußische Marine dauerte von 1657 bis 1867, aber die österreichische Marine ("die Kaiserliche und Königliche Kriegsmarine") war die erste wirkliche "berufliche" deutschsprachige Marine (von 1379 bis 1918).*

The history of the German and the Austrian navies is yet another one of my many interests. I have a collection of 333 pictures of German and Austrian naval and commercial vessels commissioned in between 1354 and 2009 displayed in my home. My paternal grandfather Wilhelm Johannes Nonnenkamp (1903-1972) served in the interwar "Reichsmarine" from 1924 until he left it for the German Customs Service in 1936, whence he retired in the 1960s. Unknown to many people, Germany (including Austria) does have a very rich maritime history. The Holy Roman Empire of the German Nation or First German Empire ("erstes Reich" or First Reich) established an Admiralty in 983. "Reich" is the German word for "empire." The Holy Roman Empire of the German Nation endured from its founding by Charlemagne (Charles the Great) in 800 until its dissolution by Napoleon Bonaparte in 1806. It was preceded by the Frankish Kingdom, which lasted from 482 until 800. Before the Frankish Kingdom came the Frankish Federation, which endured from 356 until 482. The Franks were merely one of many Germanic tribes from 260 until 356. Charlemagne was the King of the Franks, and his heirs live today in the line of the Habsburg-Lothringen Dynasty of Austria. The tradition of the German Navy lives on today in the "Deutsche Marine" of the Federal Republic of Germany (population of 83 million people) and the tradition of the Austrian Navy lives on as well in the modern "Kriegsmarine" of Croatia (home to 1.5 million bilingual German-speaking people as well as to the Croatian majority). Croatia is one of many modern nations that used to be an enthusiastic part of the old Austrian Empire. The modern Croatian "Kriegsmarine" (a term used by both Germany and Austria in the past) was established in 1991. It is the direct successor to the Yugoslavian Socialist Federal Navy of 1945-1991, which in turn succeeded the Yugoslavian Royal Navy of 1918-1945. Before the latter came the Imperial and Royal Navy of Austria-Hungary, Austria and Venice (the "Kaiserliche und Königliche Kriegsmarine"), having been first established in 1379.

## Chapter 2 (Kapitel Zwei): The Modern Federal Republic of Germany ("die Bundesrepublik Deutschland")

The modern Federal Republic of Germany (population of 83 million) has a substantial population of racial, ethnic, linguistic and religious minorities. These include the Turks (1,760,000), the Poles (1,700,000), the Russians (610,000), the Italians (541,000), the Frisians (500,000), the Croatians (350,000), the Greeks (310,000), the Gypsies (250,000), the Jehovah's Witnesses (151,000), the Jews (200,000), the Sorbs (60,000) and the Danes (60,000). The Frisians are a Germanic minority native to parts of Western Lower Saxony and Western Schleswig-Holstein. The Danes are native to Northern Schleswig, and the Sorbs are an old Slavic tribe native to Lusatia in Southeastern Saxony. Jews settled in Germany as far back as the 4th century after Christ. Gypsies are yet another older minority. Poles started emigrating to Germany for economic reasons in the 19th century. Most of the Turks, Russians, Italians, Croatians and Greeks emigrated to Germany after World War Two, and also for economic opportunity. These more recent immigrants have often been called "Guest Workers" in many nations of Western Europe.

*Die Bevölkerungszahl der Bundesrepublik Deutschland ist etwa 83 Millionen. Die größten Bevölkerungsminderheiten innerhalb der Bundesrepublik Deutschland sind die Türken/Kurden (1,76 Millionen), die Polen (1,7 Millionen), die Rußen (610,000), die Italiener (541,000), die Friesen (500,000), die Kroaten (350,000), die Griechen (310,000) und die Zigeuner (250,000). Die Friesen sind eine Volksgruppe, die im Westen Niedersachsens und im Westen Schleswig-Holsteins leben. Die Eider Dänen (60,000 Menschen) sind auch eine Volksgruppe, die in Nordschleswig wohnen. Die Sorben (auch 60,000 Menschen) sind eine westslawische Volksgruppe, die in Lausitz im Südosten Sachsens leben. Die deutschen Juden (200,000 Leute) leben in Deutschland seit dem 4. Jahrhundert nach Christus. Vor 1935 gab es mehr als 400,000 Juden im Deutschen Reich.*

## Chapter 3 (Kapitel Drei): The Modern Republic of Austria ("die Republik Österreich")

The modern Republic of Austria (8.3 million people) also has small minorities of Turks (2%), Serbs (2%), Croatians (0,8%), Slovenes (0,4%), Hungarians (0,4%), Czechs (0,2%) and Jews (0,1%). The Slovenes are native to parts of Carinthia, whereas the Hungarians are native to parts of Burgenland, and the Czechs are native to parts of Upper and Lower Austria. Jews have lived in Austria as long as in Germany itself. Most of the Turks are post-World War Two immigrants.

*Die Republik Österreich hat eine Bevölkerungszahl von ewta 8,3 Millionen Menschen. Die größten Bevölkerungsminderheiten innerhalb Österreich sind die Türken/Kurden (2% der Gesamtbevölkerung), die Serben (auch 2%), die Kroaten (0,8%), die Slowener (0,4%), die Magjaren (auch 0,4%), die Tschechen (0,2%) und die Juden (0,1%). Die Slowener sind eine Bevölkerungsgruppe innerhalb Kärnten, die Magjaren wohnen im Burgenland und die Tschechen in Ober-und Niederösterreich (nahe Böhmen). Vor 1938 gab es mehr als 200,000 Juden in Deutschösterreich.*

## Chapter 4 (Kapitel Vier): The Official Names of the German Fleets over Time ("die Namen der Deutschen Flotten")

"Deutsche Marine" has been the official name of the German Navy since German reunification in 1990; from 1956 until 1990 the Navy of Western Germany was known as the "Bundesmarine" (Federal Navy) and the Navy of Eastern Germany was known as the "Volksmarine" (Peoples' Navy). From 1945-1956 the Western Allies established the "Deutscher Minenräumdienst" (German Minesweeping Service) to clear German waters of the many mines unfortunately laid during the Second World War. The Navy of the Third German Empire ("drittes Reich" or Third Reich) was known as the "Kriegsmarine" (War Navy) from 1935-1945. The Navy of the First German Republic or Weimar Republic was known as the "Reichsmarine" from 1922-1935 and the Navy of the Second German Empire ("zweites Reich" or Second Reich) was known as the "Kaiserliche Marine" (Imperial Navy) from 1871-1922. The term "Weimar Republic" came into being because the First German Republic was proclaimed in the city of Weimar in the State of Thuringia. The North German Federation ("Norddeutscher Bund") had a Federal Navy ("Norddeutsche Bundesmarine") from 1866-1871, but this was basically the Prussian Navy under a new name. The Prussian Navy is discussed below, after my discussion of the Austrian Navy.

**Die Flagge der Reichsmarine (von 1933 bis 1935) / The Flag of the Reichsmarine (as used from 1933 until 1935) and the Imperial Navy Jack (as used from 1867 to 1922) in black, white and red**

*Seit der deutschen Wiedervereinigung im Jahre 1990 heißt die Marine in Deutschland die "Deutsche Marine." Von 1956 bis 1990 hieß die Marine in Westdeutschland die "Bundesmarine," und die Marine in Ostdeutschland die "Volksmarine." Von 1945 bis 1956 gab es in Westdeutschland einen "Deutschen Minenräumdienst." Die "Kriegsmarine" des Dritten Reiches dauerte von 1935 bis 1945. Vorher war es die "Reichsmarine" von 1922 bis 1935. Die "Kaiserliche Marine" des Zweiten Deutschen Reiches dauerte von 1871 bis 1922. Vorher war es die "Norddeutsche Bundesmarine" von 1867 bis 1871. Die Marine vom Königreich Preußen dauerte von 1701 bis 1867. Vorher gab es eine Marine des Herzogtum Brandenburgs von 1618 bis 1701. Die Hanseatische Marine von Hamburg und Lübeck dauerte von 1267 bis 1618. Eine neue Kroatische Kriegsmarine gibt es seit 1991. Davor gab es eine Jugoslawische Sozialistische Bundesmarine von 1945 bis 1991. Das Königreich Jugoslawien hatte eine Königliche Marine von 1918 bis 1945. Die "Kaiserliche und Königliche Kriegsmarine" von Österreich-Ungarn, Österreich und Österreich-Venedig dauerte von 1379 bis 1918. Die Admiralität des Heiligen Römischen Reiches der Deutschen Nation (800-1806) wurde im Jahre 983 gegründet. Das Königreich Franken dauerte von 482 bis 800, und der Fränkische Bund von 358 bis 482. Vorher gab es sehr viele Germanische Stämme wie die Franken, die Sachsen, die Friesen, die Bayern, die Angeln, die Sueben, die Thüringer, die Vandalen, die Langobarden, die Jüten, die Burgunden, die Goten, die Salier, die Markomannen, und so weiter.*

## Chapter 5 (Kapitel Fünf): German and Austrian Ship Name Histories ("die Geschichte der Deutschen und der Österreichischen Patennamen")

I have written about 1,936 of the unique ship and boat names used within the German, West German, East German, Brandenburg-Prussian, Hanseatic League, Holy Roman, Austro-Hungarian, Austrian and Austro-Venetian Navies, and within the HAPAG-Lloyd, HAPAG, North German Lloyd, Austrian Lloyd and Austro-Americana Shipping Lines built and commissioned in between the years of 1354 and 2010. Ships and boats with planned names are included in my histories, as well (even if they never came around to receiving their unique names, such as the many larger combat vessels of the famous "Z-Plan," including planned battlecruisers, battleships, aircraft cruisers and aircraft carriers). My narrative does include most of the major "named" naval vessels of more than 10 tons full load displacement. I have chosen to give equal importance and coverage to the historical navies of Austria, because Austria established the first true "national" German-speaking navy in 1379. The German-speaking navies of the Hanseatic League cities actually go back even further in time (specifically to the year 1267), but the each Hanseatic League City had its own such force. Furthermore, data on ships so old is much harder to locate. The largest German-speaking Hanseatic League cities are Hamburg, Bremen, Lübeck and Rostock. The Admiralty of the Holy Roman Empire of the German Nation was established in the year 983.

*Es möge hinreichen das über 1,936 von den einmaligen Schiffs-und Bootspatennamen der Deutschen, West-Deutschen, Ost-Deutschen, Brandenburgisch-Preußischen, Hanseatischen, Heilig-Römischen, Österreichisch-Ungarischen, Österreichischen, Österreichisch-Venedigschen Marinen zu erwähnen - sowie über HAPAG-Lloyd, HAPAG, den Norddeutschen Lloyd, den Österreichischen Lloyd, die Austro-Americana Linie und die Donau Dampfschiffs-Gesellschaft. Kriegsschiffe-und Boote mit "geplanten" Patennamen sind hier auch, obwohl viele davon nie gebaut oder getauft wurden. Solche Einheiten waren Mitglieder des berühmten "Z-Plan" der Zwischenkriegsjahre – wie die Schlachtkreuzer der "O-Klaße," die Schlachtschiffe der "H-Klaße," die Flugzeugträger der "Graf Zeppelin" Klaße, die Großflugzeugkreuzer und die Flugdeckkreuzer. Erwähnt wird auch fast alle Kriegseefahrzeuge, die mehr als 10 Tonnen Einsatzverdrängung hatten.Der Österreichischen Marine wird genausoviel Wichtigkeit wie der Deutschen Marine zu geben, weil die Österreicher die erste wirkliche berufliche deutschsprachige Marine im Jahre 1379 gegründet haben. Die Hanseatische Marine von Hamburg, Lübeck und Wismar ist eigentlich älter (sie wurde im Jahre 1267 gegründet), aber Tatsachen über Schiffe und Boote, die so alt sind, sind sehr schwierig zu finden. Deutschlands größte Hansestädte sind nun Hamburg, Bremen, Lübeck und Rostock. Die Admiralität des Ersten Deutschen Reiches wurde im Jahre 983 gegründet.*

The flag used by the Imperial and Royal (Austrian) Navy was the red, white and red tricolor of 3 horizontal stripes. Yet another red, white and red tricolor of 3 horizontal stripes was placed off-center toward the left within the large central (white) stripe. Above this smaller red, white and red tricolor was the Habsburg Crown. This flag was used as the official flag of the Imperial and Royal Navy from 1786 until the "end" of the Habsburg Monarchy in November 1918. It was also used as the flag of the Austrian Merchant Marine (civilian commercial vessels) from 1786 until 1869, when the Habsburg Monarchy became the "dual" Monarchy of Austria-Hungary. It was the official flag of the Archduchies of both Upper and Lower Austria from 960 until November 1918. The "national" flag of the Habsburg Monarchy was the black and yellow flag of 2 horizontal stripes, in continual use from 973 until November of 1918. It is still used by Austrian, Hungarian, Czech, Slovak, Slovene and Croatian monarchists to this very day. The tricolor of the Imperial and Royal Austrian Navy is likewise still used by the members of the Austrian Naval League to this very day.

*Die Reichskriegsflagge der Kaiserlichen und Königlichen Kriegsmarine Österreichs war rot, weiß und rot. Im weißen Streifen der Flagge war noch eine kleinere Fahne, die auch rot-weiß-rot war. Über der kleinen Fahne war die Kaiserliche und Königliche Habsburgische Krone. Diese Fahne war die amtliche Fahne der Kaiserlichen und Königlichen Kriegsmarine von 1786 bis zum Ende der Habsburger Monarchie im November 1918. Sie wurde auch gebraucht als Flagge der Österreichischen Handelsmarine von 1786 bis 1869, als die Habsburger Monarchie die "Doppelmonarchie" Österreich-Ungarns entstand. Die selbe Flagge war auch die amtliche Flagge der Erzherzogtüme Ober-und Niederösterreichs von 960 bis November 1918. Sie ist immer noch im Gebrauch bei den Monarchisten in Österreich, Ungarn, Tschechien, Slowakei, Slowenien und Kroatien. Die Trikolore der Kaiserlichen und Königlichen Kriegsmarine ist noch im Gebrauch bei den Mitgliedern des Österreichischen Marinebunds.*

The total cumulative number of vessels in the German and Austrian Navies is a most impressive 53,526. This number includes 125 modern battleships, 31 heavy or armored cruisers, 147 light or small cruisers, 103 gunboats, 1,699 torpedo boats, 132 airships ("Zeppelin" airships), 8,421 submarines, 1,513 auxiliary warships, 958 corvettes, 7,093 fast attack craft, 3,750 minesweepers, 25,000 armed fishing boats, 2,978 transporters or landing ships, 9 tenders, 4 survey ships, 250 destroyers, 24 aircraft carriers, 274 frigates and 1,015 training ships.

*Die Gesamtzahl der Einheiten der Deutschen und Österreichischen Marine kommt auf imposante 53,526 Seefahrzeuge, einschliesslich 125 moderne Schlachtschiffe, 31 Schwere oder Große Kreuzer, 147 Leichte oder Kleine Kreuzer, 103 Kanonenboote, 1,699 Torpedoboote, 132 Luftschiffe, 8,421 Unterseeboote, 1,513 Hilfsschiffe, 958 Korvetten, 7,093 Schnellboote, 3,750 Minensuchboote, 25,000 Kriegsfischkutter, 2,978 Transporter oder Landungsboote, 9 Versorger, 4 Aufklärungsschiffe, 250 Zerstörer, 24 Flugzeugträger 274 Fregatten und 1,015 Schulschiffe.*

Many German destroyers were never named, but merely numbered.  Likewise, most German torpedo boats, torpedo recovery vessels, submarines, sloops, corvettes, fast attack craft (formerly called "motor torpedo boats"), minesweepers, motor minesweepers (very small minesweepers), motor fishing vessels, ferries and transport vessels were never "named" – but merely numbered with "call" or "pennant" numbers.

*Viele deutsche Zerstörer wurden nicht mit Patennamen getauft, sondern nur mit Nummern.  Ebenfalls wurden die meisten deutschen Torpedoboote, Unterseeboote, Geleitboote, Korvetten, Schnellboote, Minensuchboote, Kriegsfischkutter und Landungsboote nicht mit Patennamen, sondern nur mit Nummern benannt.*

One might refer to the Austrian Navy of 1369 to 1849 as "Austrian-Venetian," to the Austrian Navy of 1849 to 1867 as "Austrian" and to the Austrian Navy of 1867 to 1918 as "Austro-Hungarian."  Prior to 1849, most Austrian naval personnel were ethnic Italians.  From 1849 until 1867, ethnic Germans were in the majority.  In 1867, Hungary obtained virtually equal status with Austria within the Habsburg empire.  Many Magyars (Hungarians), Czechs, Moravians, Slovaks, Slovenes, Poles, Ruthenians (Ukrainians), Romanians, Bosnians, and especially Croatians joined the Navy.  The Croatians of Dalmatia are especially well-suited to be professional sailors (much like the Germans of East Frisia, North Frisia, Schleswig-Holstein, Bremen, Bremerhaven, Hamburg, Lübeck, Mecklenburg and Pomerania).  Technical specifications and histories for the much older wooden sailing vessels are harder to find.  For the Austrian Navy of the Adriatic Sea, I can go back to 1628 with partial technical specifications on a few such named vessels.  For the Hanseatic Navies of Northern Germany, I can go back as far as 1354 with a few ship types and names.

*Von 1369 (d.h. 10 Jahre bevor die Kaiserliche und Königliche Kriegsmarine gegründet wurde) bis 1848 war die Österreichische Marine eigentlich die Marine von "Österreich-Venedig," weil die Mehrheit des Marinepersonals eigentlich italienisch war. Nach der sogenannten Revolutionen von 1848 war die Mehrheit des österreichischen Marinepersonals Deutsch. Ab 1867, kam die Mehrheit des Personals aus Mittel-und Osteuropa, d.h. aus Ungarn, Tschechien, Slowakei, Slowenien, Kroatien, Bosnien-Herzegowina, Galizien, Lodomerien, Siebenbürgen, Banat und Weißruthenien. Die Kroaten aus Dalmatien waren besonders gute Seeleute, genauso wie die Leute aus Friesland, Schleswig-Holstein, Bremen, Bremerhaven (ehemals "Wesermünde"), Hamburg, Lübeck, Lauenburg, Mecklenburg, Pommern, Preußen und Kurland. Technische Daten für ältere Segelschiffe und Segelboote sind natürlich schwierig zu finden. Für die Kaiserliche und Königliche Kriegsmarine Österreichs kann man bis 1628 zurückgehen. Für die Hanseatische Marine von Hamburg, Lübeck und Wismar geht es bis 1354 zurück.*

In terms of modern maritime technology, vessels of 1,000 tons full load displacement or more are considered to be worthy for deployment upon the high seas, whereas smaller vessels are generally considered to be suited mostly for coastal use. There are of course exceptions in either direction. One may find larger vessels or barges suited for use only on rivers or lakes, and smaller vessels seaworthy enough to cross the great oceans and seas of the world. The largest designs for German battleships went up to a world-record 141,500 tons full load displacement (the "H-44" design of 1944). Modern German battlecruisers displaced up to 43,000 tons full load (the "Gneisenau" conversion project). Modern German armored ships ("Panzerschiffe" in German) until 1945 displaced up to 25,689 tons full load (of the "Kreuzer-P" project of the Z-Plan). German heavy cruisers up to 1945 displaced up to 19,800 tons full load (the last planned ship of the "Admiral Hipper" class), and German light cruisers up to 1945 displaced as much as 12,165 tons full load. Modern German frigates displace from 1,841 to 6,800 tons full load. Modern German corvettes may displace anywhere from 394 tons up to 1,840 tons full load. German fast attack craft (formerly called "motor torpedo boats") are considered to be large and rapid patrol craft. They displace anywhere from 74 up to 393 tons full load. Small German and Austrian patrol boats tend to be considerably slower, and displace less than 74 tons. They may be as small as 10 tons for river and/or lake duty.

*Heutzutage sind Schiffe mit einer Einsatzverdrängung von 1,000 oder mehr Tonnen hauptsächlich "Hochsee-Einheiten." Die meisten Schiffe und Boote mit einer Einsatzverdrängung von weniger als 1,000 Tonnen sind hauptsächlich für Binnenfahrt, d.h. an den Küsten, auf den Flüßen und auf den Binnenseen. Es gibt natürlich viele Ausnamen, d.h. kleinere Einheiten, die auf Hochsee ganz fähig sind, und auch größere Einheiten, die nur für Binnenfahrt gemeint sind. Die größten geplanten Kriegschiffe der Deutschen Marine waren die letzten Einheiten der "H-Klaße." Das geplante Schlachtschiff "H-44" von 1944 sollte eine Einsatzverdrängung von 141,500 Tonnen haben. Das ist wesentlich größer als die größten Atomkraft-Flugzeugträger der heutigen Amerikanischen Marine. Der größte deutsche Schlachtkreuzer war das geplante "Gneisenau" Konversionprojekt, mit einer Einsatzverdrängung von 43,000 Tonnen. Das größte deutsche Panzerschiff war das "Kreuzer-P" Projekt des Z-Plans, mit einer Einsatzverdrängung von 25,689 Tonnen. Der größte deutsche Schwere Kreuzer war die geplante "Lützow" der "Admrial Hipper" Klaße, mit einer Einsatzverdrängung von 19,800 Tonnen. Die größten deutschen Leichten Kreuzer waren die zwei Beuteschiffe des zweiten Weltkrieges aus Holland, nämlich die "Eendracht" und die "De Zeven Provincien," beide mit einer Einsatzverdrängung von 12,165 Tonnen. Die zwei Schiffe gehören nun Peru. Moderne deutsche Fregatten haben eine Einsatzverdrängung von 1,841 bis auf 6,800 Tonnen. Die geplante "Thüringen" und die geplante "Baden-Württemberg" der "F125-Klaße" werden je eine Einsatzverdrängung von 6,800 Tonnen haben. Moderne deutsche Korvetten haben eine Einsatzverdrängung von 394 bis auf 1,840 Tonnen. Die fünf Mitglieder der neuen "Braunschweig-Klaße" haben eine Einsatzverdrängung von je 1,840 Tonnen. Moderne deutsche Schnellboote haben eine Einsatzverdrängung von 74 bis auf 393 Tonnen, und moderne deutsche und österreichische Patrouillenboote haben eine Einsatzverdrängung von 10 bis auf 73 Tonnen.*

It may be somewhat difficult for most of us to imagine today, but when the Englishman Sir Francis Drake circumnavigated the globe from 1577 to 1580, his state-of-the-art wooden sailing battleship "H.M.S. Golden Hind" had a standard displacement of a mere 102 tons. Today, most of us would be apprehensive to sail around the globe in so "small" a vessel – small by our modern criteria.

*Vielleicht ist es für uns heute ein bischen schwierig vorzustellen, aber als der Engländer Sir Francis Drake seine Weltreise zwischen 1577 un 1580 machte, hatte sein Segel-Linienschiff "H.M.S. Golden Hind" eine Einsatzverdrängung von nur 102 Tonnen. Heutzutage wäre das ganz klein, aber damals war das ein ganz modernes und großes Schlachtschiff.*

## Chapter 6 (Kapitel Sechs): The Austrian Navy ("Die Österreichische Marine")

*Bis 1866 war die größte Marine im deutschsprachigen Raum die "Kaiserliche und Königliche Kriegsmarine" Österreichs. Die wichtigsen Marinestüztpunkte waren in Venedig, Triest, Polei (heute "Pula" in Kroatien), Sankt Veit am Pflaumb (heute "Rijeka" in Kroatien), Spalato (heute "Split" in Kroatien), Sibenning (heute "Sibenik" in Kroatien) und Cattaro (heute "Kotor" in Montenegro). Damals, war die Mehrheit der Bevölkerung dieser Gegend italienisch sowie kroatisch, mit einer Deutschen Minderheit. Die österreichische Marineakademie war usprünglich im Jahre 1802 in Venedig gegründet, und mußte dann im Jahre 1854 nach Sankt Veit am Pflaumb versetzt werden, weil Venedig leider von Italien annektiert wurde. Im Krieg von 1848 waren mindstens 30% der Italiener Österreichtreu. Die wichtigsten Flaggenoffiziere in der Geschichte der "Kaiserlichen und Königlichen Kriegsmarine" Österreichs sowie Österreich-Ungarns waren Großadmiral Anton Johann Freiherr von Haus, Admiral Maximilian Njegovan (aus Kroatien), Admiral Rudolf Ludwig Raimund Heinrich Alfons Graf von Montecuccoli, Admiral Hermann Freiherr von Spaun, Admiral Maximilian Freiherr Daublebsky von Sterneck zu Ehrenstein, Admiral Friedrich von Pöck, Admiral Anton Michael Freiherr Bourguignon von Baumberg, Admiral Alfred Freiherr von Koudelka, Admiral Erzherzog Franz Ferdinand von Habsburg-Lothringen (im Sarajevo in Juni 1914 ermordet), Admiral Julius von Ripper, Vizeadmiral Franz von Holub und Vizeadmiral Karl Kailer von Kaltenfels.Der bedeutendste Held der Flaggenoffiziere war Vizeadmiral Wilhelm Josef von Tegetthoff, der die italienische Kriegsflotte bei Lissa im Jahre 1866 besiegte. Als Marineoffizier war Admiral Miklos Horthy de Nagybánya aus Ungarn hervorragend (er hat die italienische sowie die britische Kriegsflotte bei der Otrantostraße im Jahre 1917 angegriffen), aber nach dem ersten Weltkrieg blieb er seinem ehemaligen Kaiser Karl von Habsburg-Lothringen nicht treu. Kaiser Karl wollte 1921 nach Ungarn zurückkehren, aber Miklos Horthy als Staatsoberhaupt von Ungarn hat das verhindert. Andere Vizeadmirale in der Geschichte der k.u.k. Kriegsmarine waren Jospeh Wachtel von Elbenbruck, Karl Lanjus von Wellenburg, Maximilian Franz Freiherr von Pitner, Karl Seidensacher, Franz Ritter von Keil, Erzherzog Ferdinand Max von Habsburg-Lothringen (eventuell als Kaiser von Mexiko in 1867 leider ermordet) und Ludwig von Fautz.*

The most powerful German state up to 1866 was Austria, and she had her own "Kaiserliche und Königliche Kriegsmarine" (Imperial and Royal War Navy) from 1379 until the unfortunate defeat of the Habsburg Monarchy in 1918. The Battle

Flag used by the Imperial and Royal War Navy (a red, white and red tricolor of horizontal stripes, featuring the Habsburg Crown in the middle of the central white stripe) was officially used from 1786 until 1918. The same flag was used as the official Austrian merchant marine flag from 1786 until 1869. This flag was also used as the official flag of the Archduchies of Upper and Lower Austria from 960 until 1918. The national flag in use was the one with the horizontal black & yellow stripes of the Habsburg Monarchy from 973 until 1918. The Austrian Navy had major bases in Adriatic coastal cities such as Venice ("Venedig" in German or "Venezia" in Italian), Triest ("Trieste" in Italian), Pula ("Polei" in German or "Pola" in Italian), Fiume ("Sankt Veit am Pflaumb" in German), Split ("Spalato" in Italian), Sebenico ("Sibenning") and Cattaro. The majority of the population in these coastal cities was Italian and Croatian, with a German-speaking minority as well. The modern Republic of Austria is today a landlocked nation with 8.3 million German-speaking people. The Austrian Naval Academy ("Marineakademie") was founded in 1802. This is where the elite of officer candidates received their military leadership and seamanship training. Originally in Venice (Austria used to enjoy sovereignty over most of what is today modern Italy), it was moved to Fiume ("Sankt Veit am Pflaumb" in German, or "Rijeka" in Croatian) in 1854. Perhaps the internationally most famous graduate of this great academy was the eventual Korvettenkapitän (a Commander in the Austrian Navy) Georg Ritter von Trapp, whose family became immortalized in Rodgers and Hammerstein's "The Sound of Music" (this was made into a 3-hour feature film by 20th Century Fox in 1965). Another famous graduate of this school was Vizeadmiral (or Vice Admiral) Wilhelm Josef von Tegetthoff, who was the victorious commander of the Austrian fleet in the Battle of Lissa against Italy in 1866. In this battle, he became famous for the "ramming" technique (the ramming of an enemy ship with the bow of one's own warship). Because of this, most surface warships were constructed with so-called "ram bows" (a portruding armored frontal bulge located below the waterline of the ship) until about the time of the First World War.

*Zwischen 1369 (d.h. 10 Jahren vor der Gründung der "Kaiserlichen und Königlichen Kriegsmarine" Österreichs) und 1848 (als viele Revolutionen sowie Kriege leider nach Europa gekommen sind), hat die k.u.k. Kriegsmarine 962 Schiffe und Seefahrzeuge in Einsatz gesetzt. Diese Seefahrzeuge waren hauptsächlich Segelschiffe und Segelboote, ohne Dampfkraft. Damals waren die Seefahrzeuge wesentlich kleiner als heute. Zum Beispiel war die Einsatzverdrängung Österreichs 7 größte Segelfregatten der "S.M.S. Principessa di Bologna" Klaße vom Jahre 1810 nur je 1,570 Tonnen. Bis 1848, war die Mehrheit der Offiziere sowie der Matrosen bei der k.u.k. Kriegsmarine Österreichs italienisch. Nach 1848, war die Mehrheit des Marinepersonals deutsch. Im großen und ganzen waren die verschiedenen Völker des habsburgischen Reiches zu Österreich und ihren gemeinsamen Kaiser ganz treu. Es gab Deutsche, Magyaren, Tschechen, Mähren, Schlesier, Slowaken, Polen, Italiener, Slowener, Kroaten, Serben, Montenegriner, Rumänen, Weißruthenier (d.h. Ukrainer), sowie alle Konfeßionen – Katholiken, Protestanten, Orthodoxen, Juden und Mohammedaner. Diese verschinden Völker haben gemeinsam gegen die Feinde des gemeinsamen Vaterlandes gekämpft, und heute ruhen diese gefallenen Helden auch zusammen.*

In between 1369 (ten years before the "official" creation of an Austrian Navy in Triest, which is now part of Italy) and 1848 (the year when war and revolution came to much of Europe, including to Italy), the Imperial and Royal Austrian Navy deployed a total of 962 vessels of various types. During this time, the Austrian Navy was known as the "Austro-Venetian Navy," because the largest naval base was in the city of Venice ("Venedig" in German), and most of the manpower in the navy was Italian-speaking. These were the days of sailing ships, before steam power. 24 of their largest ships were wooden "ships-of-the-line," or battleships. Over the many years of recorded history, ships have been growing ever larger due to new and improved technologies. Up to 1848, a majority of the men who served in the Imperial and Royal Austrian Navy were ethnic Italians, but after 1848 it shifted to the ethnic Germans. Many of the most qualified rank and file sailors were Croatians right up to 1918. People from all over the vast Habsburg empire served faithfully in the navy, including Czechs, Moravians, Silesians, Slovaks, Poles, Slovenes, Ruthenians (Ukrainians), Magyars (Hungarians), Romanians, Bosnian Muslims and Orthodox Serbs. All religions of the empire were represented as well, including the majority Roman Catholics, Evangelical Lutherans, Calvinist Protestants, Eastern Orthodox, Jews and Muslims. These men served, fought and died side by side, evidence of which one sees today in Austrian naval cemeteries where they rest side by side. A few notes on the official name of the Austrian Navy. "Imperial" refers to the fact that the Habsburg Austrian Monarch was an Emperor of Empires such as Rome, Germany and later Austria itself. "Royal" refers to the fact that he was a King of Kingdoms such as Bohemia, Galicia, Lodomeria, Hungary, Croatia and Slavonia. Going down the list of his noble titles, he was also an Archduke of Lower Austria (of which the city of Vienna is the capital) and of Upper Austria (ironically the birthplace of Adolf Hitler in April 1889). Hitler left Austria for Germany in 1913, where he joined the Bavarian Army in 1914 and served in World War One. Hitler eventually persecuted the members of the Habsburg family after the German annexation of Austria in 1938. He feared the Habsburgs, and drove most of them out of Austria at least for the duration of World War Two. The Habsburg Monarch was also a Duke of the Duchies of Carinthia, Carniola, Salzburg, Silesia and Styria. In addition to this, the Habsburg Monarch held the noble titles of Margraviate of the March of Moravia and Prince of the Principality of the Tyrol.

*Die "Kaiserliche und Königliche Kriegsmarine" war die Marine von Österreich. Der Kaiser von Österreich und das Heilige Römische Reich der Deutschen Nation kam aus dem Kaiserlichen Hause Habsburg-Lothringen. Der Kaiser war auch König von Böhmen, Galizien, Lodomerien, Ungarn, Kroatien und Slavonien. Er war auch Erzherzog von Niederösterreich ("Österreich unter der Enns") und Oberösterreich ("Österreich ob der Enns"). Er war Herzog von Kärnten, Krain, Salzburg, Schlesien, und Steiermark. Er war auch Markgraf von Mähren sowie Prinz von Tirol.*

Going down the list of ships (progressively smaller than the wooden battleships) were 35 sailing cruisers, 33 sailing brigs, 37 sailing brigantines, 104 coastal warships, 79 sailing pinnaces, 20 swimming batteries, 10 sailing galleons and many smaller vessels. The fleet had many auxiliary craft as well, including 69 transporters and 83 ships of the famous Danube River Flotilla. In between 1369 and 1849, the Imperial and Royal Austrian Navy engaged in no fewer than 47 sea, river or lake battles. Their opponents were various former states in modern day Italy, the Ottoman Empire, Germany, Switzerland, Greece and North Africa. The Navy was victorious in 27 of the 47 encounters, or 57% of the total battles.

*Zwischen 1369 und 1848 hatte die Kaiserliche und Königliche Kriegsmarine Österreichs insgesamt 24 Segel-Linienschiffe, 35 Segelkreuzer (d.h. Segelfregatten und Segelkorvetten), 33 Segelbriggs, 37 Segelbrigantinen, 104 Küstenschiffe, 79 Segelpenichen, 20 Schwimmende Batterien, 10 Segelgaleonen sowie viele kleinere Kriegschiffe und Boote. Es gab auch viele Hilfsschiffe, wie die 69 Transportschiffe, sowie die 83 Einheiten der berühmten Donauflottille. Zwischen 1369 und 1849 hatte die Kaiserliche und Königliche Kriegsmarine an mindestens 47 Seeschlächten teilgenommen. 27 mal war die K.u.K. Kriegsmarine siegreich, d.h. an 57% der Seeschlächte.*

## Chapter 7 (Kapitel Sieben): The Prussian Navy ("Die Preußische Marine")

The second most powerful German state until 1866 was the Kingdom of Brandenburg-Prussia, which had its own navy since 1657.  Prussia had naval bases in the Baltic Sea coastal cities such as Memel, Königsberg, Pillau, Elbing, Danzig, Zoppot, Hela, Kolberg, Swinemünde and Stettin.  This region was turned over to both Poland and Russia after World War Two.  The former German provinces of Pomerania, Silesia, West Prussia, Masuria and Posen are in modern Poland, which is still home to 8 million German-speaking people.  Northern East Prussia is part of Russia, and Russia itself is still home to more than 17.8 million German-speaking people today.  Most of them are descendants of German immigrants who emigrated to Russia during the time of Empress Catherine the Great of Russia.  Even current Prime Minister Vladimir Putin of Russia, his wife and their two young daughters speak fluent German.  The two Putin girls attend a German school in Moscow.

**Die Flagge der Marine von Brandenburg-Preußen (von 1657 bis 1701) / The Flag of the Navy of Brandenburg-Prussia (as used from 1657 until 1701)**

*Bis 1866 war das zweitmächtiges Land im ganzen Deutschen Reich das Königriech Preußen. Die Marinehäfen des Königreich Preußens waren in Seehäfen wie Memel, Königsberg, Pillau, Elbing, Danzig, Zoppot, Hela, Kolberg, Swinemünde und Stettin. Es gibt immer noch 8 Millionen Menschen, die in Polen Deutsch sprechen. Die ehemaligen deutschen Provinzen von Hinterpommern, Schlesien, Westpreußen, Posen, Masuren und das Ermland liegen heute in Polen. Nordostpreußen gehört nun Rußland, das Memelland gehört Litauen und das Kurland gehört Lettland. Es gibt immer noch 17,8 Millionen Menschen in Rußland, die Deutsch sprechen. Viele Deutsche sind nach Rußland im 18. Jahrhundert ausgewandert. Wladimir Putin (der Ministerpräsident von Rußland), seine Ehefrau und ihre zwei jungen Töchter sprechen alle Deutsch. Die zwei Putin-Mädchen besuchen in Moskau eine Deutsche Schule.*

The cities of the Hanseatic League along the North German coast (such as Hamburg, Bremen, Lübeck, Rostock, Stralsund and Wismar) had numerous warships as well. In the days of wooden sailing ships, the differences between naval and commercial ships were no where near as pronounced as they are today. Commercial ships had to be rather heavily armed due to the rough and tough nature of the maritime world.

**Die Flagge der Preußischen Marine (von 1817 bis 1867) / The Flag of the Prussian Navy (as used from 1817 until 1867)**

*Die Deutschen Hansestädte (besonders Hamburg, Lübeck und Wismar) hatten auch viele gute Kriegsschiffe. Zur Zeit der Segelschiffe gab es eigentlich zwischen Kriegsschiffen und Handelsschiffen nicht viele Unterschiede. Damals war es wirklich notwendig, Handelsschiffe zu bewaffnen.*

The Hanseatic League ("die Hansa") was a trading guild formed in the Middle Ages, in the year 1267. Cities all over Northern Europe joined the league to protect their commercial interests, especially for the purposes of overseas trade. The Hanseatic League was closely tied to the Teutonic Knights, who were an order of Germanic Knights in the Middle Ages. Knightly Orders were founded for both military and religious reasons. The Teutonic Knights colonized much of Eastern Europe, setting up German colonies in the form of cities and rural communities. They also Christianized the peoples of modern countries such as Poland, Lithuania, Latvia and Estonia. Many Slavic tribes (such as the Wends, the Sorbs, the Lusatians, the Pomeranians, the Silesians, the Kassubians and the Masurians) as well as Baltic tribes such as the Prussians became Germanized in both culture and language.

**Marinegarnisonskirche Wilhelmshaven im Jahre 1933 / Evangelical-Luthern Naval Garrison Church in Wilhelmhaven in 1933 – Nonnenkamp Family Archives**

*Die Deutsche Hanse wurde im Mittelalter, nämlich im Jahre 1267, gegründet. Die Mitgliederstädte der Deutschen Hanse waren eventuell in ganz Mitteleuropa und Nordeuropa zu finden. Die Ritterorden des Deutschen Reiches waren mit der Deutschen Hanse eng verbündet. Die deutschen Ritterorden haben die deutsche Sprache, die deutsche Kultur das Christentum nach Mittel-und Osteuropa gebracht. Viele westslawische und baltische Stämme, wie die Sorben, die Pommern, die Schlesier, die Masuren und die Preußen, wurden germanisiert.*

**Die Gebrüder Nonnenkamp aus Oldenburg im Jahre 1936 / The Nonnenkamp brothers of Oldenburg in 1936 (from top left to lower right): Heinz, Georg, Franz, Otto, Wilhelm and August – Nonnenkamp Family Archives**

The German Naval Academy ("Marineschule") was founded in the city of Mürwik near Germany's largest Baltic Sea Naval Base of Kiel in 1910. Kiel is actually Germany's second largest naval base after the city of Wilhelmshaven, which is located in the German Bay ("Deutsche Bucht") of the North Sea. Grand Admiral Karl Dönitz led the last government of the Third Reich in Mürwik, Kiel in May 1945, when the primary concern was moving fleeing ethnic German civilians West. The Navy did this job admirably, saving the lives of 2 million ethnic Germans who moved mostly into modern day Western Germany. Grand Admiral Karl Dönitz joined the German Navy as a young officer, and served in the Adriatic and Mediterranean theaters during World War One. He was initially stationed aboard the small cruiser "S.M.S. Breslau," which served as an escort to the battlecruiser "S.M.S. Goeben." "Breslau" is the capital city of the province of Silesia, which is now part of Poland. Prior to 1740, Silesia belonged to Austria. Prussia took Silesia away from Austria after she defeated Austria during the War of the Austrian Succession. August Karl von Goeben was a Prussian General who lived from 1816 until 1880, and who served in the Prussian wars fought against Denmark, Austria, Bavaria, Württemberg, Saxony, Hanover, Baden, Hesse-Darmstadt, Holstein, Nassau and France from 1864 until 1871. The two ships were sent from Germany to Turkey before World War One, and their daring sortie ensured Ottoman Turkey's entry into the war on the side of the Central Powers. The Central Powers were Germany, Austria-Hungary, Bulgaria and the Ottoman Empire (Turkey). "S.M.S. Breslau" was sunk in the Aegean Sea in January 1918, while "S.M.S. Goeben" served in the Turkish Navy until she was scrapped in 1974. Karl Dönitz served aboard submarines during World War One, and remained in the German Navy after the war. He commanded the new light cruiser "Emden" (commissioned in 1925) and was appointed commander of Germany's reborn submarine fleet in 1935. Upon the retirement of Grand Admiral Erich Raeder in 1943, Karl Dönitz was made a Grand Admiral (a 5 star admiral) and Commander in Chief of the "Kriegsmarine." Erich Raeder had been Commander in Chief of the German Navy from 1928 until 1943. Both of these fine men survived World War Two, Grand Admiral Raeder passing away in 1960 and Grand Admiral Dönitz passing away in 1980.

**Mein Urgroßvater Carl Friedrich Rudolph im Jahre 1900 / My great-grandfather Carl Friedrich Rudolph (the father-in-law of Wilhelm Johannes Nonnenkamp) in the uniform of the Army of the Grand Duchy of Oldenburg in 1900 – Nonnenkamp Family Archives**

*Die Marineschule Mürwik (die elite Offiziersschule der Deutschen Marine) wurde im Jahre 1910 von Kaiser Wilhelm II gegründet. Mürwik liegt bei Kiel, und Kiel ist nach Wilhelmshaven der zweitgrößte Marinehafen Deutschlands. Großadmiral Karl Dönitz hat die letzte Regierung des dritten Reiches in Mürwik geleitet. Damals hatte die Kriegsmarine 2 Millionen Deutsche Flüchtlinge aus den deutschen Ostgebieten gerettet. Im Ersten Weltkrieg diente Karl Dönitz auf dem Kleinen Kreuzer "S.M.S. Breslau," sowie auf Unterseeboote im Mittelmeer.*

*Nach dem Ersten Weltkrieg war Karl Dönitz Kommandeur des neuen Leichten Kreuzers "Emden" (getauft im Jahre 1925). Im Jahre 1935 wurde er "Führer der Unterseeboote" der neuen Deutschen Kriegsmarine. Als Großadmiral Erich Raeder 1943 in den Ruhestand ging, wurde Karl Dönitz zum Großadmiral befördert. Großadmiral Erich Raeder ist im Jahre 1960 gestorben, und Großadmiral Karl Dönitz starb im Jahre 1980.*

## Chapter 8 (Kapitel Acht): The Modern German Navy / HAPAG-Lloyd / Austrian Lloyd ("die Deutsche Marine und die Deutsch-Österreichische Reedereien")

The "Deutsche Marine" is today the ninth largest Navy in the world in terms of commissioned warships (76) while Croatia's Navy ranks 62nd. There are 193 independent countries in the world. Germany's civilian merchant fleet is even more prominent, with 2,616 ocean-going vessels of more than 1,000 tons each and 4,812 coastal vessels of less than 1,000 tons each. Of the ocean-going fleet, 2,321 of the ships are over 10,000 tons each. Add to this Austria's fleet of 37 ocean-going vessels and 190 coastal & river vessels. Germany's best known and largest shipping company is of course HAPAG-Lloyd of Hamburg, which was formed due to a corporate merger in 1970. They rank number five (5) in the world after the Maersk Line of Denmark, MSC of Switzerland, CMA-CGM of France and Evergreen of Taiwan (the Republic of China). Their hometown of Hamburg is the world's ninth largest port after Singapore, Shanghai (in China), Hong Kong (also in China), Shenzen (yet again in China), Pusan (in South Korea), Rotterdam (in the Netherlands), Dubai (in the United Arab Emirates) and Kaohsiung (in Taiwan, the "Republic of China").

**Die Flagge der Kaiserlichen Marine (von 1867 bis 1922) / The Flag of the Imperial German Navy (as used from 1867 until 1922)**

*Die Deutsche Marine ist die 9. größte Marine der Welt, und auf der selben Rangliste ist die Kriegsmarine Kroatiens Nummer 62. Die Deutsche Marine hat 76 "aktive" Kriegsschiffe, und noch 62 in Reserve (138 Seefahrzeuge insgesamt). Die deutsche Handelsflotte ist die drittgrößte Flotte der Welt, mit 2,321 größeren Hochsee-Einheiten (mit einer Einsatzverdrängung von mehr als 10,000 Tonnen pro Schiff). Die Österreichische Handelsflotte hat 37 Schiffe. HAPAG-Lloyd ist die größte Reederei Deutschlands, und ist Nachvolger von HAPAG (aus Hamburg) und der Norddeutsche Lloyd (aus Bremen). Die zwei größten Schiffe von HAPAG-Lloyd sind die "Savannah Express" (2005) und die "Houston Express" (2005), mit einer Einsatzverdrängung von je 108,180 Tonnen. Beide Einheiten haben eine Höchstgeschwindigkeit von 25,4 Knoten. Das drittgrößte Schiff von HAPAG-Lloyd ist die "Columbo Express" (auch im Jahre 2005 getauft) mit einer Einsatzverdrängung von 104,400 Tonnen und einer maximalen Geschwindigkeit von 25 Knoten.*

1-2.) Their two largest vessels register 108,180 tons each. These are the container vessels and sister ships "Savannah Express" (2005) and "Houston Express" (2005), named after the large cities in the American states of Georgia and Texas, respectively. They have a top speed of 25,4 knots.

3.) HAPAG-Lloyd's next largest vessel is the container ship "Columbo Express" (2005), named after the city in Sri Lanka. She displaces 104,400 tons and can make up to 25 knots.

## HAPAG-Lloyd

HAPAG-Lloyd was formed as a merger between HAPAG of Hamburg ("Hamburg-Amerika Packetfahrt, A.G.") and Norddeutscher ("North German" in English) Lloyd of Bremen, Germany in 1970. HAPAG was founded in 1847 and the North German Lloyd was established in 1857. Today, HAPAG-Lloyd operates a fleet of 59 commercial vessels. Their parent company operates a commercial airline with more than 120 aircraft, in addition to 3,500 travel agencies, 79 tour operators in 18 countries plus 12 hotel brands in 28 countries with 285 hotels and 163,000 guest beds.

*HAPAG-Lloyd entstand im Jahre 1970 aus einer Fusion von HAPAG ("Hamburg-Amerika Packetfahrt, A.G.) und dem Norddeutschen Lloyd aus Bremen. HAPAG war im Jahre 1847, und der Norddeutsche Lloyd im Jahre 1857 gegründet. Heute hat HAPAG-Lloyd 59 Schiffe, 120 Flugzeuge, 3,500 Reisebüros, 79 Reiseführer in 18 Ländern sowie 285 Hotels in 28 Ländern.*

## "Hamburg-Amerika Packetfahrt, A.G." (HAPAG)

HAPAG operated 331 commercial vessels from the time of their founding on May 27, 1847 until their merger with, or purchase of, the North German Lloyd shipping line in 1970. The Hamburg-based merchants who founded HAPAG in 1847 included Adolph Godeffroy, F. Laiesz, H.J. Merck, Carl Woermann and August Bolten. HAPAG was the largest and best known of all German shipping companies.

*Zwischen 1847 und 1970 hatte HAPAG 331 Handels-und Passagierschiffe. Die Kaufmänner Adolph Godeffroy, F. Laiesz, H.J. Merck, Carl Woermann und August Bolten haben HAPAG am 27. Mai 1847 gegründet.*

1.) HAPAG's largest ship and most luxurious passenger liner ever was the "S/S Bismarck" (commissioned in 1914) of 56,551 tons total displacement, which was built by the Blohm & Voss A.G. Shipyard in Hamburg. These civilian passenger vessels are not to be confused with similarly-named combat vessels of the German Navy. This great ship was unfortunately confiscated by the British in 1920 as war reparations for World War One. This was the sole ship owned by HAPAG to be named after former Prussian and German Chancellor (Prime Minister) Otto von Bismarck.

*HAPAG's größte Schiff und deren größtes Passagierschiff war die "S/S Bismarck," die im Jahre 1914 getauft wurde. Die "S/S Bismarck" hatte eine Einsatzverdrängung von 56,551 Tonnen, und wurde von Blohm und Voss, A.G. in Hamburg gebaut. Sie hatte eine Höchstgeschwindigkeit von 23,5 Knoten und hatte Platz für 2,145 Passagiere (750 Erste Klaße, 545 Zweite Klaße und 850 Dritte Klaße). Nach dem Ersten Weltkrieg haben die Engländer die schöne "S/S Bismarck" von Deutschland leider beschlagnahmt. Sie ist am 29. September 1940 in Rosyth (Schottland) ausgebrannt.*

2-3.) The container ships "S/S Hamburg Express" (1972) and "S/S Tokio Express" (1972) each displace up to 55,600 tons full load, and were both absorbed into the merged HAPAG-Lloyd shipping line after the fusion with the North German Lloyd of Bremen in 1970. They were likely launched by 1970, but not commissioned and placed into active service until 1972. "Tokio" is the German spelling of the Japanese city of Toyko, which is the most populous metropolitan area on earth.

*Die beiden Containerschiffe "S/S Hamburg Express" (1972) und "S/S Tokio Express" (1972) haben eine Einsatzverdrängung von je 55,600 Tonnen. Die zwei Schiffe gehören immer noch dem HAPAG-Lloyd.*

4.) The famous passenger liner "S/S Vaterland" (1914) displaced up to 54,282 tons full load, and was built by the Blohm & Voss A.G. Shipyard in Hamburg. "Vaterland" is of course the German name for "Fatherland." The ship was unfortunately confiscated by the Americans in 1917, when the United States declared war on the German Empire. She had been interned in the port of New York since the outbreak of World War One in 1914. This was the 1st ship owned by HAPAG to be named after the German Fatherland.

*Das berühmte und große Passagierschiff "S/S Vaterland" (1914) hatte eine Einsatzverdrängung von 54,282 Tonnen, und wurde von Blohm und Voss, A.G. in Hamburg gebaut. Das Schiff wurde von den Amerikanern im Jahre 1917 beschlagnahmt, als Amerika Krieg an Deutschland erklärte. Die "S/S Vaterland" wurde am Anfang des Ersten Weltkrieges im Jahre 1914 im Hafen von Neu York interniert.*

5.) The "S/S Imperator" (1913) displaced up 52,117 tons and was confiscated by the British in 1919 as war reparations for World War One. She was built by the A.G. Vulkan Shipyard in Hamburg. We must remember that shipping companies are just like any other private companies. Their unfortunate owners were financially ruined during two world wars, with many of their ships being confiscated in foreign ports, sunk by Allied navies and then with their surviving ships confiscated from them as war booty after the end of armed hostilities. This is yet another example of the cruelty and unfairness of war, and once again demonstrates just some of the horrific consequences of the reckless foreign policies pursued by Kaiser Wilhelm II in 1914 and by Adolf Hitler in 1939. This was the sole ship owned by HAPAG to be named "Imperator," which means "Emperor" in Latin.

*Das berühmte Passagierschiff "S/S Imperator" (1913) hatte eine Einsatzverdrängung von 52,117 Tonnen, und wurde von A.G. Vulkan in Hamburg gebaut. Das Schiff wurde von den Engländern nach dem Ersten Weltkrieg beschlagnahmt.*

6.) A new passenger liner named "S/S Vaterland" was commissioned in 1940. She displaced 41,000 tons full load, and was built by the Blohm & Voss A.G. Shipyard in Hamburg. She was bombed and sunk at her berth during an Allied air raid in 1944, raised and then scrapped in 1949. This was the 2nd ship owned by HAPAG to be named after the German Fatherland.

*Das zweite Passagierschiff "S/S Vaterland" (1940) hatte eine Einsatzverdrängung von 41,000 Tonnen, und wurde bei Blohm und Voss A.G. in Hamburg gebaut. Das Schiff wurde in einem Luftangriff auf Hamburg im Jahre 1944 versenkt, später aufgehoben, und endlich im Jahre 1949 verschrottet.*

7.) The container ship "S/S Sydney Express" (1970) displaces up to 33,100 tons full load, and was absorbed into the new merged HAPAG-Lloyd fleet after the corporate union with the North German Lloyd shipping line in 1970.

*Das Containerschiff "S/S Sydney Express" (1970) hat eine Einsatzverdrängung von 33,100 Tonnen, und gehört immer noch dem HAPAG-Lloyd.*

8.) The passenger liner "S/S Kaiserin Auguste Victoria" (1906) displaced up to 24,581 tons full load, and was built by the A.G. Vulkan Shipyard in Stettin, Pomerania. She was unfortunately confiscated by the British in 1919 as war reparations after World War One. She was named for the German Empress Kaiserin Augusta Victoria Friederike Luise Feodora Jenny of Schleswig-Holstein-Sonderburg-Augustenburg (1858-1921), who was the wife of German Emperor Kaiser Wilhelm II. The Kaiser of course led the Hohenzollern Dynasty, while his wife came from a branch of the Oldenburg Dynasty. The latter dynasty is the root of the Royal Houses of Denmark, Norway, Sweden, Greece, Russia, Schleswig-Holstein and of course the Grand Duchy of Oldenburg in Germany. Both Schleswig and Holstein used to be Duchies in Northern Germany, just South of the Danish border. This ship was the sole one owned by HAPAG to be named after the Empress of Germany.

*Das Passagierschiff "S/S Kaiserin Auguste Victoria" (1906) hatte eine Einsatzverdrängung von 24,581 Tonnen, und wurde bei A.G. Vulkan in Stettin (Hinterpommern) gebaut. Das Schiff wurde von den Engländern nach dem Ersten Weltkrieg im Jahre 1919 leider beschlagnahmt. Kaiserin Augusta Victoria Friederike Luise Feodora Jenny von Schleswig-Holstein-Sonderburg-Augustenburg (1858-1921) war die erste Ehefrau von Kaiser Wilhelm II. Schleswig-Holstein-Sonderburg-Augustenburg gehört das Haus Oldenburg. Die Monarchen von Dänemark, Norwegen, Schweden, Griechenland, Rußland, Schleswig-Holstein und natürlich auch Oldenburg stammen aus dem Großherzogtum Oldenburg in Nordwestdeutschland.*

9.) The passenger liner "S/S Amerika" (1905) displaced up to 22,225 tons full load, and was built by the Harland & Wolff, Limited Shipyard in Belfast, Northern Ireland. She was confiscated by the Americans in 1917, when US President Wilson and the United States Congress declared war upon Imperial Germany, Austria-Hungary, Bulgaria and the Ottoman Turkish Empire. She had been interned in the port of New York since the outbreak of World War One in 1914. She was the sole ship owned by HAPAG to be named after America.

*Das Passagierschiff "S/S Amerika" (1905) hatte eine Einsatzverdrängung von 22,225 Tonnen, und wurde bei Harland und Wolff, Limited in Belfast (Nordirland) gebaut. Das Schiff wurde leider von den Amerikanern im Jahre 1917 beschlagnahmt, als die Amerikaner Krieg an Deutschland, Österreich-Ungarn, Bulgarien und das Ottomanische Reich (die Türkei) erklärten. Die "S/S Amerika" wurde seit Anfang des Ersten Weltkrieges im Jahre 1914 im Hafen von Neu York interniert.*

10-13.) The 4 sister ships and passenger liners "S/S Albert Ballin" (1923), "S/S Deutschland" (1923), "S/S Hamburg" (1925) and "S/S New York" (1927) each displaced up to 21,455 tons, and were built by the Blohm & Voss Shipyard in Hamburg. Mr. Albert Ballin was a very talented German-Jewish executive who managed HAPAG from 1888 until his unfortunate suicide in 1918. He ended his own life in dispair, due to the fact that World War One had ruined his company financially. So many German ships had either been sunk or merely confiscated at war's end by the victorious and vindictive Western allies. The liner "Albert Ballin" survived World War Two, but was confiscated by the Soviet Union in 1949 as war reparations. She had been unfortunately renamed "S/S Hansa" by the Nazis in 1935, due to the fact that Albert Ballin was a German-Jew. She was the sole ship owned by HAPAG to be named after Mr. Ballin.

*Die vier Schwester-Passagierschiffe "S/S Albert Ballin" (1923), "S/S Deutschland" (1923), "S/S Hamburg" (1925) und "S/S New York" (1927) hatten eine Einsatzverdrängung von je 21,455 Tonnen, und wurden alle bei Blohm und Voss in Hamburg gebaut. Herr Albert Ballin war der begabte deutschjüdische Direktor HAPAG-Lloyds, der die Firma von 1888 bis 1918 geleitet hat. Im Jahre 1918 hatte er Selbstmord begangen, weil die Firma nach dem Ende des Ersten Weltkrieges ruiniert war. Das Passagierschiff "S/S Albert Ballin" wurde von den Nationalsozialisten im Jahre 1935 "S/S Hansa" wegen der Judenverfolgung umbenannt. Das Schiff überlebte den Zweiten Weltkrieg, und wurde von Sowjetrußland im Jahre 1949 beschlagnahmt.*

This "S/S Deutschland" was the 4th ship owned by HAPAG to be named after Germany. She was sunk at her berth in Lübeck during an Allied air raid in 1945, raised and then scrapped in 1948.

*Das Passagierschiff "S/S Deutschland" (1923) wurde bei einem Luftangriff auf Lübeck im Jahre 1945 versenkt, später geborgen und dann endlich im Jahre 1948 verschrottet.*

The liner "S/S Hamburg" survived World War Two, and was confiscated by the Soviet Union in 1950 as part of war reparations. She was the 2nd ship owned by HAPAG to be named after their home town of Hamburg, which is Germany's largest seaport.

*Das Passagierschiff "S/S Hamburg" (1925) hat der Zweite Weltkrieg überlebt, aber sie wurde von Sowjetrußland im Jahre 1950 beschlagnahmt.*

The liner "S/S New York" was sunk at her berth during an Allied air raid on Kiel in 1945, raised and then scrapped in 1948. She was the sole ship owned by HAPAG to be named after the great American city of New York.

*Das Passagierschiff "S/S New York" (1927) wurde bei einem Luftangriff auf Kiel im Jahre 1945 versenkt, später geborgen und dann im Jahre 1948 verschrottet.*

14-15.) The passenger liners "S/S Resolute" (1920) and "S/S Reliance" (1920) displaced up to 19,980 tons each, and were built by the Bremer Vulkan A.G. Shipyard in Vegesack and by the J.C. Tecklenborg A.G. Shipyard in Geestemünde (Bremerhaven), respectively. They were the sole ships owned by the HAPAG line to carry these English names. "S/S Resolute" was sold to new owners in 1935, and "S/S Reliance" was turned over the British as part of war reparations after her commissioning, returned to HAPAG in 1926, burned out due to an accidental fire in 1938 and then finally scrapped.

*Die zwei Passagierschiffe "S/S Resolute" (1920) und "S/S Reliance" (1920) hatten eine Einsatzverdrängung von je 19,980 Tonnen, und wurden bei dem Bremer Vulkan A.G. in Vegesack und von J.C. Tecklenborg in Geestemünde (in Bremerhaven, vormals "Wesermünde") gebaut. "S/S Resolute" wurde im Jahre 1935 verkauft. "S/S Reliance" wurde im Jahre 1938 verschrottet.*

16-17.) The passenger liners "S/S President Grant" (1907) and "S/S President Lincoln" (1907) each displaced up to 18,168 tons full load, and were both built by the Harland & Wolff, Limited Shipyard of Belfast, Northern Ireland. They were the sole ships owned by the HAPAG line to be named after these two American Presidents. They were both interned in the port of New York upon the outbreak of World War One in 1914, and unfortunately confiscated by the Americans upon their declaration of war upon Imperial Germany in 1917.

*Die beiden Passagierschiffe "S/S President Grant" (1907) und "S/S President Lincoln" (1907) hatten eine Einsatzverdrängung von je 18,168 Tonnen, und wurden bei Harland und Wolff, Limited in Belfast (Nordirland) gebaut. Sie waren im Hafen von Neu York am Anfang des Ersten Weltkrieges im Jahre 1914 interniert, und dann im Jahre 1917 von den Amerikanern beschlagnahmt. Die ehemaligen amerikanischen Präsidenten Grant und Lincoln gehörten zur Republikanischen Partei.*

18-19.) The passenger liners "S/S Cleveland" (1909) and "S/S Cincinnati" (1909) each displaced up to 16,960 tons full load, and were both built by the Blohm & Voss A.G. Shipyard in Hamburg. They were the sole ships owned by the HAPAG line to be named after the two cities in the State of Ohio. Many German immigrants settled in Ohio and other states of the American Midwest, and Americans of German ancestry are still the largest ethnic group in the USA. "S/S Cleveland" was confiscated by the Americans as part of war reparations after World War One in 1919, but actually returned to HAPAG in 1926. She was removed from service in 1933 and scrapped shortly thereafter. "S/S Cincinnati" was interned in the port of Boston, Massachusetts upon the outbreak of World War One in 1914, and unfortunately confiscated by the Americans after their declaration of war upon Imperial Germany in 1917.

*Die beiden Passagierschiffe "S/S Cleveland" (1909) und "S/S Cincinnati" (1909) hatten eine Einsatzverdrängung von je 16,960 Tonnen, und wurden bei Blohm und Voss A.G. in Hamburg gebaut. Die zwei Städte Cleveland und Cincinnati liegen im US-Bundesland Ohio, wo viele Bürger deutscher Abstammung leben. Die Deutschamerikaner sind immer noch die größte Bevölkerungsgruppe der USA, mit einer Stärke von etwa 63,5 Millionen Menschen. Die "S/S Cleveland" wurde im Jahre 1933 verschrottet, und die "S/S Cincinnati" wurde von den Amerikanern im Jahre 1917 beschlagnahmt. Das Schiff "S/S Cincinnati" wurde im Hafen von Boston (US-Bundesland Massachusetts) am Anfang des Ersten Weltkrieges im Jahre 1914 interniert.*

20-21.) The passenger liners "S/S St. Louis" (1929) and "S/S Milwaukee" (1929) each displaced up to 16,732 tons full load, and were built by the Bremer Vulkan A.G. Shipyard in Vegesack and by the Blohm & Voss A.G. Shipyard in Hamburg, respectively. They were the sole ships owned by the HAPAG line to be named after the large respective cities in the American states of Missouri and Wisconsin. Both states have very large numbers of people of German descent. In fact, Wisconsin has the largest German population percentage of of any American state at an amazing 63%. "S/S St. Louis" was sunk at her berth in Kiel during an Allied air raid in 1944, raised in 1950 and then scrapped. "S/S Milwaukee" was unfortunately confiscated by the British in 1945 as part of war reparations after World War Two.

*Die beiden Passagierschiffe "S/S St. Louis" (1929) und "S/S Milwaukee" (1929) hatten eine Einsatzverdrängung von je 16,732 Tonnen, und wurden bei dem Bremer Vulkan A.G. in Vegesack (die "St. Louis") und bei Blohm und Voss A.G. in Hamburg auf Kiel gelegt (die "Milwaukee"). Die Stadt St. Louis liegt im US-Bundesstaat Missouri und die Stadt Milwaukee liegt im US-Bundesstaat Wisconsin. Sehr viele deutsche Einwanderer haben in Missouri und Wisconsin gesiedelt. Heute sind 63% der Bevölkerung Wisconsins deutscher Abstammung. Das Schiff "S/S St. Louis" wurde in einem Luftangriff auf Kiel im Jahre 1944 versenkt, später geborgen und dann im Jahre 1950 verschrottet. Das Schiff "S/S Milwaukee" wurde von den Engländern im Jahre 1945 leider beschlagnahmt.*

22.) The passenger liner "S/S Deutschland" (1900) displaced up to 16,703 tons full load, and was built by the A.G. Vulkan Shipyard in Stettin, Pomerania. She was thus the third ship owned by the HAPAG line to be named after Germany. She was renamed "S/S Victoria Luise" in 1911, and renamed yet again as "S/S Hansa" in 1920. She was removed from service in 1925, and scrapped shortly thereafter.

*Das Passagierschiff "S/S Deutschland" (1900) hatte eine Einsatzverdrängung von 16,703 Tonnen, und wurde bei der A.G. Vulkan in Stettin (Hinterpommern) gebaut. Sie war für HAPAG die zweite "S/S Deutschland." Das Schiff wurde von Sowjetrußland im Jahre 1946 leider beschlagnahmt.*

23.) The passenger liner "S/S Patria" (1938) displaced up to 16,595 tons full load, and was built by the Deutsche Werft A.G. Shipyard in Hamburg. She was thus the second ship owned by the HAPAG line to be named "Patria," which is the Latin word for "Fatherland." She was unfortunately confiscated by the Soviet Union in 1946 as part of war reparations after World War Two.

*Das Passagierschiff "S/S Patria" (1938) hatte eine Einsatzverdrängung von 16,595 Tonnen, und wurde bei der Deutschen Werft A.G. in Hamburg gebaut. Das Schiff wurde auch von Sowjetrußland im Jahre 1946 leider beschlagnahmt.*

24-25.) The container ships "S/S Elbe Express" (1968) and "S/S Alster Express" (1968) displace up to 14,071 tons full load, and were both taken into the new merged fleet of HAPAG-Lloyd upon the merger with the North German Lloyd shipping line in 1970. Each ship is named after a major German river which flows through the city of Hamburg.

*Die beiden Containerschiffe "S/S Elbe Express" (1968) und "S/S Alster Express" (1968) haben eine Einsatzverdrängung von je 14,071 Tonnen, und gehören immer noch dem HAPAG-Lloyd.*

26-29.) The four freighters "S/S Ludwigshafen" (1970), "S/S Erlangen" (1970), "S/S Leverkusen" (1970) and "S/S Hoechst" (1970) displace up to 13,073 tons each, and were all absorbed into the HAPAG-Lloyd fleet after the merger with the North German Lloyd shipping line. The first three vessels are named after German cities, while the fourth unit is named after a German corporation. "S/S Ludwigshafen" is the sole ship of her name ever to be owned by HAPAG, while "S/S Erlangen" is the second ship of her name to be owned by HAPAG. "S/S Leverkusen" is the third ship of her name to be owned by HAPAG, whereas "S/S Hoechst" is the second ship owned by HAPAG to be named after this famous German company.

*Die vier Frachter "S/S Ludwigshafen" (1970), "S/S Erlangen" (1970), "S/S Leverkusen" (1970) und "S/S Hoechst" (1970) haben eine Einsatzverdrängung von je 13,073 Tonnen. Die vier Schiffe gehören immer noch dem HAPAG-Lloyd.*

30-33.) The four passenger liners "S/S Pennsylvania" (1897), "S/S Pretoria" (1898), "S/S Patricia" (1899) and "S/S Graf Waldersee" (1899) displaced up to 13,023 tons each. "S/S Pennsylvania" (1897) was built by the Harland & Wolff, Limited Shipyard in Belfast, Northern Ireland, was interned in the port of New York upon the outbreak of World War One in 1914, and was unfortunately confiscated by the Americans upon their declaration of war upon Imperial Germany in 1917. She was the sole ship owned by HAPAG to be named after the American State of Pennsylvania, which received America's very first German immigrants in 1683. They were Amish members of the Mennonite religion, who unfortunately fled Germany due to religious persecution. They came from the City of Krefeld, and settled in Philadelphia to found Germantown, Pennsylvania.

*Die vier Passagierschiffe "S/S Pennsylvania" (1897), "S/S Pretoria" (1898), "S/S Patricia" (1899) und "S/S Graf Waldersee" (1899) hatten eine Einsatzverdrängung von je 13,023 Tonnen. Die "S/S Pennsylvania" wurde bei Harland und Wolff, Limited in Belfast (Nordirland) auf Kiel gelegt. Am Anfang des Ersten Weltkrieges im Jahre 1914 wurde sie im Hafen von Neu York interniert. Als die Amerikaner im Jahre 1917 Krieg an das Deutsche Reich erklärten, wurde sie leider beschlagnahmt. Die erste richtige "Gruppe" Einwanderer aus Deutschland sind im Jahre 1683 auf dem englischen Segelschiff "Concord" von Deutschland nach Philadelphia (im US-Bundesstaat Pennsylvanien) angekommen. Sie waren 13 Amish-Mennoniten Familien aus Krefeld, oder deutsche Baptisten, die "Germantown," Pennsylvanien am 6. Oktober 1683 gegründet haben. Heute gibt es 1,478,540 Mennoniten, 227,000 Amish-Mennoniten, 50,000 Hutterit-Mennoniten, 207,526 Brethren-Mennoniten und 620,987 Deutsche Baptisten. Diese Leute führen ein einfaches Leben, sind sehr religiös, sehr fleißig, sehr erfolgreich, und bestehen oft aus Familien mit vielen Kindern. Drei deutsche Männer (mit den Familiennamen Unger, Keffer und Volday) sind in Jamestown, Virginien im Jahre 1607 angesiedelt. Der Deutsche Peter Minnewit aus Wesel wurde als Governeur von Manhattan (Neu Amsterdam, später "New York" genannt) im Jahre 1626 ernannt. Nach 1664 war der Deutsche Jacob Leisler aus Frankfurt der neue Governeur von holländisch Neu Amsterdam. Einige Deutsche haben sich auch in den englischen Kolonien von Neu York, Maryland und Virginien vor 1683 angesiedelt. Auf Deutsch würde Maryland "Marialand" heißen, und Virginien "Jungfrauland."*

"S/S Pretoria" (1898) was built by the Blohm & Voss A.G. Shipyard in Hamburg, and was unfortunately confiscated by the Americans as part of war reparations after World War One in 1919. She was the sole ship owned by HAPAG to be named after the city in South Africa, which is a country home to many people of German descent. Roughly 40% of the Afrikaner population of South Africa is of German origin, being Calvinist Protestants who fled Europe due to religious persecution in the 17th century.

*Das Passagierschiff "S/S Pretoria" (1898) wurde bei Blohm und Voss A.G. in Hamburg auf Kiel gelegt, und wurde nach dem Ersten Weltkrieg im Jahre 1919 von den Amerikanern leider beschlagnahmt. Die Stadt Pretoria liegt in Südafrika. Die weiße Volksgruppe der "Afrikaner" oder "Kapholländer" ist etwa 40% deutscher Abstammung.*

"S/S Patricia" (1899) was built by the A.G. Vulkan Shipyard in Stettin, Pomerania. She was unfortunately confiscated by the Americans as part of war reparations after World War One in 1919. She was the 1st ship with this name owned by the HAPAG line.

*Das Passagierschiff "S/S Patricia" (1899) wurde bei der A.G. Vulkan in Stettin (Hinterpommern) auf Kiel gelegt, und wurde nach dem Ersten Weltkrieg im Jahre 1919 von den Amerikanern leider beschlagnahmt.*

"S/S Graf Waldersee" (1899) was built by the Blohm & Voss Shipyard in Hamburg. She was also unfortunately confiscated by the Americans as part of war reparations after World War One in 1919. She was the only ship owned by HAPAG to carry this particular name.

*Das Passagierschiff "S/S Graf Waldersee" (1899) wurde bei Blohm und Voss in Hamburg auf Kiel gelegt, und wurde nach dem Ersten Weltkrieg im Jahre 1919 von den Amerikanern leider auch beschlagnahmt.*

## "Norddeutscher Lloyd" (North German Lloyd)

The North German Lloyd operated 141 commercial vessels from the time of its establishment on February 20, 1857 until the corporate merger with HAPAG in 1970. The company was founded in Bremen, Germany by Messers. Hermann Heinrich Meyer and Eduard Crüsemann. Their ships sailed from Bremerhaven to ports such as New York, Baltimore, Savannah, Galveston, Havana, Rio de Janeiro, Marseille, Alexandria, Bangkok, Singapore, Hong Kong, Swatow, Shanghai, Manila, Cebu, Tokyo and Sydney. Employment totalled 22,000 people. The North German Lloyd was Germany's second largest shipping company, being surpassed only by the HAPAG shipping line of Hamburg.

*Der Norddeutsche Lloyd wurde von den Herren Hermann Heinrich Meyer und Eduard Crüsemann am 20. Februar 1857 in Bremen gegründet. Von 1857 bis zur Fusion mit HAPAG hatte der Norddeutsche Lloyd 141 Seefahrzeuge. Der Norddeutsche Lloyd war Deutschlands zweigrößte Reederei, mit 22,000 Angestellten in Bremen, Bremerhaven, Neu York, Baltimore, Savannah, Galveston, Havana, Rio de Janeiro, Marseille, Alexandria, Bangkok, Singapur, Hongkong, Swatow, Schanghai, Manila, Cebu, Tokio und Sydney.*

1.) Their largest ship was the passenger liner "S/S Europa" (1929), which displaced 49,746 tons. She was built by the Blohm & Voss Shipyard in Hamburg, and was the first "S/S Europa to be commissioned by the North German Lloyd. The German Navy took this ship over during World War Two, and planned to convert it into an auxiliary aircraft carrier. Had she been coverted into a carrier, her displacement would have been increased to 56,500 tons full load. She could make up to 26,5 knots and had a range of 10,000 nautical miles. She was to have been armed with 42 combat aircraft, including 24 Messerschmitt Bf-109 Fighters and 18 Junkers Ju-87 Dive Bombers.  After World War Two she was confiscated by the French as war reparations, where she was renamed "S/S Liberte."  She was finally scrapped in 1962.

*Das Passagierschiff "S/S Europa" (1929) war das größte Schiff des Norddeutschen Lloyds, und hatte eine Einsatzverdrängung von 49,746 Tonnen. Das Schiff wurde bei Blohm und Voss in Hamburg gebaut.  Während des Zweiten Weltkrieges hatte die Deutsche Kriegsmarine es vor, die "S/S Europa" als Hilfsflugzeugträger umzubauen.  Leider wurde das nie gemacht, weil die Marine auf Hitlers "Rangliste" immer ganz am Ende war.  Die SS, das Wehrmacht-Heer und die Luftwaffe waren für Hitler und seine Regierung immer wichtiger als die Kriegsmarine.  Aber in Wirklichkeit war die Deutsche Kriegsmarine doch allerwichtig.  Die Amerikaner, die Engländer und die Sowjetrußen haben das Deutsche Reich immer als den mächtigsen Feind gesehen – noch stärker und gefährlicher als Japan.  Die Amerikaner aber besonders die Engländer haben die Deutsche Kriegsmarine, und besonders die deutsche Unterseebootwaffe als Hauptfeind gesehen – gefährlicher als die Waffen-SS, das Wehrmacht-Heer und die Luftwaffe zusammen.  Der geplante Hilfsflugzeugträger "Europa" (1942) sollte eine Einsatzverdrängung von 56,500 Tonnen haben – d.h. mehr als die "Tirpitz" oder die "Bismarck."  Sie hatte eine maximale Geschwindigkeit von 26,5 Knoten und eine Reichweite von 10,000 Seemeilen.  Sie sollte mit 42 Flugzeugen (24 Messerschmitt Bf-109 Jagdflugzeuge und 18 Junkers Ju-87 Sturzkampfbombenflugzeuge mit Torpedos) bewaffnet sein.  Nach dem Zweiten Weltkrieg wurde die "S/S Europa" von den Franzosen leider beschlagnahmt, und als "S/S Liberte" umbenannt.  Sie wurde endlich im Jahre 1962 verschrottet.*

2.)  The second largest ship in the history of the North German Lloyd was the passenger liner "S/S Bremen" (1929).  She was built by the A.G. Weser Shipyard in Bremen.  This particular "S/S Bremen" was the fourth ship of this name for the North German Lloyd.  She displaced 51,656 tons, and was destroyed due to an accidental fire in 1941.

*Das zweitgrößte Schiff des Norddeutschen Lloyds war die "S/S Bremen" (1929) mit einer Einsatzverdrängung von 51,656 Tonnen.  Dieses Passagierschiff wurde bei der A.G. Weser in Bremen gebaut, und war die vierte "Bremen" des Norddeutschen Lloyds.  Das Schiff verbrannte im Jahre 1941 und wurde kurz danach verschrottet.*

3.)  The third largest ship of the North German Lloyd was the passenger liner "S/S Columbus" (1914), which displaced up to 33,526 tons full load.  She was the first ship of the North German Lloyd to be named after the great explorer Christopher

Columbus, and was built by the F. Schichau Shipyard in Danzig, West Prussia. She was confiscated by the British in 1921 as war reparations, and renamed "S/S Homeric" in their service.

*Das drittgrößte Schiff des Norddeutschen Lloyds war das Passagierschiff "S/S Columbus" (1914). Sie hatte eine Einsatzverdrängung von 33,526 Tonnen, und wurde bei F. Schichau in Danzig (Westpreußen) gebaut. Sie wurde leider nach dem Ersten Weltkrieg von den Engländern im Jahre 1921 beschlagnahmt, und als "S/S Homeric" umbenannt.*

4.)  The fourth largest ship of the North German Lloyd was the passenger liner "S/S Columbus" (1924), which displaced 32,354 tons.  She was built by the F. Schichau Shipyard of Danzig, West Prussia, and was the second passenger liner of the North German Lloyd to carry this great name.  She was unfortunately overseas upon the start of World War Two in September 1939.  She tried to make a run for Germany from the Mexican port of Veracruz, but was hunted down by a British destroyer in late 1939.  Her crew scuttled her before the British were able to board her, and all her men except two were rescued by an American cruiser. They were taken to Ellis Island next to New York City (technically in New Jersey), after which most of the men traveled by train to San Francisco.  Some of the men with valid immigration papers chose to remain in the United States. After detention on Angel Island in San Francisco Bay, the men sailed to Japan – then an ally of Germany.  While in Japan, many of the men fought for the German war effort by serving aboard merchant ships, armed auxiliary cruisers and even submarines.  Some of the men even made it back to Germany aboard such vessels.  One of these was the armed merchantman "Anneliese Essberger," which managed to sail from Japan to German-occupied France in 1941.

*Das viertgrößte Schiff des Norddeutschen Lloyds war das Passagierschiff "S/S Columbus" (1924) mit einer Einsatzverdrängung von 32,354 Tonnen.  Sie wurde bei F. Schichau in Danzig (Westpreußen) gebaut, und war die zweite "Columbus" des Norddeutschen Lloyds.  Am Anfang des Zweiten Weltkrieges war sie leider in Veracruz, Mexiko.  Sie versuchte nach Deutschland zurückzukehren, aber leider ist das nicht gelungen.  Sie hat sich selbst versenkt, weil sie sich nicht an einen Englischen Zerstörer übergeben wollte.  Ihre Mannschaft wurde von einem Amerikanischen Kreuzer gerettet, und wurde nach Ellis-Insel (im Hafen von Neu York) gebracht.  Dann sind die meisten Besatzungsmitglieder nach San Francisco (in Kalifornien) mit der Eisenbahn gereist.  Danach sind die Deutschen Seemänner nach Japan gereist, wo sie auf deutschen Hilfskreuzern und Unterseebooten im Zweiten Weltkrieg gedient haben.  Dem deutschen Dampfer*

*"S/S Anneliese Essberger" ist es gelungen Frankreich von Japan im Jahre 1941 zu erreichen.*

5.)  The fifth largest ship of the North German Lloyd was the fifth passenger liner named "T/S Bremen" (1939) by them, after the Hanseatic City of Bremen in Northern Germany.  She was built by the Chantiers et Ateliers de St. Nazaire Shipyard in France.  She displaced 32,336 tons, and it was aboard this ship that my parents and I sailed from New York to Bremerhaven and back in 1967.  She was originally known as the "T/S Pasteur" while in French service.  The North German Lloyd purchased her in 1959.  While on her way to the breakers in Taiwan in 1980, the "Bremen" unfortunately sunk in the Indian Ocean.  The prefix "T/S" stands for "Turbine Ship."

*Das fünfgrößte Schiff des Norddeutschen Lloyds war das Passagierschiff "T/S Bremen" (1939).  Sie hatte eine Einsatzverdrängung von 32,336 Tonnen, und wurde bei Chantiers et Ateliers de Sankt Nazaire (in Frankreich) gebaut.  Sie war die fünfte "Bremen" des Norddeutschen Lloyds, und wurde im Jahre 1959 von den Franzosen gekauft.  Die drei anderen "Bremen" des Norddeutschen Lloyds wurden in den Jahren 1858, 1897 und 1922 getauft.  Im Jahre 1967 sind meine Eltern und ich von Neuyork nach Bremerhaven und zurück auf dem Turbinenschiff "T/S Bremen" gereist.  "T/S" bedeutet "Turbinenschiff," und "S/S" bedeutet "Dampfschiff" auf Englisch.*

**Passagierschiff / Passenger Liner "T/S Bremen" (1939) – Nonnenkamp Family Archives (as seen in 1967)**

6.) The passenger liner "S/S George Washington" (1909) displaced 25,570 tons. She was built by the A.G. Vulcan Shipyard in Stettin, Pomerania. Like so many German vessels, she was unfortunately overseas when World War One began in 1914. The Americans confiscated her in 1917, when the United States declared war upon Germany.

*Das Passagierschiff "S/S George Washington" (1909) hatte eine Einsatzverdrängung von 25,570 Tonnen, und wurde von der A.G. Vulcan in Stettin (Hinterpommern) gebaut. Sie war leider am Anfang des Ersten Weltkrieges in Amerika interniert, wie so viele andere deutsche Schiffe. Die Kaiserliche Marine Deutschlands war leider nicht groß genug, die Meere der Welt zu beherrschen. Damals hatte das Deutsche Reich nach England die zweitgrößte Marine der Welt. Die "George Washington" wurde von den Amerikanern im Jahre 1917 beschlagnahmt, als Amerika Krieg an das Deutsche Reich erklärte. George Washington war General und Feldherr während des amerikanischen Unabhängigkeitskrieges (1774 bis 1783), und der erste Präsident der USA von 1789 bis 1797. Er und sein Vizepräsident John Adams gehörten der Föderalistischen Partei an, Vorgänger der heutigen Republikanischen Partei. George Washington kam aus dem US-Bundesstaat Virginien, und John Adams kam aus dem US-Bundesstaat Massachusetts.*

7.) A new passenger liner named "S/S Europa" was commissioned in 1953. She displaces 21,514 tons and still exists today. She was built by De Schelde N.V. Shipyard in Vlissingen, the Netherlands. Originally, she was known as "S/S Kungsholm." In 1965, she was purchased by the North German Lloyd. In 1970, she was absorbed into the fleet of HAPAG-Lloyd after their merger with the North German Lloyd. She was the 2nd ship to be named "S/S Europa" by the North German Lloyd.

*Das zweite Passagierschiff "S/S Europa" (1953) hat eine Einsatzverdrängung von 21,514 Tonnen, und wurde bei De Schelde N.V. in Vlissingen (Niederlande) gebaut. Sie wurde von den Holländern im Jahre 1965 gekauft, und gehört seit 1970 dem HAPAG-Lloyd.*

8.) The passenger liner "S/S Kaiser Wilhelm II" (1903) displaced 19,361 tons full load. She was built by AG Vulcan in Stettin, Pomerania, which has been part of modern Poland since May 1945. She was interned in the port of New York upon the start of World War One in August 1914, and finally confiscated by the USA upon the American declaration of war upon Imperial Germany in April 1917. She was of course named after the German Emperor William II of the Hohenzollern Dynasty of Brandenburg-Prussia, who reigned from 1888 until his abdication in

November 1918. She was the second ship of the North German Lloyd to be named after Kaiser Wilhelm II.

*Das Passagierschiff "S/S Kaiser Wilhelm II" (1903) hatte eine Einsatzverdrängung von 19,361 Tonnen, und wurde bei der A.G. Vulkan in Stettin (Hinterpommern) gebaut. Sie wurde am Anfang des Ersten Weltkrieges im Hafen von Neu York interniert, und dann im Jahre 1917 von den Amerikanern beschlagnahmt.*

9.) The passenger liner "S/S Kronprinzessin Cecilie" (1907) displaced 19,360 tons full load, and was a sister ship of "S/S Kaiser Wilhelm II." She was built by AG Vulkan in Stettin, Pomerania, which is situated on the Baltic Sea coast. She was named after the wife of Crown Prince William of the Hohenzollern Dynasty, who would have become German Emperor "Kaiser Wilhelm III" upon the death of his father in 1941 – had the Royal family not been forced to abdicate in November 1918. This ship was interned in the port of Boston, Massachusetts upon the outbreak of World War One in August 1914, and finally confiscated by the USA upon the American declaration of war upon Imperial Germany in April 1917.

*Das Passagierschiff "S/S Kronprinzessin Cecilie" (1907) hatte eine Einsatzverdrängung von 19,360 Tonnen, und wurde bei der A.G. Vulkan in Stettin (Hinterpommern) gebaut. Kronprinzessin Cecilie war die Ehefrau von Kronprinz Wilhelm von Brandenburg-Preußen. Sein Vater Kaiser Wilhelm II von Brandenburg-Preußen ist in Holland im Jahre 1941 gestorben, und Kronprinz Wilhelm ist in Deutschland im Jahre 1951 gestorben. Das Schiff wurde am Anfang des Ersten Weltkrieges im Hafen von Boston (US-Bundesstaat Massachusetts) interniert, und dann von den Amerikanern im Jahre 1917 beschlagnahmt.*

10.) The passenger liner "S/S München" (1920) displaced 18,940 tons full load, and was built at the AG Weser yard in Bremen, Germany (the second largest seaport in Germany after Hamburg). She was named after the city of Munich, which is the capital of the German State of Bavaria. She was the 1st ship of the North German Lloyd to be named after the city of Munich. In 1923, she was confiscated by the United Kingdom as delayed war reparations for World War One, and renamed "S/S Ohio."

*Das Passagierschiff "S/S München" (1920) hatte eine Einsatzverdrängung von 18,940 Tonnen, und wurde bei der A.G. Weser in Bremen gebaut. Sie wurde nach dem Ersten Weltkrieg im Jahre 1923 von den Engländern leider beschlagnahmt.*

11.) The passenger liner "S/S Berlin" (1925) displaced 18,600 tons full load, and was built by Armstrong, Whitworth & Company in Newcastle (the United Kingdom). She served until 1966, when she was scrapped. She was the fourth ship of the North German Lloyd to be named after the city of Berlin. Berlin has been the capital of modern Germany since 1871, and was the capital of the Kingdom of Prussia since 1701. Originally, she had been known as "S/S Gripsholm." The North German Lloyd purchased her in 1955, where she served for 11 years.

*Das Passagierschiff "S/S Berlin" (1925) hatte eine Einsatzverdrängung von 18,600 Tonnen, und wurde bei Armstrong, Whitworth and Company in Newcastle (England) gebaut. Sie diente bis 1966, und wurde danach verschrottet. Sie war die vierte "Berlin" des Norddeutschen Lloyds.*

12.) The passenger liner "S/S Scharnhorst" (1935) displaced up to 18,184 tons full load, and was built by the A.G. Weser Shipyard in Bremen. She was interned in the port of Kobe, Japan in 1939 due to outbreak of World War Two, and then purchased by the Japanese in 1942. The Japanese coverted her into an auxiliary aircraft carrier, in which role she was sunk by the American submarine "U.S.S. Spadefish" Northeast of Shanghai, China on November 17, 1944. She was the second "S/S Scharnhorst" to be commissioned by the North German Lloyd, and was named after a great general of the Prussian Army. He was one of the Prussian leaders who was instrumental in creating the modern Prussian-German General Staff.

*Das Passagierschiff "S/S Scharnhorst" (1935) hatte eine Einsatzverdrängung von 18,184 Tonnen, und wurde bei der A.G. Weser in Bremen gebaut. Sie wurde von den Japanern im Jahre 1942 gekauft, weil sie am Anfang des Zweiten Weltkrieges im Hafen von Kobe lag. Die Japanische Marine hat sie zu einem Hilfsflugzeugträger umgebaut. Sie wurde am 17. November 1944 vor Schanghai von dem amerikanischen Unterseeboot "U.S.S. Spadefish" torpediert.*

13.) The passenger liner "S/S Gneisenau" (1935) displaced up to 18,160 tons full load, and was built by the A.G. Weser Shipyard in Bremen. She was sunk by a mine in the Baltic Sea on May 2, 1943. Before this, the German Navy wanted to convert her into an auxiliary aircraft carrier. She could make up to 21 knots, and had a range of 9,000 nautical miles. Had she ever been coverted into a carrier, she would have been armed with 24 combat aircraft (including 12 Messerschmitt Me-109 Fighters and 12 Junkers Ju-87 Dive Bombers). She was the 2nd "S/S Gneisenau" to be commissioned by the North German Lloyd, and was named after another great general of the Prussian Army.  He was a contemporary of Scharnhorst.

*Das Passagierschiff "S/S Gneisenau" (1935) hatte eine Einsatzverdrängung von 18,160 Tonnen, und wurde bei der A.G. Weser in Bremen gebaut.  Sie wurde leider am 2. Mai 1943 von einem Minentreffer in der Ostsee gesunken.  Vorher wollte die Deutsche Kriegsmarine die "S/S Gneisenau" als einen Hilfsflugzeugträger umbauen, aber das ist leider nie geschehen.  Sie hatte eine maximale Geschwindigkeit von 21 Knoten, und eine Reichweite von 9,000 Seemeilen.  Als Flugzeugträger sollte sie mit 24 Flugzeugen bewaffnet werden (12 Messerschmitt Bf-109 Jagdflugzeuge und 12 Junkers Ju-87 Sturzkampfbombenflugzeuge mit Torpedos).*

14.)  The passenger liner "S/S Potsdam" (1935) displaced up to 17,528 tons full load, and was built by the Blohm & Voss Shipyard in Hamburg.  She was yet another passenger liner which the German Navy planned to convert into an auxiliary aircraft carrier, but did not.  She was confiscated by the British as war reparations as late as 1954, and was scrapped by 1976.  The planned coversion into a carrier would have raised her total displacement to 23,500 tons and given her 24 combat aircaft (12 Messerschmitt Me-109 Fighters and 12 Junkers Ju-87 Dive Bombers).  She could make up to 21 knots and had a range of 9,000 nautical miles.

*Das Passagierschiff "S/S Potsdam" (1935) hatte eine Einsatzverdrängung von 17,528 Tonnen, und wurde bei Blohm und Voss in Hamburg gebaut.  Die Deutsche Kriegsmarine hatte es auch vor, die "S/S Potsdam" als einen Hilfsflugzeugträger umzubauen, aber das ist auch leider nie geschehen.  Als Flugzeugträger sollte sie eine Einsatzverdrängung von 23,500 Tonnen haben.  Ihre maximale Geschwindigkeit war 21 Knoten, und sie hatte eine Reichweite von 9,000 Seemeilen.  Sie sollte mit 24 Flugzeugen bewaffnet werden (12 Messerschmitt Bf-109 Jagdflugzeuge und 12 Junkers Ju-87 Sturzkampfbombenflugzeuge mit Torpedos).  Das Schiff wurde von den Engländern im Jahre 1954 leider beschlagnahmt.  Nach dem Zweiten Weltkrieg ging es Großbrittanien eigentlich nicht gut – der Staat war pleite, und das Weltreich der Engländer wurde immer kleiner.  Im Jahre 1952 hatte schon Westdeutschland eine Wirtschaft so groß wie des Deutschen Reiches von 1937.*

15.)  The passenger liner "S/S Berlin" (1909) displaced up to 17,324 tons full load, and was built by the A.G. Weser Shipyard in Bremen.  She was the second passenger liner of the North German Lloyd to be named after the city of Berlin.

She was confiscated by the British as war reparations in 1919, and renamed "S/S Arabic" in British service.

*Das Passagierschiff "S/S Berlin" (1909) hatte eine Einsatzverdrängung von 17,324 Tonnen, und wurde bei der A.G. Weser in Bremen gebaut. Sie war die zweite "Berlin" des Norddeutschen Lloyds. Sie wurde nach dem Ersten Weltkrieg im Jahre 1919 von den Engländern beschlagnahmt, und als "S/S Arabic" umbenannt.*

16.) The passenger liner "S/S Prinz Friedrich Wilhelm" (1907) displaced up to 17,082 tons full load, and was built by the J.C. Tecklenborg A.G. Shipyard of Geestemünde. She was confiscated by the British as war reparations in 1919, where she was renamed "S/S Montlaurier."

*Das Passagierschiff "S/S Prinz Friedrich Wilhelm" (1907) hatte eine Einsatzverdrängung von 17,082 Tonnen, und wurde bei der J.C. Tecklenborg A.G. in Geestemünde (Bremerhaven, vormals "Wesermünde") gebaut. Sie wurde nach dem Ersten Weltkrieg im Jahre 1919 von den Engländern beschlagnahmt, und as "S/S Montlaurier" umbenannt.*

17.) The passenger line "S/S Berlin" (1925) displaced up to 15,286 tons full load, and was built by the Bremer Vulkan A.G. Shipyard in Vegesack. She was the third passenger liner of the North German Lloyd to be named after the city of Berlin. She was confiscated by the Soviet Union as war reparations in 1948, where she was renamed "S/S Admiral Nachimov."

*Das Passagierschiff "S/S Berlin" (1925) hatte eine Einsatzverdrängung von 15,286 Tonnen, und wurde bei der Bremer Vulkan A.G. in Vegesack gebaut. Sie war die dritte "Berlin" des Norddeutschen Lloyds. Sie wurde nach dem Zweiten Weltkrieg im Jahre 1948 von Sowjetrußland beschlagnahmt, und als "S/S Admiral Nachimov" umbenannt.*

18.) The passenger liner "S/S Kronprinz Wilhelm" (1901) displaced up to 14,908 tons full load, and was built by the A.G. Vulcan Shipyard in Stettin, Pomerania. She was named after the heir to the throne of Imperial Germany, who would have become German Emperor in 1941 upon the death of his father Kaiser Wilhelm II – had the monarchy not been abolished in November 1918. She was interned in the port of Newport News, Virginia in 1915, and confiscated by the Americans upon their declaration of war upon Germany and the Central Powers in 1917.

*Das Passagierschiff "S/S Kronprinz Wilhelm" (1901) hatte eine Einsatzverdrängung von 14,908 Tonnen, und wurde bei der A.G. Vulcan in Stettin (Hinterpommern) gebaut. Sie wurde im Hafen von Newport News, Virginien im Jahre 1915 interniert, und von den Amerikanern im Jahre 1917 beschlagnahmt.*

19.) The passenger liner "S/S Kaiser Wilhelm der Grosse" (1897) displaced up to 14,349 tons full load, and was built by the A.G. Vulcan Shipyard in Stettin, Pomerania. She was sunk very early in World War One by the British cruiser "H.M.S. Highflyer." She was named after German Emperor Kaiser Wilhelm I of the Hohenzollern Dynasty, who reigned from 1861 until his death in 1888.

*Das Passagierschiff "S/S Kaiser Wilhelm der Große" (1897) hatte eine Einsatzverdrängung von 14,349 Tonnen, und wurde bei der A.G. Vulcan in Stettin (Hinterpommern) gebaut. Sie wurde früh im Ersten Weltkrieg von dem Englischen Kreuzer "H.M.S. Highflyer" gesunken. Kaiser Wilhelm I "der Große" war der Vater von Kaiser Wilhelm II. Er war König von Brandenburg-Preußen von 1861 bis 1888, und Deutscher Kaiser von 1871 bis 1888.*

20.) The passenger liner "S/S Zeppelin" (1915) displaced up to 14,167 tons full load, and was built by the Bremer Vulkan A.G. Shipyard in Vegesack (which is a suburb of the city of Bremen). She was confiscated by the British in 1923 as war reparations, and renamed "S/S Ohio" in their service. Count Zeppelin was the man who designed the lighter-than-air ships which bore his name. The first generation of 132 airships were built starting before World War One until shortly before the start of World War Two. A new generation of safer and more sophisticated airships is being built today in the very same place – near Lake Constance, or the "Bodensee" in Southern Germany.

*Das Passagierschiff "S/S Zeppelin" (1915) hatte eine Einsatzverdrängung von 14,167 Tonnen, und wurde bei dem Bremer Vulkan A.G. in Vegesack gebaut. Sie wurde im Jahre 1923 von den Engländern nach dem Ersten Weltkrieg beschlagnahmt, und als "S/S Ohio" umbenannt. Bis 1938 wurden insgesamt 132 von den Zeppelin Luftschiffen gebaut. Vor und während des Ersten Weltkrieges wurden die Zeppelin Luftschiffe von der Kaiserlichen Marine benutzt.*

21.) The passenger liner "S/S Stuttgart" (1924) displaced up to 13,367 tons full load, and was built by the A.G. Vulcan Shipyard in Stettin, Pomerania. She was sunk by an Allied air attack while in the port city of Gotenhafen (now known as "Gdynia" in Poland) in West Prussia in 1943. She was the third ship of the North German Lloyd to be named after the city of Stuttgart, which used to be the capital of the old Duchy of Swabia in Southwestern Germany.

*Das Passagierschiff "S/S Stuttgart" (1924) hatte eine Einsatzverdrängung von 13,367 Tonnen, und wurde bei der A.G. Vulcan in Stettin (Hinterpommern) gebaut. Sie wurde in einem Luftangriff auf Gotenhafen im Jahre 1943 gesunken. Sie war die dritte "Stuttgart" des Norddeutschen Lloyds.*

22.) The passenger liner "S/S München" (1923) displaced up to 13,325 tons full load, and was built by the A.G. Vulcan Shipyard in Stettin, Pomerania. She was sunk by an Allied torpedo close to the end of World War Two in 1945. She was the third ship of the North German Lloyd to be named after the Bavarian capital city of Munich. She had been renamed by them as "S/S General von Steuben" in 1931 and again as "S/S Steuben" in 1938. General von Steuben was a Prussian Army general who emigrated to the United States, and who lead American Army troops during the Revolutionary War against Britain.

*Das Passagierschiff "S/S München" (1923) hatte eine Einsatzverdrängung von 13,325 Tonnen, und wurde bei der A.G. Vulcan in Stettin (Hinterpommern) gebaut. Sie wurde von den Alliierten kurz vor dem Ende des Zweiten Weltkrieges torpediert. Sie war die dritte "München" des Norddeutschen Lloyds," aber wurde als "S/S General von Steuben" im Jahre 1931 umbenannt. General von Steuben war Preußischer Heeresoffizier, der im Amerikanischen Befreiungskrieg (1774-1783) auf der Seite Amerikas gegen England gekämpft hatte.*

23.) The passenger liner "S/S Grosser Kurfürst" (1900) displaced up to 13,183 tons full load, and was built by the F. Schichau Shipyard in Danzig, West Prussia. She was interned in the port of New York upon the outbreak of World War One in 1914, and then confiscated by the Americans upon their declaration of war upon Imperial Germany and the nations of the Central Powers in 1917.

*Das Passagierschiff "S/S Großer Kurfürst" (1900) hatte eine Einsatzverdrängung von 13,183 Tonnen, und wurde bei F. Schichau in Danzig (Westpreußen) gebaut. Sie wurde im Hafen von Neu York am Anfang des Ersten Weltkrieges im Jahre 1914 interniert, und wurde von den Amerikanern im Jahre 1917 beschlagnahmt.*

24.) The passenger liner "S/S Kaiser Friedrich" (1898) displaced up to 12,481 tons full load, and was built by the F. Schichau Shipyard in Danzig, West Prussia. She was named after German Emperor Friedrich III, who reigned for a very short period in 1888 before he died of cancer. He was the son of Kaiser Wilhelm I "the Great" and the father of Kaiser Wilhelm II. This ship was actually sold before World War One to the French shipping line "Cie. de Navigation Sudatlantique," and renamed "S/S Burdigala" by its new owners.

*Das Passagierschiff "S/S Kaiser Friedrich" (1898) hatte eine Einsatzverdrängung von 12,481 Tonnen, und wurde bei F. Schichau in Danzig (Westpreußen) gebaut. Sie wurde nach dem Preußisch-Deutschen Kaiser Friedrich III benannt. Er war der Sohn von Kaiser Wilhelm I "der Große" und auch der Vater von Kaiser Wilhelm II. Er war Kaiser für nur ein paar Monate im Jahre 1888, weil er schon sehr krank war und leider an Krebs starb.*

25.) The passenger liner "S/S Sierra Cordoba" (1924) displaced up to 11,469 tons full load, and was built by the Bremer Vulkan A.G. Shipyard in Vegesack, which is a suburb of the city of Bremen. She was the second ship of the North German Lloyd to be named after this Spanish mountain range. She was confiscated by the British in 1946 as war reparations, and was destroyed in an accidental fire in 1948.

*Das Passagierschiff "S/S Sierra Cordoba" (1924) hatte eine Einsatzverdrängung von 11,469 Tonnen, und wurde beim Bremer Vulkan A.G. in Vegesack gebaut. Sie war die zweite "Sierra Cordoba" des Norddeutschen Lloyds. Sie wurde nach dem Zweiten Weltkrieg im Jahre 1946 von den Engländern beschlagnamt, und verbrannte im Jahre 1948.*

26.) The passenger line "S/S Sierra Morena" (1924) displaced up to 11,430 tons full load, and was built by the Bremer Vulkan A.G. Shipyard in Vegesack, which is a suburb of the Hanseatic City of Bremen. She was taken over by the National Socialist government organ "KdF" ("Kraft durch Freude" or "Strength through Joy" in English) and renamed "S/S Der Deutsche." "KdF" produced the Volkswagen Beetle from 1935 until 1945.

*Das Passagierschiff "S/S Sierra Morena" (1924) hatte eine Einsatzverdrängung von 11,430 Tonnen, und wurde beim Bremer Vulkan A.G. in Vegesack gebaut. Im Jahre 1933 wurde sie von der nationalsozialistischen "KdF" ("Kraft durch Freude") übernommen. Die KdF Organisation gehörte zur damaligen deutschen "Arbeitsfront" der NSDAP.*

27.) The passenger liner "S/S Sierra Ventana" (1923) displaced up to 11,392 tons full load, and was built by Bremer Vulkan A.G. in Vegesack, which is a suburb of the city of Bremen. She was the second ship of the North German Lloyd to be named after this particular mountain range in Spain. She was sold to new owners in 1935.

*Das Passagierschiff "S/S Sierra Ventana" (1923) hatte eine Einsatzverdrängung von 11,392 Tonnen, und wurde beim Bremer Vulkan A.G. in Vegesack gebaut.*

*Sie war die zweite "Sierra Ventana" des Norddeutschen Lloyds," und wurde im Jahre 1935 verkauft.*

28.) The passenger liner "S/S Princess Alice" (1900) displaced up to 10,911 tons full load, and was built by the A.G. Vulcan Shipyard in Stettin, Pomerania. She had been commissioned as "S/S Kiautschou" by the HAPAG Shipping line of Hamburg in 1900, and was purchased and renamed by the North German Lloyd of Bremen in 1904. Her initial name from HAPAG was in honor of Germany's Crown Colony in China. Unfortunately, she was in an American port in 1917, and was confiscated by the Americans upon their declaration of war upon Imperial Germany and the nations of the Central Powers Alliance (the other countries being Austria-Hungary, Bulgaria and the Ottoman Turkish Empire).

*Das Passagierschiff "S/S Princess Alice" (1900) hatte eine Einsatzverdrängung von 10,911 Tonnen, und wurde bei der A.G. Vulcan in Stettin (Hinterpommern) gebaut. Ursprünglich wurde sie "S/S Kiautschao" von der HAPAG getauft, und dann wurde sie an den Norddeutschen Lloyd verkauft. Sie wurde im Jahre 1917 von den Amerikanern beschlagnahmt. "Kiautschao" war die deutsche Kronkolonie in China – die Stadt Tsingtau und der Provinz Schantung.*

29.) The passenger liner "S/S Prinzess Irene" (1900) displaced up to 10,881 tons full load, and was built by the A.G. Vulcan Shipyard in Stettin, Pomerania. She was renamed "S/S Bremen" in 1923, thus becoming the 3rd vessel of the North German Lloyd to be named after their famous home town. In 1928, she was renamed yet again as "S/S Karlsruhe," becoming the second ship of the North German Lloyd to be named after the capital of the German State of Baden. She was scrapped in 1932, after 32 years of service to the North German Lloyd shipping line.

*Das Passagierschiff "S/S Prinzess Irene" (1900) hatte eine Einsatzverdrängung von 10,881 Tonnen, und wurde bei der A.G. Vulcan in Stettin (Hinterpommern) gebaut. Sie wurde als "S/S Bremen" im Jahre 1923 umbenannt, und war dadurch die dritte "Bremen" des Norddeutschen Lloyds. Im Jahre 1928 wurde sie dann als "S/S Karlsruhe" umbenannt. Die Stadt Karlsruhe war Hauptstadt des ehemaligen Großherzogtum Badens.*

30.) The passenger liner "S/S Barbarossa" (1897) displaced up to 10,769 tons full load, and was built by the Blohm & Voss A.G. Shipyard in Hamburg. She was interned in the port of New York upon the outbreak of World War One in 1914, and confiscated by the Americans upon their declaration of war upon Imperial

Germany in 1917. She was named after the former German Emperor Friedrich Barbaroßa ("Frederick the Red Beard" in English) from the Middle Ages.

*Das Passagierschiff "S/S Barbaroßa" (1897) hatte eine Einsatzverdrängung von 10,769 Tonnen, und wurde bei Blohm und Voss A.G. in Hamburg gebaut. Sie wurde am Anfang des Ersten Weltkrieges im Jahre 1914 im Hafen von Neu York interniert, und dann im Jahre 1917 von den Amerikanern beschlagnahmt. Friedrich I "Barbaroßa" war von März 1152 bis Juni 1190 Deutscher Kaiser. Bei seiner Krönung in Frankfurt und Aachen kamen die Farben "Schwarz-Rot-Gold" zum ersten Mal im Gebrauch. Er war auch Herzog von Schwaben, und gehörte zum Haus Hohenstaufen.*

31.) The passenger liner "S/S König Albert" (1899) displaced up to 10,643 tons full load, and was built by the A.G. Vulcan Shipyard in Stettin, Pomerania. She was interned in the port of Genoa, Italy upon the outbreak of World War One in 1914, and then confiscated by the Italians upon their declaration of war upon Austria-Hungary (Germany's ally) in 1915. She was named after King Albert of Saxony, a large Central German state.

*Das Passagierschiff "S/S König Albert" (1899) hatte eine Einsatzverdrängung von 10,463 Tonnen, und wurde bei der A.G. Vulcan in Stettin (Hinterpommern) gebaut. Sie war am Anfang des Ersten Weltkrieges im Jahre 1914 im Hafen von Genua interniert, und wurde dann von den Italienern im Jahre 1915 beschlagnahmt, als Italien Krieg an Österreich-Ungarn und Deuschland erklärte. Albert war von Oktober 1873 bis Juni 1902 König von Sachsen.*

32.) The passenger liner "S/S Königin Luise" (1897) displaced up to 10,566 tons full load, and was built by the A.G. Vulcan Shipyard in Stettin, Pomerania. She was confiscated by the British in 1919 as war reparations after World War One.

*Das Passagierschiff "S/S Königin Luise" (1897) hatte eine Einsatzverdrängung von 10,566 Tonnen, und wurde bei der A.G. Vulcan in Stettin (Hinterpommern) auf Kiel gelegt. Sie wurde im Jahre 1919 nach dem Ersten Weltkrieg von den Engländern beschlagnahmt.*

33.) The passenger liner "S/S Bremen" (1897) displaced up to 10,522 tons full load, and was built by the F. Schichau Shipyard in Danzig, West Prussia. She was the second ship of the North German Lloyd shipping line to be named after their home town. She was unfortunately confiscated by the British in 1919 as war reparations after World War One.

*Das Passagierschiff "S/S Bremen" (1897) hatte eine Einsatzverdrängung von 10,522 Tonnen, und wurde bei F. Schichau in Danzig (Westpreußen) auf Kiel gelegt. Sie war die zweite "Bremen" des Norddeutschen Lloyds, und wurde nach dem Ersten Weltkrieg im Jahre 1919 von den Engländern beschlagnahmt.*

34.) The passenger liner "S/S Friedrich der Grosse" (1896) displaced up to 10,531 tons full load, and was built by the A.G. Vulcan Shipyard in Stettin, Pomerania. She was named after the Prussian King Frederick the Great of the Hohenzollern Dynasty. She was interned in the port of New York upon the outbreak of World War One in 1914, and unfortunately confiscated by the Americans upon their declaration of war upon Imperial Germany in 1917.

*Das Passagierschiff "S/S Friedrich der Große" (1896) hatte eine Einsatzverdrängung von 10,531 Tonnen, und wurde bei der A.G. Vulcan in Stettin (Hinterpommern) auf Kiel gelegt. Sie wurde am Anfang des Ersten Weltkrieges im Hafen von Neu York im Jahre 1914 interniert, und dann im Jahre 1917 von den Amerikanern beschlagnahmt.*

35.) The passenger liner "S/S Main" (1900) displaced up to 10,067 tons full load, and was built by the Blohm & Voss Shipyard in Hamburg. She was named after the German river which flows through the city of Frankfurt. She was thus the second ship of the North German Lloyd to be named after this great river. She was interned in the port of Baltimore, Maryland upon the outbreak of World War One in 1914, and unfortunately confiscated by the Americans upon their declaration of war upon Imperial Germany in 1917.

*Das Passagierschiff "S/S Main" (1900) hatte eine Einsatzverdrängung von 10,067 Tonnen, und wurde bei Blohm und Voss in Hamburg auf Kiel gelegt. Sie war die zweite "Main" des Norddeutschen Lloyds. Am Anfang des Ersten Weltkrieges wurde sie im Hafen von Baltimore (US-Bundesstaat Maryland) interniert, und dann im Jahre 1917 von den Amerikanern beschlagnahmt.*

36.) The passenger liner "S/S Rhein" (1899) displaced up to 10,058 tons full load, and was built by the Blohm & Voss Shipyard in Hamburg. She was named after Germany's most famous river, which flows through cities such as Cologne and Bonn. She was also thus the second ship of the North German Lloyd to carry this great name. She was unfortunately confiscated by the British in 1919 as war reparations after World War One.

*Das Passagierschiff "S/S Rhein" (1899) hatte eine Einsatzverdrängung von 10,058 Tonnen, und wurde bei Blohm und Voss in Hamburg auf Kiel gelegt. Sie war die zweite "Rhein" des Norddeutschen Lloyds, und wurde nach dem Ersten Weltkrieg im Jahre 1919 von den Engländern beschlagnahmt.*

37.) The passenger liner "S/S Neckar" (1901) displaced up to 9,835 tons full load, and was built by the J.C. Tecklenborg A.G. Shipyard in Geestemünde, which is a suburb of Bremerhaven. She was interned in the port of Baltimore, Maryland upon the outbreak of World War One in 1914, and was unfortunately confiscated by the Americans upon their declaration of war upon Imperial Germany in 1917.

*Das Passagierschiff "S/S Neckar" (1901) hatte eine Einsatzverdrängung von 9,835 Tonnen, und wurde bei J.C. Tecklenborg A.G. in Geestemünde (in Bremerhaven, vormals "Wesermünde") auf Kiel gelegt. Sie wurde am Anfang des Ersten Weltkrieges im Jahre 1914 im Hafen von Baltimore (US-Bundesstaat Maryland) interniert, und dann im Jahre 1917 von den Amerikanern beschlagnahmt.*

38.) The passenger liner "S/S Prinz Ludwig" (1906) displaced up to 9,630 tons full load, and was built by the A.G. Vulcan Shipyard in Stettin, Pomerania. She was unfortunately confiscated by the British in 1920 as war reparations for World War One.

*Das Passagierschiff "S/S Prinz Ludwig" (1906) hatte eine Einsatzverdrängung von 9,630 Tonnen, und wurde bei der A.G. Vulcan in Stettin (Hinterpommern) auf Kiel gelegt. Sie wurde nach dem Ersten Weltkrieg im Jahre 1920 von den Engländern beschlagnahmt.*

39.) The passenger liner "S/S Crefeld" (1922) displaced up to 9,573 tons full load, and was built by the Flensburger Schiffbau-Gesellschaft in Schleswig-Holstein. She was named after the city of Crefeld (now spelled "Krefeld) in North Rhine-Westphalia, thus being the second ship owned by the North German Lloyd to be named after this city. She was interned in the port of Massaua, Eritrea upon the outbreak of World War Two in 1939 (then part of the Italian Colony of Somaliland and Ethiopia), and then scuttled by her crew in 1941 to prevent her from falling into British hands. The British had conquered all of Italian East Africa by November 27, 1941.

*Das Passagierschiff "S/S Crefeld" (1922) hatte eine Einsatzverdrängung von 9,573 Tonnen, und wurde bei der Flensburger Schiffbau-Gesellschaft in Schleswig-Holstein auf Kiel gelegt. Am Anfang des Zweiten Weltkrieges wurde sie im Hafen von Massaua, Eritrea (eine italienische Kolonie) interniert, und dann im Jahre 1941 selbst versenkt. Die Engländer haben Italienisch Ostafrika am 27. November 1941 erobert.*

40.) The passenger liner "S/S Fulda" (1924) displaced up to 9,492 tons full load, and was built by the A.G. Weser Shipyard in Bremen. She was named after the city of Fulda in the German State of Hesse, thus being the second ship owned by the North German Lloyd to be named after this city. She was interned in the port of Dairen in Northeast China upon the outbreak of World War Two in 1939, and then sold to Japan (an ally of Germany during World War Two) in 1940.

*Das Passagierschiff "S/S Fulda" (1924) hatte eine Einsatzverdrängung von 9,492 Tonnen, und wurde bei der A.G. Weser in Bremen auf Kiel gelegt. Sie war die zweite "Fulda" des Norddeutschen Lloyds. Am Anfang des Zweiten Weltkrieges wurde sie im Hafen von Dairen, China interniert (damals war Dairen von den Japanern besetzt), und dann im Jahre 1940 wurde sie an die Japaner verkauft.*

41.) The passenger liner "S/S Werra" (1923) displaced up to 9,475 tons full load, and was built by the A.G. Weser Shipyard in Bremen. She was named after a German river, which has its source in the mountains of the state of Thuringia in Central Germany. She was thus the second ship owned by the North German Lloyd to be named after the Werra River. She was sold to new owners in 1935.

*Das Passagierschiff "S/S Werra" (1923) hatte eine Einsatzverdrängung von 9,475 Tonnen, und wurde bei der A.G. Weser in Bremen auf Kiel gelegt. Sie war die zweite "Werra" des Norddeutschen Lloyds, und wurde im Jahre 1935 verkauft.*

42.) The passenger liner "S/S Weser" (1922) displaced up to 9,450 tons full load, and was built by the A.G. Weser Shipyard in Bremen. She was named after a river in Northwestern Germany, which flows through cities such as Bremen, Bremerhaven and Nordenham on the North Sea Coast. She was thus the third ship owned by the North German Lloyd to be named after their home town river. She was removed from service in 1933, and scrapped thereafter.

*Das Passagierschiff "S/S Weser" (1922) hatte eine Einsatzverdrängung von 9,450 Tonnen, und wurde bei der A.G. Weser in Bremen auf Kiel gelegt. Sie war die dritte "Weser" des Norddeutschen Lloyds, und wurde im Jahre 1933 verschrottet.*

43.) The passenger liner "S/S Coblenz" (1924) displaced up to 9,449 tons full load, and was built by the A.G. Weser Shipyard in Bremen. She was named after the city of Coblenz in the Rhineland-Palatinate (now spelled "Koblenz"), which is situated on both the Rhine and Mosel rivers. She was thus the second ship owned by the North German Lloyd to be named after the city of Koblenz. She was sold to new owners in 1935.

*Das Passagierschiff "S/S Coblenz" (1924) hatte eine Einsatzverdrängung von 9,449 Tonnen, und wurde bei der A.G. Weser in Bremen auf Kiel gelegt. Sie war die zweite "Coblenz" des Norddeutschen Lloyds, und wurde im Jahre 1935 verkauft.*

44.) The passenger liner "S/S Saarbrücken" (1924) displaced up to 9,429 tons full load, and was built by the A.G. Weser Shipyard in Bremen. She was named after the city of Saarbrücken in the Saarland, and was thus the sole ship of this name to be owned by the North German Lloyd. She was sold to new owners in 1935.

*Das Passagierschiff "S/S Saarbrücken" (1924) hatte eine Einsatzverdrängung von 9,429 Tonnen, und wurde bei der A.G. Weser in Bremen auf Kiel gelegt. Sie wurde im Jahre 1935 verkauft.*

45.) The passenger liner "S/S Trier" (1924) displaced up to 9,415 tons full load, and was built by the A.G. Weser Shipyard in Bremen. She was named after the City of Trier, which is situated on the River Mosel in the Rhineland-Palatinate. Trier is one of the oldest cities in Germany, having been founded by the Romans in 16 B.C. This vessel was thus the second ship owned by the North German Lloyd to be named after Trier. She was sold to new owners in 1936.

*Das Passagierschiff "S/S Trier" (1924) hatte eine Einsatzverdrängung von 9,415 Tonnen, und wurde bei der A.G. Weser in Bremen auf Kiel gelegt. Sie war die zweite "Trier" des Norddeutschen Lloyds, und wurde im Jahre 1936 verkauft. Trier ist eine der ältesten Städte, wenn nicht die älteste Stadt Deutschlands. Die Stadt wurde im Jahre 16 vor Christus von den Römern gegründet.*

46.) The passenger liner "S/S Köln" (1922) displaced up to 9,265 tons full load, and was built by the Bremer Vulkan A.G. Shipyard in Vegesack, which is a suburb of Bremen. She was named after the large German City of Cologne, which is located on the River Rhine in the State of North Rhine-Westphalia. Cologne proper is Germany's fourth largest city, but it forms the nucleus of Germany' largest metropolitan region – with more than 11,8 million inhabitants. It is also one of Germany's oldest cities, having been founded by the Romans in

38 B.C. "S/S Köln" was the third ship owned by the North German Lloyd to be named after the great city of Cologne. She was stranded by accident of the Norrland coast of Sweden (opposite Finland) in 1940, and scrapped thereafter.

*Das Passagierschiff "S/S Köln" (1922) hatte eine Einsatzverdrängung von 9,265 Tonnen, und wurde beim Bremer Vulkan A.G. in Vegesack auf Kiel gelegt. Sie war die dritte "Trier" des Norddeutschen Lloyds. Sie strandete vor der schwedischen Küste im Jahre 1940 und wurde kurz danach verschrottet. Die Stadt Köln ist Deutschlands viertgrößte Stadt, aber die Metropole Köln ist Deutschlands größte Metropole mit mehr als 11,8 Millionen Einwohnern. Köln ist auch eine der ältesten Städte Deutschlands, die im Jahre 38 vor Christus von den Römern gegründet wurde.*

47.) The passenger liner "S/S Derfflinger" (1908) displaced up to 9,060 tons full load, and was built by the F. Schichau Shipyard in Danzig, West Prussia. She was named after Georg von Derfflinger (1606-1695), who served as a Field Marshall in the Brandenburg-Prussian Army. She was the sole ship owned by the North German Lloyd to be named after him, was removed from service in 1932 and was scrapped shortly thereafter.

*Das Passagierschiff "S/S Derfflinger" (1908) hatte eine Einsatzverdrängung von 9,060 Tonnen, und wurde bei F. Schichau in Danzig (Westpreußen) auf Kiel gelegt. Das Schiff wurde im Jahre 1932 verschrottet. Georg von Derfflinger (1606-1695) war Feldmarschall von Brandenburg-Preußen.*

48.) The passenger liner "S/S Bülow" (1906) displaced up to 9,028 tons full load, and was built by the J.C. Tecklenborg A.G. Shipyard in Geestemünde, which is a suburb of Bremerhaven. She was named after Friedrich Wilhelm Freiherr von Bülow (1755-1816), who served as a Prussian General during the Napoleonic Wars. She was thus the sole ship owned by the North German Lloyd to be named after him. She was interned in the port of Lisbon, Portugal upon the outbreak of World War One in 1914, and unfortunately confiscated by the Portuguese upon their declaration of war upon Imperial Germany in 1916.

*Das Passagierschiff "S/S Bülow" (1906) hatte eine Einsatzverdrängung von 9,028 Tonnen, und wurde bei J.C. Tecklenborg A.G. in Geestemünde (in Bremerhaven, vormals "Wesermünde") auf Kiel gelegt. Am Anfang des Ersten Weltkrieges war das Schiff in Lissabon interniert, und dann im Jahre 1916 beschlagnahmt, als Portugal Krieg an das Deutsche Reich erklärte. Friedrich Wilhelm Freiherr von Bülow (1755-1816) war preußischer General während der napoleonischen Kriege.*

49.) The passenger liner "S/S Kleist" (1907) displaced up to 8,950 tons full load, and was built by the F. Schichau Shipyard in Danzig, West Prussia. She was named after Friedrich Graf Kleist von Nollendorf (1762-1823), a Prussian Field Marshal who served during the Napoleonic Wars. She was thus the sole ship owned by the North German Lloyd to be named after him. She was unfortunately confiscated by the British as war reparations in 1920 after World War One.

*Das Passagierschiff "S/S Kleist" (1907) hatte eine Einsatzverdrängung von 8,950 Tonnen, und wurde bei F. Schichau in Danzig (Westpreußen) auf Kiel gelegt. Das Schiff wurde nach dem Ersten Weltkrieg im Jahre 1920 von den Engländern beschlagnahmt. Friedrich Graf Kleist von Nollendorf (1762-1823) war preußischer Generalfeldmarschall während der napoleonischen Kriege.*

50.) The passenger liner "S/S Yorck (1906) displaced up to 8,901 tons full load, and was built by the F. Schichau Shipyard in Danzig, West Prussia. She was named after Hans David Ludwig Graf Yorck von Wartenburg (1759-1830), who served as a Prussian Field Marshall during the Napoleonic Wars. She was thus the only ship owned by the North German Lloyd to be named after him. She was taken out of service in 1933, and scrapped shortly thereafter.

*Das Passagierschiff "S/S Yorck" (1906) hatte eine Einsatzverdrängung von 8,901 Tonnen, und wurde bei F. Schichau in Danzig (Westpreußen) auf Kiel gelegt. Das Schiff wurde im Jahre 1933 verschrottet. Hans David Ludwig Graf Yorck von Wartenburg (1759-1830) war preußischer Generalfeldmarschall während der napoleonischen Kriege.*

51.) The passenger liner "S/S Prinz Eitel Friedrich" (1904) displaced up to 8,865 tons full load, and was built by the A.G. Vulcan Shipyard in Stettin, Pomerania. She was named after Prinz ("Prince") Eitel Friedrich of Prussia (1883-1942), who was a son of the German Emperor Kaiser Wilhelm II of the Hohenzollern Dynasty. She was thus the only ship owned by the North German Lloyd to be named after him. She was interned in the port of Newport News, Virginia in 1915, and unfortunately confiscated by the Americans upon their declaration of war upon Imperial Germany in 1917.

*Das Passagierschiff "S/S Prinz Eitel Friedrich" (1904) hatte eine Einsatzverdrängung von 8,865 Tonnen, und wurde bei der A.G. Vulcan in Stettin (Hinterpommern) auf Kiel gelegt. Am Anfang des Ersten Weltkrieges war das Schiff im Hafen von Newport News (US-Bundesstaat Virginien) interniert, und wurde dann im Jahre 1917 beschlagnahmt. Prinz Eitel Friedrich von Brandenburg-Preußen (1883-1942) war Sohn von Kaiser Wilhelm II.*

52.) The passenger liner "S/S Lützow" (1908) displaced up to 8,818 tons full load, and was built by the A.G. Weser Shipyard in Bremen. She was named after Ludwig Adolf Wilhelm Freiherr von Lützow (1782-1834), a Prussian Lieutenant General who served during the Napoleonic Wars. He became famous for establishing and leading the "Freikorps Lützow," a voluntary cavalry corps which served during the war against France. She was thus the only ship owned by the North German Lloyd to be named after him. She was taken out of service in 1932, and scrapped shortly thereafter.

*Das Passagierschiff "S/S Lützow" (1908) hatte eine Einsatzverdrängung von 8,818 Tonnen, und wurde bei der A.G. Weser in Bremen auf Kiel gelegt. Ludwig Adolf Wilhelm Freiherr von Lützow (1782-1834) war preußischer Generalleutnant während der napoleonischen Kriege. Berühmt war er als Kommandeur des "Freikorps Lützow," ein Freiwillige-Reiterkorps, das gegen die Franzosen gekämpft hatte.*

53. The passenger liner "S/S Goeben" (1907) displaced up to 8,792 tons full load, and was built by the A.G. Weser Shipyard in Bremen. She was named after August Karl von Goeben (1816-1880), a Prussian infantry General who served during the Franco-Prussian war of 1870-1871. She was thus the only ship owned by the North German Lloyd to be named after him. She was unfortunately confiscated by France as war reparations after World War One in 1920, and renamed "S/S Rousillon" in their service.

*Das Passagierschiff "S/S Goeben" (1907) hatte eine Einsatzverdrängung von 8,792 Tonnen, und wurde bei der A.G. Weser in Bremen auf Kiel gelegt. August Karl von Goeben (1816-1880) war preußischer Infanteriegeneral während des Deutsch-Französischen Krieges (1870-1871). Nach dem Ersten Weltkrieg im Jahre 1920 wurde das Schiff von den Franzosen beschlagnahmt, und als "S/S Rousillon" umbenannt.*

## "Österreichischer Lloyd" (Austrian Lloyd) and the "Austro-Americana" Shipping Line

1.) Österreichischer Lloyd Ship Management of Vienna, Austria (known in English as the Austrian Lloyd) has an even larger ship – the 123,000 ton bulk carrier "M/S Salzburg," which was commissioned in 1977. She can make up to 15,2 knots. Salzburg is both a city and a province within Austria; in the days of the Habsburg Monarchy, the province of Salzburg was a Duchy of the Habsburg family. The Austrian Lloyd is one of world's oldest existing shipping lines, having been founded in the city of Triest (now part of Italy) in 1836. Today, they operate a fleet of 37 commercial vessels. Prior to the outbreak World War One in 1914, the two large Austrian steamship companies (these being the Austrian Lloyd and the Austro-Americana Line) owned a grand total of 278 vessels. The prefix "M/S" stands for "Motor Ship."

*Österreichischer Lloyd Ship Management aus Wien hat das größte Schiff im deutschsprachigen Raum: das Containerschiff "M/S Salzburg" (1977) mit einer Einsatzverdrängung von 123,000 Tonnen. Sie hat eine maximale Geschwindigkeit von 15,2 Knoten. "M/S" bedeutet "Motorschiff." Vor 1919 hieß das Land Salzburg "das Herzogtum Salzburg." Der Österreichische Lloyd ist eine der ältesten Reedereien der Welt, die in Triest im Jahre 1836 gegründet wurde. Heute hat die Reederei 37 Handelsschiffe. Vor dem Ersten Weltkrieg hatte der Österreichische Lloyd und die Austro-Americana Linie insgesamt 278 Handelsschiffe.*

2.) The second largest ship of the Austrian Lloyd is the 66,157-ton bulk carrier "M/S Tirol," commissioned in 1976. Her top speed is 14 knots. The "Tyrol" (English spelling) is a province within modern Austria. The South Tyrol (or "Alto Adige" in Italian) has been part of Italy since the Treaty of Versailles ended the First World War in 1919. The modern South Tyrol is 74% German and Romansch speaking, and merely 26% Italian-speaking. Romansch is a small language more closely related to Latin than any other language now in use. Most Romansch-speakers reside in Southeastern Switzerland today.

*Das zweitgrößte Schiff des Österreichischen Lloyds ist das Containerschiff "M/S Tirol" (1976), mit einer Einsatzverdrängung von 66,157 Tonnen und einer maximalen Geschwindigkeit von 14 Knoten. Südtirol (gehört seit 1919 zu Italien) ist heute 74% Deutsch-und Dolomitenladinisch-sprachig, und nur 26% italienisch. Dolomitenladinisch ist eine romanische Sprache, die von 30,000 Menschen im Norden Italiens gesprochen wird. Dolomitenladinisch ist Rätoromanisch sehr ähnlich. Rätoromanisch wird in Graubünden (in der Schweiz) gesprochen. Nordtirol und Osttirol liegen in Österreich. Vor 1919 hieß Tirol "die Gefürstete Grafschaft Tirol und das Land Vorarlberg."*

3.) The third largest ship of the Austrian Lloyd today is the 44,600-ton multi-purpose bulk carrier "M/S Alberg," commissioned in 1978. Her maximum speed is 16 knots. She sails the high seas, going as far as Australia.

*Das drittgrößte Schiff des Österreichischen Lloyds ist das Containerschiff "M/S Arlberg" (1978) mit einer Einsatzverdrängung von 44,600 Tonnen und einer maximalen Geschwindigkeit von 16 Knoten. Die "Arlberg" ist ein Hochseeschiff das zwischen Europa und Australien verkehrt. Das Schiff wurde nach dem Arlberg Paß genannt, ein verkehrswichtiger Paß im Alpengebirge (1.793 Meter über dem Adriatischen Meeresspiegel) gelegen zwischen den modernen österreichischen Bundesländern Vorarlberg und Tirol. Der wirtschaftlichen Bedeutung entsprechend, tragen viele Orte an den Paßzugängen den Zusatz "am Alberg." Mit dem Tourismus am Alberg hat sich der Begriff auch als Marke für eine Tourismusregion (vor allem als Wintersportgebiet) etabliert.*

4.) The fourth largest ship of the Austrian Lloyd is a modern cruise liner named "M/V Orient Queen," of 16,000 tons maximum displacement and commissioned in 1968. She sails mostly in the Mediterranean Sea, from her home port in Lebanon. The prefix "M/V" stands for "Motor Vessel."

*Das viertgrößte Schiff des Österreichischen Lloyds ist das Passagierschiff / Vergnügungsdampfer "M/V Orient Queen" (1968) mit einer Einsatzverdrängung von 16,000 Tonnen. Sie ist hauptsächlich im Mittelmeer unterwegs, da ihr Heimathafen im Libanon liegt. "M/V" bedeutet "Motor Vessel" auf Englisch, oder "Motorfahrzeug" auf Deutsch. "Orient Queen" bedeutet "Königin des Morgenlandes / des Ostens" auf Deutsch.*

5.) The fifth largest vessel in the history of the Austrian Lloyd was never completed due to the sad outbreak of World War One. The passenger liner "S/S Kaiserin Elisabeth" was to have displaced 15,500 tons. She was to have been named after the assassinated Empress of Austria-Hungary, the late wife of then Emperor Francis Joseph I (who reigned from 1848 until his death in 1916). The beloved Empress "Sisi" was murdered by an anarchist while on holiday in Geneva, Switzerland in 1898. The incomplete ship to be named after her was scrapped on the slipway after World War One. The prefix "S/S" stands for "Steamship."

*Das fünfgrößte Schiff des Österreichischen Lloyds war das nie getaufte Passagierschiff "S/S Kaiserin Elisabeth." Sie sollte eine Einsatzverdrängung von 15,500 Tonnen haben, aber war wegen des Ersten Weltkrieges nie vom Stapel gelaufen. Elisabeth von Bayern war die beliebte Ehefrau des Kaisers Franz Josef I von Habsburg-Lothringen, die tragisch auf Urlaub in Genf von einem italienischen Anarchisten im Jahre 1898 ermordet wurde. Das Schiff wurde kurz nach dem Ersten Weltkrieg verschrottet.*

6.) The sixth largest civilian ship in the history of the Austria was the passenger liner "S/S Kaiser Franz Josef I" (1912), which displaced 12,567 tons. She belonged to the Austro-Americana Line, which was founded in the city of Triest in 1903. This was obviously a much newer shipping line compared to the Austrian Lloyd, which was founded all the way back in 1836. The Austro-Americana Line began passenger services from Triest to Messina, Naples, Palermo and New York in 1904. Service to South America began in 1907. After World War One, the Austro-Americana Line was confiscated by Italy and renamed the "Cosulich Line." They merged with another Italian shipping company in 1932, and the new merged firm was in turn bought out by "Italia Societa Anonima di Navigazione" in 1937.

*Das sechsgrößte Handelsschiff Österreichs war das Passagierschiff "S/S Kaiser Franz Josef I" (1912), mit einer Einsatzverdrängung von 12,567 Tonnen. Sie gehörte der Austro-Americana Linie, die in Triest im Jahre 1903 gegründet wurde. Die Austro-Americana Linie verkehrte zwischen Triest, Messina, Neapel, Palermo und Neu York sowie Südamerika. Nach dem Ersten Weltkrieg wurde die Austro-Americana Linie leider von den Italienern beschlagnahmt, und als "Cosulich Linie" umbenannt. Im Jahre 1937 wurde die Cosulich Linie von der Italia Societa Anonima di Navigazione gekauft.*

7.) The Austro-Americana Line commissioned the 11,464-ton passenger liner "S/S Polonia" in 1899, which was named for Poland. She was sold to HAPAG of Hamburg, Germany in 1914.

*Das siebtgrößte Handelsschiff Österreichs war das Passagierschiff "S/S Polonia" (1899), die mit einer Einsatzverdrängung von 11,464 Tonnen für Polen genannt wurde. Das Schiff wurde an die HAPAG im Jahre 1914 verkauft.*

8.) Austro-Americana commissioned the 10,237-ton passenger liner "S/S Canada" in 1898. She was also sold to HAPAG of Hamburg, Germany in 1914.

*Das achtgrößte Handelsschiff Österreichs war das Passagierschiff "S/S Canada" (1898) mit einer Einsatzverdrängung von 10,237 Tonnen. Sie wurde auch an die HAPAG im Jahre 1914 verkauft.*

9.) "S/S Gablonz" (1912) was commissioned by the Austrian Lloyd, and displaced 8,448 tons full load. She was confiscated by Italy in 1919 and renamed "S/S Tevere" in 1921.

*Das neuntgrößte Handelsschiff Österreichs war das Passagierschiff "S/S Gablonz" (1912) mit einer Einsatzverdrängung von 8,448 Tonnen. Nach dem Ersten Weltkrieg wurde sie leider von den Italienern im Jahre 1919 beschlagnahmt, und als "S/S Tevere" umbenannt. Die Stadt Gablonz an der*

*Neiße hat 44,822 Einwohner, und lag im kaiserlichen österreichischen Königreich Böhmen.*

10.) "S/S Marienbad" (1913) was a sister ship of "S/S Gablonz," also commissioned by the Austrian Lloyd and also displacing 8,448 tons full load. She was seized by the British in 1916, who turned her over to the French after World War One. In 1923, the French renamed her "S/S Pellerin de Latouche."

*Das Passagierschiff "S/S Marienbad" (1913) war ein Schwesterschiff der "S/S Gablonz" (1912), auch mit einer Einsatzverdrängung von 8,448 Tonnen. Die "Marienbad" wurde von den Engländern im Jahre 1916 erbeutet, und im Jahre 1923 an Frankreich gegeben. Die Franzosen hatten sie als "S/S Pellerin de Latouche" umbenannt. Die Stadt Marienbad hat 14,083 Einwohner, und lag auch im kaiserlichen österreichischen Königreich Böhmen.*

11.) "S/S Martha Washington" (1908) was commissioned by the Austro-Americana Line, and displaced 8,312 tons full load. She was interned in the port of New York upon the outbreak of World War One in 1914, and seized by the United States upon the US entry into the war in 1917. In 1932, she was turned over to the "Italia Line" of Italy, and renamed "S/S Tel Aviv." She was scrapped in 1934.

*Das Passagierschiff "S/S Martha Washington" (1908) gehörte der Austro-Americana Linie, und hatte eine Einsatzverdrängung von 8,312 Tonnen. Am Anfang des Ersten Weltkrieges wurde sie im Jahre 1914 im Hafen von Neu York interniert, und dann im Jahre 1917 von den Amerikanern beschlagnahmt. Die Amerikaner haben sie an die "Italia Linie" im Jahre 1932 verkauft, wo sie als "S/S Tel Aviv" umbenannt wurde. Sie wurde kurz danach im Jahre 1934 verschrottet. Martha Washington war die Ehefrau von George Washington. Tel Aviv ist heute die bevölkerungsreichste Stadt Israels. Vor 1948 war Israel die britische Kolonie "Palästina." Vor 1919 gehörte Palästina (sowie Libanon, Syrien, Irak, Koweit, Jemen und Bahrain) zum Türkisch-Ottomanische Reich. Im 19. Jahrhundert gehörten zum mohammedanisch Türkisch-Ottomanischen Reich auch Ägypten, Libyen, Bulgarien, die Wallachei, Moldawien, Griechenland, Albanien, Mazedonien, Serbien, Montenegro sowie Bosnien-Herzegowina.*

**"Donau Dampf-Schiff Gesellschaft" (Danube Steamship Company)**

Today, inland waterway shipping traffic in Austria is still handled by the "Donau Dampf-Schiff Gesellschaft" (DDSG), which is even older than the Austrian Lloyd, having been founded on March 13, 1829. "DDSG" means "Danube

Steamship Company" in English. By comparison, the Cunard Steamship Company of the UK was founded in 1841. HAPAG of Hamburg, Germany was founded in 1856 and the North German Lloyd of Bremen, Germany was founded in 1857.

*Die Donau Dampf-Schiff Gesellschaft (DDSG) ist noch älter als der Österreichische Lloyd. Die DDSG wurde am 13. März 1829 gegründet, und ist die älteste Reederei der Welt. In den Binnengewäßern Österreichs gibt es immer noch 190 aktive Handelsschiffe. Die bekanntesten Schiffe der DDSG ist das "Dampfschiff Schönbrunn," "M/S Stadt Wien," "M/S Stadt Passau," "M/S Vindobona" ("Vindobona" is lateinisch für Wien), "M/S Maria," "M/S Wachau" und "M/S Austria."*

Since 1983, the fleet of the Danube Steamship Company has included the likes of "Dampfschiff Schönbrunn" (named after one of the main Habsburg family palaces), "M/S Stadt Wien" (named after the Austrian capital city of Vienna), "M/S Stadt Passau" (named after the German city of Passau in Lower Bavaria, which is situated on the Danube River), "M/S Vindobona" (the Latin name for Vienna), "M/S Maria" (named after the Blessed Virgin Mary, the Mother of God), "M/S Wachau" (named after the valley Wachau in Lower Austria, which is situated on the Danube River) and "M/S Austria" (the Latin and English name of "Österreich" in German). These very fine small ships transport passengers in comfort among Austria's numerous inland waterways. The Danube Steamship Company's fleet consists of 190 inland waterway ships today.The term "Lloyd" for shipping companies comes from Lloyd's of London, which is one of the oldest insurance companies in the world.

## Chapter 9 (Kapitel Neun): Germany – an Industrial and Maritime Giant ("Wirtschaftsmacht und Seemacht Deutschland")

When one includes both ocean-going and inland-waterway commercial vessels, Germany has the 5th largest commercial fleet on earth (after Mainland China, Russia, the USA and the Netherlands). When one ranks just ocean-going fleets, Germany ranks 4th largest in the world (after Panama, Greece and Japan). Since the High Middle Ages (the 1300s), more than 63,000 vessels have been built in German and Austrian shipyards – both civilian and military. These include more than 25,000 fishing vessels, 10,000 merchantmen, 8,000 submarines, 7,000 fast attack craft, 3,000 minesweepers, 2,000 transport vessels, 1,000 torpedo boats, 1,000 auxiliary naval vessels and 1,000 sailing vessels.

*Deutschland ist heute bestimmt eine große Seemacht. Deutschland hat nach China, Rußland, Amerika und dem Niederland die fünfgrößte Handelsflotte der Welt. Die Hochseehandelsflotte Deutschlands ist nach Panama, Griechenland und Japan auf der Weltrangliste Nummer vier. Seit dem Hochmittelalter sind aus Deutschlands sowie Österreichs Werften mehr als 63.000 Seefahrzeuge vom Stapel gelaufen. Eingerechnet damit sind mehr als 25.000 Fischkutter, 10.000 Handelsschiffe, 8.000 Unterseeboote, 7.000 Schnellboote, 3.000 Minensuchboote, 2.000 Transportschiffe, 1.000 Torpedoboote, 1.000 Hilfskriegsschiffe sowie 1.000 Segelschiffe.*

Modern Germany is the undisputed "industrial locomotive" behind the European Union (EU). The European Union now has an economy even larger than that of the United States, with a Gross Domestic Product (GDP) worth in excess of US $16 trillion per year. Germany is nothing short of an economic superpower, albeit unfortunately still a "political dwarf" since May 7, 1945.

*Deutschland hat die größte Wirtschaft Europas, und Europas Wirtschaft ist nun größer als Amerikas Wirtschaft. Auf der Weltrangliste ist Europa Nummer eins, Amerika Nummer zwei, Japan Nummer drei, China Nummer vier, Kanada Nummer fünf, Brasilien Nummer sechs, Rußland Nummer sieben und Indien Nummer acht. Aber die Mitgliedschaft in der EU (Europäische Union) ist für Deutschland nicht zum Vorteil, und finanziell ist es zu kostspielig. Deutschland ist auch seit dem 7. Mai 1945 (der Waffenstillstand in Mitteleuropa) bedauerlicherweise ein "politischer Zwerg."*

By comparison, the nominal value of the Gross Domestic Product (GDP) of the United States is over US $13 Trillion per year. The USA now has the second largest economy in the world after the European Union (EU). Japan ranks third (over US $4 Trillion) and Mainland China is fourth (more than US $3 Trillion). Those remaining economies producing in excess of US $1 Trillion per year include Canada, Brazil, Russia and India.

### Why Commercial and Naval Fleets? / Warum eine Handelsmarine sowie eine Kriegsmarine?

The answer to this is simple: fully 90% of the goods in the world are transported by sea, and 95% of foreign trade is done by water. Without commercial and naval fleets, the world would return to the Stone Age – or worse. In the entire world today, there exist 297,256 civilian vessels (of these, 30,936 units are of more than 10,000 tons each – the rest go all the way down to small coastal and inland waterway units). These civilian vessels are protected by a mere 3,155 navy and coast guard vessels – and this figure includes both combat vessels and auxiliary vessels (active duty and reserve units included). One must keep in mind that auxiliary military vessels are more often than not former civilian vessels, not really meant for combat. They have little or no protective armor plating, little or no armament and often times even no electronic warfare capability (radar and sonar). Reserve combat vessels are usually old and obsolete – no match for their modern counterparts in armament, electronic countermeasures and/or speed. Among active duty military vessels, only combat ships (and usually not boats, with the exception of submarines) are suited for operations on the high seas of the world. The ratio of civilian to military vessels worldwide is thus an astounding 94 to 1, clearly demonstrating how vulnerable civilian maritime traffic can be to armed conflict, be it from hostile nation-states or due to piracy.

*Warum hat Deutschland eine große Handelsmarine, und warum soll Deutschland noch wieder eine große "Hochseeflotte," d.h. eine große Kriegsmarine haben? Die Antwort ist das Ausmaß des Außenhandels: 90 prozent aller Handelsgüter werden über die Meere, Seen und Flüße transportiert, und mit dem Außenhandel (noch wichtiger für Deutschland und Mitteleuropa) sind 95 prozent der Güter über die Gewäßer transportiert. Das Dasein einer Deutschen Handelsmarine und Deutschen Kriegsmarine erklärt sich deswegen von selbst. Ohne Welthandel im heutigen Maße würden wir uns in die Steinzeit versetzt fühlen. Weltweit gibt es heute 297,256 Handelsschiffe und Handelsboote. Davon haben 30,936 Schiffe mehr als je 10,000 Tonnen Einsatzverdrängung (Waßerverdrängung). Der großen Anzahl der Welthandelsflotte steht eine "Kriegsflotte" von nur 3,155 Einheiten gegenüber. Und außerdem sind einige Schiffe der internationalen "Kriegsflotte" überhaupt nicht "Gefechtsfähig." Nicht alle Hilfsschiffe, Einsatzgruppenversorger, Öltanker, Transportschiffe, Landungsschiffe, Aufklärungsschiffe, Minensuchboote sowie Schulschiffe sind völlig*

*Einsatzbereit. Zur Zeit der beiden Weltkriege (1914 bis 1918 und 1939 bis 1945) haben die sogenannten westlichen Allierten (hauptsächlich Großbrittanien und die Vereinigten Staaten von Amerika) den Handel mit Deutschland und Mitteleuropa, sowie Japan, leider zum großen Teil erfolgreich blockiert. Und heute haben wir wieder große "Piratenflotten" in Ländern wie Somalien in Ostafrika.*

The largest navy in the world today is of course the United States Navy, with 622 vessels of all types. 280 of these are active duty combat vessels. Ships in the American Navy are also larger compared to those of other modern navies. In fact, the gross tonnage of the American Navy is more than that of next 17 navies combined.

*Die größte Kriegsmarine der Welt seit 1942 ist die Marine der Vereinigten Staaten von Amerika. Die Amerikanische Marine hat heute 622 Seefahrzeuge, davon sind 280 aktive Kampfschiffe und Kampfboote, mit einer gesamten Waßerverdrängung größer als die der nächsten 17 Marineländer.*

The second largest navy in the world today is that of Russia, with 577 vessels of all types. In third place is Mainland China, with 265 vessels. Japan is in 4th place with 112 vessels. North Korea is in 5th place with 101 vessels, and India is in 6th place with 92 vessels. The Royal Navy of England is in 7th place with 91 commissioned vessels. The Royal Navy is obviously the second largest navy within NATO, or the North Atlantic Treaty Organization. France is in 8th place with 83 vessels and the German Navy is of course in 9th place with 76 commissioned vessels. France is no longer a "full member" of NATO, while the Federal Republic of Germany is.

*Die zweitgrößte Marine der Welt ist in Rußland, mit 577 Seefahrzeugen. Nummer drei ist China mit 265 Seefahrzeugen. Nummer vier ist Japan mit 112, Nummer fünf ist Nordkorea mit 101, Nummer sechs ist Indien mit 92, Nummer sieben ist Großbrittanien mit 91, und Nummer acht ist Frankreich mit 83 Seefahrzeugen. Auf der Weltrangliste steht die Bundesrepublik Deutschland auf Platz neun, mit 76 getauften Marineschiffen und Marinebooten. Innerhalb der NATO hat Deutschland nach Amerika und England die drittgrößte Marine. Frankreich ist seit 1966 kein volles NATO Mitglied. Aber wie auch bei der EU ist die NATO nicht von besonderen Vorteilen für Deutschland und Mitteleuropa. Deutschland und Mitteleuropa sollten auf guter und besserer Zusammenarbeit mit Rußland und Asien bauen. Der ehemalige "Dreikaiserbund" vom Deutschen Reich, Österreich-Ungarn und dem Tsarenreich könnte als Vorbild dienen. Fürst Otto von Bismarck sagte schon, daß die Zukunft Deutschlands im Osten liegt.*

Other modern navies rank as follows in terms of total commissioned combat and non-combat vessels: 10) Turkey (72 vessels), 11) Taiwan (71 vessels), 12) Italy (65 vessels), 13) South Korea (64 vessels), 14) Spain (57 vessels), 15) Indonesia (56 vessels), 16) Greece (49 vessels), 17) México (49 vessels), 18) Brazil (48 vessels), 19) Poland (31 vessels), 20) Argentina (29 vessels), 21) Iran (28 vessels), 22) Australia (27 vessels), 23) the Netherlands (25 vessels), 24) Pakistan (25 vessels), 25) Egypt (25 vessels), 26) Thailand (24 vessels), 27) Sweden (23 vessels), 28) Canada (22 vessels), 29) Chile (20 vessels), 30) the Ukraine (19 vessels), 31) Portugal (19 vessels), 32) Venezuela (17 vessels), 33) Romania (17 vessels), 34) Peru (16 vessels), 35) the Philippines (15 vessels), 36) Norway (15 vessels), 37) Denmark (14 vessels), 38) Colombia (14 vessels), 39) Malaysia (12 vessels), 40) Ecuador (12 vessels), 41) Saudi Arabia (11 vessels), 42) Singapore (11 vessels), 43) Vietnam (10 vessels), 44) South Africa (9 vessels), 45) Bangladesh (7 vessels), 46) Bulgaria (7 vessels), 47) Algeria (7 vessels), 48) Israel (7 vessels), 49) Oman (6 vessels), 50) Libya (6 vessels), 51) Uruguay (6 vessels), 52) New Zealand (5 vessels), 53) Finland (5 vessels), 54) Serbia (5 vessels), 55) Morocco (5 vessels), 56) Yemen (4 vessels), 57) Belgium (4 vessels), 58) Syria (3 vessels), 59) Ireland (3 vessels), 60) Myanmar (3 vessels), 61) the United Arab Emirates (3 vessels), 62) Austria-Croatia (3 vessels), 63 ) Cuba (2 vessels), 64) Kenya (2 vessels), 65) Mauritania (2 vessels), 66) Tunisia (2 vessels), 67) Albania (1 vessel), 68) Bahrain (1 vessel), 69) Ivory Coast (1 vessel), 70) Gabon (1 vessel), 71) Estonia (1 vessel), 72) Mauritius (1 vessel) and 73) Nigeria (1 vessel). The remaining 120 independent nation-states have no navy, but some others do have a coast guard.

*Andere Länder haben noch weniger Marinefahrzeuge. Die Turkei mit 72 Einheiten ist Nummer 10. Taiwan/Republik China mit 71 Einheiten ist Nummer 11. Italien mit 65 Einheiten ist Nummer 12. Südkorea mit 64 Einheiten ist Nummer 13. Spanien mit 57 Einheiten ist Nummer 14. Indonesien mit 56 Einheiten ist Nummer 15. Griechenland ist auf Platz 16 mit 49 Einheiten. Mexiko ist auch auf Platz 16 mit 49 Einheiten. Brasilien ist auf Platz 18 mit 48 Einheiten. Polen ist auf Platz 19 mit 31 Einheiten. Argentinien ist auf Platz 20 mit 29 Einheiten. Iran ist auf Platz 21 mit 28 Einheiten. Australien liegt auf Platz 22 mit 27 Einheiten. Die Niederlande liegen auf Platz 23 mit 25 Einheiten. Pakistan liegt auch auf Platz 23 mit 25 Einheiten. Ägypten liegt ebenfalls auf Platz 23 mit 25 Einheiten. Thailand liegt auf Platz 26 mit 24 Einheiten. Schweden mit 23 Einheiten kommt auf Platz 27. Kanada mit 22 Einheiten kommt auf Platz 28. Chile mit 20 Einheiten kommt auf Platz 29. Die Ukraine mit 19 Einheiten kommt auf Platz 30. Portugal mit 19 Einheiten kommt auch auf Platz 30. Venezuela / "Kleinvenedig" mit 17 Einheiten kommt auf Platz 32. Rumänien mit 17 Einheiten kommt auch auf Platz 32. Peru belegt Platz 34 mit 16 Einheiten. Die Philippinen belegen Platz 35 mit 15 Einheiten. Norwegen belegt auch Platz 35 mit 15 Einheiten. Dänemark belegt Platz 37 mit 14 Einheiten. Kolumbien belegt auch Platz 37 mit 14 Einheiten. Malaysien belegt Platz 39 mit 12 Einheiten. Ekuador belegt auch Platz 39 mit 12 Einheiten. Saudiarabien mit 11 Einheiten kommt auf Platz 41. Singapur mit 11 Einheiten kommt auch auf Platz 41. Vietnam mit 10 Einheiten kommt auf Platz 43. Südafrika mit 9 Einheiten kommt auf Platz 44. Bangladesch mit 7 Einheiten kommt auf Platz 45. Bulgarien mit 7 Einheiten kommt auch auf Platz 45. Algerien mit 7 Einheiten kommt ebenfalls auf Platz 45. Israel mit auch 7 Einheiten kommt gleichfalls auf Platz 45. Oman auf Platz 49 besitzt 6 Einheiten. Libyen auch auf Platz 49 besitzt auch 6 Einheiten. Uruguay ebenfalls auf Platz 49 besitzt 6 Einheiten. Neuseeland auf Platz 52 besitzt 5 Einheiten. Finnland findet sich auch auf Platz 52 mit 5 Einheiten. Serbien ist ebenfalls auf Platz 52 mit 5 Einheiten. Marokko ist gleichfalls auf Platz 52 mit 5 Einheiten. Jemen mit 4 Einheiten finden wir auf Platz 56. Belgien mit 4 Einheiten finden wir auch auf Platz 56. Syrien mit 3 Einheiten finden wir auf Platz 58. Irland mit 3 Einheiten finden wir auch auf Platz 58. Burma mit ebenfalls 3 Einheiten finden wir auch auf Platz 58. Die Vereinigten Arabischen Emirate mit 3 Einheiten finden wir gleichfalls auf Plazt 58. Kroatien / Österreich auch mit 3 Einheiten sind auch auf Platz 58. Kuba, Kenya, Mauretanien und Tunesien mit je 2 Einheiten teilen sich auf Platz 63. Albanien, Bahrain, die Elfenbeinküste, Gabun, Estland, Mauritius und Nigerien haben je ein Kriegsschiff und kommen zusammen auf Platz 67. Andere Länder haben keine Kreigsmarine, aber vielleicht doch einige kleine Küstenschutzboote.*

## "Kronkolonien des Reiches" (Crown Colonies of the Reich)

Germany had numerous good overseas colonies in Africa, including Großfriedrichsburg (modern Ghana), Arguin (in modern Mauretania from 1685-1721), Togoland (modern Togo from 1700-1914), Kamerun (modern Cameroon from 1884-1914), German South-West Africa (modern Namibia and part of modern Botswana from 1884-1915) and German East Africa (modern Tanzania, Burundi and Rwanda, plus "Wituland" in modern Kenya and the "Kionga Triangle" in modern Mozambique from 1885-1918). The Holy Roman Empire of the German Nation colonized Venezuela ("Kleinvenedig" in German or "Small Venice" in English) in the 16th century and Austria colonized such places as Delagoa Bay in East Africa (now part of Mozambique), Calebon (near Madras, India), Banquibazar (in West Bengal), the Nicobar Islands in the Indian Ocean, the Malabar Coast of India and Sabah (now part of Malaysia) between 1722 and 1783. Austria-Hungary also held the Chinese City of Tianjin from 1898-1914 and the uninhabited island group of Franz Josef Land in the Arctic Ocean (from 1873-1926).

*Deutschland hatte vor 1919 viele wertvolle Kolonien und Schutzgebiete. In Afrika hatte Deutschland Großfriedrichsburg (heute "Ghana"), Arguin (heute in Mauretanien), Togoland, Kamerun, Deutsch-Südwestafrika (heute "Namibien"), Deutschostafrika (heute Tansania, Burundi und Ruanda), Wituland (heute in Kenia) und das Kionga Dreieck (heute in Mosambik). In Südamerika hatte Deutschland Kleinvenedig (heute "Venezuela"). Österreich hatte Delagoabucht (heute in Mosambik), Calebon (in der Nähe von Madras in Indien), Banquibazar (in West-Bangladesch), die Nicobarinseln (im Indischen Ozean), die Malabarküste (in Indien), Sabah (heute in Malaysien), die Stadt Tianjin (in China) und das Franz-Josef Land (im Arktischen Ozean).*

Brandenburg-Prussia held the Island of St. Thomas in the Virgin Islands (1685-1720), Krabbeninsel ("Crab Island" in English and held from 1689-1693) and Tertholen (1696) in the Caribbean Sea. Grossfriedrichsburg was colonized by the Brandenburg-Prussian Sailing Frigates "S.M.S. Churprinz" and "S.M.S. Mohrian" on January 1, 1683, whereas the remaining German colonies in Africa and the Pacific region were colonized in the 1800s both by the Imperial German Navy and by German merchants such as Adolf Lüderitz and Carl Peters. In fact, there is still a coastal city in Namibia today named Lüderitz. The majority of the people in the Southern part of Namibia are Khoisan Blacks (formerly called "Hottentots"), while there is still a small minority of 45,000 German-speaking people. Half of Namibia's current Black population (about 1 million souls) belong to the Evangelical-Lutheran Church of Germany, their ancestors having been converted to Christianity by German missionaries in the 1800s. Namibia's capital city is the very German-looking city of Windhuk ("Windhoek" in the Cape Dutch dialect of Afrikaans). About 1 million people of German ancestry reside in South Africa today. The Germans there comprise about 40% of the white Afrikaner population, or about 23% of white South Africans.

*Brandenburg-Preußen hatte Sankt Thomas (in den Jungfrauinseln), Krabbeninsel und Tertholen im Karibischen Meer. Großfriedrichsburg in Westafrika wurde von den Brandenburgisch-Preußischen Segelfregatten "S.M.S. Churprinz" und "S.M.S. Mohrian" am 1. Januar 1683 kolonisiert. Deutsche Kaufmänner wie Adolf Lüderitz und Carl Peters haben Länder wie Deutsch-Südwestafrika und Deutsch-Ostafrika kolonisiert. In Namibien (vormals "Deutsch-Südwestafrika") gibt es die Stadt Lüderitz wo noch viel Deutsch gesprochen wird. In Namibien gibt es etwa 45,000 Leute (etwa zweidrittel davon sind weiß), die Deutsch sprechen. Und etwa die hälfte der Bevölkerung Namibiens ist evangelisch. Die*

*Hauptstadt Namibiens ist die Stadt Windhuk ("Windhoek" auf kapholländisch oder Afrikaans). Viele Deutschstämmige Leute wohnen auch in Südafrika, wo 40% der "Afrikaner" (die weiße Stämme Südafrikas) deutsche Ahnen haben.*

German colonies in the Pacific region included the city of Tsingtau ("Tsingtao" in English) and the province of Schantung ("Shantung" in English) in China, the Northern Mariana Islands, the Marshall Islands, Micronesia, Palau, Nauru, German Samoa (now known as Samoa and held from 1899-1945) and German New Guinea (much of modern day Papua New Guinea, which was held from 1884-1914).

*Deutschlands Kronkolonien in Asien waren die Stadt Tsingtau und die Provinz Schantung in China, die Marianen-Inseln, die Marshall-Inseln, Mikronesien, Palau, Nauru, Deutsch-Samoa (West-Samoa) und Deutsch-Neuguinea (Papua Neuguinea).*

The total population of all former German and Austrian colonies today is more than 223 million people.

*Die heutige Bevölkerungszahl der ehemaligen Deutschen Kronkolonien ist mehr als 223 Millionen. Fast 92 Millionen Menschen wohnen in Tsingtau und Schantung und mehr als 55 Millionen Leute wohnen im ehemaligen Deutsch-Ostafrika. Die Bevölkerungszahl von Großfriedrichsburg (Ghana) ist nun 23 Millionen, und mehr als 17 Millionen Menschen wohnen im ehemaligen Deutsch-Westafrika (Kamerun). Mehr als 11 Millionen Leute wohnen in Tianjin, China (eine ehemalige Österreichische Kolonie), und mehr als 7 Millionen Menschen wohnen nun im ehemaligen Deutsch-Neuguinea. Die heutige Bevölkerungszahl von Togoland ist mehr als 5 Millionen, und mehr als 3 Millionen Menschen wohnen in Sabah (in Malaysien, vormals österreichisch) sowie in Arguin (in Mauretanien, vormals brandenburgisch-preußisch). Fast 2 Millionen Leute wohnen im ehemaligen Deutsch-Südwestafrika (Namibien) sowie in Betschuanaland (heute "Botswana," vormals auch deutsch).*

### Chapter 10 (Kapitel Zehn): LARGE CAPITAL SHIPS ("Große Kriegsschiffe")

### I. "Schlachtschiffe der "Kriegsmarine" (Fast Battleships of the World War II German Navy)

The largest warship ever commissioned into the German Navy was the great battleship "Tirpitz" (commissioned in 1941 and sunk by British RAF bomber aircraft in Norwegian waters in November 1944), of 52,600 tons and armed with 8-15 inch guns plus 6 aircraft and capable of more than 30 knots with her diesel engines and turbines. She was the newer sister ship of the famous 50,900-ton "Bismarck" (commissioned in 1940 and sunk in the North Sea in May 1941 by a British Royal Navy force which outnumbered her 34 to 1). The maximum steaming radius of the "Tirpitz" was 10,200 miles and that of the "Bismarck" was 9,280 miles. "Tirpitz" was scrapped in 1957, as she was in very shallow waters. "Bismarck" is a protected monument and grave site, and may not be disturbed. 1,977 German sailors went down with the "Bismarck" on May 27, 1941.

*Das größte je getaufte Kriegsschiff Deutschlands war die "Tirpitz" (1941). Das Schlachtschiff "Tirpitz" hatte eine Einsatzverdrängung von 52,600 Tonnen, und war mit 8-38 cm Schnellfeuerkanonen sowie mit 6 Flugzeugen bewaffnet. Sie hatte eine maximale Geschwindigkeit von mehr als 30 Knoten und eine Reichweite von 10,200 Seemeilen. Die "Tirpitz" war das etwas größere Schwesterschlachtschiff der sehr berühmten "Bismarck" (1940). Die "Bismarck" hatte eine Einsatzverdrängung von 50,900 Tonnen und eine Reichweite von 9,280 Seemeilen. Die mächtige "Bismarck" wurde von 34 englischen Kriegsschiffen gejagt, und leider am 27. Mai 1941 im Nordatlantik versenkt. 1,977 deutsche Seemänner sind am diesen traurigen Tag für ihr Vaterland gefallen. Die "Tirpitz" wurde von englischen Bombenflugzeugen in Norwegen im Jahre 1944 versenkt, und dann im Jahre 1957 verschrottet.*

### Ia. "Hindenburg" Class / Hindenburg Klasse (1939)

Even larger battleships were laid down by 1939, but scrapped due to the outbreak of World War Two in September 1939. The naval leadership had been told by Adolf Hitler that no war would start before 1943, so they were caught off guard due to the misplaced trust in their own country's political leaders. The bad circumstances brought about due to Hitler's reckless foreign policy forced the German Navy to concentrate primarily upon submarine construction for the duration of World War Two, because Germany's resources and her shipbuilding capability were limited. Germany was expending much more industrial capacity on behalf of her large land army and new air force, meaning the navy had last priority among Germany's military branches. Submarines were a faster and less expensive way to wage war against the vast numerical superiority of the British Royal Navy. By contrast, Germany is today the largest industrial power in all of Europe. In fact, Western Germany alone surpassed all of prewar Germany's 1939 industrial capacity as early as 1952. German shipyards can now easily outproduce those in the United Kingdom. The new capital ships were to have been the six battleships of the "Hindenburg" class of 68,000 tons each and armed with 8-16 inch guns plus 6 aircraft and capable of reaching a top speed of 30 knots with their diesel engines and turbines. Steaming radius would have been an impressive 19,000 miles on a combination of diesels and turbines.

*Die Deutsche Kriegsmarine hatte vor, noch größere und mächtigere Schlachtschiffe zu bauen. Die geplante "Hindenburg" Klaße von 1939 hätte eine Einsatverdrängung von je 68,000 Tonnen, und sollte mit 8-40,6 cm Schnellfeuerkanonen sowie mit 6 Flugzeugen bewaffnet werden. Die geplante maximale Geschwindigkeit war 30 Knoten und die geplante Reichweite war eine sehr eindrucksvolle 19,000 Seemeilen. Die Patennamen dieser geplanten Schiffe waren "Hindenburg," "Friedrich der Große," "Ludendorff," "Moltke," "Großdeutschland" und "Führer." Die "Hindenburg" und auch die "Friedrich der Große" waren auf dem Kiel gelegt, aber nicht vollendet. Sie wurden beide im Jahre 1940 schon verschrottet. Und warum? Weil das damalige Staatsoberhaupt des Großdeutschen Reiches, nämlich Adolf Hitler, einen Zweiten Weltkrieg angefangen hatte. Das Deutsche Vaterland, die Deutsche Wehrmacht, und besonders die Deutsche Kriegsmarine waren für solch einen Krieg gar nicht vorbereitet.*

Grand Admiral Alfred von Tirpitz was the commander of the German Navy at the start of World War One, and he is often credited with giving great importance to the torpedo as a major new weapon. Prince Otto von Bismarck was the Prussian and German Chancellor (or Prime Minister) from 1862 until his retirement in 1890. Paul von Hindenburg was a Field Marshall in the German Army during World War One, famous for the great victory at Tannenberg in East Prussia against the Russians in September of 1914. He also served as the President (or Head of State) of Germany from 1925 until his death in 1934.The planned sister ships of the super-battleship "Hindenburg" were have to been named "Friedrich der Grosse" (after the 18th Century King of Prussia Frederick the Great), "Ludendorff" (to be named after another famous Field Marshall of World War One who served under fellow Field Marshall Paul von Hindenburg at the Battle of Tannenberg in 1914), "Moltke" (to be named after a famous Prussian

Field Marshall of the wars of German unification in 1864, 1866 and 1870-1871), "Grossdeutschland" (to be named after the Greater German Empire) and finally "Führer" (to be named after Germany's infamous Fascist dictatorial leader Adolf Hitler, who ruled the country from 1933 to 1945). "Führer" is the German word for "leader." Adolf Hitler went down as one of the most ruthless butchers of history, after even more murderous criminals such as Chairman Mao-Tse Tung of Red China (366 million dead), Ghengis Khan of the Mongol Empire (300 million dead) and Joseph Stalin of Soviet Russia (60 million dead). Hitler's extermination camps and death squads ended the lives of 12 million souls, half of them Jewish. Perhaps the cruelest tragedy were the deaths of 680,000 loyal German and Austro-Hungarian Jews, whose ancestors had been part of the fabric of Greater Germany, Central Europe and the Balkans for more than 1,600 years – and who loyally defended the Sacred Soil of the Fatherland in every war up to and including World War One. 100,000 German Jews fought for Germany alone during World War One, and 11,000 of them gave their lives for their beloved Fatherland. The story was much the same throughout Austria-Hungary.

## Ib. Improved "Hindenburg" Classes / Neue Hindenburg Klassen (1940-1944)

Amazingly, there were actually so-called technical studies for even larger battleships compared to the 6 planned ships of the "Hindenburg" or H-class of 1939. Given Germany's industrial reality in 1939, such ideas were virtually fantasy. Furthermore, such ships would have been of limited value given the changing nature of naval warfare, with the ever-growing importance of both aircraft carriers and submarines. The plan for battleship "H-40A" in 1940 called for a vessel of 65,600 tons total displacement, armament of 6-16 inch guns in three dual turrets (two fore and one aft), 6 aircraft and a top speed of 32,2 knots. With such armament, I would call such a vessel a "super battlecruiser." The design study for battleship "H-40B" in 1940 called for a ship of 70,000 maximum displacement, armament of 8-16 inch guns, 6 aircraft and a top speed of 32,3 tons. Compared to the "H-class" of 1939, this vessel basically had more armor. Both ships designed in 1940 were to have a maximum steaming radius of 20,000 miles.

*Es gab auch Pläne für eine größere "H-Klaße," die nie auf Kiel gelegt wurden. Im Jahre 1940, gab es die "H-40A-Klaße" und auch die "H-40B-Klaße." Der erste Plan "H-40A" war für einen Schlachtkreuzer mit einer Einsatzverdrängung von 65,600 Tonnen, 6-40,6 cm Schnellfeuerkanonen, 6 Flugzeuge und einer maximalen Geschwindigkeit von 32,2 Knoten und einer Reichweite von 20,000 Seemeilen. Der zweite Plan "H-40B" war für ein Schlachtschiff mit einer*

*Einsatzverdrängung von 70,000 Tonnen, 8-40,6 cm Schnellfeuerkanonen, 6 Flugzeuge, einer maximalen Geschwindigkeit von 32,3 Knoten und auch einer Reichweite von 20,000 Seemeilen. Im Jahre 1941 gab es die noch größere "H-41 Klaße." Der Plan "H-41" war ein Schlachtschiff mit einer Einsatzverdrängung von 76,000 Tonnen, 8-40,6 cm Schnellfeuerkanonen, 6 Flugzeuge, einer maximalen Geschwindigkeit von 28,8 Knoten und auch einer Reichweite von 20,000 Seemeilen. Im Jahre 1942 gab es die "H-42 Klaße." Der Plan "H-42" war ein Schlachtschiff mit einer Einsatzverdrängung von 98,000 Tonnen (damals konnten die Werften und Häfen des Großdeutschen Reiches Einheiten größer als 98,000 Tonnen nicht unterbringen), 8-40,6 cm Schnellfeuerkanonen, 6 Flugzeuge, einer maximalen Geschwindigkeit von 32,2 Knoten und auch einer Reichweite von 20,000 Seemeilen. Geplante Schiffe wie die Klaßen "H-40A" bis "H-42" waren hautpsächlich die "Klaße H-39" (die "Hindenburg-Klaße") mit vielmehr Panzerung.*

The design study "H-41" of 1941 called for a ship of 76,000 tons, armament of 8-16 inch guns plus 6 aircraft and with a top speed of 28,8 knots. Steaming radius was to have been 20,000 miles. Once again, we are talking basically of yet heavier armor plating. Each ship's numerical designation denoted in which year its design study was completed. As the war went on, every year brought ever more bad news for Germany – making the fulfillment of such plans ever less realistic. The "H-42" of 1942 called for a fantastic 98,000 battleship (about the maximum any German shipyard could have accommodated at the time) to be armed with 8-16 inch guns, 6 aircraft and with a top speed of 32,2 knots. Radius would have been a maximum 20,000 miles. The battleship design study of 1943 was the "H-43" of a very unrealistic 120,000 tons total displacement, which would have made her the largest warship in world history – even to this very day. In fact, no German harbor could have accommodated her in World War Two. She was to have been armed with 8-20 inch guns and 6 aircraft. Such a gun caliber would also have taken her into the record books for all time, up to and including the present. Such unrealistic specifications had far more to do with Hitler's demands than they did with anyone in the German Navy itself. Radius was to have been 20,000 miles. The final battleship design study was for the "H-44" of 1944. This ship was to have displaced an absolutely amazing 141,500 tons, to have been armed with 8-20 inch guns and 9 aircraft and was to have been capable of reaching a top speed of 30,1 knots. Steaming radius was yet again 20,000 miles.

*Endlich gaben es auch die Klaßen "H-43" und "H-44." In den Jahren 1943 und 1944 war es schon extrem unrealistsch, weil das Ende des Krieges gegen das Großdeutsche Reich schon in klarer Sicht war. Der Plan "H-43" wäre ein*

*Schlachtschiff mit einer Einsatzverdrängung von 120,000 Tonnen, 8-50,8 cm Schnellfeuerkanonen, 6 Flugzeuge, einer maximalen Geschwindigkeit von etwa 30 Knoten und einer Reichweite von 20,000 Seemeilen.*

## Das Riesenschlachtschiff "H-44" (the Super-Battleship "H-44")

*Der Plan "H-44" war für ein Riesenschlachtschiff mit einer Einsatzverdrängung von 141,500 Tonnen, 8-50,8 Schnellfeuerkanonen, 9 Flugzeuge, einer maximalen Geschwindigkeit von 30,1 Knoten und einer Reichweite von 20,000 Seemeilen. Aber Schlachtschiffe sowie Schlachtkreuzer waren zu der Zeit schon veraltet. Seit 1941 waren die wichtigsten größeren Kampfschiffe Flugzeugträger. Die Deutsche Kriegsmarine von 1939 war noch nicht kampfbereit und auch nicht groß genug. Und außerdem war die Außenpolitik Adolf Hitlers extrem rücksichtslos. Die Führung der Deutschen Kriegsmarine unter Großadmiral Erich Raeder und später unter Großadmiral Karl Dönitz, sowie viele andere Offiziere der Kriegsmarine, war wohl sehr fähig, konnte sich aber nicht gegen Adolf Hitler durchsetzen.*

Adolf Hitler once said of the "Wehrmacht" (German for "armed forces") that "I have a reactionary Army, a National Socialist Air Force and a Christian and Imperial Navy." This obviously speaks very well of the German Naval leadership, for they were rather free of Nazi (National Socialist) political influence – more so than any other branch of the military service, partially due to Hitler's total ignorance of naval warfare.

## Ic. "Sovetskaja Ukraina" Class / "Sovetskaja Ukraina" Klasse (1932)

The Russian naval battleship "Sovetskaya Ukraina" (laid down in 1938 but never completed) was captured by the advancing German armed forces at Nikolaev in the Black Sea in 1941. When the Germans were forced to retreat later in the war, they destroyed the vessel in March of 1944. This would have been a very substantial battleship, which would have displaced up to 65,150 tons full load, and was to have been armed with 9-16 inch guns in three triple turrets (two fore and one aft) plus 12-6 inch guns. Top speed was planned at a very decent 29 knots. The name of the ship of course refers to the Ukraine, which is now an independent nation in Eastern Europe. Russian and Ukrainian are mutually intelligible Slavic languages, but the Ukrainian culture is significantly more Westward-looking compared to the Russian culture. Furthermore, many Ukrainians adhere to the Byzantine Rite Roman Catholic Church, as opposed to the Russian Eastern Orthodox Church. Sadly, the German occupation of the Ukraine during World War Two was extremely brutal, as it was in much of

Eastern Europe. The horrific policies of Adolf Hitler and his National Socialist Party were very bad for Germany as well, especially when one remembers that German troops were initially greeted as liberators in places such as the Ukraine and the Baltic States of Lithuania, Latvia and Estonia. In other words, this huge resevoir of goodwill towards Germany was squandered. And even in spite of this, an overwhelming number of German veterans attest to the fact that the civilians in Russia and the former Soviet Union were among the friendliest people they met abroad.

*Das sowjetrußische Schlachtschiff "Sovetskaya Ukraina" (im Jahre 1938 auf Kiel gelegt, ist aber nie vom Stapel gelaufen) wurde von den vorstürmenden Soldaten der Deutschen Wehrmacht in Nikolaev am Schwarzen Meer im Jahre 1941 erbeutet. Als die Wehrmacht sich im März 1944 aus Nikolaev zurückzog, wurde das Schiff von den Deutschen zerstört. Die geplante "Sovetskaya Ukraine" hatte eine Einsatzverdrängung von 65,150 Tonnen, und wurde mit 9-40,6 cm Schnellfeuerkanonen (in drei Drillingstürme, davon zwei vorne und einer hinten) sowie mit 12-15 cm Schnellfeuerkanonen bewaffnet. Die maximale geplante Geschwindigkeit des Schiffes war 29 Knoten. Seit 1991 ist die Ukraine ein unabhängiges Land mit etwa 46,3 Millionen Einwohnern, wovon mehr als 4,6 Millionen Deutsch sprechen. Es gibt auch Rußen, Weißrußen, Tartaren, Bulgaren, Magjaren, Polen, Juden (105,000) und auch Griechen in der Ukraine. Die meisten Ukrainer gehören entweder zur Ukrainisch-Orthodoxen oder zur Römisch-Katholischen Kirche. Als die Deutsche Wehrmacht im Juni 1941 in die Sowjetunion einmarschierte, wurden die Deutschen Soldaten zuerst als Befreier anerkannt. So war es in Litauen, Lettland, Kurland, Estland und auch der Ukraine. Aber leider hatten Männer wie Adolf Hitler, Heinrich Himmler, Reinhard Heidrich und deren SS (d.h. die "zivile" SS aber nicht die Waffen-SS) die Slawische und die Jüdische Zivilbevölkerung sehr schlecht behandelt. Die neun Abteilungen der Schutz-Staffeln (SS), die die große Mehrheit der Greueltaten "im Namen Deutschlands" eigentlich gemacht haben waren der RKFDV (Reichskommissar-SS für die Festigung Deutschen Volkstums), das RUSHA (Rass-und Siedlungs Hauptamt), die VOMI (Volksdeutsche Mittelstelle), das WVHA (Wirtschaft-und Verwaltungs Hauptamt), das RSHA (Reichsicherheits Hauptamt), die GESTAPO (Geheime Staatspolizei), die KRIPO (Kriminalpolizei), der SD (Sicherheitsdienst) und auch die "Einsatzgruppen." 225,000 Leute "dienten" in diesen neun grausamen Abteilungen der "zivilen" SS. Die 610,000 Mitglieder der Waffen-SS waren im großen und ganzen tüchtige, fähige, patriotische, treue, ernsthafte, fleißige und gute Soldaten – genauso wie beim Wehrmacht-Heer, bei der Luftwaffe und natürlich auch bei der Deutschen Kriegsmarine.*

82

*Es war sehr tragisch und auch sehr ironisch, weil so viele Deutsche Wehrmachtsangehörige die Rußen und die Ukrainer als sehr freundliche und nette Menschen angesehen haben. Von 1939 bis 1945 gab es schon 2 Millionen ausländische Freiwillige bei der Deutschen Wehrmacht, und die Hälfte davon kam aus der ehemaligen Sowjetunion. Wenn Fall "Barbaroßa" im Osten ein "Befreiungskreig" statt ein "Vernichtungskrieg" gewesen wäre, hätte das Deutsche Reich den Krieg im Osten gewonnen – genausowie im Ersten Weltkrieg, als Deutschland und Österreich-Ungarn das Rußische Tsarenreich besiegten. Damals (im Jahre 1918) kamen Polen, Litauen, Lettland, Kurland, Weißrußland sowie die Ukraine ins Deutsche Kaiserreich.*

## Id. "Gascogne" Class / "Gascogne" Klasse (1938)

The initial materials for the French naval battleship "Gascogne" and an as yet unnamed sister ship were captured by advancing German forces in June 1940. Neither ship was ever laid down. These were to have been substantial battleships, each displacing up to 48,950 tons. Armament was to have consisted of 8-15 inch guns in two quadruple turrets, one fore and one aft. Each ship would have been equipped with 2 aircraft, and top speed was planned at a very respectable 32,1 knots. The conquest of France was yet another situation badly handled by Adolf Hitler, at least as far as the German Navy was concerned. It is true that all of the French Atlantic bases were very useful for German submarines and light forces such as torpedo boats for the remainder of the war. But the Germans should have made every effort to absorb the French capital ships into the German Navy as well. Realistically, this would have at least added the modern battleships "Dunkerque" (35,500 tons) and "Strasbourg" (35,500 tons) to the German Navy. Each ship was armed with 8-13 inch guns, mounted in two forward-mounted quadruple turrets. Each ship had 4 aircraft as well, and could make up to 31 knots.

*Das geplante französische Schlachtschiff "Gascogne" (1938) wurde von den Deutschen Truppen im Jahre 1940 erbeutet. Das Schiff wurde auf Kiel gelegt, aber ist nie vom Stapel gelaufen. Die "Gascogne" (1938) und ihre unbenanntes Schwesterschlachtschiff hätten eine Einsatzverdrängung von 48,980 Tonnen gehabt, und wären mit 8-38 cm Schnellfeuerkanonen in zwei Vierlingstürmen, sowie mit zwei Flugzeugen bewaffnet worden. Die maximale Geschwindigkeit wäre 32,1 Knoten. Die erfolgreiche deutsche Eroberung von Frankreich, Belgien und Holland im Mai und Juni 1940 war eigentlich überhaupt nicht als "Blitzkrieg" geplant. Die Feldherren von Deutschland, Frankreich und England glaubten, daß es sich auch wie im Ersten Weltkrieg auswirken wird (d.h. ein Krieg von vier Jahren anstatt von vier Wochen). Deutsche Panzergenerale wie*

*Erich von Manstein und Gerd von Rundstedt haben alles "gewettet" – und deswegen haben sie "gewonnen." Mit diesem Erfolg hatte Adolf Hitler eigentlich nichts zu tun. Für die Deutsche Kriegsmarine war die Eroberung Frankreichs vom großem Vorteil. Zum ersten mal hatte Deutschland Marinestützpunkte nicht nur in Deutschland, aber nun auch von Norwegen bis zur spanischen Grenze. Leider gab es nicht genug Kampfschiffe und Kampfboote, vor allem nicht genug Unterseeboote. Im Esten Weltkrieg war Adolf Hitler ein Gefreiter, und folglich kein Kriegsherr im Sinne des Wortes. Er wurde nie als Offizier (und auch nie als Unteroffizier) ausgebildet. Als Land-und Luft "Feldherr" war er total unwissend – und für die Deutsche Kriegsmarine war er noch schlimmer. Großadmiral Erich Raeder wollte die zwei großen französischen Schlachtschiffe "Dunkerque" ("Dünkirchen" auf Deutsch) und "Strasbourg" ("Straßburg" auf Deutsch) in die Deutsche Kriegsmarine bringen, aber leider hatte der unwissende Adolf Hitler das abgelehnt. Diese Klaße hatte eine Einsatzverdrängung von 35,500 Tonnen, und wurde mit 8-33 cm Schnellfeuerkanonen sowie mit 4 Flugzeugen bewaffnet. Die maximale Geschwindigkeit war 31 Knoten.*

## II. "Schlachtschiffe / Schlachtkreuzer" (post-dreadnought Battleships / Battlecruisers)

Other famous capital ships of the "Kriegsmarine" include the 38,900-ton battleships (armed with 9-11 inch guns in triple turrets) "Scharnhorst" and "Gneisenau," named for Prussian military leaders of the Napoleonic Wars against France (fought from 1792 to 1815). These two generals are also credited with having formed the modern Prussian-German General Staff in 1807. The "Scharnhorst" was sunk in the Battle of the North Cape off Northern Norway on December 26, 1943. This was the last battle between surface warships in Europe, in which the "Scharnhorst" was outnumbered 14 to 1 against the Royal Navy of England. The "Gneisenau" survived to the final year of the war, and was to have been upgraded to carry 6-15 inch guns in triple turrets (in replacement for her 9-11 inch guns) – a conversion which unfortunately never took place due to heavy Allied air raids. "Gneisenau" was scrapped in 1951, while "Scharnhorst" is a protected grave site for the 1,803 German sailors who lost their lives in the Battle of the North Cape on December 26, 1943. Steaming radius of both ships was 10,000 miles. Note: the German Navy referred to these ships as "battleships," whereas the British referred to them as "battlecruisers." The British reasoning was the lighter-than-normal armament of 11-inch guns.

*Die zwei Schlachtschiffe "Gneisenau" (1938) und "Scharnhorst" (1939) waren Deutschlands größte aktive Kriegsschiffe am Anfang des Zweiten Weltkrieges.*

*Sie waren bestimmt sehr gute Schiffe (auf jeden Fall besser als englische Schiffe), aber leider war die Deutsche Kriegsmarine zu klein. Die "Gneisenau" und die "Scharnhort" hatten eine Einsatzverdrängung von je 38,900 Tonnen, und wurden mit 9-28 cm Schnellfeuerkanonen (in drei Drillingstürme) bewaffnet. Die "Scharnhorst" wurde am 26. Dezember 1943 von 14 englischen Kriegsschiffen am Nordkap gesunken. 1,803 Deutschen Seemänner sind am diesen tragischen und traurigen Tag für ihr Vaterland gefallen. Die Seeschlacht am Nordkap war die letzte "große" Seeschlacht Europas. Die Deutsche Kriegsmarine hatte es vor, die "Gneisenau" zu verbessern, d.h. mit 6-38 cm Schnellfeuerkanonen (auch in drei Drillingstürme), aber leider ist das nie passiert. Der Krieg ging gegen Deutschland und die Kapitulierung war schon in Sicht.*

## IIa.  "Schneidheim" Class / "Schneidheim" Klasse (1939)

3 other battlecruisers were planned but never laid down. They were to have been of similar size (38,200 tons full-load displacement) and their armament was to have been similar to the "Gneisenau" conversion project. Planned names included "Schneidheim" (named for a Holy Roman administrative area in the former Kingdom of Württemberg), "Wallenstein" (a Holy Roman and German Field Marshall who served during the Thirty Years' War, which lasted from 1618 until 1648) and a third ship for which no new name was yet proposed. The new ships were designed to make an extremely impressive 35 knots with their diesel engines and turbines, and to have a good steaming radius of 14,000 miles. The Thirty Years' was particularly devastating, in which foreign powers such as France, Denmark and Sweden decimated one-third of Germany's 17th century population, or 7 million out of 21 million Germans in 1618. This demonstrates just how political the so-called Protestant Reformation was. Habsburg attempts to reform the Holy Roman Empire of the German Nation in the late 1400s were sadly too little and too late for Germany's own geopolitical good.

*Die Deutsche Kriegsmarine hatte es vor, noch drei Schlachtkreuzer der "O-Klaße" (1939) zu bauen. Diese guten Kriegsschiffe wurden aber leider nie auf Kiel gelegt. Die Einsatzverdrängung war auf 38,200 Tonnen geplant, und die Bewaffnung war mit 9-38 cm Schnellfeuerkanonen geplant. Die maximale Geschwindigkeit wären schnelle 35 Knoten, und die Reichweite wäre um die 14,000 Seemeilen (im Gegensatz zu der "Gneisenau" oder der "Scharnhorst," mit je 10,000 Seemeilen). Mögliche Patennamen waren "Schneidheim" und "Wallenstein." "Schneidheim" lag im Königreich Württemberg im Ersten Deutschen Reich (das Heilige Römische Reich der Deutschen Nation, das von 800 bis 1806 bestand). Albrecht Wenzel Eusebius von Wallenstein (1583-1634) war Deutscher Generalfeldmarschall, der in Böhmen geboren wurde, der im Dreißigjährigen diente und fiel. Der Dreißigjährige Krieg (1618-1648) war für Deutschland verheerend – 7 Millionen Deutsche (von 21 Millionen Deutsche insgesamt) sind im Krieg gestorben. Die Protestantische "Reformation" von Martin Luther war für Deutschland schon gar nicht gut – die Einigung des Vaterlandes wurde zerstört. Aber der "religiöse" Dreißigjährige Krieg war am schlimmsten für Deutschland, weil Länder wie Frankreich, Dänemark und Schweden den religiösen Zwiespalt innerhalb Deutschlands ausgenutzt haben um Deutschland noch mehr zu schwächen. Und außerdem hatte Deutschland mit diesen Ländern keine notwendigen Schwierigkeiten, aber davon war nie die Rede. Die Weltpresse schwieg über dieses Thema und verbreitete lügenhaft vom "bösen Deutschland."*

### IIb.  "40,000-Ton" Class / "40,000-Tonnen" Klasse (1918)

A plan for a 40,000-ton battlecruiser marked the peak in Austro-Hungarian capital ship design. Obviously, the plan never came to fruition due to the bad geopolitical situation. Armament was planned at 4-16,5 inch guns in two dual turrets, one fore and one aft. Secondary armament would have consisted of 12-6 inch guns (4 of these being anti-aircraft guns) and 1-21 inch torpedo tube. Top speed was planned at a very impressive 30 knots.

*Dieser geplanter Schlachtkreuzer (von 1918) wurde aber nie gebaut. Mit einer Einsatzverdrängung von 40,000 Tonnen wäre es das größte und mächtigste geplante Kriegsschiff Österreich-Ungarns gewesen. Die Bewaffnung war mit vier 42-cm Schnellfeuerkanonen (in zwei Zwillingstürme), sowie mit zwölf 15-cm Schnellfeuerkanonen und einem 533-cm Torpedorohr geplant. Die maximale Geschwindigkeit wäre eine gute 30 Knoten gewesen.*

### IIc.  "Ersatz S.M.S. Yorck" Class / "Ersatz-Yorck" Klasse (1916)

A plan for three (3) new battlecruisers of the "Ersatz Yorck" class in 1916 and 1917 marked the pinnacle of capital ship design in World War One Germany. All three ships were actually laid down, but never launched. Each vessel was to have displaced up to 38,000 tons, and to have been armed with 8-15 inch guns in four turrets (two fore and two aft), plus 12-6 inch guns mounted in casemates. Top speed was planned at a very good 27,3 knots. Both this design and the "Mackensen" class design were to heavily influence the design for the "Scharnhorst" and the "Gneisenau" of the 1930s.

*Die drei geplanten Schlachtkreuzer der "Ersatz Yorck" Klaße von 1916 waren die letzten geplanten Großkriegsschiffe der Kaiserlichen Marine. Sie waren schon alle auf Kiel gelegt, aber sind nie vom Stapel gelaufen. Die geplante Einsatzverdrängung war 38,000 Tonnen, und die Bewaffnung war mit acht 38-cm Schnellfeuerkanonen (in vier Zwillingstürme), sowie mit zwölf 15-cm Kasemattkanonen geplant. Die maximale Geschwindigkeit wären gute 27,3 Knoten. Die "Nachfolger" der Ersatz Yorck-Klaße waren die "Gneisenau" von 1938 und die "Scharnhorst" von 1939.*

### IId. "36,000-Ton" Class / "36,000-Tonnen" Klasse (1917)

The plan for a 36,000-ton battlecruiser was the next-to-last capital ship design to come from Austria-Hungary. Primary armament would have consisted of 6-15 inch guns in three dual turrets, one mounted fore, the second mounted centrally and the last mounted aft. Secondary armament would have been 22-6 inch guns, 4 of these being anti-aircraft guns, plus 6-21 inch torpedo tubes. Torpedoes launched from larger surface ships tended to be far less accurately fired compared to those launched from destroyers, torpedo boats, fast attack craft or submarines. This decent plan never came to fruition, due to the bad geopolitical situation of Austria-Hungary.

*Die Kaiserliche und Königliche Kriegsmarine Österreich-Ungarns hatte es auch vor, einen 36,000 Tonnen Schlachtkreuzer im Jahre 1917 zu bauen. Aber dieser mächtige Schlachtkreuzer wurde nicht gebaut. Die Bewaffnung war mit sechs 38-cm Schnellfeuerkanonen (in drei Zwillingstürme), sowie mit zweiundzwanzig 15-cm und mit sechs 533-cm Torpedorohren geplant.*

### IIe. "34,000-Ton" Classes / die drei "34,000-Tonnen" Klassen (1915, 1916 and 1917)

Three separate plans for a 34,000-ton battlecruiser marked the first plans for such ships to come from Austria-Hungary. Each of the three plans called for the same secondary armament (18-6 inch guns, 18-3,5 inch guns and 6-21 inch torpedo tubes) as well as the same very good speed (30 knots). Primary armament is where the three plans differed. The first plan of 1915 called for 9-13,75 inch guns, mounted in three triple turrets (one fore, one central and one aft). The second plan of 1916 called for 8-13,75 inch guns, mounted in four dual turrets (two fore and two aft). The final plan of 1917 called for 6-15 inch guns, mounted in three dual turrets (one fore, one central and one aft). These were all very advanced designs, but they never came to fruition due to Austria-Hungary's unfavorable geopolitical situation – which merely became worse with every successive year of war.

*Die Kaiserliche und Königliche Kriegsmarine Österreich-Ungarns hatte drei verschiedene Pläne für Schlachtkreuzer in den Jahren 1915, 1916 und 1917, die aber auch nicht gebaut wurden. Die Einsatzverdrängung war 34,000 Tonnen, und die untergeordnete Bewaffnung war immer mit achtzehn 15-cm Kasemattkanonen, achtzehn 9-cm Schnellfeuerkanonen sowie mit sechs 533-cm Torpedorohren geplant. Im Jahre 1915 wurde die Hauptbewaffnung mit neun 35-cm Schnellfeuerkanonen (in drei Drillingstürme) geplant Im Jahre 1916 wurde die Hauptbewaffnung mit acht 35-cm Schnellfeuerkanonen (in vier Zwillingstürme) geplant. Im Jahre 1917 wurde die Hauptbewaffnung endlich mit sechs 38-cm Schnellfeuerkanonen (in drei Zwillingstürme) geplant. Aber die geopolitische Lage in Österreich-Ungarn sowie die der Mittlemächte (Deutschland, Bulgarien und das Ottomanische Reich) war nicht geeignet solche Pläne zu verwirklichen.*

### III. "Linienschiffe" (Ships-of-the-Line / Dreadnought Battleships and Battlecruisers of the Imperial Navy)

Admiral Reinhard Scheer commanded the Imperial German "Hochseeflotte" ("High Seas Fleet" in English) during the great Battle of Jutland on May 31, 1916 in World War One. This was the largest ever clash between dreadnought battleships, in which 101 German warships fought 151 British warships to a tactical victory (albeit a strategic stalemate). The 50% numerical advantage enjoyed by the British Royal Navy in May 1916 was to decline before the end of World War One. On April 23, 1918, the Imperial German High Seas Fleet engaged in huge sortie which took the fleet as far North as the lattitude of Stavanger, Norway. Unfortunately, the German fleet was not able to meet the combined fleets of the British Royal Navy and the U.S. Atlantic fleet. 100 German warships and 146 British and American warships went out to sea on that morning in April 1918, never to meet in battle (a 46% numerical advantage for the British, but this with the U.S. Atlantic fleet attached to them).

*Im Ersten Weltkrieg spielten die großen und mächtigen Linienschiffe und Schlachtkreuzer (aber auch die Unterseeboote) eine große und wichtige Rolle. Bei der Seeschlacht am Skagerrak am 31. Mai 1916 stand eine Minderheit von nur 101 Einheiten der Kaiserlich-Deutschen Marine einem Gegner mit 151 englischen Einheiten gegenüber. Die Engländer hatten 50 prozent mehr Kriegsschiffe (Linienschiffe, Schlachtkreuzer und Kleine Kreuzer) und andere Kriegsboote (wie zum Beispiel Panzerkreuzer, Minenleger, Zerstörer und Torpedoboote) als Deutschland. Außerdem war es zum Nachteil für die deutsche Hochseeflotte daß Kaiser Wilhelm II die Flotte nicht voll ausgenutzt hat. Am 23. April 1918 war die deutsche Hochseeflotte soweit Nord bis Stavanger, Norwegen*

*angekommen, hatte aber nicht den Gegner (die Briten
und Amerikaner) angefunden. Die englische Flotte war schon im Jahre
1918 wesentlich geschwächt und war auf Hilfe aus Amerika angewiesen. Zu der
Zeit im April bestanden die hundert große deutsche Einheiten aus Linienschiffe,
Schlachtkreuzer, Kleine Kreuzer und Torpedoboote. Dem gegenüber standen 146
Einheiten aus Großbrittanien und den Vereinigten Staaten von Amerika. Die
deutsche Flotte leidete unter einem großen Nachteil und war nicht oft im Einsatz.
Deutschland und die anderen Mittelmächte (Österreich-Ungarn, Bulgarien und
das Ottomanische Reich) leideten wegen der sehr wirksamen von den Allierten
geführten Handelsblockade. Nahrungsmittel, Gummi, Erdgas und andere
Rohstoffe waren in Deutschland und Mitteleuropa eventuell sehr knapp. Die
Deutsche Industrie produzierte sehr viele verschiede sogenannte
"Ersatz" Waren die natürlich nicht ebenmäßig mit dem originalen Gütern
waren. Zu der Zeit gab es angeblich Nahrungsmittel dem Segespäne eingemischt
waren. Hungerleiden war weit verbreitet und in vielen Fällen tödlich. Im Jahre
1917 haben die Mittelmächte das Rußische Zarenreich besiegt. Aber es war für
Deutschland leider zu spät. Eventuell führte es zu einer brutalen und blutigen
Revolution in Rußland, und anschließend zu einer gleichfalls brutalen
kommunistischen Regierung. Der Kommunismus verbreitete sich in Osteuropa,
einschließlich in Ostdeutschland, sowie in Asien, verbunden mit unzahlreichen
Verlusten unter der Bevölkerung dieser Länder. In der Zeit von 1917 und
1991 sind unter der sowjetischen Regierung mehr als 60 Millionen Menschen ums
Leben gekommen - das fünffache von dem was während der Jahre 1933 bis 1945
im nationalsozialisten Europa unter Adolf Hitler und Heinrich Himmler der Fall
war.*

I say it was unfortunate that they did not meet in battle because it was extremely bad for German Naval morale to keep the German fleet confined to port. Above all, it was bad for the civilian population of the Central Powers (Germany, Austria-Hungary, Bulgaria and the Ottoman Turkish Empire) to be blockaded into starvation by the British Royal Navy. Civilians were reduced into eating "Ersatz" food ("substitute food" in English) with ingredients such as sawdust. Meat and grains became very scarce, and one of the few staples left in larger quantities were turnips. The infantrymen at the front were unable to break the stalemate in the West from the Summer of 1914 until the Fall of 1918, largely due to the limitations of technology at the time. They had plenty of artillery and automatic machine-guns, but no tanks until Britain invented the tank toward the end of World War One. They were able to massacre each other in brutal battles such as Ypres, the Somme and Verdun, but they were unable to advance to any strategic degree. This was merely one more critical reason to have a large navy, and to use that large navy.

In August 1914 (one month after the start of World War One in the Balkan region), the British Royal Navy had 373 combat vessels either commissioned or under construction versus 227 for the German High Seas Fleet, or a 64% numerical advantage over Germany. Among the next largest navies, France had 165 vessels and Czarist Russia had 156.

At the Battle of Jutland in May 1916 (called the Battle of the Skagerrak by Germany), 151 Royal Navy ships met 101 ships of the Imperial German Navy, for a 50% British numerical advantage. British losses in this battle were 14 ships (115,025 tons) and 6,781 casualties. German losses were 11 ships (61,180 tons) and 3,058 casualties. "Skagerrak" is the Danish name for the narrow channel of water located in between the Danish Jutland peninsula and Norway. Eventually, this body of water leads from the North Sea into the Baltic Sea. By the time of Norwegian sortie of the German Navy in April 1918, the British Royal Navy could muster just 127 warships against 100 German ships (the figure of 146 Western Allied ships included 19 ships of the American Atlantic Fleet from Norfolk, Virginia). The British numerical advantage over the German Imperial High Seas Fleet had thus gone down from 64% in August 1914, to 50% in May 1916 and down again to a mere 27% by April 1918. This was yet more proof of the folly of German Kaiser Wilhelm II, who was so afraid to deploy his capital warships. He believed that Germany should "save" its capital ships to use as political bargaining chips in any future peace treaty with the Western Allies. But without using the ships in the first place, there would never be any such peace treaty. The Central Powers actually did triumph on the Eastern Front, when Russia surrendered to them on December 22, 1917. In the Treaty of Brest-Litovsk (signed on March 3, 1918), Russia surrendered Finland, Estonia, Latvia, Lithuania, Belarus (White Russia) and the Ukraine to Germany. In the Balkan region, Austria-Hungary had wanted to annex Romania (Wallachia), Serbia and Montenegro. The Ottoman Turkish Empire had wanted to regain Greece and Albania.

### IIIa. "S.M.S. Bayern" Class / "S.M.S. Bayern" Klasse (1912)

Germany's final flagship during World War One was the super-dreadnought battleship "S.M.S. Baden" (1916) – of 32,200 tons maximum displacement and armed with 8-15 inch guns plus 16-6 inch guns and capable of reaching 22 knots under full steam with her coal boilers. Steaming radius was 5,000 miles, which demonstrates just how limited coal-fired ships were compared to the future diesel and turbine-powered ships. She had three sister ships, one of which ("S.M.S. Bayern") was also commissioned into active duty service with the "Kaiserliche Marine" (Imperial Navy) in 1916. All German and Austrian warships up to 1918 carried the Imperial prefix "S.M.S." which meant "Seine Majestät Schiff" (His Majesty's Ship – He being the German and Austro-Hungarian "Kaiser" or Emperor). Her sister battleships ""S.M.S. Sachsen" and "S.M.S. Württemberg" were not completed and thus not commissioned into active duty service by November 11, 1918. The four ships were named after German states or provinces. "Bayern" is the German word for "Bavaria" and "Sachsen" is German for "Saxony." "S.M.S. Bayern" was surrendered to the British after the war and scuttled by her own German crew at the Royal Navy base of Scapa Flow in Scotland in June 1919. "S.M.S. Baden" was also surrendered after World War One, but used by the British as a target and sunk Southwest of Portsmouth, England in 1921. She still lies there to this day. "S.M.S. Sachsen" was launched in 1916 but never commissioned – the Germans scrapped her in 1921. "S.M.S. Württemberg" (named for the Kingdom of Württemberg in Southwestern Germany) was launched in 1917, never commissioned and also scrapped by the Germans in 1921. All German capital ships (i.e., large warships) up to the end of World War One were powered by coal. The British had already begun to switch to oil or diesel. Diesel fuel was preferable due to its longer range and due to the fact that a diesel-powered ship leaves much less of a "wake" in the form of less visible pollution. The Germans refrained from the use of diesel power in capital surface ships due to the fact that Germany had far less access to crude oil deposits – something which became very critical with the Allied naval blockade against Germany and her allies of Austria-Hungary, Bulgaria and Ottoman Turkey. This was less of an issue during World War Two, because Germany had access to crude oil from Romania (an ally of Germany during World War Two) and Russia (a neutral friend of Germany until 1941 and later significantly occupied by invading German troops).

*Die größten Linienschiffe der Kaiserlichen Marine waren die vier Einheiten der "S.M.S. Bayern" (1916) Klaße, mit einer Einsatzverdrängung von je 32,200 Tonnen. Allerdings wurden nur die "S.M.S. Bayern" und die "S.M.S. Baden" getauft. Die "S.M.S. Sachsen" und die "S.M.S. Württemberg" sind vom Stapel gelaufen, wurden aber nie getauft und auch nie in Dienst gestellt. Die "S.M.S. Baden" war die letzte Flaggschiff der Kaiserlichen Deutschen Marine. Die Bewaffnung eines Linienschiffes der "S.M.S. Bayern" Klaße bestand aus acht 38 cm Schnellfeuerkanonen (in vier Zwillingstürmen) sowie 16-15 cm Kasemattkanonen. Die Höchstgeschwindigkeit war mit 22 Knoten bemeßen, und die Reichweite der Schiffe waren 5,000 Seemeilen. Die "S.M.S. Sachsen" und die "S.M.S. Württemberg" wurden aber im Sinne des Versailler-Vertages nach dem Ersten Weltkrieg im Jahre 1921 verschrottet. Die "S.M.S. Bayern" wurde von ihrer deutschen Mannschaft im britischen Marinehafen von Scapa Flow im Jahre 1919 selbst versenkt. Und fast die ganze übergebende deutsche Hochseeflotte hatte sich selbst versenkt, um den "siegriechen" Engländern diese große Nachkriegsbeute nicht zu gönnen.*

### IIIb. "S.M.S. Mackensen" Class / "S.M.S. Mackensen" Klasse (1914)

Even larger dreadnought battlecruisers were launched during World War One, but never commissioned due to the end of the war. They were to have taken the place of regular battleships due to the knowledge gained by the German Navy at the Battle of Jutland on May 31, 1916. Battlecruisers had proven themselves to be far more useful compared to battleships, due to their superior speed. These included the four ships of the "S.M.S. Mackensen" class, which were to displace up to 35,300 tons and were to have been armed with 8-14 inch guns plus 14-6 inch guns. Their top speed was to have been an impressive 28,8 knots under full steam with their coal boilers, and range of action was 5,500 miles. "S.M.S. Mackensen" was launched in April 1917, and scrapped in 1924. "S.M.S. Graf Spee" was launched in September 1917 and scrapped in 1923. "S.M.S. Prinz Eitel Friedrich" and "S.M.S. Fürst Bismarck" were still on the slipways at the end of the war, and were scrapped in 1922. August von Mackensen (1849-1945) was a great German Field Marshall of World War One, who distinguished himself in victories against Russia, Romania and Serbia. Admiral Maximilian Graf von Spee (1861-1914) was the Admiral who went down with his ships at the Battle of the Falkland Islands in 1914. Prinz Eitel Friedrich (1883-1942) was a son of Kaiser Wilhelm II, the latter being the German Emperor from 1888-1918. "Fürst Bismarck" literally means "Prince Bismarck" and of course refers to the German and Prussian Chancellor Otto von Bismarck (1815-1898) who held office from 1862 until his retirement in 1890.

*Die vier Schlachtkreuzer der "S.M.S. Mackensen" (1914) Klaße waren auf Kiel gelegt, wurden aber leider nie getauft. Zur Zeit des Ersten Weltkrieges waren Schlachtkreuzer wesentlich besser als Linienschiffe weil sie verhältnismaßig schneller waren. Die Panzerung und die Bewaffnung der Schlachtkreuzer lag unter der der Linienschiffe, aber die höhere Geschwindigkeit war vorteilhafter. Die geplante Einsatzverdrängung eines Schlachtkreuzers der "S.M.S. Mackensen" Klaße lag bei 35,300 Tonnen. Die geplante Bewaffnung dieser Klaße waren acht 35,5 cm Schnellfeuerkanonen (in vier Zwillingstürmen) sowie 14-15 cm Kasemattkanonen. Und die geplante Höchstgeschwindigkeit lag bei 28,8 Knoten mit einer geplanten Reichweite von 5,500 Seemeilen. Die "S.M.S. Mackensen" ist im April 1917 vom Stapel gelaufen und wurde im Jahre 1924 verschrottet. Die "S.M.S. Graf Spee" ist im September 1917 vom Stapel gelaufen und wurde im Jahre 1923 verschrottet. Die "S.M.S. Prinz Eitel Friedrich" und die "S.M.S. Fürst Bismarck" sind nie vom Stapel gelaufen, wurden aber im Jahre 1922 verschrottet. Generalfeldmarschall August von Mackensen (1849-1945) war deutscher Feldherr im Ersten Weltkrieg (1914-1918), der die Rußen, die Rumänen und Serben siegreich geschlagen hat. Admiral Maximilian Graf von Spee (1861-1914) war Kommandeur des Deutsch-Ostasiengeschwaders am Anfang des Ersten Weltkrieges. Er fiel mit allen deutschen Kreuzern (die "S.M.S. Scharnhorst," die "S.M.S. Gneisenau," die "S.M.S. Nürnberg" und die "S.M.S. Leipzig") in der Falkland-Schlacht. Prinz Eitel Friedrich (1883-1942) war Sohn von Kaiser Wilhelm II. Fürst Otto von Bismarck (1815-1898) war Preußisch-Deutscher Kanzler (der "Eiserner Kanzler") von 1862 bis 1890.*

### IIIc. "S.M.S. Derfflinger" Class / "S.M.S. Derfflinger" Klasse (1911)

Other important dreadnought class ships during World War One were the three battlecruisers of the "S.M.S. Derfflinger" (1914) class each of which were of 31,200 tons maximum displacement and were armed with 8-12 inch guns plus 12-6 inch guns. They could make up to 25,5 knots under full steam with their coal boilers. Steaming radius was 5,300 miles. The two other ships of this class were "S.M.S. Lützow" (1915) and "S.M.S. Hindenburg" (1917). "S.M.S. Derfflinger" was named after Brandenburg-Prussian Field Marshal Georg von Derfflinger (1606-1695), who served Brandenburg-Prussia against the Holy Roman Empire of the German Nation during the Thirty Years' War (1618-1648). "S.M.S. Lützow" was named after Ludwig Adolf Wilhelm von Lützow (1782-1834), a Prussian Lieutenant General who distinguished himself as a great cavalry officer and leader of men during the final years of the Napoleonic Wars (1792-1815), and "S.M.S. Hindenburg" was of course named after the famous German Field Marshall Paul von Hindenburg (1847-1934) of World War One. "S.M.S. Lützow" was scuttled after heavy damage at the Battle of Jutland in May 1916. Both of the other ships survived World War One. "S.M.S. Derfflinger" fought at the Battle of Jutland, but "S.M.S. Hindenburg" was commissioned thereafter (in May of 1917); both ships were surrendered to the British after the war and scuttled by their own German crews at the Royal Navy base of Scapa Flow in Scotland in June 1919. The British later raised and scrapped them, "S.M.S. Hindenburg" in 1931, and "S.M.S. Derfflinger" in 1946.

*Schlachtkreuzer der "S.M.S. Derfflinger" (1911) Klaße waren leider die letzten drei getauften Schlachtkreuzer der Kaiserlichen Marine. Die Schiffe dieser Klaße hatten einer Einsatzverdrängung von je 31,200 Tonnen. Die Bewaffnung dieser Klaße bestand aus acht 30,5 cm Schnellfeuerkanonen (in vier Zwillingstürme) sowie 12-15 cm Kasemattkanonen. Die maximale Geschwindigkeit betraf 25,5 Knoten, mit einer Reichweite von 5,300 Seemeilen. Zwei weiter*

*Schlachtkreuzer dieser Klaße waren die "S.M.S. Lützow" und die "S.M.S. Hindenburg." "S.M.S. Derfflinger" und "S.M.S. Lützow" nahmen an der Seeschlacht vom Skagerrak teil am 31. Mai 1916, wo die "S.M.S. Lützow" wegen schwerer Beschädigung eigenhändig versenkt wurde. Die meisten Besatzungsmitglieder der "S.M.S. Lützow" wurden allerdings von anderen deutschen Kriegsschiffen Gott sei Dank gerettet. "S.M.S. Derfflinger" und "S.M.S. Hindenburg" überlebten beide den Ersten Weltkrieg, wurden aber eigenhändig von den Deutschen im britischen Marinehafen von Scapa Flow im Juni 1919 versenkt.*

*Georg von Derfflinger (1606-1695) war Brandenburisch-Preußischer Generalfeldmarschall zur Zeit des tragischen Dreißigjährigen Krieges, als Brandenburg-Preußen treulos mit Frankreich, Dänemark und Schweden gegen das Heilige Römische Reich Deutscher Nation in den Krieg ging. Ludwig Adolf Wilhelm von Lützow (1782-1834) war berühmter Preußischer Kavallerie-Generalleutnant zur Zeit des Napoleonischen Krieges (1792-1815). Paul von Hindenburg (1847-1934) war doch der berühmte Generalfeldmarschall von Tannenberg (1914), und später Reichspräsident der Weimarer Republik von 1925 bis 1934.*

### IIId. "S.M.S. König" Class / "S.M.S. König" Klasse (1911)

The four dreadnought battleships of the "S.M.S. König" (commissioned in 1914 and named for the King of Prussia) class were of 28,600 tons maximum displacement each and were armed with 10-12 inch guns plus 14-6 inch guns. They were the most powerful German battleships for the first two years of the First World War. They could make up to 21,3 knots under full steam with their coal boilers, and were slightly better protected (or armored) compared to the very similar "S.M.S. Kaiser" class which preceded them. Range of action was a decent 8,000 miles. The three remaining vessels of the "S.M.S. König" class were the "S.M.S. Großer Kurfürst" (1914), the "S.M.S. Markgraf" (1914) and the "S.M.S. Kronprinz Wilhelm" (1914). "S.M.S. Großer Kurfürst"was named for Prince Friedrich Wilhelm I of Brandenburg-Prussia (1620-1688). His official titles were "Prince of Brandenburg and Duke of Prussia." At the time of his rule, Brandenburg was part of the Holy Roman Empire of the German Nation. Prussia (or what later came to be known as "East Prussia") was under the sovereignty of the United Kingdom of Poland and Lithuania. Prussia was most definitely German in both culture and language, but part of a different nation-state. The United Kingdom of Poland and Lithuania was yet another great nation of the Middle Ages, which included modern Poland, Lithuania, Belarus (White Russia) and the Ukraine (Little Russia). Much like the Holy Roman Empire of the

German Nation, the United Kingdom of Poland and Lithuania was both multi-cultural and multi-lingual. The official state religion was Roman Catholicism, but other religions were respected. Most Poles and Lithuanians are Roman Catholics, whereas most White Russians are Eastern (Russian) Orthodox. The Ukrainians (the "Little Russians") are a mixture of both Byzantine (Greek) Rite Roman Catholic and Eastern (Ukrainian and Russian) Orthodox. The German Prussians and Slavic Masurians of Eastern Prussia were mostly Evangelical Lutheran, whereas the East Prussian Ermland region was mostly German-speaking Roman Catholic. In addition to this, Poland had the largest Jewish community in the world, which was largely Yiddish speaking. Yiddish is a German language written in Hebrew characters, with a highly developed grammar, vocabulary and a rich literary tradition. Prior to the Holocaust of 1939-1945, the Jewish population in modern Poland was almost 3 million strong.

*Die vier Linienschiffe der "S.M.S. König" (1911) Klaße waren bis 1916 die größten Kriegsschiffe der Kaiserlichen Marine. Sie hatten eine Einsatzverdrängung von je 28,600 Tonnen, und wurden mit zehn 30,5 cm Schnellfeuerkanonen (in fünf Zwillingstürme) sowie mit 14-15 cm Kasemattkanonen bewaffnet. Die maximale Geschwindigkeit war 21,3 Knoten, und die Reichweite war gute 8,000 Seemeilen. Das die damaligen "Kohlendampfer" wesentlich langsamer waren als die späteren und modernen Diesel-und Turbinenschiffe spricht für sich selbst. Die Reichweite der älteren Schiffe war auch nicht die wie heutzutage. Die drei anderen Mitglieder dieser wichtigen Klaße waren die "S.M.S. Großer Kurfürst" (1914), die "S.M.S. Markgraf" (1914) und die "S.M.S. Kronprinz Wilhelm" (1914). Die "S.M.S. Großer Kurfürst" wurde im Jahre 1936 verschrottet. Die drei anderen Schwesterlinienschiffe liegen immer noch im britischen Hafen von Scapa Flow, wo sie von ihren deutschen Besatzungsmitgliedern im Juni 1919 selbst versenkt wurden.*

*Der König war doch Kaiser Wilhelm II, auch König von Preußen. Preußen war von 1701 bis 1918 Königreich, und bis Mai 1945 das größte Land im Deutschen Reich. Prinz Friedrich Wilhelm I von Brandenburg-Preußen (1620-1688) war der Große Kurfürst. Damals war er Prinz von Brandenburg sowie Herzog von Preußen. Brandenburg-Preußen gehörte zum Adelhaus Hohenzollern. Hohenzollern liegt neben Württemberg, und war das Adelhaus von Brandenburg-Preußen sowie Rumänien. Ostpreußen war doch deutschsprachig, aber war Schutzgebiet von Polen.*

### Nordostpreußen in Rußland (Northeast Prussia – now part of Russia)

*Nordostpreußen (heute "Kaliningrad Oblast" oder "Königsberg Gebiet" in Rußland sowie Memelland in Litauen) und Masuren waren evangelische (Masuren ist heute noch evangelisch), aber das Ermland in Südostpreußen war (und ist heute noch) römisch-katholisch. Das Vereinigte Königreich von Polen und Litauen (1385-1791) war vormals Großmacht in Osteuropa, mit Herrschaft über Polen, Westpreußen, Posen, Galizien, Lodomerien, Litauen, Weißrußland, die Ukraine und Bukowina. Damals hatte Polen die größte jüdische Bevölkerungszahl der Welt. Im Jahre 1939 hatte Polen immer noch 3 Millionen Juden.*

### Markgrafschaft Brandenburg (the Margraviate of Brandenburg)

*Das Linienschiff "S.M.S. Markgraf" wurde für die ehemalige Markgrafschaft Brandenburg benannt. Brandenburg war Markgrafschaft von 1415 bis 1815, Herzogtum und Markgrafschaft von 1618 bis 1701, Königreich Brandenburg-Preußen von 1701 bis 1815, Provinz vom Königreich Preußens von 1815 bis 1918, Provinz des Landes Preußen von 1918 bis 1945, Land der sowjetischen Besatzungszone von 1945 bis 1949 und war aufgeteilt in mehrere Bezirke der Deutschen Demokratischen Republik (DDR) von 1952 bis 1990.*

### Kronprinz Wilhelm von Preußen (Crown Prince Wilhelm of Prussia)

*Kronprinz Wilhelm von Preußen war der älteste Sohn vom Deutschen Kaiser Wilhelm II. Kaiser Wilhelm II mußte aber abdanken im November 1918, und lebte in Holland bis er im Jahre 1941 starb. Kronprinz Wilhelm war leider Anhänger der Nationalsozialistischen Bewegung Adolf Hitlers, und starb in Deutschland im Jahre 1951. Der älteste überlebende Sohn von Kronprinz Wilhelm (Prinz Louis Ferdinand von Preußen) war Antinazi, und war während des Zweiten Weltkrieges in Nordamerika. Sein ältester Sohn Prinz Louis Ferdinand II von Preußen lebte nur von 1944 bis 1977. Der älteste Sohn von Prinz Louis Ferdinand II ist Prinz Georg Friedrich Ferdinand von Preußen (im Jahre 1976 geboren).*

"S.M.S. Markgraf" was named after a great Count of one of the Eastern Marches (i.e., new territories) of the Hohenzollern Dynasty of Brandenburg-Prussia as well – this going back even further in history. The English equivalent of this noble title is "Marquess." The Margraviate of Brandenburg was under the rule of the Hohenzollern Dynasty from 1415 until 1918. It was officially a Margraviate from 1415 until 1815. It was just a Margraviate and no more from 1415 to 1618, it was in personal union with the Duchy of Prussia from 1618 until 1701, and then in personal union with the Kingdom of Prussia from 1701 until 1815. Brandenburg was then a "Province" of the Kingdom of Prussia from 1815 until 1918, and then of the State of Prussia from 1918 until 1945. In 1945, Brandenburg came under Soviet Russian occupation after World War Two. In 1949, all former provinces within the Soviet zone of occupation were abolished and replaced with more numerous and much smaller administrative districts of the newly established Communist "German Democratic Republic," ("Deutsche Demokratische Republik" in German) which lasted from 1949-1990. With the peaceful reunification of Germany in 1990, the old provinces such as Brandenburg were once again re-established, and joined with the existing Federal Republic of Germany ("Bundesrepublik Deutschland" in German) of the West. "S.M.S. Kronprinz Wilhelm" was named for the Crown Prince of Germany, who would have become Kaiser Wilhelm III in 1941 had his father not been deposed in November 1918. Crown Prince William (his English name) lived until 1951 and was succeeded by his son Prince Louis Ferdinand of Prussia, who lived until 1994. Crown Prince William joined the Nazi Party before World War Two, but Prince Louis Ferdinand was an avid anti-Nazi who left Germany before World War Two. The current head of the House of Prussia or Hohenzollern Dynasty is Prinz Georg Friedrich Ferdinand, who was born in 1976 (Prince George Frederick Ferdinand in English), the grandson of Prince Louis Ferdinand (his father Prince Louis Ferdinand II only lived from 1944 until 1977). The four ships of this class all fought at the Battle of Jutland in May 1916 and survived World War One. They were surrendered to the Royal Navy and were scuttled by their own German crews in an act of defiance in June 1919 at the British base of Scapa Flow in Scotland. "S.M.S. Großer Kurfürst" was later raised and scrapped in 1936, but the three other ships remain at the bottom of Scapa Flow today. A Scottish company purchased the rights to raise and scrap them in 1962, but has never done so.

### IIIe. "S.M.S. Seydlitz" Class / "S.M.S. Seydlitz" Klasse (1911)

The dreadnought battlecruiser "S.M.S. Seydlitz" (commissioned in 1913) displaced 28,550 tons and was armed with 10-11 inch guns plus 12-6 inch guns. She could make up to 28,1 knots with her coal boilers at full steam and had an operating radius of 4,200 miles. She served with great distinction at the Battle of Jutland in May 1916, inflicting huge losses upon the Royal Navy of England. She survived that battle as the most heavily damaged German ship, limping back home to safety in spite of her tremendous wounds. This was a profound testament to the extremely high quality of German construction and to the skill and bravery of her officers and crewmen. She survived World War One to be surrendered to the British and to be scuttled by her own German crew at the Royal Navy base of Scapa Flow in Scotland in June 1919. She was finally raised and scrapped in 1930. She was named for Friedrich Wilhelm Freiherr von Seydlitz (1721-1773), one of the greatest cavalry generals in the history of the Prussian Army.

*Der Schlachtkreuzer "S.M.S. Seydlitz" ist im Jahre 1911 vom Stapel gelaufen, und wurde im Jahre 1913 getauft. Das Schiff hatte eine Einsatzverdrängung von 28,550 Tonnen, und war mit zehn 28 cm Schnellfeuerkanonen (in fünf Zwillingstürme) sowie mit 12-15 cm Kasemattkanonen bewaffnet. Die "S.M.S. Seydlitz" hatte eine Höchstgeschwindigkeit von 28,1 Knoten, und eine Reichweite von 4,200 Seemeilen. Bei der Seeschlacht vom Skagerrak am 31. Mai 1916 wurde sie schwer beschädigt, gelang aber sicher wieder nach Wilhelmshaven Dank ihrer leistungsfähigen Besatzung und auch letztlich wegen der unübertrefflichen Wertverarbeitung während Herstellung des Schiffes. Nach dem Ersten Weltkrieg in Juni 1919 wurde sie von ihrer deutschen Besatzung im Hafen von Scapa Flow selbst versenkt weil sie die Briten diese Kriegsbeute vorenthalten wollten. Friedrich Wilhelm von Seydlitz (1721-1773) war einer der berühmtesten Kavalleriegenerale der Preußischen Armee.*

### IIIf. "S.M.S. Kaiser" Class / "S.M.S. Kaiser" Klasse (1909)

The five dreadnought battleships of the "S.M.S. Kaiser" (1912) class were each of 27,000 tons maximum displacement, were also armed with 10-12 inch guns plus 14-6 inch guns and could make up to 23,4 knots under full steam with their coal boilers. Range of operations was a rather decent 7,900 miles. "Kaiser" of course referred to the German Emperor Kaiser Wilhelm II, who reigned from 1888 until his abdication in November 1918. The four other ships of this class were "S.M.S. Prinzregent Luitpold" (1912), "S.M.S. Friedrich der Grosse" (1912), "S.M.S. Kaiserin" (1913) and "S.M.S. König Albert" (1913). "S.M.S. Prinzregent Luitpold" was named for the heir to the throne of the Kingdom of Bavaria, a large South German state. "S.M.S. Friedrich der Grosse" was of course named after King Frederick the Great of Prussia, who won fame (or infamy, depending upon who one asks) as a successful military leader in the 18th century. "S.M.S. Kaiserin" was named for the Empress of Germany and wife of Kaiser Wilhelm II – her name was Kaiserin Augusta. "S.M.S. König Albert" was named after King Albert of Bavaria. All ships except "S.M.S. König Albert" fought at the Battle of Jutland in May 1916. They all survived World War One, and were surrendered to the British after the war. They were scuttled by their own crews in the Royal Navy base of Scapa Flow in Scotland in June 1919. Thereafter, they were raised by the British and scrapped. "S.M.S. Kaiserin" and "S.M.S. König Albert" were scrapped in 1936, and "S.M.S. Friedrich der Grosse" was scrapped in 1937.

These ships and the four that followed them were considered to be the backbone of the German Navy from 1912 until 1918, and they successfully fought against much larger English ships – a testament to very high German quality of construction and the skill and bravery of the German officers and sailors. "S.M.S. Friedrich der Grosse" served as Fleet Flagship from 1912 until 1916 (the ships of Grand Admiral Alfred von Tirpitz and Admiral Reinhard Scheer). It was Admiral Scheer who commanded the fleet at Jutland.

*Die fünf Linienschiffe der "S.M.S. Kaiser" (1909) Klaße hatten eine Einsatzverdrängung von je 27,000 Tonnen, und waren mit je zehn 30,5 cm Schnellfeuerkanonen (in fünf Zwillingstürme) sowie mit 14 15-cm Kasemattkanonen bewaffnet. Sie hatten eine Höchstgeschwindigkeit von 23,4 Knoten und eine Reichweite von 7,900 Seemeilen. Die anderen Linienschiffe dieser Klaße waren die "S.M.S. Prinzregent Luitpold" (1912), die "S.M.S. Friedrich der Große" (1912), die "S.M.S. Kaiserin" (1913) und die "S.M.S. König Albert" (1913). Alle Einheiten dieser Klaße (außer der "S.M.S. König Albert") nahmen an der großen Seeschlacht am Skagerrak im Mai 1916 teil. Diese fünf Linienschiffe überlebten den Ersten Weltkrieg, und wurden im Hafen von Scapa Flow in Juni 1919 selbst versenkt. Danach wurden sie alle von den Briten geborgen und verschrottet – die "S.M.S. Kaiserin" und die "S.M.S. König Albert" im Jahre 1936 und die "S.M.S. Friedrich der Große" im Jahre 1937.*

## Kaiser Wilhelm II (German Emperor Wilhelm II)

*"Kaiser" war doch Kaiser Wilhelm II, König von Preußen. "Kaiserin" war seine Gemahlin, die Kaiserin Augusta von Deutschland sowie die Königin von Preußen. Der "Prinzregent Luitpold" war der älteste Sohn des Königs von Bayern, und der "König Albert" war der König von Sachsen. Friedrich der Große war doch König von Preußen sowie Markgraf von Brandenburg im 18. Jahrhundert. Er war auch als der "Alte Fritz" und als der "Große Fritz" bekannt.*

**Kaiser Wilhelm II von Deutschland und Kaiser Franz Josef I von Österreich-Ungarn / Emperor William II of Germany (reigned from 1888 until 1918) and Emperor Francis Joseph of Austria-Hungary (reigned from 1848 until 1916).**

**IIIg. "S.M.S. Moltke" Class / "S.M.S. Moltke" Klasse (1909)**

The two dreadnought battlecruisers of the "S.M.S. Moltke" (1912) class were of 25,400 tons each and were armed with 10-11 inch guns plus 10-6 inch guns and could make an impressive 28,0 knots under full steam with their coal boilers. Steaming radius was 4,100 miles. Helmuth von Moltke was the senior-ranking Prussian Field Marshall during the wars of German unification. These were fought against Denmark in 1864, (sadly) against Austria in 1866 and finally against France from 1870 to 1871. Von Moltke was the first military leader in Europe to make very efficient use of modern railroads to move troops quickly, and to use the telegraph to communicate with his commanders in the field of battle. Prussian observers had learned much about these new technologies by visiting the United States during the Civil War between North and South from 1861 to 1865. The second ship in this class was the "S.M.S. Goeben" (1912), which became famous due to her sortie to Ottoman Turkey at the start of World War One. Germany thus ensured that the Ottoman Empire would enter the war on the side of the Central Powers of Germany, Austria-Hungary and Bulgaria. Both ships survived World War One. "S.M.S. Moltke" fought at the Battle of

Jutland in May 1916 and was surrendered to Britain after the war. She was scuttled by her crew while interned in the English Royal Navy Base at Scapa Flow in Scotland, raised and scrapped in 1929. "S.M.S. Goeben" served in the Turkish Navy until she was sadly scrapped in 1974. Many naval veterans in Germany wanted to save her, bring her back home to Germany and restore her as a museum. She was named for the Prussian general August Karl von Goeben, who lived from 1816 until 1880.

*Die zwei Schlachtkreuzer der "S.M.S. Moltke" (1909) Klaße hatten eine Einsatzverdrängung von je 25,400 Tonnen, und wurden mit zehn 28 cm Schnellfeuerkanonen sowie mit zehn 15 cm Kasemattkanonen bewaffnet. Die Höchstgeschwindigkeit waren gute 28 Knoten, und die Reichweite war 4,100 Seemeilen. Die "S.M.S. Moltke" diente bei der großen Seeschlacht vom Skagerrak im Mai 1916, sowie bei der Befreiung von Estland im Oktober 1917. 363 kaiserlich-deutsche Seefahrzeuge, 80 Flugzeuge, 6 Zeppelin-Luftschiffe und 25,000 Truppen des deutschen Heeres haben die Inseln von Dago, Ösel und Moon von den Rußen erobert, und dadurch den Krieg im Osten gewonnen. Nach dem Ersten Weltkrieg wurde die "S.M.S. Moltke" im britischen Hafen von Scapa Flow selbst versenkt, später geborgen und dann im Jahre 1929 verschrottet.*

**Helmuth von Moltke**

*Der ältere Helmuth von Moltke war der berühmte und fähige Preußische Feldherr in den Kriegen gegen Dänemark (1864), Österreich (1866) und Frankreich (1870-1871). Er hatte die moderne Technologie (wie die Eisenbahn und den Telegraph) in der neuen "Keßelschlacht-Taktik" ausgenutzt. Es war aber sehr bedauerlich, daß Preußen Krieg gegen den deutschsprachigen Bruderstaat Österreich führte. Ein großdeutsches Reich genausowie im Ersten Deutschen Reich (das Heilige Römische Reich der Deutschen Nation von 800 bis 1806) wäre für Deutschland besser gewesen. Die christliche Donaumonarchie des Adelhauses Habsburg-Lothringen könnte als Vorbild dienen – ein vereintes Mitteleuropa für das Deutschtum sowie für die Ungarn, die Tschechen, die Slowaken, die Slowener, die Kroaten, die Südtiroler, die Schlesier, die Galizier und die Weißruthener aus Bukowina ("Buchenland" auf deutsch).*

**Der Schlachtkreuzer "S.M.S. Goeben" / the Battlecruiser "S.M.S. Goeben"**

*Der andere Schlachtkreuzer dieser Klaße war die "S.M.S. Goeben" (1912). Am Anfang des Ersten Weltkrieges war die "S.M.S. Goeben" sowie der Kleine Kreuzer die "S.M.S. Breslau" im Mittelmeer. Für die englische Marine waren die zwei deutsche Kriegsschiffe einfach zu schnell. Es war der "S.M.S. Goeben" und der "S.M.S. Breslau" gelungen, das Ottomanische Reich zu erreichen. Die deutsche Regiergung unter Kaiser Wilhelm II hatte die "S.M.S. Goeben" an die ottomanische Türkei gegeben, und die Türken haben sich dann mit den Mittelmächten (Deutschland, Österreich-Ungarn und Bulgarien) vereinigt. Die "S.M.S. Goeben" überlebte beide Weltkriege, und wurde erst im Jahre 1974 verschrottet. Vorher hatte der Deutsche Marinebund versucht, die "S.M.S. Goeben" zu kaufen und wieder nach Deutschland zu bringen. Der Marinebund wollte die "S.M.S. Goeben" restaurieren, aber leider haben die Türken das abgelehnt. August Karl von Goeben (1816-1880) war Preußischer General, der im Deutsch-Französischen Krieg gedient hatte.*

**Schlachtkreuzer "S.M.S. Goeben" (1912) / Battlecruiser "S.M.S. Goeben" (1912) – painting by Naval artist Günther Todt (1928-2009)**

**IIIh. "S.M.S. Helgoland" Class / "S.M.S. Helgoland" Klasse (1908)**

The four German dreadnought battleships of the "S.M.S. Helgoland" (1911) class were of 24,700 tons maximum displacement each and were armed with 12-12 inch guns plus 14-6 inch guns and could make up to 21,2 knots under full steam with their coal boilers. Radius of action for these ships was 3,600 miles. "Helgoland" is an island and naval base in the German Bay of the North Sea. Her population is Frisian, which is a small Germanic tribe inhabiting the coastal region of Denmark, Germany and the Netherlands. They have a very unique language, quite different from modern German, Dutch or Danish. The island was traded to Germany by England in 1890, for which the English received the island of Zanzibar off the coast of German East Africa in return. The three remaining ships of this class were the "S.M.S. Ostfriesland" (1911), the "S.M.S. Thüringen" (1911) and the "S.M.S. Oldenburg" (1912). "Ostfriesland" is the German word for the Lower Saxon region of East Frisia, which is located in between the city of Oldenburg and the Dutch border. "Thüringen" is the German word for the German state of Thuringia. This region used to be home to a number of Saxon principalities, one of which is the ancestral home of the current Royal Family of England. During World War One, the English Royal Family adopted the surname "Windsor" due to anti-German feeling in Britain. This is not their real surname, because the male head of the family came from the Thuringian Principality of Sachsen-Coburg-Gotha. The female head of the family was descended from Queen Victoria, who came from the North German Royal House of Hanover. "Oldenburg" was a former Grand Duchy in Northern Germany, with a capital city also named Oldenburg. The current and former Royal Houses of Denmark, Norway, Greece and Russia all trace their ancestral lineage to the Royal House of the Grand Duchy of Oldenburg in Germany. The House (noble family) of Oldenburg is Evangelical Lutheran in Germany, Denmark and Norway. They are Eastern Orthodox in Greece (Greek Orthodox, specifically) and in Russia (Russian Orthodox).

*Die vier Linienschiffe der "S.M.S. Helgoland" (1908) Klaße hatten eine Einsatzverdrängung von je 24,700 Tonnen, und wurden mit 12-30,5 cm Schnellfeuerkanonen sowie mit 14-15 cm Kasemattkanonen bewaffnet. Die Höchstgeschwindigkeit war 21,2 Knoten, und die Reichweite war 3,600 Seemeilen. Diese vier Linienschiffe beteiligten sich bei der großen Seeschlacht am Skagerrak am 31. Mai 1916, und überlebten den Ersten Weltkrieg. Die anderen Mitglieder dieser Klaße waren die "S.M.S. Ostfriesland" (1911), die "S.M.S. Thüringen" (1911) und die "S.M.S. Oldenburg" (1912). Alle vier Linienschiffe der "S.M.S. Helgoland" Klaße überlebten den Ersten Weltkrieg. Die "S.M.S. Oldenburg" wurde im Jahre 1921 verschrottet, die "S.M.S. Helgoland" wurde im Jahre 1924 verschrottet und die "S.M.S. Thüringen" wurde nur im Jahre 1933 verschrottet. Die "S.M.S. Ostfriesland" wurde aber im Sinne des Versailler-Vertrages nach dem Ersten Weltkrieg an die USA gegeben. Die Amerikaner haben die "S.M.S. Ostfriesland" an der Küste vor dem US-Bundesstaat Virginien mit Luftbomben im Jahre 1921 versenkt, ein Manöver das keinen wertvollen und besonderen Eindruck bei der Führung der amerikanischen Marine hinterließ. Die kaiserlichen japanischen Streitkräfte allerdings haben davon Gebrauch gemacht am 7. Dezember 1941 im Angriff auf Pearl Harbor, Hawaii.*

## Die Adelhäuser von Oldenburg und Sachsen / the Noble Houses of Oldenburg and Saxony

*Die Adelhäuser in Norwegen, Dänemark, Griechenland und Rußland stammen alle aus dem Großherzogtum Oldenburg. Die adelige Familie des Hauses Oldenburg ist in Oldenburg, Norwegen und Dänemark evangelisch, und in Griechenland und Rußland orthodoxisch. Die adelige Familie Wettin stammt aus Sachsen und Thüringen. Die Adelhäuser in Großbrittanien, Portugal, Brasilien, Belgien, Bulgarien, Polen und Litauen stammen alle aus Sachsen und Thüringen. Die adelige Familie des Hauses Wettin ist in Deutschland evangelisch, in Bulgarien orthodoxisch, in Großbrittanien anglikanisch, und in Portugal, Brasilien, Belgien, Polen und Litauen römisch-katholisch.*

All four ships of this class fought at the Battle of Jutland in May 1916 and survived the First World War. "S.M.S. Thüringen" survived the longest, having been scrapped in 1933. "S.M.S. Helgoland" was scrapped in 1924, and "S.M.S. Oldenburg" was scrapped in 1921. "S.M.S Ostfriesland" was taken by the Americans as war booty after World War One, and sunk as a target off the coast of Virginia in 1921. The official Japanese Navy observers of this test used the knowledge they gained in the attack on Pearl Harbor, Oahu (Hawaii, USA) on December 7, 1941.

## IIIi. "Ersatz S.M.S. Monarch" Class / "Ersatz S.M.S. Monarch" Klasse (1914)

The Austro-Hungarian Navy planned four brand new dreadnought battleships in 1914, the construction of which was cancelled due to the outbreak of World War One. They were to have been somewhat larger than the four ships of the "S.M.S. Viribus Unitis" class, at 24,605 tons each. Primary armament was to have been 10-14 inch guns, mounted in four turrets (one triple and one dual turret each, fore and aft). Secondary armament was to have been 18-6 inch guns, mounted in casemates. Top speed was to have been 21 knots. But I doubt these ships were missed, because they also lacked the very critical underwater protection – torpedo bulkheads which were not present in the "S.M.S. Viribus Unitis" class. Names for two of the four planned ships had already been mentioned, including "S.M.S. Laudon" and "S.M.S. Hunyadi." Ernst Gideon Freiherr von Laudon (1717-1790) was a great Austrian Field Marshall of the Seven Years' War (1756-1763). He was of German, Latvian and Scottish descent (his surname being Scottish). "Hunyadi" was a noble family of Hungarian and Romanian ancestry, whose line died out in the 16th century.

*Die vier Linienschiffe der "Ersatz S.M.S. Monarch" Klaße der Kaiserlichen und Königlichen Kriegsmarine Österreich-Ungarns von 1914 waren auf jeden Fall geplant, aber nie auf Kiel gelegt. Mit einer geplanten Einsatzverdrängung von je 24,605 Tonnen waren sie ein bischen größer als die vier getauften Linienschiffe der "S.M.S. Viribus Unitis" Klaße. Hauptbewaffnung war mit zehn 35,5 cm Schnellfeuerkanonen, (zwei Drillingstürme und zwei Zwillingstürme) sowie mit 18-15 cm Kasemattkanonen geplant. Die geplante Höchstgeschwindigkeit lag bei 21 Knoten. Aber die Linienschiffe Österreich-Ungarns (sowie die meisten Linienschiffe außerhalb des Deutschen Reiches) hatten nicht genug Torpedoabwehrsicherung. Zwei von den vier geplanten Linienschiffe dieser Klaße hatten schon vorgeschlagene Patennamen: die "S.M.S. Laudon" und die "S.M.S. Hunyadi." Ernst Gideon Freiherr von Laudon (1717-1790) war österreichischer Generalfeldmarschall des Siebenjährigen Krieges (1756-1763). Seine Abstammung kam aus Deutschland, Lettland und Schottland. Hunyadi gehörte zu einem Adelhaus aus Ungarn und Siebenbürgen, das im 16. Jahrhundert ausgestorben ist.*

## IIIj. "S.M.S. Viribus Unitis" Class / "S.M.S. Viribus Unitis" Klasse (1911)

The four Austrian dreadnought battleships of the "S.M.S. Viribus Unitis" (1912) class were of 22,500 tons maximum displacement each and armed with 12-12 inch guns plus 12-6 inch guns and could make up to 20,8 knots under full steam with their coal boilers. Range of action was 4,200 miles – very good for ships to be confined to the Adriatic Sea. "Viribus Unitis" is Latin for "with united forces" – this was the motto of the Austrian armed forces, known as the "Kaiserliche und Königliche Wehrmacht" (Imperial and Royal Armed Forces). From 1935 to 1945, Germany also called its armed forces the "Wehrmacht" instead of the "Reichswehr," which was the official name of the German armed forces from 800 until 1935. Germany had no official armed forced from 1945 until 1956 (aside from the Federal Border Patrol ("Bundesgrenzschutz" in German) and the German Minesweeping Service ("Deutscher Minenräumdienst" in German). Since 1956, the German armed forces have been known as the Federal Armed Forces (or "Bundeswehr" in German). From 1949 until 1990, the armed forces of the former Communist East Germany were known as the National Peoples' Army ("Nationale Volksarmee" in German). The former East German Navy was known as the Peoples' Navy ("Volksmarine" in German). Since 1955, the armed forces of Austria have been known as the Federal Army (or "Bundesheer" in German). The Austrian armed forces had this same name from 1918 until 1938, when Austria was annexed by Germany.

*Die vier Linienschiffe der "S.M.S. Viribus Unitis" (1911) Klaße gehörten zur Kaiserlichen und Königlichen Kriegsmarine von Österreich-Ungarn. Sie hatten eine Einsatzverdrängung von je 22,500 Tonnen, und wurden mit 12-30,5 cm Schnellfeuerkanonen (in vier Drillingstürmen) sowie mit 12-15 cm Kasemattkanonen bewaffnet. Die Höchstgeschwindigkeit lag bei 20,8 Knoten und die Reichweite war 4,200 Seemeilen – ganz gut für Schiffe, die für das Adriatische Meer beabsichtigt waren. "Viribus Unitis" ist lateinisch für "mit vereinten Kräfte," der Wahlspruch der Kaiserlichen und Königlichen Wehrmacht. Die drei anderen Linienschiffe dieser Klaße waren die "S.M.S. Prinz Eugen" (1912), die "S.M.S. Tegetthoff" (1913) und die "S.M.S. Szent Istvan" (1915).*

## Prinz Eugen von Savoyen / Prince Eugene of Savoy

*Prinz Eugen von Savoyen (1663-1736) war ein sehr berühmter Generalfeldmarschall des Heiligen Römischen Reiches der Deutschen Nation. Prinz Eugen trat der Kaiserlichen und Königlichen Armee im Jahre 1683 bei. Im Jahre 1697 wurde er zum Oberbefehlshaber der Kaiserlichen und Königlichen Armee befördert. Prinz Eugen hatte die ottomanischen Türken im Jahre 1697 bei der Schlacht von Zenta geschlagen, als er Sarajevo in Bosnien-Herzegowina eroberte. Zur Zeit des spanischen Erbfolgkrieges (1700 bis 1714) kämpfte Prinz Eugen bei den Schlachten von Cassano und Chiari im Norditalien im Jahre 1705. Und letztlich hatte er im dritten Türkenkrieg von 1716 bis 1718 die ottomanischen Türken bei den Schlachten von Peterwardein und Temeschburg wieder geschlagen. Beim Friedensvertrag von Passarowitz im Jahre 1718 wurden Nordserbien und die kleine Wallachei an Österreich übergeben. Die Kaiserliche und Königliche Kriegsmarine hatte drei Schiffe "S.M.S. Prinz Eugen" benannt. Das erste Schiff war eine Panzerfregatte im Jahre 1863, dann ein Kasemattschiff im Jahre 1880 und letztlich ein Linienschiff im Jahre 1912. Das Linienschiff überlebte den Ersten Weltkrieg und wurde nach dem Krieg an Frankreich übergeben. Am 24. Mai 1915 hatte die "S.M.S. Prinz Eugen" den Feindeshafen von Ancona (Italien) bombardiert. Am 28. Juni 1922 hatte die französische Marine die "S.M.S. Prinz Eugen" südlich von Toulon als Zielschiff versenkt – und dort liegt sie immer noch. Im Jahre 1940 hatte die Deutsche Kriegsmarine einen Schweren Kreuzer "Prinz Eugen" getauft. Der Kreuzer überlebte den Zweiten Weltkrieg, und wurde eventuell an die amerkanische Marine übergeben. Die Amerikaner haben die "Prinz Eugen" von 1940 im Dezember 1946 in Kwajalein (in den ehemaligen Kaiserlich-Deutschen Marshall Inseln) als Zielschiff versenkt. Ihr umgekippter Rumpf ist dort immer noch leicht zu sehen, weil sie in sehr seichtem Wasser liegt. Eine von ihren Schrauben wurde von den Amerikanern an den Deutschen Marinebund zurückgegeben, und ist nun im Marine-Ehrenmal Laboe zu sehen. Die Donau Dampfschiff Gesellschaft*

*(DDSG) von Österreich hat ein neues Passagierschiff "M/S Prinz Eugen" im Jahre 1987 getauft, und sie ist immer noch im Dienst.*

**Die Linienschiffe der "S.M.S. Tegetthoff" Klasse / the Battleships of the "S.M.S. Tegetthoff" Class**

*Das Linienschiff "S.M.S. Tegetthoff" (1913) überlebte den Ersten Weltkrieg, und wurde im Jahre 1925 in La Spezia (Italien) verschrottet. Am 24. Mai 1915 hatte die "S.M.S. Tegetthoff" den Hafen von Ancona (Italien) bombardiert. Das Schiff wurde am 25. März 1919 den Italienern übergeben, und blieb bis 1923 im Hafen von Venedig. Vizeadmiral Wilhelm Joseph Freiherr von Tegetthoff hatte die königliche italienische Marine im Jahre 1866 bei der Seeschlacht von Lissa geschlagen. Zu der Zeit war die italienische Flotte die drittgrößte Marine der Welt – nach der Royal Navy von England und der US Navy von Amerika.*

**Das Linienschiff "S.M.S. Szent Istvan" / the Battleship "S.M.S. Szent Istvan"**

*Das Linienschiff "S.M.S. Szent Istvan" wurde in Sankt Veit am Pflaumb ("Fiume" auf italienisch und heute "Rijeka" auf kroatisch) im Jahre 1912 auf Kiel gelegt, ist im Jahre 1914 vom Stapel gelaufen und wurde erst im Kriegsjahr 1915 getauft und in Dienst gestellt. "Szent Istvan" ist magjarisch für Sankt Stefan, der Kirchenpatron von Ungarn. Während des Ersten Weltkrieges war die "S.M.S. Szent Istvan" fast nie im Einsatz. Am 11. Juni 1918 war sie endlich im Einsatz, wurde aber von dem italienischen Schnellboot "MAS 15" in der südlichen Adria torpediert. 89 Besatzungsmitglieder sind an diesem traurigen Tag gefallen, aber mindestens 873 wurden von anderen Kaiserlichen und Königlichen Kriegsschiffen gerettet.*

The three remaining ships of the "S.M.S. Viribus Unitis" class were the "S.M.S. Tegetthoff" (1913), the "S.M.S. Prinz Eugen" (1912) and the S.M.S. Szent Istvan" (1915). "S.M.S. Tegetthoff" was of course named after Vice Admiral Wilhelm Joseph von Tegetthoff, who was the great hero of the Battle of Lissa in 1866. "S.M.S. Prinz Eugen" (1912) was named after the great Holy Roman and German Field Marshall Prince Eugene of Savoy, who lived from 1663 until 1736. He was famous for having defeated both the Ottoman Turks and the French. Prince Eugene joined the Imperial and Royal Army in 1683, and became its supreme commander in 1697 – the same year in which the Ottoman Turks were defeated at the Battle of Zenta (leading to the capture of Sarajevo in Bosnia-Herzegovina). He commanded the Army yet again during the War of the Spanish Succession (1700-1714), when the Spanish Monarchy passed from the Habsburg

Dynasty to the Bourbon Dynasty. Prince Eugene was active in the Italian theater during the War of the Spanish Succession, at the Battles of Cassano and Chiari (both in 1705). Finally, he commanded the Army during the Third Turkish War from 1716 to 1718, defeating the Ottoman Turks at the Battles of Peterwardein and Temeschburg. He lead the conquest of Belgrade in 1717, which lead to the Peace Treaty of Passarowitz in 1718 – when Ottoman Turkey surrendered both Northern Serbia and Little Wallachia (in modern Romania) to the Austrian Empire. An Armored Sailing Frigate was named "S.M.S. Prinz Eugen" in 1863 (displacing 3,588 tons full load) as well as a Casemate Sailing Ship in 1880. "S.M.S. Szent Istvan" was named for Saint Stephen, the Patron Saint of Hungary. Both "S.M.S. Viribus Unitis" and "S.M.S. Tegetthoff" were scrapped after World War One (the latter in 1925), the former ship after she was sunk by Italian torpedos and went down with some of her crew in 1918. "S.M.S. Prinz Eugen" was taken by France as war booty after the First World War, and sunk as a target off the Southern coast of France – where she remains to this day. "S.M.S. Szent Istvan" was sunk by Italian torpedos in 1918, and went down with some of her crew in shallow waters off the Adriatic coast of Croatia. The wreck is still there, and is preserved as a national monument and grave site.

### IIIk. "S.M.S. Wolga" Class / "S.M.S. Wolga" Klasse (1912)

The completed Imperial Russian dreadnought battleship "Imperator Aleksandr III" (commissioned in 1918) was surrendered to the Imperial German Navy when Russia surrendered to Germany in 1917. She was originally named for Czar Alexander III, but the Germans renamed her after the river "Volga" ("Wolga" in German), along which many ethnic German settlers lived. She displaced 22,500 tons full load, and was armed with 12-12 inch guns plus 18-5 inch guns. She could make up to 21,4 knots with her coal boilers under full steam, but her range of operation was a mere 1,000 miles – which would have been an extreme drawback operating in the North Atlantic and beyond. She was returned to Russia after Germany's surrender to the Western Allies in November 1918, and fought on the side of the anti-communists in the Russian Civil War. She eventually escaped to France after the unfortunate Bolshevik Communist victory in Russia, where she was finally scrapped in 1936.

*Das ehemalige kaiserlich-rußische Linienschiff "Imperator Aleksandr III" (1912) wurde im Jahre 1917 an die Kaiserlich-Deutsche Marine übergeben, und dann im Jahre 1918 als die "S.M.S. Wolga" getauft. Sehr viele Wolgadeutsche wohnen seit dem 18. Jahrhundert in Rußland. Die "S.M.S. Wolga" hatte eine Einsatzverdrängung von 22,500 Tonnen, und wurde mit 12-30,5 cm Schnellfeuerkanonen sowie mit 18-13 mm Kasemattkanonen bewaffnet. Ihre*

*Höchstgeschwindigkeit war 21,4 Knoten aber ihre Reichweite war nur 1,000 Seemeilen. Man soll hierbei bedenken, daß viele russische Marinefahrzeuge nur für Einsätze auf der Ostsee gebaut wurden. Nach dem Ende des Ersten Weltkrieges wurde das Linienschiff an die Rußen zurückgegeben, wo es auf der Seite der Antikommunisten gekämpft hat. Nach dem Sieg der Bolschewisten ist es der "Imperator Aleksandr III" gelungen nach Frankreich zu entkommen. Sie wurde endlich im Jahre 1936 verschrottet.*

### IIІl. "S.M.S. Von der Tann" Class / "S.M.S. Von der Tann" Klasse (1907)

"S.M.S. Von der Tann" (1910) was the very first German dreadnought battlecruiser. She was of 21,300 tons maximum displacement and was armed with 8-11 inch guns plus 12-6 inch guns, and could make an impressive 27,4 knots under full steam with her coal boilers. Range of action was 4,400 miles. She was named for a Bavarian general who lived from 1815 until 1881. "S.M.S. Von der Tann" (1910) served at the Battle of Jutland in May 1916, was surrendered to the British after World War One and interned at the Royal Navy base of Scapa Flow in Scotland where her own crew scuttled her in June 1919. The British raised and scrapped the wreck in 1934. Battlecruisers were the ships that replaced armored, or large cruisers. They were even larger, better protected, faster and had more larger caliber guns. Battlecruisers thus made armored, or large cruisers obsolete in the first decade of the twentieth century.

*Die "S.M.S. Von der Tann" (1907) war Deutschlands erster Schlachtkreuzer. Sie hatte eine Einsatzverdrängung von 21,300 Tonnen, und wurde mit acht 28 cm Schnellfeuerkanonen (in vier Zwillingstürmen) sowie mit 12-15 cm Kasemattkanonen bewaffnet. Ihre Höchstgeschwindigkeit war gute 27,4 Knoten, und ihre Reichweite war 4,400 Seemeilen. Sie beteiligte sich bei der großen Seeschlacht vom Skagerrak am 31. Mai 1916, und wurde nach dem Ersten Weltkrieg an die Briten im November 1918 übergeben. Im Juni 1919 wurde sie von ihrer deutschen Besatzung im britischen Marinehafen von Scapa Flow (in Schottland) selbst versenkt, um den Engländern diese Kriegsbeute nicht zu gönnen. Im Jahre 1934 wurde sie eventuell geborgen und danach verschrottet.*

### IIIm. "S.M.S. Nassau" Class / "S.M.S. Nassau" Klasse (1908)

The four dreadnought battleships of the "S.M.S. Nassau" (1908) class were the very first German dreadnoughts, displaced a maximum of 20,535 tons each and were armed with 12-11 inch guns plus 12-6 inch guns. They could make up to 20,2 knots under full steam with their coal boilers and all saw action at the Battle of Jutland in May 1916. Range of action was an impressive 9,400 miles. "S.M.S.

Nassau" (1908) was named for the Duchy of Nassau, which is today part of the German State of Hessen ("Hesse" in English). Her three sister ships were "S.M.S. Westfalen" (1909), "S.M.S. Rheinland" (1910) and "S.M.S. Posen" (1910). "S.M.S. Westfalen" was named for the old Prussian province of Westphalia, now part of the German State of Northrhine-Westphalia. "S.M.S. Rheinland" was named for the old Prussian province of the Rhineland, which is today divided between the modern German States of North Rhine-Westphalia, the Rhineland-Palatinate and the Saarland. "S.M.S. Posen" was named for the old Prussian province of Posen, which is part of modern Poland. 8% of Posen's population of 5.7 million people can still speak German today. All four ships of this class survived World War One, "S.M.S. Westfalen" being scrapped as late as 1924. "S.M.S. Nassau" was scrapped in June 1920, "S.M.S. Rheinland" was scrapped in 1921, and "S.M.S. Posen" was scrapped in 1922.

**Linienschiff "S.M.S. Nassau" (1908) / Battleship "S.M.S. Nassau" (1908) – painting by Naval artist Günther Todt (1928-2009)**

*Die vier Linienschiffe der "S.M.S. Nassau" (1908) Klaße waren Deutschlands erste sogenannte "Dreadnoughts." Die "H.M.S. Dreadnought" (1905) der Royal Navy war das erste große und moderne Linienschiff der Welt. Sie hatte mehr Panzerung und mehr größere Schnellfeuerkanonen. Die anderen Linienschiffe der "S.M.S. Nassau" Klaße waren die "S.M.S. Westfalen" (1909), die "S.M.S.*

*Rheinland" (1910) und die "S.M.S. Posen" (1910). Sie hatten eine Einsatzverdrängung von je 20,535 Tonnen, und wurden mit 12-28 cm Schnellfeuerkanonen (in sechs Zwillingstürmen) sowie mit 12-15 cm Kasemattkanonen bewaffnet. Die Höchstgeschwindigkeit war 20,2 Knoten und die Reichweite war gute 9,400 Seemeilen. Diese vier Linienschiffe beteiligten sich bei der großen Seeschlacht vom Skagerrak am 31. Mai 1916, und wurden nach dem Ersten Weltkrieg endlich verschrottet – die "S.M.S. Nassau" im Jahre 1920, die "S.M.S. Rheinland" im Jahre 1921, die "S.M.S. Posen im Jahre 1922 und die "S.M.S. Westfalen" im Jahre 1924.*

Battlecruisers proved to be far more useful than battleships (they had less armor plating and fewer guns, but were faster ships – which was critical in battles). The term "dreadnought" battleship came into being in 1906, when the English Royal Navy commissioned "H.M.S. Dreadnought." She was the first "all big gun" battleship. Before this, battleships were armed with a combination of both large and medium caliber guns. After this, much more importance was given to having many more guns of very large caliber. German battleships in particular were known to have the highest quality of construction and the most accurate guns. Of special importance was the underwater protection given to German dreadnought battleships in the form of separate compartments and torpedo bulkheads. This increased the chance of survival in battle markedly, and enabled German warships to sustain much more punishment in comparison to those of other navies. The best example of this was the German battlecruiser "S.M.S. Seydlitz" which was still able to limp back home to Germany after the Battle of Jutland in May 1916. So many English ships simply exploded, whereas German ships did not.

### IV. "Linienschiffe" (Ships-of-the-Line / Pre-Dreadnought Battleships of the Imperial Navy)

The Austrian Navy had among the best pre-dreadnought battleships in the world. The most recent were the three ships of the "S.M.S. Erzherzog Franz Ferdinand" (1910) class. They were each of 15,851 tons full-load displacement, armed with 4-12 inch plus 8-9 inch guns and were capable of 20,2 knots under full steam. They were driven by coal boilers. "S.M.S. Erzherzog Franz Ferdinand" was named for Archduke Francis Ferdinand, the heir to the throne of Austria-Hungary who was tragically assassinated along with his wife in the city of Sarajevo, Bosnia-Herzegovina in June 1914. Sadly, the leaders of Europe used this incident as an excuse to start World War One, which endured from July 1914 until November 1918 and cost the lives of 70 million souls. Her sister ships were "S.M.S. Radetzky" (1911) and "S.M.S. Zrinyi" (1911). "S.M.S. Radetzky" was named for the victorious Austrian Field Marshall who defeated the Italians in

1848, while "S.M.S. Zrinyi" was named for the national hero of both Hungary and Croatia who battled the Ottoman Turks at the town of Szigetvar in 1566. The three ships bombarded the Italian coast in 1915. They survived World War One, and were scrapped in 1921 (''S.M.S. Erzherzog Franz Ferdinand'' and "S.M.S. Zrinyi") and in 1926 (''S.M.S. Radetzky'').

*Die drei Linienschiffe der österreich-ungarischen "S.M.S. Erzherzog Franz Ferdinand" (1910) Klaße waren die letzten und auch die besten sogenannten "Pre-Dreadnoughts." Sie hatten eine Einsatzverdrängung von je 15,851 Tonnen, und wurden mit vier 30,5 cm Skodageschützen (in zwei Zwillingstürmen) sowie mit acht 24 cm Skodageschützen (in vier Zwillingstürmen) bewaffnet. Die Höchstgeschwindigkeit war gute 20,2 Knoten. Die anderen Mitglieder dieser Klaße waren die "S.M.S. Radetzky" (1911) und die "S.M.S. Zrinyi" (1911). Die drei Schiffe haben Ancona, Italien im Mai 1915 bombardiert, und haben auch den Ersten Weltkrieg überlebt. Sie wurden alle im Jahre 1921 verschrottet.*

## Erzherzog Franz Ferdinand von Österreich-Este (Archduke Franz Ferdinand of Austria-Este)

*Erzherzog Franz Ferdinand von Österreich-Este (1863-1914) war Neffe und nach dem Tod von Kronprinz Erzherzog Rudolf von Österreich (1858-1889) Thronfolger von Kaiser Franz Josef I von Österreich (1830-1916). Er wurde aber auch mit seiner Gemahlin Sophie Gräfin Chotek, die Herzogin von Hohenberg (1868-1914) im Sarajevo, Bosnien-Herzegowina erschossen.*

## Josef Wenzel Graf Radetzky von Radetz

*Josef Wenzel Graf Radetzky von Radetz (1766-1858 ) war österreichischer Generalfeldmarschall, böhmischer Adeliger und wohl der bedeutendeste Heeresführer Österreichs in der ersten Hälfte des 19. Jahrhunderts. Er tratt 1784 als Kadett in das 2. Kürassierregiment ein und beteiligte sich zwischen 1788 und 1789 unter den Feldherren Lacy und Laudon am Türkenkrieg. Von 1792 bis 1795 war er auf Feldzügen gegen Napoleon in den Niederlanden und am Rhein. Zu Beginn des Feldzuges von 1805 wurde Radetzky als Generalmajor nach Italien versetzt. Für seine Leistungen in diesem Feldzug als Oberbefehlshaber des 3. Kürassierregiments erwarb er das Ritterkreuz des Militär Maria Theresia Ordens. 1809 kämpfte er im 5. Armeekorps als Befehlshaber der Vorhut bei Braunau am Inn ebenfalls mit Auszeichnung und stieg nach der Schlacht bei Aspern zum Feldmarschallleutnant auf. 1813 entwickelte er als Chef des Quartiermeisteramts den Plan zur Völkerschlacht bei Leipzig. Nach dem Friedensschluß von 1815 kam Radetzky als Divisionär nach Ödenburg in*

*Westungarn, später nach Ofen (heute Budapest) und 1821 als General der Kavallerie und Festungskommandant nach Olmütz in Mähren. Von 1831 bis 1857 war er Generalkommandant der österreichischen Armee im lombardo-venezianischen Königreich (seit 1836 im Range eines Generalfeldmarschalls). Radetzky wurde vor allem durch seine Siege in den Jahren von 1848 bis 1849 gegen Piemont-Sardinien berühmt. Erst am 28. Februar 1857, im Alter von 90 Jahren, wurde er in den Ruhestand versetzt.*

### Nikolaus Subic Zrinyi

*Zrinyi ("Serin" auf Deutsch) ist der Name eines kroatisch-ungarischen Adelgeschlechts. Nikolaus Subic Zrinyi (1508-1566) war ein kroatischer Feldherr und diente während der Herrschaft des deutschen Kaisers Ferdinand I von Österreich (1503-1564). Bei der Belagerung von Szigetvar im Südungarn ("Inselburg" auf Deutsch) im Jahre 1566 wurden fast alle kroatischen und ungarischen Verteidiger von den überlegenden ottomanischen Türken getötet. Zrinyi geriet schwer verwundet in Gefangenschaft und wurde enthauptet. Etwa 90,000 Türken mit 300 Geschützen standen nur 2,500 Kroaten mit 69 Geschützen gegenüber. Die Türken haben etwa 30,000 Soldaten verloren, und ihre Armee wurde dadurch sehr geschwächt.*

### IVa. "S.M.S. Deutschland" Class / "S.M.S. Deutschland" Klasse (1904)

The most modern German pre-dreadnought battleships were the "S.M.S. Schlesien" (1908) and her four sister ships. "Schlesien" is the German word for the former Austrian and German province of Silesia, which is now in modern day Poland (Silesia, which has a population of 8.6 million people today is still 77% German-speaking, mostly as a second language, and parts of Upper Silesia are in fact officially bilingual). Cities with large numbers of German-speaking people include Breslau, Oppeln and Kattowitz.

Each of the five ships of this class displaced a full load of 14,900 tons, were armed with 4-11 inch guns plus later with 2-88 mm anti-aircraft guns. They were capable of 18,5 knots under full steam in their coal boilers, and enjoyed an operating radius of 4,800 miles. The "S.M.S. Schlesien" and her sister ship "S.M.S. Schleswig-Holstein" survived World War One to serve as the largest ships in the postwar "Reichsmarine" until 1933. "Schleswig-Holstein" is the name of the German province on the Danish border, which Denmark finally surrendered back to Germany after the Prusso-Danish War of 1864. In modern Denmark, there are still 3 million German-speaking people (mostly as a second language). Those in North Schleswig maintain a strong German cultural and political identity, where the cities of Tondern and Apenrade are still majority German. The ethnic Danish and Frisian minorities in Schleswig-Holstein enjoy similar privileges. Like all five ships in this class, "S.M.S. Pommern" served at the Battle of Jutland in May 1916; unfortunately she went down with her crew during the night fighting. "Pommern" is the German word for the former German province of Pomerania, which was annexed to Poland in 1945. Modern Further Pomerania has a population of more than 6 million people, of whom 14% still speak German, largely as a second language. Cities with large numbers of German-speaking people today include Stettin and Kolberg.

After World War Two in May 1945, the Treaties of Yalta and Potsdam took large parts of Eastern Germany and gave them to Poland. Poland in turn lost much land in Eastern Poland to the former Soviet Union. In addition to this most unfortunate consequence of World War Two, millions of human beings were expelled from their homes and moved West. Poles from Eastern Poland moved into formerly German lands, and Germans from Eastern Germany were either expelled or murdered by advancing Soviet troops. 2 million German civilians in Eastern Germany and Eastern Europe lost their lives during the final months of World War Two. 12 million ethnic Germans from formerly Eastern Germany and Eastern Europe were expelled from their ancestral homelands between 1944 and 1950, and settled in what is today modern Germany. Since 1950, a further 4 million ethnic Germans from Eastern Europe and the former Soviet Union have emigrated as well, mostly to modern Germany. So since late 1944, fully 16 million ethnic Germans have left their ancestral homelands for the West. For the millions of ethnic Germans who remain in Eastern Europe and the former Soviet Union, the passage of time has healed wartime scars to the point where they can now once again nurture their German culture and language. Modern German-speakers in this vast region now inhabit Estonia (201,870), Kazakhstan (3,987,874), Kyrgyzstan (20,000), Croatia (1,511,000), Latvia (541), Lithuania (2,060), Moldova (7,300), Poland (8,000,000), Transylvania-Romania (150,000), Russia (17,842,300), Serbia (5,000), Slovakia (1,505,500), Slovenia (1,002,000), the Czech Republic (3,041,200), the Ukraine (4,664,742). Hungary (3,700,000) and Uzbekistan (3,000,000). In the present and in the future, it will be very good if all political jurisdictions will respect peoples' ethnicity, language, culture and faith as did such medieval states as the Holy Roman Empire of the German Nation, and the United Kingdom of Poland and Lithuania. Belligerent modern nationalism as we still know it today benefits nobody, save the tiny "elite" of the so-called "New World Order."

*Die letzten "Pre-Dreadnoughts" der kaiserlich-deutschen Marine waren die fünf Linienschiffe der "S.M.S. Deutschland" (1904) Klaße. Die anderen Mitglieder dieser Klaße waren die "S.M.S. Hannover" (1907), die "S.M.S. Pommern" (1907), die "S.M.S. Schliesien" (1908) und die "S.M.S. Schleswig-Holstein" (1908). Diese fünf Linienschiffe hatten eine Einsatzverdrängung von je 14,900 Tonnen, und wurden mit vier 28 cm Schnellfeuerkanonen (in zwei Zwillingstürmen), 14-17 cm Kasemattkanonen sowie mit 20-88 mm Flugzeugabwehrkanonen und sechs 45 cm Torpedorohren bewaffnet. Die Höchstgeschwindigkeit war 18,5 Knoten, und die Reichweite war 4,800 Seemeilen. Alle fünf Einheiten nahmen bei der großen Seeschlacht am Skagerrak am 31. Mai 1916 teil, wo die "S.M.S. Pommern" torpediert und mit 839 Besatztungsmitglieder versenkt wurde. Die vier anderen Schiffe dieser Klaße überlebten den Ersten Weltkrieg, und dienten bei der nachkriegs Reichsmarine. Die "S.M.S. Deutschland" wurde in Wilhelmshaven im Jahre 1922 verschrottet, aber die drei anderen Schiffe überlebten auch den Zweiten Weltkrieg. Die "S.M.S. Hannover" wurde in Bremerhaven im Jahre 1946 verschrottet. Die "S.M.S. Schlesien" wurde in Swinemünde im Jahre 1956 verschrottet, und die "S.M.S. Schleswig-Holstein" wurde in Gotenhafen auch im Jahre 1956 von den Polen verschrottet. Die "S.M.S. Deutschland" diente als Flaggschiff der kaiserlich-deutschen Marine von 1906 bis 1912, als sie mit der "S.M.S. Friedrich der Große" ersetzt wurde. Das ehemalige Königreich Hannover dauerte bis es das Königreich Preußen Hannover nach dem preußisch-österreichischen Krieg im Jahre 1866 annektierte. Das war nicht nett und auch nicht besonders vorteilhaft, weil ja die königliche Familie vom Königreich Hannover mit der des Vereinigten Königreich von Großbrittanien und Irland direkt verwandt waren. Die Provinz Hinterpommern gehörte bis 1945 dem Land Preußen. Heutzutage hat Hinterpommern 6 Millionen Einwohner, wovon 14% noch deutsch sprechen (besonders in Stettin und Kolberg). Es gibt viele Deutsche mit polnischer Abstammung. Eine Unzahl von Polen wandern nach Deutschland aus und passen sich der neuen Heimat leicht an. Im Mittelalter hat das Heilige Römische Deutsche Reich sowie der Deutsche Ritterorden Mittel-und Osteuropa besiedelt, germanisiert und auch zum Christentum bekehrt. Viele slawische und auch baltische Stämme wie die Pommern, die Preußen, die Sorben, die Schlesier und die Masuren waren überwiegend germanisiert. Das Herzogtum Schlesien gehört seit 1945 Polen, aber gehörte von 1742 bis 1945 dem Land Preußen.*

**Linienschiff / Battleship "S.M.S. Hannover" (1907) - courtesy of Captain (CA) George J. Albert, Jr., Army Field Historian of the California Center for Military History**

**Das Herzogtum Schlesien (the Duchy of Silesia)**

*Ursprünglich war das Herzogtum Schlesien österreichisch. Die Herzogtüme Schleswig und Holstein waren im Jahre 1864 von Preußen und Österreich endlich befreit. Für viele Jahrzehnte waren die beiden Herzogtüme unter dänischer Besatzung.*

"S.M.S. Deutschland" (named after Germany) served as fleet flagship from 1906 until 1912. The next ship to be named "Deutschland" was of course the so-called "pocket battleship" commissioned in 1933, upon which my paternal grandfather Wilhelm Johannes Nonnenkamp served from 1933 until 1936. "S.M.S. Hannover" was named for the German city of Hanover and the former Kingdom of Hanover, now part of the state of Lower Saxony ("Niedersachsen" in German). The Kingdom of Hanover was a former ally of Austria against Prussia, and sadly lost her sovereignty in 1866 when the victorious Prussians merely annexed her after the Austro-Prussian War. The Kingdom of Hanover had a dynastic union with the United Kingdom, because the English Royal Family was of the same family as the Royal Family of Hanover (the so-called "Guelphs" or "Welfen" in German). Aside from the "S.M.S. Pommern" which was lost during World War One, the remaining ships of this "S.M.S. Deutschland" class were eventually scrapped – "S.M.S. Schliesien" as late as 1956. "S.M.S. Deutschland" was scrapped in 1922, "S.M.S. Hannover was scrapped in 1946 (after World War Two), and "S.M.S. Schleswig-Holstein" was scrapped in 1947 (also after the Second World War).

## IVb. "S.M.S. Braunschweig" Class / "S.M.S. Braunschweig" Klasse (1903)

The next previous class of five German pre-dreadnought battleships were almost identical in displacement, armament and speed. These included the "S.M.S. Braunschweig" ("Brunswick" in English) which survived World War One to serve in the postwar "Reichsmarine." In fact, this was the first ship upon which my paternal grandfather Wilhelm Johannes Nonnenkamp (1903-1972) served as a young sailor in 1924.

**Linienschiff / Battleship "S.M.S. Braunschweig" (1903) – Nonnenkamp Family Archives**

*Die fünf Linienschiffe der "S.M.S. Braunschweig" (1903) Klaße waren den folgenden fünf Linienschiffen der "S.M.S. Deutschland" (1904) Klaße sehr ähnlich. Die fünf Einheiten der "S.M.S. Braunschweig" Klaße hatten eine Einsatzverdrängung von je 14,394 Tonnen, und wurden auch mit vier 28 cm Schnellfeuerkanonen (in zwei Zwillingstürmen) sowie mit 14-17 cm Kasemattkanonen bewaffnet. Die anderen Mitglieder dieser Klaße waren die "S.M.S. Hessen," die "S.M.S. Preußen," die "S.M.S. Elsaß" und die "S.M.S. Lothringen." Nur die "S.M.S. Hessen" hat bei der großen Seeschlacht am*

*Skagerrak am 31. Mai 1916 teilgenommen. Alle fünf Einheiten der "S.M.S. Braunschweig" Klaße hatten den Ersten Weltkrieg überlebt, und dienten bei der nachkriegs-Reichsmarine. Die "S.M.S. Preußen" und die "S.M.S. Lothringen" wurden im Jahre 1931 verschrottet, die "S.M.S. Braunschweig" (wo mein Großvater Wilhelm Johannes Nonnenkamp seine Reichsmarinedienstzeit im Jahre 1924 begonnen hatte) wurde im Jahre 1932 verschrottet, die "S.M.S. Elsaß" wurde im Jahre 1936 verschrottet und die "S.M.S. Hessen" wurde erst nach dem Zweiten Weltkrieg im Jahre 1950 verschrottet. Das ehemalige Herzogtum Braunschweig gehörte genau wie dem ehemaligen Königreich Hannover den Welfen. Das ehemalige Großherzogtum Hessen-Darmstadt, das Herzogtum Nassau, das Kurfürstentum Hessen-Kassel und die Freie und Reichstadt Frankfurt bildeten zusammen das moderne deutsche Bundesland Hessen. Das ehemalige Königreich Preußen war das größte Land im ehemaligen wilhelminischen deutschen Kaiserreich. Elsaß und Lothringen (seit 1945 französisch) waren wie andere moderne "französische" Gegenden ursprünglich Teile des Heiligen Römischen Reiches der Deutschen Nation. Elsaß, Lothringen, Burgund, Flandern, Savoyen, Provence und Bar waren alle deutsch. Es gibt immer noch 5,2 Millionen Menschen in Frankreich, die deutsch sprechen (besonders in Elsaß und Ostlothringen).*

Herzogtum Braunschweig (the "Duchy of Brunswick") in English existed as such from 1815 until Germany's monarchies were sadly abolished at the end of World War One in November 1918. This Duchy was a successor to Herzogtum Braunschweig-Wolfenbüttel (the "Duchy of Brunswick-Wolfenbuettel" in English), which existed from 1235 until 1815. The last Duke of Brunswick was Ernst August Christian Georg (1887-1953), who reigned from 1913 until the abdication of his throne in November 1918. He belonged to the Royal House of Hanover ("Hannover" in German), whose members (his direct relatives) used to rule the former Kingdom of Hanover and the United Kindom of Great Britain and Ireland. His eldest son was Prinz Ernst August (1914-1987), who would have inherited his father's title and position had the monarchy not been abolished in November of 1918. The eldest son of the late Prinz Ernst August (1914-1987) is Prinz Ernst August IV, who was born in 1954. He is married to Caroline, the hereditary Princess of Monaco (a daughter of the late Prince Rainier III of Monaco and his wife, the late American film actress Grace Kelly). The current Prinz Ernst August IV (born in 1954) is also a great-great grandson of the last official King of Hanover, Georg V (1819-1878). The King's full name was "Georg Friedrich Alexander Karl Ernst August." He was a first cousin of Queen Victoria of the United Kingdom of Great Britain and Ireland, and was a Duke of Cumberland in the peerage of Great Britain. He was most unfortunately deposed in 1866, when the Kingdom of Prussia abolished the Hanoverian monarchy and annexed the Kingdom of Hanover, making it a mere province within the Kingdom of Prussia. The Kingdom of Hanover had been a loyal ally of the Empire of Austria in the Austro-Prussian War of 1866. The eldest child and only son of Georg V (1819-1878) was named Ernst August (1845-1923). He would have become the King of Hanover upon the death of his father Georg V in 1878. He and his wife the Princess Thyra of Denmark had 6 children, 3 of them boys. The first son died at the age of 11 in 1912 and the second one at the age of 16 in 1901. The third son was none other than Ernst August Christian Georg (1887-1953), who reigned as the Duke of Brunswick. Thus, one can see that this family has a valid claim to both the thrones of the Kingdom of Hanover and to the Duchy of Brunswick. The four remaining ships in the "S.M.S. Braunschweig" class were "S.M.S. Elsass" (named after the province of Alsace, which is now part of France), "S.M.S. Lothringen" (named after the province of Lorraine, which is also now part of France), "S.M.S. Hessen" (named after the German state of Hesse) and "S.M.S. Preussen" (named after the province of Prussia, which is now part of Poland and Russia). There are still 5,2 million German-speaking people in modern France (primarily as a second language, but as a native German dialect in the Alsace (700,000 individuals) and in the Eastern Lorraine (400,000 people).

**Linienschiff / Battleship "S.M.S. Elsass" (im Jahre 1922 / seen here in 1922) - courtesy of Captain (CA) George J. Albert, Jr., Army Field Historian of the California Center for Military History**

Many modern provinces of France, including Alsace ("Elsass" in German), Lorraine ("Lothringen" in German), Burgundy ("Burgund" in German), Savoy ("Savoyen" in German) and Flanders ("Flandern" in German) used to belong to the Holy Roman Empire of the German Nation. The Alsace and Eastern Lorraine are still German-speaking today, and in Burgundy a majority of the population can speak German as a second language. Even in modern Savoy, 9% of the people can speak German as a second language. All five ships of this "S.M.S. Braunschweig" class were eventually scrapped – "S.M.S. Hessen" as late as 1950 (after World War Two). "S.M.S. Braunschweig" was scrapped in 1932, "S.M.S. Elsaß" was scrapped in 1936, and both "S.M.S. Preussen" and "S.M.S. Lothringen" were scrapped in 1931.

### IVc. "S.M.S. Wittelsbach" Class / "S.M.S. Wittelsbach" Klasse (1902)

The preceding class of five German pre-dreadnought battleships belonged to the "S.M.S. Wittelsbach" (1902) class, each of which displaced a maximum 12,798 tons full load, were armed with 4-9 inch guns plus 18-6 inch guns and could make up to 18,1 knots under full steam with their coal boilers. "S.M.S. Wittelsbach" (1902) was named for the Royal House of the Kingdom of Bavaria, which was an ally of Austria until 1866. "S.M.S. Wettin" (1902) was named for the Royal House of the Kingdom of Saxony, another ally of Austria until 1866. "S.M.S. Zähringen" (1902) was named for the Royal House of the Grand Duchy of Baden, yet another ally of Austria until 1866. "S.M.S. Mecklenburg" (1903) was named for the Grand Duchies of Mecklenburg-Schwerin and Mecklenburg-Strelitz in Northern Germany, both allies of the Kingdom of Prussia. "S.M.S. Schwaben" (1904) was named for the old Duchy of Swabia, of which the city of Stuttgart was the capital.

*Die fünf Linienschiffe der "S.M.S. Wittelsbach" (1902) Klaße hatten eine Einsatzverdrängung von je 12,798 Tonnen, und wurden mit vier 24 cm Schnellfeuerkanonen sowie mit 18-15 cm Kasemattkanonen bewaffnet. Die Höchstgeschwindigkeit war 18,1 Knoten. Alle fünf Einheiten dieser Klaße überlebten den Ersten Weltkrieg. Die vier anderen Mitglieder dieser Klaße waren die "S.M.S. Wettin" (1902), die "S.M.S. Zähringen" (1902), die "S.M.S. Mecklenburg" (1903) und die "S.M.S. Schwaben" (1904). Vier Schiffe wurden im Jahre 1921 verschrottet, aber die "S.M.S. Zähringen" wurde nach dem Zweiten Weltkrieg erst im Jahre 1950 verschrottet. Das Adelhaus Wittelsbach beherrschte das Königreich Bayern (mit der Pfalz) bis November 1918. Das Königreich Bayern war nach dem Königreich Preußen und dem Kaiserreich Österreich-Ungarn das drittmächtigste Land im deutschen Reich. Das Adelhaus Wittelsbach hat bis heute auch das römisch-katholische Anrecht auf den Thron von England, Schottland, Wales und Irland. Das Adelhaus Wettin beherrschte das Königreich Sachsen und die Herzogtüme von Thüringen bis November 1918, sowie das Königreich Bulgarien bis 1945. Vorher hatte das Adelhaus Wettin auch das Königreich Portugal sowie Brasilien unter sich beherrscht. Sie haben das Vereinigte Königreich von Polen und Litauen bis 1795 beherrscht. Die wettinische Linie von Sachsen-Coburg-Gotha beherrscht noch das Vereinigte Königreich von Großbrittanien und Nordirland, sowie das Königreich Belgien. Das Adelhaus Zähringen beherrschte das Großherzogtum Baden (wovon Karlsruhe die Hauptstadt war) bis November 1918. Das Adelhaus Mecklenburg ist im ehemaligen Großherzogtum Mecklenburg-Schwerin ausgestorben, und deswegen hat das Adelhaus Hohenzollern nun das Anrecht auf Mecklenburg-Schwerin. Das Adelhaus Mecklenburg-Strelitz beherrschte das Großherzogtum Mecklenburg-Strelitz bis November 1918, und existiert noch heute.*

The male line of the House of Mecklenburg-Schwerin became extinct on July 31, 2001 upon the death of Hereditary Grand Duke Friedrich Franz (1910-2001). The title passed on by inheritance to the Hohenzollern Dynasty, or the Royal House of Brandenburg-Prussia. The male line of the former Grand Duchy of Mecklenburg-Strelitz is currently held by Hereditary Grand Duke Georg Borwin, born in 1956. "S.M.S. Schwaben" was named for the old Holy Roman Duchy of Swabia in Southern Germany, which eventually became part of the Kingdom of Württemberg. Swabia is of course home to two famous German carmakers of today: both Mercedes-Benz and Porsche are based in the Swabian capital city of Stuttgart. All five ships in this class were eventually scrapped, "S.M.S. Zähringen" as late as 1950 (after World War Two). "S.M.S. Wettin," "S.M.S. Wittelsbach," "S.M.S. Schwaben" and "S.M.S. Mecklenburg" were all scrapped in 1921.

### IVd. "S.M.S. Kaiser Friedrich III" Class / "S.M.S. Kaiser Friedrich III" Klasse (1898)

The class of five pre-dreadnought battleships built immediately before the "S.M.S. Wittelsbach" class were those of the "S.M.S. Kaiser Friedrich III" (1898) class. These ships displaced a maximum of 11,785 tons each and were armed with 4-9 inch guns plus 18-6 inch guns and could make up to 17,9 knots under full steam with their coal boilers. "S.M.S. Kaiser Friedrich III" was named for the German Emperor and King of Prussia Frederick III who reigned only for a brief period during 1888 – he unfortunately died of cancer. "S.M.S. Kaiser Wilhelm II" (1900) was named after the German Emperor and King of Prussia William II who reigned from 1888 until his abdication and exile to the Netherlands in 1918. He was the eldest son of Kaiser Friedrich III, and was very instrumental in making Germany's navy second largest in the world after the Royal Navy of England.  He died in exile in 1941.  "S.M.S. Kaiser Wilhelm der Grosse" (1901) was named after German Emperor and King of Prussia William the Great, who reigned from 1861 until his death in 1888.  He was the father of Frederick III and the grandfather of William II.  "S.M.S. Kaiser Barbarossa" (1901) was named after Holy Roman and German Kaiser Friedrich I Barbarossa ("Emperor Frederick I the Red Beard" in English), who ruled from 1152 until his death in 1190.  The official occasion of the coronation of Kaiser Friedrich I Barbarossa was the first time the modern German national colors of black, red and gold were used.  These colors have been used by the German peasant rebels of 1525, by the German "Freikorps Lützow" cavalry volunteers of the Napoleonic Wars, by the Germanic Confederation (1815-1866), by the liberal democratic German revolutionaries of 1848, by ethnic German minorities in the Balkans, by the Weimar Republic (1918-1933), by the former East Germany (1949-1990) and by other countries such as Belgium and Papua New Guinea (both formerly parts of the German Empire).

*Die fünf Linienschiffe der "S.M.S. Kaiser Friedrich III" (1898) Klaße waren den folgenden fünf Linienschiffen der "S.M.S. Wittelsbach" (1902) Klaße sehr ähnlich.  Sie hatten eine Einsatzverdrängung von je 11,785 Tonnen, und wurden mit je vier 24 cm Schnellfeuerkanonen (in zwei Zwillingstürmen) sowie mit 18-15 cm Kasemattkanonen bewaffnet.  Die Höchstgeschwindigkeit war 17,9 Knoten.  Die vier anderen Mitglieder dieser Klaße waren die "S.M.S. Kaiser Wilhelm II" (1900), die "S.M.S. Kaiser Wilhelm der Große" (1901), die "S.M.S. Kaiser Barbaroßa" (1901) und die "S.M.S. Kaiser Karl der Große" (1902).  Alle fünf Linienschiffe dieser Klaße haben den Ersten Weltkrieg überstanden und wurden im Jahre 1920 verschrottet – außer der "S.M.S. Kaiser Wilhelm II," die im Jahre 1922 verschrottet wurde.  Friedrich III (1831-1888) war Deutscher Kaiser und König von Preußen für nur 99 Tage im Jahre 1888, als er an Kehlkopfkrebs starb.  Friedrichs ältester Sohn Wilhelm II (1859-1941) war Deutscher Kaiser und König von Preußen von 1888 bis zu seiner Abdankung im November 1918.  Wilhelm I "der Große" (1797-1888) war der Vater von Friedrich III (1831-1888) und der Großvater von Wilhelm II (1859-1941).  Er war König von Preußen von 1861 bis 1888 und Deutscher Kaiser von 1871 bis 1888.  Wilhelm I, Friedrich III und Wilhelm II gehörten zum Adelhaus Hohenzollern.  Kaiser Friedrich I "Barbaroßa" (1122-1190) war Herzog von Schwaben (1147-1190), Römisch-Deutscher König (1152-1190) und auch Deutscher Kaiser (1155-1190).  Er gehörte zum Adelhaus Hohenstaufen.  Bei seiner Krönung in Frankfurt am Main am 4. März 1152 waren die deutschen Nationalfarben "Schwarz-Rot-Gold" zum ersten Mal in Gebrauch.  Die männliche Linie des Adelhauses Hohenstaufen starb im Jahre 1268 aus. Die Erben des Adelhauses Hohenstaufen sind die Mitglieder des modernen Adelhauses Habsburg-Lothringen.*

## Kaiser Karl der Große (Emperor Charles the Great = "Charlemagne")

*Karl der Große (747-814) war seit dem 25. Dezember 800 in Aachen der erste Deutsche Kaiser. Er gehörte zum Adelhaus der Karolinger. Damals gehörten Frankreich, die Niederlande, die Lombardei, Rom, das Herzogtum Benevent (in Süditalien), das Spanische Mark, Böhmen, Mähren, die Schweiz, Österreich, Slowenien, Kroatien sowie Westungarn zum Deutschen Reich. Die Karolinger waren Franken, und die Franken stammen aus Nordwestdeutschland und den Niederlanden seit dem 3. Jahrhundert nach Christus. Die modernen Erben der Karolinger sind die Mitglieder des Adelhauses Habsburg-Lothringen.*

"S.M.S. Kaiser Karl der Grosse" (1902) was named after Holy Roman and German Emperor Charles the Great (Charlemagne), who ruled from 768 until his death in 814. He was King of Franconia from 768 and Holy Roman & German Emperor from 800, when the First German Empire was proclaimed in the city of Aachen. Franconia is located in Northern Bavaria. All five ships of this class were eventually scrapped, "S.M.S. Kaiser Wilhelm II" as late as 1922. "S.M.S. Kaiser Friedrich III," "S.M.S. Kaiser Wilhelm der Grosse," "S.M.S. Kaiser Karl der Grosse" and "S.M.S. Kaiser Barbarossa" were all scrapped in 1920.

## IVe. "S.M.S. Erzherzog Karl" Class / "S.M.S. Erzherzog Karl" Klasse (1906)

The three ships of the "S.M.S. Erzherzog Karl" (1906) class of the Imperial and Royal Austro-Hungarian Navy displaced a maximum 11,782 tons each and were armed with 4-9 inch plus 12-7 inch guns and could make up to 20,5 knots under full steam with their coil boilers. "Erzherzog Karl" means "Archduke Charles," who was a member of the Royal House of Habsburg, the Austrian Royal Family. A Habsburg first inherited the throne of the Holy Roman Empire of the German Empire, or the First Reich, in 1273. They were deposed from this throne in 1806 after their defeat at the hands of Napoleon Bonaparte of France. The German Empire was replaced with a Confederation of German states, although Austria continued to remain the most influential German state until their defeat at the hands of Prussia in 1866 during the Austro-Prussian War. Erzherzog Karl of Habsburg was actually a great military commander of the Napoleonic Wars against France, which lasted from 1792 until 1815. He was the first commander to defeat Napoleon at the Battle of Aspern in May 1809, and it is for this fact that he is remembered and honored. He lived from 1771 until 1847. The Habsburg family ruled Austria-Hungary until November 1918, and the former foes of

Germany and Austria-Hungary were allied to one another militarily from 1866 to 1918. The Hohenzollern leadership of Brandenburg-Prussia and later Germany was inept, but not evil. They relied too heavily upon force in their foreign policy – something they had exercised against rival German states for hundreds of years. This reckless philosophy earned them the enmity of many sovereign nations especially after Kaiser Wilhelm II came to the imperial throne of Germany in 1888. Worst of all was Kaiser Wilhelm II's loss of the political alliance forged by Chancellor Otto von Bismarck, who served as Prussian and German Chancellor from 1862 until his retirement in 1890. This was known as the "Dreikaiserbund" or "Three Emperors' League" which included Germany, Austria-Hungary and Czarist Russia. It never made any sense for Germany and Austria to earn the enmity of Russia, which had so many interests in common with them. The fall of the Christian monarchies in Germany, Austria-Hungary and Russia in 1917-1918 paved the way for harsh "peace treaties" such as the horrible Treaty of Versailles. Germany was stripped of much territory inhabited by German people, of her colonies and was slapped with massive war reparations which she could never hope to pay. Austria-Hungary fared even worse, being divided into many small countries – hence the phrase "Balkanization." Russia fared worst of all, falling into civil war and a Communist dictatorship which eventually murdered 60 million of her own people. The global economic depression which came upon the world soon thereafter (hyperinflation in Germany in 1923 and the Wall Street stock market crash in 1929) paved the way for the rise of Adolf Hitler and his National Socialist ("Nazi") Party in 1933. His policies were truly bad, and even more reckless on a global scale compared with those of the Hohenzollern Dynasty. In hindsight, nothing compares favorably with the longevity of the Holy Roman Empire of the German Nation or "First Reich" (800 to 1806) nor with the Habsburg Dynasty which endured in Austria until 1918.

**k.u.k. Linienschiff "S.M.S. Erzherzog Karl" (1903) / Austro-Hungarian Battleship "S.M.S. Erzherzog Karl" (1903) – courtesy of Herr Alexander Traiber (Freunde Historischer Schiffe – Vienna, Austria).**

*Die drei Linienschiffe der "S.M.S. Erzherzog Karl" (1906) Klaße der Kaiserlichen und Königlichen Kriegsmarine hatten eine Einsatzverdrängung von je 11,782 Tonnen, und waren mit je vier 24 cm Schnellfeuerkanonen sowie mit je 12-19 cm Schnellfeuerkanonen bewaffnet. Die Höchstgeschwindigkeit war gute 20,5 Knoten. Die zwei anderen Mitglieder dieser Klaße waren die "S.M.S. Erzherzog Friedrich" (1907) und die "S.M.S. Erzherzog Ferdinand Max" (1907). Die drei Einheiten dieser Klaße überlebten den Ersten Weltkrieg, und wurden im Jahre 1920 verschrottet. Erzherzog Karl von Österreich (1771-1847) war auch Herzog von Teschen, Feldherr und Mitglied des Adelhauses Habsburg-Lothringen. Er ist am besten dadurch in Erinnerung geblieben, weil er Napoleon Bonaparte von Frankreich die erste Niederlage auf dem Schlachtfeld zufügte. Die Schlacht bei Aspern fand am 21. und 22. Mai 1809 zwischen napoleonischen Truppen und Österreich bei den Orten Aspern und Eßling (heute Teile Wiens) statt. Erzherzog Friedrich von Österreich (1856-1936) war auch Herzog von Teschen und Heerführer im Ersten Weltkrieg. Im Ersten Weltkrieg war Friedrich von 1914 bis 1917 Armeeoberkommandant und damit Befehlshaber der gesamten Kaiserlichen und Königlichen Wehrmacht. Friedrich Ferdinand Leopold von Österreich (1821-1847) trat im Jahre 1837 in die Kaiserliche und Königliche Kriegsmarine ein und wurde bald danach Schiffskapitän. Im Jahre 1839 unternahm Erzherzog Friedrich Orientreisen. Im Jahre 1840 zeichnete er sich bei dem syrischen Feldzug der "Londoner Allianz" (Österreich, England, Rußland und das Ottomanische Reich) gegen Muhammad Ali Pascha (1769-1849) aus. Bei der Eroberung des Kastells von Sidon ("Saida" auf italienisch und deutsch) und bei der Einnahme von Sankt Jean d'Acre (heute "Akkon" in der Bucht von Haifa, Israel) erhielt er aufgrund seiner Tapferkeit den Maria Theresia-Orden verliehen. Im Jahre 1844 wurde er zum Vizeadmiral und Marineoberkommandant der Kaiserlichen und Königlichen Kriegsmarine ernannt. Er legte den Grundstein für zahlreiche Reformen und zur Umgestaltung der damals noch vollständig venezianisch orientierten Österreichischen Kriegsmarine. Im Jahre 1845 wurde er feierlich in den Johanniter Orden aufgenommen. Mit nur 26 Jahren starb Friedrich an den Folgen einer Gelbsucht.*

**k.u.k. Linienschiff "S.M.S. Erzherzog Karl (1903) / Austro-Hungarian Battleship "S.M.S. Erzherzog Karl" (1903) seen while on maneuvers – courtesy of Herr Alexander Traiber (Freunde Historischer Schiffe – Vienna, Austria)**

**Erzherzog Ferdinand Maximilian von Österreich, Kaiser von Mexiko (Archduke Ferdinand Maximilian of Austria, Emperor of México)**

*Erzherzog Ferdinand Maximilian von Österreich (1832-1867) war der jüngere Bruder von Kaiser Franz Josef I (1830-1916) aus dem Adelhaus Habsburg-Lothringen. Zur Zeit der französischen "Mexikanischen Interventionskriege" (1861-1867) wurde er von 1864 bis 1867 von Frankreich, Österreich und Belgien als Kaiser von Mexiko eingesetzt.*

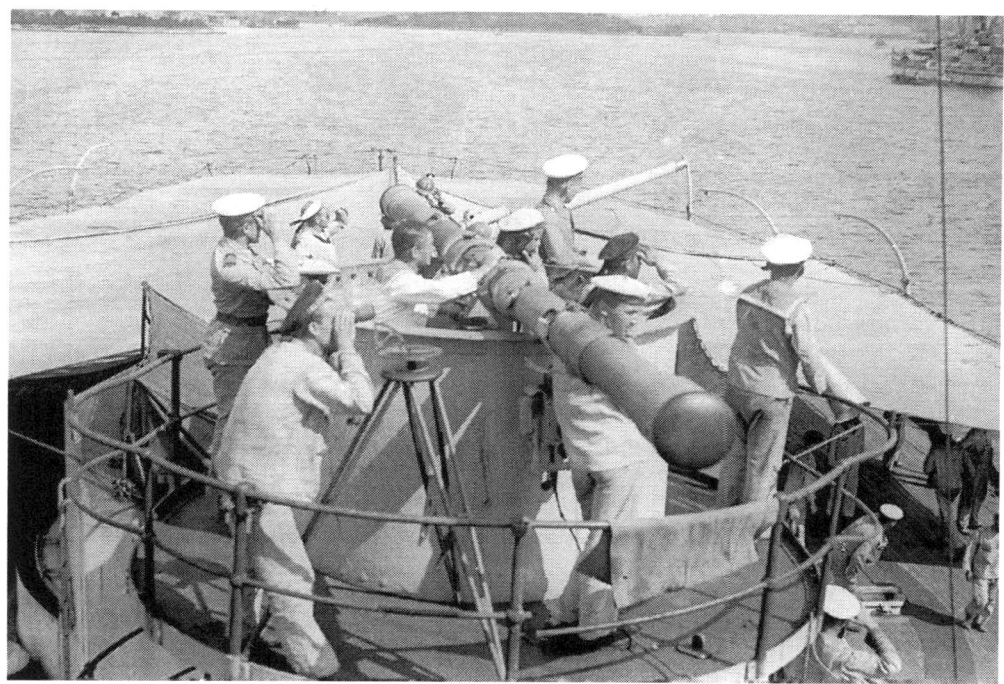

**k.u.k. Linienschiff "S.M.S. Erzherzog Karl" (1903) / Austro-Hungarian Battleship "S.M.S. Erzherzog Karl" (1903) with crew members using the rangefinder – courtesy of Herr Alexander Traiber (Freunde Historischer Schiffe – Vienna, Austria)**

**Die Reise der Segelfregatte "S.M.S. Elisabeth" (the Voyage of the Sailing Frigate "S.M.S. Elisabeth")**

*Maximilian intereßierte sich vor allem für die Seefahrt und unternahm viele Fernreisen (zum Beispiel nach Brasilien) auf der Kaiserlichen und Königlichen Segelfregatte "S.M.S. Elisabeth." Im Jahre 1854 wurde er im Alter von nur 22 Jahren zum Oberbefehlshaber der Kaiserlichen und Königlichen Kriegsmarine ernannt, welche er in den folgenden Jahren reorganisierte. 1857 erfolgte seine Hochzeit mit der belgischen Prinzeßin Charlotte, sowie seine Ernennung zum Generalgouverneur von dem Königreich Lombardei-Venedig. Als Kaiser von Mexiko wurde Ferdinand Maximilian von den Mexikanern unter Benito Juarez (1806-1872) am 14. Mai 1867 entmachtet, und wurde dann am 19. Juni 1867 mit seiner Gemahlin und seinen mexikanischen Generälen erschoßen. Seit 1867 ist Mexiko immer noch eine ziemlich korrupte Republik mit viel Armut und hohe Kriminalität.*

**k.u.k. Linienschiff "S.M.S. Erzherzog Karl" (1903) / Austro-Hungarian Battleship "S.M.S. Erzherzog Karl" (1903) with crew members hanging laundry – courtesy of Herr Alexander Traiber (Freunde Historischer Schiffe – Vienna, Austria)**

The two remaining ships of the "S.M.S. Erzherzog Karl" (1906) class were the "S.M.S. Erzherzog Friedrich" (1907) which means "Archduke Frederick" in English and the "S.M.S. Erzherzog Ferdinand Max" (1907). Erzherzog Friedrich was yet another member of the ruling Austrian House of Habsburg, who was a Field Marshall during World War One. He lived from 1856 until 1936. The second ship was named after none other than the younger brother of Austro-Hungarian Emperor Kaiser Franz Josef I (who ruled Austria from 1848 until his death in 1916). Archduke Ferdinand Maximilian was a great friend of the Imperial and Royal Austrian Navy and rose to the rank of Vice Admiral therein. He eventually moved to Mexico with his wife to become the Emperor of Mexico, where he was tragically assassinated in 1867 at the young age of 34. He was a good man, and his death was a terrible loss to the Imperial & Royal Navy, to

Austria-Hungary and to Mexico. The three ships of this class survived World War One, and were scrapped in 1920.

### IVf. "S.M.S. Brandenburg" Class / "S.M.S. Brandenburg" Klasse (1892)

The next previous class of German capital ships were actually the first "modern" pre-dreadnought battleships in the Imperial German Navy. The four ships of the "S.M.S. Brandenburg" (1892) class displaced a maximum 10,670 tons each, were armed with 6-11 inch guns plus 8-4 inch guns and could make up to 16,9 knots under full steam with their coal boilers. Their construction marked the very start of the naval arms race between Germany and Britain, which of course culminated in World War One. "Brandenburg" is the name of the German State surrounding Germany's national capital city of Berlin. The remaining ships of this class were named "S.M.S. Wörth" (1893), "S.M.S. Weissenburg" (1894) and "S.M.S. Kurfürst Friedrich Wilhelm" (1894). "Wörth" and "Weissenburg" are the names of German-speaking cities in Alsace-Lorraine, which were the sites of German victories against France during the Franco-Prussian War of 1870-1871. Kurfürst Friedrich Wilhelm (1620-1688), or "Prince Frederick William" of the House of Hohenzollern ruled Brandenburg-Prussia from 1640 until his death in 1688. He was a prince of Brandenburg and a duke of Prussia. Brandenburg-Prussia was a kingdom from 1701 until 1918, and Brandenburg alone had been an Electorate Principality within the Holy Roman Empire of the German Nation before that. Prussia had been an ethnically German Duchy under the sovereignty of the United Kingdom of Poland and Lithuania, another great medieval nation-state. The majority religion in Prussia was Evangelical Lutheran, with a Roman Catholic minority in the Ermland region. The old Duchy of Prussia eventually came to be known as "East Prussia" in modern times.

*Die vier Linienschiffe der "S.M.S. Brandenburg" (1892) Klaße waren Deutschlands erste moderne sogenannte "Pre-Dreadnoughts." Sie waren große, gepanzerte Hochseekampfschiffe ohne Segel, mit Schnellfeuerkanonen (statt mit nur Kasemattkanonen) bewaffnet. Sie hatten eine Einsatzverdrängung von je 10,670 Tonnen, und waren mit je sechs 28 cm Schnellfeuerkanonen sowie mit acht 10,5 cm Kasemattkanonen bewaffnet. Die Höchstgeschwindigkeit war 16,9 Knoten. Die drei anderen Mitglieder dieser Klaße waren die "S.M.S. Wörth" (1893), die "S.M.S. Weißenburg" (1894) und die "S.M.S. Kurfürst Friedrich Wilhelm" (1894). Alle vier Einheiten dieser Klaße nahmen im Jahre 1900 am chinesischen Boxeraufstand teil. Drei von den vier Linienschiffen dieser Klaße überstanden den Ersten Weltkrieg. Die "S.M.S. Kurfürst Friedrich Wilhelm" wurde von einem englischen Unterseeboot im Jahre 1915 torpediert. Die "S.M.S. Wörth" wurde im Jahre 1919 verschrottet, die "S.M.S. Brandenburg" wurde ein*

*Jahr später verschrottet und die "S.M.S. Weißenburg" wurde erst im Jahre 1938 verschrottet. Die Schlachten von Weißenburg (am 4. August 1870) und Wörth an der Sauer (am 6. August 1870) waren preußische Siege zur Zeit des Deutsch-Französischen Krieges (1870-1871). Kurfürst Friedrich Wilhelm I von Preußen (1620-1688) war Kurfürst von Brandenburg sowie Herzog von Preußen von 1640 bis 1688. Sein dritter Sohn, Friedrich I (1657-1713), war Kurfürst von Brandenburg, Herzog von Preußen sowie (nach dem Jahre 1701) König "in Preußen."*

All four ships of this class gained fame (or infamy if one is Chinese) in the Boxer Rebellion, when they were sent to help crush the nationalist Boxer uprising. All of the Western powers (and Japan) in China joined forces to crush the uprising – these included the USA, Britain, France, Portugal, Russia, Germany and Austria-Hungary. The Austrian commander had the greatest empathy and respect for the Chinese when he declared that if he had been one of them he would have been a Boxer (Chinese Nationalist) as well. Three of these four vessels survived World War One, with "S.M.S. Weissenburg" being scrapped as late as 1938. "S.M.S. Kurfürst Friedrich Wilhelm" was sunk by a British submarine in 1915. "S.M.S. Wörth" was scrapped in 1919, and "S.M.S. Brandenburg" was scrapped in 1920.

### IVg. "S.M.S. Habsburg" Class / "S.M.S. Habsburg" Klasse (1902)

The first and very smallest Austrian modern pre-dreadnought battleships were the three ships of the "S.M.S. Habsburg" (1902) class. They each displaced a maximum 8,823 tons, were armed with 3-9 inch guns plus 12-6 inch guns and could make up to 19,5 knots under full steam with their coal boilers. "Habsburg" is of course the name of the Royal Family of Austria, which has been headed by Prince Otto von Habsburg since 1922. He became the head of the family at age 10, when his father Kaiser Karl died in 1922. Kaiser Karl was recently beatified by the Roman Catholic Church, which means he is on his way to Sainthood. He earned this great honor because he was such a benevolent ruler of his people and tried in vain to end World War One before November 1918 – unfortunately "leaders" such as Woodrow Wilson of the United States would have none of it. Wilson wanted the war to continue until unconditional surrender and the destruction of Central Europe. "Habsburg" (spelled "Hapsburg" in English) is actually a corruption of "Habichtsburg" which was the name of the family when they owned their ancestral castle in the Canton of Aargau in Switzerland. "Habichtsburg" literally means "Castle of the Hawk" in English. The noble family of Habsburg-Lothringen can trace their ancestral lineage at least as far back as 60 B.C.

*Die drei Linienschiffe der "S.M.S. Habsburg" (1902) Klaße waren die ersten und auch die kleinsten sogenannten "Pre-Dreadnoughts" der Kaiserlichen und Königlichen Kriegsmarine. Sie hatten je eine Einsatzverdrängung von 8,823 Tonnen, und waren mit je drei 24 cm Schnellfeuerkanonen sowie mit 12-15 cm Kasemattkanonen bewaffnet. Die Höchstgeschwindigkeit waren gute 19,5 Knoten. Die zwei anderen Mitglieder dieser Klaße waren die "S.M.S. Árpád" (1903) und die "S.M.S. Babenberg" (1904). Alle drei Einheiten haben den Ersten Weltkreig überstanden, und wurden im Jahre 1923 verschrottet. Das Adelhaus Árpád herrschte über das Königreich Ungarn von 896 bis 1301, und das Adelhaus Babenberg herrschte über die Erzherzogtümer Nieder-und Oberösterreich von 976 bis 1248. Die beiden Adelhäuser sind ausgestorben, und deren Erben sind die Mitglieder des modernen Adelhauses Habsburg-Lothringen. Das Adelhaus Habsburg stammt aus der "Habichtsburg" im Kanton Aargau in der Schweiz, und kann ihren Stammbaum bis mindestens 60 Jahren vor Christus verfolgen. Das heutige Familienhaupt des Adelhauses Habsburg-Lothringen ist Prinz Otto von Habsburg (im Jahre 1912 geboren). Vormals war er CSU-Abgeordneter des europäischen Parlaments in Straßburg. Heute ist er im Ruhestand und wohnt in Bayern. Seine Gattin Prinzessin Regina ist im Jahre 2010 leider gestorben.*

Modern Switzerland was part of the Holy Roman Empire of the German Nation until the so-called "Peace Treaty" of Westphalia in 1648. Both the Netherlands and Switzerland were taken from Germany and given their "independence" by the victors of France, Denmark and Sweden – who had decimated the German population by one-third in 30 years of horrible warfare from 1618-1648. 7 million Germans died in the Thirty Years' War. The Netherlands is still home to 11.8 million German-speaking people today (the modern high Dutch language is very closely related to German) and Switzerland has another 7 million German-speaking people. The other official languages of modern Switzerland are French, Italian and Romansch. Romansch is the modern language most closely resembling Latin. The remaining ships in this class were "S.M.S. Árpád" (1903) and "S.M.S. Babenberg" (1904). "Árpád" was the name of the family and the dynasty that ruled Hungary from 896-1301, whereas "Babenberg" was the name of the family and the dynasty that ruled Austria from 976-1248, before the Habsburg dynasty inherited the Austrian lands. The Babenberg family came from Bamberg, Franconia, which is now in Northern Bavaria (Germany). The Habsburg family came from the Aargau, which is now in Switzerland. All three ships survived World War One, and were finally scrapped in 1923. Pre-dreadnought battleships of all nations were of course obsolete with the advent of the dreadnought battleships, and thus did not carry the brunt of the battle during World War One. The largest battle between pre-dreadnought battleships ever was fought between Japan and Russia at Tsushima in the Pacific in 1905. The Japanese crushed the Russian fleet in this important battle of the Russo-Japanese War. Going back even further in time, the predecessors of pre-dreadnought battleships were "ships of the line," built of wood and powered by sails in the old days, and moving up to iron construction and coil boilers by the late 19th century. Later ironclads were often known as "casemate ships" (due to their casemate guns) or simply as armored ships ("Panzerschiffe" in German) due to their protective belt armor plating. The forerunners of heavy, large or armored cruisers were known as frigates (first as sailing frigates and then as armored frigates), whereas the forerunners of light or small cruisers were known as corvettes (first as sailing and then as armored corvettes). The forerunners of modern destroyers and torpedo boats were likely smaller warships such as gunboats, cannon-boats, dispatch boats and "Avisos" (Spanish for cruising or scouting vessels). Rivers and lakes were often patrolled by armored monitors, small vessels with large guns but shallow draughts.

### IVh. "S.M.S. Renown" Class / "S.M.S. Renown" Klasse (1857)

"S.M.S. Renown" (1857) was a former British ship, and was the only large old-style wooden "ship of the line" ever owned by the Imperial German Navy. She was purchased from the English in 1870, being carvel-built out of oak, 74 meters long and with a maximum displacement of 5,700 tons. She had a single expansion engine, was fully rigged, had a sail area of 4,500 square meters and could make up to 10 knots. She had 2 battery decks armed with 91 cannon, built by the British Naval Arsenal at Woolwich. Her crew consisted of 42 commissioned officers and 477 enlisted men. She was scrapped in 1892 after 35 years of service.

*Das kaiserlich-deutsche Segellinienschiff "S.M.S. Renown" (1857) wurde von England im Jahre 1870 gekauft. Sie war aus Holz gebaut, war 74 Meter lang, hatte eine Segelfläche von 4,500 Quadratmeter (sowie eine einzelne Expansionsmaschine) und hatte eine Einsatzverdrängung von 5,700 Tonnen. Die Höchstgeschwindigkeit war 10 Knoten. Sie war mit 91 Kanonen bewaffnet und hatte eine Mannschaft von 42 Offizieren und 477 Matrosen. Sie wurde endlich im Jahre 1892 verschrottet.*

Germany and Austria-Hungary owned a total of 103 gunboats over the years, which ranged in size up to about 1,000 tons or so. Many of these vessels served overseas in Germany's Pacific colonies. By the time of World War One in 1914, they had become hopelessly obsolete and were thus largely scuttled by their crews at the beginning of the war. Monitors ranged in size up to about 600 tons, and were very slow due to being river and lake-based.

*Deutschland und Österreich-Ungarn haben insgesamt 103 Kanonenboote gehabt. Im Ersten Weltkrieg waren Kanonenboote schon veraltet. Die besten und auch die modernsten Kanonenboote der kaiserlich-deutschen Marine waren die sechs Einheiten der "S.M.S. Iltis" (1897) Klaße. Sie hatten je eine Einsatzverdränung von 1,048 Tonnen, und waren mit je vier 88 mm Schnellfeuerkanonen sowie mit sechs Maschinengewehren bewaffnet. Die Höchstgeschwindigkeit war 14,8 Knoten und die Reichweite war 3,080 Seemeilen. Die fünf anderen Mitglieder dieser Klaße waren die "S.M.S. Jaguar" (1899), die "S.M.S. Tiger" (1900), die "S.M.S. Luchs" (1900), die "S.M.S. Panther" (1902) und die "S.M.S. Eber" (1903). Die ersten vier Kanonenboote wurden im Kiautschou (Deutschlands Schutzgebiet in Tsingtau und Schantung, China) zwischen September und November 1914 selbst versenkt. Am Anfang des Ersten Weltkrieges lag die "S.M.S. Eber" in der Lüderitzbucht von Deutsch-Südwestafrika. Es gelang ihr allerdings nicht nach Deutschland zurück zukommen, und wurde vor Bahia (Brasilien) auch selbst versenkt. Die "S.M.S. Panther" hat den Ersten Weltkrieg überstanden, und wurde erst im Jahre 1931 verschrottet.*

## V. "Küstenpanzerschiffe" (Coastal Armored Ships)

Coastal armored ships were the true predecessors of modern pre-dreadnought battleships. They were distinguished from earlier armored casemate ships, armored frigates and wooden ships-of-the-line or battleships by having no sails. They were entirely coal-powered and used more modern guns in turrets. These guns were "rapid fire" cannon of significant caliber and would be used by all navies until the end of the Second World War as their primary surface armament. Rapid-fire cannons are called "Schnellfeuerkanonen" in German, sometimes abbreviated as "SFK."

*"Küstenpanzerschiffe" waren die Vorgänger der sogenannten "Pre-Dreadnought" Linienschiffe. Sie hatten keine Segel, und ihre Hauptbewaffnung waren Schnellfeuerkanonen (statt nur Kasemattkanonen). Die Vorgänger der Küstenpanzerschiffe waren die Kasemattschiffe, die Panzerfregatten und auch die Holzlinienschiffe – alle mit Segel und die meisten mit Kohldampfantrieb und Panzerung.*

### Va. "S.M.S. Kronprinz Erzherzog Rudolf" Class / "S.M.S. Kronprinz Erzherzog Rudolf" Klasse (1889)

"S.M.S. Kronprinz Erzherzog Rudolf" (1889) of the Austrian Navy was the largest armored coastal ship in any German Navy. She displaced a maximum 7,432 tons, was armed with 3-12 inch guns and could make up to 16 knots with her coal boilers under full steam. She was named after the initial heir to the throne of Austria-Hungary, who sadly died under suspicious circumstances before he could take the throne. He was the sole son of Austro-Hungarian Emperor Kaiser Franz Josef I, who reigned from 1848 until his death in 1916. The ship survived World War One and was scrapped thereafter.

*Das Küstenpanzerschiff "S.M.S. Kronprinz Erzherzog Rudolf" (1889) war derzeit das größte Küstenpanzerschiff der Kaiserlichen und Königlichen Kriegsmarine. Es hatte eine Einsatzverdrängung von 7,432 Tonnen und war mit drei 30,5 cm Schnellfeuerkanonen bewaffnet. Die Höchstgeschwindigkeit waren 16 Knoten. Das Schiff hat den Ersten Weltkrieg überstanden, und wurde danach verschrottet. Kronprinz Erzherzog Rudolf von Österreich-Ungarn (1858-1889) war der einzige Sohn von Kaiser Franz Josef I von Österreich (1830-1916) und Kaiserin Elisabeth von Österreich-Ungarn (1837-1898), und Erzherzog-Thronfolger von Österreich-Ungarn.*

### Vb. "S.M.S. Kronprinzessin Erzherzogin Stephanie" Class / "S.M.S. Kronprinzeßin Erzherzogin Stephanie" Klasse (1889)

"S.M.S. Kronprinz Erzherzog Rudolf" (which means Crown Prince Archduke Rudolph in English) was accompanied by "S.M.S. Kronprinzessin Erzherzogin Stephanie" (1889) which means "Crown Princess Archduchess Stephanie" in English – she was the wife, and then the widow, of young Rudolf. The ship displaced a maximum 6,830 tons, was armed with 2-12 inch guns and could make up to 17 knots under full steam with her coal boilers. This ship also survived the First World War and was scrapped thereafter.

*Das Küstenpanzerschiff "S.M.S. Kronprinzeßin Erzherzogin Stephanie" (1889) hatte eine Einsatzverdrängung von 6,830 Tonnen, und war mit zwei 30,5 cm Schnellfeuerkanonen bewaffnet. Die Höchstgeschwindigkeit waren 17 Knoten. Das Schiff hat den Ersten Weltkrieg überstanden, und wurde danach verschrottet. Stephanie von Belgien (1864-1945) war Ehefrau von Kronprinz Erzherzog Rudolf von Österreich-Ungarn (1858-1889) und dadurch auch Kronprinzeßin von Österreich-Ungarn.*

**Vc. "S.M.S. Monarch" Class / "S.M.S. Monarch" Klasse (1898)**

The next class of three Austrian armored coastal ships were somewhat smaller at 5,878 tons full load displacement per ship. They were armed with 4-9 inch guns and could make up to 17,5 knots under full steam with their coal boilers. The ships were all commissioned in 1898 and were named "S.M.S. Monarch," "S.M.S. Wien" (the German word for "Vienna") and "S.M.S. Budapest" (named after the capital city of Hungary, a country which has 3.7 million German-speaking people today). "S.M.S. Monarch" and "S.M.S. Budapest" survived World War One, and were scrapped after the war in 1921. "S.M.S. Wien" was sunk in relatively shallow water during the war and raised by the Italians thereafter. Most of her was scrapped, but the stern part of the ship with the nameplate was salvaged and can be seen in an Italian maritime museum today. Vienna is of course the capital city of Austria, and the former seat of the Habsburg Dynasty, which ruled the Holy Roman Empire of the German Nation (the First Reich) until 1806 and the Austro-Hungarian Empire until November 1918. The Habsburg family can trace its ancestral claim to the throne of Germany and Austria-Hungary all the way back to 482, when the Frankish Kingdom was proclaimed – this Kingdom became the Holy Roman Empire of the German Nation in 800, when Charles the Great ("Karl der Grosse" in German or "Charlemagne" in French) was crowned by the Pope.

*Die drei Küstenpanzerschiffe der "S.M.S. Monarch" (1898) Klaße hatten eine Einsatzverdrängung von je 5,878 Tonnen, und waren mit je vier 24 cm Schnellfeuerkanonen (in zwei Zwillingstürmen) bewaffnet. Die Höchstgeschwindigkeit war 17,5 Knoten. Die zwei anderen Mitglieder dieser Klaße waren die "S.M.S. Wien" (1898) und die "S.M.S. Budapest" (1898). Die "S.M.S. Monarch" und die "S.M.S. Budapest" überstanden den Ersten Weltkrieg, und wurden im Jahre 1921 verschrottet. Die "S.M.S. Wien" wurde am 10. Dezember 1917 von zwei italienischen Torpedoschnellbooten mit zwei Torpedos versenkt. 30 von den 435 Besatzungsmitgliedern kamen ums Leben, aber die anderen Besatzungsmitgliedern wurden von den Österreichern gerettet. Das Schiff wurde von den Italienern in den 1920er Jahren geborgen und dann verschrottet. Die Stadt Budapest ("Ofen" auf deutsch) war Hauptstadt des Königreiches Ungarns. Heute gibt es noch 3,7 Millionen deutschsprachige Einwohner in Ungarn.*

**Vd. "S.M.S. Siegfried" Class / "S.M.S. Siegfried" Klasse (1890)**

The largest class of German coastal armored ships was that of the "S.M.S. Siegfried" (1890). The 8 ships of this class each displaced a maximum 4,320 tons full load displacement and were armed with 3-9 inch guns plus 10-88 mm guns. They could make up to 15,4 knots under full steam with their coal boilers. The remaining ships were named "S.M.S. Beowulf" (1892), "S.M.S. Frithjof" (1893), "S.M.S. Hildebrand" (1893), "S.M.S. Heimdall" (1894), "S.M.S. Hagen" (1894), "S.M.S. Odin" (1896) and "S.M.S. Agir" (1896). All of these ships survived World War One, were later converted into merchant vessels after the war, and then eventually scrapped. Each ship in this class was named for characters from Norse mythology, which shows how close German culture is to the culture of Scandinavian countries such as Denmark, Norway, Sweden and Iceland. The Scandinavians are a "Germanic" people as are the Dutch, the Flemish (of Belgium), the Letzeburgers (of Luxembourg), the Frisians, the English and the Afrikaners (the Cape Dutch of South Africa). All these languages are Germanic as is Yiddish, an old Jewish language using Hebrew characters. 3 million Jews around the world still speak Yiddish, especially in countries such as the USA, Israel and Russia. There are more than 2,5 million German-speaking people each in Belgium and Sweden today. 200,000 people in Israel speak German today, mostly descendants of those who were forced to emigrate from Central Europe between 1933 and 1945. 474,000 people (virtually the entire population) in Luxembourg speak German. 1 million people in South Africa speak German today, most of them being Afrikaners of German ancestry. 3,5 million people in the United Kingdom speak German. The USA has more than 63,5 million ethnic Germans, making them the largest ethnic group in America. The largest wave of German emigration to the USA occurred in the 1840s, especially after the failed liberal revolution in Germany of 1848. Many states in the US Midwest have very large ethnic German populations. The best example is Wisconsin, where 63% of the population is of German heritage. Next comes North Dakota, where 48% of the people are ethnic Germans. In fact, the capital city of North Dakota is named "Bismarck" after German-Prussian Chancellor Otto von Bismarck. South Dakota is 47% German and Nebraska is 46% German. Iowa (home to many German Anabaptist Mennonites) is 45% German and Minnesota is 43% German. Pennsylvania is 34% German. The first German emigrants to America came from the German city of Krefeld aboard the sailing ship "Concord" in 1683, and settled in modern-day Philadelphia where they founded Germantown. Many German, Austrian, Moravian, Swiss and Dutch Anabaptists – including the Amish, the Hutterites, the Brethren, and the Quakers, all settled in Pennsylvania and beyond. They eventually expanded throughout the United States, Canada, Latin America, Africa and Asia. Some even migrated back to Central Europe. Today, there are more than 4,5 million such German Anabaptists all over the world.

*Die acht kaiserlich-deutschen Küstenpanzerschiffe der "S.M.S. Siegfried" (1890) Klaße hatten eine Einsatzverdrängung von je 4,320 Tonnen, und waren mit je drei*

*21 cm Schnellfeuerkanonen (in drei Einzeltürmen) sowie mit je zehn 88 mm Schnellfeuerkanonen (auch in Einzeltürmen) bewaffnet. Die sieben anderen Mitglieder dieser Klaße waren die "S.M.S. Beowulf" (1892), die "S.M.S. Frithjof" (1893), die "S.M.S. Hildebrand" (1893), die "S.M.S. Heimdall" (1894), die "S.M.S Hagen" (1894), die "S.M.S. Odin" (1896) und die "S.M.S. Agir" (1896). Alle Einheiten dieser Klaße überstanden den Ersten Weltkrieg, und wurden nach dem Krieg verschrottet – die "S.M.S. Odin" zuletzt im Jahre 1935. Die Patennamen dieser acht Küstenpanzerschiffe kamen aus der skandinavischen Mythologie. Die deutsche Sprache ist auch in Skandinavien weit verbreitet. 3,015,000 Leute in Dänemark, 201,870 Leute in Estland, eine Million Leute in Finnland und 2,520,000 Leute in Schweden sprechen deutsch. Vor 1919 war Nordschleswig (heute in Dänemark) ein Teil des Deutschen Reiches. Es gibt heute in Nordschleswig eine Partei der deutschen Minderheit – genauso wie der SSW (Südschleswiger Wahlverband) der dänischen und friesischen Minderheiten in Schleswig-Holstein.*

### Ve. "S.M.S. Nordland" and "S.M.S. Adler" Classes / die Klassen "S.M.S. Nordland" und "S.M.S Adler" (pre-1890 / vor 1890)

Prior German armored coastal ships were even smaller, demonstrating to us just how primitive the earliest pre-dreadnoughts were. But for their own time, they were certainly advanced merely by not having rigging & sails and in having turret guns as their primary armament instead of older casemate guns and pounders. Pounder guns were like those found on old wooden sailing ships. "S.M.S. Nordland" displaced just 3,800 tons and was armed with 3-6 inch guns, 10-20 mm guns plus 2-6 pounders. "Pounders" were just that – the shells coming out of these cannon weighed 6 pounds each in this case. In the old days, they were not even explosive! She could make 16 knots under full steam with coal power. "S.M.S. Adler" (which means "eagle" in English) was even smaller at 3,500 tons. She was armed with 2-9 inch guns, 4-6 inch guns plus 8-76 mm guns. Her top speed was also 16 knots.

*Die ersten kaiserlich-deutschen Küstenpanzerschiffe vor dem Jahre 1890 waren noch kleiner. Die "S.M.S. Nordland" hatte eine Einsatzverdrängung von 3,800 Tonnen, und war mit 3-15 cm Schnellfeuerkanonen, zehn 20 mm Schnellfeuerkanonen sowie mit zwei 6-Pfunder bewaffnet. Die Höchstgeschwindigkeit waren 16 Knoten. Das Küstenpanzerschiff "S.M.S. Adler" war noch kleiner, mit einer Einsatzverdrängung von nur 3,500 Tonnen. Sie war mit zwei 24 cm Schnellfeuerkanonen, vier 15 cm Schnellfeuerkanonen sowie mit acht 76 mm Schnellfeuerkanonen bewaffnet. Die Höchstgeschwindigkeit waren auch 16 Knoten.*

## VI. "Kasemattschiffe" (Casemate Ships)

Before the pre-dreadnought battleships and the armored coastal ships, the largest capital ships in the German and Austrian navies were the armored casemate ships, so named due to their casemate guns. Their construction included both wood and iron (thus the armor) and their propulsion included both coal boilers and sails.

*Die größten Vorgänger der sogenannten "Pre-Dreadnought" Linienschiffe waren die Kasemattschiffe. Sie waren mit Kasemattkanonen bewaffnet, waren mit Holz sowie mit Panzerung gebaut, hatten Segel und auch Kohldampfantrieb.*

## VIa. "S.M.S. Custoza" Class / "S.M.S. Custoza" Klasse (1875)

The Austrian casemate ship "S.M.S. Custoza" (1875) was named for one of Austria's great victories over the Italian nationalists in the war of 1848 to 1849. Contrary to popular belief, nationalists were never universally popular in any country. In fact, during this war roughly 30% of the Italian population fought on behalf of the Austrian side and the Habsburg Dynasty. Large segments of Southern Italy, including Sicily and Naples, wanted nothing to do with a future secular and unified Italian state. Large areas of the South Tyrol, Triest and Görz ("Gorizia" in Italian) remained loyal to Austria-Hungary right up to the end of World War One. There were also many ethnic Italians throughout the Adriatic coast of Slovenia and Croatia who remained loyal to Austria. "S.M.S. Custoza" displaced 7,609 tons and was armed with 8-10 inch casemate guns. She could make up to 14 knots and was manned by a crew of 548.

*Das Kasemattschiff "S.M.S. Custoza" (1875) der Kaiserlichen und Königlichen Kriegsmarine hatte eine Einsatzverdrängung von 7,609 Tonnen, und war mit acht 26 cm Kasemattkanonen, sechs 88 mm Schnellfeuerkanonen sowie mit zwei 70 mm Schnellfeuerkanonen bewaffnet. Die Höchstgeschwindigkeit mit Segel sowie mit Kohldampfantrieb war 14 Knoten. Sie hatte eine Besatzung von 548 Offizieren und Matrosen, und wurde im Jahre 1920 verschrottet. Custoza (vormals "Custozza") ist ein italienisches Dorf südwestlich von Verona (im Land Venedig, oder "Venezia" auf italienisch), das Schauplatz zweier Schlachten zwischen Österreich und Italien war. Am 25. Juli 1848 schlug hier Generalkommandant Johann Josef Wenzel Graf von Radetzky (1766-1858) das Heer Sardiniens unter König Albert von Sardinien-Piemont (1798-1849). Am 24. Juni 1866 besiegte Erzherzog Albrecht von Österreich (1817-1895) das bedeutend größere italienische Heer unter dem piemontesischen Oberbefehlshaber General Alfonso La Marmora (1804-1878). Die Custozzakaserne des österreichischen Heeres in*

*Neulengbach (im Sankt Pölten-Land in Niederösterreich) ist nach den Schlachten von Custozza benannt.*

## VIb. "S.M.S. Lissa" Class / "S.M.S. Lissa" Klasse (1871)

The Austrian casemate ship "S.M.S Lissa" (1871) was named for Vice Admiral Tegetthoff's great victory over the larger and more powerful Italian fleet near the island of Lissa in the Adriatic Sea in 1866. In fact, Italy's navy was ranked as the third most powerful fleet in the entire world. In my own opinion, Tegetthoff was the greatest admiral ever – he used all available ships (including those thought to be obsolete) and his battle formation literally charged the Italian fleet in the shape of a huge arrow. He split the Italian fleet in two and then destroyed it, even ramming enemy ships. He had tremendous skill and great optimism. "S.M.S. Lissa" displaced 7,086 tons and was armed with 12-9 inch casemate guns. She could make up to 13 knots and had a crew of 620 officers and enlisted men.

### Die Seeschlacht von Lissa / the Sea Battle of Lissa (1866)

*Das Kasemattschiff "S.M.S. Lissa" (1871) der Kaiserlichen und Königlichen Kriegsmarine hatte eine Einsatzverdrängung von 7,086 Tonnen, und war mit 12-23 cm Kasemattkanonen, vier Acht-Pfundern sowie mit zwei Drei-Pfunder bewaffnet. Die Höchstgeschwindigkeit mit Segel sowie mit Kohldampfantrieb war 13 Knoten, und sie hatte eine Besatzung von 620 Offizieren und Matrosen. Sie wurde im Jahre 1895 verschrottet. Im sogenannten dritten italienischen "Unabhängigkeitskrieg" gewann der Österreichische Vizeadmiral Wilhelm Freiherr von Tegetthoff (1827-1871) am 20. Juli 1866 durch Anwendung der Rammtaktik die Seeschlacht von Lissa bei der heute "Vis" (in Kroatien) genannten Insel gegen die zahlenmäßig überlegene italienische Flotte unter Admiral Carlo Pellion di Persano. Dies war die erste Seeschlacht, in der in größerem Umfang Panzerschiffe eingesetzt wurden.*

## Chapter 11 (Kapitel 11): MEDIUM CAPITAL SHIPS (Kriegsschiffe der Mittelklasse)

### VII. "Schwere Kreuzer" (Heavy Cruisers)

World War Two Heavy Cruisers included the four ships of the "Admiral Hipper" class and the three "Panzerschiffe" (armored ships which were nicknamed "Pocket Battleships" by the Western Allies) of the "Deutschland" class. The term " Pocket Battleship" is somewhat misleading, because these ships had to be much smaller than battleships according the terms of the Treaty of Versailles imposed upon Germany by the victorious Western Allies in 1919 after World War One. They were for all intents and purposes Heavy Cruisers, and were reclassified as such upon the outbreak of the Second World War in September 1939. The "Admiral Hipper" displaced 18,200 tons, was armed with 8-8 inch guns in 4 turrets plus 3 aircraft and was capable of an impressive 32,5 knots under full steam turbine power. Steaming radius was 6,800 miles. She was named for the commanding Admiral of Germany's battlecruiser squadron from World War One and survived until 1945. Her sister ship the "Blücher" (named for a Prussian Field Marshall of the Napoleonic Wars and one of the victors of the Battle of Waterloo in 1815) was unfortunately sunk during the successful German invasion and occupation of Norway in April 1940. Their sister ship the "Prinz Eugen" (named for a Field Marshall of the Holy Roman Empire of the German Nation who defeated the Turks and for a similarly-named Austrian dreadnought battleship of World War One) was handed over to the USA in 1945 and sunk as a target ship in Bikini Atoll in 1946 (a nuclear test site in which many Allied ships were also expended). The fourth ship of the "Admiral Hipper" class was launched but never completed (the "Lützow," named for a great Prussian General of the Napoleonic Wars). An earlier German battlecruiser named "S.M.S. Lützow" fought at the famous Battle of Jutland in May 1916, where she was scuttled due to heavy damage. Most of her crew was fortunately saved. Ludwig Adolf Wilhelm von Lützow was a Prussian general and hero of the Napoleonic Wars against France who lived from 1782 until 1834. His family actually came from Mecklenburg, which is North of Brandenburg-Prussia on the Baltic Sea. He formed the legendary "Freikorps Lützow" ("Free Corps Luetzow" in English) of 50,000 volunteer cavalrymen to fight the French in 1813.

*Die Zeit der Schlachtschiffe (vormals Linienschiffe, Küstenpanzerschiffe und Kasemattschiffe) ist schon vorbei. Gegen Flugzeugträger und Unterseeboote sind solche großen Einheiten nun veraltet. Die größten modernen Kriegsschiffe außer Flugzeugträger sind die Kreuzer (Schlachtkreuzer, Schwere Kreuzer und Kleine*

Kreuzer). Nur die Vereinigten Staaten von Amerika, Rußland, Frankreich und Peru haben noch Kreuzer. Die Amerikaner haben 27 Kleine Kreuzer der "U.S.S. Ticonderoga" Klaße, mit einer Einsatzverdrängung von je 9,600 Tonnen. Die Rußen haben drei Schlachtkreuzer der "Kirov" Klaße (mit einer Einsatzverdrängung von je 28,000 Tonnen), zehn Kleine Kreuzer der "Slava" Klaße (mit einer Einsatzverdrängung von je 11,490 Tonnen) und zwei Kleine Kreuzer der "Kara" Klaße (mit einer Einsatzverdränung von je 9,900 Tonnen). Die Franzosen haben einen Kleinen Kreuzer – die "Jeanne d'Arc," mit einer Einsatzverdrängung von 10,575 Tonnen. Peru hat einen Leichten Kreuzer der "De Zeven Provinciën" Klaße, mit einer Einsatzverdrängung von 12,165 Tonnen (vormals niederländisch, und auch vormals Beute der Deutschen Kriegsmarine zur Zeit des Zweiten Weltkrieges in den Niederlanden). Die letzten, die modernsten sowie die größten Schweren Kreuzer der Deutschen Marine waren fünf Einheiten der "Admiral Hipper" (1934) Klaße. Die vier anderen Mitglieder dieser Klaße waren die "Blücher" (1939), die "Prinz Eugen" (1940), die "Seydlitz" (vom Stapel gelaufen aber nie getauft) und die "Lützow" (auch vom Stapel gelaufen aber nie getauft). Die "Admiral Hipper" und die "Blücher" hatten eine Einsatzverdrängung von je 18,200 Tonnen, und die "Prinz Eugen" hatte eine Einsatzverdrängung von 18,400 Tonnen. Die Deutsche Kriegsmarine hatte es vor, die "Seydlitz" als Hilfsflugzeugträger statt als Schweren Kreuzer zu fertigen. Als Hilfsflugzeugträger war die "Seydlitz" mit einer Einsatzverdängung von 18,000 Tonnen geplant. Die geplante Einsatzverdrängung für die "Lützow" war schon 19,800 Tonnen – das größte Schiff dieser Klaße. Die Schweren Kreuzer der "Admiral Hipper" Klaße waren mit acht 20,3 cm Schnellfeuerkanonen (in vier Zwillingstürmen) sowie mit drei Flugzeugen bewaffnet. Die Höchstgeschwindigkeit war gute 33,5 Knoten. Der Schwere Kreuzer "Admiral Hipper" war zur Zeit des Zweiten Weltkrieges sehr aktiv. Im April 1945 erhielt das Schiff bei zwei Luftangriffen Bombentreffer und war nicht mehr einsatzfähig. Am 3. Mai 1945 wurde die "Admiral Hipper" von den Deutschen im Dock gesprengt. Das Schiff wurde später von den Briten abgedichtet, anschließend in die Heikendorfer Bucht geschleppt und dort gegenüber vom Leichten Kreuzer "Emden" auf Grund gesetzt. Die Abwrackung folgte im Jahre 1946. Die Schiffsglocke befindet sich im Deutschen Marine-Ehrenmal in Laboe. Der Namensvetter Admiral Franz Ritter von Hipper (1863-1932) war ein Deutscher Admiral in der Kaiserlichen Marine. Er stammt aus einer bayerischen Gastwirtschaftsfamilie. Nach der Schulzeit trat Franz Hipper mit knapp 18 Jahren im April 1881 in die Kaiserliche Marine ein. Im Herbst 1884 wurde er zum Offizier befördert und als solcher war er bis 1903 Kommandant und Flottenchef von Torpedobooten. Im Jahre 1912 wurde er zum Konteradmiral befördert, und leitete ab Oktober 1913 als Befehlshaber die Aufklärungsstreitkräfte der Hochseeflotte. Mit Ausbruch des Ersten Weltkriegs *führte er die Schlachtkreuzer der Kaiserlichen Marine erfolgreich gegen die "Royal Navy" von England. Er führte den Aufklärungsverband im Gefecht auf der Doggerbank (am 24. Januar 1915) und in der Skagerrakschlacht (am 31. Mai 1916). In der letztgenannten Schlacht wurden der "Royal Navy" schwere Verlußte zugefügt; Admiral Hipper galt danach sowohl in Deutschland als auch in Großbrittanien als großer Marineführer. Im Juni 1916 wurde er von König Ludwig III von Bayern in den erblichen bayerischen Ritterstand erhoben. Im August 1918, wurde er als Nachfolger von Admiral Reinhard Scheer zum Admiral und Chef der Deutschen Hochseeflotte ernannt. Der Schwere Kreuzer "Blücher" wurde am 20. September 1939 in Dienst gestellt. Sie hatte nur eine sehr kurze Laufbahn. Bereits bei ihrem ersten Kampfeinsatz bei der Invasion Norwegens (das "Unternehmen Weserübung") führte am 9. April 1940 zum Totalverlust des Schiffes. Das Wrack liegt heute noch an der Untergangsstelle in 90 Metern Tiefe. 830 Besatzungsmitglieder und Heeressoldaten des Landungskommandos fanden im eiskalten Wasser des Oslofjords den Tod.*

## Generalfeldmarschall Gebhardt Leberecht von Blücher (Field Marshall Gebhardt Leberecht von Blücher)

*Gebhardt Leberecht von Blücher (1742-1819) war Preußischer Generalfeldmarschall und hat sich in bedeutenden Schlachten besonders gegen Napoleon Bonaparte von Frankreich hervorgetan. Der Schwere Kreuzer "Prinz Eugen" wurde am 1. August 1940 in Dienst gestellt. Das Schiff wurde auch als "Der glückliche Prinz" oder "Das glückhafte Schiff" bezeichnet, da es verschiedene Einsätze fast unbeschadet überstand (so zum Beispiel das Unternehmen "Rheinübung" mit dem großen Schlachtschiff "Bismarck," den Kanaldurchbruch "Unternehmen Cerberus" mit den Schlachtschiffen "Scharnhorst" und "Gneisenau" und das Norwegenunternehmen "Sportpalast" (im Februar 1942). Die "Prinz Eugen" überstand den Zweiten Weltkrieg, und wurde eventuell den Amerikanern übergeben. Im Bikini-Atoll der Marschall-Inseln wurde das Schiff etwa eine Seemeile entfernt von "Nullpunkt" der als "Operation Crossroads" bekannt gewordenen Atombombenversuchsserie mit zahlreichen weiteren Versuchsschiffen (alliierte Kriegsschiffe) versenkt. Der Deutsche Marinebund bemühte sich um die Bergung und Rückführung eines der drei Propeller. Die Verhandlungen dazu wurden bis Ende des Jahres 1978 abgeschloßen. Der Propeller ist nun auf dem Gelände des Marine-Ehrenmals in Laboe aufgestellt. Eine der Torpedozielanlagen (Backbord achtern) befindet sich im Deutschen Schiff-Fahrtsmuseum Bremerhaven (vormals "Wesermünde genannt"). Prinz Eugen Franz von Savoyen-Carignan (1663-1736) war einer der berühmtesten Feldherren des Adelhauses Österreich (Habsburg) und wesentliche Stütze der Großmachtstellung Österreichs innerhalb Europas. Der Schwere*

*Kreuzer "Seydlitz" lief vom Stapel am 19. Januar 1939, wurde aber nie in Dienst gestellt. Er war mit Kriegsbeginn zu zwei Drittel fertig. Im August 1942 entschied die Deutsche Kriegsmarine, das Schiff zu einem Flugzeugträger umzubauen. Da es als Schwerer Kreuzer schon 90 Prozent fertig war, mußten umfangreiche Umbauten vorgenommen werden.*

## Schwerer Kreuzer / Hilfsflugzeugträger Seydlitz

*Wegen zunehmender Materialknappheit wurden diese Arbeiten im Januar 1943 eingestellt und die "Seydlitz" nach Königsberg in Ostpreußen geschleppt. Dort wurde sie am 10. April 1945 gesprengt. Friedrich Wilhelm Freiherr von Seydlitz-Kurzbach (1721-1773) war ein Preußischer Kavallerieoffizier. Er gilt als einer der besten Kavallerieführer Preußens.*

## Schwerer Kreuzer Lützow der "Admiral Hipper-Klasse" (Heavy Cruisers of the "Admiral Hipper" Class)

*Der Schwere Kreuzer "Lützow" lief am 1. Juli 1939 vom Stapel, wurde aber auch nie in Dienst gestellt. Das halbfertige Schiff wurde an Sowjetrußland im April 1940 verkauft, in den Hafen von Leningrad (heute wieder Sankt Petersburg genannt) geschleppt und dort weitergebaut. Zu Beginn des deutschen Rußlandfeldzuges im Juni 1941 war der Kreuzer ungefähr zu zwei Drittel fertig. Durch deutschen Beschuß erhielt der Kreuzer mehrere schwere Treffer und sank im Hafen auf Grund. Das Schiff wurde von den Rußen nach dem Krieg geborgen, aber richtig fertiggestellt wurde es nie. In der Folgezeit diente es bis zur Verschrottung im Jahre 1960 als Wohnschiff der sowjetrussischen Marine. Ludwig Adolf Wilhelm Freiherr von Lützow (1782-1834) war Preußischer Generalmajor. Er ist vor allem durch das nach ihm benannte Freikorps, die "Schwarzen Jäger," bekannt worden.*

## Captured Italian Heavy Cruisers (Beutekreuzer aus Italien)

The German Navy captured two Italian heavy cruisers in 1943. The "Bolzano" (1933) displaced 13,885 tons and was armed with 8-8 inch guns. She was named for the capital of the German-speaking South Tyrol, a former Austrian province which has been part of Italy since 1918. The German name for the city is "Bozen." Today, the German-speaking "Südtiroler Volkspartei" ("South Tyrolian Peoples' Party) governs the province from Bozen. The other captured Italian heavy cruiser was the "Gorizia" (1931), which displaced 14,560 tons and was armed with 8-8 inch guns. She was named for the capital city of the province of Gorizia, located on Italy's border with Slovenia. This was yet another former

Austrian province until 1918, the German name for it being "Görz." Today, there are 2,833,000 German-speaking people in Italy.

*Zur Zeit des Zweiten Weltkrieges hatte die Deutsche Kriegsmarine zwei italenische Schwere Kreuzer übernommen. Die "Gorizia" ("Görz" auf deutsch) wurde im Jahre 1931 getauft, und wurde im Jahre 1943 als Kriegsbeute genommen. Sie hatte eine Einsatzverdrängung von 14,560 Tonnen, und war mit acht 20,3 cm Schnellfeuerkanonen (in vier Zwillingstürmen) bewaffnet. Die Höchstgeschwindigkeit war gute 33 Knoten. Das Schiff wurde von den Engländern spät im Jahre 1943 durch Fliegerbomben versenkt, nach dem Krieg von den Italienern geborgen und dann im Jahre 1946 endlich verschrottet. Der Schwere Kreuzer "Bolzano" ("Bozen" auf deutsch) wurde im Jahre 1933 getauft, und wurde im September 1943 im Hafen von La Spezia als Kriegsbeute übernommen. Am 22. Juni 1944 wurde das Schiff von den Alliierten durch Fliegerbomben versenkt, nach dem Krieg von den Italienern geborgen und kurz danach verschrottet. Das Schiff hatte eine Einsatzverdrängung von 13,885 Tonnen, und war mit acht 20,3 cm Schnellfeuerkanonen bewaffnet. Die Höchstgeschwindigkeit war gute 35 Knoten.*

### VIII. "Panzershiffe" (Armored Ships)

The "Deutschland" class was of course famous as the largest new German capital ships built after the Treaty of Versailles. The "Deutschland" was commissioned in 1933, the "Admiral Scheer" in 1934 and the "Admiral Graf Spee" in 1936. My paternal grandfather Wilhelm Johannes Nonnenkamp (1903-1972) served aboard the "Deutschland" from 1933-1936. His first cousin from Nordenham, Lower Saxony (also named Wilhelm Nonnenkamp) served aboard the same ship as he did. My grandfather came from the city of Oldenburg which is also in Lower Saxony. The first two ships of this class survived the war, whereas the "Admiral Graf Spee" was scuttled after the Battle of the River Plate off Montevideo, Uruguay in December 1939 (she had been outnumbered by 3 British Cruisers, was low on fuel & ammunition and the German Navy believed it pointless to sacrifice her crew and/or surrender her). Her 45-year old captain Langsdorff chose to go against his orders to avoid enemy combat vessels if at all possible, and engaged 3 Royal Navy cruisers off the coast of Uruguay. This cost him fuel, ammunition, caused damage to the ship, but above all the stealth and the time he would have required to make a run back for Germany. In spite of this, during the course of 3 months (from September to December, 1939), the "Admiral Graf Spee" sunk 9 vessels and was chased or confronted by no fewer than 44 Allied ships.

**Panzerschiff Deutschland (1933) in Spanien / Armored Ship "Deutschland" (1933) in Spain - Nonnenkamp family archives**

*Die drei Panzerschiffe der "Deutschland" (1931) Klaße waren die ersten großen Einheiten der Reichsmarine, und haben die veralteten Linienschiffe der ehemaligen Kaiserlichen Marine ersetzt. Die zwei anderen Mitglieder dieser Klaße waren die "Admiral Scheer" (1934) und die "Admiral Graf Spee" (1936). Die "Deutschland" hatte eine Einsatzverdrängung von 15,900 Tonnen, aber die zwei anderen Schiffe dieser Klaße hatten je eine Einsatzverdrängung von 16,200 Tonnen. Die Hauptbewaffnung waren je sechs 28 cm Schnellfeuerkanonen (in zwei Zwillingstümen) sowie acht 15 cm Geschütze (in Einzellafetten). Die Höchstgeschwindigkeit waren gute 28 bis 28,5 Knoten.*

**Panzerschiff "Deutschland" zur See im Jahre 1935 / Armored Ship "Deutschland" on the High Seas in 1935 -Nonnenkamp family archives**

**Oberbootsmannsmaat Wilhelm Johannes Nonnenkamp**

**Segelschulschiff / Training Ship "Bremen" (1919) seen off the coast of Antwerp, Belgium – Nonnenkamp Family Archives**

My paternal grandfather Wilhelm Johannes Nonnenkamp (1903-1972) joined the interwar "Reichsmarine" of the Weimar Republic in 1924. He served aboard the pre-Dreadnought battleship "S.M.S. Braunschweig" from 1924 until 1931 – one year before the old ship was scrapped. He served aboard the training ship (a sailing vessel) "Bremen" from 1931 until 1933 (when the above photograph was taken near the port of Antwerp in Flanders / Belgium). The "Bremen" was commissioned in 1919 and still exists today, albeit in private service in Germany – no longer in the German Navy. He then served aboard the "pocket Battleship" Deutschland from the time of her commissioning in 1933 until she served in the Spanish Civil War in 1936. The "Panzerschiff Deutschland" was renamed as the Heavy Cruiser "Lützow" in 1940 and served until the end of World War Two in 1945. My grandfather served in the German Customs Service ("Zolldienst") from 1936 until his retirement in 1968. He was wounded in a border incident on the Dutch-German border before 1940, and was therefore not able to serve in active duty during World War Two. He was called to active duty in the Home Guard (the "Volkssturm") in 1945, but this did not last long as the war ended in May 1945.

**Wilhelm Johannes Nonnenkamp (1903-1972) mit "Hokko" im Jahre 1935 / Wilhelm Johannes Nonnenkamp (1903-1972) with Ship's Mascot "Hokko" the black bear in 1935 – Nonnenkamp Family Archives**

*Im Februar 1940 waren die drei Einheiten dieser Klaße als Schwere Kreuzer umklaßifiziert. Mein Großvater Wilhelm Johannes Nonnenkamp (1903-1972) diente von 1933 (die Indienstellung des Schiffes) bis 1936 auf dem Panzerschiff "Deutschland." Als 1936 in Spanien der Bürgerkrieg ausbrach, wurde die "Deutschland" zur Seeraumkontrolle in spanische Gewässer beordert. Zur Zeit des Zweiten Weltkrieges war die "Deutschland" (seit November 1939 als "Lützow" umbenannt, weil Adolf Hitler kein Schiff mit dem Namen "Deutschland" verlieren wollte) sehr aktiv, und hatte zwei feindliche Schiffe versenkt und Eins als Beute genommen. Am 16. April 1945 wurde sie von britischen Lancaster-Bombern im Hafen von Swindemünde in Hinterpommern schwer beschädigt. Sie wurde endlich von den Russen im Hafen von Königsberg in Ostpreußen im Jahre 1949 verschrottet. Die "Admiral Scheer" (1934) war auch zur Zeit des Zweiten Weltkreises sehr aktiv, und hatte 17 feindliche Schiffe versenkt. Sie wurde am 9. April 1945 nach Bombentreffern im Bauhafen der Deutschen Werke in Kiel gekentert. Der Rumpf wurde von ortsansässigen Unternehmen ausgeschlachtet (insbesondere nach Buntmetallen), und bei der Demontage der Werftanlagen mit Trümmern und Sand bedeckt und später überbaut. Die Schiffsglocke befindet sich heute im Marinemuseum in Wilhelmshaven. Reinhard Scheer (1863-1928) war Admiral der Kaiserlichen Marine. Er kommandierte die Hochseeflotte in der Skagerrakschlacht am 31. Mai 1916, eine der größten Seeschlachten der Geschichte. Die "Admiral Graf Spee" (1936) war nur am Anfang des Zweiten Weltkrieges sehr aktiv, und hatte 9 feindliche Schiffe zwischen September und Dezember 1939 versenkt. Sie war nach der Seeschlacht vor dem Rio de la Plata (am 13. Dezember gegen drei englische Kreuzer) am 17. Dezember 1939 vor der Küste Uruguays von der eigenen Besatzung, die sich in außichtsloser Lage glaubte, versenkt wurde. Ihren Namen erhielt das Schiff zu Ehren des Vizeadmirals Maximilian Johannes Maria Hubert Reichsgraf von Spee (1861-1914), der im Ersten Weltkrieg das Ostasiengeschwader befehligte.*

**Panzerschiff "Deutschland" im Marinehafen Wilhelmshaven / Armored Ship "Deutschland" in the Port of Wilhelmshaven - Nonnenkamp family archives**

The three "Deutschland" class ships displaced a maximum 16,200 tons each, were armed with 6-11 inch guns in dual turrets plus 2 aircraft and were capable of up to 28,5 knots under full steam with their diesel engines. Maximum steaming radius was an extremely impressive 21,500 miles – combat surface ships in any other navy just could not match them. Admiral Reinhard Scheer was Commander in Chief of the German Navy from 1916-1918, while Admiral Graf Spee was Commander in Chief of the German East Asia Squadron in World War One. The squadron was based in Tsingtau (China) and oversaw German colonies in Shantung (China) and the Pacific (Micronesia, Palau, Nauru, Papua New Guinea, Samoa, the Northern Marianas and the Marshall Islands). He and his ships were victorious against the British at the Battle of the Coronel in the Pacific but were later sunk by a much larger British force at the Battle of the Falkland Islands in December 1914. His two sons (junior officers) died with him on that tragic day. Admiral Graf Spee commanded two armored cruisers (also called large cruisers) which were named "S.M.S. Scharnhorst" and "S.M.S. Gneisenau" (after which their World War Two namesakes were christened). His small cruisers were named "S.M.S. Nürnberg," "S.M.S. Leipzig," "S.M.S. Köln," "S.M.S. Karlsruhe," "S.M.S. Emden" and "S.M.S. Dresden." All were named for large

German cities, and eventually all went down far from home in the face of overwhelming odds. "S.M.S. Emden" became one of the most famous warships of World War One under her chivalrous commander Korvettenkapitän (a Lieutenant Commander in the German Navy) Karl von Müller, who sunk 25 Allied ships in the Indian Ocean before he was finally defeated by H.M.A.S. Sydney at the Battle of the Cocos Islands in late 1914. "S.M.S. Emden" was hunted by 80 Allied warships – a tribute to the courage and the skill of her officers and crewmen.

**Matrose Wilhelm Johannes Nonnenkamp (1903-1972) in Bielefeld (26. August 1926) / Wilhelm Johannes Nonnenkamp (1903-1972) in the city of Bielefeld on August 26, 1926 (right hand side) – Nonnenkamp family archives.**

### VIIIa. "Kreuzer P" ("Cruiser P")

Prior to the unfortunate outbreak of World War Two in September of 1939, the German Navy's ambitious "Z" Plan called for the construction of 12 large "Panzerschiffe," which would have been extremely effective commerce raiders during time of war. Maximum displacement was to have been 25,689 tons each for the so-called "Kreuzer P" or "Cruiser P" project. Armament would have consisted of 6-11 inch guns in two triple turrets (just as in the "Deutschland" class of Panzerschiffe) plus 4-6 inch guns, 4-4 inch guns, 4-1,5 inch guns and 6 21-inch torpedos. Each ship would also have 2 Arado Ar-196 floatplanes, which was the standard aircraft aboard German surface vessels during World War Two. Top speed was to have been a very impressive 33 knots and steaming radius a record 25,000 miles – even better than that of the smaller "Deutschland" class.

*Der Plan des "Kreuzer Ps" (1939) war für 12 noch größere, bessere, und schnellere Panzerschiffe. Die geplante Einsatzverdrängung war je 25,689 Tonnen, und die geplante Bewaffnung waren je sechs 28 cm Schnellfeuerkanonen (in zwei Zwillingstürmen), vier 15 cm Geschütze, vier 10,5 cm Flugzeugabwehrkanonen, vier 3,7 cm Flugzeugabwehrkanonen sowie sechs 53,3 cm Torpedorohre und zwei Arado Ar-196 Flugzeuge. Die geplante Höchstgeschwindigkeit war gute 33 Knoten, und die geplante Reichweite war gute 25,000 Seemeilen (noch besser als die kleinere "Deutschland" Klaße). Leider wurden diese stärkeren Kriegsschiffe nie auf Kiel gelegt.*

## The "Z Plan" ("der Z-Plan")

The "Z Plan" of the German Admiralty called for Germany to have a "balanced fleet." The plan was sadly cut short by the start of the Second World War, started due to Adolf Hitler's overly aggressive, irresponsible and reckless policies. By 1948, the "Z Plan" called for Germany to have 8 aircraft carriers of the "Graf Zeppelin" class, the 4 existing battleships ("Scharnhorst," "Gneisenau," "Bismarck" and "Tirpitz"), the 6 super-battleships of the "Hindenburg" class, the 3 small Panzerschiffe of the "Deutschland" class, the 12 larger Panzerschiffe of the "Kreuzer P" class, the 5 heavy cruisers of the "Admiral Hipper" class, 24 light cruisers (the 6 existing units plus 18 planned 10,400-ton light cruisers), 36 scout cruisers (initially planned as a 5,900-ton class, but eventually upgraded to a 7,500-ton class), 70 destroyers, 90 torpedo boats and 241 submarines.

*"Z-Plan" ist die geläufige Bezeichnung für einen groß angelegten Flottenrüstungsplan, den die Deutsche Kriegsmarine unter ihrem Oberbefehlshaber Großadmiral Erich Raeder in den Jahren 1938 und 1939 entwickelte und am 27. Januar 1939 per Gesetz in Kraft gesetzt wurde. Darin vorgesehen waren zehn Schlachtschiffe (die "Scharnhorst," die "Gneisenau," die "Bismarck," die "Tirpitz" und die sechs größeren Einheiten der "H-Klaße), acht Flugzeugträger der "Graf Zeppelin" Klaße, die drei Panzerschiffe der "Deutschland" Klaße, die 12 größere Panzerschiffe der "Kreuzer P" Klaße, die fünf Schweren Kreuzer der "Admiral Hipper" Klaße, 24 Leichte Kreuzer (die "Emden," die drei Einheiten der "K-Klaße," die "Leipzig," die "Nürnberg" und 18 Einheiten der "M-Klaße"), 36 Spähkreuzer (mit einer Einsatzverdrängung von*

*je 7,500 Tonnen), 70 Zerstörer, 90 Torpedoboote und 241 Unterseeboote. Die britische Kriegserklärung gegen das Deutsche Reich am 3. September 1939 bedeutete das Ende des guten Z-Planes.*

## IX. "Panzerkreuzer" (Armored Cruisers)

Armored or large cruisers ("Grosse Kreuzer" in German) were the predecessors of the great dreadnought battlecruisers which were so important during the First World War. Most navies stopped making them during the first decade of the 20th century, because they had become obsolete. After World War One, "Heavy Cruisers" became their modern successors – they proved to be very useful ships during World War Two. By the time of the Second World War (1939-1945), battlecruisers and battleships were very similar to one another. They both required high speeds, and the American Navy actually called its newest battleships "Fast Battleships." The "U.S.S. New Jersey," "U.S.S. Missouri" and "U.S.S. Iowa" are good examples of this – they all exist in the USA as museums today (in New Jersey, Hawaii and Virginia, respectively).

*Große Kreuzer oder "Panzerkreuzer" waren die Vorgänger der modernen Schweren Kreuzer des Zweiten Weltkrieges. Panzerkreuzer waren zur Zeit des Ersten Weltkrieges schon veraltet, weil die großen Marinestreitkräften der Welt (die Royal Navy von England sowie die Deutsche Hochseeflotte) schon Schlachtkreuzer hatten. Panzerkreuzer waren zu langsam, zu klein, zu schwach (nicht genug Panzerung sowie Bewaffnung). Die modernen Schweren Kreuzer waren besser, hauptsächlich weil sie so viel schneller waren.*

## IXa. "S.M.S. Blücher" Class / "S.M.S. Blücher" Klasse (1908)

The last German armored or large cruiser was "S.M.S. Blücher" (1908). She displaced 17,500 tons (less than the new battlecruisers) and was armed with 12-8 inch guns (not as powerful as the new battlecruisers). She could make 25,8 knots, which was slower than most new battlecruisers. Unfortunately, the Imperial German Navy attached her to the first battlecruiser squadron. She was sunk at the Battle of the Dogger Bank in the North Sea in 1915, taking most of crew down with her.

## Panzerkreuzer / Armored Cruiser "S.M.S. Blücher" (1908)

*Die "S.M.S. Blücher" (1908) war Deutschlands letzter Panzerkreuzer. Sie hatte eine Einsatzverdränung von 17,500 Tonnen, und war mit 12-21 cm Schnellfeuerkanonen (davon sechs in drei Zwillingstürmen und sechs in*

*Kasemattenaufstellung) bewaffnet. Die Höchstgeschwindigkeit war nur 25,8 Knoten – besser als ältere Panzerkreuzer, aber langsamer als die Schlachtkreuzer. Sie wurde im Seegefecht auf der Doggerbank von fünf britischen Schlachtkreuzern am 24. Januar 1915 versenkt. Sie erhielt zwischen 70 und 100 Treffer. 792 Besatzungsmitglieder starben, und 260 wurden von den Briten gerettet. Gebhardt Leberecht von Blücher (1742-1819) war Preußischer Generalfeldmarshall.*

## IXb. "S.M.S. Scharnhorst" Class / "S.M.S. Scharnhorst" Klasse (1907)

The "S.M.S. Scharnhorst" and "S.M.S. Gneisenau" of 1907 each displaced 12,985 tons and were armed with 8-8 inch guns. Their top speed was 23,5 knots. After they defeated the Royal Navy at the Battle of Coronel in the Pacific, the British sent two new battlecruisers to hunt them down. They were hopelessly outclassed and outnumbered by the British fleet which sunk them at the Battle of the Falkland Islands in late 1914. Admiral Graf Spee of Germany's East Asia Squadron went down with all of his ships and most of his men, including his two sons on that tragic and sad day.

**Panzerkreuzer / Armored Cruiser "S.M.S. Scharnhorst" (1907) - courtesy of Captain (CA) George J. Albert, Jr., Army Field Historian of the California Center for Military History**

*Die zwei kaiserlich-deutschen Panzerkreuzer "S.M.S. Scharnhorst" (1907) und "S.M.S. Gneisenau" (1907) hatten eine Einsatzverdränung von je 12,985 Tonnen, und waren je mit acht 21 cm Schnellfeuerkanonen (davon vier in zwei Zwillingstürmen und vier in Kasemattenaufstellung) bewaffnet. Die Höchstgeschwindigkeit waren 23,5 Knoten. Sie gehörten zum Deutschen Ostasiengeschwader unter Vizeadmiral Maximilian Graf von Spee. Sie versenkten zwei englische Panzerkreuzer im Seegefecht bei Coronel am 1. November 1914, wurden aber von zwei englischen Schlachtkreuzern im Seegefecht bei den Falklandinseln am 8. Dezember 1914 selbst versenkt. Mehr als 2,000 Deutsche Seeleute, unter ihnen Vizeadmiral Graf von Spee und seine beiden Söhne, kamen ums Leben.*

**Panzerkreuzer / Armored Cruiser "S.M.S. Gneisenau" (1907) – courtesy of Captain (CA) George J. Albert, Jr., Army Field Historian of the California Center for Military History**

### IXc. "12,000-Ton" Class / "12,000-Tonnen" Klasse (1917)

This was the final class of planned armored, or large, cruiser in Austria-Hungary. The ship type would have displaced up to 12,000 tons full load and was to have been armed with 6-7,5 inch guns mounted in three dual turrets (one fore, one central and one aft). Secondary armament would have been comprised of 4-3,5 inch anti-aircraft guns and 2-21 inch torpedo tubes. Top speed was planned at a very impressive 35 knots. I believe that such a ship (if built and put to good use) would have served the Austro-Hungarian fleet far better than did the dreadnought battleships. This was proven in the numerous skirmishes which were fought between the Austro-Hungarians and the Western Allies (the Italians, the French and the British) in the Adriatic Sea between 1915 and 1918.

*Zur Zeit des Ersten Weltkrieges hatte die Kaiserliche und Königliche Kriegsmarine es vor, einen 12,000-Tonnen Panzerkreuzer zu bauen. Die geplante Bewaffnung waren sechs 19 cm Schnellfeuerkanonen (in drei Zwillingstürmen), vier 9 cm Flugzeugabwehrkanonen und zwei 53,3 Torpedorohre. Die geplante Höchstgeschwindigkeit war gute 35 Knoten – ganz schnell für 1917. Solche schnellen Panzerkreuzer haetten der Kaiserlichen und Königlichen Kriegsmarine von grossen Nutzen sein koennen. Aber das Schiff wurde nie auf Kiel gelegt weil die derzeitliche wirtschaftliche Lage in Österreich-Ungarn zur Zeit des Ersten Weltkrieges es verhinderte.*

### IXd. "S.M.S. Yorck" Class / "S.M.S. Yorck" Klasse (1905)

"S.M.S Yorck" (1905) and "S.M.S. Roon" (1906) each displaced 10,266 tons and were armed with 4-8 inch guns. They could make up to 21,1 knots under full steam with their coal boilers. The first ship of this class was named after the Prussian Field Marshall von Yorck, who lived from 1759 to 1830. The second ship was named after Prussian Field Marshall Albrecht Graf von Roon (1803-1879) who served during the Wars of Prussian-German Unification from 1864 to 1871. "S.M.S. Yorck" was sunk by mines in 1914, whereas "S.M.S. Roon" survived World War One and was scrapped in 1921. Late in the war, she was converted to carry 4 seaplanes as well – the first step in the direction of true aircraft carriers.

*Die zwei kaiserlich-deutschen Panzerkreuzer "S.M.S. Yorck" (1905) und "S.M.S. Roon" hatten eine Einsatzverdrängung von je 10.266 Tonnen, und waren mit je vier 21 cm Schnellfeuerkanonen bewaffnet. Die Höchstgeschwindigkeit war 21,1 Knoten. Die "S.M.S. Yorck" wurde von Minentreffern im Jahre 1914 versenkt. Die "S.M.S. Roon" überstand den Ersten Weltkrieg und wurde im Jahre 1921 verschrottet. Vor dem Ende des Ersten Weltkrieges, wurde die "S.M.S. Roon" as Seeflugzeugträger für vier Seeflugzeuge umgebaut – Deutschlands erster "Flugzeugträger." Johann David Ludwig Graf Yorck von Wartenburg (1759-1830) war ein Preußischer Generalfeldmarschall und der Gründer des Adelgeschlechts Yorck von Wartenburg. Albrecht Theodor Emil Graf von Roon (1803-1879) war ein Preußischer General und Minister, und kurzzeitig Preußischer Ministerpräsident.*

### IXe. "S.M.S. Friedrich Carl" Class / "S.M.S. Friedrich Carl" Klasse (1903)

"S.M.S. Friedrich Carl" (1903) and "S.M.S. Prinz Adalbert" (1904) were named after members of the Royal House of Brandenburg-Prussia, or the Hohenzollern Dynasty. Each ship displaced 9,875 tons and was armed with 10-6 inch guns. They could make up to 20,5 knots under full steam with their coal boilers. The first ship was sunk by mines in 1914 and the second ship by a British submarine in 1915.

**Panzerkreuzer / Armored Cruiser "S.M.S. Friedrich Carl" (1903)**

*Die zwei kaiserlich-deutschen Panzerkreuzer "S.M.S. Friedrich Carl" (1903) und "S.M.S. Prinz Adalbert" (1904) hatten eine Einsatverdrängung von je 9,875 Tonnen, und waren mit zehn 15 cm Schnellfeuerkanonen bewaffnet. Die Höchstgeschwindigkeit war 20,5 Knoten. Die "S.M.S. Friedrich Carl" wurde von Minentreffern im Jahre 1914 versenkt, und die "S.M.S. Prinz Adalbert" wurde von einem englischen Unterseeboot im Jahre 1915 torpediert. Prinz Friedrich Carl Nikolaus von Preußen (1828-1885) war Preußischer Generalfeldmarschall und auch der jüngere Bruder von Kaiser Wilhelm II. Prinz Heinrich Wilhelm Adalbert von Preußen (1811-1873) war ein Sohn von Prinzessin Marianne (1785-1846) und Prinz Friedrich Wilhelm Karl von Preußen (1783-1851). Prinz Adalbert war Deutscher Admiral.*

Prinz Adalbert ("Albert" in English) of Prussia lived from 1811 until 1873. He was a member of the Royal House of Brandenburg-Prussia, or the Hohenzollern Dynasty. His father was one Prinz Wilhelm ("Prince William" in English), this Prinz Wilhelm being the youngest brother of King Friedrich Wilhelm III ("Frederick Willam III" in English) of Prussia. King Friedrich Wilhelm III of Prussia lived from 1770 until 1840, and reigned as King of Prussia from 1797 until his death in 1840.Prinz Adalbert of Prussia (1811-1873) served in the Prussian Army from 1826 until 1848 (this meant he joined the army at the age of 15, which was not unusual in those days), and then in the Prussian Navy from 1848 until 1871.

**IXf. "S.M.S. Prinz Heinrich" Class / "S.M.S. Prinz Heinrich" Klasse (1902)**

"S.M.S. Prinz Heinrich" (1902) was named after the younger brother of Kaiser Wilhelm II of Germany. She displaced 9,806 tons and was armed with 2-6 inch guns. She could make up to 19,9 knots under full steam. She survived World War One, and was scrapped in 1920.

**Panzerkreuzer / Armored Cruiser "S.M.S. Prinz Heinrich" (1902)**

*Der kaiserlich-deutsche Panzerkreuzer "S.M.S. Prinz Heinrich" (1902) hatte eine Einsatzverdrängung von 9,806 Tonnen, und war mit zwei 15 cm Schnellfeuerkanonen (in einem Zwillingsturm) bewaffnet. Die Höchstgeschwindigkeit war 19,9 Knoten. Das Schiff überstand den Ersten Weltkrieg, und wurde im Jahre 1920 verschrottet. Prinz Albert Wilhelm Heinrich von Preußen (1862-1929) war Großadmiral der Kaiserlichen Marine und Bruder Kaiser Wilhelms II.*

Prinz Heinrich ("Prince Henry) of Prussia lived from 1862 until 1929, and he served in the Imperial German Navy from 1877 until 1918. He commanded the First Torpedo Boat Division from 1887-1888, the Imperial Yacht "S.M.S. Hohenzollern" from 1888-1889 and the cruiser "S.M.S. Irene" from 1889-1896. Thereafter, he commanded other ships such as the armored coastal ship "S.M.S. Beowulf," the armored corvette "S.M.S. Sachsen" and the pre-dreadnought battleship "S.M.S. Wörth." He was promoted to the rank of Grossadmiral ("Grand Admiral" in English) in 1909 (a 5-star admiral in the German Navy). He commanded the German naval forces the Baltic Sea during World War One (1914-1918).

### IXg. "S.M.S. Sankt Georg" Class / "S.M.S. Sankt Georg" Klasse (1905)

"S.M.S. Sankt Georg" (1905) was Austria's largest armored cruiser, displacing up to 8,070 tons full load. She was armed with 4-9 inch guns plus 12-7 inch guns and could make up to 22 knots with her coal boilers under full steam. She was named after Saint George, a hero and martyr of the early Christian Church who died in 303. He died under the persecution of Christians lead by Roman Emperor Diocletan. Legend has it that Saint George was the famed "dragon slayer." In Austria, Saint George is the patron saint of the Tyrol. The ship survived World War One and was scrapped by 1923.

*Der Panzerkreuzer "S.M.S. Sankt Georg" (1905) war der größte Panzerkreuzer der Kaiserlichen und Königlichen Kriegsmarine. Sie hatte eine Einsatzverdrängung von 8,070 Tonnen, und war mit vier 24 cm Schnellfeuerkanonen (in zwei Zwillingstürmen) und 12 19-cm Schnellfeuerkanonen bewaffnet. Die Höchstgeschwindigkeit war 22 Knoten. Sie überstand den Ersten Weltkrieg, und wurde im Jahre 1923 verschrottet. Das Schiff wurde nach Sankt Georg benannt, ein frühzeitiger Held und Martyrer des Christentums, der im Jahre 303 starb. Sankt Georg starb zur Zeit der Christenverfolgung vom Römischen Kaiser Diocletan. Eine Legende besagt, dass Sankt Georg auch "Drachentotschläger" war. Sankt Georg ist auch der Schutzheiliger von Tirol.*

### IXh. "S.M.S. Sachsen" Class / "S.M.S. Sachsen" Klasse (1877)

The Imperial German Navy's "S.M.S. Sachsen" (1877) class of armored corvettes totally outclassed previous armored sailing corvettes, so I am including them in the category of armored, protected or large cruisers. These 4 ships had no rigging or sails. "S.M.S. Sachsen" (1877) was built by the A.G. Vulcan Shipyard in Stettin, Pomerania in July 1877, and was followed by her sister ships "S.M.S.

Bayern" (1878) in May 1878, "S.M.S. Württemberg" (1878) in November 1878 and "S.M.S. Baden" (1880) in July 1880. The 3 latter ships were all built by the Imperial Shipyard in Kiel, Schleswig-Holstein. All ships were named after states of Imperial Germany, displaced up to 7,800 tons full load, were 98 meters long, and could make up to 14 knots. Their twin 4-blade screws were driven by 2 single expansion engines, and they were staffed by crews of 32 commissioned officers and 285 enlisted men. Each ship had wrought iron armor plating, and was armed with 6 26-cm guns, 6 8,7-cm ring cannon, 8 3,7-cm revolving cannon plus 2 torpedo tubes. They survived World War One, and were scrapped as late as 1940 after about 60 years of service.

*Die vier kaiserlich-deutschen Panzerkorvetten der "S.M.S. Sachsen" (1877) Klaße waren eigentlich vielmehr als Panzerkreuzer, und nicht wie Segelpanzerkorvetten. Die vier Einheiten dieser Klaße hatten keine Segel. Die drei anderen Mitglieder dieser Klaße waren die "S.M.S. Bayern" (1878), die "S.M.S. Württemberg" (1878) und die "S.M.S. Baden" (1880). Sie hatten eine Einsatzverdrängung von je 7,800 Tonnen und waren je 98 Meter lang. Die Höchstgeschwindigkeit war 14 Knoten. Sie hatten eine Besatzung von je 32 Offiziere und 285 Matrosen. Die Bewaffnung waren je sechs 26 cm Schnellfeuerkanonen, sechs 8,7 cm Ringkanonen, acht 3,7 cm Turmkanonen und zwei Torpedorohre. Alle vier Schiffe dieser Klaße überstanden den Ersten Weltkrieg, und wurden im Jahre 1940 (zur Zeit des Zweiten Welkrieges) verschrottet.*

### IXi. "S.M.S. Kaiser Karl VI" Class / "S.M.S. Kaiser Karl VI" Klasse (1900)

"S.M.S. Kaiser Karl VI" (1900) was Austria's second largest armored cruiser, displacing up to 6,970 tons full load. She was armed with 2-9 inch guns and could make up to 20 knots under full steam with her coal boilers. She was named after Holy Roman and German Emperor Kaiser Karl VI of Habsburg (Charles VI in English), who was the father of Empress Maria Theresia of Habsburg. Holy Roman and German Emperor Charles VI was married to Elisabeth Christine of Braunschweig ("Brunswick" in English), and he reigned from 1711 until his death in 1740. The ship survived World War One and was scrapped by 1923.

*Der Panzerkreuzer "S.M.S. Kaiser Karl VI" (1900) war der zweitgrößte Panzerkreuzer der Kaiserlichen und Königlichen Kriegsmarine. Sie hatte eine Einsatzverdrängung von 6,970 Tonnen und war mit zwei 24 cm Schnellfeuerkanonen bewaffnet. Die Höchstgeschwindigkeit war 20 Knoten. Sie wurde nach dem Heilig-Römischen und Deutschen Kaiser Karl VI von Österreich benannt. Seine Gattin war Elisabeth Christine von Braunschweig. Er war*

*Deutscher Kaiser von 1711 bis er im Jahre 1740 starb. Seine Nachfolgerin war seine Tochter die Kaiserin und Königin Maria Theresia von Österreich, vom Adelhaus Habsburg-Lothringen.*

## IXj. "S.M.S. Kaiserin Augusta" Class / "S.M.S. Kaiserin Augusta" Klasse (1895)

The seven ships of the "S.M.S. Kaiserin Augusta" (1895) class comprised Germany's first armored cruisers. They replaced the old armored frigates, which had been powered both by sails and by steam. The seven new ships displaced between 6,318 and 6,791 tons each, were armed with up to 2-9 inch guns, 6-6 inch guns plus 4-4 inch guns and could make up to 21,6 knots under full steam with their coal boilers. Kaiserin Augusta of the Grand Duchy of Sachsen-Weimar-Eisenach (1811-1890) was the wife of Kaiser Wilhelm I der Grosse ("William I the Great" in English) and thus the German Empress and the Queen of Prussia. The other ships in this class were "S.M.S. Hertha" (1898), "S.M.S. Freya" (1898), "S.M.S. Vineta" (1899), "S.M.S. Hansa" (1899), S.M.S. Victoria Louise" (1899) and "S.M.S. Fürst Bismarck" (1900). All seven ships survived World War One, "S.M.S. Victoria Louise" being scrapped as late as 1923. Hertha, Freya and Vineta are female first names. "Hansa" refers to the old Hanseatic League of the Middle Ages. Victoria Louise (1892-1980) was a daughter of Kaiser Wilhelm II of Germany and thus a Princess of Prussia. "Fürst Bismarck" was named after Prince (and later Prussian & German Chancellor) Otto von Bismarck.

*Die sieben kaiserlich-deutschen Panzerkreuzer der "S.M.S. Kaiserin Augusta" (1895) Klaße waren Deutschlands erste Panzerkreuzer. Sie waren die Nachfolger der Segelpanzerfregatten, und hatten selbst keine Segel mehr. Die Einsatzverdrängung dieser sieben Einheiten war zwischen 6,318 und 6,791 Tonnen. Die Bewaffnung waren je zwei 24 cm Schnellfeuerkanonen, sechs 15 cm Schnellfeuerkanonen und vier 10,5 cm Schnellfeuerkanonen. Die Höchstgeschwindigkeit war 21,6 Knoten. Kaiserin Augusta von Preußen (1811-1890) war die Gattin von Kaiser Wilhelm I "der Große" von Preußen, und wurde im Großherzogtum Sachsen-Weimar-Eisenach geboren. Die sechs anderen Mitglieder dieser Klaße waren die "S.M.S. Hertha" (1898), die "S.M.S. Freya" (1898), die "S.M.S. Vineta" (1899), die "S.M.S. Hansa" (1899), die "S.M.S. Victoria Louise" (1899) und die "S.M.S. Fürst Bismarck" (1900). Prinzessin Victoria Louise (1892-1980) war eine Tochter von Kaiser Wilhelm II. Fürst Bismarck war Reichskanzer Otto von Bismarck.*

**Panzerkreuzer "S.M.S. Victoria Louise" in Neu York im Jahre 1909 / Armored Cruiser "S.M.S. Victoria Louise" on the Hudson River in 1909 - courtesy of Captain (CA) George J. Albert, Jr., Army Field Historian of the California Center for Military History**

### IXk. "S.M.S. Kaiserin und Königin Maria Theresia" Class / "S.M.S. Kaiserin und Königin Maria Theresia" Klasse (1894)

"S.M.S. Kaiserin und Königin Maria Theresia" (1894) was Austria's first and smallest armored cruiser at 6,096 tons full load displacement. She was armed with 2-9 inch guns and could make up to 19 knots under full steam with her coal boilers. She survived World War One and was scrapped by 1923. She was named after Holy Roman and German Empress Maria Theresia of Austria (1717-1780), or the Habsburg Dynasty. She came to the throne of the Holy Roman Empire of the German Nation (the First Reich) upon the death of her father Kaiser Karl VI. Since Holy Roman and German law only allowed male monarchs to rule the country, the Habsburgs had to change the law with the help of the Reichstag, or the German parliament. Some foreign countries and one rebellious German State in particular (Brandenburg-Prussia, of course) used this as a flimsy excuse to wage war upon the Empire when she came to the throne in 1740. The War of the Austrian Succession cost the Habsburg Monarchy the German State of Silesia, which was surrendered to Prussia. Silesia remained in Prussian-German hands until 1945, when it was surrendered to Poland. The official name of the Habsburg family has been "Habsburg-Lothringen" ("Hapsburg-Lorraine" in English) since Maria Theresia married Franz I Stephan von Lothringen ("Francis I Stephen of Lorraine" in English) in 1736. This was due to the fact that the Habsburg line had no more male heirs at the time of her marriage. Maria Theresia ruled as Holy Roman and German Empress from 1740 until 1745, when she turned the Imperial title over to her husband (and consort). Her consort Franz I Stephan von Lothringen ruled as Holy Roman and German Emperor from 1745 until his death in 1765. Their eldest son Josef II ("Joseph II" in English) inherited the Imperial title in 1765, and ruled as Holy Roman and Geman Emperor until his death in 1790.

*Der Panzerkreuzer "S.M.S. Kaiserin und Königin Maria Theresia" (1894) war der erste und auch der kleinste Panzerkreuzer der Kaiserlichen und Königlichen Kriegsmarine. Sie hatte eine Einsatzverdrängung von 6,096 Tonnen, und war mit zwei 24 cm Schnellfeuerkanonen bewaffnet. Die Höchstgeschwindigkeit war 19 Knoten. Das Schiff überstand den Ersten Weltkrieg, und wurde im Jahre 1923 verschrottet. Maria Theresia von Österreich (1717-1780) war eine Fürstin aus dem Hause Habsburg. Die regierende Erzherzogin von Österreich und Königin von Ungarn und Böhmen (1740-1780) war die Ehefrau des Römisch-Deutschen Kaisers Franz I Stephan von Lothringen (1708-1765) und sie war auch Kaiserin des Heiligen Römischen Reiches der Deutschen Nation (das Erste Deutsche Reich).*

Josef II was thus the 61st consecutive monarch in the noble line of Franconian Kings, Holy Roman and German Emperors since the Merovingian House of King Clovis I came to the throne in 482. The Merovingian House held the throne from 482 until its male line died out in 679. The throne was then inherited by the Carolingian House, which held it until its male line died out in 911. The throne then passed to the Franconian House until 919. The House of Saxony was the next noble house to inherit the throne, and held the throne until its male line died out in 1024. The subsequent noble houses to inherit this great throne were the Franconian-Salian House (1024-1138), the House of Hohenstaufen (1138-1273) and finally the great House of Habsburg, which still endures to this very day.

## X. "Segelfregatten" (Sailing Frigates)

Before Heavy Cruisers, and the Large / Armored Cruisers before them, came the old sailing frigates. First they were made of wood, and then they became armored. Before the Hohenzollern Dynasty of Brandenburg-Prussia forged a second German empire in 1871 (the Second Reich), the largest German navy belonged to the Habsburg-Lothringen Dynasty of Austria, which held the Imperial Throne of the first German empire (or First Reich) – which lasted from 800 until 1806.

*Die Vorgänger der Panzerkreuzer waren die Panzerfregatten und die Segelfregatten. Vor 1866 hatte Österreich die beste und auch die größte Kriegsmarine im deutschsprachigem Raum.*

### Xa. "S.M.S. Kaiser" Class / "S.M.S. Kaiser" Klasse (1872)

The Imperial German armored sailing frigates "S.M.S. Kaiser" (1872) and "S.M.S. Deutschland" (1872) were two first-rate ships armed with casemate guns. They were built by the firm of Bermuda Brothers in Poplar (the United Kingdom), and were thus among the last large capital German warships built abroad. Each ship displaced up to 7,600 tons full load, was 89 meters long, had a single expansion engine, was fully rigged and had a sail area of 1,623 square meters. They could make up to 14,5 knots, and their armament consisted of 8 26-cm ring cannon. Their crews were comprised of 32 commissioned officers and 568 enlisted men. "S.M.S. Kaiser" served as the fleet flagship, and the new German Emperor Kaiser Wilhelm II made his first state voyage in her to Saint Petersburg (Russia), Stockholm (Sweden) and Copenhagen (Denmark) upon his ascension to the Imperial Throne in 1888. These vessels were scrapped after 1904.

*Die zwei kaiserlich-deutschen Panzerfregatten "S.M.S. Kaiser" (1872) und "S.M.S. Deutschland" (1872) wurden in England gebaut. Sie hatten eine Einsatzverdrängung von je 7,600 Tonnen, waren je 89 Meter lang und hatten ein Segelbereich von je 1,623 Quadratmeter. Die Höchstgeschwindigkeit mit Segel und Dampfantrieb war 14,5 Knoten. Sie waren mit je acht 26 cm Kasemattkanonen bewaffnet, und hatten eine Besatzung von je 32 Offiziere und 568 Matrosen. Die "S.M.S. Kaiser" war Flottenflaggschiff als der neue Kaiser Wilhelm II Sankt Petersburg, Stockholm und Kopenhagen im Jahre 1888 besuchte. Die beiden Schiffe dieser Klaße wurden im Jahre 1904 verschrottet.*

### Xb. "S.M.S. Preussen" Class / "S.M.S. Preußen" Klasse (1873)

The 3 Imperial German armored sailing frigates "S.M.S. Preussen" (1873), "S.M.S. Friedrich der Grosse" (1874) and "S.M.S. Großer Kurfürst" (1875) displaced 6,821 tons each, and were 96 meters long. "S.M.S. Preussen" was built by the A.G. Vulkan Shipyard of Stettin, Pomerania and was named after the Kingdom of Prussia. "S.M.S. Friedrich der Grosse" was built by the Imperial Shipyard in Kiel, Schleswig-Holstein and was named after Prussian King

Frederick the Great. "S.M.S. Großer Kurfürst" was built by the Imperial Shipyard in Germany's great naval base of Wilhelmshaven, in the Grand Duchy of Oldenburg. Their armored protection consisted of teak planking clad in wrought iron, and their propulsion system was a German-made single expansion engine. Their crews were comprised of 46 commissioned officers and 454 enlisted men each. Each ship had 3 masts, a sail area of 1,834 square meters and could make up to 14 knots. "S.M.S. Preussen" was scrapped in Wilhelmshaven in 1919 after 46 years of service. "S.M.S. Friedrich der Grosse" was scrapped in Rönnebeck in 1920 after 46 years of service as well. Unfortunately, "S.M.S. Grosser Kurfürst" was lost in a collision with "S.M.S. König Wilhelm" during formation exercises off the coast of Folkestone in the English Channel in 1878. Due to oversight, the bulkheads were not closed and the ship sank with 269 men.

*Die drei kaiserlich-deutschen Panzerfregatten der "S.M.S. Preußen" (1873) Klaße hatten eine Einsatzverdrängung von je 6,821 Tonnen, und waren je 96 Meter lang. Die zwei anderen Mitglieder dieser Klaße waren die "S.M.S. Friedrich der Große" (1874) und die "S.M.S. Großer Kurfürst" (1875). Sie hatten eine Besatzung von je 46 Offiziere und 454 Matrosen, hatten je drei Masten und ein Segelbereich von je 1,834 Quadratmeter. Die "S.M.S. Preußen" wurde in Wilhelmshaven im Jahre 1919 verschrottet. Die "S.M.S. Friedrich der Große" wurde in Roennebeck im Jahre 1920 verschrottet. Die "S.M.S. Grosser Kurfürst" wurde leider in einem Manöverunfall im Ärmelkanal im Jahre 1878 verloren. 269 Besatzungsmitglieder dabei kamen ums Leben.*

## Xc. "S.M.S. Erzherzog Albrecht" Class / "S.M.S. Erzherzog Albrecht" Klasse (1874)

"S.M.S. Erzherzog Albrecht" (1874) was among the last of Austria-Hungary's armored frigates, or "Panzerfregatten" in German. She displaced 5,994 tons and was made of both wood and iron. She was armed with 2-9 inch guns and could make up to 13 knots with a combination of coil boilers and sails. Her crew consisted of 580 officers and men. She was named after Austrian Archduke Albert (1817-1895), who was a great military leader and hero in the war against Italy in 1866. Unfortunately, the Austrian military leaders who fought against Prussia on Austria's Northern frontier were not so talented, so the war was lost and Prussia became the most influential German state. The Northern theater of the Austro-Prussian war was fought in Lower Saxony, Saxony proper and in Bohemia and Moravia. Austria's German allies included the likes of the Kingdom of Bavaria, the Kingdom of Saxony, the Kingdom of Württemberg, the Kingdom of Hanover and the Grand Duchy of Baden. The Kingdom of Prussia was allied to the Kingdom of Italy.

*Die Panzerfregatte "S.M.S. Erzherzog Albrecht" (1874) hatte eine Einsatzverdrängung von 5,994 Tonnen, und war mit zwei 24 cm Kasemattkanonen bewaffnet. Die Höchstgeschwindigkeit mit Segel und Dampfantrieb war 13 Knoten. Die Besatzung war 580 Offiziere und Matrosen. Erzherzog Albrecht Friedrich Rudolf von Österreich (1817-1895) war Herzog von Teschen, großer Feldherr (Generalfeldmarschall sowie Generalinspekteur der Österreich-Ungarischen Armee) und Held im Krieg gegen Italien im Jahre 1866. Er besiegte die Italiener in der Schlacht bei Custoza am 24. Juni 1866. Das Kaiserreich Österreich, das Königreich Bayern, das Königreich Sachsen, das Königreich Württemberg, das Königreich Hannover und das Großherzogtum Baden haben gegen das Königreich Preußen im Norden den Krieg leider verloren. Die Zukunft wird zeigen, daß Preußens Sieg fuer Großdeutschland nicht vorteilhaft war. Das Zweite Deutsche Reich der Preußen dauerte nur von 1871 bis 1918. Der Erste Weltkrieg war für Deutschland und Österreich-Ungarn überhaupt auch nicht von großen Nutzen, und das Dritte Deutsche Reich von 1933 bis 1945 war für Mitteleuropa noch weniger von Vorteil. Die Auswirkungen des Zweiten Weltkrieges waren für Mitteleuropa am schlimmsten, und die moderne Nachkriegswelt von heute ist total korrupt. Die sogenannten "Siegesmächte" von Nordamerika und Westeuropa sind in finanziellen Nöten, und das Wirtschaftswesen im Westen steht vor Bankrott.*

**Xd. "S.M.S. Adria" Class / "S.M.S. Adria" Klasse (1873)**

"S.M.S. Adria" (1873) displaced 3,956 tons and was named after the Adriatic Sea, Austria-Hungary's outlet to the wide world. She was also made of wood and iron, and was thus an armored sailing frigate. She was armed with 15-6 inch guns and could make up to 13 knots with a combination of her coal boilers and sails. 453 officers and men manned this ship.

*Die Panzerfregatte "S.M.S. Adria" (1873) hatte eine Einsatzverdrängung von 3,956 Tonnen, und war mit 15 15-cm Kasemattkanonen bewaffnet. Die Höchstgeschwindigkeit mit Segel und Dampfantrieb war 13 Knoten, und die Besatzung des Schiffes war 453 Offiziere und Matrosen. Die Häfen des Adriatischen Meeres waren für Österreich-Ungarn sehr wichtig. Die wichtigsten Adriahäfen sind Triest, Gafers (heute "Koper" in Slowenien), Polei (heute "Pula" in Kroatien), Sankt Veit am Plaumb (heute "Rijeka" in Kroatien), Ploce, Zara (heute "Zadar" in Kroatien), Spalato (heute "Split" in Kroatien), Ragusa (heute "Dubrovnik" in Kroatien) und Cattaro (heute "Kotor" in Montenegro).*

### Xe. "S.M.S. Vulkan" Class / "S.M.S. Vulkan" Klasse (1878)

"S.M.S. Vulkan" (1878) displaced 3,600 tons and was armed with 8-8 inch guns. She was yet another armored frigate, and could make up to 13 knots with her coal boilers and sails. She had a crew of 431 officers and men. "Vulkan" is merely one German word for "volcano."

*Die Panzerfregatte "S.M.S. Vulkan" (1878) hatte eine Einsatzverdrängung von 3,600 Tonnen, und war mit acht 21 cm Kasemattkanonen bewaffnet. Die Höchstgeschwindigkeit war 13 Knoten mit Segel und Dampfantrieb, und die Besatzung des Schiffes war 431 Offiziere und Matrosen.*

### Xf. "S.M.S. Kaiser Max" Class / "S.M.S. Kaiser Max" Klasse (1863)

The foursome of "S.M.S. Kaiser Max" (1863), "S.M.S. Prinz Eugen" (1863), "S.M.S. Feuerspeier" (1863) and "S.M.S. Don Juan d'Austria" (1863) displaced 3,588 tons each and were armed with 8-8 inch guns. They were armored frigates and could make up to 11,5 knots with their coal boilers and sails. Each vessel had a crew of 400 officers and men. "S.M.S. Kaiser Max" was named after Holy Roman and German Emperor (Kaiser) Maximilian II of the Habsburg Dynasty, who reigned from 1564 until 1576. Prince Eugene of Savoy was a very famous Field Marshall of the Holy Roman Empire of the German Nation, known for his victory over the Ottoman Turks. "Feuerspeier" is the real German word for "volcano." "S.M.S. Don Juan d'Austria" was named after the great Holy Roman and German Admiral who lived from 1547 to 1578. He was a son of the Holy Roman and German Emperor (Kaiser) Charles V (or "Karl V" in German), who reigned from 1519 until 1556. Don Juan of Austria became famous for his great naval victory at the Battle of Lepanto in 1571, when the "Holy League" alliance defeated the larger fleet of Ottoman Turkey. The Holy League deployed 212 warships versus 286 Ottoman warships. Casualties were 12 ships and 8,000 dead & wounded for the Holy League versus an astounding 187 ships and 30,000 dead, wounded and captured Turks.

*Die vier Panzerfregatten der "S.M.S. Kaiser Max" (1863) Klaße hatten eine Einsatzverdrängung von je 3,588 Tonnen, und waren mit je acht 21 cm Kasemattkanonen bewaffnet. Die Höchstgeschwindigkeit war 11,5 Knoten mit Segel und mit Dampfantrieb, und die Besatzungen waren je 400 Offiziere und Matrosen. Die drei anderen Mitglieder dieser Klaße waren die "S.M.S. Prinz Eugen" (1863), die "S.M.S. Feuerspeier" (1863) und die "S.M.S. Don Juan d'Austria" (1863).*

## Maximilian von Österreich, Römisch-Deutscher Kaiser (Maximilian of Austria, Holy Roman and German Emperor)

*Maximilian von Österreich (1527-1576) war Kaiser des Heiligen Römischen Reiches der Deutschen Nation von 1564 bis er im Jahre 1576 starb. Prinz Eugen Franz von Savoyen-Carignan (1663-1736) war einer der berühmtesten Feldherren des Adelhauses Habsburg und wesentliche Stütze der Großmachtstellung Österreichs innerhalb Europa. Johann von Österreich, oder "Don Juan d'Austria" (1547-1578) auf spanisch, war Oberbefehlshaber der spanisch-habsburgischen Flotte und auch Statthalter der spanisch-habsburgischen Niederlande (heute "Belgien"). Johann von Österreich fuehrte die Kriegsflotte der Heiligen Liga (Kriegsschiffe aus Spanien, Venedig, Savoyen, Genua, Malta, Toskana sowie päpstliche Schiffe) am 7. Oktober 1571 siegreich in der Seeschlacht von Lepanto gegen die Osmanischen Türken, nachdem sie in den Wochen vorher dauernd auf einander gewartet haben. Diese Seeschlacht war die letzte Seeschlacht, die mit Galeeren ausgetragen worden ist. 212 Kriegsschiffe des Reiches besiegten 286 osmanische türkische Kriegsschiffe. Das Reich hatte 12 Schiffe und 8,000 Seeleute verloren, aber die osmanischen Türken haben 187 Schiffe und 30,000 Seeleute verloren.*

### Xg. "S.M.S. Salamander" Class / "S.M.S. Salamander" Klasse (1862)

"S.M.S. Salamander" (1862) displaced 3,027 tons and was armed with 10-7 inch guns. She was yet another armored frigate and could make 11 knots with her coal boilers and sails. Her crew consisted of 346 officers and enlisted men.

*Die Panzerfregatte "S.M.S. Salamander" (1862) hatte eine Einsatzverdrängung von 3,027 Tonnen, und war mit zehn 19 cm Kasemattkanonen bewaffnet. Die Höchstgeschwindigkeit mit Segel und mit Dampfantrieb war 11 Knoten, und die Besatzung des Schiffes war 346 Offiziere und Matrosen.*

### Xh. "S.M.S. Schwarzenberg" Class / "S.M.S. Schwarzenberg" Klasse (1854)

"S.M.S. Schwarzenberg" (1854) displaced 2,614 tons and was armed with 6-60 pounders. She could make 11 knots with her coal boilers sails, and her crew consisted of 547 officers and men. The older the ship, the more labor intensive it was to keep it going – hence the larger crews of older ships compared to new ships. This ship was named after the great Austrian Field Marshall Karl Philipp zu Schwarzenberg (1771-1820) who helped lead the Allied forces to victory against Napoleon Bonaparte of France at the Battle of Leipzig in 1813. 310,000 Allied troops defeated 210,000 French troops in this historic battle. France suffered 76,000 casualties versus 54,000 Allied casualties. The Allied nations represented in the battle were Austria, Prussia, Russia and Sweden. Leipzig is a German city located in Saxony.

*Die Panzerfregatte "S.M.S. Schwarzenberg" (1854) hatte eine Einsatzverdrängung von 2,614 Tonnen, und war mit sechs 60 Pfundern bewaffnet. Die Höchstgeschwindigkeit mit Segel und mit Dampfantreib war 11 Knoten, und die Besatzung des Schiffes war 547 Offiziere und Matrosen. Diese älteren Schiffe benötigten mehr Seeleute als heutzutage. Karl Philipp Fuerst zu Schwarzenberg (1771-1820) war Österreichischer Generalfeldmarschall und Botschafter in Paris. Fürst zu Schwarzenberg stand seit 1788 im österreichischen Militärdienst und wurde nach der Teilnahme am Türkenkrieg im Jahre 1789 und am Ersten Koalitionskrieg gegen Frankreich im Jahre 1796 zum Generalmajor befördert. Auch in den folgenden Jahren an den Kriegen gegen das revolutionäre und napoleonische Frankreich beteiligt, wurde er 1805 Vizepräsident des Hofkriegrats. Nach dem Frieden von Schönbrunn im Jahre 1810 als österreichischer Botschafter nach Paris entsandt, leitete Schwarzenberg die Verhandlungen über die Eheschliessung Napoleon Bonapartes mit Erzherzogin Marie Louise von Habsburg-Lothringen, die Tochter des Kaisers Franz I von Österreich. Im Rußlandfeldzug führte er 1812 das österreichische Hilfskorps der Großen Armee Napoleons. Nach dem Waffenstillstand mit Rußland und dem vergeblichen Versuch, zwischen Frankreich und Rußland zu vermitteln, erhielt Schwarzenberg 1813 den Oberbefehl (im Auftrag des Fürsten von Metternich) über die verbündeten Streitkräfte gegen Napoleon. Er befehligte die Hauptarmee in der Leipziger Völkerschlacht im Jahre 1813 und zog als Feldmarschall 1814 siegreich in Paris ein; 1815 wurde er Präsident des Hofkriegsrats. In Leipzig haben 310,000 Truppen aus Österreich, Preußen, Sachsen und Rußland 210,000 französische Truppen besiegt. Die siegreichen Verbündeten haben 54,000 Soldaten verloren, und die besiegten Franzosen haben 76,000 Soldaten verloren.*

### Xi. "S.M.S. Graf Dandolo" Class / "S.M.S. Graf Dandolo" Klasse (1859)

"S.M.S. Graf Dandolo" (1859) was the smallest of the Austrian armored sailing frigates at just 1,697 tons full load displacement. She was armed with 14-6 inch guns and could make only 10 knots. Her crew consisted of 294 officers and enlisted men. She was named after a famous Austrian count who had an Italian surname – a Vice Admiral who served as the Commander-in-Chief of the Imperial and Royal Navy from 1847 to 1848. Vice Admiral Graf Dandolo was the 48th Commander-in-Chief of the Navy since 1369. The Holy Roman Empire of the German Nation established an Admiralty in 983. In between 983 and 1369, the Commander-in-Chief of the German Navy was perhaps the Emperor (i.e., Kaiser) himself, or an Admiral of one of the Hanseatic League Cities of Northern Germany (such as Hamburg or Lübeck). All countries, including Germany and Austria, have minorities of people from many diverse places who of course blend into the social fabric of the country and become loyal citizens for many generations. The Holy Roman Empire of the German Nation was majority ethnic German, but it had substantial minorities of other people such as the Frisians, Dutch, Flemings, Walloons, French, Jews, Gypsies, Italians, Romansch, Poles, Sorbs, Wends, Czechs, Moravians, Slovaks, Silesians, Masurians, Lithuanians, Kashubians, Slovenes, Croats, Bosnians, Montenegrins, Magyars, Romanians, Serbs, Ruthenians and Danes. The small size of the "S.M.S. Graf Dandolo" illustrates how the old sailing frigates evolved into armored or large cruisers, and finally into heavy cruisers. The last heavy cruiser to be laid down but not commissioned by the German Navy was the "Lützow" which was launched in 1939. She would have displaced 19,800 tons and was to have been armed with 8-8 inch guns.

*Die Panzerfregatte "S.M.S. Graf Dandolo" (1859) hatte eine Einsatzverdrängung von 1,697 Tonnen, und war mit 14 15-cm Kasemattkanonen bewaffnet. Die Höchstgeschwindigkeit war 10 Knoten, und die Besatzung des Schiffes war 294 Offiziere und Matrosen. Zwischen 1847 und 1848 war Vizeadmiral Graf Dandolo der Oberbefehlshaber der Kaiserlichen und Königlichen Kriegsmarine.*

## Xj. "S.M.S. Principessa di Bologna" Class / "S.M.S. Principessa di Bologna" Klasse (1810)

This class of wooden sailing frigates belonged to the "Austrian-Venetian" Navy. Each vessel displaced up to 1,570 tons full load, and was built out of oak. They were 47,0 meters long, with a beam of 11,9 meters. There were 8 ships in this class:

*Die acht Segelfregatten (ohne Panzerung und ohne Dampfantrieb) der "S.M.S. Principessa di Bologna" (1810) Klaße hatten eine Einsatzverdrängung von je 1,570 Tonnen, und waren aus Eichenholz gebaut. Sie waren je 47 Meter lang, und hatten eine Breite von je 11,9 Meter.*

1.) "S.M.S. Principessa di Bologna" was launched in Venice on September 3, 1811. She was armed with 44 cannons, and was scrapped in 1826.

*Die "S.M.S. Principessa di Bologna" lief am 3. September 1811 in Venedig vom Stapel und war mit 44 Kanonen bewaffnet. Das Schiff wurde im Jahre 1826 verschrottet.*

2.) "S.M.S. Austria" was launched in Venice on August 15, 1812. She made an overseas voyage to Brazil during 1817-1818, and was scrapped in 1827.

*Die "S.M.S. Austria" lief am 15. August 1812 in Venedig vom Stapel und reiste nach Brasilien zwischen 1817 und 1818. Das Schiff wurde im Jahre 1827 verschrottet.*

3.) "S.M.S. Augusta" was launched in Venice on November 7, 1815. She joined "S.M.S. Austria" on the 1817-1818 voyage to Brazil, and was scrapped in 1826.

*Die "S.M.S. Augusta" lief am 7. November 1815 in Venedig vom Stapel und reiste mit der "S.M.S. Austria" nach Brasilien zwischen 1817 und 1818. Das Schiff wurde im Jahre 1826 verschrottet.*

4.) "S.M.S. Ebe" was launched in Venice on July 14, 1821. In between 1833-1834, she undertook a voyage to transport political refugees from the port of Triest to New York, USA. She was scrapped in 1848.

*Die "S.M.S. Ebe" lief am 14. Juli 1821 in Venedig vom Stapel. Zwischen 1833 und 1834 hat sie italienische politische Flüchtlinge von Triest nach Neu York gebracht. Das Schiff wurde im Jahre 1848 verschrottet.*

5.) "S.M.S. Guerriera" was launched in Venice on September 12, 1829. She joined "S.M.S. Ebe" in transporting political refugees from the Austrian port of Triest to safety in New York during 1833-1834. She partook in military operations during the Morocco Crisis of 1838, and did likewise off Saida (now called "Sidon") in Lebanon during 1840. During the war of 1848-1849, she blockaded revolutionary forces off Venice. After the war, she was converted to use as a barracks ship. She was scrapped in 1858.

*Die "S.M.S. Guerriera" lief am 12. September 1829 in Venedig vom Stapel. Zwischen 1833 und 1834 hatte sie mit der "S.M.S. Ebe" italienische politische Flüchtlinge von Triest nach Neu York gebracht. Im Jahre 1838 hatte sie österreichische Marineinfanteristen an der Küste von Marokko unterstützt, und ebenso im Jahre 1840 an der Küste von Saida im Libanon. Zur Zeit des Krieges in Italien zwischen 1848 und 1849 hatte sie die feindliche Truppen an der Küste von Venedig blockiert. Sie wurde nach dem Krieg als Wohnschiff gebraucht, und wurde endlich im Jahre 1858 verschrottet.*

6.) "S.M.S. Medea" was launched in Venice on August 7, 1827. She immediately became the fleet flagship. In between 1829-1830, she served off Morocco and in

Arab ports where Austrian troops were deployed. In between 1833-1834, she joined her sister frigates "S.M.S. Guerriera" and "S.M.S. Ebe" in transporting Italian political refugees from Triest to New York. She was scrapped by 1842.

*Die "S.M.S. Medea" lief am 7. August 1827 in Venedig vom Stapel und wurde bald danach Flottenflaggschiff. Zwischen 1829 und 1830 hatte sie österreichische Marineinfanteristen an der Küste von Marokko unterstützt. Zwischen 1833 und 1834 hatte sie mit der "S.M.S. Guerriera" und der "S.M.S. Ebe" italienische politische Flüchtlinge von Triest nach Neu York transportiert. Das Schiff wurde im Jahre 1842 verschrottet.*

7.) "S.M.S. Venere" was launched in Venice on June 12, 1832. In between 1848-1849, she joined "S.M.S. Guerriera" in blockading revolutionary forces off the port of Venice. in 1849, she undertook a voyage to England. In 1850, she sailed to Lisbon and Madeira, Portugal. She was scrapped in 1872.

*Die "S.M.S. Venere" lief am 12. Juni 1832 in Venedig vom Stapel. Zwischen 1848 und 1849 hatte sie mit der "S.M.S. Guerriera" feindliche Truppen an der Küste von Venedig blockiert. Im Jahre 1849 reiste sie nach England, und im Jahre 1850 reiste sie nach Madeira, Portugal. Das Schiff wurde im Jahre 1872 verschrottet.*

8.) "S.M.S. Adria" was launched in Venice on February 20, 1819. In between 1820-1822, she undertook a voyage to China. From 1828 until 1830, she served off the coast of Morocco, where Austrian naval infantry were deployed. From 1850 to 1851, she made a voyage to the North Sea and to the Baltic Sea. In between 1857 and 1858, she made an even longer overseas voyage to South America and South Africa. She was finally scrapped in 1870.

*Die "S.M.S. Adria" lief am 20. Februar 1819 in Venedig vom Stapel. Zwischen 1820 und 1822 reiste sie nach China. Zwischen 1828 und 1830, hatte sie österreichische Marineinfanteristen an der Küste von Marokko unterstützt. Zwischen 1850 und 1851 reiste sie zur Nordsee und zur Ostsee. In den Jahren 1857 und 1858 ist sie nach Südamerika und Südafrika gereist. Das Schiff wurde im Jahre 1870 verschrottet.*

**Xk. "S.M.S. Novara" Class / "S.M.S. Novara" Klasse (1845)**

The great wooden sailing frigate "S.M.S. Novara" was laid down in Venice in February of 1845, launched in April 1850 and finally commissioned into the service of the Imperial and Royal Austrian Navy on November 4, 1850. She displaced up to 2,630 tons full load, and was armed with 4-60 pounders, 28-30 pounders, 2-6 inch guns, 1-4,7 inch gun plus 1-6 pounder cannon. In 1854, she sailed to England. In between 1857 and 1859, she gained fame as the very first German warship to circumnavigate the globe. In 1862, she received coal boilers and screws in addition to her sails. She became a hulk in 1876, a gunnery training ship in 1881 and she was finally scrapped in 1899 after a fruitful life of 54 years in the navy.

*Die "S.M.S. Novara" (im Jahre 1845 auf Kiel gelegt, und nach der Schlacht bei Novara im Jahre 1849 benannt) war eine Segelfregatte aus Österreich, die die Novara-Expedition von 1857 bis 1859 unternahm. Später brachte sie Erzherzog Ferdinand Maximilian von Österreich im Mai 1864 nach Veracruz, wo er zum Kaiser von Mexiko gekrönt wurde. Nach seiner Absetzung und Erschießung wurde der Leichnam Erzherzog Ferdinand Maximilians auf ihr wieder zurück über den Atlantik gebracht. Bei der Ausschiffung des Sarges am Anlegesteg von Schloß Miramare wurde Maximilians Lieblingslied "La Paloma" gespielt. Zum Andenken an dieses traurige Ereignis beschloßen die anwesenden Marineoffiziere, dass La Paloma von nun ab auf österreichischen Kriegsschiffen nie mehr erklingen soll. Diese Tradition wird bis heute von traditionsbewussten österreichischen Seglern eingehalten und wird auch bei den Kursen zur Erlangung des Segelpatents unter „Seemannschaft" vorgetragen. Die "S.M.S. Novara" hatte eine Einsatzverdrängung von 2,630 Tonnen, und war mit vier 60 Pfundern, 28-30 Pfundern, zwei 15-cm Kanonen, eine 12-cm Kanone und einen sechs Pfunder bewaffnet. Sie hatte eine Besatzung von 447 Offiziere und Matrosen.*

She had a crew of at least 447 officers and enlisted men, was 165 feet long, had a beam of 44 feet and a draught of 19 feet. Her sail area was 18,291 square feet, and her living space was just 5,685 square feet – giving one an idea of just how little space there was for such a large crew. She was equipped with a distillery, which turned salty seawater into perfectly healthy drinking water. She was also equipped with a shower for her crew, demonstrating how advanced she was for her time – and how seriously the Austrian Navy took the maintance of good personal hygiene.

### Circumnavigation of the Globe (1857-1859) / die erste deutsche Weltumsegelung (von 1857 bis 1859)

Her circumnavigation of the globe was the brainchild of His Imperial Highness Archduke Ferdinand Maximilian, the Commander-in-Chief of the Imperial and Royal Austrian Navy. Its purpose was for the expansion of scientific knowledge, to expand Austria's commercial ties, and of course to train the officers, cadets and sailors of the navy. The commander of the ship during the course of this famous and noble voyage was Kontreadmiral Bernhard Aloys Freiherr von Wüllerstorf und Urbair, who lived to the age of 67. The voyage would traverse 51,686 nautical miles, make 25 ports of call, spend 551 days at sea and 298 days in various ports around the world. A sponsor of this great undertaking who was not able to go along due to his advanced age and frail health was the illustrious Prussian-German naturalist and explorer, Friedrich Wilhelm Heinrich Alexander Freiherr von Humboldt (1769-1859). He prayed to "Almighty God, that His blessing may rest upon this great and noble enterprise, to the honor of our common German Fatherland!"

*Die "Novara Expedition" von 1857 bis 1859 war die erste großangelegte wißenschaftliche Weltumsegelungsmission der österreichischen Kriegsmarine sowie die eines deutschen Kriegsschiffes. Sie wurde von der Segelfregatte "S.M.S. Novara" (1845) durchgeführt und stand unter dem Kommando von Kontreadmiral Bernhard Aloys Freiherr von Wüllerstorf und Urbair. Die von der "Kaiserlichen Akademie der Wissenschaften in Wien" vorbereitete und von Fachgelehrten unter Leitung des Geologen Ferdinand von Hochstetter und des Zoologen Georg von Frauenfeld begleitete Forschungsreise zeitigte international beachtete Resultate. Die Fregatte verließ 30. April 1857 Triest, segelte über Gibraltar, Madeira (Portugal), Rio de Janeiro (Brasilien) zum Kap der Guten Hoffnung (Südafrika). Im Indischen Ozean besuchte die Expedition vom 19. November bis 6. Dezember 1857 die Inseln Sankt Paul und Amsterdam. Es ging dann weiter über Ceylon (heute "Sri Lanka") und Madras (Indien) nach Singapur. Die nächsten Stationen der Reise waren Java, Manila (die Philippinen), Honkong, Schanghai (China) und die Salomon-Inseln. Am 5. November 1858 erreichte sie Sydney (Australien), von wo aus Auckland (Neuseeland) und Tahiti (französisch-Polynesien) angelaufen wurden. Die Rückreise führte über Valparaiso (Chile) und um das Kap Hoorn noch zu den Azoren (Portugal). Am 26. August 1859, nachdem 10,600 Seemeilen zurückgelegt wurden, lief die Novara nach der ersten deutschen Weltumrundung wieder in Triest ein.*

### Pola, Triest and Gibraltar / von Österreich bis Gibraltar

The escorts of "S.M.S. Novara" included the wooden sailing corvette "S.M.S. Caroline," commanded by Fregattenkapitän Kohen, and the steamship "S.M.S. Santa Lucia," commanded by Fregattenkapitän von Littrow. They departed the great Austrian Naval Base of Pola (known as "Pula" in modern Croatian or as "Polei" in the German language), on March 15, 1857. They laid anchor in the

Austrian Naval Base of Triest on March 17, and after fitting out finally departed upon their global journey on April 30, 1857. They passed the Austrian Adriatic port of Ragusa on May 2nd, and left the Adriatic on May 3rd. They passed the Sicilian port of Messina on May 8th, and laid anchor for the first time at the British Royal Navy base of Gibraltar on May 20th, where they remained as welcome visitors for 10 days.

### Funchal (Madeira) and Rio de Janeiro (Brazil) / von Madeira bis Brasilien

"S.M.S. Novara" and her escorts departed the British port of Gibraltar on May 30, 1857 and arrived in the port of Funchal in the Portuguese colony of Madeira on June 8. The climate of the Madeira island group is very moderate, never getting either too hot or too cold. Unfortunately, the region was very impoverished in 1857. It was originally settled as a penal colony, and later imported slaves from Africa. "S.M.S. Novara" left her two escorts to continue the remainder of the journey on her own. They returned to Austria, while she went on to Rio de Janeiro in Brazil, where she lowered her anchor on August 4, 1857. At the time, Brazil's population consisted of just 8 million souls, 250,000 of whom inhabited Rio de Janeiro. The ethnic German colony in Rio de Janeiro already had 3,000 inhabitants (most of them Evangelical Lutherans from Prussia, who settled in Brazil as early as 1821). Another German colony was founded by the engineer Julius Friedrich Köhler in the city of Petropolis on July 30, 1845. By 1857, Petropolis had 2,500 ethnic Germans, mostly with roots from Baden and the Rhineland. "S.M.S. Novara" departed Rio de Janeiro for Cape Town, South Africa on August 31, 1857.

### Cape Town (South Africa) / Kapstadt in Südafrika

"S.M.S. Novara" visited the Cape Colony of South Africa from October 1-26, 1857. This was originally settled on behalf of the Netherlands by Jan van Riebeck in 1652, and then taken away from the Netherlands by the United Kingdom of Great Britain and Ireland in 1815 (after the Napoleonic Wars). In 1857, the Cape Colony had a population of 280,000 souls, 30,000 of whom lived in Cape Town. About half of the population was white (mostly British), with the remainder being Cape Malays, Bushmen and Hottentots. The Cape Malays originally came from the Dutch East Indies, now known as Indonesia. Bushmen and Hottentots are now called "Khoisan" blacks, being of a separate racial sub-group in comparison to the majority Bantu blacks of Central and (Northern) South Africa. One of the first German settlers in South Africa was a Mr. Rathfelder from Württemberg, who established his new home in the town of Constantia. Another wave of German immigration came after the Crimean War in 1856.

Soldiers of the German Legion under General Suttersheim (who fought on the side of the British and their French, Ottoman Turkish and Sardinian allies) settled in "British Cafraria" in the Cape Colony of South Africa.

**St. Paul and Amsterdam Islands (Southern Indian Ocean)**

The next stop for "S.M.S. Novara" were the two basically uninhabited islands of St. Paul and Amsterdam in the Southern Indian Ocean, which now belong to France. Both islands are very small in land area, and the climate in this region is known to be cold, humid and often severe. In the 19th century, the islands were only frequented by fishermen and whalers as a rest stop and as a place where they could preserve their catch. "S.M.S. Novara" remained at St. Paul Island from November 17 until December 6, 1857, where her crew conducted scientific experiments and took geographic readings. At the time, 3 fishermen were living on the island. In spite of the harsh climate, it was very suitable for growing crops such as turnips, corn, wheat and barley. The "S.M.S. Novara" was off the coast of the much smaller Amsterdam Island (which had no human habitation whatsoever) from December 7-8, 1857. It was much harder to land there, because one required very rare calm seas in which a small boat could be launched from the sailing frigate. After this, the expedition headed due North toward the Indian subcontinent.

**Point de Galle (Ceylon) and Madras (India) / von Ceylon bis Indien**

"S.M.S. Novara" docked at the port of Point de Galle, Ceylon on January 8, 1858. "Ceylon" is the former name for the modern country of Sri Lanka, located off the Southern coast of India. At the time, it was like India also a British colony. Unlike India (which is majority Hindu), Ceylon is majority Buddhist. During the visit to Ceylon, crew members and scientists from the "S.M.S. Novara" made inland journeys to Colombo (the capital city) and to the tallest mountains on the island. The frigate departed Point de Galle on January 16, 1858 and docked at the port of Madras, India on January 30, where they remained until February 10, 1858.

**Indian Ocean and Southeast Asia (the Dutch East Indies and the Spanish Philippine Islands) / Indonesien und die Philippinen**

"S.M.S. Novara" landed in the Nicobar Islands in the Indian Ocean on February 23, 1858. This group of Islands had been claimed as an Austrian Colony on April 1, 1778 by Fregattenkapitän Bennet of the Sailing Ship "S.M.S. Joseph und Theresia." Bennet landed on the Northeast side of Kar-Nicobar, in the settlement of New Denmark. The Nicobar Islands had previously been an isolated outpost of the Kingdom of Denmark. "S.M.S. Novara" left the Nicobar Islands on March 26, 1858 and landed in the British Colony of Singapore on April 15, 1858. At the time, Singapore had 100,000 inhabitants, of whom 60,000 were already ethnic Chinese. The ship departed Singapore on April 21, 1858 and landed in Batavia, the capital city of Java and the Dutch East Indies, on May 5, 1858. Batavia (now known as Jakarta) had a population of 70,000 souls and the Island of Java 10 million souls. "S.M.S. Novara" departed Java on May 29, 1858 and arrived in the port of Cavite (7 nautical miles from Manila and also on the Island of Luzon) on June 18, 1858. The Philippines ("Las Islas Filipinas" in Spanish) had been ruled by Spain since 1521. De Facto rule in the Philippines rested in the hands of four Roman Catholic Orders – the Augustinians, the Dominicans, the Franciscans and the Recoletos (who were a branch of the Augustinians). The population of the Philippines in 1858 was 3,359,864 souls – merely 3 percent of the ethnic Filipino population today. The population of Metropolitan Manila in 1858 was merely 10,000 within the walled city and 140,000 in Binondo, or 150,000 total. The major economic commodities in the Philippine economy of 1858 were tobacco (manufacture of "Cigarillos"), hemp (used for making rope and rigging for sailing ships) and sugar. The Philippines were ruled by a Spanish-appointed Governor-General until 1898. Provincial government and the provincial judiciary were headed by an "Alcalde Mayor" or "Gobernador." Departmental administrators were directly below them were known as "Gobernadorcillos," and below these were the "Cabezas" or Parish Justices.

### Hong Kong, Shanghai and the Pacific / Hong Kong und Schanghai

"S.M.S. Novara" departed Manila on June 25, 1858 and docked in the British Colony of Hong Kong on July 5, 1858, where the Austrians remained until July 18, 1858. Hong Kong was already a thriving commercial port, albeit very new and much smaller than it is today (much the same situation as in Singapore, another British Colony in Asia which was specifically developed almost from scratch). Hong Kong had 80,000 inhabitants in 1858. The Austrians arrived in the port of Shanghai, China on July 25, 1858. At the time, Old Shanghai had 250,000 inhabitants and the entire Shanghai area had a population of 400,000 people. The entire Chinese Empire (or "Middle Kingdom," as it was called by the Chinese) had a population of 420 million souls – then as now the most populous country on earth. One of China's most serious problems at the time was the opium trade, mostly conducted by the British. "S.M.S. Novara" departed Shanghai on August 11, 1858 and arrived in Guaham (now the American territory of "Guam") and the Marianne Archipelago (now the American Commonwealth of the Northern Mariana Islands) on August 27, 1858. At the time, both Guam and the Marianas (in addition to the rest of Micronesia, Palau and Nauru) were all Spanish Colonies. "S.M.S Novara" arrived at Puynipet Island (now known as "Pohnpei" in the Federated States of Micronesia) on September 16, 1858. In 1858, Puynipet Island had just 2,000 inhabitants, compared to 34,000 today. "S.M.S. Novara" departed Micronesia and sighted the Solomon Islands on October 8, 1858. They remained in the Solomon Islands for more than one week, and then resumed their voyage to Sydney, Australia where they arrived on November 5, 1858.

**Australia / Australien**

"S.M.S Novara" visited Sydney, Australia from November 5 until December 7, 1858. Australia had been established as a penal colony by the British in 1788. It was thought that convicts would have a much greater chance of rehabilitation and eventually leading a productive life in a colony as opposed to being incarcerated in Britain. They would work for a number of years, with part of their earnings going to the state and the remainder saved for them until their release. It was hoped that eventual family life would make them solid citizens of Australia, which it did. By 1858, metropolitan Sydney had 93,000 inhabitants. The state of New South Wales (of which Sydney is the largest city) had a population of 350,000 and all of British Australia (with the exception of Tasmania and New Zealand) had 1.4 million souls. New South Wales ceased to be a penal colony in 1840, at which time 21 percent of its population was comprised of convicts. In other words, most new immigrants to Australia were already free people. The ethnic German population in New South Wales in 1858 amounted to 7,000 individuals, or about two percent of the total population. Most of the Germans had come from the Rheingau wine-growing region near Wiesbaden, Lorch and Frankfurt in Hesse. They brought their agricultural and wine-growing skills with them, establishing farms and vineyards along the Hunter, Clarence and Brisbane Rivers in New South Wales.

**New Zealand / Neuseeland**

The next port of call for "S.M.S. Novara" was Auckland, New Zealand from December 22, 1858 until January 8, 1859. At the time, New Zealand had 129.392 inhabitants, of whom 57 percent were whites and 43 percent were the native Maori Pacific Islanders. The largest city of Auckland had a population of 16,315. 58 percent of the inhabitants of this British colony were males, illustrating the fact that European settlement was still in its very early stages. Men often immigrated before their wives and children, sending for their spouses and families when they were more settled financially. New Zealand in 1859 already had a small ethnic German population which comprised about 0.5 percent of the entire colony, or about 700 individuals. The ethnic German population in modern New Zealand is 200,000 strong, or 4.6 percent of the country. The geologist of the Novara Expedition (Dr. Hochstetter) stayed behind for nine months to complete an extensive survey of the southern part of the North Island at the request and at the expense of the New Zealand government.

## Tahiti (French Polynesia) and Pitcairn / Französisch Polynesien und Pitcairn

"S.M.S. Novara" visited Papeete, Tahiti (now the capital city of French Polynesia) from January 11-28, 1859. The population of the island of Tahiti at the time was just 5,988, down from an estimated 16,000 upon its discovery by Europeans in 1797. As in many places around the world, non-European populations had little or no immunity to diseases brought by the newcomers. Upon departing Tahiti, the Novara Expedition passed within one hundred nautical miles of Pitcairn Island, famous because of the true story of the "Mutiny of H.M.S. Bounty." Due to overpopulation, the people of Pitcairn were moved initially to Tahiti in March 1831 (whence they came with the British mutineers in 1789), and then to Norfolk Island (a British colony) in May 1856. The descendants of the Bounty mutineers were not happy in Tahiti, so the British government moved them to the larger Norfolk Island. In 1858, 60 of the 219 Pitcairn Islanders on Norfolk Island chose to return home to Pitcairn. The soil on Norfolk Island had proven to be less than fertile for agriculture.

## Valparaiso, Chile and Back Home to Austria / von Chile und wieder nach Österreich

"S.M.S. Novara" anchored in Valparaiso, Chile from April 17 until May 11, 1859. The rest of the voyage took the sailing frigate around dangerous Cape Horn and back to Austria via the Falkland Islands, Patagonia, La Plata (where they encountered a hurricane), the Equator, the Island of St. Helena, the Sargasso Sea, the Azores, Gibraltar, the Mediterranean Sea and the Adriatic Sea. In the Adriatic, they visited the Austrian port of Ragusa (now known as "Dubrovnik" in modern Croatia) before returning home to Triest on August 26, 1859.

The scientists of the Novara Expedition temporarily left the ship to complete an overland trip from Valparaiso, Chile to Bolivia, Peru and the Isthmus of Panama. Chile had a population of about one million people, of whom 60,000 were in Valparaiso. Panama City had roughly 9,000 inhabitants. From here, Dr. Karl Scherzer (a botanist) and other Austrian scientists went on to the Atlantic coast of Panama, St. Thomas in the then Danish Virgin Islands, and finally aboard the British passenger vessel "R.M.S. Magdalena" to London and Southampton,

England. The "Magdalena" had 163 passengers most of whom were on holiday. The steamship "Behar" took the Austrian party on to the port of Gibraltar, where they rejoined the sailing frigate "S.M.S. Novara." The global circumnavigation had been unfortunately sped up due to the new war between France and Austria. France and the Kingdom of Sardinia in northwestern Italy were attempting to unite the Italian peninsula by force of arms. Their opponents were the Kingdom of the Two Sicilies in southern Italy (Naples and Sicily), the Papal States in central Italy and the Habsburg-Este kingdoms and duchies of northeastern Italy (Lombardy-Venetia, Modena, Tuscany and Parma). The regions of Gorizia ("Görz" in German), the Isonzo (now in modern Slovenia), Trient and the South Tyrol were Austrian Habsburg-Lothringen (Lorraine) lands. Autonomous sentiments still live in the hearts of many of the people in modern Italy. Autonomous political parties currently receive 84 percent of the popular votes in the South Tyrol, 60 percent in Trient, 29 percent in Venetia, 22 percent in Lombardy, 18 percent in the Aosta Valley, 14 percent in Friuli, 13 percent in Piedmont, 5 percent in Emilia-Romagna and in Liguria and one percent in Tuscany – more than 150 years after the war launched by France and Sardinia.

## Xl. "S.M.S. Eckernförde" Class / "S.M.S. Eckernförde" Klasse (1843)

The sailing frigate "S.M.S. Eckernförde" (commissioned in Copenhagen, Denmark in 1843) was captured by the German Navy during the war against Denmark in 1848. In this war, the States of the Germanic Confederation waged war to liberate the German-speaking Duchies of Schleswig and Holstein from Danish control. This goal was not reached in 1848, but had to wait until the next war against Denmark in 1864. Austria waged war in 1848 against revolutionary nationalist uprisings in Italy, the Balkans and the Carpathian mountain region. Austria won control over Bukovina, Banat, Vojvodina and Croatia during this war. "S.M.S. Eckernförde" displaced up to 1,300 tons full load, and was carvel-built of oak with copper. She had no engines, but could make up to 15 knots with her sails. She was armed with 2-60 pounders, 26-long 24 pounders and 20-short 24 pounders. She finished her career in the Royal Prussian Navy, where she made many overseas voyages as a training vessel from 1864 until 1870. She then served as a floating barracks in Kiel from 1870 until 1880, and finally as a coal hulk from 1880 until 1891. She was scrapped in Kiel in 1891.

*Die "S.M.S. Eckernförde" (1843) war eine Segelfregatte, die ursprünglich unter dänischer Flagge fuhr, doch 1849 erbeutet und 1852 an das Königreich Preußen versteigert wurde. Sie hatte eine Einsatzverdrängung von 1,300 Tonnen, und war mit zwei 60 Pfundern, 26 langen 24 Pfundern und 20 kurzen 24 Pfundern bewaffnet. Die Höchstgeschwindigkeit unter Segel (ohne Dampfantrieb) war gute*

*15 Knoten. Bei einem Seegefecht am 5. April 1849 im Schleswig-Holsteinischen Krieg (1848-1849) gelang es durch den Beschuß der Küstenbatterien bei Eckernförde, die dänische Besatzung der Segelfregatte "S.M.S. Gefion" zur Aufgabe zu zwingen. Das Schiff konnte wegen des ungünstigen Windes die Bucht nicht verlaßen und sich so auch nicht dem feindlichen Feuer entziehen. Daraufhin wurde es erobert, repariert und dann auf Seiten des Deutschen Bundes (1815-1866) unter dem Namen "S.M.S. Eckernförde" wieder in Dienst gestellt. 1852 nach der Auflösung der gesamtdeutschen "Reichsmarine" (1848-1852) wurde das Schiff zusammen mit der Radfregatte "S.M.S. Barbaroßa" von Preußen ersteigert und unter ihrem alten Namen "S.M.S. Gefion" in Dienst gestellt. Ab 1870 lag die "S.M.S. Gefion" als Wohnschiff in Kiel. Sie wurde dann wiederum am 5. April 1880 aus der Liste der Kriegsschiffe gestrichen und die Außerdienststellung erfolgte am 5. Mai. Der Rumpf wurde als Kohlenhulk genutzt und im Sommer 1891 bei der Kaiserlichen Werft in Kiel abgewrackt. Die Galionsfigur der Gefion befindet sich heute im neuen Rathaus von Eckernförde, eine Nachbildung dient im Kurpark als Brunnenfigur. Auch der Anker des Schiffes ist im Kurpark zu sehen.*

## Xm. "S.M.S. Bellona" Class / "S.M.S. Bellona" Klasse (1842)

The sailing frigate "S.M.S. Bellona" was launched in Venice on April 21, 1842. She displaced up to 1,260 tons full load, and was armed with 44 cannon. In between 1842 and 1843, she made a training voyage to England. From 1844 until 1845, she took another cruise to England and the Azores. From 1848 to 1849, she partook in the Austrian Naval blockade of revolutionary nationalist Italian forces in Venice. In 1851, she made a voyage to Madeira, Portugal and the West Indies. She became a hulk in 1868 and was scrapped by 1903. "Bellona" is the pagan Roman goddess of war, perhaps related to Mars, the pagan god of war. Her temple lay outside of the protective walls of the Imperial city of Rome.

*Die Segelfregatte "S.M.S. Bellona" lief am 21. April 1842 in Venedig vom Stapel. Sie hatte eine Einsatzverdrängung von 1,260 Tonnen, und war mit 44 Kanonen bewaffnet. Zwischen 1842 und 1843 machte sie eine Ausbildungsreise nach England. Zwischen 1844 und 1845, reiste sie wieder nach England und auch nach den Azoren. Zwischen 1848 und 1849 hat sie feindliche Truppen an der Küste von Venedig blockiert. Im Jahre 1851 reiste sie nach Madeira sowie nach Westindien (das Karibische Meer). Ab 1868 wurde das Schiff als Hulk benutzt, und die "S.M.S. Bellona" wurde im Jahre 1903 verschrottet – nach 61 Jahren Dienstzeit. "Bellona" war die heidnische römische Kriegsgöttin, die mit Mars, dem heidnisch römischen Kriegsgott, verwandt war.*

## Xn. "S.M.S. Erzherzog Johann" Class / "S.M.S. Erzherzog Johann" Klasse (1839)

The sister German sailing frigates "S.M.S. Erzherzog Johann" (1839) and "S.M.S. Barbarossa" (1840) each displaced up to 1,135 tons full load. They had no engines, but could make up to 9 knots with their sails. They were built of oak, and rigged as barques (although the "S.M.S. Barbarossa" was re-rigged as a brig after 1852). "S.M.S. Erzherzog Johann" was scrapped in 1857.

*Die zwei deutschen Segelfregatten "S.M.S. Erzherzog Johann" (1839) und "S.M.S. Barbaroßa" (1840) hatten eine Einsatzverdrängung von je 1,135 Tonnen und waren aus Eichenholz gebaut. Die Höchstgeschwindigkeit war 9 Knoten (nur mit Segel – diese Schiffe hatten keinen Dampfantrieb). Sie wurden im Jahre 1857 verschrottet.*

## Xo. "S.M.S. Adria" Class / "S.M.S. Adria" Klasse (1786)

The old wooden sailing frigate "S.M.S. Adria" displaced up to 420 tons full load. Her construction began in Venice on May 17, 1797, and she was finally launched on June 6, 1803. She had an uneventful career, and was scrapped by 1815. She was 40 meters long, and had a maximum beam of 10,2 meters. She was built out of oak, and her armament consisted of 26-12 Pounders plus 4-6 Pounders. She had a crew of 284 commissioned officers and enlisted men.

*Die vier Segelfregatten der "S.M.S. Adria" (1786) Klasse waren vielleicht die kleinsten Segelfregatten der Kaiserlichen und Königlichen Kriegsmarine. Sie hatten eine Einsatzverdrängung von je nur 420 Tonnen, waren je 40 Meter lang und hatten eine Breite von je 10,2 Meter. Sie waren aus Eichenholz gebaut, und waren mit je 26 12-Pfundern sowie mit vier Sechs-Pfundern bewaffnet. Die Besatzungen waren je 284 Offiziere und Matrosen. Die "S.M.S. Adria" wurde am 17. Mai 1797 in Venedig auf Kiel gelegt, aber lief vom Stapel nur am 6. Juni 1806. Sie wurde im Jahre 1815 verschrottet.*
*Die drei anderen Mitglieder dieser Klaße waren die "S.M.S. Austria" (1797), die "S.M.S. Pallade" (1786) und die "S.M.S. Aquila" (1797). Die "S.M.S. Austria" lief am 21. September 1803 in Venedig vom Stapel und wurde im Jahre 1814 verschrottet. Die "S.M.S. Pallade" wurde im Jahre 1786 auf Kiel gelegt, und wurde im Jahre 1802 verschrottet – sie ist nie vom Stapel gelaufen. Die "S.M.S. Aquila" wurde im Jahre 1797 auf Kiel gelegt, und lief am 21. September 1800 vom Stapel. Sie wurde im Jahre 1806 verschrottet.*

"S.M.S. Austria" was a wooden sailing frigate and a sister ship to "S.M.S. Adria." Her keel was laid down on the same date as that of "S.M.S. Adria," and she shared the same technical specifications as well. She was launched in Venice on September 21, 1803. She also had an uneventful career, and was scrapped by 1814. "S.M.S. Pallade" was yet another wooden sailing frigate and sister ship to "S.M.S. Adria" and "S.M.S. Austria." Her construction commenced in 1786. Her career was also uneventful, and she was scrapped in 1802 – never having been launched. "S.M.S. Aquila" started construction in Venice at the same time as "S.M.S. Adria" and "S.M.S. Austria." She was actually launched earlier, on September 21, 1800. Her career was uneventful, and she was scrapped after 1806.

## Chapter 12 (Kapitel 12): SMALL CAPITAL SHIPS ("Kleinere Kriegsschiffe")

### XI. "Leichte Kreuzer" (Light Cruisers)

Other important vessels the Navy deployed during World War Two were six modern light cruisers (the "Emden," the three ships of the "Königsberg" class and the two ships of the "Leipzig" class), more than 50 modern destroyers and over 80 modern torpedo boats (basically smaller destroyers).  They were of course christened after their famous World War One namesakes.  Of their counterparts during World War One, Armored Cruisers proved to be obsolete (hence the step up to Battlecruisers), whereas Small Cruisers were useful scouts that evolved into modern light cruisers.  Small torpedo boats evolved into modern destroyers from the 1880s to the great war of 1914-1918.

*Die nächsten wichtigen Kriegsschiffe waren die Leichten Kreuzer.  Zur Zeit des Zweiten Weltkrieges gab es sechs moderne Leichte Kreuzer – die "Emden," die drei Mitglieder der "Königsberg" Klaße, die "Leipzig" und die "Nürnberg."  Die Deutsche Kriegsmarine hatte auch mehr als 50 moderne Zerstörer und mehr als 80 moderne Torpedoboote.*

### XIa. "Nürnberg" Class / "Nürnberg" Klasse (1935)

The "Nurnberg" (1935) was the final German light cruiser to be commissioned.  She displaced 9,040 tons and was armed with 9-6 inch guns in triple turrets plus 2 aircraft.  She could make up to 32 knots with her diesel engines and turbines.  Steaming radius was 5,700 miles.  Her crew consisted of 896 officers and men.  She survived World War Two and was handed over to the Soviet Union as war booty thereafter.  She served in the Soviet Navy until 1961, when she was decommissioned and scrapped.  The famous interwar (i.e., between World Wars One and Two) "Z-Plan" of German Navy had plans for thirty-six 7,500-ton scout cruisers (to be armed with 6-6 inch guns in 3 dual turrets) and eighteen 10,400-ton light cruisers (to be armed with 8-6 inch guns in 4 dual turrets) which never materialized due to the premature outbreak of World War Two.  Steaming radius was to have been 12,000 miles and 8,000 miles, respectively.

*Die "Nürnberg" (1935) war Deutschlands letzter getaufter Leichter Kreuzer.  Sie hatte eine Einsatzverdrängung von 9,040 Tonnen, und war mit neun 15 cm Schnellfeuerkanonen (in drei Drillingstürmen, eine vorne und zwei achtern) sowie mit zwei Flugzeuge bewaffnet.  Die Höchstgeschwindigkeit mit Dieselantrieb sowie mit Turbinenantrieb war gute 32 Knoten, und die Reichweite war 5,700*

*Seemeilen. Die Besatzung des Schiffes war 896 Offiziere und Matrosen. Die "Nürnberg" überstand den Zweiten Weltkrieg, und wurde an Sowjetrußland übergeben. Sie diente bei der sowjetrußischen Marine bis sie im Jahre 1961 verschrottet war. Der Z-Plan von Januar 1939 hatte es auch vor, mehr Leichte Kreuzer für Deutschland zu bauen. Die 18 Leichten Kreuzer der "M-Klaße" hatten eine geplante Einsatzverdrängung von je 10,400 Tonnen, und die geplante Bewaffnung waren je acht 15 cm Schnellfeuerkanonen (in vier Zwillingstürmen, zwei vorne und zwei achtern). Die geplante Reichweite waren je 8,000 Seemeilen. Es gab auch 36 Spähkreuzer mit einer geplanten Einsatzverdrängung von je 7,500 Tonnen. Die geplante Bewaffnung waren je sechs 15 cm Schnellfeuerkanonen (in drei Drillingstürmen, eine vorne und zwei achtern). Die geplante Reichweite waren gute je 12,000 Seemeilen. Diese geplanten Kriegsschiffe wurden aber nie auf Kiel gelegt, weil die rücksichtslose Außenpolitik Adolf Hitlers einen Zweiten Weltkrieg im September 1939 angefangen hat.*

The German naval leadership was caught off guard by Hitler's reckless foreign policy, and was forced to "shift gears" and to concentrate primarily on submarine construction for the remainder of World War Two. Hitler had promised them no armed conflict prior to 1943, and certainly no armed conflict with the United Kingdom and the United States of America. Germany's then-limited resources were thus turned away from surface ship construction.

## XIb. "Leipzig" Class / "Leipzig" Klasse (1931)

The "Leipzig" (1931) displaced 8,382 tons and was armed with 9-6 inch guns in triple turrets plus 2 aircraft. She could make a good 32 knots with her diesel engines and turbines. Radius of operations was 5,700 miles. Crew size was 850 officers and men. All of her three gun turrets were placed on a center line. In the K-class, the two aft turrets were "staggered" to increase their firing angles. This was later deemed not necessary, hence the change in the "Leipzig." The "Leipzig" was named after a large German city in Saxony and especially after her famous World War One namesake. She survived the Second World War and was scuttled in the North Sea by the British in December 1946.

*Der Leichte Kreuzer "Leipzig" (1931) war Deutschlands zweitletzter getaufter Leichter Kreuzer, und hatte eine Einsatzverdrängung von 8,382 Tonnen. Sie war mit neun 15 cm Schnellfeuerkanonen (in drei Drillingstürmen, eine vorne und zwei achtern) sowie mit zwei Flugzeuge bewaffnet. Die Höchstgeschwindigkeit mit Dieselantrieb sowie mit Turbinenantrieb war gute 32 Knoten, und die Reichweite war 5,700 Seemeilen. Die Besatzung des Schiffes war 850 Offiziere und Matrosen. Das Schiff überstand den Zweiten Weltkrieg, und wurde von den Engländern in der Nordsee im Dezember 1946 versenkt.*

## XIc. "Königsberg" Class / "Königsberg" Klasse (1929)

The so-called "K-Class" of three light cruisers followed the "Emden." The "Königsberg" (1929) and her sisters "Karlsruhe" (1929) and "Köln" (1930) each displaced 8,130 tons and were armed with 9-6 inch guns in modern triple turrets plus 2 aircraft. Small and light cruisers before this class were always armed with guns in single turrets. These ships could make a good 32,5 knots with their diesel engines and turbines. Steaming radius was a very impressive 18,000 miles in this class. The crew of each ship consisted of 820 officers and men. All 3 ships were named after large German cities in general and after their illustrious World War One counterparts in particular. "Königsberg" and "Karlsruhe" were unfortunately lost during the successful German invasion of Norway in April 1940. "Köln" survived until 1945 and was scrapped after World War Two. "Königsberg" was raised and scrapped after the war.

*Die drei Leichten Kreuzer der "K-Klaße" (1929) waren die "Königsberg" (1929), die "Karlsruhe" (1929) und die "Köln" (1930). Sie hatten eine Einsatzverdrängung von je 8,130 Tonnen, und waren mit je neun 15 cm Schnellfeuerkanonen (in drei Drillingstürmen, eine vorne und zwei achtern) sowie mit zwei Flugzeuge bewaffnet. Die Höchstgeschwindigkeit war gute 32,5 Knoten mit Dieselantrieb sowie mit Turbinenantrieb, und die Reichweite war sehr gute 18,000 Seemeilen. Die Besatzung eines Schiffes der "K-Klaße" war 820 Offiziere und Matrosen. Die "Königsberg" und die "Karlsruhe" gingen zur Zeit der erfolgreichen Norwegeninvasion im April 1940 leider verloren. Die "Köln" überstand den Zweiten Weltkrieg, und wurde kurz danach verschrottet. Die "Königsberg" wurde geborgen und nach dem Zweiten Weltkrieg auch verschrottet.*

The city of Königsberg (now called "Kaliningrad" in Russian) was once the capital of the German State of East Prussia. Modern East Prussia is divided between both Russia and Lithuania (the Northern half) and Poland (the Southern half). The Polish part includes the regions of Masuria and the Ermland. Masuria is inhabited by the Evangelical-Lutheran Slavic Masurian people, and the Ermland is an old Roman Catholic German region. The Lithuanian part includes the narrow Memelland region in the far North. The Polish part of Southern East Prussia has a population of 1,427,091 people in 2008.

### XId. "Emden" Class / "Emden" Klasse (1925)

Germany's first post-World War One light cruiser was the "Emden" (1925). She was very similar to the last class of small cruiser from the end of World War One in terms of armament, speed and crew size. In fact, the only differences between them were that she had two smoke stacks instead of four, that she was diesel-powered instead of coal-powered and that a large amount of welding was used in her construction in order to reduce the weight of the ship by a few hundred tons. She was used to "show the flag" overseas between the two world wars, and was often used to train new sailors and officer candidates. She survived until 1945 and was scrapped after World War Two. She was of course named after the very famous "S.M.S. Emden" of World War One. She displaced 6,990 tons and could steam up to 5,300 miles. Her top speed was 29 knots. She was armed with 8-6 inch guns in single turrets, and was manned by a crew of 630 commissioned officers and enlisted sailors.

*Der Leichte Kreuzer "Emden" (1925) war Deutschlands erster neuer Leichter Kreuzer nach dem Ersten Weltkrieg. Sie war den letzten deutschen Kleinen Kreuzern des Ersten Weltkrieges sehr ähnlich. Die neue "Emden" hatte zwei statt vier Schornsteine, und Dieselantrieb sowie Turbinenantrieb statt Kohlendampfantrieb. Bis September 1939 wurde sie sehr oft als Schulschiff benuetzt. Das Schiff überstand den Zweiten Weltkrieg, und wurde nach dem Ende des Krieges verschrottet. Sie hatte eine Einsatzverdrängung von 6,990 Tonnen, war mit acht 15 cm Schnellfeuerkanonen (in Einzeltürmen) bewaffnet, und hatte eine Besatzung von 630 Offiziere und Matrosen.*

### XIe. Captured Dutch Light Cruisers / Niederländische Beutekreuzer

Germany also had the possession of numerous captured enemy light cruisers during the course of World War Two. These included the two Dutch light cruisers "De Zeven Provincien" and "Eendracht," each of 12,165 tons displacement, which were not actually launched until 1953. Today, both ships belong to the Peruvian Navy under different names – and they have been substantially modernized since their original commissioning in the Dutch Navy.

*Die zwei niederländischen Leichten Kreuzer "De Zeven Provincien" und "Eendracht" wurden als Beuteschiffe zur Zeit des Zweiten Weltkrieges beschlagnahmt. Im Jahre 1940 waren sie schon auf Kiel gelegt, aber sie liefen vom Stapel nur nach dem Ende des Zweiten Weltkrieges im Jahre 1953, als sie wieder den Niederländern gehörten. Die zwei Schiffe wurden nach Peru verkauft, wo eins immer noch ist. Ein Schiff ist noch im Gebrauch, und das andere wurde schon verschrottet. Die Einsatzverdrängung der "Almirante Grau" (die ehemalige "De Zeven Provincien") ist 12,165 Tonnen. Die Bewaffnung des Schiffes besteht aus acht SSM (Schiffabwehr-Raketen), acht 15,2 cm Schnellfeuerkanonen (in zwei Zwillingstürmen vorn), acht Bofors 57 mm Flugzeugabwehrkanonen, acht Bofors 40 mm Flugzeugabwehrkanonen sowie drei Hubschrauber. Die Höchstgeschwindigkeit des Schiffes ist gute 32 Knoten.*

### XIf. Captured Italian Light Cruisers / Italienische Beutekreuzer

In 1943, the German Navy captured a good number of Italian light cruisers. These included the "Vesuvio" (1941) and the "Etna" (1942), each of 6,096 tons total displacement and armed with 6-5 inch guns. Both ships were named for volcanos in Italy, survived World War Two and were scrapped in 1945.

*Als Italien im Jahre 1943 Krieg an das Deutsche Reich erklärte, hatte die Deutsche Kriegsmarine viele italienische Kriegsschiffe als Beute genommen. Die zwei Spähkreuzer "Vesuvio" (1941) und "Etna" (1942) hatten eine Einsatzverdrängung von je 6,096 Tonnen, und waren mit je sechs 13,5 cm Schnellfeuerkanonen (in drei Drillingstürmen) sowie mit zehn 6,5 cm Schnellfeuerkanonen bewaffnet. Die Höchstgeschwindigkeit war gute 28 Knoten. Die zwei Schiffe überstanden den Zweiten Weltkrieg, und wurden nach dem Ende des Krieges verschrottet.*

The 4 other captured Italian light or scout cruisers included the "Ciao Mario" (1941), the "Cornelio Silla" (1941), the "Giulio Germanico" (1941) and the "Ottaviano Augusto" (1942). Each ship in this class displaced 5,420 tons and was armed with 8-5 inch guns. They were all named after heroes of the old Roman Empire. "Ciao Mario" was scuttled by the Germans in 1944, "Cornelio Silla" was sunk in an Allied air raid in 1944, "Giulio Germanico" survived World War Two and was scrapped in 1971, and "Ottaviano Augusto" was sunk in an Allied air attack in late 1943.

*Die vier Spähkreuzer "Ciao Mario" (1941), "Cornelio Silla" (1941), "Giulio Germanico" (1941) und "Ottaviano Augusto" (1942) hatten eine Einsatzverdrängung von je 5,420 Tonnen, und waren mit je acht 13,5 cm Schnellfeuerkanonen (in vier Zwillingstürmen, zwei vorne und zwei achtern) sowie mit acht 3,7 cm Flugzeugabwehrkanonen bewaffnet. Diese vier Schiffe wurden als Kriegsbeute im Jahre 1943 von Italien übernommen, und waren nach Helden des Römischen Reiches ernannt. Die "Ciao Mario" wurde von den Deutschen im Jahre 1944 selbst versenkt. Die "Cornelio Silla" wurde von Fliegerbomben im Jahre 1944 versenkt. Die "Giulio Germanico" überstand den*

*Zweiten Weltkrieg, und wurde erst im Jahre 1971 verschrottet. Die "Ottaviano Augusto" wurde durch Fliegerbomben im Jahre 1943 versenkt.*

## XII. "Kleine Kreuzer" (Small Cruisers)

The small cruisers used before and during World War One were the successors of the old armored and sailing corvettes. All of these ships were used heavily for scouting duty, to go ahead of the main battle fleet and to search for the enemy. They were smaller than armored or large cruisers, and had little protective armor plating. On the other hand, they were larger and more powerful compared to destroyers or torpedo boats. They were also the most common navy vessels used to serve abroad on foreign missions, training cruises or on colonial duty. Thus, they followed closely in the footsteps of their predecessors, the old armored or sailing corvettes.

*Die Kleinen Kreuzer waren die Nachfolger der Panzerkorvetten und der Segelkorvetten, und auch die Vorgänger der modernen Leichten Kreuzer. Sie hatten wenig Panzerung, keine Segel und dienten als Spähkreuzer. Sie waren auch ziemlich schnell, und stärker als Zerstörer oder Torpedoboote. Sie haben sehr oft gedient im Ausland – genau wie die Panzerkorvetten und die Segelkorvetten.*

## XIIa. "S.M.S. Cöln II" Class / "S.M.S. Cöln II" Klasse (1916)

The last class of 14 German small cruisers during World War One included the likes of the "S.M.S. Wiesbaden" (1917) and the "S.M.S. Dresden" (1918). They were named after large German cities, and namesake small cruisers which were lost earlier during the war. Dresden is of course the capital city of the German State of Saxony. Each ship displaced up to 7,486 tons full load, was armed with 8-6 inch guns in single turrets plus 3-88 mm anti-aircraft guns and could make an impressive 29,3 knots under full steam with their coal boilers. Such speed is still good for today's standards! Both ships survived World War One. "S.M.S. Wiesbaden" was scrapped by Germany in the 1920s along with 8 other incomplete cruisers of this class and "S.M.S. Dresden" was surrendered to the British and scuttled by her German crew at the Royal Navy base of Scapa Flow in Scotland in June 1919 along with 4 other completed cruisers of this class. The first German "Light Cruiser" (new nomenclature) after World War One was the "S.M.S. Emden" of 1925. She was a virtual copy of these ships, with the only differences being fewer smoke stacks (two versus four), diesel power (versus coal power) and more hull welding (to reduce weight). Names of the 12 remaining ships of this modern class were "S.M.S. Königsberg II" (1916), "S.M.S. Emden

II" (1916), "S.M.S. Karlsruhe II" (1916), "S.M.S. Nürnberg II" (1917), "S.M.S. Cöln II" (1917), "S.M.S. Magdeburg II" (1917), "S.M.S. Leipzig II" (1918), "S.M.S. Rostock II" (1918), "S.M.S. Frauenlob II" (1918), "S.M.S. Ersatz Cöln" (1918), "S.M.S. Ersatz Emden" (1918) and "S.M.S. Ersatz Karlsruhe" (1918).

*Die 14 Mitglieder der "S.M.S. Cöln II" (1916) Klaße waren die letzten, die größten und die besten Kleinen Kreuzer der Kaiserlichen Marine. Die 13 anderen Einheiten dieser Klaße waren die "S.M.S. Königsberg II" (1916), die "S.M.S. Emden II" (1916), die "S.M.S. Karlsruhe II" (1916), die "S.M.S. Wiesbaden" (1917), die "S.M.S. Nürnberg II" (1917), die "S.M.S. Magdeburg II" (1917), die "S.M.S. Dresden" (1918), die "S.M.S. Leipzig II" (1918), die "S.M.S. Rostock II" (1918), die "S.M.S. Frauenlob II" (1918), die "S.M.S. Ersatz Cöln" (1918), die "S.M.S. Ersatz Emden" (1918) und die "S.M.S. Ersatz Karlsruhe" (1918). Sie hatten je eine Einsatzverdrängung von 7,486 Tonnen, und waren mit je acht 15 cm Schnellfeuerkanonen (in Einzeltürmen) sowie mit drei 88 mm Flugzeugabwehrkanonen bewaffnet. Die Höchstgeschwindigkeit war mit Kohldampfantrieb sehr gute 29,3 Knoten – immer noch gut heutzutage. Alle Einheiten dieser Klaße wurden auf Kiel gelegt, viele liefen vom Stapel, aber die meisten wurden nie getauft. Fast alle Mitglieder dieser Klaße wurden in den 1920er Jahren verschrottet – außer fünf Schiffe, die in Scapa Flow in Schottland von den eigenen deutschen Besatzungen im Juni 1919 versenkt wurden.*

"Cöln" is merely an antiquated German spelling of the modern "Köln," or the large city of Cologne in the Rhineland. The city of Cologne proper has a population of 991,395 people today. It is the 4th largest German city after Berlin, Hamburg and Munich, but forms the largest metropolitan region in Germany with population of 11,817,132 people in 2008.

### XIIb. "S.M.S. Graudenz" Class / "S.M.S. Graudenz" Klasse (1914)

"S.M.S. Graudenz" (1914) and "S.M.S. Regensburg" (1915) displaced 6,382 tons each and were armed with 7-6 inch guns plus 2-88 mm anti-aircraft guns. They could make a good 27,5 knots under full steam with their coal boilers. Both were named after large German cities. Graudenz was in Eastern Germany (now part of Poland) and Regensburg is in Bavaria in Southern Germany. Regensburg is the former home of the Reichstag (parliament) of the Holy Roman Empire of the German Nation, or First Reich which endured from 800 to 1806. Both ships survived World War One. "S.M.S. Graudenz" was scrapped in 1937 and "S.M.S. Regensburg" was scuttled by the Germans off their occupied French naval base of Lorient in 1944, where she remains to this day.

*Die zwei Kleinen Kreuzer "S.M.S. Graudenz" (1914) und "S.M.S. Regensburg" (1915) hatten eine Einsatzverdrängung von je 6,382 Tonnen, und waren mit sieben 15 cm Schnellfeuerkanonen sowie mit zwei 88 mm Flugzeugabwehrkanonen bewaffnet. Die Höchstgeschwindigkeit war mit Kohldampfantrieb gute 27,5 Knoten – immer noch gut für heute. Die zwei Schiffe überstanden den Ersten Weltkrieg. Die "S.M.S. Graudenz" wurde im Jahre 1937 verschrottet, und die "S.M.S. Regensburg" wurde von den Deutschen in Lorient, Frankreich im Jahre 1944 selbst versenkt.*

### XIIc. "S.M.S. Stralsund" Class / "S.M.S. Stralsund" Klasse (1912)

"S.M.S Stralsund" (1912) displaced 5,587 tons and was armed with 7-6 inch guns plus 2-88 mm anti-aircraft guns. She could make an impressive 28,2 knots under full steam with her coal boilers – also a good top speed for a warship of today! Stralsund is a coastal city on the Baltic Sea, in the modern German State of Mecklenburg-Vorpommern ("Mecklenburg-Near Pomerania" in English). The ship survived World War One and was scrapped in 1935.

*Der Kleine Kreuzer "S.M.S. Stralsund" (1912) hatte eine Einsatzverdrängung von 5,587 Tonnen, und war mit sieben 15 cm Schnellfeuerkanonen (in Einzeltürmen) sowie mit zwei 88 mm Flugzeugabwehrkanonen bewaffnet. Die Höchstgeschwindigkeit mit Kohldampfantrieb war gute 28,2 Knoten – immer noch gut für heute. Das Schiff überstand den Ersten Weltkrieg, und wurde im Jahre 1935 verschrottet.*

### XIId. "S.M.S. Oldenburg" Class / "S.M.S. Oldenburg" Klasse (1884)

"S.M.S. Oldenburg" (1884) was a single member class of Imperial German armored corvette, but she was built without any rigging and sails – making her very modern for her time. It is for this reason that I include her among the small cruisers. She was built by the A.G. Vulcan Shipyard in the port city of Stettin, Pomerania. She was a casemated ship armed with 8 24-cm and 2 8,7-cm ring cannon, and her crew was comprised of 34 commissioned officers plus 355 enlisted men. She displaced up to 5,249 tons full load,, was 80 meters long, and she was powered by 2 double expansion engines driving twin 3-blade screws – giving her a top speed of up to 14 knots. She was scrapped in 1919 after 35 years of service. She was named after the Grand Duchy of Oldenburg, which was located in Northwestern Germany.

*Die Panzerkorvette "S.M.S. Oldenburg" (1884) war ein Einzelschiff ohne Segel – ganz modern zu der Zeit. Sie wurde beim A.G. Vulcan in Stettin, Hinterpommern gebaut. Sie war mit acht 24 cm Kasemattkanonen sowie mit zwei 8,7 cm Ringkanonen bewaffnet, und hatte eine Besatzung von 34 Offiziere und 355 Matrosen. Sie hatte eine Einsatzverdrängung von 5,249 Tonnen, war 80 Meter lang und die Höchstgeschwindigkeit mit Kohldampfantrieb war 14 Knoten. Sie wurde im Jahre 1919 verschrottet – nach 35 Jahren Dienstzeit.*

## XIIe. "S.M.S. Strassburg" Class / "S.M.S. Straßburg" Klasse (1912)

"S.M.S. Strassburg" (1912) and "S.M.S. Breslau" (1912) each displaced 5,281 tons and were armed with up to 8-6 inch guns, 2-88 mm anti-aircraft guns and 2-50 cm torpedo tubes. They could make up to 27,5 knots under full steam with their coal boilers. "S.M.S. Strassburg" survived World War One and was scrapped in 1947. She was named after the capital city of Strassburg in the German State of Elsass-Lothringen ("Alsace-Lorraine") which is now part of France. Strassburg ("Strasbourg" in French) is the seat of the modern European Parliament, the primary legislative body of the European Union. "S.M.S. Breslau" was sunk by mines in the Aegean Sea in January 1918.

*Die zwei Kleinen Kreuzer "S.M.S. Straßburg" (1912) und "S.M.S. Breslau" (1912) hatten eine Einsatzverdrängung von je 5,281 Tonnen, und waren mit je acht 15 cm Schnellfeuerkanonen (in Einzeltürmen), zwei 88 mm Flugzeugabwehrkanonen und zwei 50 cm Torpedorohre bewaffnet. Die Höchstgeschwindigkeit mit Kohldampfantrieb war gute 27,5 Knoten – immer noch gut für heute. Die "S.M.S. Breslau" wurde durch Minentreffer im ägaischen Meer in Januar 1918 versenkt. Die "S.M.S. Straßburg" überstand den Ersten Weltkrieg sowie den Zweiten Weltkrieg, und wurde im Jahre 1947 verschrottet.*

## XIIf. "S.M.S. Pillau" Class / "S.M.S. Pillau" Klasse (1914)

"S.M.S. Pillau" (1914) and "S.M.S. Elbing" (1915) each displaced up to 5,252 tons and were armed with 8-6 inch guns plus 4-2 inch guns. They could make up to 27,5 knots with their coal boilers under full steam. Both ships were named for coastal cities and German naval bases in the old German Province of East Prussia ("Ostpreußen" in German), which today is divided between Poland (Southern half including Ermland and Masuria regions) and Russia (Northern half now named "Kaliningrad Oblast" or "Königsberg Region"). "S.M.S. Pillau" survived World War One and was scrapped in 1944. "S.M.S. Elbing" was heavily damaged and then scuttled by her German crew at the Battle of Jutland in May 1916 – fortunately the vast majority of her crew was rescued and transferred to other German warships.

*Die Kleinen Kreuzer "S.M.S. Pillau" (1914) und die "S.M.S. Elbing" (1915) hatten eine Einsatzverdrängung von je 5,252 Tonnen, und waren mit je acht 15 cm Schnellfeuerkanonen (in Einzeltürmen) sowie mit vier 5,2 cm Schnellfeuerkanonen bewaffnet. Die Höchstgeschwindigkeit mit Kohldampfantrieb war gute 27,5 Knoten – immer noch gut für heute. Die "S.M.S. Elbing" wurde bei der Seeschlacht am Skagerrak am 31. Mai 1916 schwer beschädigt, und wurde von ihrer deutschen Besatzung selbst versenkt. Die große Mehrheit der Besatzung wurde von anderen deutschen Kriegsschiffen gerettet. Die "S.M.S. Pillau" überstand den Ersten Weltkrieg, und wurde im Jahre 1944 verschrottet.*

## XIIg. "S.M.S. Frankfurt" Class / "S.M.S. Frankfurt" Klasse (1915)

"S.M.S. Frankfurt" (1915) displaced a maximum 5,200 tons and was armed with 8-6 inch guns plus 4-2 inch guns and could make up to 27,5 knots with her coal boilers under full steam. Any speed of 26 knots and above is still considered good for the combat ships of modern navies around the world. She was named for the German city of Frankfurt, which is today the capital of the modern German State of Hessen ("Hesse" or "Hessia" in English) and the seat of the European Central Bank. Frankfurt is also Germany's banking capital, home to large banks such as Deutsche Bank and Dresdner Bank. The ship survived World War One, and was surrendered to the USA as war booty thereafter. The Americans sunk her as a target vessel in a test off the coast of Cape Henry in 1921.

*Der Kleine Kreuzer "S.M.S. Frankfurt" (1915) hatte eine Einsatzverdrängung von 5,200 Tonnen, und war mit acht 15 cm Schnellfeuerkanonen (in Einzeltürmen) sowie mit vier 5,2 cm Schnellfeuerkanonen bewaffnet. Die Höchstgeschwindigkeit mit Kohldampfantrieb war gute 27,5 Knoten. Eine maximale Geschwindigkeit von 26 oder mehr Knoten ist für moderne Kriegsschiffe immer noch ganz gut. Die "S.M.S. Frankfurt" überstand den Ersten Weltkrieg, und wurde an die USA übergeben. Sie wurde als Zielschiff der amerikanischen Marine an der Küste von Virginien im Jahre 1921 versenkt.*

## XIIh. "S.M.S. Kolberg" Class / "S.M.S. Kolberg" Klasse (1910)

"S.M.S. Kolberg" (1910) displaced 4,915 tons and was armed with 6-6 inch guns plus 2-88 mm anti-aircraft guns. She could make up to 26,3 knots with her coal boilers under full steam. She was named after the city of Kolberg in the old German Province of Pomerania, which since 1945 has been part of Poland.

Kolberg and Pomerania lie along the Baltic Sea coast. The ship survived World War One, and was scrapped in 1929.

*Der Kleine Kreuzer "S.M.S. Kolberg" (1910) hatte eine Einsatzverdrängung von 4,915 Tonnen, und war mit sechs 15 cm Schnellfeuerkanonen (in Einzeltürmen) sowie mit zwei 88 mm Flugzeugabwehrkanonen bewaffnet. Die Höchstgeschwindigkeit mit Kohldampfantrieb war gute 26,3 Knoten. Das Schiff überstand den Ersten Weltkrieg, und wurde im Jahre 1929 verschrottet. Die Stadt Kolberg liegt in Hinterpommern (seit 1945 in Polen). Die Bevölkerungszahl von Hinterpommern ist heute 6,025,877, wovon 14 Prozent immer noch deutsch als eine zweite Sprache sprechen. Die deutschsprechende Bevölkerung von Ostpommern ist hauptsächlich in Stettin und auch in Kolberg zu finden.*

Further Pomerania's current population in modern Poland is 6,025,877, of whom 14% can still speak German as a second language. The German-speaking minority of Eastern Pomerania is primarily resident in the cities of Stettin and Kolberg. Pomerania ranges from the German-Polish border near the Oder River to just West of the city of Danzig in the East (now called "Gdansk" in Polish).

## XIIi. "S.M.S. Mainz" Class / "S.M.S. Mainz" Klasse (1909)

"S.M.S. Mainz" (1909) displaced 4,889 tons and was armed with 12-4 inch guns plus 4-2 inch guns. One can notice the less powerful armament of an older small cruiser such as this. She could make up to 26,8 knots under full steam with her coal boilers and was named after the German city of Mainz. Sadly, she was sunk by British battlecruisers in the Battle of Helgoland on August 28, 1914. She carried Germany's first flag officer (i.e., an admiral) to die in World War One down with her. The German Navy had only small cruisers out to sea on that fateful day. When the battle commenced, the large and powerful German battlecruisers were unfortunately pinned down behind the Jade Estuary (the outlet of the Wilhelmshaven Naval Base) due to the low tide.

*Der Kleine Kreuzer "S.M.S. Mainz" (1909) hatte eine Einsatzverdrängung von 4,889 Tonnen, und war mit 12-10,5 cm Schnellfeuerkanonen (in Einzeltürmen) sowie mit vier 5,2 cm Schnellfeuerkanonen bewaffnet. Man soll beachten, das die älteren Kleinen Kreuzer weniger Bewaffnung hatten. Die Höchstgeschwindigkeit des Schiffes war gute 26,8 Knoten. Die meisten Kriegsschiffe am Ende des Ersten Weltkrieges haben noch Kohldampfantrieb benützt. Die "S.M.S. Mainz" wurde von englischen Schlachtkreuzern bei der Seeschlacht von Helgoland am 28. August 1914 leider versenkt. Die Kaiserliche Marine hat drei Kleine Kreuzer, ein Torpedoboot, Konteradmiral Leberecht Maass und 700 Seeleute verloren. 400 deutsche Seeleute wurden von den Engländern als Kriegsgefangene gerettet. Die Englaender haben nur 35 Seeleute verloren, weil die mächtigen deutschen Schlachtkreuzer behindert waren, weil während der Ebbe das Wasser der Jade eine Ausfahrt unmöglich machte.*

## XIIj. "S.M.S. Kaiser Franz Josef I" Class / "S.M.S. Kaiser Franz Josef I" Klasse 1890)

The Austrian small cruisers "S.M.S. Kaiser Franz Josef I" (1890) and "S.M.S. Kaiserin Elisabeth" (1892) displaced 4,566 tons each and were armed with 8-6 inch guns plus 2-3 inch guns. They could make up to 19 knots under full steam, which illustrates how older cruisers were considerably slower. They were named for the ruling Emperor Franz Josef I (1830-1916) and his wife Empress Elisabeth (1837-1898) of Austria-Hungary, who were of the Habsburg-Lothringen Dynasty. The first ship of this class survived World War One and was scrapped after the war, while "S.M.S. Kaiserin Elisabeth" was scuttled in the German colony of Tsingtau in China in 1914. She was deemed too obsolete to fight, which would have been suicidal for her crew. The men fought alongside the Germans in trying to defend Tsingtau against the vastly more numerous Japanese and British invaders. They surrendered in late 1914, and most of them spent numerous horrific years in Japanese and Australian captivity. The Australian camps were particularly brutal, and many Austrian survivors only made it back home to Austria, Hungary, Czechoslovakia and Yugoslavia in 1920.

*Die zwei Kleinen Kreuzer "S.M.S. Kaiser Franz Josef I" (1890) und "S.M.S. Kaiserin Elisabeth" (1892) hatten eine Einsatzverdrängung von je 4,566 Tonnen, und waren mit je acht 15 cm Schnellfeuerkanonen (in Einzeltürmen) sowie mit zwei 7,0 cm Schnellfeuerkanonen bewaffnet. Die Höchstgeschwindigkeit mit Kohldampfantrieb waren nur 19 Knoten. Hier kann man beachten, wie die älteren Kleinen Kreuzer auch wesentlich langsamer waren. Die "S.M.S. Kaiser Franz Josef I" überstand den Ersten Weltkrieg und wurde im Oktober 1919 verschrottet. Die "S.M.S. Kaiserin Elisabeth" war am Anfang des Ersten Weltkrieges im deutschen Schutzgebiet von Tsingtau. Sie wurde von ihrer eigenen österreichischen Besatzung versenkt, weil sie schon zu veraltet für den Krieg war. Ihre Besatzung hatte mit den deutschen Kameraden Tsingtau gegen die britische und die japanische Übermacht verteidigt, bis sie sich im Spätjahr 1914 übergaben. Die Kriegsgefangenschaft in Japan war nicht schlecht, aber in Australien war die Kriegsgefangenschaft sehr brutal. Die Deutschen sind nur im Jahre 1919 wieder nach Deutschland gekommen, aber die Österreicher, die Ungarn, die Tschechen, die Slowaken, die Slowener und die Kroaten wurden erst im Jahre 1920 aus der Kriegsgefangenschaft entlaßen. Franz Josef I von*

*Oesterreich (1830-1916) war der zweitletzte Kaiser von Österreich sowie König von Ungarn von 1848 bis er im Jahre 1916 starb. Sein Nachfolger war Karl I Franz Josef Ludwig Hubert Georg Maria (1887-1922), der letzte Kaiser von Österreich, sowie König von Ungarn, Böhmen, Dalmatien, Kroatien, Slavonien, Galizien, Lodomerien, Illyrien und Jerusalem. Elisabeth Aumalie Eugenie, Herzogin in Bayern (1837-1898), wurde auch "Sisi" oder "Sissi" genannt. Sie war Base (die Cousine) ersten Grades von Franz Josef I, und auch seine Gattin. Der Nachfolger von Kaiser Karl ist sein ältester Sohn Otto von Habsburg-Lothringen (am 20. November 1912 geboren und jetzt im Ruhestand in Bayern). Seit den 1. Januar 2007 ist das neue Oberhaupt des Adelhauses Habsburg-Lothringen Ottos ältester Sohn Karl von Habsburg-Lothringen (am 11. Januar 1961 in Bayern geboren). Karl von Habsburg-Lothringen is Souveraen, Großmeister und Ritter des Ordens vom Goldenen Vlies. Er ist auch Träger des Großkreuzes des Souveränen Malteser-Ritterordens und Ehrenritter des Deutschen Ordens. Er ist seit 1986 Präsident der habsburgischen "Paneuropa-Union," und seit 2002 Generaldirektor der "Organisation der nicht-repräsentierten Nationen und Völker" (UNPO). Karl von Habsburg-Lothringen ist mit Francesca Thyßen-Bornemisza de Kaszon verheiratet. Das Ehepaar und ihre drei Kinder wohnen seit 2005 in Wien. Ihre Kinder heißen Eleonore, Ferdinand Zvonimir (der Thronfolger, der am 21. Juni 1997 in Salzburg geboren wurde) und Gloria.*

## XIIk. "S.M.S. Irene" Class / "S.M.S. Irene" Klasse (1887)

The 2 Imperial German cruising corvettes "S.M.S. Irene" (1887) and "S.M.S. Prinzess Wilhelm" (1887) were built without any rigging and sails – thus do I include them here among other small cruisers. They were both steel ships, each 104 meters long, displacing up to 4,271 tons full load, capable of up to 18 knots, being powered by 2 double expansion engines driving twin screws. "S.M.S. Irene (1887) was built by the A.G. Vulcan Shipyard in Stettin, Pomerania, while "S.M.S. Prinzess Wilhelm" (1887) was built by the Germania Shipyard in Kiel, Schleswig-Holstein. Both vessels were armed with 14 15-cm ring cannon, and were scrapped in 1921 and 1922, respectively (after up to 35 years of service in the German Navy).

*Die zwei kaiserlich-deutschen Kreuzerkorvetten "S.M.S. Irene" (1887) und "S.M.S. Prinzeß Wilhelm" (1887) wurden ohne Segel gebaut, und waren deswegen mehr als Kleine Kreuzer. Sie hatten eine Einsatzverdrängung von je 4,271 Tonnen, waren je 104 Meter lang, und die Höchstgeschwindigkeit mit Dampfantrieb waren 18 Knoten. Die "S.M.S. Irene" wurde beim A.G. Vulcan in Stettin (Hinterpommern) gebaut, und die "S.M.S. Prinzeß Wilhelm" wurde bei*

*Germania in Kiel gebaut. Die Bewaffnung dieser Klaße waren je 14-15 cm Ringkanonen. Diese Schiffe überstanden den Ersten Weltkrieg, und wurden zwischen 1921 und 1922 verschrottet.*

### XIII. "S.M.S. Saida" Class / "S.M.S. Saida" Klasse (1914)

The three Austrian small cruisers "S.M.S. Saida" (1914), "S.M.S. Helgoland" (1914) and "S.M.S. Novara" (1915) displaced 4,010 tons each, were armed with 9-4 inch guns plus one 2 inch gun and could make up to 27 knots under full steam with their coal boilers. All three ships survived World War One and were scrapped after the war. "S.M.S. Saida" and "S.M.S. Helgoland" were taken by Italy as war booty, and scrapped in 1937 after their service in the Italian Navy. "S.M.S. Novara" was taken by France as war booty, and was scrapped by the Germans in 1942, after she was captured by Germany in 1940. In comparison to dreadnought battleships, battlecruisers and armored cruisers, small cruisers saw much more action during World War One. Both heads of state and admirals were afraid to lose the larger ships, and a new weapon (the submarine with her deadly torpedos) changed naval warfare forever. In hindsight, navies should have had many more small cruisers, destroyers, torpedo boats and submarines – and fewer of the large ships. Another new weapon of World War One (the airplane) would make battleships and battlecruisers obsolete by the time of World War Two. The aircraft carrier would eventually replace the battleship as the most important type of capital navy ship – a fact which still holds true today.

*Die drei Mitglieder der "S.M.S. Saida" (1914) Klaße hatten eine Einsatzverdrängung von je 4,010 Tonnen, und waren mit je neun 10,0 cm Schnellfeuerkanonen (in Einzeltürmen) sowie mit einer 4,7 cm Schnellfeuerkanone bewaffnet. Die Höchstgeschwindigkeit mit Dampfantrieb war gute 27 Knoten. Die zwei anderen Einheiten dieser Klaße waren die "S.M.S. Helgoland" (1914) und die "S.M.S. Novara" (1915). Alle drei Schiffe überstanden den Ersten Weltkrieg. Die "S.M.S. Saida" und die "S.M.S. Helgoland" wurden nach dem Ersten Weltkrieg an Italien übergeben, und wurden im Jahre 1937 verschrottet. Die "S.M.S. Novara" wurde nach dem Ersten Weltkrieg an Frankreich übergeben, und dann im Jahre 1940 von der Deutschen Kriegsmarine beschlagnahmt. Sie wurde dann im Jahre 1942 verschrottet. Alle drei Schiffe waren zur Zeit des Ersten Weltkriegs sehr aktiv.*

### XIIm. "S.M.S. Stuttgart" Class / "S.M.S. Stuttgart" Klasse (1908)

"S.M.S. Stuttgart" (1908) displaced 4,002 tons and was armed with 4-4 inch guns and 3 seaplanes, which made her Germany's first warship to be armed with aircraft. She could make up to 23 knots with her coal boilers under full steam. She was named after the German city of Stuttgart, which is the traditional capital of the former Duchy of Swabia. Stuttgart is still home to the companies building both Mercedes-Benz and Porsche cars today. The ship survived World War One and was scrapped in 1920.

*Der Kleine Kreuzer "S.M.S. Stuttgart" (1908) hatte eine Einsatzverdrängung von 4,002 Tonnen, und war mit vier 10,5 cm Schnellfeuerkanonen (in Einzeltürmen) bewaffnet. Die Höchstgeschwindigkeit mit Dampfantrieb war 23 Knoten. Sie wurde als Deutschlands erster Flugbootträger umgebaut, und wurde auch mit 3 Flugboote ausgerüstet. Das Schiff überstand den Ersten Weltkrieg, und wurde im Jahre 1920 verschrottet.*

## XIIn. "S.M.S. Admiral Spaun" Class / "S.M.S. Admiral Spaun" Klasse (1910)

The Austrian small cruiser "S.M.S. Admiral Spaun" (1910) displaced 4,000 tons and was armed with 7-4 inch guns and one 2 inch gun. She could make up to 27 knots under full steam with her coal boilers, and survived World War One to be scrapped thereafter. She was named after Austrian Admiral Hermann Freiherr von Spaun (1833-1919). He joined the Austrian Navy in 1850, and served in the war against France and the Kingdom of Sardinia in 1859. He also served in the war against Denmark in 1864, and in the war against Italy and the Kingdom of Prussia in 1866. Admiral von Spaun retired from the Navy in 1904.

*Der Kleine Kreuzer "S.M.S. Admiral Spaun" (1910) hatte eine Einsatzverdrängung von 4,000 Tonnen, und war mit sieben 10,0 cm Schnellfeuerkanonen (in Einzeltürmen) sowie mit einer 4,7 cm Schnellfeuerkanone bewaffnet. Die Höchstgeschwindigkeit mit Dampfantrieb war gute 27 Knoten. Das Schiff überstand den Ersten Weltkrieg, und wurde im Jahre 1922 von den Engländern verschrottet. Admiral Hermann Freiherr von Spaun (1833-1919) diente bei der Kaiserlichen und Königlichen Kriegsmarine von 1850 bis er im Jahre 1904 in den Ruhestand ging. Er diente im Krieg gegen Frankreich und das Königreich Sardinien im Jahre 1859, gegen das Königreich Dänemark im Jahre 1864, und gegen das Königreich Italian sowie das Königreich Preußen im Jahre 1866.*

## XIIo. "S.M.S. Stettin" Class / "S.M.S. Stettin" Klasse (1907)

"S.M.S. Stettin" (1907) displaced 3,822 tons and was armed with 10-4 inch guns plus 8-2 inch guns. She could make up to 25,2 knots under full steam with her coal boilers, and was named after Stettin, the capital city of Pomerania now part of modern Poland since 1945.  She survived World War One and was scrapped in 1920.

*Der Kleine Kreuzer "S.M.S. Stettin" (1907) hatte eine Einsatzverdrängung von 3,822 Tonnen, und war mit zehn 10,5 cm Schnellfeuerkanonen (in Einzeltürmen) sowie mit acht 5,2 cm Schnellfeuerkanonen bewaffnet.  Die Höchstgeschwindigkeit mit Dampfantrieb war 25,2 Knoten.  Das Schiff überstand den Ersten Weltkrieg und wurde im Jahre 1920 verschrottet.  Die Hansestadt Stettin war bis Mai 1945 die Hauptstadt von Pommern.*

## XIIp. "S.M.S. Bremen" Class / "S.M.S. Bremen" Klasse (1902)

The 12 small cruisers similar to "S.M.S. Danzig" (1907) displaced up to 3,783 tons each and were armed with 10-4 inch guns plus 2-45 cm torpedo tubes. They could make up to 25,2 knots under full steam with their coal boilers.  Danzig is a large port city in East Prussia, now part of modern Poland under the Polish name of "Gdansk."  Other ships in this class of 12 units included the "S.M.S. München" (named after the Bavarian capital city of Munich), the "S.M.S. Emden" (which gained fame due to her heroic raiding cruise in the Indian Ocean in 1914), the "S.M.S. Dresden" (which was sunk by British cruisers in the Pacific at Isla Juan Fernandez or "Robinson Crusoe" Island in 1914), the "S.M.S Königsberg" (which was scuttled by her own crew in the Rufiji River Delta in German East Africa to prevent her from being useful to the British), the "S.M.S. Nürnberg" (which was sunk by the British at the Battle of the Falkland Islands in 1914), the "S.M.S. Leipzig" (same fate as "S.M.S. Nürnberg"), the S.M.S. Karlsruhe (same fate as "S.M.S. Nürnberg") and finally the "S.M.S. Köln" (sunk by the British off Trinidad & Tobago in 1914).  Other ships of the class were of course "S.M.S. Bremen" (commissioned in 1904), "S.M.S. Berlin" (1905), "S.M.S. Hamburg" (1904) and "S.M.S. Lübeck" (1905).

**Kleiner Kreuzer / Small Cruiser "S.M.S. Emden" (1908) – painting by Naval artist Günther Todt (1928-2009)**

*Die 12 Kleinen Kreuzer der "S.M.S. Bremen" (1902) Klaße hatten eine Einsatzverdrängung von je 3,783 Tonnen, und waren mit je zehn 10,5 cm Schnellfeuerkanonen (in Einzeltürmen) sowie mit zwei 45 cm Torpedorohre bewaffnet. Die Höchstgeschwindigkeit mit Dampfantrieb war 25,2 Knoten. Die 11 anderen Mitglieder dieser zahlreichen und sehr berühmten Klaße waren die "S.M.S. Danzig," die "S.M.S. München," die "S.M.S. Emden" (1908), die "S.M.S. Dresden," die "S.M.S. Königsberg," die "S.M.S. Nürnberg," die "S.M.S. Leipzig," die "S.M.S. Köln," die "S.M.S. Berlin," die "S.M.S. Hamburg" und die "S.M.S. Lübeck." Die "S.M.S. Emden" unter Kapitän zur See Karl von Müller hatte 30 feindliche Schiffe im Indischen Ozean im Jahre 1914 versenkt. 80 feindliche Kriegsschiffe haben die "S.M.S. Emden" entweder gejagt oder auch bekämpft. Die "S.M.S. Königsberg" wurde von ihrer eigenen Besatzung in Deutsch-Ostafrika versenkt. Die "S.M.S. Nürnberg" und die "S.M.S. Leipzig" fielen bei der Falklandschlacht im Jahre 1914 (sie gehörten zum Deutschlands Ostasiengeschwader unter Vizeadmiral Maximilian Johannes Maria Hubert Reichsgraf von Spee). Die "S.M.S. Dresden" wurde von ihrer eigenen Besatzung bei Isla Juan Fernandez (oder "Robinson Kreuznauer Insel") im Südpazifischen*

*Ozean versenkt.  Die "S.M.S. Köln" wurde von der britischen Marine in der Nähe von Trinidad und Tobago im Jahre 1914 versenkt.*

**Kleiner Kreuzer / Small Cruiser "S.M.S. Leipzig" (1906) – courtesy of Captain (CA) George J. Albert, Jr., Army Field Historian of the California Center for Military History (shown flying the Kaiser's Standard – mit Kaiserflagge)**

**XIIq. "S.M.S. Arcona" Class / "S.M.S. Arcona" Klasse (1902)**

The "S.M.S. Arcona" (1902) displaced 3,180 tons and was armed with 8-4 inch guns plus 2-50 cm torpedo tubes.  She could make up to 21,5 knots under full steam with her coal boilers and was one of Germany's earliest modern small cruisers along with her sister ships.  She was named after Cape Arcona, which lies along the German Baltic Sea Coast in the modern State of Mecklenburg-Vorpommern ("Mecklenburg-Near Pomerania" in English).

*Der Kleine Kreuzer "S.M.S. Arcona" (1902) hatte eine Einsatzverdrängung von 3,180 Tonnen, und war mit acht 10,5 cm Schnellfeuerkanonen (in Einzeltürmen) sowie mit zwei 50 cm Torpedorohre bewaffnet.  Die Höchstgeschwindigkeit mit Dampfantrieb war 21,5 Knoten.  Das Schiff überstand den Ersten Weltkrieg, und diente auch bei der nachkriegs Reichsmarine. Sie wurde von ihrer eigenen Besatzung am 3. Mai in 1945 in Wilhelmshaven versenkt, nach dem Ende des Zweiten Weltkrieges geborgen und im Jahre 1949 endlich verschrottet.*

## XIIr. "S.M.S. Niobe" Class / "S.M.S. Niobe" Klasse (1900)

The "S.M.S. Niobe" (1900) displaced 2,963 tons and was armed with 10-4 inch guns plus 2-50 cm torpedo tubes. She could make up to 22,1 knots with under full steam with her coal boilers and belonged to the very first class of German small cruisers. Steaming radius was 4,000 miles. The 7 other ships in this class of 8 units were "S.M.S. Gazelle" (1900), "S.M.S. Nymphe" (1900), "S.M.S. Thetis" (1901), "S.M.S. Ariadne" (1901), "S.M.S. Amazone" (1901), "S.M.S. Medusa" (1901) and "S.M.S. Frauenlob" (1903). "Gazelle" is of course an animal, and the rest of the ships were named after figures from classical mythology with the exception of "Frauenlob." "Frauenlob" literally means "for the praise of women." The very first "S.M.S. Frauenlob" was a sailing vessel of the Prussian Navy, donations for which were collected from women all over the Kingdom of Prussia. "S.M.S. Gazelle" survived World War One and was scrapped in 1920. "S.M.S. Niobe" survived World War One to fight again in World War Two, where she was lost in the Adriatic in November 1943. "S.M.S. Nymphe" survived World War One and was scrapped in 1932. "S.M.S. Thetis" survived the great war as well, and was finally scrapped in 1930. "S.M.S. Ariadne" was sunk off the East Frisian coast of Germany in August 1914. "S.M.S. Amazone" survived both world wars and was scrapped in 1954. "S.M.S. Medusa" survived World War One to be lost very late in World War Two, in May 1945. "S.M.S. Frauenlob" was sunk by a British cruiser at the Battle of Jutland in May 1916.

*Die acht Kleinen Kreuzer der "S.M.S. Niobe" (1900) Klaße hatten je eine Einsatzverdrängung von 2,963 Tonnen, und waren mit je zehn 10,5 cm Schnellfeuerkanonen (in Einzeltürmen) sowie mit zwei 50 cm Torpedorohre bewaffnet. Die Höchstgeschwindigkeit mit Kohldampfantrieb war 22,1 Knoten, und die Reichweite war 4,000 Seemeilen. Die sieben anderen Mitglieder dieser Klaße waren die "S.M.S. Gazelle" (1900), die "S.M.S. Nymphe" (1900), die "S.M.S. Thetis" (1901), die "S.M.S. Ariadne" (1901), die "S.M.S. Amazone" (1901), die "S.M.S. Medusa" (1901) und die "S.M.S. Frauenlob" (1903). Die meisten Patennamen dieser Klaße kamen aus der klaßischen Mythologie. Die erste "S.M.S. Frauenlob" war ein Segelschiff der Königlichen Preußischen Marine. Die Geld dafür wurde von Frauen über ganz Preußen gesammelt. Die "S.M.S. Niobe" überstand den Ersten Weltkrieg, aber wurde im Jahre 1943 im Adriatischen Meer versenkt. Die "S.M.S. Gazelle" überstand den Ersten*

Weltkrieg, und wurde im Jahre 1920 verschrottet. Die "S.M.S. Nymphe" überstand den Ersten Weltkrieg, und diente bei der nachkriegs Reichsmarine. Sie wurde im Jahre 1932 verschrottet. Die "S.M.S. Thetis" überstand den Ersten Weltkrieg, und diente auch bei der nachkriegs Reichsmarine. Sie wurde im Jahre 1930 verschrottet. Die "S.M.S. Ariadne" wurde am Anfang des Ersten Weltkrieges im August 1914 an der Küste von Ostfriesland versenkt. Die "S.M.S. Amazone" überstand den Ersten sowie den Zweiten Weltkrieg, und wurde erst im Jahre 1954 verschrottet. Die "S.M.S. Medusa" überstand den Ersten und fast den Zweiten Weltkrieg – sie wurde im Mai 1945 versenkt. Die "S.M.S. Frauenlob" wurde bei der Skagerrakschlacht am 31. Mai 1916 von den Engländern versenkt.

## XIIs. "S.M.S. Aspern" Class / "S.M.S. Aspern" Klasse (1900)

The Austrian small cruiser "S.M.S. Aspern" (1900) displaced 2,625 tons and was armed with 8-5 inch guns plus 10-2 inch guns and could make up to 22 knots under full steam with her coal boilers. She was named for the Austrian victory against the French at the town of Aspern in Austria in May 1809. Austrian Archduke Charles of the Habsburg Dynasty ("Erzherzog Karl" in German) handed Napoleon Bonaparte of France his first real defeat in a war which began in 1792. The tide would truly not be turned until Napoleon's retreat from Moscow began in 1812, and final victory would not be won until the Battle of Waterloo in what is now Belgium in 1815. Napoleon Bonaparte was born on the island of Corsica, which although part of France is much closer to Italy in terms of both language and culture. The ship survived World War One and was scrapped after the war.

Der Kleine Kreuzer "S.M.S. Aspern" (1900) hatte eine Einsatzverdrängung von 2,625 Tonnen, und war mit acht 12 cm Schnellfeuerkanonen (in Einzeltürmen) sowie mit zehn 4,7 cm Schnellfeuerkanonen bewaffnet. Die Höchstgeschwindigkeit mit Kohldampfantrieb war 22 Knoten. Das Schiff überstand den Ersten Weltkrieg, und wurde im Jahre 1922 verschrottet. Erzherzog Karl Ludwig Johann Joseph Laurentius von Österreich (1771-1847) war Herzog von Teschen, grosser Feldherr und Mitglied des Adelhauses Habsburg-Lothringen. Er ist am besten dadurch in Erinnerung geblieben, daß er Napoleon Bonaparte von Frankreich die erste Niederlage bei Aspern (heute ein Teil von Wien) im Mai 1809 auf dem Schlachtfeld zufügte.

## XIIt. "S.M.S. Szigetvár" Class / "S.M.S. Szigetvár" Klasse (1901)

The Austrian small cruiser "S.M.S. Szigetvár" (1901) displaced 2,562 tons and was armed with 8-5 inch guns and could make up to 22 knots under full steam with her coal boilers.  She was named for the Hungarian and Croatian battle against the Ottoman Turks at the town of Szigetvár ("Inselburg" in German which means "island castle" in English) in Southern Hungary in 1566.  The Austrians, Hungarians and Croatians were wiped out (they had a much smaller force), but the "victory" cost Ottoman Turkey so much in men and material that the Turks never truly recovered from this costly victory of theirs.  The Hungarian-Croatian military leader in this battle was their shared national hero Miklos Zrinyi.

*Der Kleine Kreuzer "S.M.S. Szigetvar" (1901) hatte eine Einsatzverdrängung von 2,562 Tonnen, und war mit acht 12 cm Schnellfeuerkanonen (in Einzeltürmen), zehn 4,7 cm Schnellfeuerkanonen, zwei Maschinengewehre sowie mit zwei 45 cm Torpedorohre bewaffnet.  Die Besatzung des Schiffes war 17 Offiziere und 290 Matrosen.  Das Schiff überstand den Ersten Weltkrieg, und wurde im Jahre 1923 verschrottet.  Die Schlacht von Szigetvar ("Inselburg" auf deutsch) in Südungarn im Jahre 1566 ist sehr berühmt, weil die Ungarn und die Kroaten unter deren Nationalheld Miklos Subic Zrinyi den osmanischen Türken viel gekostet haben.  Die Türken haben "gewonnen" sozusagen, aber der Preis war zu hoch.  Fast alle 2,500 Ungarn und Kroaten gingen verloren, aber die osmanischen Türken haben 30,000 Soldaten und auch ihren Feldherrn Sultan Suleyman den Prächtigen verloren.*

## XIIu. "S.M.S. Zenta" Class / "S.M.S. Zenta" Klasse (1899)

The Austrian small cruiser "S.M.S. Zenta" (1899) displaced 2,313 tons and was armed with 8-5 inch guns plus 10-2 inch guns.  She could make up to 21,8 knots and was one of the last small cruisers to be powered both by coal boilers (steam engines) and by auxiliary rigging and sails.  She was sunk early in World War One in August 1914, when she was on patrol in the Southern Adriatic Sea.  Virtually the entire French fleet (complete with 12 battleships, and armored cruisers in addition to the battleships) plus numerous British cruisers and destroyers surprised and sunk her – a grand total of 61 enemy warships.  Her officers and crew were very courageous against a much larger enemy, and many of them died that day.  Many were also taken prisoner and sent to a POW camp in Montenegro, where they were eventually liberated by advancing Austrian troops more than one year later.  She was named for the Austrian victory over Ottoman Turkey in 1697 at the town of Zenta ("Senta" in Serbo-Croatian") in Serbia.  The

Austrians were lead by the legendary Holy Roman and German Field Marshall Prince Eugene of Savoy, who eventually had one Austrian dreadnought battleship (1912) and one German Heavy Cruiser (1940) named after him. The Province of Savoy is now part of France, but used to belong to the Holy Roman Empire of the German Nation.

*Der Kleine Kreuzer "S.M.S. Zenta" (1899) hatte eine Einsatzverdrängung von 2,313 Tonnen, und war mit acht 12 Schnellfeuerkanonen, zehn 4,7 cm Schnellfeuerkanonen, zwei Maschninengewehre sowie mit zwei 45 cm Torpedorohre bewaffnet. Die Besatzung des Schiffes war 17 Offiziere und 290 Matrosen. Die Höchstgeschwindigkeit mit Dampfantrieb sowie mit Segel (sie war der letzte Kleine Kreuzer der Kaiserlichen und Königlichen Kriegsmarine, der mit Segel gebaut wurde) war 21,8 Knoten. Sie wurde am Anfang des Ersten Weltkrieges am 16. August 1914 im südlichen Adriatischen Meer versenkt. Eine sehr große feindliche Flotte von 61 französischen und englischen Kriegsschiffen hatte sie gejagt und bekämpft. Dabei waren 12 Schlachtschiffe, sowie mehrere Panzerkreuzer und Zerstörer. 179 Österreichische Seeleute gingen verloren, aber die anderen wurden von den Alliierten als Kriegsgefangene gerettet. Im Jahre 1916 wurden die Gefangenen von ihren Österreichischen Armeekameraden in Montenegro befreit. Der Generalfeldmarschall Prinz Eugen Franz von Savoyen-Carignan (1663-1736) hat die ottomanischen Türken bei der Schlacht von Zenta in Serbien im Jahre 1697 zerschlagen.*

## XIIv. "S.M.S. Carola" Class / "S.M.S. Carola" Klasse (1880)

The "S.M.S. Carola" (1880) class of Imperial German flush-decked and fully rigged sailing corvettes were among the last of their kind, and foretold the coming era of small (unarmored) cruisers – hence my decision to include them at the end of this section as opposed to including them in the section immediately following this one. There were a total of 6 ships in this class, the others of which were "S.M.S. Olga," "S.M.S. Marie" (1881), "S.M.S. Sophie" (1881), "S.M.S. Alexandrine" (1885) and "S.M.S. Arcona" (1885). They were rigged as barques, and had 1,200 square meters of sail area each. Each ship displaced from 2,147 to 2,361 tons, and was from 76 up to 81 meters long. They were all built by A.G. Vulcan of Stettin, Pomerania.

*Die sechs kaiserlich-deutschen Segelkorvetten der "S.M.S. Carola" (1880) Klaße waren Kleine Kreuzer. Die Einsatzverdrängung dieser Schiffe war zwischen 2,147 und 2,361 Tonnen. Sie waren je zwischen 76 und 81 Meter lang, und hatten ein Segelbereich von je 1,200 Quadratmeter. Sie wurden alle beim A.G. Vulcan in Stettin (Hinterpommern) gebaut. Die fünf anderen Mitglieder dieser Klaße waren die "S.M.S. Olga" (1880), die "S.M.S. Marie" (1881), die "S.M.S. Sophie" (1881), die "S.M.S. Alexandrine" (1885) und die "S.M.S. Arcona" (1885).*

### XIIw. "S.M.S. Nixe" Class / "S.M.S. Nixe" Klasse (1885)

The single Imperial German flush-decked sailing corvette "S.M.S. Nixe" (1885) was also fully rigged, had a sail area of 1,580 square meters, was 63 meters long and displaced up to 1,781 tons full load. She was launched by the Imperial Shipyard in Danzig, West Prussia in July of 1885 and also foretold the soon-coming era of small cruisers.

*Die kaiserlich-deutsche Segelkorvette "S.M.S. Nixe" (1885) war auch ein Kleiner Kreuzer. Sie hatte eine Einsatzverdrängung von 1,781 Tonnen, war 63 Meter lang, und hatte ein Segelbereich von 1,580 Quadratmeter. Sie wurde in Danzig, Westpreußen gebaut.*

### XIIx. "S.M.S. Bussard" Class / "S.M.S. Bussard" Klasse (1888)

The "S.M.S. Bussard" (1888) class of 6 Imperial German small cruisers each displaced up to 1,600 tons full load, were 83 meters long, and were armed with gun-turrets at the bow and at the stern. With the exception of later unarmed sailing vessels intended just for training purposes, these were pretty much the final German Navy ships built to take rigging and sails. All the ships within this class were named after different types of birds, and all were built at the Imperial Shipyard in Wilhelmshaven. The 5 remaining members of this class were named "S.M.S. Falke" (1891), "S.M.S. Seeadler" (1892), "S.M.S. Condor" (1892), "S.M.S. Cormoran" (1892) and "S.M.S. Geier" (1894).

*Die sechs kaiserlich-deutschen Kleinen Kreuzer der "S.M.S. Bussard" (1888) Klaße hatten eine Einsatzverdrängung von je 1,600 Tonnen, waren je 83 Meter lang, und hatten Kohldampfantrieb sowie Segel. Die fünf anderen Mitglieder dieser Klaße waren die "S.M.S. Falke" (1891), die "S.M.S. Seeadler" (1892), die "S.M.S. Condor" (1892), die "S.M.S. Cormoran" (1892) und die "S.M.S. Geier" (1894). Sie wurden alle in Wilhelmshaven gebaut.*

### XIIy. "S.M.S. Blitz" Class / "S.M.S. Blitz" Klasse (1882)

The "S.M.S. Blitz" (1882) of 2 Imperial German dispatch boats were also fully rigged and foretold the immediately coming era of small, mostly unarmored cruisers. "S.M.S. Blitz" (German for "lightning") and her sister ship "S.M.S.

Pfeil" (German for "arrow") were both launched in 1882. Each ship was fully rigged as a schooner, displaced up to 1,486 tons full load and was 78 meters long.

*Die zwei kaiserlich-deutschen Segelschooner "S.M.S. Blitz" (1882) und "S.M.S. Pfeil" (1882) waren auch Kleine Kreuzer. Sie hatten eine Einsatzverdrängung von je 1,486 Tonnen und waren je 78 Meter lang.*

### XIIz. "S.M.S. Schwalbe" Class / "S.M.S. Schwalbe" Klasse (1887)

The 2 Imperial German small cruisers "S.M.S. Schwalbe" (German for the type of bird known as a "swallow") and "S.M.S. Sperber" (German for "sparrow") were both launched in 1887, displaced up to 1,111 tons full load, were rigged fore and aft as barques and were each 70 meters in length. They were built by the Imperial Shipyard in the great (and largest) German naval base of Wilhelmshaven, located in the Grand Duchy of Oldenburg.

*Die zwei Kleinen Kreuzer "S.M.S. Schwalbe" (1887) und "S.M.S. Sperber" (1887) waren Deutschlands kleinste Kleine Kreuzer. Sie hatten eine Einsatzverdrängung von je 1,111 Tonnen, waren je 70 Meter lang und hatten Kohldampfantrieb sowie Segel. Sie wurden in Wilhelmshaven (im Großherzogtum Oldenburg) gebaut.*

### XIII. "Segelkorvetten" (Sailing Corvettes)

Just as sailing frigates evolved into armored or large cruisers, so did sailing corvettes evolve into small cruisers. Method of construction was similar. These ships were originally made of wood if one goes far back enough in time, and then they eventually were built of both iron and wood – hence the later term "armored" corvettes.

*Die Segelkorvetten waren die Vorgänger der Kleinen Kreuzer. Am Anfang waren sie aus Holz ohne Panzerung gebaut, und mit Segel aber ohne Kohldampfantrieb gebaut.*

### XIII (1) "S.M.S. Hansa" Class / "S.M.S. Hansa" Klasse (1872)

"S.M.S. Hansa" (1872) was an armored and screw-driven sailing corvette, having been launched at the Imperial Shipyard in Danzig, West Prussia. This Imperial German ship was built out of iron-clad teak, was 73 meters long, and displaced up to 3,950 tons full load. She was powered by a single expansion engine, was fully rigged, had a sail area of 1,760 square meters and could make up to 13 knots. Her crew consisted of 28 commissioned officers and 371 enlisted men. She was armed with 8 21-cm ring cannon. She sailed from Kiel to South America and back from 1878 to 1880. She then served as a harbor guard ship, and as a living quarters after 1888. She was scrapped in the port of Swinemünde (near Stettin), Pomerania in 1906.

*Die Panzerkorvette "S.M.S. Hansa" (1872) wurde in Danzig, Westpreußen gebaut. Sie hatte eine Einsatzverdrängung von 3,950 Tonnen, war 73 Meter lang, hatte ein Segelbereich von 1,760 Quadratmeter, und eine Höchstgeschwindigkeit (mit Segel und mit Kohldampfantrieb) von 13 Knoten. Die Besatzung des Schiffes war 28 Offiziere und 371 Matrosen, und sie hatte eine Bewaffnung von acht 21 cm Ringkanonen. Zwischen 1878 und 1880 reiste sie von Kiel nach Südamerika und zurück. Nach 1888 wurde sie als Wohnschiff der Kaiserlichen Marine benutzt. Sie wurde in Swinemünde (Hinterpommern) im Jahre 1906 verschrottet.*

### XIII (2) "S.M.S. Bismarck" Class / "S.M.S. Bismarck" Klasse (1877)

The protected (armored) 3-masted sailing corvettes of the "S.M.S. Bismarck" (1877) class each displaced 3,300 tons full load, were 84 meters long, were fitted with a single expansion engine, were fully rigged and had a sail area of 2,210 square meters. Their crews consisted of 18 commissioned officers, 46 officer candidates (cadets) and 386 enlisted sailors. Armament was comprised of up to 14 15-cm ring cannon and two 88 mm rapid-firing cannon. The Imperial German Navy commissioned 7 ships in this class, including the "S.M.S. Blücher" (1877), the "S.M.S. Moltke" (1877), the "S.M.S. Stosch" (1878), the "S.M.S. Gneisenau" (1879), the "S.M.S. Stein" (1879) and the "S.M.S. Charlotte" (1885). "S.M.S. Stosch" (which was named after a Prussian Admiral), was launched by the A.G. Vulkan Shipyard of Stettin, Pomerania and served overseas until 1886 – when she partook in the German conquest of the Island of Zanzibar and established the Imperial Crown Colony of German East Africa (modern day Tanzania, Burundi and Rwanda). She was converted into a training ship in 1891, and finally scrapped in 1907.

*Die sieben Segelkorvetten der "S.M.S. Bismarck" (1877) Klaße hatten eine Einsatzverdrängung von je 3,300 Tonnen, waren je 84 Meter lang, hatten ein Segelbereich von je 2,210 Quadratmeter, und eine Besatzung von je 18 Offiziere, 46 Offiziersanwaerter (Kadetten) und 386 Matrosen. Die Bewaffnung waren je 14 15-cm Ringkanonen und zwei 88 mm Schnellfeuerkanonen. Die sechs anderen Mitglieder dieser Klaße waren die "S.M.S. Blücher" (1877), die "S.M.S. Moltke" (1877), die "S.M.S. Stosch" (1878), die "S.M.S. Gneisenau" (1879), die "S.M.S. Stein" (1879) und die "S.M.S. Charlotte" (1885). Die "S.M.S. Stosch" wurde* beim A.G. Vulkan in Stettin (Hinterpommern) gebaut, und diente im Ausland bis 1886. Ihre Besatzung hat Zanzibar fuer Deutschland genommen, und dann auch Deutsch-Ostafrika (Tansania, Burundi und Ruanda) etabliert. Nach 1891 wurde sie als Schulschiff benutzt, und sie wurde endlich im Jahre 1907 verschrottet. Albrecht von Stosch (1818-1896) war Deutscher Admiral von 1872 bis er im Jahre 1883 in den Ruhestand ging. Die "S.M.S. Moltke" und die "S.M.S. Gneisenau" wurde bei der Kaiserlichen Werft in Danzig, Westpreußen gebaut. Sie dienten auch oft im Ausland. Die "S.M.S. Moltke" wurde erst im Jahre 1920 verschrottet (nach 43 Jahren Dienstzeit), aber die "S.M.S. Gneisenau" ging leider am 16. Dezember 1900 in einem Sturm an der Küste von Malaga (Südspanien) mit Kapitän zur See Kretschmann und 41 Besatzungsmitgliedern verloren. Die Masten des versenkten Schiffes waren fuer viele Jahren danach immer noch sichtbar. Die "S.M.S. Gneisenau" hatte auch in Kamerun (im Jahre 1884) und Zanzibar (im Jahre 1885) gedient. Die "S.M.S. Charlotte" diente im Ausland bis 1897, und danach wurde sie als Schulschiff benutzt. Sie wurde im Jahre 1909 verschrottet. Die "S.M.S. Stein" wurde beim A.G. Vulkan in Stettin, Hinterpommern gebaut. Sie diente im Ausland bis 1888, und diente danach als Schulschiff, bis sie im Jahre 1908 verschrottet wurde. Baron Heinrich Friedrich Karl Reichsfreiherr vom und zum Stein (1757-1831) war Preußischer Staatsmann.

"S.M.S. Moltke" and "S.M.S Gneisenau" (named after famous generals of the Prussian Army) were both built by the Imperial Shipyard in Danzig, West Prussia. They also served overseas for much of their careers, "S.M.S. Moltke" being srapped in 1920 after 43 years of service. "S.M.S. Gneisenau" was unfortunately lost in a storm off the coast of Malaga on December 16, 1900 – along with 41 of her crew members (including her commander, Captain Kretschmann). The wrecked ship's masts were still visible many years later. She had served in German colonial missions off the coasts of both Cameroon in 1884 and Zanzibar in 1885. "S.M.S. Charlotte" served abroad until 1897, when she was converted into a training ship. She was scrapped in 1909. "S.M.S. Stein" (1879) was built by A.G. Vulcan of Stettin, Pomerania. She served overseas until 1888, and then became a training ship for naval cadets and cabin boys until she was scrapped in 1908. She was named after Baron Heinrich Friedrich Karl Reichsfreiherr vom und zum Stein (1757-1831), a famous Prussian statesman who introduced reforms which paved the way for the formation of the Second German Empire in 1871. He promoted the abolition of serfdom and the establishment of a modern municipal system of city governments. He came from an old Franconian family in Northern Bavaria, but was himself born on his family's estate in Hessen-Nassau. He attended the university in Göttingen, and then entered the Prussian civil service.

### XIII (3) "S.M.S. Ariadne" Class / "S.M.S. Ariadne" Klasse (1871)

The 3 flush-decked sailing corvettes "S.M.S. Ariadne" (1871), "S.M.S. Freya" (1874) and "S.M.S. Luise" (1874) were built by the Imperal (German) Shipyard in Danzig, West Prussia. Each ship displaced up to 1,692 tons full load, was 68 meters long and ran on a double expansion engine. They were fully rigged, had a sail area of 1,582 square meters and could make up to 14 knots. The crew of each vessel consisted of 13 commissioned officers and 220 enlisted men. Armament was comprised of 6 15-cm ring cannon and 2 12-cm ring cannon. "S.M.S. Luise" served in East Asia from 1875 until 1880, then for 2 years in South America, and as a training ship from 1885 to 1888. She was scrapped in Hamburg in 1897.

*Die drei Segelkorvetten der "S.M.S. Ariadne" (1871) Klaße hatten eine Einsatzverdrängung von je 1,692 Tonnen, waren je 68 Meter lang, hatten ein Segelbereich von je 1,582 Quadratmeter, eine Besatzung von je 13 Offiziere und 220 Matrosen, und eine Bewaffnung von je sechs 15 cm Ringkanonen und zwei 12 cm Ringkanonen. Die Höchstgeschwindigkeit mit Segel und Kohldampfantrieb war 14 Knoten. Die zwei anderen Mitglieder dieser Klaße waren die "S.M.S. Freya" (1874) und die "S.M.S. Luise" (1874). Alle drei Schiffe wurden bei der Kaiserlichen Werft in Danzig, Westpreußen gebaut. Die "S.M.S. Luise" diente von 1875 bis 1880 in Ostasien, für zwei Jahren in Südamerika und dann von 1885 bis 1888 als Schulschiff. Sie wurde in Hamburg im Jahre 1897 verschrottet.*

### XIII (4) "S.M.S. Delta" Class / "S.M.S. Delta" Klasse (1871)

The beautiful Austrian sailing corvettes "S.M.S. Delta" (1871), "S.M.S. Frundsberg" (1873) and "S.M.S. Aurora" (1874) each displaced 1,343 tons and were armed with 4-6 inch guns. They could make 11,5 knots and saw a good deal of overseas duty to "show the flag" and to train young naval cadets of the Imperial and Royal Naval Academy located at Sankt Veit am Pflaumb ("Fiume" in Italian and "Rijeka" as it is now called in Croatia). Rijeka is still 5% German-speaking today. Delta merely denotes the fourth letter in the Greek alphabet, while Georg ("George" in English) von Frundsberg was a famous German knight who lived from 1473 until 1528. He was one of Emperor Charles V's most highly decorated soldier-knights. During World War Two, the elite 10th Panzer Division (armored division) of the Waffen-SS was named after him as well. This elite division distinguished itself in desperate battles such as Lemberg (Eastern Front, 1944), Normandy (France, 1944), Arnhem (the Netherlands, 1944) and the Ardennes (Belgium & Luxembourg, 1944-1945). One often overlooks the sad fact that front line soldiers were often no more than teenagers, who had to grow up and die too fast – long before "their time."

*Die drei Segelkorvetten der "S.M.S. Delta" (1871) Klaße hatten eine Einsatzverdrängung von je 1,343 Tonnen, und waren mit je vier 15,2 cm Kanonen und einer 66 mm Kanone bewaffnet. Die Höchstgeschwindigkeit mit Segel und Kohldampfantrieb war 11,5 Knoten, und die Besatzungen waren je 203 Offiziere und Matrosen. Die "S.M.S. Delta" überstand den Ersten Weltkrieg, und wurde im Jahre 1920 in Polei (heute Pula in Kroatien) verschrottet. Die "S.M.S. Frundsberg" überstand den Ersten sowie den Zweiten Weltkrieg, und wurde im Jahre 1945 in Sibenning (heute Sibenik in Kroatien) verschrottet. Die "S.M.S. Aurora" überstand den Ersten Weltkrieg, und wurde im Jahre 1927 auch in Sibenning verschrottet. Diese drei Korvetten wurden auch als Schulschiffe fuer die Kaiserliche und Königliche Marineakademie in Sankt Veit am Pflaumb (heute Rijeka in Kroatien) benutzt. Etwa 5 Prozent der Bevölkerung in Sankt Veit am Pflaumb spricht immer noch deutsch. Georg von Frundsberg (1473-1528) war ein Süddeutscher Soldat und Landsknechtführer im kaiserlich-habsburgischen Dienst. Er gilt als einer der wichtigsten deutschen Infanterietaktiker und Kriegsunternehmer der frühen Neuzeit. Sein Name ist eng verbunden mit den Kämpfen der Habsburger, insbesondere mit Kaiser Karl V. Zur Zeit des Zweiten Weltkrieges gab es eine elite 10. SS-Panzerdivision "Frundsberg" der Waffen-SS, die in Schlachten wie Lemberg (Ostfront im Jahre 1944), Normandie (Westfront in Frankreich zwischen Juni und August 1944), Arnheim (Westfront in Holland zwischen September und November 1944) und den Ardennen (Westfront in Belgien und Luxemburg zwischen Dezember 1944 und Januar 1945) sich gegen die Übermacht der Alliierten sehr gut verteidigen konnte.*

## XIII (5) "S.M.S. Corona" Class / "S.M.S. Corona" Klasse (1812)

The wooden sailing corvette "S.M.S. Corona" was launched in Venice on February 20, 1819. Construction commenced in 1812, but in June of 1815 her planned name was changed to "S.M.S. Adria." One day after she was launched, she was renamed as "S.M.S. Carolina" on February 21, 1819. She displaced up to 914 tons full load, and was armed with 20-36 Pounders plus 4-12 Pounders. She was manned by a crew of 220 officers and enlisted men. In between 1820 and 1822, she undertook a voyage to China. From 1828 to 1830, she was attached to the Morocco Division of the Austrian Navy, providing support to Austrian Naval Infantry deployed in North Africa. The deployment was to combat pirates who had attacked Austrian commercial ships. In August of 1849, she was renamed yet again as "S.M.S. Lombardia." From 1850 until 1851, she made a voyage to the North Sea and into the Baltic Sea. In between 1857 and 1858, she took her final overseas voyage to South America and to South Africa. She was retired from active duty service in 1864 and was finally scrapped in 1870.

*Die Segelkorvette "S.M.S. Corona" wurde im Jahre 1812 in Venedig auf Kiel gelegt, und lief am 20. Februar 1819 vom Stapel. Sie hatte eine Einsatzverdrängung von 914 Tonnen, und war mit 20-36 Pfundern sowie mit vier 12 Pfundern bewaffnet. Die Besatzung des Schiffes war 220 Offiziere und Matrosen. Diese älteren Schiffe hatten Segel aber kein Kohldampfantrieb. Zwischen 1820 und 1822 reiste sie nach China. Zwischen 1828 und 1830 diente sie an der Küste von Marokko, wo sie Österreichische Marinesoldaten unterstützt hatte. Es gab Piraten, die Österreichische Handelsschiffe in Nordafrika angegriffen haben. Im August 1849 wurde sie als "S.M.S. Lombardia" umbenannt. Zwischen 1850 und 1851 reiste sie zur Nordsee und auch zur Ostsee. Zwischen 1857 und 1858 reiste sie nach Südamerika und auch nach Südafrika. Sie wurde erst im Jahre 1870 verschrottet, nach einer langen und guten Dienstzeit von 51 Jahren.*

## XIII (6) "S.M.S. Carolina" Class / "S.M.S. Carolina" Klasse (1808)

The earlier wooden sailing corvette also bearing the name "S.M.S. Carolina" was launched in Venice on March 12, 1808. She displaced up to 810 tons full load, was built out of oak, and was armed with 24-18 Pounders plus 2-12 Pounders. She was 41 meters long and had a maximum beam of 11,9 meters. In 1815, she partook in the Austrian naval blockade of Arcona (on the Italian Adriatic coast). This was during the war against Napoleonic France, when French troops were occupying Italian soil. She was scrapped in 1818.

*Die Segelkorvette "S.M.S. Carolina" (1808) lief am 12. März 1808 in Venedig vom Stapel. Sie hatte eine Einsatzverdrängung von 810 Tonnen, war aus Eichenholz gebaut, war 41 Meter lang und hatte eine Breite von 11,9 Meter. Sie war mit 24-18 Pfundern sowie mit zwei 12 Pfundern bewaffnet. Im Jahre 1815 am Ende der napoleonischen Kriege hatte sie die Stadt Arcona an der westlichen Adriatischen Küste blockiert. Sie wurde bald nach dem Ende des Krieges im Jahre 1818 verschrottet.*

## XIII (7) "S.M.S. Veloce" Class / "S.M.S. Veloce" Klasse (1834)

The wooden sailing corvette "S.M.S. Veloce" was launched in Venice on April 24, 1834. She displaced up to 718 tons full load, was built of oak, and was armed with 4-24 Pounders plus 20-18 Pounders. She had a crew of 238 officers and enlisted men. She was 41 meters long and had a maximum beam of 10,4 meters. She was renamed as "S.M.S. Diana" on November 19, 1849. She had an uneventful career, became a hulk in 1869 and was scrapped in 1870. "Diana" was yet another pagan Roman goddess, equivalent to the pagan Greek goddess "Artemis." They were the protectors of pregnant women.

*Die Segelkorvette "S.M.S. Veloce" lief am 24. April 1834 in Venedig vom Stapel. Sie hatte eine Einsatzverdrängung von 718 Tonnen, war aus Eichenholz gebaut, war 41 Meter lang und hatte eine Breite von 10,4 Meter. Sie war mit vier 24 Pfundern sowie mit 20-18 Pfundern bewaffnet. Die Besatzung des Schiffes bestand aus 238 Offiziere und Matrosen. Sie wurde am 19. November 1849 als "S.M.S. Diana" umbenannt, wurde als Hulk im Jahre 1869 umgebaut, und wurde im Jahre 1870 verschrottet. Diana war eine heidnische römische Göttin der Schwangerschaft.*

## XIII (8) "S.M.S. Sirena" Class / "S.M.S. Sirena" Klasse (1838)

The wooden sailing corvette "S.M.S. Sirena" was launched in Venice on October 12, 1838. She displaced up to 594 tons full load, and was built of oak. She was armed with 4-9 Pounders plus 16-36 Pounders. She had a crew of 140 officers and enlisted men. She was planned with the name "S.M.S. Sirena," but actually launched with the name "S.M.S. Clemenza." On November 19, 1849, she was renamed yet again as "S.M.S. Minerva." She was scrapped in 1893. "Sirena" is Italian for "siren" in English, this coming from the classical story of the Odyssey (song number XII). The "sirens" were the people who inhabited a particular island in Greek mythology. The sirens represented the dangerous fascination which the sea has always held for mankind. "Minerva" is the Roman goddess of war, and the protector of the craftsman. The pagan feast of Minerva in ancient Rome was held on March 19.

*Die Segelkorvette "S.M.S. Sirena" lief am 12. Oktober 1838 in Venedig vom Stapel. Sie hatte eine Einsatzverdrängung von 594 Tonnen, war aus Eichenholz gebaut, war mit vier 9 Pfundern sowie mit 16-36 Pfundern bewaffnet, und hatte eine Besatzung von 140 Offiziere und Matrosen. Am 19. November 1849 wurde sie als "S.M.S. Minerva" umbenannt, und sie wurde im Jahre 1893 (nach eine Dienstzeit von 55 Jahren) verschrottet. Minerva war eine heidnische römische Göttin des Krieges, und auch die Schutzerin von Handwerkern.*

## XIII (9) "S.M.S. Abbondanza" Class / "S.M.S. Abbondanza" Klasse (1828)

The wooden sailing corvette "S.M.S. Abbondanza" was launched in Venice on June 19, 1828. She displaced up to 430 tons full load, and was built out of oak. She was 34 meters long, and had a maximum beam of 6,9 meters. She was armed with 18-12 Pounders. In 1829, she was part of the "Morocco Division" of the

Imperial and Royal Austrian Navy, supporting Austrian naval infantry engaged in combating pirates. In 1831, she blockaded the insurgent city of Ancona on the Adriatic coast of Italy. She met her tragic end on the night of April 10, 1833. She was sailing back to Austria from Constantinople (now called "Istanbul" in Turkey). She was caught and stranded in a heavy storm by the Italian port of Brindisi. The ship was a total loss, but fortunately here entire crew was rescued.

*Die Segelkorvette "S.M.S. Abbondanza" lief am 19. Juni 1828 in Venedig vom Stapel, und war auch aus Eichenholz gebaut. Sie hatte eine Einsatzverdrängung von 430 Tonnen, war 34 Meter lang und hatte eine Breite von 6,9 Meter. Sie war mit 18-12 Pfundern bewaffnet. Im Jahre 1829 diente sie in der "Marokkodivision" der Kaiserlichen und Königlichen Kriegsmarine, die arabische Piraten bekämpfte. Im Jahre 1831 hat sie die feindliche Stadt Arcona im westlichen Adriatischen Meer blockiert. Die "S.M.S Abbondanza" strandete am 10. April 1833 in einem Sturm an der Küste von Brindisi. Das Schiff ging verloren, aber die ganze Besatzung wurde gerettet.*

### XIII (10) "S.M.S. Cesaria" Class / "S.M.S. Cesaria" Klasse (1829)

"S.M.S. Cesaria" was laid down in Venice in 1829, and launched on June 13, 1833. She was renamed as "S.M.S. Titania" on November 19, 1849, and stripped of her armament in 1859. She was used as a blockade ship in that year, and scuttled at the entrance to Venice harbor during armed hostilities in Italy. She was then raised and scrapped in 1860. She displaced up to 247 tons, which demonstrates just how small some old wooden sailing corvettes were. She was 28,6 meters long, and had a maximum beam of 7,3 meters. She was built out of oak, and her armament consisted of 10-12 Pounders. She was manned by a crew of 64 commissioned officers and enlisted men. The Italian word "Cesaria" means "Cesar," or "Emperor" in English. The German equivalent is "Kaiser," and the Russian word is "Czar." The Italian word "Titania" is "Titanic" in English. The Titans of Classical Mythology were the children of Uranos and Gaia, thus being the offspring of the first divine generation. This generation ruled, before Zeus and the Olympians took their power away from them. There were 13 Titans, being Hesiod, Kronos, Okeanos, Koios, Kreios, Hyperion, Iapetos, Theia, Themis, Mnemosyne, Phoibe, Tethys and Rheia.

*Die Segelkorvette "S.M.S. Cesaria" wurde in Venedig im Jahre 1829 auf Kiel gelegt, und lief am 13. Juni 1833 vom Stapel. Am 19. November 1849 wurde sie als "S.M.S. Titania" umbenannt. Sie wurde im Jahre 1859 als Blockadeschiff im Hafen von Venedig selbst versenkt, im Jahre 1860 geborgen und dann verschrottet. Sie hatte eine Einsatzverdrängung von nur 247 Tonnen, und war*

vielleicht die kleinste Segelkorvette der Kaiserlichen und Königlichen
Kriegsmarine. Sie war 28,6 Meter lang, hatte eine Breite von 7,3 Meter und war
aus Eichenholz gebaut. Sie war mit zehn 12-Pfundern bewaffnet, und hatte eine
Besatzung von 64 Offiziere und Matrosen. "Cesaria" ist auf deutsch "Kaiser."
"Titania" kommt aus der klaßischen Mythologie. Sie waren die Kinder von
Uranos und Gaia, und waren die erste Generation der heidnischen Götter. Die
13 Kinder von Uranos und Gaia waren die Herrscher der Welt, bevor sie von
Zeus und den Olympianern entmachtet wurden. Diese 13 Kinder hießen Hesiod,
Kronos, Okeanos, Koios, Kreios, Hyperion, Iapetos, Theia, Themis, Mnemosyne,
Phoibe, Tethys und Rheia.

### Chapter 13 (Kapitel 13): XIII (11) Smaller and Older Sailing Ships of the Austrian Navy / Kleinere und ältere Kriegsschiffe der Österreichischen Kriegsmarine

1.) "S.M.S. Pilade" was a wooden sailing brig launched in Venice on May 1, 1849. A brig was smaller than a contemporary corvette of its time, and this ship displaced up to 485 tons full load. She was renamed "S.M.S. Plyades" on November 19, 1849. She was converted into a transport vessel in 1861, and became just a hulk in 1868. She was scrapped in 1872. She was 32,4 meters long and had a maximum beam of 9,8 meters. She was built out of oak, and was armed with 4-12 Pounders plus 12-24 Pounders. She had a crew of 100 commissioned officers and enlisted men. The "Plyades" were the 7 sisters, who were the daughters of Atlas in pagan Greek mythology. Brigs were warships smaller than either wooden sailing frigates or wooden sailing corvettes. They had just 2 main masts, compared to frigates and corvettes, which had 3 main masts.

*Die größten Holzsegelschiffe der Kaiserlichen und Königlichen Kriegsmarine waren die Linienschiffe. Sie hatten eine Einsatzverdrängung zwischen 1,878 und 5,194 Tonnen. Danach kamen die Segelfregatten, die als moderne Schwere Kreuzer benutzt wurden. Die Segelfregatten der Kaiserlichen und Königlichen Kriegsmarine hatten eine Einsatzverdrängung von mindestens 420 Tonnen, und die größten davon waren größer als die kleinsten Linienschiffe. Nach den Segelfregatten kamen die Segelkorvetten, die als moderne Leichte Kreuzer benutzt wurden. Die Segelkorvetten der Kaiserlichen und Königlichen Kriegsmarine hatten eine Einsatzverdrängung von mindestens 247 Tonnen, und die größten davon waren größer als die kleinsten Segelfregatten. Nach den Segelkorvetten kamen die Segelbriggs des Adriatischen Meeres. Sie waren Hochsee-Segler zwischen 170 und 500 Tonnen, mit zwei Masten mit Rahsegeln und Gaffelsegel am Großmast. Die Segelbriggs der Kaiserlichen und Königlichen Kriegsmarine wurden als moderne Fregatten oder Zerstörer der Deutschen Marine benutzt. Das Segelbrigg "S.M.S. Pilade" lief am 1. Mai 1849 in Venedig vom Stapel. Sie hatte eine Einsatzverdrängung von 485 Tonnen, war aus Eichenholz gebaut, war 32,4 Meter lang und hatte eine Breite von 9,8 Meter. Sie war mit vier 12 Pfundern sowie mit 12-24 Pfundern bewaffnet. Die Besatzung des Schiffes war 100 Offiziere und Matrosen. Am 19. November 1849 wurde sie als "S.M.S. Plyades" umbenannt. Sie wurde im Jahre 1861 als Transportschiff umgebaut, im Jahre 1868 als Hulk umgebaut, und wurde im Jahre 1872 verschrottet. Die "Plyades" waren die sieben Töchter von Atlas aus der klassischen griechischen Mythologie.*

2.) "S.M.S. Fenice" was a wooden sailing "Galiot" (a sailing ship usually somewhat smaller than a brig, being narrow and fast by design) launched in Venice on March 26, 1812. At first, she was assigned to various duties including fleet, post (mail delivery), transport and guard. By 1829, she had been converted into a sailing brig. She was renamed "S.M.S. Usaro" on August 1, 1829, and immediately deployed to support Austrian naval infantry in Morocco – who were sent to North Africa to combat pirates. These Arab pirates had attacked commercial shipping, including from Austria. From 1836 to 1837, she transported Italian political refugees from the Austrian port of Triest (these unfortunate people likely came from North Central and Northwestern Italy) to safety in New York. In August of 1849, she was renamed as "S.M.S. Il Crociato" and again as "S.M.S. Hussar" on November 19, 1849. She then served in the fleet and as a training vessel, being retired in 1868 and scrapped in 1870. She displaced up to 462 tons full load, was built of oak, was 32 meters long and had a maximum beam of just 8,8 meters. Initially, she was armed with 16-12 Pounders; later, this was changed to 12-18 Pounders. Her crew consisted of 100 commissioned officers and enlisted men. "Hussars" were of course cavalrymen in the Imperial Austrian Army. The German name for this type of sailing vessel is "Goelette."

*Die Segelgoelette "S.M.S. Fenice" lief am 26. März 1812 in Venedig vom Stapel. Eine Segelgoelette ist ein Hochseeschiff kleiner als ein Segelbrigg gebaut, mit Schonertakelung und starkem Fall der Masten nach achtern. Die Bauart der Segelgoeletten war sehr schlank, und sie waren deswegen schnellere Segler. Die "S.M.S. Fenice" hatte eine Einsatzverdrängung von 462 Tonnen, war aus Eichenholz gebaut, war 32 Meter lang und hatte eine Breite von 8,8 Meter. Zuerst war sie mit 16-12 Pfundern bewaffnet; später war sie mit 12-18 Pfundern umgebaut. Die Besatzung des Schiffes bestand aus 100 Offiziere und Matrosen. Sie wurde am 1. August 1829 als "S.M.S. Usaro" umbenannt, und diente kurz danach an der Küste von Marokko, wo sie Österreichische Marineinfanteristen gegen arabische Piraten unterstüzte. Die arabischen Piraten haben Österreichische Handelsintereßen angegriffen. Zwischen 1836 und 1837 hat sie italienische politische Flüchtlinge von Triest nach Neu York gebracht. Im August 1849 wurde sie als "S.M.S. Il Crociato" umbenannt, und kurz danach am 19. November 1849 endlich als "S.M.S. Hussar" umbenannt. Sie wurde als Schulschiff benutzt, bis sie im Jahre 1870 verschrottet wurde. Die "Husaren" waren die berühmten Kavalleriesoldaten der Kaiserlichen und Königlichen Armee.*

3.) "S.M.S. San Marco" (Italian for "Saint Mark") was a wooden sailing brig launched in Venice on May 20, 1826. In 1827, she was upgraded to a corvette, and renamed "S.M.S. Adria." She displaced up to 450 tons full load, and was armed with 20-12 Pounders, 1-6 Pounder plus 4-1 Pounders. She was manned by a crew of 168 commissioned officers and enlisted men. She was built out of oak, had a length of 34,5 meters and a maximum beam of 9,1 meters. From 1828 to 1830, she was attached to the Morocco Division of the Imperial and Royal Austrian Navy, supporting Austrian Naval Infantry deployed to hunt down Arab pirates. In 1835, she took Italian political refugees from the Austrian port of Triest to safety in New York. In between 1848 and 1849, she partook in the Austrian naval blockade of Venice, when that Austrian port was occupied by revolutionary Italian nationalists. In 1852, she was down-graded to service as a floating coal hulk. She was finally scrapped in 1859.

*Das Segelbrigg "S.M.S. San Marco" lief am 20. Mai 1826 in Venedig vom Stapel. Im Jahre 1827 wurde sie als Segelkorvette umgebaut, und als "S.M.S. Adria" umbenannt. Eine Segelkorvette ist ein Hochseeschiff kleiner als eine Segelfregatte, jedoch mit deren Takelung. Es ist ein Vollschiff mit einfachen Marssegeln, Bram-und Oberbramsegeln, an Fock-oder Großmast nur Stag-, jedoch keine Graffelsegel, und mit etwa 18 Kanonen (Pfundern) bewaffnet. In der Adria und im Mittelmeer waren sie auch auf Riemenantrieb eingerichtet. Sie wurden als Aufklärungs-, Konvoi-und Kaperschiffe benutzt. Die "S.M.S. Adria" hatte eine Einsatzverdrängung von 450 Tonnen, war aus Eichenholz gebaut, war 34,5 Meter lang und hatte eine Breite von 9,1 Meter. Sie war mit 20-12 Pfundern sowie mit einem Sechs-Pfunder und vier Ein-Pfundern bewaffnet. Die Besatzung des Schiffes bestand aus 168 Offiziere und Matrosen. Zwischen 1828 und 1830 hat sie Österreichische Marineinfanteristen gegen arabischen Piraten an der Küste von Marokko unterstuzt. Im Jahre 1835 hat sie italienische politische Flüchtlinge von Triest nach Neu York gebracht. Zwischen 1848 und 1849 hat sie Venedig blockiert, als Venedig zur Zeit von italienischen Nationalisten übernommen wurde. Im Jahre 1852 wurde sie als Kohlenhulk umgebaut, und sie wurde endlich im Jahre 1859 verschrottet.*

4.) A sister ship of "S.M.S. San Marco" was the brig "S.M.S. Emo," launched in Venice on June 3, 1826. She was also converted and upgraded to a wooden sailing corvette in 1826. She was immediately renamed "S.M.S. Lipsia." In 1834, she transported Italian political refugees from the Austrian port of Triest to safety in New York. In between 1847 and 1848, she underwent repair work in the Austrian port of Venice. From March 1848 until August 1849, she was captured and used by revolutionary Italian nationalists under the new and temporary name "Independenza." She was then re-taken by the Austrians, and promptly renamed "S.M.S. Leipzig," after the great German city in the Kingdom of Saxony (an ally of Habsburg Austria). She was scrapped in 1860.

*Das Segelbrigg "S.M.S. Emo" war ein Schwesterschiff vom Segelbrigg "S.M.S. San Marco." Sie lief am 3. Juni 1826 in Venedig vom Stapel, wurde auch im Jahre 1826 als Segelkorvette umgebaut, und wurde bald danach als "S.M.S. Lipsia" umbenannt. Im Jahre 1834 hat sie italienische politische Flüchtlinge von Triest nach Neu York gebracht. Zwischen März 1848 und August 1849 wurde sie von feindlichen italienischen Nationalisten beschlagnahmt, und als die "Independenza" umbenannt. Im August 1849 wurde sie von den Österreichern befreit, und als die "S.M.S. Leipzig" umbenannt. Leipzig lag im Königreich Sachsen, das mit dem Kaiserreich Österreich verbündet war.*

5.) "S.M.S. Sparviero" was a wooden sailing brig. Construction in Venice commenced during 1805, and the vessel was launched as "S.M.S. Principessa Augusta" ("Princess Augusta" in English) on November 27, 1806. During the Napoleonic Wars, she partook in the Austrian naval blockade of the Italian city of Ancona, on the Adriatic coast. She was scrapped in 1836. For technical specifications, please see the end of the following paragraph under her sister ship "S.M.S. Otello."

*Das Segelbrigg "S.M.S. Sparviero" wurde in Venedig im Jahre 1805 auf Kiel gelegt, und lief am 27. November 1806 als "S.M.S. Principessa Augusta" vom Stapel. Sie hatte eine Einsatzverdrängung von 450 Tonnen, war aus Eichenholz gebaut, war 34 Meter lang und hatte eine Breite von 9,1 Meter. Sie war mit 18-9 Pfundern bewaffnet, und ihre Besatzung bestand aus 120 Offiziere und Matrosen. Zur Zeit der napoleonischen Kriege (bis 1815) hatte sie die feindliche Stadt Ancona an der westlichen Küste des Adriatischen Meeres blockiert. Sie wurde im Jahre 1836 verschrottet.*

6.) A sister ship to "S.M.S. Sparviero" was the wooden sailing brig "S.M.S. Otello." Her construction began in 1812 in Venice, and she was finally launched as "S.M.S. Veloce" in May of 1818. In 1827, she was converted into a sailing corvette. She was retired and reassigned to be a coal carrier in 1837, and finally scrapped by 1839. She displaced up to 450 tons full load, was 34 meters long and had a maximum beam of 9,1 meters. She was built out of oak, and was armed with 18-9 Pounders. Her crew consisted of 120 commissioned officers and enlisted men.

*Das Segelbrigg "S.M.S. Otello" war ein Schwesterschiff der "S.M.S. Sparviero." Sie wurde im Jahre 1812 in Venedig auf Kiel gelegt, und lief im Mai 1818 als die "S.M.S. Veloce" vom Stapel. Im Jahre 1827 wurde sie als Segelkorvette umgebaut. Sie wurde im Jahre 1837 als Kohlenhulk umgebaut, und dann im Jahre 1839 verschrottet.*

7.) The wooden sailing brig "S.M.S. Orione" displaced up to 391 tons. Her keel was laid in Venice in 1809, and she was launched on January 29, 1812. She was built of oak, was 29,3 meters long and had a maximum beam of 8,5 meters. Her armament consisted of 2-12 Pounders and 14-24 Pounders. She had a crew of 112 commissioned officers and enlisted men. She was renamed "S.M.S. Oreste" on October 27, 1832. From 1848 until 1849, she partook in the blockade of revolutionary nationalist forces in Venice. She was renamed yet again as "S.M.S. Orestes" on November 19, 1849, and was finally scrapped in 1856. In classical mythology, "Orion" was a very large hunter, and also the son of Poseidon. "Oreste" was the son of Agamemnon, and the brother of Elektra in pagan Greek mythology.

*Das Segelbrigg "S.M.S. Orione" wurde im Jahre 1809 in Venedig auf Kiel gelegt, und lief am 29. Januar 1812 vom Stapel. Sie hatte eine Einsatzverdrängung von 391 Tonnen, war aus Eichenholz gebaut, war 29,3 Meter lang und hatte eine Breite von 8,5 Meter. Sie war mit zwei 12 Pfundern sowie mit 14-24 Pfundern bewaffnet, und ihre Besatzung bestand aus 112 Offiziere und Matrosen. Am 27. Oktober 1832 wurde sie als die "S.M.S. Oreste" umbenannt. Zwischen 1848 und 1849 hat sie feindliche italienische Nationalisten an der Küste von Venedig blockiert. Am 19. November 1849 wurde sie als die "S.M.S. Orestes" umbenannt, und sie wurde im Jahre 1856 verschrottet (nach eine Dienstzeit von 44 Jahren). "Orion" war in der klaßischen heidnischen griechischen Mythologie ein großer Jäger, und auch der Sohn von Poseidon. "Oreste" war der Sohn von Agamemnon, und auch der Bruder von Elektra.*

8.) The wooden sailing brig "S.M.S. Montecuccoli" was a sister ship of "S.M.S. Orione," having been laid down in Venice in 1809. She was launched on March 22, 1817. In 1848 and 1849, she also partook in the blockade of revolutionary nationalist forces in Venice. She was retired as a hulk in 1868, and scrapped by 1872. "Montecuccoli" was a great noble ethnic Italian family from which many good Austrian naval officers came.

*Das Segelbrigg "S.M.S. Montecuccoli" war ein Schwesterschiff der "S.M.S. Orione." Sie wurde im Jahre 1809 in Venedig auf Kiel gelegt, und lief am 22. März 1817 vom Stapel. Zwischen 1848 und 1849 hatte sie auch feindliche italienische Nationalisten an der Küste von Venedig blockiert. Im Jahre 1868 wurde sie als Kohlenhulk umgebaut, und sie wurde endlich im Jahre 1872 verschrottet (nach einer Dienstzeit von 55 Jahren). Montecuccoli ist der Name einer bedeutenden aus dem Herzogtum Modena stammenden Familie. Stammsitz war die Burg Montecuccoli ("Kuckucksberg" auf deutsch) in Modena, Italien. Alfonso Montecuccoli war Admiral des Großherzogtums Toskana, der im Jahre*

*1607 eine kleine Kriegsflotte gegen die Türken geführt hat. Girolamo Montecuccoli (1583-1643) war Geheimkämmerer des Großherzogs von Toskana und Kommandant über dessen deutsche Leibgarde, und später Minister und Rat Leopolds V von Tirol. Ernesto Montecuccoli (1582-1633) war General des Heiligen Römischen Reiches der Deutschen Nation zur Zeit des Dreißigjährigen Krieges.*

## Raimondo Montecuccoli

*Raimondo Montecuccoli (1609-1680) war Österreichischer Generalfeldmarschall des Heiligen Römischen Reiches der Deutschen Nation, sowie Diplomat und Staatsmann. Leopold Philipp Fürst Montecuccoli (1662-1698) war ein kaiserlich-habsburgischer Feldmarschall-Leutnant (wie ein Generalleutnant des deutschen Heeres) des Heiligen Römischen Reiches der Deutschen Nation, und ein Sohn von Raimondo Montecuccoli. Rudolf Ludwig Raimund Heinrich Alfons Graf von Montecuccoli (1843-1922) war Admiral der Kaiserlichen und Königlichen Kriegsmarine sowie Flottenkommandant von 1904 bis 1913 (als Flottenkommandant war er der Nachfolger von Admiral Hermann Freiherr von Spaun).*

9.) The wooden sailing brig "S.M.S. Jena" was named for a German city in the region of Thuringia. This region was home to numerous Saxon duchies of the noble Wettin family. She displaced up to 390 tons, was 32 meters long and had a maximum beam of 8,8 meters. Her armament consisted of 2-12 Pounders and 14-24 Pounders. She had a crew of 112 commissioned officers and enlisted men. She was launched in Venice on November 25, 1806, and was renamed as "S.M.S. Veneto" in 1815. "Veneto" is the province of which the city of Venice is the capital. From 1828 until 1829, she was part of the "Morocco Division" of the Imperial and Royal Austrian Navy, providing support to Austrian naval infantry combating Arab pirates. In between 1848 and 1849, she partook in the Austrian naval blockade of revolutionary nationalist forces in Venice. On May 11, 1849, she was renamed yet again as "S.M.S. Pola," after the new Austrian naval base located in Croatia. She was retired as a hulk in 1868, and scrapped in 1870.

*Das Segelbrigg "S.M.S. Jena" lief am 25. November 1806 in Venedig vom Stapel. Sie hatte eine Einsatzverdrängung von 390 Tonnen, war 32 Meter lang, hatte eine Breite von 8,8 Meter und ihre Besatzung bestand aus 112 Offiziere und Matrosen. Die Bewaffnung des Schiffes war zwei 12 Pfundern sowie 14-24 Pfundern. Im Jahre 1815 wurde sie als die "S.M.S. Venento" umbenannt. Zwischen 1828 und 1829 diente sie bei der "Marokko-Division" der Kaiserlichen und Königlichen Kriegsmarine, um Österreichische Marineinfanteristen gegen arabische Piraten zu unterstützen. Zwischen 1848 und 1849 hat sie feindliche italienische Nationalisten an der Küste von Venedig blockiert. Am 11. Mai 1849 wurde sie als die "S.M.S. Pola" umbenannt. Sie wurde im Jahre 1868 als Kohlenhulk umgebaut, und wurde endlich im Jahre 1870 verschrottet (nach einer langen und guten Dienstzeit von 64 Jahren).*

10.) The wooden sailing brig "S.M.S. Indiano" was a sister ship of "S.M.S. Jena." She was launched in Venice during 1808, and severely damaged on a voyage within the Adriatic Sea on May 21, 1820. The navy was unable to salvage her to any useful degree, and therefore scrapped her by September of that same year.

*Das Segelbrigg "S.M.S. Indiano" war ein Schwesterschiff der "S.M.S. Jena." Sie lief im Jahre 1808 in Venedig vom Stapel, aber wurde am 21. Mai 1820 im Adriatischen Meer sehr schwer beschädigt. Leider war es nicht möglich das Schiff zu reparieren, und deswegen wurde es im September 1820 verschrottet.*

11.) The wooden sailing brig "S.M.S. Pallade" displaced up to 391 tons full load. She was built out of oak, was 32 meters long and had a maximum beam of 8,8 meters. Her armament consisted of 4-9 Pounders and 12-24 Pounders. She was manned by a crew of 100 commissioned officers and enlisted men. Her keel was laid down in Venice in 1834, and she was launched on October 16, 1838 as "S.M.S. Venezia" (the Italian word for "Venice"). Prior to her launching, she was actually renamed as "S.M.S. Pilade." She was assigned to Austrian fleet duties for the next 10 years, and was then renamed yet again as "S.M.S. Triest" on May 11, 1848. Triest was yet another very important Austrian Naval Base. From 1848 to 1849, she partook in the Austrian naval blockade of revolutionary nationalist forces in Venice. In 1849, she blockaded the Italian port city of Ancona for the same reason. She was sold to the breakers for scrapping in 1856.

*Das Segelbrigg "S.M.S. Pallade" wurde in Venedig im Jahre 1834 auf Kiel gelegt, und lief am 16. Oktober 1838 als die "S.M.S. Venezia" vom Stapel. Sie hatte eine Einsatzverdrängung von 391 Tonnen, war 32 Meter lang, hatte eine Breite von 8,8 Meter und eine Besatzung von 100 Offiziere und Matrosen. Die Bewaffnung des Schiffes bestand aus vier Neun-Pfundern sowie 12-24 Pfundern. Sie wurde 11. Mai 1848 als die "S.M.S. Triest" umbenannt. Zwischen 1848 und 1849 hat sie feindliche italienische Nationalisten an der Küste von Venedig sowie Ancona blockiert. Sie wurde im Jahre 1856 verschrottet.*

12.) "S.M.S. Tritone" was a sister ship of "S.M.S. Pallade." Her keel was laid down in Venice in 1834, and she was launched on April 30, 1836. She was assigned to Austrian fleet duties for the next 12 years, and was then renamed as

"S.M.S. San Marco" in August of 1849. On November 19, 1849, she renamed yet again as "S.M.S. Triton" (the German version of "Tritone"). She met her unfortunate end on May 9, 1859, when she was destroyed due to a munitions explosion in the Lacroma Canal in the Eastern Adriatic. Triton was the son of Poseidon and Amphitrite, half man and half fish (from pagan Greek mythology).

*Das Segelbrigg "S.M.S. Tritone" war ein Schwesterschiff der "S.M.S. Pallade." Sie wurde in Venedig im Jahre 1834 auf Kiel gelegt, und lief am 30. April 1836 vom Stapel. Im August 1849 wurde sie als die "S.M.S. San Marco" umbenannt, und am 19. November 1849 wurde sie wieder als die "S.M.S. Triton" umbenannt. Am 9. Mai 1859 wurde sie leider durch einen Explosionsunfall im Lacroma-Kanal in der östlichen Adria zerstört. In der heidnischen griechischen Mythologie war Triton der Sohn von Poseidon und Amphitrite. Triton war halb Mann und halb Fisch.*

13.) "S.M.S. Saida" (the Italian and the German name for the city of "Sidon" in Lebanon) was a wooden sailing "Galiot" ("Goelette" in German) which displaced up to 344 tons full load. She was built out of oak, was 28 meters long, and had a maximum beam of 8,4 meters. Her armament consisted of 6-30 Pounders, and she was manned by a crew of 68 commissioned officers and enlisted men. Her keel was laid down in Venice in 1852, and she was launched on March 24, 1855. She was assigned to numerous duties within the Imperial and Royal Austrian Navy, including as a "Station Ship," a training vessel and to a combat "Eskadré" (this is actually a French word; the German equivalent is "Geschwader," or "Squadron" in English). In 1872, she was upgraded to a wooden sailing brig. She met her unfortunate end on November 20, 1874, when she was stranded and wrecked in a storm on the Southern coast of Italy.

*Die Segelgoelette "S.M.S. Saida" wurde in Venedig im Jahre 1852 auf Kiel gelegt, und lief am 24. März 1855 vom Stapel. Sie hatte eine Einsatzverdrängung von 344 Tonnen, war aus Eichenholz gebaut, war 28 Meter lang, hatte eine Breite von 8,4 Meter und ihre Besatzung bestand aus 68 Offiziere und Matrosen. Die Bewaffnung des Schiffes bestand aus sechs 30 Pfundern. Im Jahre 1872 wurde sie als Segelbrigg umgebaut. Am 20. November 1874 strandete sie in einem Sturm an der südlichen Küste von Italien und ging verloren.*

14.) The wooden sailing battery "S.M.S. Mongibello" was laid down in Venice in 1835, and launched on October 14, 1844. She was retired in 1868, and converted into a floating hulk. She met her end on December 12, 1908, when she was assisting in recovery efforts for the new destroyer "S.M.S. Huszar." She was stranded in a storm in the Gulf of Cattaro, in the Southeastern Adriatic Sea. She displaced up to 268 tons, was 26 meters long, had a maximum beam of 8,1 meters and a maximum draught of 1,8 meters. She was constructed out of oak, and her armament consisted of 1-80 Pounder, 4-36 Pounders and 2-18 Pounders. She was manned by a crew of 53 commissioned officers and enlisted men.

*Die Segelbatterie "S.M.S. Mongibello" wurde in Venedig im Jahre 1835 auf Kiel gelegt, und lief am 14. Oktober 1844 vom Stapel. Sie hatte eine Einsatzverdrängung von 268 Tonnen, war aus Eichenholz gebaut, war 26 Meter lang, hatte eine Breite von 8,1 Meter und eine Besatzung von 53 Offiziere und Matrosen. Die Bewaffnung des Schiffes bestand aus vier 36 Pfundern sowie zwei 18 Pfundern. Im Jahre 1868 wurde sie als Kohlenhulk umgebaut. Am 12. Dezember 1908 strandete sie und ging verloren am Golf von Cattaro als sie versuchte der neue Zerstörer "S.M.S. Huszar" zu bergen.*

15.) A sister ship of "S.M.S. Mongibello" was "S.M.S. Vesuvio," named after an Italian volcano. She was also laid down in Venice in 1835, and launched on October 31, 1844. She was retired in 1868, and converted into a steam dredger in 1873. She was finally scrapped in 1915, after an impressive 80 years of service in the Austrian Navy.

*Die Segelbatterie "S.M.S. Vesuvio" war ein Schwesterschiff der "S.M.S. Mongibello." Sie wurde in Venedig im Jahre 1835 auf Kiel gelegt, und lief am 31. Oktober 1844 vom Stapel. Im Jahre 1873 wurde sie als Dampfbaggerschiff umgebaut. Sie wurde endlich im Jahre 1915 verschrottet – nach einer langen und guten Dienstzeit von 71 Jahren.*

16.) The wooden sailing battery "S.M.S. Fermo" was laid down in Venice in 1836, and launched on June 8, 1846. She was retired in 1868, and converted into a guard hulk. She was converted yet again into a coal carrier in 1877, and then into a pontoon crane vessel in 1887. She was finally scrapped in 1897. She displaced up to 251 tons, and was built out of oak. She was 23 meters long, and had a maximum beam of 8,5 meters. Her armament consisted of 2-36 Pounders, 8-18 Pounders and 8-3 Pounders. She was manned by a crew of 54 commissioned officers and enlisted men.

*Die Segelbatterie "S.M.S. Fermo" wurde in Venedig im Jahre 1836 auf Kiel gelegt, und lief am 8. Juni 1846 vom Stapel. Im Jahre 1868 wurde sie als Wachhulk umgebaut, und im Jahre 1877 wurde sie als Kohlenträger umgebaut. Sie wurde im Jahre 1897 verschrottet, nach einer Dienstzeit von 51 Jahren. Sie hatte eine Einsatzverdrängung von 251 Tonnen, war aus Eichenholz gebaut, war 23 Meter lang und hatte eine Breite von 8,5 Meter. Die Bewaffnung des Schiffes bestand aus zwei 36 Pfunder, acht 18 Pfunder und acht Drei-Pfunder. Sie hatte eine Besatzung von 54 Offiziere und Matrosen.*

17.) The sister ship of "S.M.S. Fermo" was "S.M.S. Forte," which was laid down in Venice in 1836. She was launched on July 8, 1846. She was retired in 1868, and converted into a hulk. The rest of her history was identical to that of her sister ship.

*Die Segelbatterie "S.M.S. Forte" war ein Schwesterschiff der "S.M.S. Fermo." Sie wurde in Venedig im Jahre 1836 auf Kiel gelegt, und lief am 8. Juni 1846 vom Stapel. Sie wurde auch im Jahre 1868 als Hulk umgebaut, und wurde auch im Jahre 1897 verschrottet.*

18.) "S.M.S. Dragone" was a wooden sailing "Galiot" (the German word for this type of vessel is "Goelette"), built of oak and displacing up to 214 tons. Her keel was laid down in Venice in 1806, and she was launched on July 26, 1808. She was actually taken by Austria from the Italians, where she had the name "Volteggiatore." She was originally part of the Italian Adriatic Division, and was taken over by Austria on April 25, 1814, at which time she became an Imperial Yacht for the Habsburg Monarch. In 1819, she was renamed as "S.M.S. Cesaria," and she was scrapped by 1829. She was 27,6 meters long, and had a maximum beam of 6,9 meters. Her armament consisted of 10-6 Pounders, and she was manned by a crew of 62 commissioned officers and enlisted men. "Dragone" is the Italian word for "dragon" in English, or "Drache" in German.

*Die Segelgoelette "S.M.S. Dragone" wurde in Venedig im Jahre 1806 auf Kiel gelegt, und lief am 26. Juli 1808 vom Stapel. Sie hatte eine Einsatzverdrängung von 214 Tonnen, war aus Eichenholz gebaut, war 27,6 Meter lang und hatte eine Breite von 6,9 Meter. Die Bewaffnung des Schiffes bestand aus zehn Sechs Pfundern, und sie hatte eine Besatzung von 62 Offiziere und Matrosen. Sie wurde von feindlichen italienischen Nationalisten beschlagnahmt, und als die "Volteggiatore" umbenannt. Als sie von den Österreichern am 25. April 1814 befreit wurde, wurde sie als die Kaiserliche und Königliche Jacht umgebaut. Im Jahre 1819 wurde sie als die "S.M.S. Cesaria" umbenannt, und sie wurde im Jahre 1829 verschrottet.*

19.) A sister ship of "S.M.S. Dragone" was "S.M.S. Fenice." Her keel was laid down in 1811 in Venice, and she was launched on March 26, 1812. She was originally Italian, having been taken over by the Imperial and Royal Austrian Navy on April 25, 1814. She was assigned to fleet, postal (mail delivery), transport and guard duties over the course of her career. In 1829, she was converted into a wooden sailing brig. She was renamed "S.M.S. Ussaro" on August 1, 1829, and immediately attached to the Austrian Morocco Division, supporting Austrian Naval Infantry sent to combat Arab pirates. This lasted until 1830. From 1836 until 1837, she joined other Austrian naval vessels in transporting Italian political refugees from the Austrian port of Triest to safety in New York. In March of 1848, she was renamed as "Il Crociato" in the service of revolutionary nationalist Italians who temporarily captured her from the Austrian Navy. This did not last long, and upon her return to Austria, she was renamed yet again as "S.M.S. Hussar" on November 19, 1849. She served for many years as a training vessel in the Austrian Navy, being retired in 1868 and scrapped in 1870. A "Hussar" was a cavalryman in the Imperial and Royal Austrian Army.

*Die Segelgoelette "S.M.S. Fenice" war ein Schwesterschiff der "S.M.S. Dragone." Sie wurde in Venedig im Jahre 1811 auf Kiel gelegt, und lief am 26. März 1812 vom Stapel. Sie wurde auch von feindlichen italienischen Nationalisten beschlagnahmt, und wurde auch am 25. April 1814 von den Österreichern wieder befreit. Im Jahre 1829 wurde sie als die "S.M.S. Ussaro" umbenannt, und diente bei der "Marokko-Division" der Kaiserlichen und Königlichen Kriegsmarine, wo sie Österreichische Marineinfanteristen gegen arabische Piraten unterstützt hatte. Zwischen 1836 und 1837 hat sie italienische politische Flüchtlinge von Triest nach Neu York gebracht. Im Jahre 1848 wurde sie wieder von feindlichen italienischen Nationalisten beschlagnahmt, und als die "Il Crociato" umbenannt. Nach ihrer zweiten Befreiung durch die Österreicher, wurde sie am 19. November 1849 als die "S.M.S. Hussar" umbenannt. Dann wurde sie als Schulschiff benutzt, bevor sie im Jahre 1870 verschrottet wurde – nach einer Dienstzeit von 58 Jahren.*

20.) Yet another sister ship of "S.M.S. Dragone" was "S.M.S. Sfinge." Her keel was laid down in Venice in 1829, and she was launched on July 15 of that same year. She was immediately assigned to fleet and postal delivery duties within the Imperial and Royal Austrian Navy. Between 1848 and 1849, she partook in the Austrian naval blockade of revolutionary nationalist forces in Venice. In August of 1849, she was renamed as "S.M.S. Sfinx," and reassigned back to the Austrian fleet. She was converted into a coal hulk in 1854, and scrapped by 1860. This ship was of course named after the Sphinx of Egypt, a kingly symbol of a half-man, half-lion beast. In Classical Mythology, the Sphinx was the offspring of yet another hybrid beast.

*Die Segelgoelette "S.M.S. Sfinge" war das zweite Schwesterschiff der "S.M.S. Dragone." Sie lief am 15. Juli 1829 in Venedig vom Stapel. Zwischen 1848 und 1849 hatte sie feindliche italienische Nationalisten an der Küste von Venedig blockiert. Im Jahre 1849 wurde sie als die "S.M.S. Sfinx" umbenannt. Sie wurde im Jahre 1854 als Kohlenhulk umgebaut, und wurde im Jarhe 1860 verschrottet.*

21.) Still another sister ship of "S.M.S. Dragone" was "S.M.S. Vigilante." Her keel was laid down in Venice in 1837, and her planned name was changed to "S.M.S. Virtuosa" in 1839. From March 1848 until August 1849, she was captured by revolutionary nationalist forces in Venice, but not completed. In August 1849, she was finally retaken by her original Austrian owners. Her planned name was changed yet again to "S.M.S. Aretina" on November 18, 1849, and she was finally launched into active service as "S.M.S. Arethusa" on November 4, 1850. She served as both a station and as a training vessel in the Imperial and Royal Austrian Navy before her retirement in 1882. She was then used and sunk as a target vessel for Torpedoboot V (i.e., the fifth torpedo boat to be commissioned into the Austrian Navy) on September 16, 1882 – after which she was raised and scrapped. The names of this ship went first from "vigilante" to "the virtuous one." "Arethusa" was a beautiful Nymph (a well-woman of Classical Mythology), being the daughter of Atlas. One day as she was bathing in a river, the pagan god Alpheios of that river fell in love with her. Arethusa fled from the river, and sought refuge with the goddess Artemis on the Island of Ortygia. Alpheios then changed himself into a river, and followed Arethusa through the sea so that he could be with his beloved.

*Die Segelgoelette "S.M.S. Vigilante" war das dritte Schwesterschiff der "S.M.S. Dragone." Sie wurde im Jahre 1837 in Venedig auf Kiel gelegt, und lief endlich am 4. November 1850 als die "S.M.S. Arethusa" am Stapel. Sie wurde als Schulschiff benutzt, bevor sie als Zielschiff am 16. September 1882 benutzt wurde. Sie wurde von dem Torpedoboot V (das fuenfte Torpedoboot der Kaiserlichen und Königlichen Kriegsmarine) torpediert – nachdem sie geborgen und verschrottet wurde. Arethusa war eine schöne Nymphe der klaßischen heidnischen Mythologie. Sie war auch die Tochter von Atlas. Eines Tages badete sie im Fluß, als sich der heidnische Gott Alpheois in sie verliebte. Arethusa ist dann sofort geflohen, um sich mit der Göttin Artemis auf der Insel Ortygia zu verstecken. Alpheios ist nach seiner Verliebten Arethusa gelaufen, und ist selbst ein Fluß geworden um mit ihr zu sein.*

22.) "S.M.S. Enrichetta" was a wooden sailing Galiot ("Goelette" in German), laid down in Venice in 1825. She was launched on April 7, 1826. From 1828 to 1829, she was part of the Morocco Division of the Imperial and Royal Austrian Navy, sent to help Austrian naval infantry in combating Arab pirates. Thereafter, she was reassigned to fleet, postal delivery and customs duties. She was scrapped in 1845. She was 27,3 meters long, and had a maximum beam of 6,8 meters. Her armament consisted of 14-12 Pounders, and she was manned by a crew of 87 commissioned officers and enlisted men. She was constructed out of oak, she displaced up to 207 tons and her name of course is a girl's first name.

*Die Segelgoelette "S.M.S. Enrichetta" wurde im Jahre 1825 in Venedig auf Kiel gelegt, und lief am 7. April 1826 vom Stapel. Sie hatte eine Einsatzverdrängung von 207 Tonnen, war aus Eichenholz gebaut, war 27,3 Meter lang und hatte eine Breite von 6,8 Meter. Die Bewaffnung des Schiffes bestand aus 14-12 Pfundern, und sie hatte eine Besatzung von 87 Offiziere und Matrosen. Zwischen 1828 und 1829 diente sie bei der "Marokko-Division" der Kaiserlichen und Königlichen Kriegsmarine, um Österreichische Marineinfanteristen gegen arabische Piraten zu unterstützen. Sie wurde im Jahre 1845 verschrottet.*

23.) "S.M.S. Elisabetta" was a wooden sailing Galiot ("Goelette" in German) laid down in Venice in 1826, and launched on August 4, 1826. She was immediately assigned to fleet, postal delivery and station duties within the Imperial and Royal Austrian Navy. In 1849, she partook in the Austrian naval blockade of revolutionary nationalist rebels in Venice. In August 1849, her name was Germanized to "S.M.S. Elisabeth" in honor of the new Empress of Austria, Elizabeth of Bavaria (the wife of Emperor Franz Josef I of Habsburg-Lothringen). She then served as a training ship, until she was retired in 1857. Thereafter, she was used as a coal hulk until being scrapped sometime after 1860. She displaced up to 206 tons, was built out of oak, was 27,3 meters long and had a maximum beam of 6,8 meters. Her armament consisted of 8-12 Pounders, and she was manned by a crew of 63 commissioned officers and enlisted men.

*Die Segelgoelette "S.M.S. Elisabetta" wurde im Jahre 1826 in Venedig auf Kiel gelegt, und lief am 4. August 1826 vom Stapel. Sie hatte eine Einsatzverdrängung von 206 Tonnen, war aus Eichenholz gebaut, war 27,3 Meter lang, und hatte eine Breite von 6,8 Meter. Die Bewaffung des Schiffes bestand aus acht 12 Pfundern, und sie hatte eine Besatzung von 63 Offiziere und Matrosen. Im Jahre 1849 hat sie feindliche italienische Nationalisten an der Küste von Venedig blockiert. Im August 1849 wurde sie als "S.M.S. Elisabeth," nach der neuen Kaiserin Österreichs, umbenannt. Sie wurde dann als Schulschiff benutzt, und wurde im Jahre 1860 verschrottet.*

24.) "S.M.S. Bravo" was a wooden brig-schooner laid down in Venice in 1833, and launched on June 30, 1834. She was immediately assigned to tender and postal delivery duties within the Imperial and Royal Austrian Navy. She was upgraded into a full brig in 1842, and was briefly captured by rebellious Italian nationalist forced in Venice from March 1848 until August 1849. Upon her return to the Austrian Navy, she became a training vessel. She lived a long and productive life, only being scrapped in 1903 after an impressive 70 years of service in the Austrian Navy. She was built out of oak, was 25 meters long and had a maximum beam of 7 meters. Her armament consisted of 2-1 Pounders and 6-8 Pounders. She was manned by a crew of 46 commissioned officers and enlisted men, and had a maximum displacement of 200 tons.

*Der Segelbriggschooner "S.M.S. Bravo" wurde im Jahre 1833 in Venedig auf Kiel gelegt, und lief am 30. Juni 1834 vom Stapel. Sie hatte eine Einsatzverdrängung von 200 Tonnen, war aus Eichenholz gebaut, war 25 Meter lang und hatte eine Breite von 7 Meter. Die Bewaffnung des Schiffes bestand aus zwei Ein-Pfundern und sechs Acht-Pfundern, und sie hatte eine Besatzung von 46 Offiziere und Matrosen. Im Jahre 1842 wurde sie als Segelbrigg umgebaut. Zwischen März 1848 und August 1849 wurde sie von feindlichen italienischen Nationalisten beschlagnahmt. Nach ihrer Befreiung wurde sie als Schulschiff der Kaiserlichen und Königlichen Kriegsmarine benutzt. Sie wurde erst im Jahre 1903 verschrottet, nach einer langen und guten Dienstzeit von 69 Jahren.*

25.) A sister ship of "S.M.S. Bravo" was "S.M.S. Dromedario." She was laid down in Venice in 1836, and was launched on April 15, 1837. She was immediately assigned to tender duties within the Imperial and Royal Austrian Navy (supplying other warships, that is). She was upgraded into a full brig in 1845. In between 1848 and 1849, she partook in the Austrian naval blockade of Italian nationalist rebels in Venice. On November 19, 1849 she was renamed "S.M.S. Dromedar." She returned to being a wooden sailing tender, and was retired in 1877. Thereafter, she served as a coal hulk until she was finally scrapped in 1893 after 57 years of service in the Austrian Navy.

*Der Segelbriggschooner "S.M.S. Dromedario" war ein Schwesterschiff der "S.M.S. Bravo." Sie wurde im Jahre 1836 in Venedig auf Kiel gelegt, und lief am 15. April 1837 vom Stapel. Im Jahre 1845 wurde als Segelbrigg umgebaut. Zwischen 1848 und 1849 hat sie feindliche italienische Nationalisten an der Küste von Venedig blockiert. Am 19. November 1849 wurde sie als die "S.M.S. Dromedar" umbenannt. Danach wurde sie als Versorgungsschiff benutzt, und sie wurde erst im Jahre 1893 verschrottet – nach einer Dienstzeit von 56 Jahren.*

26.) "S.M.S. Madonna dell'Assunta" was an armed wooden sailing merchantman, originally belonging to the Woinowich Shipping Company of Triest. On December 15, 1759 she commenced operations as a merchant raider against the navy of Brandenburg-Prussia, the most powerful German state after her native Austria. She was damaged in this role in 1760, and thereafter returned to her original civilian owners. She was built out of oak, displaced up to 200 tons, and was armed with between 6 and 8 guns. She was named after the Assumption of the Blessed Virgin Mary into Heaven, or the fourth Glorious Mystery of the Rosary.

*Das Hilfssegelschiff "S.M.S. Madonna dell'Assunta" war nur vom 15. Dezember 1759 bis irgendwann im Jahre 1760 im Dienst der Kaiserlichen und Königlichen Kriegsmarine. Sie gehörte der Reederei Woinowich aus Triest, und wurde im Handelskrieg gegen Brandenburg-Preußen benutzt. Sie hatte eine Einsatzverdrängung von 200 Tonnen, und war mit sechs bis acht Kanonen bewaffnet. Sie wurde nach der Annahme der Gesegneten Jungfrau Maria (das vierte prachtvolle Geheimnis des Rosenkranzes) benannt.*

27.) "S.M.S. Artemisia" was a wooden sailing Galiot ("Goelette" in German) laid down in Venice in 1839, and launched on September 15, 1851. Upon her commissioning into the Imperial and Royal Austrian Navy, her name was altered somewhat to "S.M.S. Arthemisia." She was immediately assigned to both fleet and training duties. In 1866, she was converted into an ammunition hulk. Surprisingly, she was upgraded into a full wooden sailing brig in 1869. She was then used as a training vessel for young naval cadets until her retirement and scapping in 1902. She was built out of oak, displaced up to 185 tons, was 26 meters long, had a maximum beam of 7,5 meters and was armed with 1-18 Pounder plus 8-12 Pounders. Her crew consisted of 69 commissioned officers and enlisted men. Arthemisia was the daughter of Zeus and Leto, and the twin sister of Apollon from Classical Mythology. The author Homer described her as the "sovereign of the animals," and as the "Lioness of Women." She also represented motherhood and fertility. Her famous pagan temple is located in Ephesus.

*Die Segelgoelette "S.M.S. Artemesia" wurde im Jahre 1839 in Venedig auf Kiel gelegt, und lief am 15. September 1851 als die "S.M.S. Arthemisia" vom Stapel. Sie hatte eine Einsatzverdrängung von 185 Tonnen, war aus Eichenholz gebaut, war 26 Meter lang und hatte eine Breite von 7,5 Meter. Die Bewaffnung des Schiffes bestand aus einem 18 Pfunder sowie acht 12 Pfundern, und sie hatte eine Besatzung von 69 Offiziere und Matrosen. Im Jahre 1866 wurde sie als Munitionshulk umgebaut, und dann im Jahre 1869 wurde sie als Segelbrigg umgebaut. Danach wurde sie als Schulschiff benutzt, bis sie im Jahre 1902 verschrottet wurde – nach einer Dienstzeit von 51 Jahren. Arthemisia war die Tochter von Zeus und Leto, und der Zwilling von Apollon aus der klassischen Mythologie.*

28.) "S.M.S. Delfino" was a wooden brig-schooner laid down in Venice in 1834 and launched on May 21, 1835. She was immediately assigned to tender and postal delivery duties within the Imperial and Royal Austrian Navy. She was then upgraded into a full wooden sailing brig in 1845. She was renamed as "S.M.S. Delphin" on November 19, 1849 and spent the rest of her naval career as a training vessel. She was finally sold to the breakers in 1856. She displaced up to 181 tons, was built out of oak, was 24,9 meters long and had a maximum beam of 6,8 meters. Her armament consisted of 4-6 Pounders and 6-12 Pounders. She was manned by a crew of 56 commissioned officers and enlisted men. Her name means "dolphin" in English (she had the Italian name from 1835 until 1849, and the German name thereafter).

*Der Segelbriggschooner "S.M.S. Delfino" wurde im Jahre 1834 in Venedig auf Kiel gelegt, und lief am 21. Mai 1835 vom Stapel. Sie hatte eine Einsatzverdrängung von 181 Tonnen, war aus Eichenholz gebaut, war 24,9 Meter lang und hatte eine Breite von 7,5 Meter. Die Bewaffnung des Schiffes bestand aus vier Sechs Pfundern sowie Sechs 12 Pfundern, und sie hatte eine Besatzung von 56 Offiziere und Matrosen. Im Jahre 1845 wurde sie als Segelbrigg umgebaut, und am 19. November 1849 wurde sie als die "S.M.S. Delphin" umbenannt. Danach wurde sie als Schulschiff benutzt, bis sie im Jahre 1856 verschrottet wurde.*

29.) "S.M.S. Camäleonte" was a wooden brig-schooner laid down in Venice in 1832 and launched on July 6, 1833. She was immediately assigned to tender and postal delivery duties within the Imperial and Royal Austrian Navy. In 1845, she was upgraded into a full wooden sailing brig. In between March of 1848 and August of 1849, she was captured by revolutionary nationalist rebels in Italy. Thereafter, she was retaken by her own Austrian forces. On November 19, 1849, her name was Germanized to "S.M.S. Chamäleon." The English translation is "chameleon," which is a type of lizard. For the remainder of her career, she was used as a training vessel. She was finally scrapped in 1905, after an impressive 73 years of service in the Austrian Navy. She displaced up to 168 tons, was built out of oak, was 23,4 meters long and had a maximum beam of 6,7 meters. Her armament consisted of 4-6 Pounders and 6-12 Pounders. She was manned by a crew of 56 commissioned officers and enlisted men.

*Der Segelbriggschooner "S.M.S. Camäleonte" wurde im Jahre 1832 in Venedig auf Kiel gelegt, und lief am 6. Juli 1833 vom Stapel. Sie hatte eine Einsatzverdrängung von 168 Tonnen, war aus Eichenholz gebaut, war 23,4 Meter lang und hatte eine Breite von 6,7 Meter. Die Bewaffnung des Schiffes bestand aus vier Sechs Pfundern sowie sechs 12 Pfundern, und sie hatte eine Besatzung von 56 Offiziere und Matrosen. Im Jahre 1845 wurde sie als Segelbrigg umgebaut. Zwischen März 1848 und August 1849 wurde sie von feindlichen italienischen Nationalisten beschlagnahmt. Als sie wieder österreichisch würde, wurde sie am 19. November 1849 als die "S.M.S. Chamäleon" umbenannt. Danach wurde sie als Schulschiff benutzt, bis sie im Jahre 1905 verschrottet wurde – nach einer langen und guten Dienstzeit von 72 Jahren.*

30.) The sister ship of "S.M.S. Camäleonte" was "S.M.S. Fido." Her keel was laid down in Venice in 1833, and she was launched on August 23, 1834. She was also assigned to tender and postal delivery duties within the Imperial and Royal Austrian Navy, and was similarly upgraded into a full wooden sailing brig in 1845. Her career was considerably shorter than that of her sister ship, being scrapped in 1868. "Fido" is merely the Italian word for "loyal" in English or "treu" in German.

*Der Segelbriggschooner "S.M.S. Fido" war ein Schwesterschiff der "S.M.S. Camäleonte." Sie wurde im Jahre 1833 in Venedig auf Kiel gelegt, und lief am 23. August 1834 vom Stapel. Im Jahre 1845 wurde sie als Segelbrigg umgebaut, und sie wurde im Jahre 1868 verschrottet. "Fido" ist auf deutsch "treu."*

31.) "S.M.S. Divina Providenza" was a wooden sailing "Trabaccolo" ("Trabakel" in German). This type of ship was a robust sort of smaller sailing vessel, mainly built for transport duties. She was a civilian vessel temporarily taken into the Imperial and Royal Austrian Navy from 1802 until 1806. She went back to her civilian life in February 1806. She was built out of oak and displaced up to 112 tons. While in naval service, she was armed with 2-12 Pounders and 2-6 Pounders. Her crew consisted of 27 officers and men. Her name means "Divine Providence" in English.

*Das Segeltrabakel "S.M.S. Divina Providenza" war ein Handelsschiff, das zwischen 1802 und 1806 in der Kaiserlichen und Königlichen Kriegsmarine diente. Sie hatte eine Einsatzverdrängung von 112 Tonnen, war aus Eichenholz gebaut, und hatte eine Besatzung von 27 Offiziere und Matrosen. Die Bewaffnung des Schiffes bestand aus zwei 12 Pfundern sowie zwei Sechs Pfundern. Das Segeltrabakel war ein robust gebautes kleineres Segelfahrzeug fuer Transportzwecke, mit zwei Masten mit Lateinsegeln und zwei Klüvern, für weite Reisen zusätzlich Rahsegel am Fockmast. Das Segeltrabakel war das gebräuchlichste Segelfahrzeug der Adria-Küstenfahrt, mit einer Einsatzverdrängung zwischen 15 und 115 Tonnen. Bei der Kaiserlichen und Königlichen Kriegsmarine waren sie zur Versorgung der heimischen Küstenstationen und Schiffsabteilungen im Ausland benutzt.*

32.) "S.M.S. Camello" was a wooden sailing "Trabaccolo" ("Trabakel" in German) built and launched in Venice in 1804. She served as a transport vessel from 1805 until 1809, and was then sold to civilian owners. She displaced up to 111 tons, was built out of oak, and was armed with 4 guns (2-18 Pounders and 2-6 Pounders). Her crew consisted of 27 officers and men.

*Das Segeltrabakel "S.M.S. Camello" lief im Jahre 1804 in Venedig vom Stapel. Sie hatte eine Einsatzverdrängung von 111 Tonnen, und war aus Eichenholz gebaut. Die Bewaffnung des Schiffes bestand aus zwei 18 Pfundern sowie zwei Sechs Pfundern, und sie hatte eine Besatzung von 27 Offiziere und Matrosen. Im Jahre 1809 wurde sie verkauft.*

33.) "S.M.S. La Lippa" was a wooden sailing "Trabaccolo" ("Trabakel" in German). She was laid down in Venice in 1820, and launched on October 25, 1821. On November 26 of the same year, she was renamed as "S.M.S. Dromedario." She was assigned to transport duties within the Imperial and Royal Austrian Navy, and was scrapped in 1837. She was built out of oak, displaced up to 110 tons, was 24,7 meters long and had a maximum beam of 6,2 meters. She was unarmed, and had a crew of 24 officers and men.

*Das Segeltrabakel "S.M.S. La Lippa" wurde im Jahre 1820 in Venedig auf Kiel gelegt, und lief am 25. Oktober 1821 vom Stapel. Am 26. November 1821 wurde sie als die "S.M.S. Dromedario" umbenannt. Sie hatte eine Einsatzverdrängung von 110 Tonnen, war aus Eichenholz gebaut, war 24,7 Meter lang und hatte eine Breite von 6,2 Meter. Sie hatte keine Bewaffnung, und hatte eine Besatzung von 24 Offiziere und Matrosen. Sie wurde im Jahre 1837 verschrottet.*

34.) "S.M.S. Bravo" was a wooden sailing "Trabaccolo" ("Trabakel" in German). She was purchased from civilian owners in 1800, and served as a transport vessel in the Imperial and Royal Austrian Navy until 1809, when she was sold back to civilian owners. She displaced up to 102 tons, was built out of oak, and was armed with 6 guns (2-14 Pounders and 4-9 Pounders). Her crew consisted of 50 commissioned officers and enlisted men. "Bravo" is the Italian word for "brave," "clever," "smart," "skilled," "nice" or "well done" in English. Today, this would be considered to be a small vessel. Even when she was new, she was a small naval vessel. But many hundreds of years ago, the famous English wooden sailing battleship "H.M.S. Golden Hind" had the exact same displacement as the Austrian "S.M.S. Bravo" when the former circumnavigated the globe from 1577 to 1580. The English vessel had a crew of 70, was 31 meters long, had a beam of 6 meters and a draught of 2,7 meters. She was armed with 18 guns and could make up to 3 knots under good conditions.

*Das Segeltrabakel "S.M.S. Bravo" wurde im Jahre 1800 von der Kaiserlichen und Königlichen Kriegsmarine gekauft, und im Jahre 1809 wieder verkauft. Sie hatte eine Einsatzverdrängung von 102 Tonnen, war aus Eichenholz gebaut, und hatte eine Besatzung von 50 Offiziere und Matrosen. Die Bewaffnung des Schiffes bestand aus zwei 14 Pfundern sowie vier Neun Pfundern. "Bravo" ist auf deutsch "brav." Heutzutage ist ein Schiff (oder Boot) von einer 102 Tonnen Einsatzverdrängung ziemlich klein. Als das englische Linienschiff "H.M.S. Golden Hind" in den Jahren zwischen 1577 bis 1580 eine Weltumsegelung machte, war es genauso groß (oder klein) wie das österreichische Segeltrabakel "S.M.S. Bravo von 1800. Das englische Linienschiff "S.M.S. Golden Hind" hatte eine Einsatzverdrängung von 102 Tonnen, war 31 Meter lang, hatte eine Breite von 6 Meter und ein Tiefgang von 2,7 Meter. Sie war mit 18 Kanonen bewaffnet, hatte eine Besatzung von 70 Offiziere und Matrosen, und ihre Höchstgeschwindigkeit (nur mit Segel) war 3 Knoten.*

35.) "S.M.S. Dromedario" was a wooden sailing "Trabaccolo" ("Trabakel" in German). She was purchased from civilian owners in 1804, and served as a transport vessel in the Imperial and Royal Austrian Navy until 1809, when she was sold back to civilian owners. She displaced up to 90 tons, was built out of oak, and was armed with 4 guns (2-12 Pounders and 2-6 Pounders). Her crew consisted of 27 commissioned officers and enlisted men, and her name refers to a type of animal.

*Das Segeltrabakel "S.M.S. Dromedario" wurde im Jahre 1804 von der Kaiserlichen und Königlichen Kriegsmarine gekauft, und im Jahre 1809 wieder verkauft. Sie hatte eine Einsatzverdrängung von 90 Tonnen, war aus Eichenholz gebaut, und hatte eine Besatzgung von 27 Offiziere und Matrosen. Die Bewaffnung des Schiffes bestand aus zwei 12 Pfundern sowie zwei Sechs Pfundern.*

36.) "S.M.S. San Andrea" was a wooden sailing "Trabaccolo" ("Trabakel" in German). She was purchased from civilian owners in 1802, and served as a transport vessel in the Imperial and Royal Austrian Navy until February 5, 1806, when she was sold to Italy. She displaced up to 89 tons, was built out of oak, and was unarmed. Her name translates to "Saint Andrew" in English, "Sankt Andreas" in German or "San Andrés" in Spanish.

*Das Segeltrabakel "S.M.S. San Andrea" wurde im Jahre 1802 von der Kaiserlichen und Königlichen Kriegsmarine gekauft, und am 5. Februar 1806 wieder verkauft. Sie hatte eine Einsatzverdrängung von 89 Tonnen, war aus Eichenholz gebaut, und hatte keine Bewaffnung.*

37.) "S.M.S. Calypso" was a wooden sailing cannon-sloop ("Kanonierschaluppe" in German) laid down in Venice in 1831, and launched on May 24, 1832. She was briefly captured by rebellious nationalist troops in Venice from March of 1848 until August of 1849, and then returned to the Imperial and Royal Austrian Navy. The remainder of her naval career was uneventful, being scrapped by 1858. She displaced up to 81 tons, was built out of oak, was 19,5 meters long, had a maximum beam of 5,1 meters and a draught of 2,2 meters. She was armed with 7 guns, including 1-24 Pounder, 4-4 Pounders and 2-3 Pounders. Her crew consisted of 33 commissioned officers and enlisted men.

*Die Segelkanonierschaluppe "S.M.S. Calypso" wurde im Jahre 1831 in Venedig auf Kiel gelegt, und lief am 24. Mai 1832 vom Stapel. Sie hatte eine Einsatzverdrängung von 81 Tonnen, war aus Eichenholz gebaut, war 19,5 Meter lang, hatte eine Breite von 5,1 Meter und ein Tiefgang von 2,2 Meter. Die Bewaffnung des Schiffes bestand aus einem 24 Pfunder, vier Vier Pfundern sowie zwei Drei Pfundern, und sie hatte eine Besatzung von 33 Offiziere und Matrosen. Sie wurde zwischen März 1848 und August 1849 von feindlichen italienischen Nationalisten beschlagnahmt, und wurde im Jahre 1858 verschrottet. Die Segelkanonierschaluppe war ein Ruderkanonenboot mit Hilfsbesegelung, infolge starker Bauart mit langer Lebensdauer. Sie war auch ein flaches und niedriges Seefahrzeug nach spanischem Muster, mit einem durchgehenden Oberdeck, ein Mast mit Gaffelsegel, manchmal mit Rahsegel und einem kleinen Yawlmast achtern, später nur mit Lateinsegel.*

38.) "S.M.S. Costanza" was sister ship of "S.M.S. Calypso." She was laid down in Venice in 1832, and launched on October 13th of that same year. Her career was uneventful, being scrapped by 1857.

*Die Segelkanonierschaluppe "S.M.S. Costanza" war ein Schwesterschiff der "S.M.S. Calypso." Sie wurde im Jahre 1832 in Venedig auf Kiel gelegt, und lief am 13. Oktober 1832 vom Stapel. Sie wurde im Jahre 1857 verschrottet, nach einer Dienstzeit von 25 Jahren.*

39.) "S.M.S. Viennese" was a sister ship of both "S.M.S. Calypso" and "S.M.S. Costanza." She was laid down in Venice in 1832, and launched on November 13th of that same year. She was briefly captured by revolutionary nationalist rebels in Venice from March of 1848 until August of 1849, and then returned to the Imperial and Royal Austrian Navy. The remainder of her career was uneventful, being scrapped by 1860. Her name means refers to someone who is from the Austrian capital city of Vienna. The name of the city is "Wien" in German and "Vindebona" in Latin.

*Die Segelkanonierschaluppe "S.M.S. Viennese" war das zweite Schwesterschiff der "S.M.S. Calypso." Sie lief am 13. November 1832 in Venedig vom Stapel, und wurde zwischen März 1848 und August 1849 von feindlichen italienischen Nationalisten beschlagnahmt. Sie wurde im Jahre 1860 verschrottet, nach einer Dienstzeit von 28 Jahren.*

40.) "S.M.S. Calliope" was another sister ship of "S.M.S. Calypso," "S.M.S. Costanza" and "S.M.S. Viennese." Her keel was laid down in Venice in 1832, and she was launched on March 26, 1833. Her career within the Imperial and Royal Austrian Navy was uneventful. She was converted into a coal barge in 1858, and scrapped by 1860.

*Die Segelkanonierschaluppe "S.M.S. Calliope" war das dritte Schwesterschiff der "S.M.S. Calypso." Sie wurde im Jahre 1832 in Venedig auf Kiel gelegt, und lief am 26. März 1833 vom Stapel. Sie wurde im Jahre 1858 als Kohenhulk umgebaut, und wurde im Jahre 1860 verschrottet.*

41.) "S.M.S. Danae" was yet another sister ship of "S.M.S. Calypso," "S.M.S. Costanza," "S.M.S. Viennese" and "S.M.S. Calliope." Her keel was laid down in Venice in 1832, and she was launched on January 11, 1834. In between March of 1848 and August of 1849, she was captured by rebellious Italian nationalist forces in Venice. Thereafter, she returned to the Imperial and Royal Austrian Navy. She was converted into a coal barge in 1858, and scrapped by 1860. In Classical Mythology, the name of this vessel referred to the 50 daughters of the Egyptian King Danaos. The girls did not want to marry their cousins, so they fled their country in the company of their father. They moved to Argos, but their cousins followed them. They were thus forced to marry their cousins, but they each received the gift of a dagger from their royal father. The girls promised to kill their new husbands, which 49 of the 50 sisters did on their common wedding night. The last sister (Hypermnestra) helped her new spouse Lynkeus escape with his life. The first 49 sisters were captured and made to atone for their crimes for the remainder of their lives.

*Die Segelkanonierschaluppe "S.M.S. Danae" war das vierte Schwesterschiff der "S.M.S. Calypso." Sie wurde im Jahre 1832 in Venedig auf Kiel gelegt, und lief am 11. Januar 1834 vom Stapel. Zwischen März 1848 und August 1849 wurde sie von feindlichen italienischen Nationalisten beschlagnahmt. Sie wurde als Kohlenhulk im Jahre 1858 umgebaut, und wurde im Jahre 1860 verschrottet. Die "Danae" waren die 50 Töchter des Ägyptischen König Danaos aus der klassischen Mythologie. Die Mädchen wollten ihre Vettern nicht heiraten, und zogen mit ihrem Vater nach Argos um. Die Vetter liefen den Mädchen nach, um sie doch zu heiraten. 49 von den 50 Schwestern haben ihre 49 Vettern ermordet, aber die Schwester Hypermnestra hat ihren neuen Ehemann Lynkeus geholfen, sodaß er nicht ermordet wurde. Danach wurden die anderen 49 Schwestern gefangen genommen.*

42.) "S.M.S. Veneziana" was still another vessel of the prolific "S.M.S. Calypso" class. Her keel was laid down in Venice (after which she was named) in 1832, and she was launched on January 11, 1834. She was renamed "S.M.S. Veruda" on May 11, 1848. She was converted into a coal barge in 1852, and scrapped by 1857.

*Die Segelkanonierschaluppe "S.M.S. Veneziana" war das fünfte Schwesterschiff der "S.M.S. Calypso." Sie wurde im Jahre 1832 in Venedig auf Kiel gelegt, und lief am 11. Januar 1834 vom Stapel. Am 11. Mai 1848 wurde sie als die "S.M.S. Veruda" umbenannt. Im Jahre 1852 wurde sie als Kohlenhulk umgebaut, und sie wurde im Jahre 1857 verschrottet.*

43.) "S.M.S. Concordia" was another vessel belonging to the "S.M.S. Calypso" class. Her keel was laid down in Venice in 1832, and she was launched on April 22, 1834. She was also converted into a coal barge in 1858, and then scrapped by 1860. In the old pagan religion of ancient Rome, "Concordia" embodied the spirit of harmony within society. A temple in honor of Concordia was constructed in the 4th Century before Christ. The temple was located near the Forum of Rome, and its altar was at the exit of the capitol. Emperor Tiberius restored the temple, which was renamed "Corcordia Augusta." He wanted to restore the harmony within his own royal family, which was actually infamous for murderous infighting.

*Die Segelkanonierschaluppe "S.M.S. Concordia" war das sechste Schwesterschiff der "S.M.S. Calypso." Sie wurde im Jahre 1832 in Venedig auf Kiel gelegt, und lief am 22. April 1834 vom Stapel. Im Jahre 1858 wurde sie als Kohlenhulk umgebaut, und sie wurde im Jahre 1860 verschrottet.*

44.) "S.M.S. Merope" was also a member of the numerous "S.M.S. Calypso" class of sloops. Her keel was laid down in Venice in 1832, and she was launched on May 17, 1834. From March 1848 until August 1849, she was captured by rebellious nationalist Italian forces in Venice. After her return to the Imperial and Royal Austrian Navy, she was converted into a storage boat and scrapped by 1858.

*Die Segelkanonierschaluppe "S.M.S. Merope" war das siebte Schwesterschiff der "S.M.S. Calypso." Sie wurde im Jahre 1832 in Venedig auf Kiel gelegt, und lief am 17. Mai 1834 vom Stapel. Zwischen März 1848 und August 1849 wurde sie von feindlichen italienischen Nationalisten beschlagnahmt. Danach wurde sie als Lagerboot benutzt, bis sie im Jahre 1858 verschrottet wurde.*

45.) "S.M.S. Didone" was another member of the "S.M.S. Calypso" class of wooden sailing cannon-sloops within the Imperial and Royal Austrian Navy. Her keel was laid down in Venice in 1832, and she was launched on June 19, 1834. Her career was unremarkable, she being converted to coal carrying duties by 1852 and scrapped by 1860.

*Die Segelkanonierschaluppe "S.M.S. Didone" war das achte Schwesterschiff der "S.M.S. Calypso." Sie wurde im Jahre 1832 in Venedig auf Kiel gelegt, und lief am 19. Juni 1834 vom Stapel. Im Jahre 1852 wurde sie als Kohlenhulk umgebaut, und sie wurde im Jahre 1860 verschrottet.*

46.) "S.M.S. Medusa" was yet another member within the "S.M.S. Calypso" class of Austrian wooden cannon-sloops. Her keel was laid down in Venice in 1832, and she was launched on February 26, 1835. From March of 1848 until August of 1849, she was under the control of rebellious Italian nationalist forces in Venice. The remainder of her career within the Imperial and Royal Austrian Navy was not eventful – she was converted into a coal barge in 1858, and scrapped by 1860. "Medusa" became a popular ship's name in the German Navies of the future – first for sailing vessels in the Royal Prussian Navy, and later for small cruisers in the Imperial German Navy. Today, one will find names like this among modern German minesweepers.

*Die Segelkanonierschaluppe "S.M.S. Medusa" war das neunte Schwesterschiff der "S.M.S. Calypso." Sie wurde im Jahre 1832 in Venedig auf Kiel gelegt, und lief am 26. Februar 1835 vom Stapel. Zwischen März 1848 und August 1849 wurde sie von feindlichen italienischen Nationalisten beschlagnahmt. Im Jahre 1858 wurde sie als Kohlenhulk umgebaut, und sie wurde im Jahre 1860 verschrottet. Der Patenname "Medusa" ist immer noch bei der Deutschen Marine beliebt. Heute gibt es ein Minensuchboot, das "Medusa" heißt.*

47.) "S.M.S. Delfina" was also a member of the "S.M.S. Calypso" class of Austrian wooden cannon-sloops. Her keel was laid down in Venice in 1832, and she was launched on March 11, 1835. She was also captured by revolutionary nationalist Italian rebels in Venice from March 1848 until August 1849. She was scrapped in 1857, after having served as a coal barge.

*Die Segelkanonierschaluppe "S.M.S. Delfina" war das zehnte Schwesterschiff der "S.M.S. Calypso." Sie wurde im Jahre 1832 in Venedig auf Kiel gelegt, und lief am 11. März 1835 vom Stapel. Zwischen März 1848 und August 1849 wurde sie auch von feindlichen italienischen Nationalisten beschlagnahmt. Danach wurde sie als Kohlenhulk umgebaut, und sie wurde im Jahre 1857 verschrottet.*

48.) "S.M.S. Fulminante" was another member of the "S.M.S. Calypso" class of Imperial and Royal Austrian cannon-sloops. Her keel was laid down in Venice in 1835, and she was launched on September 3, 1836. She was also under the control of revolutionary nationalist Italian rebels in Venice from March of 1848 until August of 1849. She was scrapped in 1857, after having served the navy as a fresh water barge.

*Die Segelkanonierschaluppe "S.M.S. Fulminante" war das elfte Schwesterschiff der "S.M.S. Calypso." Sie wurde im Jahre 1835 in Venedig auf Kiel gelegt, und lief am 3. September 1836 vom Stapel. Zwischen März 1848 und August 1849 wurde sie auch von feindlichen italiensichen Nationalisten beschlagnahmt. Danach wurde sie als Süßwasserhulk umgebaut, und sie wurde im Jahre 1857 verschrottet.*

49.) "S.M.S. Gelosa" was yet another member of the "S.M.S. Calypso" class of Imperial and Royal Austrian cannon-sloops. Her keel was laid down in Venice in 1835, and she was launched on April 5, 1839. She was under the control of revolutionary nationalist Italian rebels in Venice from March 1848 until August 1849. Upon her return to the Austrian Navy, she was used as a barge. She was retired and scrapped in 1857.

*Die Segelkanonierschaluppe "S.M.S. Gelosa" war das zwölfte Schwesterschiff der "S.M.S. Calypso." Sie wurde im Jahre 1835 in Venedig auf Kiel gelegt, und lief am 5. April 1839 vom Stapel. Zwischen März 1848 und August 1849 wurde sie auch von feindlichen italienischen Nationalisten beschlagnahmt. Danach wurde sie als Lastkahnboot umgebaut, und sie wurde im Jahre 1857 verschrottet.*

50.) "S.M.S. Proserpina" was still another member of the "S.M.S. Calypso" class of Imperial and Royal Austrian sailing cannon-sloops. Her keel was laid down in Venice in 1832, and she was launched on December 28, 1844. She was briefly captured by revolutionary nationalist Italian rebels in the port of Venice from March 1848 until August 1849. Upon her return to Austria, she served as a coal barge (from 1864 until 1872) and then as a guard hulk (from 1872 until 1877). She was only scrapped in 1894, after 62 years of service in the Austrian Navy.

*Die Segelkanonierschaluppe "S.M.S. Proserpina" war das dreizehnte Schwesterschiff der "S.M.S. Calypso." Sie wurde im Jahre 1832 in Venedig auf Kiel gelegt, und lief erst am 28. Dezember 1844 vom Stapel. Zwischen März 1848 und August 1849 wurde sie auch von feindlichen italienischen Nationalisten beschlagnahmt. Im Jahre 1864 wurde sie als Kohlenhulk umgebaut, und sie wurde erst im Jahre 1894 verschrottet – nach einer langen und guten Dienstzeit von 50 Jahren.*

51.) "S.M.S. Stella" was also a member of the prolific "S.M.S. Calypso" class of Imperial and Royal Austrian cannon-sloops. Her keel was laid down in Venice in 1832, and she was launched on January 27, 1845. She was captured by revolutionary nationalist Italian rebels in the Austrian naval port of Venice from March 1848 until August 1849. Her career was rather brief. She was converted into a harbor-blocking guard hulk, and then scrapped by 1862.

*Die Segelkanonierschaluppe "S.M.S. Stella" war das vierzehnte Schwesterschiff der "S.M.S. Calypso." Sie wurde im Jahre 1832 in Venedig auf Kiel gelegt, und lief erst am 27. Januar 1845 vom Stapel. Zwischen März 1848 und August 1849 wurde sie von feindlichen italienischen Nationalisten beschlagnahmt. Danach wurde sie als Wachhulk umgebaut, und sie wurde im Jahre 1862 verschrottet.*

52.) "S.M.S. Pandora" was another member of the "S.M.S. Calypso" class of Imperial and Royal Austrian cannon-sloops. Her keel was laid down in Venice in 1835, and she was launched on February 10, 1845. She was also captured by revolutionary nationalist Italian troops in the then-Austrian naval port of Venice from March 1848 until August 1849. After her return to the Austrian Navy, she was retired in 1862 and then converted into an ammunition hulk. She was scrapped in 1866. In classical mythology, "Pandora" was supposedly created by the pagan gods in order to punish Prometheus, because the latter had stolen fire from the heavens.

*Die Segelkanonierschaluppe "S.M.S. Pandora" war das fünfzehnte Schwesterschiff der "S.M.S. Calypso." Sie wurde im Jahre 1835 in Venedig auf Kiel gelegt, und lief erst am 10. Februar 1845 vom Stapel. Zwischen März 1848 und August 1849 wurde sie auch von feindlichen italienischen Nationalisten beschlagnahmt. Im Jahre 1862 wurde sie als Munitionshulk umgebaut, und sie wurde im Jahre 1866 verschrottet. In der heidnischen griechischen Mythologie hat die Frau Pandora Prometheus bestraft, weil er Feuer vom Himmel gestohlen hatte. Prometheus war der Freund und der Kulturstifter der Menschheit.*

53.) "S.M.S. Tartara" was also a member of the "S.M.S. Calypso" class of Imperial and Royal Austrian wooden sailing cannon-sloops. Her keel was laid down in the Austrian naval port of Venice in 1836, and she was launched on February 19, 1845. She was briefly under the control of revolutionary nationalist Italian rebels in Venice from March 1848 until August 1849. Upon her return to Austria, she served as an ammunition hulk from 1862 until she was scrapped in 1866. In classical pagan mythology, the name of this vessel referred to the origin of the universe. "Tartara" was supposedly underneath the earth and under Hell, where he served as a prison for the enemies of the pagan gods of the first generation. Cyclops, titans and giants were among the numerous prisoners of Tartara.

*Die Segelkanonierschaluppe "S.M.S. Tartara" war das sechszehnte Schwesterschiff der "S.M.S. Calypso." Sie wurde im Jahre 1836 in Venedig auf Kiel gelegt, und lief am 19. Februar 1845 vom Stapel. Zwischen März 1848 und August 1849 wurde sie auch von feindlichen italienischen Nationalisten beschlagnahmt. Im Jahre 1862 wurde sie als Munitionshulk umgebaut, und sie wurde im Jahre 1866 verschrottet. In der heidnischen griechischen Mythologie war Tartara mit dem Ursprung des Universums verbunden. Er lebte unter der Hölle, wo er als der Kerkermeister für die Feinde der Götter der ersten Generation diente.*

54.) "S.M.S. Tremenda" was yet another member of the numerous "S.M.S. Calypso" class of Imperial and Royal Austrian wooden sailing cannon-sloops. Her keel was laid down in the Austrian naval port of Venice in 1842, and she was launched on February 22, 1845. She was briefly captured by revolutionary nationalist Italian rebels in Venice from March 1848 until August 1849. Upon her return to the Austrian Navy, she served as an ammunition barge from 1862 until she was scrapped in 1866.

*Die Segelkanonierschaluppe "S.M.S. Tremenda" was das siebzehnte Schwesterschiff der "S.M.S. Calypso." Sie wurde im Jahre 1842 in Venedig auf Kiel gelegt, und lief am 22. Februar 1845 vom Stapel. Zwischen März 1848 und August 1849 wurde sie auch von feindlichen italienischen Nationalisten beschlagnahmt. Im Jahre 1862 wurde sie als Munitionshulk umgebaut, und sie wurde im Jahre 1866 verschrottet.*

55.) "S.M.S. Galatea" was the final member of the "S.M.S. Calypso" class of Imperial and Royal Austrian wooden sailing cannon-sloops. Her keel was laid down in the Austrian naval port of Venice in 1847, and she was launched on January 27, 1849. She was under the control of revolutionary nationalist Italian rebels in Venice (while still unfinished) from March 1848 until August 1849. Upon her return to the Austrian Navy, she was used as an ammunition barge until 1864, and as a fresh water barge until she was scrapped in 1868. In classical mythology, Galatea was a nymph of the ocean. She was called into being during Homer's 18th song. She was the lover of Akis.

*Die Segelkanonierschaluppe "S.M.S. Galatea" war das achtzehnte und auch das letzte Schwesterschiff der "S.M.S. Calypso." Sie wurde im Jahre 1847 in Venedig auf Kiel gelegt, und lief am 27. Januar 1849 vom Stapel. Zwischen März 1848 und August 1849 wurde sie auch von feindlichen italienischen Nationalisten beschlagnahmt. Im Jahre 1864 wurde sie als Munitionshulk umgebaut, und sie wurde im Jahre 1868 verschrottet. In der heidnischen griechischen Mythologie war Galatea eine Nymphe des Ozeans. Sie war die Verliebte von Akis, und wurde während des 18. Liedes von Homer ernannt.*

56.) "S.M.S. Vicenza" was a wooden sailing cannon-barge (a floating battery) purchased from civilian owners in the Austrian naval port of Triest in August 1848. She was briefly deployed in the Austrian naval blockade of revolutionary nationalist Italian rebels in the occupied Austrian naval port of Venice in January 1849. She was later renamed "S.M.S. Caorle." She displaced up to 81 tons, was built out of oak, was armed with up to 10 howitzers, and had a crew of 38 commissioned officers and enlisted men.

*Die schwimmende Segelbatterie "S.M.S. Vicenza" wurde von der Kaiserlichen und Königlichen Kriegsmarine im August 1848 in Triest gekauft. Im Januar 1849 hat sie feindliche italienische Nationalisten an der Küste von Venedig blockiert. Danach wurde sie als die "S.M.S. Caorle" umbenannt. Sie hatte eine Einsatzverdrängung von 81 Tonnen, war aus Eichenholz gebaut, hatte eine Bewaffnung von zehn Kanonen, und eine Besatzung von 38 Offiziere und Matrosen.*

57.) "S.M.S. Custoza" was the sister ship of "S.M.S. Vicenza." Her naval career was identical to that of her sister ship, with the same historical dates as well. She was later renamed "S.M.S. Pirano." Custoza was named for the Battle of Custoza, in which the Imperial and Royal Austrian Army defeated the Army of the Kingdom of Sardinia from July 24-25, 1848. 33,000 Austrian troops under the leadership of Field Marshall (the equivalent of a 5-star general in the American Army) Joseph Graf Radetzky von Radetz (1766-1858) defeated 22,000 Sardinian Italians under the command of King Charles Albert of Piedmont-Sardinia (1798-1849). There was yet another Battle of Custoza in 1866, during the Prusso-Austrian War. The Austrians defeated the Italians yet again in 1866.

*Die schwimmende Segelbatterie "S.M.S. Cuztoza" war das Schwesterschiff der "S.M.S. Vicenza." Nach Januar 1849 wurde sie als die "S.M.S. Pirano" umbenannt. Es gibt zwei Schlachten von Cuztoza in Italien. Im Juli 1848 haben 33,000 Österreichische Truppen unter Generalfeldmarschall Josef Graf Radetzky von Radetz (1766-1858) 22,000 Sardinische Truppen unter König Karl Adalbert von Piemont-Sardinien (1798-1849) geschlagen. Im Deutschen Bruderkrieg von 1866 haben die Österreicher die Italiener nochmal bei Custoza besiegt.*

58.) "S.M.S. Aquila" was the first member of a class of wooden cannon-sloops in the Imperial and Royal Austrian Navy. She displaced up to 80 tons, was 17,6 meters long, had a maximum beam of 4,9 meters and a maximum draught of 1,6 meters. She was built out of oak, was armed with 1-24 Pounder and 2-1 Pounders. She was manned by a crew of 31 commissioned officers and enlisted men. These vessels were powered by a combination of sails and rudders (oars), and meant for coastal combat duty. This vessel was built in either Triest or Sankt Veit am Pflaumb ("Fiume" in Italian and Rijeka in modern Croatia) in 1788, and was used until March of 1798. Until 1849, Venice ("Venedig" in German) was the largest Austrian Navy base. Thereafter, Triest and Pola ("Polei" in German and Pula in modern Croatia) became the largest and most important Austrian naval bases. During World War One, most Austro-Hungarian capital warships were based in Polei. Sankt Veit am Plaumb was the home of the Austrian naval academy until 1918.

*Die Segelkanonierschaluppe "S.M.S. Aquila" wurde entweder in Triest oder in Sankt Veit am Pflaumb (vormals "Fiume" auf italienisch und nun "Rijieka" in Kroatien) im Jahre 1788 gebaut, und im März 1798 verkauft. Sie hatte eine Einsatzverdrängung von 80 Tonnen, war 17,6 Meter lang, hatte eine Breite von 4,9 Meter und ein Tiefgang von 1,6 Meter. Die Bewaffnung des Schiffes bestand aus einem 24-Pfunder und zwei Ein-Pfundern. Sie hatte eine Besatzung von 31 Offiziere und Matrosen. Bis 1849 war Venedig der größte österreichische Marinehafen. Die "S.M.S. Aquila" hatte sehr viele Schwesterschiffe mit ähnlichen Lebensgeschichten. Von 1849 bis 1918 waren Triest und Polei (vormals "Pola" auf italienisch und nun "Pula" in Kroatien) die größten österreichischen Marinehäfen. Zwischen 1802 und 1854 war die Marineakademie der Kaiserlichen und Königlichen Kriegsmarine in Venedig, von 1854 bis 1918 war sie in Sankt Veit am Pflaum (damals "Fiume" genannt). Die Akademie existiert heute noch in Kroatien.*

59.) "S.M.S. Centauro" was the 2nd member of the "S.M.S. Aquila" class of Imperal and Royal Austrian wooden cannon-sloops. Her naval career and historical dates were identical to those of "S.M.S. Aquila." A centaur is a creature from classical mythology, with the head and chest of a man and the body of a horse. They were known to be very wise, educated in matters of astronomy and to have the special gift of accurate prophecy.

*Die Segelkanonierschaluppe "S.M.S. Centauro" war das Schwesterschiff der "S.M.S. Aquila." Der Zentaur kommt aus der klassischen Mythologie, und war halb Mann und halb Pferd. Sie waren sehr verständig, und wußten viel von der Sternkunde sowie über Vorausdeutung.*

60.) "S.M.S Colombo" was the 3rd member of the "S.M.S. Aquila" class of Imperial and Royal Austrian wooden cannon-sloops. Her naval career and historical dates were identical to those of "S.M.S. Aquila." Colombo is the capital city of the island of Sri Lanka, located in the Indian Ocean off the Southern coast of India proper. Sri Lanka used to be known as "Ceylon."

*Die Segelkanonierschaluppe "S.M.S. Colombo" war das zweite Schwesterschiff der "S.M.S. Aquila." Colombo ist die Hauptstadt Sri Lankas (vormals "Ceylon" genannt).*

61.) "S.M.S. Corvo" was the 4th member of the "S.M.S. Aquila" class of Imperial and Royal Austrian wooden cannon-sloops. Her naval career and historical dates were identical to those of "S.M.S. Aquila."

*Die Segelkanonierschaluppe "S.M.S. Corvo" war das dritte Schwesterschiff der "S.M.S. Aquila."*

62.) "S.M.S. Dragone" was the 5th member of the "S.M.S. Aquila" class of Imperial and Royal Austrian wooden cannon sloops. Her naval career and historical dates were identical to those of "S.M.S. Aquila." "Dragone" is the Italian word for "dragon," or "Drache" in German. Dragons are creatures from mythology, known to be large, fire-breathing, flying reptiles. They were also intelligent, and known to steal and horde treasure such as jewels, precious metals and diamonds.

*Die Segelkanonierschaluppe "S.M.S. Dragone" war das vierte Schwesterschiff der "S.M.S. Aquila." Drachen kommen auch aus der klassischen Mythologie. Sie waren sehr große, feuer-spuckende, furchterregende, fliegende Reptilien. Sie waren auch sehr intelligent, und begehrten Edelsteine, Edelmetalle sowie Diamanten.*

63.) "S.M.S. India" was the 6th member of the "S.M.S. Aquila" class of Imperial and Royal Austrian wooden cannon-sloops. Her naval career and historical dates were identical to those of "S.M.S. Aquila." She was named after the empire of India, or "Indien" in German. Most of the Indian subcontinent became a colony of Britain, but there were exceptions. The Malabar Coast of India, as well as the Nicobar Islands in the Bay of Bengal, were both originally colonies of Austria and the Holy Roman Empire of the German Nation. Portugal, France and the Netherlands also had substantial colonial possessions on the Indian subcontinent and in the Indian Ocean. The Hindu faith is dominant in India, with a large minority of Muslims and substantial numbers of both Christians (especially Roman Catholics) and Sikhs as well. There are modern Indians with the surname "Borromeo," named after the famous Traditionalist Roman Catholic Cardinal from Milan, Saint Charles Borromeo.

*Die Segelkanonierschaluppe "S.M.S. India" war das fünfte Schwesterschiff der "S.M.S. Aquila." Indien war vormals eine Kronkolonie von Großbrittanien, aber andere Mächte aus Europa hatten auch Schutzgebiete in Indien. Portugal, Frankreich, die Niederlande und auch Österreich hatten Kolonien in Südwestasien. Die Malabarküste von Indien sowie die Nicobar-Inseln gehörten Österreich. Das Erzherzogtum Österreich war der wichtigste und der mächtigste Staat im Ersten Deutschen Reich (das Heilige Römische Reich der Deutschen Nation).*

64.) "S.M.S. Lira" was the 7th member of the "S.M.S. Aquila" class of Imperial and Royal Austrian wooden cannon-sloops. Her naval career and historical dates were identical to those of "S.M.S. Aquila." "Lira" is the name of the former Italian currency, in use until the unfortunate adoption of the Euro. Since the adoption of the modern Euro currency, most people in Europe have seen their incomes stagnate, while at the same time their cost of living has doubled or even tripled.

*Die Segelkanonierschaluppe "S.M.S. Lira" war das sechste Schwesterschiff der "S.M.S. Aquila." Die Lira war die ehemalige Währung Italiens. Der heutige "Euro" hat für Europa mehr Nachteile als Vorteile. Das Einkommen ist ungefähr dasselbe, aber die Lebenskosten sind nun zwei-oder dreimal so hoch wie früher.*

65.) "S.M.S. Lupo" was the 8th member of the "S.M.S. Aquila" class of Imperial and Royal Austrian wooden cannon-sloops. Her naval career and historical dates were identical to those of "S.M.S. Aquila." Lupo is now the trademark name of the smallest Volkswagen passenger car sold in Europe. In some markets, the same car now carries the trademark name of "Fox."

*Die Segelkanonierschaluppe "S.M.S. Lupo" war das siebte Schwesterschiff der "S.M.S. Aquila." Die berühmte und erfolgreiche Gruppe Volkswagen-Porsche aus Deutschland und Österreich verkauft einen Kleinwagen, der "Lupo" heißt.*

66.) "S.M.S. Pavone" was the 9th member of the "S.M.S. Aquila" class of Imperial and Royal Austrian wooden cannon-sloops.  Her naval career and historical dates were identical to those of "S.M.S. Aquila."

*Die Segelkanonierschaluppe "S.M.S. Pavone" was das achte Schwesterschiff der "S.M.S. Aquila."*

67.) "S.M.S. Delfino" was the 10th member of the "S.M.S. Aquila" class of Imperial and Royal Austrian wooden cannon-sloops.  Her naval career was identical to that of "S.M.S. Aquila," except for the fact that she was scrapped in 1797.  Her name is Italian for "dolphin" in English or "Delfin" in German.

*Die Segelkanonierschaluppe "S.M.S. Delfino" war das neunte Schwesterschiff der "S.M.S. Aquila." Ihre Lebensgeschichte war die der "S.M.S. Aquila" sehr ähnlich, aber sie wurde im Jahre 1797 verschrottet.*

68.) "S.M.S. Ercole" was the 11th member of the "S.M.S. Aquila" class of Imperial and Royal Austrian wooden cannon-sloops.  Her naval career and historical dates were identical to those of "S.M.S. Delfino."

*Die Segelkanonierschaluppe "S.M.S. Ercole" war das zehnte Schwesterschiff der "S.M.S. Aquila."*

69.) "S.M.S. Orione" was the 12th member of the "S.M.S. Aquila" class of Imperial and Royal Austrian wooden cannon-sloops.  Her naval career and historical dates were identical to those of "S.M.S. Delfino."  In classical pagan mythology, "Orion" was a very large (giant) hunter.  Orion was the son of Poseidon and Euryale, and one of the Gorgones.

*Die Segelkanonierschaluppe "S.M.S. Orione" war das elfte Schwesterschiff der "S.M.S. Aquila." Orion kommt auch aus der klassischen heidnischen Mythologie. Er war ein riesiger Jäger, und auch der Sohn von Poseidon und Euryale. Er gehörte zu den Gorgonen.*

70.) "S.M.S. Pegaso" was the 13th member of the "S.M.S. Aquila" class of Imperial and Royal Austrian wooden cannon-sloops.  Her naval career and historical dates were identical to those of "S.M.S. Delfino."  Her name ("Pegasus" in Latin) refers to the famous winged horse of classical mythology, which had its origin in Asia Minor (or modern Turkey).

*Die Segelkanonierschaluppe "S.M.S. Pegaso" war das zwölfte Schwesterschiff der "S.M.S. Aquila." Das fliegende Pferd Pegasus kommt aus der klassischen römischen Mythologie, das aus der Türkei kam.*

71.) "S.M.S. Cane" was the 14th member of the "S.M.S. Aquila" class of Imperial and Royal Austrian wooden cannon-sloops. Her keel was laid down in 1793 in either Trieste, Fiume ("Sankt Veit am Pflaumb" in German, or "Rijeka" in modern Croatia) or Porto Re. She was used until she was scrapped in 1797 – a very brief naval career of merely 4 years!

*Die Segelkanonierschaluppe "S.M.S. Cane" war das dreizehnte Schwesterschiff der "S.M.S. Aquila." Sie wurde im Jahre 1793 entweder in Triest, in Sankt Veit am Pflaumb (damals "Fiume" genannt) oder in Porto Re auf Kiel gelegt, und wurde schon im Jahre 1797 verschrottet.*

72.) "S.M.S. Ceffea" was the 15th member of the "S.M.S. Aquila" class of Imperial and Royal Austrian wooden cannon-sloops. Her naval career and historical dates were identical to those of "S.M.S. Cane," with the single exception that she was scrapped one year later in 1798.

*Die Segelkanonierschaluppe "S.M.S. Ceffea" war das vierzehnte Schwesterschiff der "S.M.S. Aquila." Ihre Lebensgeschichte und die Lebensgeschichten der folgenden Segelkanonierschaluppen waren die der "S.M.S. Cane" sehr ähnlich, aber die "S.M.S. Ceffea" wurde im Jahre 1798 verschrottet.*

73.) "S.M.S. Celsea" was the 16th member of the "S.M.S. Aquila" class of Imperial and Royal Austrian wooden cannon-sloops. Her naval career and historical dates were identical to those of "S.M.S. Cane."

*Die Segelkanonierschaluppe "S.M.S. Celsea" war das fünfzehnte Schwesterschiff der "S.M.S. Aquila."*

74.) "S.M.S. Cetta" was the 17th member of the "S.M.S. Aquila" class of Imperial and Royal Austrian wooden cannon-sloops. Her naval career and historical dates were identical to those of "S.M.S. Cane."

*Die Segelkanonierschaluppe "S.M.S. Cetta" war das sechszehnte Schwesterschiff der "S.M.S. Aquila."*

75.) "S.M.S. Dolfino" was the 18th member of the "S.M.S. Aquila" class of Imperial and Royal Austrian wooden cannon-sloops. Her naval career and historical dates were identical to those of "S.M.S. Ceffea," thus being scrapped in 1798.

*Die Segelkanonierschaluppe "S.M.S. Dolfino" war das siebzehnte Schwesterschiff der "S.M.S. Aquila." Ihre Lebensgeschichte war die der "S.M.S. Aquila" sehr ähnlich, aber sie wurde im Jahre 1798 verschrottet.*

76.) "S.M.S. Grue" was the 19th member of the "S.M.S. Aquila" class of Imperial and Royal Austrian wooden cannon-sloops. Her naval career and historical dates were identical to those of "S.M.S. Ceffea," thus being scrapped in 1798.

*Die Segelkanonierschaluppe "S.M.S. Grue" war das achtzehnte Schwesterschiff der "S.M.S. Aquila." Sie wurde im Jahre 1798 verschrottet.*

77.) "S.M.S. Pallena" was the 20th member of the "S.M.S. Aquila" class of Imperial and Royal Austrian wooden cannon-sloops. Her naval career and historical dates were identical to those of "S.M.S. Cane," being scrapped in the year 1797.

*Die Segelkanonierschaluppe "S.M.S. Pallena" war das neunzehnte Schwesterschiff der "S.M.S. Aquila," und wurde im Jahre 1797 verschrottet.*

78.) "S.M.S. Pantera" was the 21st member of the "S.M.S. Aquila" class to be named – in other words, there were numerous other Imperial and Royal Austrian wooden cannon-sloops of this particular class which never received names (just call or pennant numbers). She was laid down by the Austrians at least by March of 1798, but was taken over by the French Navy from April 1, 1806 until she was liberated in September of 1813. 1806 was the year when Napoleon Bonaparte sadly abolished the Holy Roman Empire of the German Nation (800 – 1806), and replaced it with his puppet "Confederation of the Rhine." This vessel was scrapped by 1818.

*Die Segelkanonierschaluppe "S.M.S. Pantera" war das zwanzigste genannte Schwesterschiff der "S.M.S. Aquila." Es gab mehrere Mitglieder dieser Klaße, die nie genannt wurden. Die große Mehrheit der Unterseeboote Deutschlands sowie Österreich-Ungarns hatten auch keine Patennamen, und nur Nummern. Die "S.M.S. Pantera" wurde im Jahre 1798 auf Kiel gelegt, und wurde von den Franzosen am 1. April 1806 beschlagnahmt. Im Jahre 1806 hat Napoleon Bonaparte auch das Erste Deutsche Reich (das Heilige Römische Reich der*

*Deutschen Nation) leider beendet, und mit seinem sogenannten "Rheinbund" ersetzt. Die "S.M.S. Pantera" wurde im Jahre 1818 verschrottet – drei Jahre nach Napoleon Bonaparte und Frankreich endlich besiegt wurden. Napoleons sogenanntes "Rheinbund" dauerte von 1806 bis 1815, aber der Deutsche Bund (von dem Kaiserreich Österreich beherrscht, genauso wie das Erste Deutsche Reich von 800 bis 1806) dauerte von 1815 bis 1867, als es von Preußens "Norddeutsche Bund" von 1867 bis 1871 ersetzt wurde.*

79.) "S.M.S. Corragiosa" was the 22nd member of the "S.M.S. Aquila" class of Imperial and Royal Austrian wooden cannon-sloops to be named. She was laid down at least by March of 1798, and then disarmed by November 1809. She was taken by the French Navy in 1810, and returned to Austria on December 5, 1813. She was sunk off the coast of Dalmatia (now part of modern Croatia) by accident in 1816, raised in 1818 and scrapped by 1819.

*Die Segelkanonierschaluppe "S.M.S. Corragiosa" war das einundzwanzigste genannte Schwesterschiff der "S.M.S. Aquila." Sie wurde nicht später als März 1798 auf Kiel gelegt, und wurde dann im Jahre 1809 entwaffnet. Im Jahre 1810 wurde sie von den Franzosen beschlagnahmt, und dann am 5. Dezember 1813 wurde sie von Österreich befreit. Im Jahre 1816 wurde sie in einem Unfall an der Küste von Dalmatien versenkt, im Jahre 1818 geborgen und dann endlich im Jahre 1819 verschrottet.*

80.) "S.M.S. Audace" was the 23rd member of the "S.M.S. Aquila" class of Imperial and Royal Austrian wooden cannon-sloops to be named. She was laid down in Venice 1796, and launched in December of that same year. She was briefly in the possession of the French Navy from May 17 until December 30, 1797, and then re-taken by Austria in heavily damaged condition in 1798. She was stripped of her armament in November 1809, and then sold to the French Navy in 1810. She returned yet again to Austria on December 5, 1813 and was scrapped by 1820.

*Die Segelkanonierschaluppe "S.M.S. Audace" war das zweiundzwanzigste genannte Schwesterschiff der "S.M.S. Aquila." Sie wurde im Jahre 1796 in Venedig auf Kiel gelegt, und lief im Dezember 1796 vom Stapel. Sie wurde von den Franzosen vom 17. Mai bis dem 30. Dezember 1797 beschlagnahmt, und wurde im Jahre 1798 beschädigt von den Österreichern befreit. Im Jahre 1809 wurde sie entwaffnet, und dann im Jahre 1810 an die Franzosen verkauft. Am 5. Dezember 1813 wurde sie wieder österreichisch, und sie wurde endlich im Jahre 1820 verschrottet.*

81.) "S.M.S. Adirata" was the 24th member of the "S.M.S. Aquila" class of Imperial and Royal Austrian wooden cannon-sloops to be named. She was laid down in Venice in 1797, and then briefly taken over by the French Navy before being re-taken by Austria in 1798. Her construction progressed very slowly, and she was only launched in 1805. She was disarmed in November 1809, and then sold to France in 1810. She was finally returned to Austria in the Dalmatian port of Zara (another Austrian naval base) on December 5, 1813. She met an unfortunate end in August 1820, when she was stranded in a storm near the Dalmatian port of Ragusa (yet another Austrian naval base now known as "Dubrovnik" in modern Croatia). The ship was literally broken in two.

*Die Segelkanonierschaluppe "S.M.S. Adirata" war das dreiundzwanzigste genannte Schwesterschiff der "S.M.S. Aquila." Sie wurde im Jahre 1797 in Venedig auf Kiel gelegt, und wurde für einige Monaten zwischen 1797 und 1798 beschlagnahmt. Sie wurde erst im Jahre 1805 von der Kaiserlichen und Königlichen Kriegsmarine in Dienst genommen. Im Jahre 1809 wurde sie entwaffnet, und im Jahre 1810 an den Franzosen verkauft. Am 5. Dezember 1813 wurde sie wieder im Hafen von Zara in Dalmatien wieder österreichisch. Im August 1820 strandete sie in einem Sturm an der Küste von Ragusa in Dalmatien (heute Dubrovnik in Kroatien). Das Schiff zerbrach in zwei Teile, und wurde versenkt.*

82.) "S.M.S. Vittoria" was the 25th member of the "S.M.S. Aquila" class of Imperial and Royal Austrian wooden cannon-sloops to be named. Her historical dates and naval career were virtually identical to those of "S.M.S. Adirata," with the exception being that she was merely scrapped by the year 1820. Her name is Italian for "Victoria" in English.

*Die Segelkanonierschaluppe "S.M.S. Vittoria" war das vierundzwanzigste genannte Schwesterschiff der "S.M.S. Aquila." Ihre Lebensgeschichte war die der "S.M.S. Adirata" sehr ähnlich, aber sie wurde im Jahre 1820 verschrottet.*

83.) "S.M.S. Leda" was the 26th member of the "S.M.S. Aquila" class of Imperial and Royal Austrian wooden cannon-sloops to be named. The facts about her career are unfortunately not very complete. She was in enemy (Italian) hands during the Napoleonic Wars. On April 1, 1809 she was taken over by the British sailing frigate "H.M.S. Mercury," and returned to Austria in the port of Triest (an important Austrian naval base) on April 11, 1809. In classical Greek mythology, Leda was the daughter of King Thestion and the wife of King Tyndareos of Sparta. She had an affair with the god Zeus, and bore him the children Polydeukes ("Pollux" in Latin), Helena, Kastor and Klytaimnestra.

*Die Segelkanonierschaluppe "S.M.S. Leda" war das fünfundzwanzigste genannte Schwesterschiff der "S.M.S. Aquila." Leider wissen wir nicht viel über ihre Lebensgeschichte. Zur Zeit der napoleonischen Kriege wurde sie von feindlichen italienischen Waffenverbündeten Napoleons beschlagnahmt. Am 1. April 1809 wurde sie von der britischen Segelfregatte "H.M.S. Mercury" befreit, und in Triest an Österreich zurückgegeben. In der klaßischen griechischen Mythologie war Leda die Tochter von König Thestion und auch die Ehefrau von König Tyndareos von Sparta. Obwohl sie schon verheiratet war, war Leda in den heidnischen Gott Zeus verliebt, mit dem sie die Kinder Polydeukes ("Pollux" auf lateinisch), Helena, Kastor und Klytaimnestra hatte.*

84.) "S.M.S. Ninfa" was the 27th member of the "S.M.S. Aquila" class of Imperial and Royal Austrian wooden cannon-sloops to be named. Very little is known about her history, but we do know that she was in existence in 1809.

*Die Segelkanonierschaluppe "S.M.S. Ninfa" war das sechsundzwanzigste genannte Schwesterchiff der "S.M.S. Aquila."*

85.) "S.M.S. Bellepoule" was the 28th member of the "S.M.S. Aquila" class of Imperial and Royal Austrian wooden cannon-sloops to be named. She was launched in Venice in 1795, was taken over by France in 1797, returned to Austria in 1814 and scrapped by 1816.

*Die Segelkanonierschaluppe "S.M.S. Bellepoule" war das siebenundzwanzigste genannte Schwesterschiff der "S.M.S. Aquila." Sie lief im Jahre 1795 in Venedig vom Stapel, und wurde im Jahre 1797 von den Franzosen beschlagnahmt. Im Jahre 1814 wurde sie an Österreich zurückgegeben, und sie wurde im Jahre 1816 verschrottet.*

86.) "S.M.S. Dea" was the 29th member of the "S.M.S. Aquila" class of Imperial and Royal Austrian wooden cannon-sloops to be named. She was launched in Venice in September of 1794, was taken over by France in 1797, by the Italians in 1806 and was returned to Austria in 1814. She was discovered to be unseaworthy upon her return to the Austrian Navy, and was therefore immediately sent to the breakers.

*Die Segelkanonierschaluppe "S.M.S. Dea" war das achtundzwanzigste genannte Schwesterschiff der "S.M.S. Aquila." Sie lief im Jahre 1794 in Venedig vom Stapel, und wurde im Jahre 1797 von den Franzosen beschlagnahmt. Im Jahre 1806 wurde sie von den Franzosen den Italienern gegeben. Sie wurde endlich im*

*Jahre 1814 an Österreich zurückgegeben, aber leider war sie nicht mehr seetüchtig – deswegen wurde sie verschrottet.*

87.) "S.M.S. Egida" was the 30th member of the "S.M.S. Aquila" class of Imperial and Royal Austrian wooden cannon-sloops to be named. She was launched in Venice in 1795, taken over by France in 1797, by the Italians in 1806 and was returned to Austria in 1814. She served in the Austrian Navy for 7 years prior to being scrapped in 1821.

*Die Segelkanonierschaluppe "S.M.S. Egida" war das neunundzwanzigste genannte Schwesterchiff der "S.M.S. Aquila." Sie lief im Jahre 1795 in Venedig vom Stapel, und wurde im Jahre 1797 von den Franzosen beschlagnahmt. Im Jahre 1806 wurde sie auch von den Franzosen den Italienern gegeben. Im Jahre 1814 wurde sie endlich der Kaiserlichen und Königlichen Kriegsmarine zurückgegeben, wo sie bis ihrer Verschrottung im Jahre 1821 wieder diente.*

88.) "S.M.S. Fiera" was the 31st member of the "S.M.S. Aquila" class of Imperial and Royal Austrian wooden cannon-sloops to be named. She was launched in Venice in 1794, taken over by France in 1797, by the Italians in 1806 and was returned to Austria in 1814. She served in the Austrian Navy for 6 years prior to being scrapped in 1820.

*Die Segelkanonierschaluppe "S.M.S. Fiera" war das dreißigste genannte Schwesterschiff der "S.M.S. Aquila." Sie lief im Jahre 1794 in Venedig vom Stapel, und wurde im Jahre 1797 von den Franzosen beschlagnahmt. Im Jahre 1806 wurde sie auch von den Franzosen den Italienern gegeben. Im Jahre 1814 wurde sie endlich an der Kaiserlichen und Königlichen Kriegsmarine zurückgegeben, wo sie bis ihrer Verschrottung im Jahre 1820 wieder diente.*

89.) "S.M.S. Medusa" was the 32nd member of the "S.M.S. Aquila" class of Imperial and Royal Austrian wooden cannon-sloops to be named. She was launched in Venice in 1795, was taken over by France in 1797, thereafter by the Italians, and was returned to Austria in the Dalmatian port of Zara on December 5, 1813. She served in the Austrian Navy for 4 more years prior to being sold to civilian owners in 1817. Numerous smaller ships in the German Navies of the future were to eventually carry the name "Medusa."

*Die Segelkanonierschaluppe "S.M.S. Medusa" war das einunddreißigste genannte Schwesterschiff der "S.M.S. Aquila." Sie lief im Jahre 1795 in Venedig vom Stapel, und wurde im Jahre 1797 von den Franzosen und den Italienern beschlagnahmt. Am 5. Dezember 1813 wurde sie im Hafen von Zara in Dalmatien an Österreich zurückgegeben. Im Jahre 1817 wurde sie verkauft.*

90.) "S.M.S. Tigre" was the 33rd member of the "S.M.S. Aquila" class of Imperial and Royal Austrian wooden cannon-sloops to be named. She was launched in 1804, and was eventually scrapped in 1829 after an uneventful career. Her name means "Tiger" in both German and English.

*Die Segelkanonierschaluppe "S.M.S. Tigre" war das zweiunddreißigste genannte Schwesterschiff der "S.M.S. Aquila." Sie lief im Jahre 1804 vom Stapel und wurde im Jahre 1829 verschrottet.*

91.) "S.M.S. Calypso" was the 34th member of the "S.M.S. Aquila" class of Imperial and Royal Austrian wooden cannon-sloops to be named. Her keel was laid down in Venice in 1806, and she was launched in November of 1807. She was scrapped in 1831 after an uneventful career.

*Die Segelkanonierschaluppe "S.M.S. Calypso" war das dreiunddreißigste genannte Schwesterschiff der "S.M.S. Aquila." Sie wurde im Jahre 1806 in Venedig auf Kiel gelegt, und lief im November 1807 vom Stapel. Sie wurde im Jahre 1831 verschrottet.*

92.) "S.M.S. Mantovana" was the 35th member of the "S.M.S. Aquila" class of Imperial and Royal Austrian wooden cannon-sloops to be named. She was launched in Venice in 1806, sunk by accident in 1816, raised and scrapped by 1818.

*Die Segelkanonierschaluppe "S.M.S. Mantovana" war das vierunddreißigste genannte Schwesterschiff der "S.M.S. Aquila." Sie lief im Jahre 1806 in Venedig vom Stapel, wurde im Jahre 1816 bei einem Unfall versenkt, wurde geborgen und im Jahre 1818 verschrottet.*

93.) "S.M.S. Sovrana" was the 36th member of the "S.M.S. Aquila" class of Imperial and Royal Austrian wooden cannon-sloops to be named. She suffered the same fate (and on the same dates) as her sister ship "S.M.S. Mantovana."

*Die Segelkanonierschaluppe "S.M.S. Sovrana" war das fünfunddreißigste genannte Schwesterschiff der "S.M.S. Aquila." Ihre Lebensgeschichte war die der "S.M.S. Mantovana" sehr ähnlich.*

94.) "S.M.S. Baccante" was the 37th member of the "S.M.S. Aquila" class of Imperial and Royal Austrian wooden cannon-sloops to be named. The details of her past are unfortunately very sketchy; we know she existed by 1814 and that she was scrapped by 1818.

*Die Segelkanonierschaluppe "S.M.S. Baccante" war das sechsunddreißigste genannte Schwesterschiff der "S.M.S. Aquila." Wir wissen leider nicht viel über ihre Lebensgeschichte. Sie existierte schon im Jahre 1814, und wurde im Jahre 1818 verschrottet.*

95.) "S.M.S. Battava" was the 38th member of the "S.M.S. Aquila" class of Imperial and Royal Austrian wooden cannon-sloops to be named. The details of her past are even more sketchy than those of "S.M.S. Baccante." We do know that she was in existence in 1814, when she was determined to be unseaworthy and therefore scrapped.

*Die Segelkanonierschaluppe "S.M.S. Battava" war das siebenundzwanzigste genannte Schwesterschiff der "S.M.S. Aquila." Wir wissen auch nicht viel über ihre Lebensgeschichte. Im Jahre 1814 war sie nicht mehr seefähig, und wurde deswegen verschrottet.*

96.) "S.M.S. Elvetica" was the 39th member of the "S.M.S. Aquila" class of Imperial and Royal Austrian wooden cannon-sloops to be named. As far as is known, her history was pretty much identical to that of her sister ship "S.M.S. Battava," except that she was scrapped in 1815.

*Die Segelkanonierschaluppe "S.M.S. Elvetica" war das achtundzwanzigste genannte Schwesterschiff der "S.M.S. Aquila." Ihre Lebensgeschichte war die der "S.M.S. Battava" sehr ähnlich, aber sie wurde im Jahre 1815 verschrottet.*

97.) "S.M.S. Fina" was the 40th member of the "S.M.S. Aquila" class of Imperial and Royal Austrian wooden cannon-sloops to be named. The details of her past are hard to come by, but we do know that she was based with the Austrian Navy in the port of Triest in November 1813, and that she was scrapped by 1829.

*Die Segelkanonierschaluppe "S.M.S. Fina" war das neunundzwanzigste genannte Schwesterschiff der "S.M.S. Aquila." Wir wissen leider nicht viel über ihre Lebensgeschichte, aber im Jahre 1813 war sie im Hafen von Triest stationiert, und sie wurde im Jahre 1829 verschrottet.*

98.) "S.M.S. Imperiosa" was the 41st member of the "S.M.S. Aquila" class of Imperial and Royal Austrian wooden cannon-sloops to be named. We know that she was in the Austrian Navy by 1814 at least until 1820.

*Die Segelkanonierschaluppe "S.M.S. Imperiosa" war das vierzigste genannte Schwesterschiff der "S.M.S. Aquila." Sie diente bei der Kaiserlichen und Königlichen Kriegsmarine mindestens von 1814 bis 1820.*

99.) "S.M.S. Lodola" was the 42nd member of the "S.M.S. Aquila" class of Imperial and Royal Austrian wooden cannon-sloops to be named. We know only that she was based with the Austrian Navy in the port of Triest by November 1813, and that she was sold to civilian owners in 1814.

*Die Segelkanonierschaluppe "S.M.S. Lodola" war das einundvierzigste genannte Schwesterschiff der "S.M.S. Aquila." Im November 1813 war sie im Marinehafen von Triest stationiert, und sie wurde im Jahre 1814 verkauft.*

100.) "S.M.S. Palestra" was the 43rd member of the "S.M.S. Aquila" class of Imperial and Royal Austrian wooden cannon-sloops to be named. We know only that she existed by 1814.

*Die Segelkanonierschaluppe "S.M.S. Palestra" war das zweiundvierzigste genannte Schwesterschiff der "S.M.S. Aquila." Sie existierte schon im Jahre 1814, aber mehr wissen wir leider nicht.*

101.) "S.M.S. Pelosa" was the 44th member of the "S.M.S. Aquila" class of Imperial and Royal Austrian wooden cannon-sloops to be named. We know merely that she was in existence by 1814, and that the Austrian Navy sold her to the breakers by 1819.

*Die Segelkanonierschaluppe "S.M.S. Pelosa" war das dreiundvierzigste genannte Schwesterschiff der "S.M.S. Aquila." Sie existierte schon im Jahre 1814, und sie wurde im Jahre 1819 verschrottet.*

102.) "S.M.S. Veneziana" was the 45th member of the "S.M.S. Aquila" class of Imperial and Royal Austrian wooden cannon-sloops to be named. Her history and dates were identical to those of her sister ship "S.M.S. Pelosa." Her name refers to someone who comes from the city of Venice.

*Die Segelkanonierschaluppe "S.M.S. Veneziana" war das vierundvierzigste genannte Schwesterschiff der "S.M.S. Aquila." Ihre Lebensgeschichte war die der "S.M.S. Pelosa" sehr ähnlich.*

103.) "S.M.S. Zenobia" was the 46th member of the "S.M.S. Aquila" class of Imperial and Royal Austrian wooden cannon-sloops to be named. We only know that she was in existence in 1814.

*Die Segelkanonierschaluppe "S.M.S. Zenobia" war das fünfundvierzigste genannte Schwesterschiff der "S.M.S. Aquila." Sie existierte schon im Jahre 1814, aber mehr wissen wir leider nicht.*

104.) "S.M.S. Comachiesa" was the 47th member of the "S.M.S. Aquila" class of Imperial and Royal Austrian wooden cannon-sloops to be named. She was launched in 1807, and was broken up in the port of Ancona in 1815.

*Die Segelkanonierschaluppe "S.M.S. Comachiesa" war das sechsundvierzigste genannte Schwesterschiff der "S.M.S. Aquila." Sie lief im Jahre 1807 vom Stapel, und sie wurde in Ancona im Jahre 1815 verschrottet.*

105.) "S.M.S. Gelosa" was the 48th member of the "S.M.S. Aquila" class of Imperial and Royal Austrian wooden cannon-sloops to be named. Her keel was laid down in Venice in 1817, and she was launched on June 7, 1818. She was eventually used as a target vessel (i.e., as target practice for other Austrian naval vessels), and scrapped by 1835.

*Die Segelkanonierschaluppe "S.M.S. Gelosa" war das siebenundvierzigste genannte Schwesterschiff der "S.M.S. Aquila." Sie wurde in Venedig im Jahre 1817 auf Kiel gelegt, und lief am 7. Juni 1818 vom Stapel. Eventuell wurde sie als Zielschiff benutzt, und sie wurde im Jahre 1835 verschrottet.*

106.) "S.M.S. Pandora" was the 49th member of the "S.M.S. Aquila" class of Imperial and Royal Austrian wooden cannon-sloops to be named. Her keel was laid down in Venice in 1817, and she was launched on July 25, 1818. Her naval career was uneventful, and she was scrapped by 1836.

*Die Segelkanonierschaluppe "S.M.S. Pandora" war das achtundvierzigste genannte Schwesterschiff der "S.M.S. Aquila." Sie wurde in Venedig im Jahre 1819 auf Kiel gelegt, und lief am 12. Dezember 1820 vom Stapel. Sie wurde im Jahre 1842 verschrottet.*

107.) "S.M.S. Tremenda" was the 50th member of the "S.M.S. Aquila" class of Imperial and Royal Austrian wooden cannon-sloops to be named. Her keel was laid down in Venice in 1819, and she was launched on December 12, 1820. Her naval career was uneventful, and she was scrapped by 1842.

*Die Segelkanonierschaluppe "S.M.S. Tremenda" war das neunundvierzigste genannte Schwesterschiff der "S.M.S. Aquila." Sie wurde in Venedig im Jahre 1819 auf Kiel gelegt, und lief am 12. Dezember 1820 vom Stapel. Sie wurde auch im Jahre 1842 verschrottet.*

108.) "S.M.S. Fulminante" was the 51st member of the "S.M.S. Aquila" class of Imperial and Royal Austrian wooden cannon-sloops to be named. Her keel was laid down in Venice in 1820, and she was launched on December 21, 1820. Her naval career was uneventful, and she was scrapped by 1835.

*Die Segelkanonierschaluppe "S.M.S. Fulminante" war das fünfzigste genannte Schwesterschiff der "S.M.S. Aquila." Sie wurde in Venedig im Jahre 1820 auf Kiel gelegt, und lief am 21. Dezember 1820 vom Stapel. Sie wurde im Jahre 1835 verschrottet.*

109.) "S.M.S. Tartara" was the 52nd member of the "S.M.S. Aquila" class of Imperial and Royal Austrian wooden cannon-sloops to be named. Her keel was laid down in 1819 in Venice, and she was launched on December 28, 1820. Her naval career was uneventful, and she was scrapped by 1836.

*Die Segelkanonierschaluppe "S.M.S. Tartara" war das einundfünfzigste genannte Schwesterschiff der "S.M.S. Aquila." Sie wurde in Venedig im Jahre 1819 auf Kiel gelegt, und lief am 28. Dezember 1820 vom Stapel. Sie wurde im Jahre 1836 verschrottet.*

110.) "S.M.S. Galatea" was the 53rd and final member of the "S.M.S. Aquila" class of Imperial and Royal Austrian wooden cannon-sloops to be named. Her keel was laid down in Venice in 1824, and she was launched on August 29, 1826. Her naval career was uneventful, and she was scrapped by 1847.

*Die Segelkanonierschaluppe "S.M.S Galatea" war das zweiundfünfzigste und letzte genannte Schwesterschiff der "S.M.S. Aquila." Sie wurde in Venedig im Jahre 1824 auf Kiel gelegt, und lief am 29. August 1826 vom Stapel. Sie wurde im Jahre 1847 verschrottet.*

111.) "S.M.S. Ercole" was a wooden sailing trabaccolo ("Trabakel" in German) of the Imperial and Royal Austrian Navy. She displaced up to 80 tons, was built out of oak and was not armed due to the fact that she began her career as a civilian vessel. She was taken over by the navy and used for transport duties from 1802 to 1806. She was stranded in the Gulf of Medolino on November 3, 1806.

*Das Segeltrabakel "S.M.S. Ercole" war ein Einzelschiff. Sie hatte eine Einsatzverdrängung von 80 Tonnen, war aus Eichenholz gebaut und hatte keine Bewaffnung. Ursprünglich war sie Zivilschiff, und sie gehörte der Kaiserlichen und Königlichen Kriegsmarine nur von 1802 bis sie am 3. November 1806 am Golf von Medolino (heute Medulin in Istrien, Kroatien) strandete und versank. Auf deutsch heißt Istrien auch "Küstenland."*

**Chapter 14 (Kapitel 14): XIII (12) The Smallest Sailing Vessels of the Austro-Venetian Navy (less than 80 tons displacement) / die kleinsten Segelfahrzeuge der Österreichischen Kriegsmarine (weniger als 80 Tonnen)**

*Die kleinsten genannten Segelfahrzeuge der Kaiserlichen und Königlichen Kriegsmarine (weniger als 80 Tonnen Einsatzverdrängung):*

1.) "S.M.S. Saetta" was a wooden sailing battery, laid down in Venice in 1835 and launched on March 12, 1845. She was taken over by revolutionary nationalist Italian rebels in Venice from March 1848 until August 1849. Thereafter, she was liberated and returned to the Imperial and Royal Austrian Navy. She was converted into an ammunition barge in 1871, and into a mine-carrying barge in 1908. She displaced up to 76 tons, was built out of oak, was 17,5 meters long, had a maximum beam of 5,2 meters and a draught of 1,3 meters. She was armed with 1-36 Pounder, 1-18 Pounder and 4-24 Pounders. Her crew consisted of 39 commissioned officers and enlisted men.

*Die Segelbatterie "S.M.S. Saetta" wurde in Venedig im Jahre 1835 auf Kiel gelegt, und lief am 12. März 1845 vom Stapel – zehn Jahre nach der Kiellegung. Zwischen März 1848 und August 1849 wurde sie von feindlichen italienischen Nationalisten beschlagnahmt. Im Jahre 1871 wurde sie als Munitionshulk umgebaut, und dann im Jahre 1908 wurde sie als Minenträger umgebaut. Sie hatte eine Dienstzeit von vielleicht 73 Jahren. Sie hatte eine Einsatzverdrängung von 76 Tonnen, war aus Eichenholz gebaut, war 17,5 Meter lang, hatte eine Breite von 5,2 Meter und ein Tiefgang von 1,3 Meter. Die Bewaffnung des Schiffes bestand aus einem Ein-Pfunder, einem 18-Pfunder und vier 24-Pfundern. Sie hatte eine Besatzung von 39 Offiziere und Matrosen.*

2.) "S.M.S San Francesco delle Vigne" (1802) was a "trabaccolo" (a "Trabakel" in German) of 75 tons displacement. She was used for transport duties within the Austrian Navy, and was surrendered to the Italian allies of Napoleonic France on February 4, 1806.

*Das Segeltrabakel "San Francesco delle Vigne" (1802) hatte eine Einsatzverdrängung von 75 Tonnen. Sie wurde als Transportfahrzeug benutzt, und wurde am 4. Februar 1806 an Frankreich übergeben.*

3.) "S.M.S. Agile" (1815) was a pinnace (called a "Peniche" in German) laid down in Venice, and launched on April 26, 1816. She was scrapped in 1832.

*Die Segelpeniche "S.M.S. Agile" (1815) lief am 26. April 1816 in Venedig vom Stapel, und wurde im Jahre 1832 verschrottet. Eine Segelpeniche war eine verbesserte Segelkanonierschaluppe nach französischen Plänen, jedoch leichter, schärfer und hochbordiger gebaut, deshalb seetüchtiger und besser besegelt. Infolge guter und starker Bauart hatten die Segelpenichen eine längere Lebensdauer. Sie waren als Topsegelschoner getakelt, in drei Größenklaßen und wurden als Stations-und Kurierschiffen benutzt.*

4.) "S.M.S. Amazone" (1815) was the 2nd member of the "S.M.S. Agile" class of pinnaces, laid down in Venice. She was launched on August 16, 1816 and she was scrapped in 1839.

*Die Segelpeniche "S.M.S. Amazone" (1815) war ein Schwesterschiff der "S.M.S. Agile." Sie lief am 16. August 1816 in Venedig vom Stapel, und wurde im Jahre 1839 verschrottet.*

5.) "S.M.S. Ninfa" (1817) was the 3rd member of the "S.M.S. Agile" class of pinnaces, laid down in Venice. She was launched on April 4, 1818. She was stranded in a storm off the coast of Pirano on January 31, 1839. The wreck was scrapped in February 1839.

*Die Segelpeniche "S.M.S. Ninfa" (1817) war das zweite Schwesterschiff der "S.M.S. Agile." Sie lief am 4. April 1818 in Venedig vom Stapel, und strandete am 31. Januar 1839 in einem Sturm an der Küste von Pirano (heute Piran in Slowenien). Im Februar 1839 wurde sie verschrottet.*

6.) "S.M.S. Sirena" (1817) was the 4th member of the "S.M.S. Agile" class of pinnaces, and was laid down in Venice in 1817. She was launched on April 4, 1818, and she served in the Austrian Navy until she was scrapped in the year 1832.

*Die Segelpeniche "S.M.S. Sirena" (1817) war das dritte Schwesterschiff der "S.M.S. Agile." Sie wurde in Venedig im Jahre 1817 auf Kiel gelegt, und lief am 4. April 1818 vom Stapel. Sie wurde im Jahre 1832 verschrottet.*

7.) "S.M.S. Aspide" (1817) was the 5th member of the "S.M.S. Agile" class of wooden sailing pinnaces, and was laid down in Venice in 1817. She was launched on June 27, 1818, and she served the Imperial and Royal Austrian Navy until being scrapped in 1833.

*Die Segelpeniche "S.M.S. Aspide" (1817) war das vierte Schwesterschiff der "S.M.S. Agile." Sie wurde in Venedig im Jahre 1817 auf Kiel gelegt, und lief am 27. Juni 1818 vom Stapel. Sie wurde im Jahre 1833 verschrottet.*

8.) "S.M.S. Baccante" (1817) was the 6th member of the "S.M.S. Agile" class of wooden sailing pinnaces in the Austrian Navy, and was laid down in Venice in 1817. She was launched on September 2, 1818, and she served until being scrapped in 1833.

*Die Segelpeniche "S.M.S. Baccante" (1817) war das fünfte Schwesterschiff der "S.M.S. Agile." Sie wurde in Venedig im Jahre 1817 auf Kiel gelegt, und lief am 2. September 1818 vom Stapel. Sie wurde im Jahre 1833 verschrottet.*

9.) "S.M.S. Costante" (1819) was the 7th member of the "S.M.S. Agile" class of wooden sailing pinnaces, and was launched in Venice on November 19, 1819. She served in the Imperial and Royal Austrian Navy until being scrapped in 1841.

*Die Segelpeniche "S.M.S. Costante" (1819) war das sechste Schwesterschiff der "S.M.S. Agile." Sie lief am 19. November 1819 in Venedig vom Stapel, und wurde im Jahre 1841 verschrottet.*

10.) "S.M.S. Furiosa" (1819) was the 8th member of the "S.M.S. Agile" class of wooden sailing pinnaces, and was launched in Venice on November 27, 1819. She served in the Imperial and Royal Austrian Navy until being scrapped in 1834.

*Die Segelpeniche "S.M.S. Furiosa" (1819) war das siebte Schwesterschiff der "S.M.S. Agile." Sie lief am 27. November 1819 in Venedig vom Stapel, und wurde im Jahre 1834 verschrottet.*

11.) "S.M.S. Sentinella" (1819) was the 9th member of the "S.M.S. Agile" class of wooden sailing pinnaces, and was launched in Venice on May 23, 1820. She served in the Imperial and Royal Austrian Navy until being scrapped in 1832.

*Die Segelpeniche "S.M.S. Sentinella" (1819) war das achte Schwesterschiff der "S.M.S. Agile." Sie lief am 23. Mai 1820 in Venedig vom Stapel, und wurde im Jahre 1832 verschrottet.*

12.) "S.M.S. Gloriosa" (1821) was the 10th member of the "S.M.S. Agile" class of wooden sailing pinnaces, and was launched in Venice in 1821. We have no further data about her service in the Imperial and Royal Austrian Navy.

*Die Segelpeniche "S.M.S. Gloriosa" (1821) war das neunte Schwesterschiff der "S.M.S. Agile." Sie lief im Jahre 1821 in Venedig vom Stapel, aber weiteres ist uns leider nicht bekannt.*

13.) "S.M.S. Lince" (1821) was the 11th member of the "S.M.S. Agile" class of wooden sailing pinnaces, and was launched in Venice on June 4, 1821. She served in the Imperial and Royal Austrian Navy until being scrapped in 1839.

*Die Segelpeniche "S.M.S. Lince" (1821) war das zehnte Schwesterschiff der "S.M.S. Agile." Sie lief am 4. Juni 1821 in Venedig vom Stapel, und wurde im Jahre 1839 verschrottet.*

14.) "S.M.S. Palma" (1821) was the 12th member of the "S.M.S. Agile" class of wooden sailing pinnaces, and was launched in Venice on June 4, 1821. She served in the Imperial and Royal Austrian Navy until be scrapped in 1841.

*Die Segelpeniche "S.M.S. Palma" (1821) war das elfte Schwesterschiff der "S.M.S. Agile." Sie lief am 4. Juni 1821 in Venedig vom Stapel, und wurde im Jahre 1841 verschrottet.*

15.) "S.M.S. Astuta" (1821) was the 13th member of the "S.M.S. Agile" class of wooden sailing pinnaces, and was launched in Venice on August 27, 1821. She served in the Imperial and Royal Austrian Navy until being scrapped in 1835.

*Die Segelpeniche "S.M.S. Astuta" (1821) war das zwölfte Schwesterschiff der "S.M.S. Agile." Sie lief am 27. August 1821 in Venedig vom Stapel, und wurde im Jahre 1835 verschrottet.*

16.) "S.M.S. Ecate" (1821) was the 14th member of the "S.M.S. Agile" class of wooden sailing pinnaces, and was launched in Venice on September 6, 1821. She served in the Imperial and Royal Austrian Navy until being scrapped in 1837.

*Die Segelpeniche "S.M.S. Ecate" (1821) war das dreizehnte Schwesterschiff der "S.M.S. Agile." Sie lief am 6. September 1821 in Venedig vom Stapel, und wurde im Jahre 1837 verschrottet.*

17.) "S.M.S. Vestale" (1821) was the 15th member of the "S.M.S. Agile" class of wooden sailing pinnaces, and was launched in Venice in 1821. She was stranded and lost off the coast of Syra, Venice on October 1, 1822.

*Die Segelpeniche "S.M.S. Vestale" (1821) war das vierzehnte Schwesterschiff der "S.M.S. Agile." Sie lief im Jahre 1821 in Venedig vom Stapel, und strandete am 1. Oktober 1822 in der Nähe von Syra an der Küste von Venedig.*

18.) "S.M.S. Anfitrite" (1824) was the 16th member of the "S.M.S. Agile" class of wooden sailing pinnaces, and was launched in Venice on July 15, 1824. She served in the Imperial and Royal Austrian Navy until being scrapped in 1839.

*Die Segelpeniche "S.M.S. Anfitrite" (1824) war das fünfzehnte Schwesterschiff der "S.M.S. Agile." Sie lief am 15. Juli 1824 in Venedig vom Stapel, und wurde im Jahre 1839 verschrottet.*

19.) "S.M.S. Diana" (1824) was the 17th member of the "S.M.S. Agile" class of wooden sailing pinnaces, and was launched in Venice on August 18, 1824. She served in the Imperial and Royal Austrian Navy until being scrapped in 1843.

*Die Segelpeniche "S.M.S. Diana" (1824) war das sechszehnte Schwesterschiff der "S.M.S. Agile." Sie lief am 18. August 1824 in Venedig vom Stapel, und wurde im Jahre 1843 verschrottet.*

20.) "S.M.S. Leda" (1827) was the 18th member of the "S.M.S. Agile" class of wooden sailing pinnaces, and was launched in Venice on September 27, 1827. In 1847, she was converted into a coal barge, and then in 1857, into fresh water-carrying barge number 22.

*Die Segelpeniche "S.M.S. Leda" (1827) war das siebzehnte Schwesterschiff der "S.M.S. Agile." Sie lief am 27. September 1827 in Venedig vom Stapel, und wurde im Jahre 1847 als Kohlenhulk umgebaut. Im Jahre 1857 wurde sie als Süßwaßerlastkahn Nummer 22 umgebaut. Sie hatte eine Dienstzeit von vielleicht 91 Jahren.*

21.) "S.M.S. Cerere" (1826) was the 19th member of the "S.M.S. Agile" class of wooden sailing pinnaces, and was launched in Venice on December 1, 1827. In 1849, her name was changed to "S.M.S. Ceres." In 1857, she was converted into fresh water-carrying barge number 18.

*Die Segelpeniche "S.M.S. Cerere" (1826) war das achtzehnte Schwesterschiff der "S.M.S. Agile." Sie lief am 1. Dezember 1827 in Venedig vom Stapel, und wurde im Jahre 1849 als die "S.M.S. Ceres" umbenannt. Im Jahre 1857 wurde sie als Süßwaßerlastkahn Nummer 18 umgebaut. Sie hatte eine Dienstzeit von vielleicht 91 Jahren.*

22.) "S.M.S. Pallade" (1827) was the 20th member of the "S.M.S. Agile" class of wooden sailing pinnaces, and was launched in Venice on December 10, 1827. She was briefly captured by Italian nationalist rebels in Venice from March 1848 until August 1849. Upon her return to the Imperial and Royal Austrian Navy in 1849, her name was changed to "S.M.S. Pallas." In 1857, she was converted into coal-carrying barge number 13.

*Die Segelpeniche "S.M.S. Pallade" (1827) war das neunzehnte Schwesterschiff der "S.M.S. Agile." Sie lief am 10. Dezember 1857 in Venedig vom Stapel, und wurde zwischen März 1848 und August 1849 von feindlichen italienischen Nationalisten beschlagnahmt. Danach wurde sie als die "S.M.S. Pallas" umbenannt. Im Jahre 1857 wurde sie als Süßwaßerlastkahn Nummer 13 umgebaut. Sie hatte eine Dienstzeit von vielleicht 91 Jahren.*

23.) "S.M.S. Sibilla" (1827) was the 21st member of the "S.M.S. Agile" class of wooden sailing pinnaces, and was launched in Venice on April 5, 1828. In 1849, her name was changed to "S.M.S. Sibylle." In 1858, she was converted into cargo boat number 37.

*Die Segelpeniche "S.M.S. Sibilla" (1827) war das zwanzigste Schwesterschiff der "S.M.S. Agile." Sie lief am 5. April 1828 in Venedig vom Stapel, und wurde im Jahre 1849 als die "S.M.S. Sibylle" umbenannt. Im Jahre 1858 wurde sie als Frachtboot Nummer 37 umgebaut. Sie hatte eine Dienstzeit von vielleicht 90 Jahren.*

24.) "S.M.S. Tetide" (1827) was the 22nd member of the "S.M.S. Agile" class of wooden sailing pinnaces, and was launched in Venice on April 26, 1828. In 1849, her name was changed to "S.M.S. Thetis." In 1857, she was converted into coal-carrying barge number 11.

*Die Segelpeniche "S.M.S. Tetide" (1827) war das einundzwanzigste Schwesterschiff der "S.M.S. Agile." Sie lief am 26. April 1828 in Venedig vom Stapel, und wurde im Jahre 1849 als die "S.M.S. Thetis" umbenannt. Im Jahre 1857 wurde sie als Kohlenhulk Nummer 11 umgebaut. Sie hatte eine Dienstzeit von vielleicht 90 Jahren.*

25.) "S.M.S. Minerva" (1827) was the 23rd and final named member of the "S.M.S. Agile" class of wooden sailing pinnaces, and was launched in Venice on June 18, 1828. In 1843, her named was changed to "S.M.S. Modesta." In 1852, she was converted into a coal-carrying hulk. In October 1854, she was sunk at her berth in the Dalmatian port of Zara due to an accident. After unsuccessful attempts to raise her in 1855, she was blown up.

*Die Segelpeniche "S.M.S. Minerva" (1827) war das zweiundzwanzigste und letzte genannte Schwesterschiff der "S.M.S. Agile." Sie lief am 18. Juni 1828 in Venedig vom Stapel, und im Jahre 1843 wurde sie als die "S.M.S. Modesta" umbenannt. Im Jahre 1852 wurde sie als Kohlenhulk umgebaut. Im Oktober 1854 wurde sie bei einem Unfall im Marinehafen Zara versenkt. Die Versuche, das Boot im Jahre 1855 zu bergen blieben ohne Erfolg.*

26.) "S.M.S. Morlacca" (1829) was the first member of a brand new class of wooden sailing pinnaces, and was launched in Venice on February 22, 1831. In 1857, she was converted into cargo boat number 12. The boats of this class displaced 72 tons each, were 19 meters long, had a beam of 4,9 meters and a draught of 2,3 meters. Like all Austrian wooden sailing vessels, they were built out of oak. Their armament consisted of 5 cannon (1-12 Pounder, 2-4 Pounders and 2-1 Pounders). The crew was comprised of 26 commissioned officers and enlisted men.

*Die Segelpeniche "S.M.S. Morlacca" (1829) lief am 22. Februar 1831 in Venedig vom Stapel, und wurde im Jahre 1857 als Frachtboot Nummer 12 umgebaut. Sie hatte eine Einsatzverdrängung von 72 Tonnen, war aus Eichenholz gebaut, war 19 Meter lang, hatte eine Breite von 4,9 Meter und einen Tiefgang von 2,3 Meter. Die Bewaffnung des Schiffes bestand aus fünf Kanonen (einem 12-Pfunder, zwei Vier-Pfundern und zwei Ein-Pfunder). Sie hatte eine Besatzung von 26 Offiziere und Matrosen. Sie hatte eine Dienstzeit von vielleicht 87 Jahren.*

27.) "S.M.S. Brenta" (1829) was the 2nd member of the "S.M.S. Morlacca" class of wooden sailing pinnaces, and was launched in Venice on March 1, 1831. In 1857, she was converted into coal depot boat number 8.

*Die Segelpeniche "S.M.S. Brenta" (1829) war ein Schwesterschiff der "S.M.S. Morlacca." Sie lief am 1. März 1831 in Venedig vom Stapel, und im Jahre 1857 wurde sie als Kohlendepotboot Nummer 8 umgebaut. Sie hatte eine Dienstzeit von vielleicht 87 Jahren.*

28.) "S.M.S. Laibach" (1830) was the 3rd member of the "S.M.S. Morlacca" class of wooden sailing pinnaces, and was launched in Venice on September 17, 1831. In 1857, she was converted into cargo boat number 28. She was named after the capital city of the Duchy of Carniola (called "Herzogtum Krain" in German), which is still the capital city of modern Slovenia. About half the people in modern Slovenia speak German as a second language.

*Die Segelpeniche "S.M.S. Laibach" (1830) war das zweite Schwesterschiff der "S.M.S. Morlacca." Sie lief am 17. September 1831 in Venedig vom Stapel, und im Jahre 1857 wurde sie als Frachtboot Nummer 28 umgebaut. Sie hatte eine Dienstzeit von vielleicht 87 Jahren. Die Stadt Laibach war die Hauptstadt des Herzogtums Krain, und ist heute die Hauptstadt Sloweniens – wo immer noch die Hälfte der Gesamtbevölkerung deutsch spricht.*

29.) "S.M.S. Salona" (1831) was the 4th member of the "S.M.S. Morlacca" class of wooden sailing pinnaces, and was launched in Venice on March 17, 1832. She was briefly captured by Italian nationalist rebels in Venice from March 1848 until being liberated by Austrian forces in August 1849. She was scrapped in 1863.

*Die Segelpeniche "S.M.S. Salona" (1831) war das dritte Schwesterschiff der "S.M.S. Morlacca." Sie lief am 17. März 1832 in Venedig vom Stapel, und wurde zwischen März 1848 und August 1849 von feindlichen italienischen Nationalisten beschlagnahmt. Sie wurde im Jahre 1863 verschrottet.*

30.) "S.M.S. Iride" (1831) was the 5th member of the "S.M.S. Morlacca" class of wooden sailing pinnaces, and was launched in Venice on August 1, 1832. In 1849, whe was renamed "S.M.S. Iris." In 1858, she was converted into cargo boat number 41. In 1866, she was converted yet again to carry coal.

*Die Segelpeniche "S.M.S. Iride" (1831) war das vierte Schwesterschiff der "S.M.S. Morlacca." Sie lief am 1. August 1832 in Venedig vom Stapel, und im Jahre 1849 wurde sie als die "S.M.S. Iris" umbenannt. Im Jahre 1858 wurde sie als Lastboot Nummer 41 umbenannt, und im Jahre 1866 wurde sie als Kohlenhulk umgebaut. Sie hatte eine Dienstzeit von vielleicht 86 Jahren.*

31.) "S.M.S. Agile" (1832) was the 6th member of the "S.M.S. Morlacca" class of wooden sailing pinnaces, and was launched in Venice on January 19, 1833. In 1857, she was converted into fresh water-carrying barge number 19.

*Die Segelpeniche "S.M.S. Agile" (1832) was das fünfte Schwesterschiff der "S.M.S. Morlacca." Sie lief am 19. Januar 1833 in Venedig vom Stapel, und wurde im Jahre 1857 als Süßwaßerlastkahn Nummer 19 umgebaut. Sie hatte eine Dienstzeit von vielleicht 85 Jahren.*

32.) "S.M.S. Aquila" (1831) was the 7th member of the "S.M.S. Morlacca" class of wooden sailing pinnaces, and was launched in Venice on September 2, 1833. In 1857, she was converted into cargo boat number 33.

*Die Segelpeniche "S.M.S. Aquila" (1831) war das sechste Schwesterschiff der "S.M.S. Morlacca." Sie lief am 2. September 1833 in Venedig vom Stapel, und im Jahre 1857 wurde sie als Frachtboot Nummer 33 umgebaut. Sie hatte eine Dienstzeit von vielleicht 85 Jahren.*

33.) "S.M.S. Sirena" (1833) was the 8th member of the "S.M.S. Morlacca" class of wooden sailing pinnaces, and was launched in Venice on October 17, 1833. In 1849, her name was changed to "S.M.S. Sirene." In 1854, she was converted into a fresh water-carrying barge (pennant number not known).

*Die Segelpeniche "S.M.S. Sirena" (1833) war das siebte Schwesterschiff der "S.M.S. Morlacca." Sie lief am 17. Oktober 1833 in Venedig vom Stapel, und im Jahre 1849 wurde sie als die "S.M.S. Sirene" umbenannt. Im Jahre 1854 wurde sie als Süßwaßerlastkahn umgebaut (Nummer nicht bekannt). Sie hatte eine Dienstzeit von vielleicht 85 Jahren.*

34.) "S.M.S. Baccante" (1833) was the 9th member of the "S.M.S. Morlacca" class of wooden sailing pinnaces, and was launched in Venice on December 7, 1833. In 1857, she was converted into coal hulk number 10. She was scrapped in 1861.

*Die Segelpeniche "S.M.S. Baccante" (1833) war das achte Schwesterschiff der "S.M.S. Morlacca." Sie lief am 7. Dezember 1833 in Venedig vom Stapel, und im Jahre 1857 wurde sie als Kohlenhulk Nummer 10 umgebaut. Sie wurde im Jahre 1861 verschrottet.*

35.) "S.M.S. Sentinella" (1833) was the 10th member of the "S.M.S. Morlacca" class of wooden sailing pinnaces, and was launched in Venice on February 5, 1834. In 1852, she was converted into a barge. In 1857, she was converted yet again into cargo boat number 21. Thereafter (unknown year) she was converted into a fresh water-carrying barge.

*Die Segelpeniche "S.M.S. Sentinella" (1833) war das neunte Schwesterschiff der "S.M.S. Morlacca." Sie lief am 5. Februar 1834 in Venedig vom Stapel, und im Jahre 1852 wurde sie als Lastkahn umgebaut. Im Jahre 1857 wurde sie als Frachtboot Nummer 21 umgebaut, und danach als Süßwaßerlastkahn umgebaut. Sie hatte eine Dienstzeit von vielleicht 84 Jahren.*

36.) "S.M.S. Aspide" (1833) was the 11th member of the "S.M.S. Morlacca" class of wooden sailing pinnaces, and was launched in Venice on May 7, 1834. In 1849, her name was changed to "S.M.S. Aspis." In 1858, she was converted into cargo boat number 42.

*Die Segelpeniche "S.M.S. Aspide" (1833) war das zehnte Schwesterschiff der "S.M.S. Morlacca." Sie lief am 7. Mai 1834 in Venedig vom Stapel, und im Jahre 1849 wurde sie als die "S.M.S. Aspis" umbenannt. Im Jahre 1858 wurde sie als Frachtboot Nummer 42 umgebaut. Sie hatte eine Dienstzeit von viellecht 84 Jahren.*

37.) "S.M.S. Elena" (1834) was the 12th member of the "S.M.S. Morlacca" class of wooden sailing pinnaces, and was launched in Venice on September 18, 1834. In 1858, she was converted into cargo boat number 40. Thereafter (year of conversion unknown), she was converted yet again into a coal carryer.

*Die Segelpeniche "S.M.S Elena" (1834) war das elfte Schwesterschiff der "S.M.S. Morlacca." Sie lief am 18. September 1834 in Venedig vom Stapel, und im Jahre 1858 wurde sie als Frachtboot Nummer 40 umgebaut. Danach wurde sie als Kohlenhulk umgebaut. Sie hatte eine Dienstzeit von vielleicht 84 Jahren.*

38.) "S.M.S. Furiosa" (1834) was the 13th member of the "S.M.S. Morlacca" class of wooden sailing pinnaces, and was launched in Venice on December 13, 1834. She was captured by Italian nationalist rebels in 1848, and was sunk in a skirmish with Imperial and Royal Austrian coastal batteries on June 13, 1848. This happened off the coast of Caorle, Venice and she was blown to bits in the process of the battle.

*Die Segelpeniche "S.M.S. Furiosa" (1834) war das zwölfte Schwesterschiff der "S.M.S. Morlacca." Sie lief am 13. Dezember 1834 in Venedig vom Stapel, und wurde im März 1848 von feindlichen italienischen Nationalisten beschlagnahmt. Am 13. Juni 1848 wurde sie von österreichischen Küstenbatterien in der Nähe von Caorle (Venedig) versenkt.*

39.) "S.M.S. Astuta" (1835) was the 14th member of the "S.M.S. Morlacca" class of wooden sailing pinnaces, and was launched in Venice on August 6, 1836. In 1866, she was converted into an ammunition depot boat. She was scrapped in 1868.

*Die Segelpeniche "S.M.S. Astuta" (1835) war das dreizehnte Schwesterschiff der "S.M.S. Morlacca." Sie lief am 6. August 1836 in Venedig vom Stapel, und wurde im Jahre 1866 als Munitionsdepotboot umgebaut. Sie wurde im Jahre 1868 verschrottet.*

40.) "S.M.S. Ecate" (1837) was the 15th member of the "S.M.S. Morlacca" class of wooden sailing pinnaces, and was launched in Venice on July 19, 1838. In 1849, she was renamed "S.M.S. Hecate." In 1866, she was converted into an ammunition depot boat.

*Die Segelpeniche "S.M.S. Ecate" (1837) war das vierzehnte Schwesterschiff der "S.M.S. Morlacca." Sie lief am 19. Juli 1838 in Venedig vom Stapel, und wurde im Jahre 1848 als die "S.M.S. Hecate" umbenannt. Im Jahre 1866 wurde sie als Munitionsdepotboot umgebaut. Sie hatte eine Dienstzeit von vielleicht 80 Jahren.*

41.) "S.M.S. Vestale" (1837) was the 16th member of the "S.M.S. Morlacca" class of wooden sailing pinnaces, and was launched in Venice on January 18, 1839. In 1857, she was converted into coal barge number 9.

*Die Segelpeniche "S.M.S. Vestale" (1837) war das fünfzehnte Schwesterschiff der "S.M.S. Morlacca." Sie lief am 18. Januar 1839 in Venedig vom Stapel, und wurde im Jahre 1857 als Kohlenhulk Nummer 9 umgebaut. Sie hatte eine Dienstzeit von vielleicht 79 Jahren.*

42.) "S.M.S. Amazone" (1838) was the 17th member of the "S.M.S. Morlacca" class of wooden sailing pinnaces, and was launched in Venice on June 26, 1839. She was briefly captured by Italian nationalist rebels from March 1848 until August 1849. She was stranded off the coast of Veruda, Venice on July 2, 1854 and scrapped shortly thereafter.

*Die Segelpeniche "S.M.S. Amazone" (1838) war das sechszehnte Schwesterschiff der "S.M.S. Morlacca." Sie lief am 26. Juni 1839 in Venedig vom Stapel, und wurde zwischen März 1848 und August 1849 von feindlichen italienischen Nationalisten beschlagnahmt. Am 2. Juli 1854 strandete sie an der Küste von Veruda (Venedig) und kurz danach wurde sie verschrottet.*

43.) "S.M.S. Ninfa" (1839) was the 18th member of the "S.M.S. Morlacca" class of wooden sailing pinnaces, and was launched in Venice on August 31, 1839. In 1852, she was converted into coal hulk number 14.

*Die Segelpeniche "S.M.S. Ninfa" (1839) war das siebzehnte Schwesterschiff der "S.M.S. Morlacca." Sie lief am 31. August 1839 in Venedig vom Stapel, und wurde im Jahre 1852 als Kohlenhulk Nummer 14 umgebaut. Sie hatte eine Dienstzeit von vielleicht 79 Jahren.*

44.) "S.M.S. Bocchese" (1839) was the 19th member of the "S.M.S. Morlacca" class of wooden sailing pinnaces, and was launched in Venice on November 30, 1839. In 1858, she was converted into cargo boat number 36.

*Die Segelpeniche "S.M.S. Bocchese" (1839) war das achtzehnte Schwesterschiff der "S.M.S. Morlacca." Sie lief am 30. November 1839 in Venedig vom Stapel, und im Jahre 1858 wurde sie als Frachtboot Nummer 36 umgebaut. Sie hatte eine Dienstzeit von ungefähr 79 Jahren.*

45.) "S.M.S. Lince" (1839) was the 20th member of the "S.M.S. Morlacca" class of wooden sailing pinnaces, and was launched in Venice on February 9, 1841. In 1849, she was renamed "S.M.S. Linx." In 1858, she was converted into cargo boat number 45.

*Die Segelpeniche "S.M.S. Lince" (1839) war das neunzehnte Schwesterschiff der "S.M.S. Morlacca." Sie lief am 9. Februar 1841 in Venedig vom Stapel, und wurde im Jahre 1849 als die "S.M.S. Linx" umbenannt. Im Jahre 1858 wurde sie zum Frachtboot Nummer 45 umgebaut. Sie hatte eine Dienstzeit von fast 77 Jahren.*

46.) "S.M.S. Anfitrite" (1839) was the 21st member of the "S.M.S. Morlacca" class of wooden sailing pinnaces, and was launched in Venice on November 16, 1841. In 1858, she was converted into cargo boat number 38.

*Die Segelpeniche "S.M.S Anfitrite" (1839) war das zwanzigste Schwesterschiff der "S.M.S. Morlacca." Sie lief am 16. November 1841 in Venedig vom Stapel, und im Jahre 1858 wurde sie zum Frachtboot Nummer 38 umgebaut. Sie hatte eine Dienstzeit von zirka 77 Jahren.*

47.) "S.M.S. Najade" (1839) was the 22nd member of the "S.M.S. Morlacca" class of wooden sailing pinnaces, and was launched in Venice on December 23, 1841. She was converted into a general-purpose hulk in 1875. In 1901, she was converted into coal barge number K60 – and she was still in service as late as 1911, 72 years after her keel was laid down.

*Die Segelpeniche "S.M.S. Najade" (1839) war das einundzwanzigste Schwesterschiff der "S.M.S. Morlacca." Sie lief am 23. Dezember 1841 in Venedig vom Stapel, und im Jahre wurde sie zum Hulk umgebaut. Im Jahre 1901 wurde sie zum Kohlenhulk Nummer K.60 umgebaut. Sie hatte eine Dienstzeit von nahezu 77 Jahren.*

48.) "S.M.S. Palma" (1841) was the 23rd member of the "S.M.S. Morlacca" class of wooden sailing pinnaces, and was launched in Venice on February 21, 1843. She was briefly captured by Italian nationalist rebels from March 1848 until August 1849. In 1857, she was converted into coal barge number 6. In 1859, she was converted yet again into a munitions-carrying boat.

*Die Segelpeniche "S.M.S. Palma" war das zweiundzwanzigste Schwesterschiff der "S.M.S. Morlacca." Sie lief am 21. Februar 1843 in Venedig vom Stapel. Zwischen März 1848 und August 1849 wurde sie von feindlichen italienischen Nationalisten beschlagnahmt. Im Jahre 1857 wurde sie zum Kohlenhulk Nummer 6 umgebaut, und im Jahre 1859 wurde sie als Munitionsboot umgebaut. Sie hatte eine Dienstzeit von vielleicht 75 Jahren.*

49.) "S.M.S. Costante" (1841) was the 24th member of the "S.M.S. Morlacca" class of wooden sailing pinnaces, and was launched in Venice on April 10, 1843. In 1857, she was converted into the fresh water-carrying barge number 20.

*Die Segelpeniche "S.M.S. Costante" (1841) war das dreiundzwanzigste Schwesterschiff der "S.M.S. Morlacca." Sie lief am 10. April 1843 in Venedig vom Stapel, und im Jahre 1857 wurde sie zum Süßwaßerlastkahn Nummer 20 umgebaut. Sie hatte eine Dienstzeit von ungefähr 75 Jahren.*

50.) "S.M.S. Diana" (1843) was the 25th and final named member of the "S.M.S. Morlacca" class of wooden sailing pinnaces, and was launched in Venice on July 27, 1844. In 1857, she was converted into coal barge number 7. She was stranded off the coast of Caroman-Venetien, Venice in December 1859. In 1860, she was raised and scrapped.

*Die Segelpeniche "S.M.S. Diana" (1843) war das vierundzwanzigste und letzte genannte Schwesterschiff der "S.M.S. Morlacca." Sie lief am 27. Juli 1844 in Venedig vom Stapel, und im Jahre 1857 war sie zum Kohenhulk Nummer 7 umgebaut. Im Dezember 1859 strandete sie an der Küste von Caroman (Venedig), und im Jahre 1860 wurde sie geborgen und verschrottet.*

51.) "S.M.S. Brenta" (1811) was the first member of another class of wooden sailing pinnaces in the Imperial and Royal Austrian Navy. She and her sister vessels were captured from the Italian allies of Napoleonic France, and entered the Austrian Navy in the Gulf of Cattaro (in modern day Montenegro) in

September of 1813. She was scrapped in 1829. She displaced 67 tons, was 19 meters long, had a beam of 4,6 meters and a draught of 1,9 meters. Like all wooden sailing vessels in the Austrian Navy, she was built out of oak. She and her sister vessels were built in Venice, were armed with just one 12-Pounder cannon, and were manned by a crew of 27 commissioned officers and enlisted sailors.

*Die Segelpeniche "S.M.S. Brenta" (1811) und ihre Schwesterschiffe wurden von den italienischen Waffenverbündeten Frankreichs im September 1813 beschlagnahmt, und von der Kaiserlichen und Königlichen Kriegsmarine Österreichs eingenommen. Die "S.M.S. Brenta" hatte eine Einsatzverdrängung von 67 Tonnen, war 19 Meter lang, hatte eine Breite von 4,6 Meter und einen Tiefgang von 1,9 Meter. Sie wurde in Venedig aus Eichenholz gebaut. Ihre Bewaffnung bestand aus einem 12-Pfunder, und sie hatte eine Besatzung von 27 Offiziere und Matrosen. Sie wurde im Jahre 1829 verschrottet.*

52.) "S.M.S. Bocchese" (1811) was the 2nd member of the "S.M.S. Brenta" class of wooden sailing pinnaces. She was scrapped in 1839.

*Die Segelpeniche "S.M.S. Bocchese" (1811) war ein Schwesterschiff der "S.M.S. Brenta." Sie wurde im Jahre 1839 verschrottet.*

53.) "S.M.S. Gliuta" (1811) was the 3rd member of the "S.M.S. Brenta" class of wooden sailing pinnaces, and was commissioned into the Imperial and Royal Austrian Navy in the Dalmatian port of Zara on December 5, 1813. She was scrapped in 1821.

*Die Segelpeniche "S.M.S. Gliuta" (1811) war das zweite Schwesterschiff der "S.M.S. Brenta." Sie war im Kriegshafen Zara in Dalmatien (Kroatien) stationiert, und wurde im Jahre 1821 verschrottet.*

54.) "S.M.S. Laibach" (1811) was the 4th member of the "S.M.S. Brenta" class of wooden sailing pinnaces, and was commissioned into the Austrian Navy in the Dalmatian port of Zara on December 5, 1813. She was scrapped in 1830. She was named after the capital city of the Duchy of Carniola (called "Herzogtum Krain" in German), which is still the capital city of modern-day Slovenia. About half the population in Slovenia speaks German today.

*Die Segelpeniche "S.M.S. Laibach" (1811) war das dritte Schwesterschiff der "S.M.S. Brenta." Sie war auch im Kriegshafen Zara in Dalmatien (Kroatien) stationiert, und wurde im Jahre 1830 verschrottet.*

55.) S.M.S. Morlacca" (1811) was the 5th member of the "S.M.S. Brenta" class of wooden sailing pinnaces, and was commissioned into the Austrian Navy in the Dalmatian port of Zara on December 5, 1813.  She was scrapped in 1827.

*Die Segelpeniche "S.M.S. Morlacca" (1811) war das vierte Schwesterschiff der "S.M.S. Brenta."  Sie war auch im Kriegshafen Zara in Dalmatien (Kroatien) stationiert, und wurde im Jahre 1827 verschrottet.*

56.) "S.M.S. Narenta" (1811) was the 6th member of the "S.M.S. Brenta" class of wooden sailing pinnaces, and was commissioned into the Austrian Navy in the Dalmatian port of Zara on December 5, 1813.  She was scrapped during the decade of the 1820s (specific year not known).

*Die Segelpeniche "S.M.S. Narenta" (1811) war das fünfte Schwesterschiff der "S.M.S. Brenta."  Sie war auch im Kriegshafen Zara in Dalmatien (Kroatien) stationiert, und wurde in den 1820er Jahren verschrotiet.*

57.) "S.M.S. Ragusa" (1811) was the 7th member of the "S.M.S. Brenta" class of wooden sailing pinnaces, and was commissioned into the Austrian Navy in the Dalmatian port of Zara on December 5, 1813.  The Dalmatian port city of Ragusa is now known as "Dubrovnik" in modern Croatia.

*Die Segelpeniche "S.M.S. Ragusa" (1811) war das sechste Schwesterschiff der "S.M.S. Brenta."  Sie war auch im Kriegshafen Zara in Dalmatien (Kroatien) stationiert, und hatte eine Dienstzeit von vielleicht 107 Jahren.  Die Hafenstadt Ragusa nennt sich heute "Dubrovnik" in Kroatien.*

58.) "S.M.S. Rovignese" (1811) was the 8th member of the "S.M.S. Brenta" class of wooden sailing pinnaces, and was commissioned into the Austrian Navy in the Dalmatian port of Zara on December 5, 1813.  She was scrapped in 1827.

*Die Segelpeniche "S.M.S. Rovignese" (1811) war das siebte Schwesterschiff der "S.M.S. Brenta."  Sie war auch im Kriegshafen Zara in Dalmatien (Kroatien) stationiert, und wurde im Jahre 1827 verschrottet.*

59.) "S.M.S. Salona" (1811) was the 9th member of the "S.M.S. Brenta" class of wooden sailing pinnaces, and was commissioned into the Austrian Navy in the Dalmatian port of Zara on December 5, 1813.  She was scrapped in 1831.

*Die Segelpeniche "S.M.S. Salona" (1811) war das achte Schwesterschiff der "S.M.S. Brenta." Sie war auch im Kriegshafen Zara in Dalmatien (Kroatien) stationiert, und wurde im Jahre 1831 verschrottet.*

60.) "S.M.S. Triestina" (1811) was the 10th member of the "S.M.S. Brenta" class of wooden sailing pinnaces, and was commissioned into the Austrian Navy in the Dalmatian port of Zara on December 5, 1813. She was scrapped in 1826.

*Die Segelpeniche "S.M.S. Triestina" (1811) war das neunte Schwesterschiff der "S.M.S. Brenta." Sie war auch im Kriegshafen Zara in Dalmatien (Kroatien) stationiert, und wurde im Jahre 1826 verschrottet.*

61.) "S.M.S. Aspide" (1811) was the 11th member of the "S.M.S. Brenta" class of wooden sailing pinnaces. She was not kept by the Austrians for long, and was both commissioned and scrapped in 1814.

*Die Segelpeniche "S.M.S. Aspide" (1811) war das zehnte Schwesterschiff der "S.M.S. Brenta." Sie existierte überhaupt nicht lange. Sie lief vom Stapel und wurde schon im Jahre 1814 verschrottet.*

62.) "S.M.S. Bianca" (1812) was the 12th member of the "S.M.S. Brenta" class of wooden sailing pinnaces, and was commissioned into the Austrian Navy in 1814. She was scrapped in 1819.

*Die Segelpeniche "S.M.S. Bianca" (1812) war das elfte Schwesterschiff der "S.M.S. Brenta." Sie wurde im Jahre 1814 getauft und wurde schon im Jahre 1819 verschrottet.*

63.) "S.M.S. Bionda" (1812) was the 13th member of the "S.M.S. Brenta" class of wooden sailing pinnaces, and was commissioned into the Austrian Navy in 1814. She was scrapped in 1824.

*Die Segelpeniche "S.M.S. Bionda" (1812) war das zwölfte Schwesterschiff der "S.M.S. Brenta." Sie wurde im Jahre 1814 getauft und wurde schon im Jahre 1824 verschrottet.*

64.) "S.M.S. Elena" (1812) was the 14th member of the "S.M.S. Brenta" class of wooden sailing pinnaces, and was commissioned into the Austrian Navy in 1814. She was scrapped in 1833.

*Die Segelpeniche "S.M.S. Elena" (1812) war das dreizehnte Schwesterschiff der "S.M.S. Brenta." Sie wurde im Jahre 1814 getauft und dann im Jahre 1833 verschrottet.*

65.) "S.M.S. Fiamma" (1812) was the 15th member of the "S.M.S. Brenta" class of wooden sailing pinnaces, and was commissioned into the Austrian Navy in 1814. She was scrapped in 1819.

*Die Segelpeniche "S.M.S. Fiamma" (1812) war das vierzehnte Schwesterschiff der "S.M.S. Brenta." Sie wurde im Jahre 1814 getauft und wurde schon im Jahre 1819 verschrottet.*

66.) "S.M.S. Fiumana" (1811) was the 16th member of the "S.M.S. Brenta" class of wooden sailing pinnaces, and was commissioned into the Austrian Navy in 1814. She was scrapped in 1829.

*Die Segelpeniche "S.M.S. Fiumana" (1811) war das fünfzehnte Schwesterschiff der "S.M.S. Brenta." Sie wurde im Jahre 1814 getauft und im Jahre 1829 verschrottet.*

67.) "S.M.S. Lubna" (1811) was the 17th member of the "S.M.S. Brenta" class of wooden sailing pinnaces, and was commissioned into the Austrian Navy in 1814. She was scrapped sometime after 1816.

*Die Segelpeniche "S.M.S. Lubna" (1811) war das sechszehnte Schwesterschiff der "S.M.S. Brenta." Sie wurde im Jahre 1814 getauft und schon nach 1816 verschrottet.*

68.) "S.M.S. Sdobba" (1811) was the 18th member of the "S.M.S. Brenta" class of wooden sailing pinnaces, and was commissioned into the Austrian Navy in 1814. She was scrapped in 1824.

*Die Segelpeniche "S.M.S. Sdobba" (1811) war das siebzehnte Schwesterschiff der "S.M.S. Brenta." Sie wurde im Jahre 1814 getauft und im Jahre 1824 verschrottet.*

69.) "S.M.S. Trevisana" (1811) was the 19th and final named member of the "S.M.S. Brenta" class of wooden sailing pinnaces, and was commissioned into the Austrian Navy in 1814. She was stranded and wrecked in 1818 (location not known).

*Die Segelpeniche "S.M.S. Trevisana" (1811) war das achtzehnte und letzte genannte Schwesterschiff der "S.M.S. Brenta." Sie wurde im Jahre 1814 getauft und strandete im Jahre 1818 (der Ort der Strandung ist unbekannt).*

70.) "S.M.S. Fortunato" (1833) was a "trabaccolo" (called a "Trabakel" in German), laid down in Venice and launched on September 2, 1833. She was assigned to transport duties in the Imperial and Royal Austrian Navy, and was briefly captured by Italian nationalist rebels in Venice from March 1848 until August 1849. She was scrapped in 1862. She displaced 60 tons, was 18 meters long and had beam of 5,9 meters. Like all Austrian wooden sailing vessels, she was built out of oak.

*Das Segeltrabakel "S.M.S. Fortunato" lief am 2. September 1833 in Venedig vom Stapel. Zwischen März 1848 und August 1849 wurde sie von feindlichen italienischen Nationalisten beschlagnahmt. Sie wurde im Jahre 1862 verschrottet. Sie hatte eine Einsatzverdrängung von 60 Tonnen, war aus Eichenholz gebaut, war 18 Meter lang und hatte eine Breite von 5,9 Meter.*

71.) "S.M.S. Fedele" (1833) was the only named sister vessel of "S.M.S. Fortunato," and was laid down in Venice. She was launched on November 9, 1833, and was assigned to transport duties in the Austrian Navy. The remainder of her service was identical to that of "S.M.S. Fortunato."

*Das Segeltrabakel "S.M.S. Fedele" (1833) war das einzige genannte Schwesterboot der "S.M.S. Fortunato." Sie lief am 9. November 1833 in Venedig vom Stapel, und ihre Lebensgeschichte war die der "S.M.S. Fortunato" sehr ähnlich.*

72.) "S.M.S. Intrepido" (1830) was the sole wooden sailing "trabaccolo" (called a "Trabakel" in German) in her class, and was used as a transport vessel. She was laid down in Venice in 1830, and was launched on July 30, 1831. She was briefly captured by Italian nationalist rebels in Venice from March 1848 until August 1849, and was scrapped in 1862. She displaced 58 tons, was 18 meters long, and had a beam of 5,9 meters. She was built out of oak, and had a crew of just 9 officers and men.

*Das Segeltrabakel "S.M.S. Intrepido" (1830) war ein Einzelboot. Sie wurde im Jahre 1830 in Venedig auf Kiel gelegt, und lief am 30. Juli 1831 vom Stapel. Zwischen März 1848 und August 1849 wurde sie von feindlichen italienischen Nationalisten beschlagnahmt. Sie wurde im Jahre 1862 verschrottet. Sie hatte eine Einsatzverdrängung von 58 Tonnen, war 18 Meter lang, hatte eine Breite von*

*5,9 Meter, war aus Eichenholz gebaut, und hatte eine Besatzung von 9 Offiziere und Matrosen.*

73.) "S.M.S. Rondine" (1828) was the first member of yet another class of wooden sailing pinnaces, and was built in Venice. She was launched on October 25, 1828, and was briefly captured by Italian nationalist rebels in Venice from March 1848 until August 1849. In late 1849, she was renamed "S.M.S. Schwalbe" (which means the bird type "swallow" in German). In 1858, she was converted into cargo boat number 43. In 1861, she was converted again, and this time into a mine-carrying barge. In 1866, she was assigned to harbor guard duties. She and her sisters displaced 56 tons each, were 17,6 meters long, had a beam of 4,2 meters and a draught of 1,6 meters. Like all wooden sailing vessels from Austria, she was built out of oak. She was armed with 3 cannon (1-12 Pounder and 2-1 Pounders) and had a crew of 26 commissioned officers and enlisted men.

*Die Segelpeniche "S.M.S. Rondine" (1828) lief am 25. Oktober 1828 in Venedig vom Stapel. Zwischen März 1848 und August 1849 wurde sie von feindlichen italienischen Nationalisten beschlagnahmt. Spät im Jahr 1849 wurde sie als "S.M.S. Schwalbe" umbenannt. Im Jahre 1858 wurde sie zum Frachter Nummer 43 umgebaut. Im Jahre 1861 wurde sie zum Minenträger umgebaut, und nach 1866 wurde sie für den Hafenwachtdienst benutzt. Sie hatte eine Dienstzeit von ungefähr 90 Jahren. Sie hatte eine Einsatzverdrängung von 56 Tonnen, war aus Eichenholz gebaut, war 17,6 Meter lang, hatte eine Breite von 4,2 Meter und einen Tiefgang von 1,6 Meter. Ihre Bewaffnung bestand aus einem 12-Pfunder und zwei Ein-Pfundern. Sie hatte eine Besatzung von 26 Offiziere und Matrosen.*

74.) "S.M.S. Volpe" (1828) was the 2nd member of the "S.M.S. Rondine" class of wooden sailing pinnaces, and was built in Venice. She was launched on December 18, 1828, and was briefly captured by Italian nationalist rebels in Venice from March 1848 until August 1849. In 1853, she was converted into the coal-carrying hulk number 15. On September 19, 1861 she was sunk due to an accident near Kumbor in the Gulf of Cattaro (in modern day Montenegro). She was raised and scrapped in December 1861.

*Die Segelpeniche "S.M.S. Volpe" (1828) war ein Schwesterboot der "S.M.S. Rondine." Sie lief am 18. Dezember 1828 in Venedig vom Stapel. Zwischen März 1848 und August 1849 wurde sie von feindlichen italienischen Nationalisten beschlagnahmt. Im Jahre 1853 wurde sie zum Kohlenhulk Nummer 15 umgebaut. Am 19. September 1861 wurde sie bei einem Unfall im Golf von Cattaro (heute*

"Kotor" in Montenegro) versenkt. Im Dezember 1861 wurde sie geborgen und verschrottet.

75.) "S.M.S. Lampreda" (1828) was the 3rd member of the "S.M.S. Rondine" class of wooden sailing pinnaces, and was built in Venice. She was launched on January 13, 1829, and was briefly captured by Italian nationalist rebels in Venice from March 1848 until August 1849. In 1857, she was converted into general-purpose barge number 25.

*Die Segelpeniche "S.M.S. Lampreda" (1828) war das zweite Schwesterboot der "S.M.S. Rondine." Sie lief am 13. Januar 1829 in Venedig vom Stapel. Zwischen März 1848 und August 1849 wurde sie von feindlichen italienischen Nationalisten beschlagnahmt. Im Jahre 1857 wurde sie zum Lastkahn Nummer 25 umgebaut. Sie hatte eine Dienstzeit von fast 89 Jahren.*

76.) "S.M.S. Serpe" (1828) was the 4th member of the "S.M.S. Rondine" class of wooden sailing pinnaces, and was built in Venice. She was launched on March 7, 1829, and was briefly captured by Italian nationalist rebels in Venice from March 1848 until August 1849. In late 1849, she was renamed "S.M.S. Schlange" (which means "snake" in German). In 1858, she was converted into cargo boat number 39.

*Die Segelpeniche "S.M.S. Serpe" (1828) war das dritte Schwesterboot der "S.M.S. Rondine." Sie lief am 7. März 1829 in Venedig vom Stapel, und wurde zwischen März 1848 und August 1849 von feindlichen italienischen Nationalisten beschlagnahmt. Spät im Jahr 1849 wurde sie als die "S.M.S. Schlange" umbenannt. Im Jahre 1858 wurde sie zum Frachter Nummer 39 umgebaut. Sie hatte eine Dienstzeit von zirka 89 Jahren.*

77.) "S.M.S. Leggera" (1829) was the 5th and final named member of the "S.M.S. Rondine" class of wooden sailing pinnaces, and was built in Venice. She was launched on October 8, 1829, and was briefly captured by Italian nationalist rebels in Venice from March 1848 until August 1849. In 1854, she was converted into general-purpose barge number VI. In 1857, her pennant or "call" number was changed to 26.

*Die Segelpeniche "S.M.S. Leggera" (1829) war das vierte und letzte genannte Schwesterboot der "S.M.S. Rondine." Sie lief am 8. Oktober 1829 in Venedig vom Stapel, und wurde zwischen März 1848 und August 1849 von feindlichen italienischen Nationalisten beschlagnahmt. Im Jahre 1854 wurde sie zum*

*Lastkahn Nummer VI umgebaut, und im Jahre 1857 wurde sie als Lastkahn Nummer 26 umbenannt. Sie hatte eine Dienstzeit von nahezu 89 Jahren.*

78.) "S.M.S. Andromaca" (1829) was the first member of another class of wooden sailing pinnaces, and was built in Venice. She was launched on Feburary 28, 1830, and was briefly captured by Italian nationalist rebels in Venice from March 1848 until August 1849. In late 1849, she was renamed "S.M.S. Andromache." In 1857, she was converted into coal-carrying barge number 27. She displaced 44 tons, was 16,3 meters long, had a beam of 3,9 meters and a draught of 1,5 meters. Like all wooden sailing vessels from Austria, she was built out of oak. She was armed with one 12-Pounder cannon, and had a crew of 26 commissioned officers and enlisted men.

*Die Segelpeniche "S.M.S. Andromaca" (1829) lief am 28. Februar 1830 in Venedig vom Stapel, und wurde zwischen März 1848 und August 1849 von feindlichen italienischen Nationalisten beschlagnahmt. Spät im Jahr 1849 wurde sie als die "S.M.S. Andromache" umbenannt. Im Jahre 1857 wurde sie zum Kohlenhulk Nummer 27 umgebaut. Sie hatte eine Dienstzeit von vielleicht 88 Jahren. Sie hatte eine Einsatzverdrängung von 44 Tonnen, war aus Eichenholz gebaut, war 16,3 Meter lang, hatte eine Breite von 3,9 Meter und einen Tiefgang von 1,5 Meter. Ihre Bewaffnung bestand aus einem 12-Pfunder, und sie hatte eine Besatzung von 26 Offiziere und Matrosen.*

79.) "S.M.S. Zaira" (1831) was the 2nd and final member of the "S.M.S. Andromaca" class of wooden sailing pinnaces, and was built in Venice. She was launched on September 1, 1831, and was briefly captured by Italian nationalist rebels in Venice from March 1848 until August 1849. In 1858, she was converted into cargo boat number 44.

*Die Segelpeniche "S.M.S. Zaira" (1831) war das einzige Schwesterboot der "S.M.S. Andromaca." Sie lief am 1. September 1831 in Venedig vom Stapel, und wurde auch zwischen März 1848 und August 1849 von feindlichen italienischen Nationalisten beschlagnahmt. Im Jahre 1858 wurde sie zum Frachter Nummer 44 umgebaut. Sie hatte eine Dienstzeit von ungefähr 87 Jahren.*

80.) "S.M.S. Amico" (1848) was the first member of a class of wooden sailing "trabaccolos" (called a "Trabakel" in German), and was a former merchant vessel purchased by the Austrian Navy. She was assigned to the "Ruderflottille Friaul" (which means "Rudder Flottilla Friuli" in English), which was located off the coast of Triest. She displaced 44 tons, was unarmed, was built out of oak and had a crew of just 7 officers and men.

*Das Segeltrabakel "S.M.S. Amico" (1848) hatte eine Einsatzverdrängung von 44 Tonnen, war aus Eichenholz gebaut, hatte keine Bewaffnung, und hatte eine Besatzung von nur 7 Offiziere und Matrosen. Sie gehörte zur Ruderflottille Friaul an der Küste von Triest. Sie hatte eine Dienstzeit von fast 70 Jahren.*

81.) "S.M.S. Guglielmo" (1842) was the 2nd and final member of the "S.M.S. Amico" class of wooden sailing trabaccolos. She was built in Rovigno (a Croatian port in Istria), and was assigned to the "Ruderflottille Friaul" after 1849. This basically involved transport and harbor duties. She was scrapped after 1862.

*Das Segeltrabakel "S.M.S. Guglielmo" (1842) war das einzige Schwesterboot der "S.M.S Amico." Sie wurde in Rovigno im Istrien (Kroatien) gebaut, und gehörte auch nach 1849 zur Ruderflottille Friaul. Sie wurde im Jahre 1862 verschrottet.*

82.) "S.M.S. Vulcano" (1848) was a wooden sailing "trabaccolo" of 29 tons displacement. She was also assigned to the "Ruderflottille Friaul" after 1849. She was built out of oak, and was not armed.

*Das Segeltrabakel "S.M.S. Vulcano" (1848) hatte eine Einsatzverdrängung von 28 Tonnen, war aus Eichenholz gebaut, war 12,4 Meter lang, hatte eine Breite von 4,5 Meter und einen Tiefgang von 1,6 Meter. Sie gehörte auch zur Ruderflottille Friaul an der Küste von Triest. Sie wurde im Jahre 1859 verkauft.*

83.) "S.M.S. Fiorentino" (1848) was another wooden sailing "trabaccolo," and of 28 tons displacement. She was also part of the "Ruderflottille Friaul" off the coast of Triest after 1849, and was sold to civilian owners in 1859. She was 12,4 meters long, had a beam of 4,5 meters, a draught of 1,6 meters and was built out of oak.

*Das Segeltrabakel "S.M.S. Fiorentino" (1848) hatte eine Einsatzverdrängung von 28 Tonnen, war aus Eichenholz gebaut, war 12,4 Meter lang, hatte eine Breite von 4,5 Meter und einen Tiefgang von 1,6 Meter. Sie gehörte auch zur Ruderflottille Friaul an der Küste Triests, und wurde im Jahre 1859 verkauft.*

84.) "S.M.S. Vincitore" (1843) was built in Rovigno, and was a wooden sailing "trabaccolo" of 27 tons displacement. She was also assigned to the "Ruderflottille Friaul," and was scrapped after 1866. She was built out of oak, and was not armed.

*Das Segeltrabakel "S.M.S. Vincitore" (1843) wurde in Rovigno im Istrien (Kroatien) gebaut, hatte eine Einsatzverdrängung von 27 Tonnen, war aus*

*Eichenholz gebaut, und hatte keine Bewaffnung. Sie gehörte auch der Ruderflottille Friaul an der Küste Triests, und wurde im Jahre 1866 verschrottet.*

85.) "S.M.S. Santa Eufemia" (1848) was a wooden sailing "trabaccolo" of 23 tons displacement. She was part of the "Ruderflottille Friaul" until 1856. She was built out of oak, and was unarmed.

*Das Segeltrabakel "S.M.S. Santa Eufemia" (1848) hatte eine Einsatzverdrängung von 23 Tonnen, und gehörte bis 1856 zur Ruderflottille Friaul an der Küste von Triest. Sie war aus Eichenholz gebaut, und hatte keine Bewaffnung.*

86.) "S.M.S. Elvira" (1832) was the first member of a class of wooden sailing "piroges," built in Venice. She was scrapped in 1843. She displaced just 19 tons, was 14 meters long, had a beam of 3,5 meters and a very shallow draught of 0,5 meters. She was built out of oak, and was armed with 1-24 Pounder cannon. Most of her numerous sister vessels were briefly captured by Italian nationalist rebels in Venice from March 1848 until August 1849 (they are numbered immediately below):

*Die Segelpiroge "S.M.S. Elvira" (1832) wurde in Venedig auf Kiel gelegt, und wurde im Jahre 1843 verschrottet. Sie hatte eine Einsatzverdrängung von 19 Tonnen, war 14 Meter lang, hatte eine Breite von 3,5 Meter und einen Tiefgang von 0,5 Meter. Sie war aus Eichenholz gebaut und ihre Bewaffnung bestand aus einem 24-Pfunder. Die Mehrheit ihrer Schwesterfahrzeuge wurden zwischen März 1848 und August 1849 von den feindlichen italienischen Nationalisten beschlagnahmt. Eine Segelpiroge ist ein leichtes, flaches Lagunenfahrzeug mit Segel-und Riemenantrieb, mit einem Mast mit Lateinsegel und acht Riemen. Sie waren sehr zahlreich, und wurden immer wieder für Stations-und Zolldienst, auch auf Flüssen, nachgebaut.*

87.) "S.M.S. Adelaide" (1839) was launched on April 15, 1846 and kept in the Imperial and Royal Austrian Navy until 1861.

*Die Segelpiroge "S.M.S. Adelaide" (1839) lief am 15. April 1846 vom Stapel und wurde im Jahre 1861 verkauft.*

88.) "S.M.S. Attiva" (1839) was launched on April 15, 1846 and scrapped after 1860.

*Die Segelpiroge "S.M.S. Attiva" (1839) lief am 15. April 1846 vom Stapel und wurde nach 1860 verschrottet.*

89.) "S.M.S. Bianca" (1834) was launched on April 30, 1846 and scrapped after 1860.

*Die Segelpiroge "S.M.S. Bianca" lief am 30. April 1846 vom Stapel und wurde nach 1860 verschrottet.*

90.) "S.M.S. Bilancia" (1834) was launched on April 30, 1846 and scrapped after 1864.

*Die Segelpiroge "S.M.S. Bilancia" (1834) lief am 30. April 1846 vom Stapel und wurde nach 1864 verschrottet.*

91.) "S.M.S. Celia" (1834) was launched on April 23, 1846 and attached to the "Gardaseeflottille" ("Lake Garda Flottilla" in German) after 1856.

*Die Segelpiroge "S.M.S. Celia" (1834) lief am 23. April 1846 vom Stapel und gehörte nach 1856 zur Gardaseeflottille.*

92.) "S.M.S. Civetta" (1838) was launched on April 17, 1846 and was converted into cargo boat number 29 in 1857.

*Die Segelpiroge "S.M.S. Civetta" (1838) lief am 17. April 1846 vom Stapel und wurde im Jahre 1857 als Frachter Nummer 29 umgebaut. Sie hatte eine Dienstzeit von vielleicht 72 Jahren.*

93.) "S.M.S. Colomba" (1834) was launched on April 24, 1846 and was scrapped after 1859.

*Die Segelpiroge "S.M.S. Colomba" (1834) lief am 24. April 1846 vom Stapel und wurde nach 1859 verschrottet.*

94.) "S.M.S. Conchiglia" (1840) was launched on September 4, 1844 and was part of the "Gardaseeflottille" until 1864.

*Die Segelpiroge "S.M.S. Conchiglia" (1840) lief am 4. September 1844 vom Stapel und gehörte bis 1864 zur Gardaseeflottille.*

95.) "S.M.S. Curiosa" (1833) was launched on August 20, 1844 and scrapped after 1859.

*Die Segelpiroge "S.M.S. Curiosa" (1833) lief am 20. August 1844 vom Stapel und wurde nach 1859 verschrottet.*

96.) "S.M.S. Eleonora" (1833) was launched on August 9, 1844 and was attached to the "Gardaseeflottille" until 1864.

*Die Segelpiroge "S.M.S. Eleonora" (1833) lief am 9. August 1844 vom Stapel und gehörte bis 1864 zur Gardaseeflottille.*

97.) "S.M.S. Elvira" (1833) replaced the lead member of this class when she was launched on August 8, 1844. She was assigned to the Tagliamento River until 1866, which lies in between Triest and Venice.

*Die Segelpiroge "S.M.S. Elvira" (1833) lief am 8. August 1844 vom Stapel, und diente bis 1866 auf dem Tagliamento Fluß (zwischen Triest und Venedig).*

98.) "S.M.S. Erminia" (1834) was launched on May 5, 1846 and scrapped after 1860.

*Die Segelpiroge "S.M.S. Erminia" (1834) lief am 5. Mai 1846 vom Stapel und wurde nach 1860 verschrottet.*

99.) "S.M.S. Eulalia" (1839) was launched on August 22, 1844 and scrapped after 1866.

*Die Segelpiroge "S.M.S. Eulalia" (1839) lief am 22. August 1844 vom Stapel und wurde nach 1866 verschrottet.*

100.) "S.M.S. Euridice" (1833) was launched on October 24, 1844 and scrapped after 1866.

*Die Segelpiroge "S.M.S. Euridice" (1833) lief am 24. Oktober 1844 vom Stapel und wurde nach 1866 verschrottet.*

101.) "S.M.S. Gemma" (1833) was launched on August 27, 1844 and scrapped after 1860.

*Die Segelpiroge "S.M.S. Gemma" (1833) lief am 27. August 1844 vom Stapel und wurde nach 1860 verschrottet.*

102.) "S.M.S. Generosa" (1831) was launched May of 1832 and scrapped after 1859.

*Die Segelpiroge "S.M.S. Generosa" (1831) lief im Mai 1832 vom Stapel und wurde nach 1859 verschrottet.*

103.) "S.M.S. Gentile" (1832) was launched on August 23, 1832 and scrapped after 1860.

*Die Segelpiroge "S.M.S. Gentile" (1832) lief am 23. August 1832 vom Stapel und wurde nach 1860 verschrottet.*

104.) "S.M.S. Giusta" (1831) was launched in August of 1832 and scrapped after 1860.

*Die Segelpiroge "S.M.S. Giusta" (1831) lief im August 1832 vom Stapel und wurde nach 1860 verschrottet.*

105.) "S.M.S. Gloriosa" (1831) was launched in September of 1832 and scrapped after 1864.

*Die Segelpiroge "S.M.S. Gloriosa" (1831) lief im September 1832 vom Stapel und wurde nach 1864 verschrottet.*

106.) "S.M.S. Grave" (1833) was launched in March of 1839 and scrapped after 1860.

*Die Segelpiroge "S.M.S. Grave" (1833) lief im März 1839 vom Stapel und wurde nach 1860 verschrottet.*

107.) "S.M.S. Graziosa" (1833) was launched on May 9, 1845 and scrapped after 1860.

*Die Segelpiroge "S.M.S. Graziosa" (1833) lief am 9. Mai 1845 vom Stapel und wurde nach 1860 verschrottet.*

108.) "S.M.S. Guglia" (1833) was launched on August 7, 1844 and scrapped after 1860.

*Die Segelpiroge "S.M.S. Guglia" (1833) lief am 7. August 1844 vom Stapel und wurde nach 1860 verschrottet.*

109.) "S.M.S. Ingegnosa" (1833) was launched on August 3, 1844 and scrapped after 1860.

*Die Segelpiroge "S.M.S. Ingegnosa" (1833) lief am 3. August 1844 vom Stapel und wurde nach 1860 verschrottet.*

110.) "S.M.S. Lodola" (1833) was launched on July 30, 1844 and scrapped after 1860.

*Die Segelpiroge "S.M.S. Lodola" (1833) lief am 30. Juli 1844 vom Stapel und wurde nach 1860 verschrottet.*

111.) "S.M.S. Maga" (1833) was launched on August 20, 1844 and was converted into cargo boat number 34 in 1857.

*Die Segelpiroge "S.M.S. Maga" (1833) lief am 20. August 1844 vom Stapel und wurde im Jahre 1857 als Frachter Nummer 34 umgebaut. Sie hatte eine Dienstzeit von ungefähr 74 Jahren.*

112.) "S.M.S. Matilde" (1833) was launched on August 23, 1844 and scrapped after 1860.

*Die Segelpiroge "S.M.S. Matilde" (1833) lief am 23. August 1844 vom Stapel und wurde nach 1860 verschrottet.*

113.) "S.M.S. Mosca" (1833) was launched on April 11, 1846 and scrapped after 1859.

*Die Segelpiroge "S.M.S. Mosca" (1833) lief am 11. April 1859 vom Stapel und wurde nach 1859 verschrottet.*

114.) "S.M.S. Nereide" (1833) was launched on September 3, 1844 and scrapped after 1860.

*Die Segelpiroge "S.M.S. Nereide" (1833) lief am 3. September 1844 vom Stapel und wurde nach 1860 verschrottet.*

115.) "S.M.S. Niobe" (1834) was launched on March 12, 1845 and scrapped after 1860.

*Die Segelpiroge "S.M.S. Niobe" (1834) lief am 12. März 1845 vom Stapel und wurde nach 1860 verschrottet.*

116.) "S.M.S. Perla" (1833) was launched on February 25, 1845 and was attached to the "Gardaseeflottille" in 1856.

*Die Segelpiroge "S.M.S. Perla" (1833) lief am 25. Februar 1845 vom Stapel und gehörte ab 1856 zur Gardaseeflottille.*

117.) "S.M.S. Pernice" (1833) was launched on May 5, 1845 and scrapped after 1859.

*Die Segelpiroge "S.M.S. Pernice" (1833) lief am 5. Mai 1845 vom Stapel und wurde nach 1859 verschrottet.*

118.) "S.M.S. Perseverante" (1833) was launched on February 8, 1845 and scrapped after 1860.

*Die Segelpiroge "S.M.S. Perseverante" (1833) lief am 8. Februar 1845 vom Stapel und wurde nach 1860 verschrottet.*

119.) "S.M.S. Placida" (1833) was launched on May 7, 1846, attached to the "Gardaseeflottille" in 1856 and scrapped after 1860.

*Die Segelpiroge "S.M.S. Placida" (1833) lief am 7. Mai 1846 vom Stapel und gehörte zwischen 1856 und 1860 zur Gardaseeflottille; danach wurde sie verschrottet.*

120.) "S.M.S. Pomona" (1834) was launched on March 13, 1845, attached to the "Gardaseeflottille" in 1856 and scrapped after 1860.

*Die Segelpiroge "S.M.S. Pomona" (1834) lief am 13. März 1845 vom Stapel und gehörte zwischen 1856 und 1860 zur Gardaseeflottille; danach wurde sie verschrottet.*

121.) "S.M.S. Sagace" (1834) was launched on February 25, 1845 and scrapped after 1860.

*Die Segelpiroge "S.M.S. Sagace" (1834) lief am 25. Februar 1845 vom Stapel und wurde nach 1860 verschrottet.*

122.) "S.M.S. Susanna" (1833) was launched on April 23, 1845, attached to the "Gardaseeflottille" in 1856 and scrapped after 1860.

*Die Segelpiroge "S.M.S. Susanna" (1833) lief am 23. April 1845 vom Stapel, und gehörte zwischen 1856 und 1860 zur Gardaseeflottille; danach wurde sie verschrottet.*

123.) "S.M.S. Temeraria" (1833) was launched on August 30, 1844 and scrapped after 1860.

*Die Segelpiroge "S.M.S. Temeraria" (1833) lief am 30. August 1844 vom Stapel und wurde nach 1860 verschrottet.*

124.) "S.M.S. Teresa" (1833) was launched on October 1, 1844 and scrapped after 1866.

*Die Segelpiroge "S.M.S. Teresa" (1833) lief am 1. Oktober 1844 vom Stapel und wurde nach 1866 verschrottet.*

125.) "S.M.S. Tigre" (1833) was launched on January 29, 1845 and scrapped after 1860.

*Die Segelpiroge "S.M.S. Tigre" (1833) lief am 29. Januar 1845 vom Stapel und wurde nach 1860 verschrottet.*

126.) "S.M.S. Tortosa" (1833) was launched on September 3, 1844 and scrapped after 1860.

*Die Segelpiroge "S.M.S. Tortosa" (1833) lief am 3. September 1844 vom Stapel und wurde nach 1860 verschrottet.*

127.) "S.M.S. Umile" (1833) was launched on February 7, 1845 and scrapped after 1866.

*Die Segelpiroge "S.M.S. Umile" (1833) lief am 7. Februar 1845 vom Stapel und wurde nach 1866 verschrottet.*

128.) "S.M.S. Urania" (1833) was launched on October 1, 1844 and scrapped after 1860.

*Die Segelpiroge "S.M.S. Urania" (1833) lief am 1. Oktober 1844 vom Stapel und wurde nach 1860 verschrottet.*

129.) "S.M.S. Valente" (1834) was launched on August 3, 1844 and scrapped after 1860.

*Die Segelpiroge "S.M.S. Valente" (1834) lief am 3. August 1844 vom Stapel und wurde nach 1860 verschrottet.*

130.) "S.M.S. Vespa" (1834) was launched on September 20, 1846 and scrapped after 1860.

*Die Segelpiroge "S.M.S. Vespa" (1834) lief am 20. September 1846 vom Stapel und wurde nach 1860 verschrottet.*

131.) "S.M.S. Virginia" (1834) was launched on September 21, 1846 and scrapped after 1860.

*Die Segelpiroge "S.M.S. Virginia" (1834) lief am 21. September 1846 vom Stapel und wurde nach 1860 verschrottet.*

132.) "S.M.S. Vivace" (1834) was launched on September 19, 1846 and scrapped after 1860.

*Die Segelpiroge "S.M.S. Vivace" (1834) lief am 19. September 1846 vom Stapel und wurde nach 1860 verschrottet.*

133.) "S.M.S. Zenobia" (1834) was the final named member of the "S.M.S. Elvira" class of wooden sailing piroges, and was launched in Venice on September 24, 1846.  She was scrapped after 1860.

*Die Segelpiroge "S.M.S. Zenobia" (1834) war das letzte genannte Segelfahrzeug der "S.M.S. Elvira" Klaße.  Sie wurde im Jahre 1834 in Venedig auf Kiel gelegt, und lief am 24. September 1846 vom Stapel.  Sie wurde nach 1860 verschrottet.*

### Chapter 15 (Kapitel 15): XIII (13) Older Sailing Ships of the Austrian Navy (for which exact tonnage is not available) / Ältere Segelschiffe der Österreichischen Kriegsmarine (ohne technische Daten)

An Admiralty was established in the Holy Roman Empire of the German Nation by Kaiser Otto III in A.D. 983. Even before this time, the Empire and the Frankish Kingdom from which it descended had to defend itself from maritime threats launched by the Frisians, the Normans and the predecessors of the Moors (from what is now modern Mauritania). In the 10th century, the Empire was expanding toward the North and the East, where Slavic tribes were being Germanized and Christianized. This meant a German naval presence in the Baltic Sea. From the 11th to the 13th centuries, German vessels departing from the North Sea and its tributaries took part in the Christian Crusades in the Holy Land. The main German states with naval vessels in the North Sea (the German Bay or "Deutsche Bucht" in German) and the Baltic Sea (called the "East Sea" or "Ostsee" in German) were the Hanseatic Cities such as Hamburg, Bremen, Lübeck, Kiel, Rostock, Stralsund, Wismar, Greifswald, Anklam, Demmin, Wolgast, Stettin and Königsberg.

*Die deutsche Admiralität (das heißt: die Admiralität des Deutschen Reiches, oder genauer des Heiligen Römischen Reiches der Deutschen Nation – auch "Das Erste Deutsche Reich") wurde im Jahre 983 von Kaiser Otto III gegründet. Das Deutsche Reich selbst wurde im Jahre 800 in Aachen gegründet. Der Vorgänger des Deutschen Reiches war das Königreich der Franken (die modernen germanischen Nachfolger der Franken sind die Franken in Nordbayern). Die Kriegsmarine des Ersten Deutschen Reiches mußte sich im Westen gegen die Friesen, die Normannen, und auch gegen die islamischen Mauren verteidigen. Im Osten haben die Deutschen die westlichen slawischen und baltischen Stämme erobert, germanisiert und zum Christentum bekehrt. Die Kriegsmarine des Reiches mußte Deutschlands Interessen in der Ostsee verteidigen. Zwischen dem 11. und den 13. Jahrhundert hatten die Kriegsschiffe des Deutschen Reiches die christlichen Kreuzfahrer zum heiligen Land transportiert. Die deutschen Hansestädte wie Hamburg, Bremen, Lübeck, Kiel, Rostock, Stralsund, Wismar, Stettin und Königsberg hatten die meisten, die besten und auch die größten deutschen Kriegsschiffe.*

After the 13th century, the then Habsburg Archduchy of Austria became the premier naval state within the Holy Roman Empire of the German Nation. The earliest Austrian naval port was that of Triest, which voluntarily placed itself under the protection of Austria on August 31, 1369. It was already an important commercial seaport with valuable business in shipping the likes of lumber, salt, oil and fish. Other important and powerful states in the Adriatic Sea in those days included Görz ("Gorizia" in Italian), Istria, the Republic of Venedig ("Venezia" in Italian or "Venice" in English) and Dalmatia on the modern coast of Croatia.

*Nach dem 13. Jahrhundert hatte das Erzherzogtum Österreich die größte und auch die beste Kriegsmarine im Ersten Deutschen Reich. Am 31. August 1369 hat sich der Kriegshafen Triest freiwillig unter Österreichs Schutz gestellt. Als Handelshafen war Triest für ganz Mitteleuropa (für Güter wie Holz, Salz, Öl und Fisch) schon sehr wichtig. Im Jahre 1374 wurden Istrien ("Küstenland" auf deutsch) und Krain auch österreichisch. Im Jahre 1440 wurde das Kriegsmarinearsenal Wien gegründet. In der Donaustadt Wien wurden die ersten österreichischen Galeeren gebaut. Die Soldaten des Deutschen Reiches haben die Stadt Preßburg von den Ungarn befreit. Zwischen 1441 und 1446 wurden die ersten vier Galeeren in Dienst gestellt. Sie hatten eine Einstaztverdrängung von je 200 Tonnen, zwei bis drei Masten mit Lateinsegel, und waren wie Ramkreuzer gebaut. Sie hatten je bis 70 Riemen, mit drei bis fünf Matrosen pro Riemen. Zwischen 1458 und 1488 wurden neun mehr Galeeren in Dienst gestellt. Die Verlußte im Krieg gegen Ungarn waren ziemlich hoch, aber die neue Donauflottille war für Österreich sehr wichtig. Eventuell wurde Ungarn auch ein treues Teil des habsburgischen Reiches.*

In 1374, Austria gained the neighboring territories of Istria (named "Küstenland" or "coastal land" in German) and Carniola (called "Krain" in German). In the year 1440, an arsenal for building river-going warships was founded in the Austrian capital city of Vienna (called "Wien" in German). The city of Vienna is located right along the river Danube (called the "Donau" in German). The first warships to be constructed in Vienna were galleys, for use against Hungarian forces near the river city of Pressburg (now known as "Bratislava" in modern Slovakia). Such galleys were commissioned into the new Imperial and Royal Austrian Navy in 1441, 1442, 1443 and 1446. The ship type of the Galley had been constructed by countries within the Mediterranean Sea region since about A.D. 1000. The largest vessels displaced up to 200 tons, and their primary armament was the ram, located at the tip of the bow below the waterline. They would have up to 70 oars, with each oar being manned by 3 to 5 crew members. In addition to the oars, 2 to 3 masts with lateen sails would provide auxiliary propulsion. In addition to the all-important ram-bow, the ships would carry catapults which were mounted fore and aft on widely overhanging platforms. Such ships were used by Mediterranean navies as their primary capital warships until the 16th century. Additional galleys were commissioned into the Imperial and Royal Austrian Navy in 1458, 1459, 1476, 1477, 1478, 1480, 1482, 1485 and

1488. Losses in combat against the Hungarians were very high, but the new Danube Flottilla was an important force operation in unison with the Imperial and Royal Austrian Army. Eventually, Hungary would be subdued and become an important and loyal part of the Habsburg Empire. The many older wooden sailing vessels for which technical data (such as definitive displacement in tons) is unfortunately sketchy include Ships-of-the-Line (battleships), Frigates, Brigs, Brigantines, Pinnaces, Floating Batteries, Galleys, Galleons, Avisos (scouts), Sloops and Transporters. Their information follows immediately below.

## XIII (14) Austro-Venetian "Ships-of-the-Line" (Wooden Battleships for which exact tonnage is not available) / Österreichische Segellinienschiffe (ohne technische Daten)

"Ships-of-the-Line" (or plural "Linienschiffe" in German) were the great capital ships of yesterday. They evolved into the battleships, dreadnought battleships and fast battleships of the modern era. They grew out of the great galleons of antiquity, and were not replaced until rendered obsolete by the modern aircraft carrier.

*Für die älteren Kriegsschiffe und Segelfahrzeuge des Ersten Deutschen Reiches haben wir leider nicht genug technische Daten. Die größten Kriegsschiffe waren zuerst die Galeeren, und dann die Linienschiffe. Linienschiffe, Schlachtschiffe und Schlachtkreuzer waren die wichtigsten Kriegsschiffe bis den Zweiten Weltkrieg. Bis zum Ende des Zweiten Weltkrieges waren die größten Kriegsschiffe die Schlachtschiffe.*

1.) The oldest Austrian "Ship-of-the-Line," or wooden sailing battleship, was "S.M.S. San Leopoldo," which was part of the Austro-Venetian Navy from at least 1713 until 1733. She had been purchased from the Navy of the Kingdom of Naples, and was scrapped early due to decay. She was armed with 50 cannon, and built out of oak. We do not know what her official displacement was, but ships of this caliber could have been anywhere from 1,879 tons up to 5,194 tons in size. Her name refers to "Saint Leopold" in English, who was a favorite patron saint of the House of Habsburg. The name had been used for male members of the Habsburg Dynasty since the time of Archduke Leopold, who was martyred at the hands of Swiss rebels in June of 1386. The original lands of the Habsburg Dynasty were located at the castle "Habichtsburg" ("the Castle of the Hawk" in English), which is still located in the Swiss Canton of Aargau today.

*Das erste Segellinienschiff der Kaiserlichen und Königlichen Kriegsmarine Österreichs war die "S.M.S. San Leopoldo." Sie wurde von der Kriegsmarine des*

*Königreiches Neapel gekauft, und diente von 1713 bis sie im Jahre 1733 verschrottet wurde. Sie war aus Eichenholz gebaut, und ihre Bewaffnung bestand aus 50 Kanonen. Die Segellinienschiffe der Kaiserlichen und Königlichen Kriegsmarine hatten je eine Einsatzverdrängung von 1,879 bis 5,194 Tonnen. Sankt Leopoldus ist der Lieblingsschutzheilige des Adelhauses Habsburg. Der erste Erzherzog Leopold von Österreich fiel im Jahre 1386 gegen schweizerische Aufständige. Der Ursprung des Adelhauses Habsburg ist das Schloß "Habichtsburg" im schweizerischen Kanton Aargau.*

2.) "S.M.S. Santa Barbara" was commissioned into the Austrian Navy in 1716, but sold to the Navy of the Kingdom of Naples in 1718. The Kingdom of Naples was an old ally of Austria, which encompassed the Southern third of Italy. She was built out of oak.

*Das Segellinienschiff "S.M.S. Santa Barbara" wurde im Jahre 1716 getauft. Im Jahre 1718 hat die Kaiserliche und Königliche Kriegsmarine Österreichs die "S.M.S. Santa Barbara" an das Königreich Neapel verkauft. Das Königreich Neapel (Süditalien und Sizilien) und das Erzherzogtum Österreich waren miteinander verbündet.*

3.) "S.M.S. San Carlo" was commissioned into the Austrian Navy in 1718. She had originally belonged to the Navy of the Kingdom of Naples, and was named after Saint Charles Borromeo of Milan. She was built out of oak, and was armed with 70 cannon. She was decommissioned in 1735 and scrapped in the port of Triest in 1737 due to early decay.

*Das Segellinienschiff "S.M.S. San Carlo" wurde im Jahre 1718 getauft. Sie wurde von dem Königreich Neapel gekauft, war aus Eichenholz gebaut, und war mit 70 Kanonen bewaffnet. Sie wurde im Jahre 1737 in Triest verschrottet. "San Carlo Borromeo" war Sankt Karl Borromäus (1538-1854) von Mailand in Norditalien. Er war ein Kardinal und ist ein Heiliger der Römisch-Katholischen Kirche. Er stammte aus dem italienischen Adelsgeschlecht der Borromeo. Er war der Sohn von Giberto Borromeo (der Graf von Arona) und Margherita de Medici. Arona liegt am Lago Maggiore ("Langensee" auf deutsch).*

4.) "S.M.S. Kaiser Karl VI" was laid down in the port of Triest in 1725, and commissioned into the Austrian Navy on September 28, 1726. We believe she was sold to the breakers in Venice on December 30, 1738. Like all other Austrian wooden sailing vessels, she was built out of oak. She was named after Holy Roman and German Emperor ("Kaiser") Karl VI, who reigned from 1711 until

1740. He was married to Elisabeth Christine von Braunschweig, and they were the parents of future Empress ("Kaiserin") Maria Theresia.

*Das Segellinienschiff "S.M.S. Kaiser Karl VI" wurde im Jahre 1725 in Triest auf Kiel gelegt, und lief am 28. September 1726 vom Stapel. Sie war aus Eichenholz gebaut. Am 30. Dezember 1738 wurde sie verkauft, und danach wurde sie verschrottet. Der Heilig-Römische und Deutsche Kaiser Karl VI Franz Josef Wenzel Balthasar Anton Johann Ignaz von Österreich (1685-1740) regierte von 1711 bis er im Jahre 1740 starb. Seine Ehefrau war Elisabeth Christine von Braunschweig-Wolfenbüttel (1691-1750), und deren Tochter war die zukünftige Kaiserin und Königin Maria Theresia von Österreich (1717-1780).*

5.) "S.M.S. Triest" was laid down in the port after which she was named in 1725, and commissioned into the Austrian Navy in 1728. She met the same eventual fate as her sister ship "S.M.S. Kaiser Karl VI."

*Das Segellinienschiff "S.M.S. Triest" wurde im Jahre 1725 in Triest auf Kiel gelegt, und wurde im Jahre 1728 getauft. Ihre Lebensgeschichte war die des Schwesternschiffes "S.M.S. Kaiser Karl VI" sehr ähnlich.*

6.) "S.M.S. San Luis" was commissioned in 1733, and met with the same fate as her sister ships "S.M.S. Kaiser Karl VI" and "S.M.S. Triest."

*Das Segellinienschiff "S.M.S. San Luis" wurde im Jahre 1733 getauft. Ihre Lebensgeschichte war die des Schwesternschiffes "S.M.S. Kaiser Karl VI" sehr ähnlich.*

7.) "S.M.S. San Michele" was laid down in 1733, launched in 1734, and met with the same eventual fate as her sister ships of the "S.M.S. Kaiser Karl VI" class.

*Das Segellinienschiff "S.M.S. San Michele" wurde im Jahre 1733 auf Kiel gelegt, und lief im 1734 vom Stapel. Ihre Lebensgeschichte war die des Schwesternschiffes "S.M.S. Kaiser Karl VI" sehr ähnlich.*

8.) "S.M.S. Santa Elisabetta" was laid down in 1734, launched in 1735, and met with the same eventual fate as her sister ships of the "S.M.S. Kaiser Karl VI" class.

*Das Segellinienschiff "S.M.S. Santa Elisabetta" wurde im Jahre 1734 auf Kiel gelegt, und lief im 1735 vom Stapel. Ihre Lebensgeschichte war die des Schwesternschiffes "S.M.S. Kaiser Karl VI" sehr ähnlich.*

9.) "S.M.S. Diamante" was laid down in Venice in 1798, and launched on January 19, 1806. At first, she was taken over by the Italians, but later returned on Austria on April 25, 1814. She was scrapped by 1825.

*Das Segellinienschiff "S.M.S. Diamante" wurde im Jahre 1798 in Venedig auf Kiel gelegt, und lief am 19. Januar 1806 vom Stapel. Sie wurde von den italienischen Waffenverbündeten Napoleons beschlagnahmt, und wurde erst am 25. April 1814 an Österreich zurückgegeben. Sie wurde im Jahre 1825 verschrottet.*

10.) "S.M.S. Leoni" was laid down in Venice in 1798, but never completed. She was damaged during the Napoleonic Wars, and scrapped in 1805.

*Das Segellinienschiff "S.M.S. Leoni" wurde im Jahre 1798 in Venedig auf Kiel gelegt, wurde aber nie fertiggestellt. Zur Zeit der napoleonischen Kriege wurde sie beschädigt, und sie wurde im Jahre 1805 verschrottet.*

11.) "S.M.S. Coronati" had the same history as her sister ship "S.M.S. Leoni."

*Das Segellinienschiff "S.M.S. Coronati" hatte eine Lebensgeschichte die der ihres Schwesternschiffes die "S.M.S. Leoni" sehr ähnlich war.*

12.) "S.M.S. Laharpe" was launched in Venice on July 23, 1797. She was armed with 74 cannon, and was built out of oak. Initially, she was confiscated by the French Navy due to the Napoleonic Wars. She was returned to the Austrian Navy on November 14, 1799, and was used as a prison hulk after 1803. She was then confiscated by the Italians (allies of Napoleon Bonaparte) on January 19, 1806. She was once again returned to her rightful Austrian owners in Venice on April 25, 1814, and was scrapped by 1815.

*Das Segellinienschiff "S.M.S. Laharpe" lief am 23. Juli 1797 in Venedig vom Stapel. Sie war aus Eichenholz gebaut, und war mit 74 Kanonen bewaffnet. Sie wurde von den Franzosen beschlagnahmt, und wurde am 14. November 1799 an Österreich zurückgegeben. Sie wurde bis 1803 als Gefängnishulk benutzt. Am 19. Januar 1806 wurde sie von den italienischen Waffenverbündeten Napoleons beschlagnahmt, und wurde erst am 25. April 1814 an Österreich zurückgegeben. Sie wurde im Jahre 1815 verschrottet.*

13.) "S.M.S. Beyrand" was launched in Venice on July 17, 1797, and was confiscated by the French Navy due to the Napoleonic Wars. On August 16,

1799, she was sunk by Austrian and Russian artillery. The Austrians recovered their former ship in July 1800, and scrapped her by 1802.

*Das Segellinienschiff "S.M.S. Beyrand" lief am 17. Juli 1797 in Venedig vom Stapel, und wurde von den Franzosen sofort beschlagnahmt. Am 16. August 1799 wurde sie von österreichischer und rußischer Artillerie versenkt. Im Juli 1800 wurde sie von den Österreichern geborgen, und dann im Jahre 1802 verschrottet.*

14.) "S.M.S. Stengel" was built and launched in Venice in 1797. She was confiscated by the French Navy on May 17, 1797 due to the Napoleonic Wars. The Austrian Navy recaptured her in Ancona (on the Italian side of the Adriatic Sea) on November 14, 1799. She was cannibalized for spare parts by the Austrians in the port of Venice in 1800, converted into a pontoon vessel and renamed "S.M.S. Megera" in 1805. On January 19, 1806 she was confiscated by the Italians, where she spent the rest of her days.

*Das Segellinienschiff "S.M.S. Stengel" lief im Jahre 1797 in Venedig vom Stapel. Am 17. Mai 1797 wurde sie von den Franzosen beschlagnahmt. Am 14. November 1799 hatte die Kaiserliche und Königliche Kriegsmarine die "S.M.S. Stengel" im Kriegshafen von Ancona befreit. Im Jahre 1800 hatten die Österreicher das Schiff für Ersatzteile benutzt, danach als Pontonschiff umgebaut, und im Jahre 1805 als die "S.M.S. Megera" umbenannt. Am 19. Januar 1806 wurde sie von den italienischen Waffenverbündeten Napoleons beschlagnamt, und sie wurde nie wieder zurückgegeben.*

15.) "S.M.S. Saturno" was laid down in Venice in 1812, but never completed. In December 1815, her named was changed to "S.M.S. Emo." She was finally scrapped while only 45% complete in 1823. She was to have been armed with 80 cannon.

*Das Segellinienschiff "S.M.S. Saturno" wurde im Jahre 1812 in Venedig auf Kiel gelegt, aber sie wurde nie fertiggestellt. Im Dezember 1815 wurde sie als die "S.M.S. Emo" umbenannt. Im Jahre 1823 wurde sie verschrottet trotzdem sie nur 45 Prozent fertiggestellt war. Ihre geplante Bewaffnung war 80 Kanonen.*

16.) "S.M.S. Castiglione" was laid down in Venice in 1811, and launched on August 2, 1812. Unfortunately, she caught fire and was burned while still in port on September 14, 1814. Thereafter, her remains were scrapped. She was armed with 74 cannon, built out of oak, was 59 meters long, and had a maximum beam of 15,5 meters. Her armament was on 2 decks, and she was manned by a crew of 580 commissioned officers and sailors.

*Das Segellinienschiff "S.M.S. Castiglione" wurde im Jahre 1811 in Venedig auf Kiel gelegt, und lief am 2. August 1812 vom Stapel. Am 14. September 1814 fiel sie einem Feuer zum Opfer und wurde danach verschrottet. Ihre Bewaffnung bestand aus 74 Kanonen. Sie war aus Eichenholz gebaut, war 59 Meter lang, hatte eine Breite von 15,5 Meter und eine Besatzung von 580 Offiziere und Matrosen.*

17.) "S.M.S. San Bernardo" was was a sister ship of "S.M.S. Castiglione," and had the same history with the same dates.

*Das Segellinienschiff "S.M.S. San Bernardo" war ein Schwesterschiff der "S.M.S. Castiglione," und ihre Lebensgeschichte war die der "S.M.S. Castiglione" sehr ähnlich.*

18.) "S.M.S. Duquesne" was laid down in Venice in 1811, and was launched as "S.M.S. Cesare" on December 7, 1815. She was never commissioned, and was scrapped in 1820 while only 90% complete. She was a member of the "S.M.S. Castiglione" class of wooden sailing battleships.

*Das Segellinienschiff "S.M.S. Duquesne" wurde im Jahre 1811 in Venedig auf Kiel gelegt, und lief am 7. Dezember 1815 als die "S.M.S. Cesare" vom Stapel. Sie wurde nie in Dienst gestellt, und wurde im Jahre 1820 verschrottet – als sie fast 90 Prozent fertiggestellt war. Sie gehörte zur "S.M.S. Castiglione" Klaße.*

19.) "S.M.S. Montenotte" was laid down in Venice in 1810, but was never launched or commissioned. Her name was changed to "S.M.S. Kulm" on June 11, 1814, but she was scrapped while just 60% complete in 1818. She was also a member of the "S.M.S. Castiglione" class of Austrian wooden sailing battleships.

*Das Segellinienschiff "S.M.S. Montenotte" wurde im Jahre 1810 in Venedig auf Kiel gelegt, aber sie lief nie vom Stapel. Am 11. Juni 1814 wurde sie als die "S.M.S. Kulm" umbenannt. Im Jahre 1818 wurde sie verschrottet, als sie schon 60 Prozent fertiggestellt war. Sie gehörte auch zur "S.M.S. Castiglione" Klaße. Zwischen den 29. und den 30. August 1813 haben 60.000 Truppen aus Österreich, Preußen und Rußland 32.000 Soldaten des napoleonischen Frankreichs bei der Schlacht von Kulm in Nordböhmen besiegt. Die Verlusste der Sieger waren 11.000 Mann und die Verlusste der Franzosen waren 18.000 Soldaten (5.000 davon gefallen oder verwundet und 13.000 davon gefangen genommen).*

20.) "S.M.S. Arcole" was laid down in Venice in 1811, but was also never launched or commissioned into service. Her planned name was changed to

"S.M.S. Tonante" on June 11, 1814, but she was scrapped while just 20% complete in 1821. She was yet another member of the "S.M.S Castiglione" class of Austrian wooden sailing battleships.

*Das Segellinienschiff "S.M.S. Arcole" wurde im Jahre 1811 in Venedig auf Kiel gelegt, aber sie lief nie vom Stapel. Am 11. Juni 1814 wurde sie als die "S.M.S. Tonante" umbenannt. Im Jahre 1821 wurde sie verschrottet, als sie nur 20 Prozent fertiggestellt war. Sie gehörte auch zur "S.M.S. Castiglione" Klaße.*

21.) "S.M.S. Sigmaring" was laid down in Venice in 1810, but was also not launched or commissioned into active duty service. Her planned name was changed to "S.M.S. Hanau" on June 11, 1814, but she was scrapped while only 20% complete in 1826. She was part of the "S.M.S. Castiglione" class of Austro-Venetian wooden sailing battleships.

*Das Segellinienschiff "S.M.S. Sigmaring" wurde im Jahre 1810 in Venedig auf Kiel gelegt, aber sie lief nie vom Stapel. Am 11. Juni 1814 wurde sie als die "S.M.S. Hanau" umbenannt. Im Jahre 1826 wurde sie verschrottet, als sie nur 20 Prozent fertiggestellt war. Sigmaringen liegt in Baden-Württemberg. Das Schloß Sigmaringen war auch als "Hohenzollernschloß" bekannt. "Hohenzollern-Sigmaringen" ist die schwäbisch römisch-katholisch gebliebene Linie der Hohenzollern, ein altes deutsches Adelsgeschlecht. Hanau die Stadt der Gebrüder Grimm liegt im Gebiet östlich vom Rhein-Main an der Mündung Kinzig und Main. Im 19. Jahrhundert war Hanau ein Zentrum der demokratischen Bewegung in Deutschland.*

22.) "S.M.S. Severo" was laid down in Venice in 1807, and was launched as "S.M.S. Rigeneratore" on July 7, 1811. Her name reverted to "S.M.S. Severo" on June 11, 1814, when she served as an Admiral's flagship in Venice. In 1823, she was converted into a Frigate, and renamed yet again as "S.M.S. Bellona." She was armed with 56 cannon, and served in the Levant-Eskadre (squadron) of the Austro-Venetian Navy. She was scrapped in 1831.

*Das Segellinienschiff "S.M.S. Severo" wurde im Jahre 1807 in Venedig auf Kiel gelegt, und lief am 7. Juli 1811 als die "S.M.S. Rigeneratore" vom Stapel. Am 11. Juni 1814 wurde sie wieder als die "S.M.S. Severo" umbenannt, als sie als das Flaggschiff des Admirals diente. Im Jahre 1823 wurde sie als eine Segelfregatte umgebaut, und als die "S.M.S. Bellona" umbenannt. Ihre Bewaffnung bestand aus 56 Kanonen, und sie diente bei der "Levant-Eskadré" der Kaiserlichen und Königlichen Kriegsmarine (bei der kaiserlich deutschen*

*Marine wurden die Eskadrén "Geschwader" benannt). Die "S.M.S. Bellona" wurde im Jahre 1831 verschrottet.*

23.) "S.M.S. Reale Italiano" was laid down in Venice in 1807, and was launched on August 15, 1812. She was disarmed in 1814, and converted into a Frigate. After she was renamed as "S.M.S. Italiano" (meaning "the Italian" in English) in 1829, she served as both a training vessel and as harbor guard ship. In 1835, she was retired and used as a target vessel, finally being scrapped in 1836. She had been armed with 74 cannon.

*Das Segellinienschiff "S.M.S. Reale Italiano" wurde im Jahre 1807 in Venedig auf Kiel gelegt, und lief am 15. August 1812 vom Stapel. Im Jahre 1814 wurde sie als eine Segelfregatte umgebaut. Im Jahre 1829 wurde sie als die "S.M.S. Italiano" umbenannt, nachdem sie als Schulschiff und Hafenwachtschiff diente. Im Jahre 1835 wurde sie als Zielschiff benutzt, und sie wurde im Jahre 1836 verschrottet. Zwischen 1812 und 1814 bestand ihre Bewaffnung aus 74 Kanonen, danach wurde sie aber entwaffnet.*

24.) "S.M.S. Lombardo" was laid down in Venice in 1810, but never launched or commissioned. She was scrapped while just 30% complete in 1830. She was a sister ship of "S.M.S. Reale Italiano."

*Das Segellinienschiff "S.M.S. Lombardo" wurde im Jahre 1810 in Venedig auf Kiel gelegt, aber sie lief nie vom Stapel. Sie wurde im Jahre 1830 verschrottet, als sie nur 30 Prozent fertiggestellt war. Sie war ein Schwesterschiff der "S.M.S. Reale Italiano."*

### XIII (15) Austro-Venetian Frigates (for which exact tonnage is not available) / Österreichische Segelfregatten (ohne technische Daten)

Wooden sailing frigates (with a single ship called a "Segelfregatte" in German) within the old Imperial and Royal Austrian Navy ranged in size from 420 tons to 1,878 tons displacement. Even Danube river frigates were not necessarily small; "S.M.S. Sankt Leopoldus" of 1716 had 3 masts and 2 cannon decks. Both wooden sailing frigates and wooden sailing corvettes were warships with 3 main masts. Eventually, frigates grew larger than corvettes. The former evolved into the large, heavy and armored cruisers of the modern era. The latter evolved into the small and light cruisers of the modern era, also known by their Spanish name of "Avisos," or "scouts."

*Die Segelfregatten der Kaiserlichen und Königlichen Kriegsmarine hatten eine Einsatzverdrängung von je zwischen 420 und 1,878 Tonnen. Auch die berühmten Donaufregatten waren nicht klein. Zum Beispiel, hatte die "S.M.S. Sankt Leopoldus" von 1716 drei Masten und zwei Kanonendecks. Segelfregatten und Segelkorvetten hatten drei Masten, aber die Segelfregatten waren größer. Die Segelfregatten waren die Schweren Kreuzer, und die Segelkorvetten waren die Leichten Kreuzer von gestern.*

1.) The wooden Danube sailing frigate "S.M.S. Santa Anna" was built and launched in Vienna in 1692. She served in the naval war against Ottoman Turkey, and was disarmed in 1699 – likely to be sold to civilian commercial interests. She was 44,3 meters long, built out of oak, armed with 60 cannon on 2 decks (40 heavy cannon and 20 light cannon), and her crew consisted of 210 commissioned officers and enlisted men. She was named after the mother of the Blessed Virgin Mary, who was the wife of Saint Joachim. Her sister 7 ships were:

*Die Donaufregatte "S.M.S. Santa Anna" lief im Jahre 1692 in Wien vom Stapel. Sie diente im Krieg gegen die ottomanische Türkei. Im Jahre 1699 wurde sie entwaffnet und als Handelsschiff verkauft. Sie war 44,3 Meter lang, war aus Eichenholz gebaut, war mit 60 Kanonen auf zwei Decks bewaffnet (40 schwere Kanonen und 20 leichte Kanonen) und sie hatte eine Besatzung von 210 Offiziere und Matrosen. Sie hatte sieben Schwesterschiffe. "Santa Anna" war die Mutter der Jungfrau Maria, und auch die Ehefrau von Sankt Joachim.*

2.) "S.M.S. Sankt Gabriel" (1692): same history. She was named after the Archangel Gabriel who appeared to the Blessed Virgin Mary, who said "Hail Mary, full of Grace, Blessed art Thou amongst women, and Blessed is the Fruit of Thy Womb, Jesus." It was He who told her of the coming Virgin Birth of Our Lord and Savior Jesus the Christ (the Messiah).

*Die Donaufregatte "S.M.S. Sankt Gabriel" (1692) hatte eine Lebensgeschichte die der ihres Schwesternschiffes "S.M.S. Santa Anna" sehr ähnlich war. Der Erzengel Gabriel (zu deutsch "Held Gottes") ist der zweite der vier Erzengel und wird in der Bibel in dem Buch Daniel und im Evangelium nach Lukas erwähnt. Er gilt als Ausleger von Visionen und als Bote Gottes. Er nimmt auch im Islam eine wichtige Rolle ein.*

3.) "S.M.S. Santa Maria" (1692): same history. She was named after the Blessed Virgin Mary, the Mother of God (Our Lord and Savior Jesus Christ).

*Die Donaufregatte "S.M.S. Santa Maria" (1692) hatte eine Lebensgeschichte die der ihres Schwesternschiffes "S.M.S. Santa Anna" sehr ähnlich war. Die Jungfrau Santa Maria war die Mutter von Jesus Christus, die Ehefrau von Sankt Josef, und die Tochter von Sankt Joachim und Santa Anna.*

4.) "S.M.S. Sankt Michael" (1692): same history. She was named after the senior Archangel of Heaven, who came to his position after Lucifer rebelled and was cast down into Hell by God the Father. It is Saint Michael who will defeat Satan (the "Adversary," and the new name of the former "Lucifer," or "angel of light"), after the angel of darkness is crushed by the Blessed Virgin Mary (as foretold in the Book of Genesis, Chapter 3, Verse 15).

*Die Donaufregatte "S.M.S. Sankt Michael" (1692) hatte eine Lebensgeschichte die der ihres Schwesternschiffes "S.M.S. Santa Anna" sehr ähnlich war. Der Erzengel Michael (auf deutsch "Wer ist wie Gott?") ist ein in der Bibel erwähnter Erzengel, der für Anhänger aller drei Abrahamitischen Relgionen von Bedeutung ist. Den Christen gilt er vor allem als Bezwinger Satans und Seelenwäger am Tag des Jüngsten Gerichts. Er ist seit der siegreichen Schlacht auf dem Lechfeld am 10. August 955 Schutzpatron des Heiligen Römischen Reiches sowie des modernen Deutschlands.*

5.) "S.M.S. Sankt Salvator" (1692): same history. She was named after our "Holy Savior," Jesus the Christ (Messiah) of Nazareth.

*Die Donaufregatte "S.M.S. Sankt Salvator" (1692) hatte eine Lebensgeschichte die der ihres Schwesternschiffes "S.M.S. Santa Anna" sehr ähnlich war. "Sankt Salvator" ist der Heilige Erlöser Jesus Christus.*

6.) "S.M.S. Heiliger Erlöser" was laid down in Vienna in 1692 and launched in 1693. She was sunk due to an accidental munitions explosion off the coast of Esseg (now known as "Osijek" in Croatia) on December 15, 1695. Her name means "Holy Redeemer" in English, she thus having been named after Our Lord and Savior Jesus Christ.

*Die Donaufregatte "S.M.S. Heiliger Erlöser" wurde im Jahre 1692 in Wien auf Kiel gelegt, und lief im Jahre 1693 vom Stapel. Am 15. Dezember 1695 versank sie bei einem Munitionsunglück an der Küste von Esseg (nun "Osijek" in Kroatien).*

7.) "S.M.S. Sankt Joseph" (1693) served with her sister Frigates in the war against Ottoman Turkey. She was scuttled by her own crew on August 17, 1696 at the mouth of the River Theiss (the longest tributary river of the Danube), in order to prevent her from falling into enemy hands. This extreme measure was taken because Turkish forces had effectively blocked her escape. She was of course named after Saint Joseph, the Foster Father of Our Lord and Savior Jesus Christ, who was also the husband of the Blessed Virgin Mary.

*Die Donaufregatte "S.M.S. Sankt Joseph" (1693) diente mit ihren Schwesterschiffen im Krieg gegen die ottomanische Türkei. Am 17. August 1696 wurde sie an der Theißmündung (der längste Nebenfluß der Donau) selbst versenkt, weil die Kaiserliche und Königliche Kriegsmarine das Schiff nicht an den ottomanischen Türken aufgeben wollte. Die ottomanische Armee hat ihre Flucht aber blockiert. Sankt Josef war der Ehemann der Jungfrau Maria, und auch der Stiefvater von Jesus Christus.*

8.) "S.M.S. Sankt Leopold" (1693) had the same history and the same unfortunate fate as her sister ship "S.M.S. Sankt Joseph." She was named after one of the favorite Patron Saints of the Habsburg Monarchy.

*Die Donaufregatte "S.M.S. Sankt Leopold" (1693) hatte eine Lebensgeschichte die der ihres Schwesternschiffes "S.M.S. Sankt Joseph" sehr ähnlich war.*

9.) "S.M.S. Sankt Carolus Borromäus" (1716) was the first Imperial and Royal Austrian wooding sailing frigate of the class following the "S.M.S. Santa Anna" class. She was named after Saint Charles Borromeo, a great Roman Catholic Cardinal from Milan, Italy (called "Mailand" in German). She was armed with 30 cannon, and served in the war against Ottoman Turkey from 1716 to 1717. She was 42 meters long, had a maximum beam of 8,8 meters, was built out of oak, and had a crew of 150 commissioned officers and enlisted men (plus a contingent of up to 320 Austrian Marine troops). This was a very prolific class of Danube Frigates, and the histories of her many sister ships follow immediately below:

*Die Donaufregatte "S.M.S. Sankt Carolus Borromäus" (1716) diente bis 1717 mit ihren Schwesterschiffen im Krieg gegen die ottomanische Türkei. Sie war 42 Meter lang, hatte eine Breite von 8,8 Meter, war aus Eichenholz gebaut, war mit 30 Kanonen bewaffnet, und sie hatte eine Besatzung von 150 Offiziere und Matrosen und 320 Marineinfanteristen.*

10.) "S.M.S. Sankt Franciscus" (1716): same history. She was named after Saint Francis of Assisi.

*Die Donaufregatte "S.M.S. Sankt Franciscus" (1716) hatte eine Lebensgeschichte die der ihres Schwesternschiffes "S.M.S. Sankt Carolus Borromäus" sehr ähnlich war. Franz von Assisi (gebürtig Giovanni Battista Bernardone, 1181-1226) versuchte streng und bis ins Einzelne nach dem Vorbild des Jesus von Nazaret zu leben (sogenannte "Imitatio Christi"). Diese Lebensweise zog gleichgesinnte Gefährten und Nachahmer an. Franz gründete den Orden der "Minderen Brüder" und war Mitbegründer des Frauenordens der Klarissen. Er ist ein Heiliger der Römisch-Katholischen Kirche.*

11.) "S.M.S. Sankt Josephus" (1716): same history. She was named after Saint Joseph, the Foster Father of Our Lord and Savior Jesus Christ.

*Die Donaufregatte "S.M.S. Sankt Josephus" (1716) hatte eine Lebensgeschichte die der ihres Schwesternschiffes "S.M.S. Sankt Carolus Borromäus" sehr ähnlich war.*

12.) "S.M.S. Sankt Leopoldus" (1716): same history. She was named after one of the favorite Patron Saints of the Habsburg Monarchy, a member of the family who was martyred in a battle in Switzerland in the 14th century. He was defending their ancestral home castle known as the "Habichtsburg" (the "castle of the hawk" in English). The Habsburg family surname is derived from the name of this castle.

*Die Donaufregatte "S.M.S. Sankt Leopoldus" (1716) hatte eine Lebensgeschichte die der ihres Schwesternschiffes "S.M.S. Sankt Carolus Borromäus" sehr ähnlich war.*

13.) "S.M.S. Santa Elisabeth" (1716): same history. She was named after Saint Elizabeth, the first degree cousin of the Blessed Virgin Mary, and the mother of Saint John the Baptist.

*Die Donaufregatte "S.M.S. Santa Elisabeth" (1716) hatte eine Lebensgeschichte die der ihres Schwesternschiffes "S.M.S. Sankt Carolus Borromäus" sehr ähnlich war. "Elisabet" war gemäß der biblischen Erzählung des Neuen Testaments die Mutter Johannes des Taufers. Nach dem Lukasevangelium stammte sie aus dem Geschlecht Aarons, nach dessen Stamm-Mutter Elischeba sie genannt war. Sie war mit dem Priester Zacharias verheiratat. Die Ehe blieb lange kinderlos, da Elisabet unfruchtbar war, bis der Engel Gabriel Zacharias die Geburt eines Sohnes voraußagte, den er Johannes nennen sollte. Weiter erwähnt wird Elisabet bei der Heimsuchung Marias (ihre Base oder ihre Kusine) und bei der Geburt von Johannes des Taufers.*

14.) "S.M.S. Santa Maria" (1716): same history as her sister ships of the "S.M.S. Sankt Carolus Borromäus" class, but with the proud distinction that she served as the Admiral's flagship.  She was named after the Blessed Virgin Mary, the Mother of God (Our Lord and Savior Jesus the Christ of Nazareth).

*Die Donaufregatte "S.M.S. Santa Maria" (1716) hatte eine Lebensgeschichte die der ihres Schwesternschiffes "S.M.S. Sankt Carolus Borromäus" sehr ähnlich war.  Sie war auch das Flaggschiff des Admirals.*

15.) "S.M.S. Sankt Stephanus" (1716): same history.

*Die Donaufregatte "S.M.S. Sankt Stephanus" (1716) hatte eine Lebensgeschichte die der ihres Schwesternschiffes "S.M.S. Sankt Carolus Borromäus" sehr ähnlich war.  Stephanus (1-40) ist laut dem Neuen Testament ein Diakon der Jerusalemer Urgemeinde.  Er gilt als erster christlicher Martyrer.  Aus der Namensgebung läßt sich schließen, daß er vermutlich hellenistischer Herkunft war.  Seit 560 Jahren nach Christus sind seine Gebeine angeblich in der Krypta von San Lorenzo fuori le mura in Rom neben denen des römischen Archidiakons Laurentius bestattet.*

16.) "S.M.S. Sankt Eugenius" (1716): same history.

*Die Donaufregatte "S.M.S. Sankt Eugenius" (1716) hatte eine Lebensgeschichte die der ihres Schwesternschiffes "S.M.S. Sankt Carolus Borromäus" sehr ähnlich war.  Eugen I wurde am 10. August 654 als Nachfolger von Martin I zum Pabst gewählt.  Sein Name bedeutet aus dem Griechischen übersetzt "der Edelgeborene."  Er wurde als Heiliger der Römisch-Katholischen Kirche kanonisiert.  Das Patronatsfest ist an seinem Todestag, also am 2. Juni (er ist im Jahre 657 gestorben).*

17.) "S.M.S. Sankt Johannes Capistranus" (1716): this ship was completed too late in time for the war against Ottoman Turkey (it was commissioned in 1718), so it never saw any combat.  It was named after Saint John Capistrano.

*Die Donaufregatte "S.M.S. Sankt Johannes Capistranus" (1716) war ein Schwesterschiff der "S.M.S. Sankt Carolus Borromäus."  Sie wurde im Jahre 1718 getauft, und diente deswegen nicht im Krieg gegen die ottomanische Türkei, da der Krieg schon beendet war.  Johannes Capistranus (1386-1456), eigentlich "Giovanni da Capistrano," war ein in seiner Zeit weithin berühmter Wanderprediger, Heerführer und Inquisitor.*

18.) "S.M.S. Santa Theresia" (1716): this was the final ship in the "S.M.S. Sankt Carolus Borromäus" class of Imperial and Royal Austrian Danube wooden sailing frigates. She was also commissioned too late (1718) to partake in the war against Ottoman Turkey, so she never saw combat.

*Die Donaufregatte "S.M.S. Santa Theresia" (1716) war das letzte Schwesterschiff der "S.M.S. Sankt Carolus Borromäus." Sie wurde im Jahre 1718 getauft, und diente deswegen auch nicht im Krieg gegen die ottomanische Türkei, da der Krieg schon beendet war. Theresia von Avila, eigentlich "Teresa Sanchez de Cepeda y Ahumada" (1515-1582) war Karmelitin und Mystikerin, Kirchenlehrerin und Heilige.*

19.) "S.M.S. Arciduchessa Teresa" (1733) was armed with 30 cannon. Her keel was laid down in Triest, and she was launched on October 15, 1735.

*Die Segelfregatte "S.M.S. Arciduchessa Teresa" (1733) lief am 15. Oktober 1735 in Triest vom Stapel, und war mit 30 Kanonen bewaffnet. Maria Theresia von Österreich (1717-1780) war eine Fürstin aus dem Adelhaus Habsburg. Die regierende Erzherzogin von Österreich und Königin von Ungarn, Böhmen, Dalmatien, Kroatien, Slavonien, Galizien und Lodomerien (1740-1780) zählte zu den prägenden Monarchen der Ära des Aufgeklärten Absolutismus. Sie war Ehefrau des Römisch-Deutschen Kaisers Franz I Stephan von Lothringen (insofern Kaiserin) und Mitregentin ihres Sohnes Kaiser Josephs II. Ihr Gatte stützte sich maßgeblich auf ihre Hausmacht.*

20.) "S.M.S. Sankt Carl" (1735) was also armed with 30 cannon. She was built and launched in Belgrade, the modern-day capital of Serbia. She partook in a war against Ottoman Turkey, which occupied Serbia for many years. For a very short time, Serbia was occupied by Austria. In fact, Austria held both Northern Serbia (where Belgrade is located) and Little Wallachia (Western Romania) from 1718 until the Turks took these areas back in 1739. On November 10, 1737 the crew of "S.M.S. Sankt Carl" scuttled their ship off the coast of Orschowa (now known as "Orsova" in Southwestern Romania) to prevent her from falling into enemy hands. An unsuccessful attempt was made to salvage her in 1738. The 14 frigates of the "S.M.S. Sankt Carl" class were built out of oak, and with a shallow draught (no more than 2,2 meters). They had 2 decks, and could accommodate up to 320 marine infantrymen. The regular crew consisted of about 38 commissioned officers and enlisted sailors (this was of course in addition to the Austrian marines).

*Die Donaufregatte "S.M.S. Sankt Carl" (1735) lief im Belgrad vom Stapel, und war auch mit 30 Kanonen bewaffnet. Sie diente im Krieg gegen die ottomanische Türkei. Am 10. November 1737 wurde sie an der Donauküste von Orschowa (nun "Orsova" in Südwestrumänien) eigenhändig versenkt, weil die Kaiserliche und Königliche Kriegsmarine das Schiff nicht an die ottomanischen Türken aufgeben wollten. Im Jahre 1738 versuchten die Österreicher ohne Erfolg das Schiff zu bergen. Die 14 Donaufregatten der "S.M.S. Sankt Carl" Klaße waren aus Eichenholz gebaut, hatten einen Tiefgang von nur 2,2 Meter, hatten zwei Kanonendecks und hatten je eine Besatzgung von 38 Offiziere und Matrosen sowie 320 Marineinfanteristen. Zwischen 1718 und 1739 waren Nordserbien und die Kleine Wallachei (Südwestrumänien) ein Teil des habsburgischen Reiches.*

21.) "S.M.S. Santa Elisabeth" (1735) was also built in Belgrade. She was scuttled by her own crew for the same reason and in the same location as her sister ship "S.M.S. Sankt Carl." The Turkish forces actually succeeded in salvaging and removing the vessel for their own use.

*Die Donaufregatte "S.M.S. Santa Elisabeth" (1735) hatte eine Lebensgeschichte die der ihres Schwesternschiffes "S.M.S. Sankt Carl" sehr ähnlich war, aber die ottomanische Türken haben es geschafft das Schiff zu bergen und für die eigene Kriegsmarine gegen Österreich zu benutzen.*

22.) "S.M.S. Sankt Francesco" (1736) was also laid down and launched in Belgrade. She was scuttled by her crew at the mouth of the River Temesch on July 24, 1739 in order to prevent her from falling into Ottoman Turkish hands. This is located in modern-day Western Romania.

*Die Donaufregatte "S.M.S. Sankt Francesco" (1736) war ein Schwesterschiff der "S.M.S. Sankt Carl." Am 24. Juli 1739 wurde sie an der Temeschmündung in der Kleinen Wallachei selbst versenkt, weil die Kaiserliche und Königliche Kriegsmarine das Schiff nicht an die ottomanischen Türken aufgeben wollten.*

23.) "S.M.S. Santa Theresa" (1736) was also built in Belgrade. She met the same fate on the same day as that of her sister ship "S.M.S. Sankt Francesco."

*Die Donaufregatte "S.M.S. Santa Theresa" (1736) gehörte auch zur "S.M.S. Sankt Carl" Klaße. Sie hatte eine Lebensgeschichte die der ihres Schwesternschiffes "S.M.S. Sankt Francesco" sehr ähnlich war.*

24.) "S.M.S. Sankt Stephano" (1736) was laid down in Belgrade, but never launched or completed.

*Die Donaufregatte "S.M.S. Sankt Stephano" (1736) wurde auch in Belgrad auf Kiel gelegt, lief aber nie vom Stapel. Sie gehörte auch zur "S.M.S. Sankt Carl" Klaße.*

25.) "S.M.S. Aquila Imperiale" (1737) was laid down and launched in Vienna. She partook in the campaign against Ottoman Turkey until 1739. In 1738, this frigate was renamed "S.M.S. Unbefleckte Empfängnis," which means "Immaculate Conception" in English. This Roman Catholic Dogma refers to the fact that the Blessed Virgin Mary was herself born without the taint of original sin, which the rest of the human race inherits from the transgression of Adam and Eve committed in the Garden of Eden 6,000 years ago.

*Die Donaufregatte "S.M.S. Aquila Imperiale" (1737) lief in Wien vom Stapel. Sie gehörte auch zur "S.M.S. Sankt Carl" Klaße. Im Jahre 1738 wurde sie als die "S.M.S. Unbefleckte Empfängnis" umbenannt. Zwischen 1737 und 1739 diente sie im Krieg gegen die ottomanische Türkei. Das Unbefleckte Empfängnis (auf lateinisch "immaculata conceptio") ist ein Römisch-Katholisches Glaubensdogma, das nicht mit der Jungfraugeburt verwechselt werden darf. Ein eigenes kirchliches Fest, das der Erwählung Marias im Mutterleib gedenkt, lässt sich bereits im 9. Jahrhundert nachweisen. Nach der Lehre von dem Unbefleckten Empfängnis wurde die Gottesmutter Maria von jedem Makel der Erbsünde bewahrt, jedoch auf natürliche Weise von ihrer Mutter empfangen und geboren. Damit errettete Gott Maria vom allerersten Augenblick ihres Lebens an vor der Macht der Sünde.*

26.) "S.M.S. Il Leone" (1737) was also built in Vienna, and had a similar career to her sister ship "S.M.S. Aquila Imperiale." In 1738, this frigate was renamed "S.M.S. Sankt Leopoldo."

*Die Donaufregatte "S.M.S Il Leone" (1737) lief in Wien vom Stapel, und gehörte auch zur "S.M.S. Sankt Carl" Klaße. Im Jahre 1738 wurde sie als die "S.M.S. Sankt Leopoldo" umbenannt. Sie hatte eine Lebensgeschichte die der ihres Schwesternschiffes "S.M.S. Aquila Imperiale" sehr ähnlich war.*

27.) "S.M.S. Il Tritone" (1737) was also built in Vienna, and had a similar career to her sister ships "S.M.S. Aquila Imperiale" and "S.M.S. Il Leone." In 1738, this frigate was renamed "S.M.S. Sankt Michael."

*Die Donaufregatte "S.M.S. Il Tritone" (1737) lief in Wien vom Stapel, und gehörte auch zur "S.M.S. Sankt Carl" Klaße. Im Jahre 1738 wurde sie als die*

*"S.M.S. Sankt Michael" umbenannt. Sie hatte eine Lebensgeschichte die der ihres Schwesternschiffes "S.M.S. Aquila Imperiale" sehr ähnlich war.*

28.) "S.M.S. Il Cavallo Marino" (1737) was also built in Vienna, and had a similar career to her sister frigates "S.M.S. Aquila Imperiale," "S.M.S. Il Leone" and "S.M.S. Il Tritone." In 1738, this frigate was renamed "S.M.S. Sankt Josephus."

*Die Donaufregatte "S.M.S. Il Cavallo Marino" (1737) lief in Wien vom Stapel, und gehörte auch zur "S.M.S. Sankt Carl" Klaße. Im Jahre 1738 wurde sie als die "S.M.S. Sankt Josephus" umbenannt. Sie hatte eine Lebensgeschichte die der ihres Schwesternschiffes "S.M.S. Aquila Imperiale" sehr ähnlich war.*

29.) Another "S.M.S. Sankt Carl" was built in Belgrade, and launched in 1738. This was to replace the wooden sailing frigate of the same name, which was lost in 1737.

*Die Donaufregatte "S.M.S. Sankt Carl" (1738) lief in Belgrad vom Stapel. Sie war ein Ersatzschiff für die erste Donaufregatte "S.M.S. Sankt Carl," die am 10. November 1737 selbst versenkt wurde.*

30.) Another "S.M.S. Santa Elisabeth" was built and launched in Vienna in 1739. She also fought against the Ottoman Turks. This was to replace the wooden sailing frigate of the same name, which was lost in 1737.

*Die Donaufregatte "S.M.S. Santa Elisabeth" (1739) lief in Wien vom Stapel, und gehörte auch zur "S.M.S. Sankt Carl" Klaße. Sie diente im Krieg gegen die ottomanische Türkei, und war ein Ersatzschiff für die erste Donaufregatte "S.M.S. Santa Elisabeth," die auch am 10. November 1737 selbst versenkt wurde.*

31.) "S.M.S. Santa Maria Anna" was built and launched in Vienna in 1739; she also fought against the Ottoman Turks.

*Die Donaufregatte "S.M.S. Maria Anna" (1739) lief in Wien vom Stapel, und diente auch im Krieg gegen die ottomanische Türkei. Das Schiff gehörte zur "S.M.S. Sankt Carl" Klaße. Maria (auf aramäisch "Mariam") ist im Neuen Testament die Mutter des Jesus Christus von Nazaret. Sie lebte nach Mark 1,9 unter anderen als gläubige Jüdin mit ihrem Ehemann Josef und weiteren Angehörigen in der Kleinstadt Nazaret in Galiläa. Als Gottesgebärerin, die Jesus Christus als Jungfrau empfing und gebar, wird sie im Römisch-Katholizismus und in der Östlichen Orthodoxie verehrt. Im Protestantismus wird die*

*Jungfraugeburt überwiegend dogmatisch anerkannt, die Verehrung Marias als Gottesmutter jedoch hauptsächlich (aber nicht ausschließlich) abgelehnt. Die Heilige Anna (auf hebräisch "Hannah), die Mutter Marias war laut mehreren apokryphen Evangelien des 2. bis 6. Jahrhunderts die Großmutter von Jesus Christus.*

32.) "S.M.S. Santa Catharina" was built and launched in Vienna in 1739; she also fought against the Ottoman Turks.

*Die Donaufregatte "S.M.S. Santa Catharina" (1739) lief in Wien vom Stapel, und diente im Krieg gegen die ottomanische Türkei. Sie gehörte auch zur "S.M.S. Sankt Carl" Klaße. Die Heilige Catharina von Siena ("Caterina Benincasa" als 23. Kind eines verarmten Adeligen geboren, der sich als Wollfärber den Lebensunterhalt verdienen mußte) lebte von 1347 bis 1380, und war eine italienische Mystikerin und Kirchenlehrerin.*

33.) "S.M.S. Sankt Francesco de Paula" was built and launched in Vienna in 1739; she also fought against the Ottoman Turks. This was the 14th and final member of the "S.M.S. Sankt Carl" class of Imperial and Royal Austrian wooden sailing frigates.

*Die Donaufregatte "S.M.S. Francesco de Paula" (1739) lief in Wien vom Stapel, und war das letzte Schiff der "S.M.S. Sankt Carl" Klaße. Sie diente auch im Krieg gegen die ottomanische Türkei.*

34.) "S.M.S. Maria Theresia" (1765) was laid down in Kosterneuburg and launched on April 14, 1769. Until August 1769 she was based in Peterwardein. She partook in a war against Ottoman Turkey from 1788-1791, where she served as the Admiral's flagship. She was sold to civilian owners thereafter. She was of course named after the Holy Roman and German Empress Maria Theresia of the House of Habsburg. From this point onward, the House has been known as "Habsburg-Lothringen," due to Maria Theresia's marriage to Francis I of Lothringen (or "Lorraine" in English). Francis I was also the Grand Duke of Tuscany, which came into the Habsburg inheritance through his relationship. This vessel did not have any sister ships.

*Die Donaufregatte "S.M.S. Maria Theresia" (1765) lief am 14. April 1769 in Klosterneuburg (bei Wien) vom Stapel, und war ein Einzelschiff. Bis 1769 war sie in Peterwardein (bei Neusatz in Wojwodina) stationiert. Zwischen 1788 und 1791 diente sie als Flaggschiff des Admirals im Krieg gegen die ottomanische Türkei.*

35.) "S.M.S. Aurora" (1765) was armed with 30 cannon, and was launched in Sankt Veit am Pflaumb ("Fiume" in Italian or "Rijeka" in modern Croatia) on September 10, 1766. In 1770, she was sold to the Italian State of Tuscany.

*Die Segelfregatte "S.M.S. Aurora" (1765) lief am 10. September 1766 in Sankt Veit am Pflaumb (heute "Rijeka" in Kroatien) vom Stapel, und war mit 30 Kanonen bewaffnet. Im Jahre 1770 wurde sie an das Großherzogtum Toskana (mit Österreich verbündet) verkauft. Die Großherzogen Toskanas kamen aus den Adelhäusern Medici, Bourbon-Parma und eventuell auch Habsburg-Lothringen.*

36.) "S.M.S. Stella Mattutina" (1765) was a sister ship of "S.M.S. Aurora," and was also launched in Sankt Veit am Pflaumb on September 7, 1768. She was also sold to the Italian State of Tuscany in 1770.

*Die Segelfregatte "S.M.S. Stella Mattutina" (1765) war ein Schwesterschiff der "S.M.S. Aurora," und lief am 7. September 1768 in Sankt Veit am Pflaumb vom Stapel. Im Jahre 1770 wurde sie auch an das Großherzogtum Toskana verkauft.*

37.) "S.M.S. Etruria" (1767) was another sister ship of "S.M.S. Aurora" and "S.M.S. Stella Mattutina." She was launched in Sankt Veit am Pflaumb (the future location of the Austrian Naval Academy) in 1769. The Imperial and Royal Austrian Naval Academy was founded by Archduke Charles of Habsburg-Lothrigen (1771-1847) in 1802. This wooden sailing frigate served both Austria and the Grand Duchy of Tuscany, which came into the Habsburg-Lothringen inheritance.

*Die Segelfregatte "S.M.S. Etruria" (1767) war auch ein Schwesterschiff der "S.M.S. Aurora," und lief im 1769 in Sankt Veit am Pflaumb vom Stapel. Die Marineakademie der Kaiserlichen und Königlichen Kriegsmarine liegt in Sankt Veit am Pflaumb, und wurde im Jahre 1802 in Venedig von Erzherzog Karl von Österreich (1771-1847) gegründet. Die "S.M.S. Etruria" wurde eventuell auch an das Großherzogtum Toskana verkauft.*

38.) "S.M.S. L'Austria" (1799) was armed with 22 cannon, and was a former merchantman purchased by the Imperal and Royal Austrian Navy. She was fitted out in the port of Livorno on the Ligurian Sea as "corsair" to raid enemy merchant shipping off the Italian Riviera. She was sold back to civilian owners in July 1800.

*Die Segelfregatte "S.M.S. L'Austria" (1799) wurde in Livorno am Ligurischen Meer gebaut, und war mit 22 Kanonen bewaffnet. Im Juli 1800 wurde sie als*

*Handelsschiff verkauft. Bevor Napoleon Bonaparte Norditalien angegriffen hat, gab es Staaten wie das Königreich Sardinien, die Republik Venedig, und die Herzogtüme Parma, Modena, Lucca sowie das Großherzogtum Toskana und die Päpstlichen Staaten. Die sogenannten Republiken Cisalpine (Mailand) und Ligurien (Genua sowie Livorno) waren nichts mehr als Satelliten Frankreichs.*

39.) "S.M.S La Costanza" (1805) was armed with 12 cannon, and was yet another former merchantman purchased by the Austrian navy. She was assigned to port defense duties, and was sold back to civilian owners in 1806.

*Die Segelfregatte "S.M.S. La Costanza" (1805) wurde auch im Jahre 1806 als Handelsschiff verkauft. Sie war mit 12 Kanonen für den Handelskrieg bewaffnet.*

40.) "S.M.S. Felsenburg" (1805) was armed with 9 cannon, and was a former merchant vessel purchased by the Austrian navy. She was assigned to convoy and transport duties before being sold back to civilian owners in 1806.

*Die Segelfregatte "S.M.S. Felsenburg" (1805) wurde auch im Jahre 1806 als Handesschiff verkauft. Sie war mit 9 Kanonen als Geleitschiff und Transporter bewaffnet. Eine Felsenburg ist eine mittelalterliche Burg, bei der natürliche Felsenformationen unmittelbar in die Wehranlagen einbezogen sind und den Aufbau der Anlage prägen. Topographisch gehören Felsenburgen zur Gruppe der Höhenburgen.*

41.) "S.M.S. L'Utilita" (1805) was another former merchantman purchased by the Austrian navy, and used for convoy duties (as a convoy lead ship) and the defense of commerce before being sold back to civilian owners.

*Die Segelfregatte "S.M.S. Armonia" (1809) war auch ein ehemaliges Handelsschiff, das eventuell wieder als Handelsschiff verkauft wurde.*

42.) "S.M.S. Armonia" (1809) was still another former merchantman purchased by the Imperial and Royal Austrian Navy, and kept for a short while before being sold back to civilian owners.

*Die Segelfregatte "S.M.S. Armonia" (1809) war auch ein ehemaliges Handelsschiff, das eventuell wieder als Handelsschiff verkauft wurde.*

43.) "S.M.S. Strela" (1808) was captured from the Napoleonic French Navy, which had in turn captured the ship from the Imperial Russian Navy during the retreat of the latter from the Adriatic Sea. She was armed with 24 cannon, and was based first in Triest and then in Venice.  She was sold to civilian owners in August 1814.

*Die Segelfregatte "S.M.S. Strela" (1808) wurde von den Franzosen beschlagnamt, und in die Kaiserliche und Königliche Kriegsmarine eingenommen.  Davor haben die Franzosen das Schiff von den Russen beschlagnahmt, als es Rußland im Adriatischen Meer diente.  Das Schiff war mit 24 Kanonen bewaffnet, und war von der Kaiserlichen und Königlichen Kriegsmarine Österreichs in Triest und eventuell in Venedig stationiert.  Im August 1814 wurde sie als Handelsschiff verkauft.*

### XIII (16) Austro-Venetian Brigs (for which exact tonnage is not available) / Österreichische Segelbriggs (ohne technische Daten)

A "brig" (called a "Brigg" in German) was a 2-masted and square-rigged wooden sailing ship, smaller than either a frigate or a corvette (which had 3 masts).  Brigs within the Imperial and Royal Austrian Navy ranged in size from 168 up to 485 tons displacement.

*Die Segelbriggs der Kaiserlichen und Königlichen Kriegsmarine Österreichs hatten eine Einsatzverdrängung von je zwischen 168 und 485 Tonnen.  Segelbriggs haben zwei Masten (die Segelfregatten und die Segelkorvetten sind noch größer, und haben drei Masten).*

1.) "S.M.S. Achilles" (1793) was part of the Austrian Navy from 1793 until at least 1815 (the end of the Napoleonic Wars).

*Das Segelbrigg "S.M.S. Achilles" (1793) diente mindestens bis 1815.*

2.) "S.M.S. Distruzione" (1784) was launched in Venice.  She was armed with 16 cannon, and was confiscated by the French Navy on May 17, 1797.  Her new French crew scuttled her on December 30, 1797, and the Austrians raised her on January 18, 1798.  She was repaired and renamed "S.M.S. Orione" in 1802, now armed with just 12 cannon.  On January 19, 1806 she was turned over to France's Italian allies.

*Das Segelbrigg "S.M.S. Distruzione" (1784) lief in Venedig vom Stapel, und war mit 16 Kanonen bewaffnet.  Am 17. Mai 1797 wurde das Schiff von den Franzosen beschlagnahmt, und am 30. Dezember 1797 wurde die "S.M.S. Distruzione" von den Franzosen selbst versenkt.  Am 18. Januar 1798 hatten die Österreicher das Schiff geborgen, und im Jahre 1802 als die "S.M.S. Orione" umbenannt.  Die*

*"S.M.S. Orione" war mit nur 12 Kanonen umgebaut, und am 19. Januar 1806 wurde sie von den italienischen Verbündeten Frankreichs endlich beschlagnahmt.*

3.) "S.M.S. Oreste" was commissioned no later than 1797, and was armed with 18 cannon. The French Navy confiscated her from Austria on May 17, 1797, and scuttled her off the coast of Venice on December 30, 1797. The Austrians raised the ship on January 18, 1798, repaired and then recommissioned her in 1799. From 1803-1805, she undertook a mission to Cadiz, Spain and then to Morrocco. In November 1809, she was sold to civilian owners.

*Das Segelbrigg "S.M.S. Oreste" (1797) war mit 18 Kanonen bewaffnet. Am 17. Mai 1797 wurde sie auch von den Franzosen beschlagnahmt, und am 30. Dezember 1797 auch von den Franzosen selbst versenkt. Am 18. Januar 1798 hatten die Österreicher das Schiff geborgen und im Jahre 1799 wieder getauft. Zwischen 1803 und 1805 reiste die "S.M.S. Oreste" nach Cadiz in Spanien und auch nach Marokko. Im November 1809 wurde sie als Handelsschiff verkauft.*

4.) "S.M.S. Pilade" (1797) had the same history and dates as her sister sailing brig "S.M.S. Oreste."

*Das Segelbrigg "S.M.S. Pilade" (1797) hatte eine Lebensgeschichte die der ihres Schwesternschiffes "S.M.S. Oreste sehr ähnlich war.*

5.) "S.M.S. Polluce" was armed with 16 cannon, and was launched in Venice in 1791 under the orginal name "S.M.S. Castore." The French Navy confiscated her from Austria on May 17, 1797 and renamed her yet again as "S.M.S. Rivoli." In 1799, the Austrians recaptured her from the French in the port of Ancona, on the Italian Adriatic coast. She then reverted to her old name of "S.M.S. Polluce." On January 19, 1806 she was turned over to France's Italian allies. She was scrapped by 1812.

*Das Segelbrigg "S.M.S. Polluce" lief im Jahre 1791 in Venedig ursprünglich als die "S.M.S. Castore" vom Stapel. Am 17. Mai 1797 wurde sie von den Franzosen beschlagnahmt, und als die "S.M.S. Rivoli" umbenannt. Im 1799 wurde sie von den Österreichern im Hafen von Ancona zurückgenommen, und wieder als die "S.M.S. Polluce" umbenannt. Am 19. Januar 1806 wurde sie von den italienischen Waffenverbündeten Frankreichs beschlagnahmt, und im Jahre 1812 wurde sie verschrottet.*

6.) "S.M.S. Faceto" was purchased from civilian owners in 1804, but sold back later in the same year.

*Das Segelbrigg "S.M.S. Faceto" wurde als Handelsschiff im Jahre 1804 verkauft. Das Schiff hatte keine Bewaffnung, weil sie vorher auch ein Handelsschiff war.*

7.) "S.M.S. L'Oracolo" had the same history and dates as her sister sailing brig "S.M.S. Faceto." She had been armed with 14 cannon.

*Das Segelbrigg "S.M.S. L'Oracolo" hatte eine Lebensgeschichte die der ihres Schwesternschiffes "S.M.S. Faceto" sehr ähnlich war, aber sie war mit 14 Kanonen bewaffnet.*

8.) "S.M.S. Il Bizarro" was armed with 12 cannon, and was purchased from civilian owners in 1805. She was sold back to the same owners in 1806.

*Das Segelbrigg "S.M.S. Il Bizarro" war ein ehemaliges Handelsschiff, das im Jahre 1805 gekauft wurde. Sie war mit 12 Kanonen bewaffnet. Im Jahre 1806 wurde sie wieder als Handelsschiff verkauft.*

9.) "S.M.S. Castore" was armed with 20 cannon, and was laid down in Venice in 1804. In August 1805, she was launched with the new name "S.M.S. Eolo." She was briefly assigned to the Austrian fleet, and then sold to civilian owners in November 1809.

*Das Segelbrigg "S.M.S. Castore" wurde im Jahre 1804 in Venedig auf Kiel gelegt, und lief im August 1805 als die "S.M.S. Eolo" vom Stapel. Sie war mit 20 Kanonen bewaffnet. Im November 1809 wurde sie als Handelsschiff verkauft.*

10.) "S.M.S. Assur" was armed with 4 cannon. She was purchased from civilian owners in July 1806, and then renamed as "S.M.S. Delfino" on August 30, 1806. She was briefly assigned to the Imperial and Royal Austrian fleet, and then sold back to civilian owners in November 1809.

*Das Segelbrigg "S.M.S. Assur" war mit 4 Kanonen bewaffnet. Im Juli 1806 wurde das Handelsschiff von der Kaiserlichen und Königlichen Kriegsmarine gekauft, und am 30. August 1806 als die "S.M.S. Delfino" umbenannt. Im November 1809 wurde sie wieder als Handelsschiff verkauft.*

11.) "S.M.S. Cesare" (1814) was captured from the Italian allies of Napoleonic France. She was armed with 16 cannon, and was not kept in the Imperial and Royal Austrian Navy for very long before being sold to civilian owners.

*Das Segelbrigg "S.M.S. Cesare" (1814) wurde von den italienischen Waffenverbündeten Frankreichs weggenommen. Sie war mit 14 Kanonen bewaffnet, und wurde als Handelsschiff verkauft.*

12.) "S.M.S. Eridano" (1806) was built overseas, and was captured by the Imperial and Royal Austrian Navy during the Napoleonic Wars. She was armed with 16 cannon, and was scrapped after June 1816.

*Das Segelbrigg "S.M.S. Eridano" (1806) wurde von den Franzosen weggenommen. Sie war mit 16 Kanonen bewaffnet, und wurde im Juni 1816 verschrottet.*

13.) "S.M.S. Mamelucco" (1808) was laid down in Venice in 1808, and launched on August 17, 1811. She was armed with 10 cannon, and was captured from the Italian allies of Napoleonic France. She was renamed "S.M.S. Ussaro" on May 5, 1815, and was renamed yet again as "S.M.S. Fenice" after modernization on February 18, 1829. She was briefly under the control of Italian nationalist rebels in Venice from March 1848 until August 1849. After the Austrians got her back, she was renamed yet another time as "S.M.S. Phönix." She was scrapped in 1855, after 47 years of service.

*Das Segelbrigg "S.M.S. Mamelucco" (1808) wurde in Venedig auf Kiel gelegt, und lief am 17. August 1811 vom Stapel. Sie war mit zehn Kanonen bewaffnet, und wurde von den italienischen Waffenverbündeten Frankreichs übernommen. Am 5. Mai 1815 wurde sie als die "S.M.S. Ussaro" umbenannt, und nach einer Modernisierung am 18. Februar 1829 als die "S.M.S. Fenice" umbenannt. Zwischen März 1848 und August 1849 wurde sie von feindlichen italienischen Nationalisten beschlagnahmt. Danach wurde sie als die "S.M.S. Phönix" umbenannt. Im Jahre 1855 wurde sie verschrottet – nach einer Dienstzeit von 44 Jahren.*

14.) "S.M.S. Waxel" (1814) was captured from the Italian allies of Napoleonic France, but not kept by the Austrians for very long. She was sold to civilian owners on August 29, 1814.

*Das Segelbrigg "S.M.S. Waxel" (1814) wurde von den italienischen Waffenverbündeten Frankreichs beschlagnahmt, und am 29. August 1814 als Handelsschiff verkauft.*

15.) "S.M.S. Ciclope" (1809) was also captured from the Italian allies of Napoleonic France, and was sold to civilian owners in 1814. She had been based in the port of Triest and was active off the coast of Istria (called "Küstenland" in German, or "coastal land" in English).

*Das Segelbrigg "S.M.S. Ciclope" (1809) wurde auch von den italienischen Waffenverbündeten Frankreichs beschlagnahmt, und im Jahre 1814 als Handelsschiff verkauft. Bei der Kaiserlichen und Königlichen Kriegsmarine Österreichs war sie in Triest stationiert, und an der Küste von Istrien ("Küstenland" auf deutsch) im Einsatz.*

16.) "S.M.S. Mercurio" (1809) had an identical history to her sister ship "S.M.S. Ciclope."

*Das Segelbrigg "S.M.S. Mercurio" (1809) hatte eine Lebensgeschichte die der ihres Schwesternschiffes "S.M.S. Ciclope" sehr ähnlich war.*

17.) "S.M.S. Castellano" (1848) was a former Venetian merchantman, captured by the Imperial and Royal Austrian Navy. She was scuttled in order to help block the harbor entrance to Venice, later raised and then scrapped in 1850.

*Das Segelbrigg "S.M.S. Castellano" (1848) war ein ehemaliges Handelsschiff aus Venedig. Sie wurde von der Kaiserlichen und Königlichen Kriegsmarine in der Hafeneinfahrt von Venedig selbst versenkt, um den Hafen zu blockieren. Im Jahre 1850 wurde sie geborgen und dann verschrottet.*

18.) "S.M.S. Febo" (1849) was captured from the Italian nationalist rebels, and then converted into a coal depot ship in 1850.

*Das Segelbrigg "S.M.S. Febo" (1849) wurde von den feindlichen italienischen Nationalisten beschlagnahmt, und im Jahre 1850 als Kohlendepotschiff umgebaut.*

## XIII (17) Austro-Venetian Brigantines (for which exact tonnage is not available) / Österreichische Segelbrigantinen (ohne technische Daten)

A "brigantine" (with the same name in German, but capitalized like all German nouns) was a sort of smaller brig. A brig was a wooden sailing warship with 2 main masts, thus being somewhat smaller than either wooden sailing frigates or wooden sailing corvettes, which had 3 main masts. Brigantines within the Imperial and Royal Austrian Navy displaced from 185 up to 462 tons.

*Eine Segelbrigantine ist etwas kleiner als ein Segelbrigg, aber hat auch zwei Masten. Die Segelbrigantinen der Kaiserlichen und Königlichen Kriegsmarine Österreichs hatten eine Einsatzverdrängung von je zwischen 185 und 462 Tonnen.*

1.) "S.M.S. König David" (1628) was part of a contingent of 24 warships of the "Imperial Armada of the Baltic Sea" during the 30 Years' War of 1618-1648. They were based in the port cities of Wismar and Rostock. She was named after King David of Israel from the Old Testament of the Holy Bible.

*Die Segelbrigantine "S.M.S. König David" (1628) gehörte der Kaiserlichen Armada der Ostsee zur Zeit des Dreißigjährigen Krieges (1618-1648). Es gab 24 Österreichische Kriegsschiffe, die in den Kriegshäfen von Wismar und Rostock stationiert waren.*

2.) "S.M.S. Gran Rodolfo" (1764) was armed with 20 cannon, and was a former merchantman purchased by the Imperial and Royal Austrian Navy. She partook in convoy duties, protecting Austrian shipping traffic from Algerian pirates. She was later sold back to civilian owners.

*Die Segelbrigantine "S.M.S. Graf Rodolfo" (1764) war mit 20 Kanonen bewaffnet, und war ein ehemaliges Handelsschiff. Sie wurde als Geleitschiff gegen algerische Piraten benutzt. Danach wurde sie wieder als Handelsschiff verkauft.*

3.) "S.M.S. La Sacra Famiglia" (1764) was armed with 12 cannon, and had a history very similar to her sister ship "S.M.S. Gran Rodolfo." She was named after the Holy Family of Saint Joseph, the Blessed Virgin Mary and Jesus Christ.

*Die Segelbrigantine "S.M.S. La Sacra Famiglia" (1764) war mit 12 Kanonen bewaffnet, und sie hatte eine Lebensgeschichte die der ihres Schwesternschiffes "S.M.S. Graf Rodolfo" sehr ähnlich war. Die Mitglieder der Heiligen Familie waren Sankt Josef, die Jungfrau Maria und Jesus Christus von Nazaret.*

4.) "S.M.S. Il Vincitore" (1778) was armed with 12 cannon, and originally belonged to David's Shipping Company of Sankt Veit am Pflaumb (called "Fiume" in Italian and "Rijeka" in modern Croatia). She was briefly purchased by the Imperial and Royal Austrian Navy to guard her home port, but was deemed to be unsuited to this task and thereby resold to her civilian owners. Sankt Veit am Plaumb was the home of the Naval Academy of the Imperial and Royal Austrian Navy, which endured until the sad end of the Habsburg-Lothringen Monarchy in November 1918.

*Die Segelbrigantine "S.M.S. Il Vincitore" (1778) war mit 12 Kanonen bewaffnet, und gehörte ursprünglich der Reederei David in Sankt Veit am Pflaumb (heute Rijeka in Kroatien). Sie wurde von der Kaiserlichen und Königlichen Kriegsmarine als Hafenschutzschiff benutzt, und wurde bald wieder an die Reederei David verkauft.*

5.) "S.M.S. Le Ferme" (1784) was armed with with 20 cannon, and was built in the Austrian Netherlands (modern-day Belgium). In 1786, she sailed to Triest, which became her new home port. She was active in the Imperial and Royal Austrian Navy at least until July 1794.

*Die Segelbrigantine "S.M.S. La Ferme" (1784) war mit 20 Kanonen bewaffnet, und wurde in den Österreichischen Niederlanden (heute Belgien) gebaut. Im Jahre 1786 reiste sie nach Triest, und war dort stationiert. Sie wurde kurz nach Juli 1794 verschrottet.*

6.) "S.M.S. Le Just" (1784) was also armed with 20 cannon, and also came from the Austrian Netherlands (modern-day Belgium). She accompanied her sister ship "S.M.S. Le Ferme" to Triest in 1786, and was sold to civilian owners in July 1791.

*Die Segelbrigantine "S.M.S. Le Just" (1784) hatte eine Lebensgeschichte die der ihres Schwesternschiffes "S.M.S. La Ferme" sehr ähnlich war, aber sie wurde als Handelsschiff im Jahre 1791 verkauft.*

7.) "S.M.S. Le Fort" (1784) was a sister ship of "S.M.S. Le Ferme" and "S.M.S. Le Just." Unlike her two sister ships, she remained in the Austrian Netherlands (modern-day Belgium).

*Die Segelbrigantine "S.M.S. Le Fort" (1784) gehörte zur "S.M.S. La Ferme" Klaße. Sie blieb in den Österreichischen Niederlanden (heute Belgien).*

8.) "S.M.S. Cesare Augusto" (1788) was a former merchantman, briefly purchased by the Imperial and Royal Austrian Navy for use in a war against Ottoman Turkey. She was assigned to coastal protection duties before being sold back to civilian owners in November 1788.

*Die Segelbrigantine "S.M.S. Cesare Augusto" (1788) war ein ehemaliges Handelsschiff, die in den Krieg gegen die ottomanische Türkei benutzt wurde. Im November 1788 wurde sie wieder als Handelsschiff verkauft.*

9.) "S.M.S. Citta di Vienna" (1788) was identical to and had the same history as her sister ship "S.M.S. Cesare Augusto." She was named after the city of Vienna, capital of the Habsburg-Lothringen empire.

*Die Segelbrigantine "S.M.S. Citta di Vienna" (1788) hatte eine Lebensgeschichte die der ihres Schwesternschiffes "S.M.S. Cesare Augusto" sehr ähnlich war.*

10.) "S.M.S. San Giovanni" (1788) was identical to and had the same history as her sister ships "S.M.S. Cesare Augusto" and "S.M.S. Citta di Vienna."

*Die Segelbrigantine "S.M.S. San Giovanni" (1788) hatte eine Lebensgeschichte die der ihres Schwesternschiffes "S.M.S. Cesare Augusto" sehr ähnlich war.*

11.) "S.M.S. Agile" (1791) was armed with 8 cannon, and was built in Venice. She was briefly captured by the French Navy from May 17 until December 30, 1797, before being retaken by the Austrians on January 18, 1798. She was damaged while under French authority, partially repaired and launched in 1805. She was then assigned to commerce protection and harbor defense duties within the Imperial and Royal Austrian Navy.

*Die Segelbrigantine "S.M.S. Agile" (1791) war mit acht Kanonen bewaffnet, und wurde in Venedig gebaut. Zwischen den 17. Mai und den 30. Dezember 1797 wurde sie von den Franzosen beschlagnahmt, bevor sie am 18. Januar 1798 von den Österreichern zurückerobert wurde. Die Brigantine wurde von der Kaiserlichen und Königlichen Kriegsmarine repariert und danach im Jahre 1805 in Dienst gestellt. Danach wurde sie als Geleitschiff sowie als Hafenverteidigungsschiff benutzt.*

12.) "S.M.S. Indagatore" (1797) was armed with 8 cannon, and was built in Venice. She was captured by the Napoleonic French Navy on May 17, 1797 and damaged on December 30, 1797 before being launched. The Austrians recaptured her on January 18, 1798 but did not resume working on her until 1805. She was launched in September 1805, and then assigned to coastal protection, harbor defense and convoy duties. She was sold to civilian owners in 1810.

*Die Segelbrigantine "S.M.S. Indagatore" (1797) hatte eine Lebensgeschichte die der ihres Schwesternschiffes "S.M.S. Agile" sehr ähnlich war, aber sie wurde als Handelsschiff im Jahre 1810 verkauft.*

13.) "S.M.S. Cibelle" (1790) was armed with 12 cannon, and was built in Venice. She was captured from the Italian allies of Napoleonic France, and launched on

May 17, 1790. The French Navy recaptured her off the island of Corfu on July 23, 1797, while the Austrians got her back again off the port of Ancona on November 14, 1799. She was then assigned to courier, trade protection and port defense duties. The Italians retook her from the Austrians on January 19, 1806, and she finally went back to Austria near the end of the Napoleonic Wars in 1814. She was later renamed "S.M.S. Dalmato," and was reassigned to salvaging duties. She remained in the Imperial and Royal Austrian Navy at least until September 1820.

*Die Segelbrigantine "S.M.S. Cibelle" (1790) war mit 12 Kanonen bewaffnet, und wurde in Venedig gebaut. Sie wurde von den italienischen Waffenverbündeten Frankreichs beschlagnahmt, und lief am 17. Mai 1790 im Dienst der Kaiserlichen und Königlichen Kriegsmarine vom Stapel. Am 23. Juli 1797 hatten die Franzosen das Schiff an der Küste von Korfu zurückerobert. Am 14. November 1799 hatten dann die Österreicher das Schiff an der Küste von Ancona von den Franzosen zurückerobert. Danach wurde sie als Transportschiff, als Geleitschiff sowie als Hafenverteidigungsschiff benutzt. Am 19. November 1806 wurde sie von der italienischen Waffenverbündeten Frankreichs nochmals beschlagnahmt. Im Jahre 1814 wurde sie endlich wieder von Österreich beschlagnamt, und als die "S.M.S. Dalmato" umbenannt. Danach wurde sie als Bergungsschiff benutzt, bis sie im September 1820 verschrottet wurde.*

14.) "S.M.S. Arabo" (1799) was a former armed merchantman captured from the Italians and the French.

*Die Segelbrigantine "S.M.S. Arabo" (1799) war ein ehemaliges bewaffnetes französisches und italienisches Handelssschiff, das von den Österreichern beschlagnahmt wurde.*

15.) "S.M.S. Merope" (1796) was launched in Venice on June 25, 1796. She was also captured from the Italian allies of the Napoleonic French. The French Navy retook her off the coast of Genoa from May 17, 1797 until the Austrians captured her yet again on June 4, 1800. She remained in the Imperial and Royal Austrian Navy at least until 1822.

*Die Segelbrigantine "S.M.S. Merope" (1796) lief am 25. Juni 1796 in Venedig vom Stapel. Bei der Kiellegung war sie italienisch, bei dem Stapellauf österreichisch, und am 17. Mai 1797 wurde sie an der Küste von Genua von den Franzosen beschlagnahmt. Am 4. Juni 1800 wurde sie endlich von Kaiserlichen und Königlichen Kriegsmarine zurückerobert und im Jahre 1822 wurde sie verschrottet.*

16.) "S.M.S. La Francesca" (1805) was a former merchantman purchased by the Imperial and Royal Austrian Navy. She briefly partook in commerce protection and harbor defense duties before being resold to civilian owners in 1806.

*Die Segelbrigantine "S.M.S. La Francesca" (1805) war ein ehemaliges Handelsschiff, das von der Kaiserlichen und Königlichen Kriegsmarine gekauft wurde. Sie wurde als Geleitschiff und als Hafenverteidigungsschiff benutzt, bevor sie im Jahre 1806 wieder als Handelsschiff verkauft wurde.*

17.) "S.M.S. La Solidita" (1805) had a history identical to that of her sister ship "S.M.S. La Francesca."

*Die Segelbrigantine "S.M.S. La Solidita" (1805) hatte eine Lebensgeschichte die der ihres Schwesternschiffes "S.M.S. La Francesca" sehr ähnlich war.*

18.) "S.M.S. La Gioja" (1805) was another armed former merchantman. She was overpowered by 3 French corsairs while escorting 5 Austrian merchant ships near the Adriatic island of Lissa on December 5, 1805. She and the 5 civilian vessels capitulated to the French Navy.

*Die Segelbrigantine "S.M.S. La Gioja" (1805) war ein ehemaliges bewaffnetes Handelsschiff. Am 5. Dezember 1805 wurde sie und fünf österreichische Handelsschiffe von drei französischen Korsaren in der Nähe von Lissa erobert.*

19.) "S.M.S. La Viaggiatrice" (1805) was armed with 28 cannon, and was a former merchantman not kept for very long by the Imperial and Royal Austrian Navy.

*Die Segelbrigantine "S.M.S. La Viaggiatrice" (1805) war mit 28 Kanonen bewaffnet, und war auch ein ehemaliges Handelsschiff. Sie war nicht lange bei der Kaiserlichen und Königlichen Kriegsmarine.*

20.) "S.M.S. Iride" (1813) was another former merchantman confiscated from the Italian allies of Napoleonic France upon the Austrian liberation of the port of Triest in November 1813. She was assigned to commerce protection and transport duties within the Imperial and Royal Austrian Navy, and then sold to civilian owners in August 1814.

*Die Segelbrigantine "SM.S. Iride" (1813) war ein ehemaliges Handelsschiff, das im November 1813 von den italienischen Waffenverbündeten Frankreichs im neulich befreiten Hafen von Triest beschlagnahmt wurde. Sie wurde als*

*Geleitschiff sowie als Transportschiff benutzt, und dann als Handelsschiff im August 1814 verkauft.*

21.) "S.M.S. Nina" (1807) was built in the United States, and taken from the Italian allies of Napoleonic France upon the Austrian liberation of the port of Triest in November 1813. She was renamed as "S.M.S. Arianna," and assigned to commerce protection, transport, fleet, training and postal delivery duties within the Imperial and Royal Austrian Navy. She was scrapped in 1839, after 32 years of service.

*Die Segelbrigantine "S.M.S. Nina" (1807) wurde in den Vereinigten Staaten gebaut, und wurde auch im November 1813 von den italienischen Waffenverbündeten Frankreichs im neulich befreiten Hafen von Triest beschlagnahmt. Sie wurde als die "S.M.S. Arianna" umbenannt, und diente als Geleitschiff, als Transportschiff, als Flottenschiff sowie als Schulschiff. Im Jahre 1839 wurde sie verschrottet, nach einer Dienstzeit von 32 Jahren.*

22.) "S.M.S. Aurora" (1814) was taken from the Italian allies of Napoleonic France on April 25, 1814. She was assigned to postal delivery and station duties within the Imperial and Royal Austrian Navy, and scrapped in 1844.

*Die Segelbrigantine "S.M.S. Aurora" (1814) wurde am 25. April 1814 von den italienischen Waffenverbündeten Frankreichs beschlagnahmt. Sie wurde als Postschiff sowie als Stationsschiff benutzt, und wurde im Jahre 1844 verschrottet – nach einer Dienstzeit von 30 Jahren.*

23.) "S.M.S. Gloria" (1806) was armed with 10 cannon, and was built in Venice. She was launched in March of 1807, and taken from the Italian allies of Napoleonic France on April 25, 1814. On May 20, 1815 she was renamed as "S.M.S. Vigilante," and assigned to commerce protection, transport, fleet, training and postal delivery duties within the Imperial and Royal Austrian Navy. She was scrapped in 1836.

*Die Segelbrigantine "S.M.S. Gloria" (1806) war mit zehn Kanonen bewaffnet, und wurde in Venedig gebaut. Sie lief im März 1807 vom Stapel, und wurde am 25. April 1814 von den italienischen Waffenverbündeten Frankreichs beschlagnahmt. Am 20. Mai 1815 wurde sie als die "S.M.S. Vigilante" umbenannt, wurde als Geleitschiff, als Transportschiff, als Flottenschiff, als Schulschiff sowie als Postschiff bei der Kaiserlichen und Königlichen Kriegsmarine benutzt. Sie wurde im Jahre 1836 verschrottet, nach einer Dienstzeit von 29 Jahren.*

24.) "S.M.S. Aretusa" (1811) was armed with 10 cannon, and was also built in Venice. She was launched on April 15, 1812, and taken from the Italian allies of Napoleonic France on April 25, 1814. She was assigned to fleet, training and customs duties within the Imperial and Royal Austrian Navy. She was scrapped in 1843.

*Die Segelbrigantine "S.M.S. Aretusa" (1811) war mit zehn Kanonen bewaffnet, und wurde in Venedig gebaut. Sie lief am 15. April 1812 vom Stapel, und wurde am 25. April 1814 von den italienischen Waffenverbündeten Frankreichs beschlagnahmt. Sie wurde als Flottenschiff, als Schulschiff sowie als Zollschiff bei der Kaiserlichen und Königlichen Kriegsmarine benutzt. Sie wurde im Jahre 1843 verschrottet, nach einer Dienstzeit von 31 Jahren.*

25.) "S.M.S. Amora" (1815) was in the Austrian Navy, but unfortunately we have no further details about her history of service therein.

*Die Segelbrigantine "S.M.S. Amora" (1815) diente bei der Kaiserlichen und Königlichen Kriegsmarine Österreichs, aber mehr ist uns leider nicht bekannt.*

**XIII (18) Austro-Venetian Cannon Sloops (for which exact tonnage is not available) / Österreichische Segelkanonierschaluppen (ohne technische Daten)**

A cannon sloop (called a "Kanonierschaluppe" in German) was cannon boat with a rudder and sails. They were well-built, and were known for their longevity. They were designed to be flat and low, and were first seen in Spain. In the Imperial and Royal Austrian Navy, a cannon-sloop would have displaced from 80 to 81 tons.

*Die Segelkanonierschaluppen der Kaiserlichen und Königlichen Kriegsmarine hatten eine Einsatzverdrängung von je zwischen 80 un 81 Tonnen.*

1.) "S.M.S. Schwalbe" (1849) was built in Triest, and was launched on June 20, 1849. "Schwalbe" is the German word for the bird known in English as a "swallow." She was in service until 1851, when she was stripped of her armament.

*Die Segelkanonierschaluppe "S.M.S. Schwalbe" (1849) lief am 20. Juni 1849 in Triest vom Stapel, und diente bis sie im Jahre 1851 entwaffnet wurde.*

2.) "S.M.S. Italiana" (1849) was built in Venice, and was launched on August 27, 1849. She was captured from Italian nationalist rebels, and absorbed into the Imperial and Royal Austrian Navy.

*Die Segelkanonierschaluppe "S.M.S. Italiana" (1849) lief am 27. August 1849 in Venedig vom Stapel, und wurde von feindlichen italienischen Nationalisten beschlagnahmt.*

### XIII (19) Austro-Venetian Pinnaces (for which exact tonnage is not available) / Österreichische Segelpenichen (ohne technische Daten)

A "pinnace" (called a "Peniche" in German) was a small and light sailing vessel used to guide larger warships. They were better than wooden cannon-sloops, and were first seen in France. In comparison to sloops, they were lighter, sharper, more seaworthy and equipped with more effective sails. They were also used for courier duties. In the Imperial and Royal Austrian Navy, a pinnace would have displaced from 44 up to 72 tons.

*Die Segelpenichen der Kaiserlichen und Königlichen Kriegsmarine Österreichs hatten eine Einsatzverdrängung von je zwischen 44 und 72 Tonnen.*

1.) "S.M.S. Tartara" (1848) was only part of the Austrian Navy from 1848 until 1849.

*Die Segelpeniche "S.M.S. Tartara" (1848) diente bei der Kaiserlichen und Königlichen Kriegsmarine nur bis 1849.*

2.) "S.M.S. Neitra" (1848) was purchased by the Imperial and Royal Austrian Navy in 1848, and was scrapped in 1861.

*Die Segelpeniche "S.M.S. Neitra" (1848) diente bis sie im Jahre 1861 verschrottet wurde.*

3.) "S.M.S. Furiosa" (1849) was built in Triest, and was scrapped in 1859.

*Die Segelpeniche "S.M.S. Furiosa" (1848) lief in Triest vom Stapel, und wurde im Jahre 1859 verschrottet.*

### XIII (20) Austro-Venetian Floating Batteries (for which exact tonnage is not available) / Österreichische Schwimmende Batterieen (ohne technische Daten)

The wooden sailing battery (called a "schwimmende Batterie" in German) was the predecessor of the more modern armorclad monitor or even the gunboat. These were small vessels, intended for coastal, river and lake usage.

*Die schwimmenden Segelbatterien der Kaiserlichen und Königlichen Kriegsmarine waren die Vorgänger der späteren Kanonenboote. Sie waren ziemlich klein, und dienten hauptsächlich an den Küsten, auf Flüßen und auf Binnenseen.*

1.) "S.M.S. Vulcano" was purchased from civilian owners in late September 1797, and then armed for the defense of the Austrian naval port of Triest. In January 1798, she was sold back to her civilian owners. This vessel was named "volcano" in Italian, the language of the majority of officers and servicemen within the Imperial and Royal Austrian Navy until 1848, when German became the majority language.

*Die Segelbatterie "S.M.S. Vulcano" wurde im September 1797 gekauft, und war als Hafenverteidiger bewaffnet. Sie wurde schon wieder im Januar 1798 verkauft.*

2.) "S.M.S. Bucintoro" was armed with 12 cannon, and had been launched in Venice in 1728. She was briefly captured by the French Navy from July 17 until December 30, 1797. The Austrians got her back on January 18, 1798, renamed her "S.M.S. Idra" in 1805, but lost her again to France's Italian allies on January 19, 1806. She was returned to Austria for the final time on April 25, 1814, and was finally scrapped in 1824 – after an incredible 96 years of service.

*Die Segelbatterie "S.M.S. Bucintoro" war mit 12 Kanonen bewaffnet, und lief im Jahre 1728 in Venedig vom Stapel. Zwischen den 17. Juli und den 30. Dezember 1797 wurde sie von den Franzosen beschlagnahmt. Am 18. Januar 1798 wurde sie wieder österreichisch, aber am 19. Januar 1806 wurde sie von den italienischen Waffenverbündeten Frankreichs beschlagnahmt. Am 25. April 1814 wurde sie endlich wieder österreichisch, und sie wurde im Jahre 1824 verschrottet – nach einer langen Dienstzeit von 96 Jahren.*

3.) "S.M.S. Obusiera" (1840) was built in Venice, but we have no further details about her.

*Die Segelbatterie "S.M.S. Obusiera" (1840) wurde in Venedig gebaut, aber mehr ist uns leider nicht bekannt.*

## XIII (21) Austro-Venetian Galiots (for which exact tonnage is not available) / Österreichische Segelgaleotten (ohne technische Daten)

A "galiot" (called a "Galeotte" in German) was a smaller type of wooden sailing galley. They had one or two masts, and about 20 oars, using both sails and oars for propulsion. Warships of this type usually carried between 2 and 12 smaller cannon, and between 50 and 150 commissioned officers and enlisted men. They could displace anywhere from 50 to 300 tons, and were common in the Holy Roman Empire of the German Nation.

*Die Segelgaleotten der Kaiserlichen und Königlichen Kriegsmarine Österreichs waren etwas kleiner als die Segelgaleeren. Eine Segelgaleotte hatte einen oder zwei Masten, ungefähr 20 Riemen, war mit zwei bis zwölf Kanonen bewaffnet, und hatte eine Besatzung von 50 bis 150 Offiziere und Matrosen. Sie hatten eine Einsatzverdrängung von je zwischen 50 und 300 Tonnen, und waren im Ersten Deutschen Reich sehr zahlreich.*

1.) "S.M.S. Azzardo" was armed with 12 cannon, and was purchased by the Austrian Navy in 1797. She served to protect commercial shipping in the Northern Adriatic Sea at least until 1799. The ships of this class were built out of oak, were 31 meters long, had a maximum beam of 6,3 meters and a draught of 1,1 meters. They could accommodate up to 97 commissioned officers and enlisted men, and had up to 36 oars per vessel.

*Die Segelgaleotte "S.M.S. Azzardo" war mit 12 Kanonen bewaffnet, und wurde im Jahre 1797 gekauft. Sie diente in der nördlichen Adria mindestens bis 1799. Sie war aus Eichenholz gebaut, war 31 Meter lang, hatte eine Breite von 6,3 Meter und einen Tiefgang von 1,1 Meter. Sie hatte eine Besatzung von 97 Offiziere und Matrosen, und hatte bis 36 Riemen.*

2.) "S.M.S. Cacciatrice" was a sister ship of "S.M.S. Azzardo," and had a very similar history.

*Die Segelgaleotte "S.M.S. Cacciatrice" hatte eine Lebensgeschichte die der ihres Schwesternschiffes "S.M.S. Azzardo" sehr ähnlich war.*

3.) "S.M.S. Colomba" was a sister ship of both "S.M.S. Azzardo" and "S.M.S. Cacciatrice," and had an identical history of service and dates.

*Die Segelgaleotte "S.M.S. Colomba" hatte eine Lebensgeschichte die der ihres Schwesternschiffes "S.M.S. Azzardo" sehr ähnlich war.*

4.) "S.M.S. Dalmatina" was yet another member of the "S.M.S. Azzardo" class of Austrian wooden sailing galiots. Her history and dates of service were the same as those of her 3 earlier sister ships.

*Die Segelgaleotte "S.M.S. Dalmatina" hatte eine Lebensgeschichte die der ihres Schwesternschiffes "S.M.S. Azzardo" sehr ähnlich war.*

5.) "S.M.S. Pirogue" was also a member of the "S.M.S. Azzardo" class of Austrian wooden sailing galiots. Her history and dates of service were identical to those of her 4 earlier sister ships.

*Die Segelgaleotte "S.M.S. Pirogue" hatte eine Lebensgeschichte die der ihres Schwesternschiffes "S.M.S. Azzardo" sehr ähnlich war.*

6.) "S.M.S. Valerosa Risoluzione" was another member of the "S.M.S. Azzardo" class of Imperial and Royal Austrian wooden sailing galiots. Her history and dates of service were the same as those of her 5 earlier sisters ships.

*Die Segelgaleotte "S.M.S. Valerosa Risoluzione" hatte eine Lebensgeschichte die der ihres Schwesternschiffes "S.M.S. Azzardo" sehr ähnlich war.*

7.) "S.M.S. Speranza" was the 7th named member of the "S.M.S. Azzardo" class of Imperial and Royal Austrian wooden sailing galiots. Her history and dates of service were identical to those of her 6 earlier sister ships.

*Die Segelgaleotte "S.M.S. Speranza" hatte eine Lebensgeschichte die der ihres Schwesternschiffes "S.M.S. Azzardo" sehr ähnlich war.*

8.) "S.M.S. Stella" was the 8th named member of the "S.M.S. Azzardo" class of Imperial and Royal Austro-Venetian wooden sailing galiots. Her history and dates of service were the same as those of her 7 earlier sister ships.

*Die Segelgaleotte "S.M.S. Stella" hatte eine Lebensgeschichte die der ihres Schwesternschiffes "S.M.S. Azzardo" sehr ähnlich war.*

9.) "S.M.S. Buon Destino" was the 9th member of the "S.M.S. Azzardo" class of Imperial and Royal Austro-Venetian wooden sailing galiots. She was launched in Venice in May 1796, and also served to protect commercial shipping traffic in the Northern Adriatic Sea after July 1797. On January 19, 1806 she was turned over to France's Italian allies, who had temporarily defeated German and Austrian forces in the Napoleonic Wars.

*Die Segelgaleotte "S.M.S. Buon Destino" war das neunte Mitglied der "S.M.S. Azzardo" Klaße. Sie lief im Mai 1796 in Venedig vom Stapel, und diente auch als Geleitschiff in der nördlichen Adria. Am 19. Januar 1806 wurde sie von den italienischen Waffenverbündeten Frankreichs beschlagnahmt.*

10.) "S.M.S. Diana" was the 10th member of the "S.M.S. Azzardo" class of Imperial and Royal Austro-Venetian wooden sailing galiots. She was launched in Venice in May 1796, and was surrendered to the French Navy from May 17 until December 30, 1797. The Austrians recaptured her in damaged condition on January 18, 1798. They repaired and relaunched her that same year, and used her to block the harbor entrance into Venice until 1805. She was again surrendered on January 19, 1806 – this time to France's Italian allies in the Napoleonic Wars.

*Die Segelgaleotte "S.M.S. Diana" war das zehnte Mitgleid der "S.M.S. Azzardo" Klaße. Sie lief im Mai 1796 in Venedig vom Stapel. Zwischen den 17. Mai und den 30. Dezember 1797 wurde sie von den Franzosen beschlagnahmt, und am 18. Januar 1798 wurde sie wieder österreichisch. Sie wurde von der Kaiserlichen und Königlichen Kriegsmarine repariert, und diente bis 1805 in Venedig als Hafenverteidiger. Am 19. Januar 1806 wurde sie von den italienischen Waffenverbündeten beschlagnahmt.*

11.) "S.M.S. Isabella" was the 11th member of the "S.M.S. Azzardo" class of Imperial and Royal Austro-Venetian wooden sailing galiots. She was armed with 6 cannon, and was a former merchant vessel. In July 1799, she was converted into a "corsair," which is an armed vessel intended to raid commercial shipping. She was sold back to civilian owners in November 1799.

*Die Segelgaleotte "S.M.S. Isabella" war das elfte Mitglied der "S.M.S. Azzardo" Klaße. Sie war mit sechs Kanonen bewaffnet, und war ein ehemaliges Handelsschiff. Im Juli 1799 wurde sie als Korsar umgebaut, um am Handelskrieg teilzunehmen. Im November 1799 wurde sie wieder als Handelsschiff verkauft.*

12.) "S.M.S. Klenau" was the 12th member of the "S.M.S. Azzardo" class of Imperial and Royal Austrian wooden sailing galiots, and the sole member of this class to be given a German name. Her history and specifications were identical to those of her sister ship "S.M.S. Isabella," with the exception that she was armed with just 2 cannon as opposed to 6.

*Die Segelgaleotte "S.M.S. Klenau" hatte eine Lebensgeschichte die der ihres Schwesternschiffes "S.M.S. Isabella" sehr ähnlich war, aber sie war mit nur zwei Kanonen bewaffnet. Johann von Klenau (1758-1819) war österreichischer General. Er trat 1775 als Leutnant in ein Infanterieregiment ein. Er wurde 1778 Rittmeister bei den "Chevaux-legers" (leichte Reiter), 1788 Major, 1795 wegen seiner Tapferkeit im französischen Krieg (namentlich am 27. Juli 1794 vor Lüttich und am 24. September 1795 bei Handschuhsheim bei Heidelberg) Oberst und 1797 Generalmajor. Nachdem er sich besonders 1799 in Italien durch sein Feldherrntalent hervorgetan hat, wurde er bald im Jahre 1800 zum Feldmarschall-Leutnant befördert. Während der Napoleonischen Kriege schlug er Pierre Francois Charles Augereau bei Lauf und wurde 1805 in Ulm gefangen genommen. 1809 führte er in der Schlacht bei Aspern die Vorhut der 4. und 5. Kolonne und in der Schlacht bei Wagram an Stelle Hillers das 6. Armeekorps mit Auszeichnung. Danach kämpfte er in der Völkerschlacht bei Leipzig, wo er den Kolmberg bei Wachau am 16. Oktober 1813 erfolgreich verteidigte. Er nahm am 11. November 1813 die Stadt Dresden durch Kapitulation und ging dann mit seinem Korps nach Italien. Im Jahre 1815 wurde er kommandierender Feldmarschall-Leutnant in Brünn in Mähren.*

13.) "S.M.S. Principe Carlo" was the 13th named member of the "S.M.S. Azzardo" class of Imperial and Royal Austrian wooden sailing galiots. Her history and specifications were identical to those of her two sister ships "S.M.S. Isabella" and "S.M.S. Klenau," with the exception that she was armed with 4 cannon.

*Die Segelgaleotte "S.M.S. Principe Carlo" war das dreizehnte Mitglied der "S.M.S. Azzardo" Klaße. Sie hatte eine Lebensgeschichte die der ihres Schwesternschiffes "S.M.S. Isabella" ähnlich war, aber sie war mit vier Kanonen bewaffnet.*

14.) "S.M.S. Intrapresa" was the 14th and final named member of the "S.M.S. Azzardo" class of Imperial and Royal Austrian wooden sailing galiots. Her keel was laid down in Venice in 1804, and she was launched on May 21, 1805. She was assigned to escort (protect) Austrian commercial vessels for 4 years. During the Austrian retreat from the port of Triest on May 15, 1809, she was damaged and became unseaworthy.  The French occupation forces repaired her by 1810, and recommissioned her as "L'Enterprise."  During the Allied campaign to liberate the Illyrian Peninsula from French rule, she was burned and gutted by her French crew to prevent her from falling into the hands of the British Royal Navy.

*Die Segelgaleotte "S.M.S. Intrapresa" war das vierzehnte und letzte genannte Mitglied der "S.M.S. Azzardo" Klaße.  Sie wurde im Jahre 1804 in Venedig auf Kiel gelegt, und lief am 21. Mai 1805 vom Stapel.  Sie wurde als Geleitschiff für vier Jahre benutzt, aber bei dem österreichischen Rückzug vor Triest am 15. Mai 1809 wurde sie beschädigt und war nicht mehr seefähig.  Die Franzosen hatten das Schiff beschlagnahmt, und als die "L' Enterprise" umbenannt.  Als die Franzosen am Ende der Napoleonischen Kriege aus Illyrien ("Küstenland" auf deutsch) zurückzogen, wurde das Schiff selbst versenkt, damit es nicht der britischen Kriegsmarine in die Hände fiel.*

15.) "S.M.S. Arciduca Giovanni" (1815) was attached to the "Gardaseeflottille" ("Lake Garda Flottilla" in English) of the Imperial and Royal Austrian Navy, and was sold to civilian owners in 1838.

*Die Segelgaleotte "S.M.S. Arciduca Giovanni" (1815) gehörte zur Gardaseeflottille, und wurde im Jahre 1838 als Handelsschiff verkauft.*

## XIII (22) Austro-Venetian Chebeks (for which exact tonnage is not available) / Österreichische Segelschebeken (ohne technische Daten)

A chebek (called a "Schebek" in German) was a very thin, or narrow, and very fast sailing vessel with 2 or 3 masts.  The Austrian vessels were built out of oak, and were up to 23,7 meters long, with a maximum beam of 6,8 meters and a draught of 2 meters.  They had a maximum crew of 75 commissioned officers and enlisted men.

*Eine Segelschebeke ("Sciabecchino" auf italienisch) ist ein leichtes, flottes Segelfahrzeug – auch bei schwachem Wind.  Es hat zusätzlich Riemenantrieb, und ist gut manövrierfähig.  Es ist auch lang und schmal, ist sehr scharf gebaut, und ist besonders gut zum Kreuzen und zum leichten Kriegsdienst.  Es hat zwei bis drei Masten mit Lateinsegel und Klüver, und Fockmast Fall nach vorne.*

1.) "S.M.S. Colloredo" was armed with 14 cannon, and was built in the German-speaking port city of Zengg in 1788.  She had a busy career of combat service in the Imperial and Royal Austrian Navy, before she was surrendered to France's Italian allies on January 19, 1806.

*Die Segelschebeke "S.M.S. Colloredo" war mit 14 Kanonen bewaffnet, und wurde im Jahre 1788 in Zengg (heute "Senj" in Kroatien) gebaut. Sie war sehr oft im Einsatz, bevor sie am 16. Januar 1806 an den italienischen Waffenverbündeten Frankreichs übergeben wurde.*

2.) "S.M.S. Henricy" was the 2nd member of the "S.M.S. Colloredo" class of Imperial and Royal Austrian chebeks. Her history in the service of the Austrian navy was identical to that of her sister ship, she also being surrendered to France's Italian allies on the same day. On July 5, 1806 one Russian frigate and two Russian brigs captured her in a bloodless operation off San Giorgio di Lesina in the Adriatic Sea.

*Die Segelschebeke "S.M.S. Henricy" war das zweite Mitglied der "S.M.S. Colloredo" Klaße. Sie hatte eine Lebensgeschichte die der ihres Schwesternfahrzeuges "S.M.S. Colloredo" sehr ähnlich war, aber am 5. Juli 1806 wurde sie von einer russischen Segelfregatte und zwei Segelbriggs an der Küste von San Giorgio di Lesina erobert.*

3.) "S.M.S. Agamemnone" was the 3rd member of the "S.M.S. Colloredo" class of Imperial and Royal Austrian wooden sailing chebeks. She was armed with 12 cannon, and was built in Venice in 1797. On November 18, 1800 she was stranded and lost off Cervia in the Adriatic Sea.

*Die Segelschebeke "S.M.S. Agamemnone" war das dritte Mitglied der "S.M.S. Colloredo" Klaße. Sie war mit 12 Kanonen bewaffnet, und wurde im Jahre 1797 in Venedig gebaut. Am 18. November 1800 strandete sie an der Küste von Cervia an der westlichen Adria, und wurde deswegen versenkt.*

4.) "S.M.S. Ardito il Grande" was the 4th member of the "S.M.S. Colloredo" class of Imperial and Royal Austrian wooden sailing chebeks. She was armed with 16 cannon, and was built in Venice in 1794. She was surrendered to Napoleonic France's Italian allies on January 19, 1806.

*Die Segelschebeke "S.M.S. Ardito il Grande" war das vierte Mitglied der "S.M.S. Colloredo" Klaße. Sie war mit 16 Kanonen bewaffnet, und wurde im Jahre 1794 in Venedig gebaut. Am 19. Januar 1806 wurde sie von den italienischen Waffenverbündeten Frankreichs beschlagnahmt.*

5.) "S.M.S. Ardito il Piccolo" was the 5th member of the "S.M.S. Colloredo" class of Imperial and Royal Austrian wooden sailing chebeks. She was armed with 8 cannon, and was built in Venice in 1791. She was surrendered to Napoleonic France's Italian allies on January 19, 1806.

*Die Segelschebeke "S.M.S. Ardito il Piccolo" war das fünfte Mitglied der "S.M.S. Colloredo" Klaße. Sie war mit acht Kanonen bewaffnet, und wurde im Jahre 1791 in Venedig gebaut. Am 19. Januar 1806 wurde sie von den italienischen Waffenverbündeten Frankreichs beschlagnahmt.*

6.) "S.M.S. Corriere" was the 6th member of the "S.M.S. Colloredo" class of Imperial and Royal Austrian wooden sailing chebeks. She was armed with 8 cannon, and was built in Venice in 1794. She was surrendered to Napoleonic France's Italian allies on January 19, 1806.

*Die Segelschebeke "S.M.S. Corriere" war das sechste Mitglied der "S.M.S. Colloredo" Klaße. Sie war mit acht Kanonen bewaffnet, und wurde im Jahre 1794 in Venedig gebaut. Am 19. Januar 1806 wurde sie von den italienischen Waffenverbündeten Frankreichs beschlagnahmt.*

7.) "S.M.S. Diocleziano" was the 7th member of the "S.M.S. Colloredo" class of Imperial and Royal Austrian wooden sailing chebeks. She was built in Venice in 1771, and had very active service until she was converted into a prison hulk in 1801. She was scrapped in 1803.

*Die Segelschebeke "S.M.S. Diocleziano" war das siebte Mitglied der "S.M.S. Colloredo" Klaße. Sie wurde im Jahre 1771 in Venedig gebaut, und war sehr oft im Einsatz bis sie im Jahre 1801 als Gefängnishulk umgebaut wurde. Sie wurde im Jahre 1803 verschrottet, nach einer Dienstzeit von 32 Jahren.*

8.) "S.M.S. Emilio" was the 8th member of the "S.M.S. Colloredo" class of Imperial and Royal Austrian wooden sailing chebeks. She was built in Venice in 1793, and had very active service until being converted into a hulk in 1803. She was used to help block the harbor entrance into Venice in 1805, and was surrendered to Napoleonic France's Italian allies on January 19, 1806.

*Die Segelschebeke "S.M.S. Emilio" war das achte Mitglied der "S.M.S. Colloredo" Klaße. Sie wurde im Jahre 1793 in Venedig gebaut, und war sehr oft im Einsatz bis sie im Jahre 1803 als Gefängnishulk umgebaut wurde. Im Jahre 1805 nahm sie an Venedigs Hafenverteidigung teil, aber am 19. Januar 1806 wurde sie von den italienischen Waffenverbündeten Frankreichs beschlagnahmt.*

9.) "S.M.S. Enea" was the 9th member of the "S.M.S. Colloredo" class of Imperial and Royal Austrian wooden sailing chebeks. She was built in Venice in 1795, and had very active service until being converted into a hulk in 1803. She was surrendered to Napoleonic France's Italian allies on January 19, 1806.

*Die Segelschebeke "S.M.S. Enea" war das neunte Mitglied der "S.M.S. Colloredo" Klaße. Sie wurde im Jahre 1795 in Venedig gebaut, und war sehr oft im Einsatz bis sie im Jahre 1803 als Hulk umgebaut wurde. Am 19. Januar 1806 wurde sie von den italienischen Waffenverbündeten Frankreichs beschlagnahmt.*

10.) "S.M.S. Intrepido" was the 10th member of the "S.M.S. Colloredo" class of Imperial and Royal Austrian wooden sailing chebeks. She was armed with 18 cannon, and was built in Venice in 1794. She was surrendered to Napoleonic France's Italian allies on January 19, 1806.

*Die Segelschebeke "S.M.S. Intrepido" war das zehnte Mitglied der "S.M.S. Colloredo" Klaße. Sie war mit 18 Kanonen bewaffnet, und wurde im Jahre 1794 in Venedig gebaut. Am 19. Januar 1806 wurde sie von den italienischen Waffenverbündeten Frankreichs beschlagnahmt.*

11.) "S.M.S. Lampo" was the 11th member of the "S.M.S. Colloredo" class of Imperial and Royal Austrian wooden sailing chebeks. She was armed with 12 cannon, and was built in Venice in 1795. She was surrendered to Napoleonic France's Italian allies on January 19, 1806.

*Die Segelschebeke "S.M.S. Lampo" war das elfte Mitglied der "S.M.S. Colloredo" Klaße, wurde in Venedig gebaut und war mit 12 Kanonen bewaffnet. Am 19. Januar 1806 wurde sie von den italienischen Waffenverbündeten Frankreichs beschlagnahmt.*

12.) "S.M.S. Nord" was the 12th member of the "S.M.S. Colloredo" class of Imperial and Royal Austrian wooden sailing chebeks, and the first member of this class to have a German name. "Nord" is the German word for "North." She was built in Venice in 1794, and had active service until being scrapped in 1803.

*Die Segelschebeke "S.M.S. Nord" war das zwölfte Mitglied der "S.M.S. Colloredo" Klaße. Sie wurde in Venedig im Jahre 1794 gebaut, und wurde im Jahre 1803 verschrottet.*

13.) "S.M.S. Prudente" was the 13th member of the "S.M.S. Colloredo" class of Imperial and Royal Austrian wooden sailing chebeks. She was built in Venice in

1793, was armed with 8 cannon, and was used to help block the harbor entrance into Venice in 1805. She was surrendered to Napoleonic France's Italian allies on January 19, 1806.

*Die Segelschebeke "S.M.S. Prudente" war das dreizehnte Mitglied der "S.M.S. Colloredo" Klaße. Sie wurde im Jahre 1793 in Venedig gebaut, war mit acht Kanonen bewaffnet, und verteidigte im Jahre 1805 den Hafen von Venedig. Am 19. Januar 1806 wurde sie von den italienischen Waffenverbündeten Frankreichs beschlagnahmt.*

14.) "S.M.S. Re Pirro" was the 14th member of the "S.M.S. Colloredo" class of Imperial and Royal Austrian wooden sailing chebeks, and was also armed with 14 cannon. She was built in Venice in 1789, and had a very active naval career filled with convoy, courier and transport duties. She was surrendered to Napoleonic France's Italian allies on January 19, 1806. In 1849, she was still active – albeit as a civilian commerce vessel (an impressive 60 years after her launching).

*Die Segelschebeke "S.M.S. Re Pirro" war das vierzehnte Mitglied der "S.M.S. Colloredo" Klaße. Sie war mit 14 Kanonen bewaffnet, wurde im Jahre 1789 in Venedig gebaut, und war als Geleitfahrzeug sowie als Transportfahrzeug sehr aktiv. Am 19. Januar 1806 wurde sie von den italienischen Waffenverbündeten Frankreichs beschlagnahmt. Im Jahre 1849 war sie immer noch als Handelsfahrzeug unterwegs – 60 Jahre nach dem Stapellauf.*

15.) "S.M.S. Staffeta" was the 15th member of the "S.M.S. Colloredo" class of Imperial and Royal Austrian wooden sailing chebeks, and was armed with 8 cannon. In 1805, she was used to help block the harbor entrance into Venice. She was surrendered to Napoleonic France's Italian allies on January 19, 1806.

*Die Segelschebeke "S.M.S. Staffeta" war das fünfzehnte Mitglied der "S.M.S. Colloredo" Klaße. Sie war mit acht Kanonen bewaffnet, und im Jahre 1805 verteidigte sie den Hafen von Venedig. Am 19. Januar 1806 wurde sie von den italienischen Waffenverbündeten Frankreichs beschlagnahmt.*

16.) "S.M.S. Tigre" was the 16th member of the "S.M.S. Colloredo" class of Imperial and Royal Austrian wooden sailing chebeks, and was commissioned into the Austrian navy in July 1797. She was built in Venice, and entered active duty service off the coast of Dalmatia. "Tigre" is the Italian word for "tiger."

*Die Segelschebeke "S.M.S. Tigre" war das sechszehnte Mitglied der "S.M.S. Colloredo" Klaße, und wurde im Juli 1797 getauft. Sie wurde in Venedig gebaut, und diente an der Küste von Dalmatien in Kroatien.*

17.) "S.M.S. Tritone" was the 17th member of the "S.M.S. Colloredo" class of Imperial and Royal Austrian wooden sailing chebeks, and was armed with 18 cannon. She was built in Venice, and was commissioned into the Austrian navy in July 1797. She served off the coast of Dalmatia, and was used to blockade the harbor entrance into Venice in 1805. She was surrendered to Napoleonic France's Italian allies on January 19, 1806.

*Die Segelschebeke "S.M.S. Tritone" war das siebzehnte Mitglied der "S.M.S. Colloredo" Klaße. Sie war mit 18 Kanonen bewaffnet, wurde in Venedig gebaut, und wurde im Juli 1797 getauft. Sie diente hauptsächlich an der Küste von Dalmatien in Kroatien, verteidigte aber im Jahre 1805 den Hafen von Venedig. Am 19. Januar 1806 wurde sie von den italienischen Waffenverbündeten Frankreichs beschlagnahmt.*

18.) "S.M.S. Trionfante" was the 18th member of the "S.M.S. Colloredo" class of Imperial and Royal Austrian wooden sailing chebeks, and was armed with 3 cannon. She was built in Venice, and was commissioned into the Austrian navy in July 1797. She served off the coast of Dalmatia, and was scrapped by 1803.

*Die Segelschebeke "S.M.S. Trionfante" war das achtzehnte Mitglied der "S.M.S. Colloredo" Klaße. Sie war mit drei Kanonen bewaffnet, wurde in Venedig gebaut, und wurde im Juli 1797 getauft. Sie diente an der Küste von Dalmatien in Kroatien, und wurde im Jahre 1803 verschrottet.*

19.) "S.M.S. Arzilio" was the 19th named member of the "S.M.S. Colloredo" class of Imperial and Royal Austrian wooden sailing chebeks, and was built in Venice in 1797. She was scrapped by 1803.

*Die Segelschebeke "S.M.S. Arzilio" war das neunzehnte genannte Mitglied der "S.M.S. Colloredo" Klaße. Sie wurde im Jahre 1797 in Venedig gebaut, und wurde im Jahre 1803 verschrottet.*

20.) "S.M.S. Proserpina" was the 20th named member of the "S.M.S. Colloredo" class of Imperial and Royal Austrian wooden sailing chebeks, and was armed with 3 cannon. She was commissioned into the Austrian navy in July 1797, and initially served off the coast of Dalmatia. She was confiscated almost immediately by the French Navy, and was held by them until December 30, 1797

– when she was recaptured by the Austrians. She was sold to civilian owners in 1803, then came into the Italian Navy allied to Napoleonic France, and was once again returned to Austria on April 25, 1814.

*Die Segelschebeke "S.M.S. Proserpina" war das zwanzigste genannte Mitglied der "S.M.S. Colloredo" Klaße, und war mit drei Kanonen bewaffnet. Sie wurde im Juli 1797 getauft, und wurde bis zum 30. Dezember 1797 von den Franzosen unter Beschlagnahme gehalten, als sie dann von der Kaiserlichen und Königlichen Kriegsmarine befreit wurde. Im Jahre 1803 wurde sie als Handelsfahrzeug verkauft, wurde aber kurz danach von den italienischen Waffenverbündeten Frankreichs beschlagnahmt. Am 25. April 1814 wurde sie endlich wieder österreichisch.*

21.) "S.M.S. Chasteler" was the 21st named member of the "S.M.S. Colloredo" class of Imperial and Royal Austrian wooden sailing chebeks, and was armed with 16 cannon. She was a former merchant vessel, taken into the Austrian navy and armed as a "corsair" to attack enemy merchant shipping. She served in this capacity from July until November of 1799, after which she was sold back to her civilian owners.

*Die Segelschebeke "S.M.S. Chasteler" war das einundzwanzigste genannte Mitglied der "S.M.S. Colloredo" Klaße, und war mit 16 Kanonen bewaffnet. Sie war ein ehemaliges Handelsfahrzeug, und diente zwischen Juli und November 1799 als Korsar bei der Kaiserlichen und Königlichen Kriegsmarine. Danach wurde sie wieder als Handelsfahrzeug verkauft.*

22.) "S.M.S. D'Aspre" was the 22nd named member of the "S.M.S. Colloredo" class of Imperial and Royal Austrian wooden sailing chebeks, and was armed with 6 cannon. She was a former merchantman, purchased by the Austrian navy for use as a "corsair," to raid enemy merchant shipping. She served in this capacity for the brief period from July until November of 1799, after which she was sold back to her civilian owners.

*Die Segelschebeke "S.M.S. D'Aspre" war das zweiundzwanzigste genannte Mitglied der "S.M.S. Colloredo" Klaße, und war mit sechs Kanonen bewaffnet. Sie hatte eine Lebensgeschichte die der ihres Schwesternfahrzeuges "S.M.S. Chasteler" sehr ähnlich war.*

23.) "S.M.S. Melas" was the 23rd named member of the "S.M.S. Colloredo" class of Imperial and Royal Austrian wooden sailing chebeks, and was armed with 3 cannon. She was a former merchantman, purchased by the Austrian navy for use as a "corsair," to raid enemy merchant shipping. She served in this capacity for the brief period from July until November of 1799. On December 25, 1799, she became part of the Imperial and Royal Austrian "Flottilla of the Riviera," with coastal patrol and convoy duties in the Ligurian Sea. The Italian Riviera is East of the French Riviera, and North of the Island of Corsica.

*Die Segelschebeke "S.M.S. Melas" war das dreiundzwanzigste genannte Mitglied der "S.M.S. Colloredo" Klaße, und war mit drei Kanonen bewaffnet. Sie hatte eine Lebensgeschichte die der ihres Schwesternfahrzeuges "S.M.S. Chasteler" sehr ähnlich war, aber ab den 25. Dezember 1799 gehörte sie zur ligurischen "Rivierenflottille" der Kaiserlichen und Königlichen Kriegsmarine.*

24.) "S.M.S. Suwaroff" was the 24th named member of the "S.M.S. Colloredo" class of Imperial and Royal Austrian wooden sailing chebeks, and was armed with 3 cannon. She was a former merchantman, purchased by the Austrian navy for use as a "corsair," to raid enemy merchant shipping. She served in this capacity for the brief period from July until November of 1799, after which she was sold back to her civilian owners. She was also stationed in Livorno on the Ligurian Sea, in the Grand Duchy of Tuscany. The Grand Duchy of Tuscany was initially ruled by the Medici family (related to the Borromeo family of Milan, Italy and to the Vitaliani family of Padua, Italy) from 1569 until 1737. It then passed to the Habsburg-Lothringen Dynasty, where it remained until 1860. The Grand Duchy of Tuscany is still rightfully claimed by the House of Habsburg-Lothringen.

*Die Segelschebeke "S.M.S. Suwaroff" war das vierundzwanzigste genannte Mitglied der "S.M.S. Colloredo" Klaße, und war mit drei Kanonen bewaffnet. Sie hatte eine Lebensgeschichte die der ihres Schwesternfahrzeuges "S.M.S. Melas" sehr ähnlich war. Die "Rivierenflottille" der Kaiserlichen und Königlichen Kriegsmarine war in Livorno stationiert. Livorno und Ligurien gehörte zum Großherzogtum Toskana. Von 1569 bis 1737 beherrschte die Familie Medici das Großherzogtum Toskana. Ab 1737 gehörte Toskana zum Adelshaus Habsburg-Lothringen.*

25.) "S.M.S. Monnier" was the 25th named member of the "S.M.S. Colloredo" class of Imperial and Royal Austrian wooden sailing chebeks, and was armed with 4 cannon. She was initially a Neapolitan merchantman (the Kingdom of Naples endured from 1285 until 1816), until the French Navy converted her into a "corsair" in 1799. She was captured by the Austrian navy on November 14, 1799.

*Die Segelschebeke "S.M.S. Monnier" war das fünfundzwanzigste genannte Mitglied der "S.M.S. Colloredo" Klaße, und war mit vier Kanonen bewaffnet. Ursprünglich war sie ein Handelsfahrzeug aus Neapel. Im Jahre 1799 wurde sie als Korsar von den Franzosen beschlagnahmt, aber am 14. November 1799 wurde sie von der Kaiserlichen und Königlichen Kriegsmarine beschlagnahmt.*

26.) "S.M.S. Eugenio" was the 26th and final named member of the "S.M.S. Colloredo" class of Imperial and Royal Austrian wooden sailing chebeks, and was armed with 5 cannon. Initially, she belonged to the Italian allies of Napoleonic France. The Austrian navy captured her on April 25, 1814 and then sold to civilian owners in August 1814.

*Die Segelschebeke "S.M.S. Eugenio" war das sechsundzwanzigste und letzte genannte Mitglied der "S.M.S. Colloredo" Klaße, und war mit fünf Kanonen bewaffnet. Ursprünglich gehörte sie zu den italienischen Waffenverbündeten Frankreichs. Am 25. April 1814 wurde sie von der Kaiserlichen und Königlichen Kriegsmarine beschlagnahmt, und im August 1814 als Handelsfahrzeug verkauft.*

### XIII (23) Austro-Venetian Marteganes (for which exact tonnage is not available) / Österreichische Segelmarteganen (ohne technische Daten)

A "martegane" (same name in German, but capitalized like all German nouns) was a sharply built wooden sailing vessel of about 110 tons displacement, and with 2 to 3 masts. Marteganes were similar to chebeks, but with fuller forms. They were armed with anywhere from 4 to 14 light cannon, and had a crew of 27 to 70 commissioned officers and enlisted men.

*Eine Segelmartegane ("Martegana" auf italienisch) ist ein scharf gebauter Segler von etwa 110 Tonnen Einsatzverdrängung, mit zwei bis drei Masten und Lateinsegeln, manchmal auch mit Klüver. Eine Segelmartegane ist einer Segelschebeke sehr ähnlich, mit 12 bis 14 Kanonen bewaffnet und mit einer Besatzung von 40 bis 70 Offiziere und Matrosen.*

1.) "S.M.S. Julie" was was armed with 4 cannon, and was formerly a French vessel. The Imperial and Royal Austrian Navy captured her from the Napoleonic French Navy on November 14, 1799. She was lost in a storm off the coast of Ancona on August 8, 1800.

*Die Segelmartegane "S.M.S. Julie" war mit vier Kanonen bewaffnet, und wurde am 14. November 1799 von den Franzosen beschlagnahmt. Am 8. August 1800 wurde sie in einem Sturm vor Ancona versenkt.*

2.) "S.M.S. Nereide" was armed with 14 cannon, and was also captured from the Napoleonic French Navy on November 14, 1799.  She had been launched by the French in the port of Marseilles in 1787.  The Imperial and Royal Austrian Navy renamed her "S.M.S. Teti" on February 13, 1802, and assigned her to convoy duties.  She was surrendered to Napoleonic France's Italian allies on January 19, 1806.

*Die Segelmartegane "S.M.S. Nereide" war mit 14 Kanonen bewaffnet, und wurde auch am 14. November 1799 von den Franzosen beschlagnahmt.  Sie lief im Jahre 1787 in Marseilles vom Stapel, und wurde am 13. Februar 1802 als die "S.M.S. Teti" umbenannt.  Danach diente sie als Geleitfahrzeug, bis sie am 19. Januar 1806 von den italienischen Waffenverbündeten Frankreichs beschlagnahmt wurde.*

3.) "S.M.S. Teti" was armed with 14 cannon, and was also originally part of the French Navy.  She had been launched in Marseilles in 1792, and was taken over by the Imperial and Royal Austrian Navy on November 14, 1799.  She was initially assigned to port defense and convoy duties.  She was renamed "S.M.S. Nereide" on February 13, 1802 (thus exchanging names with martegane number 2 on my list).  She was used as a transport vessel until she was surrendered to Napoleonic France's Italian allies on January 19, 1806.

*Die Segelmartegane "S.M.S. Teti" war mit 14 Kanonen bewaffnet, und lief im Jahre 1792 in Marseilles vom Stapel.  Am 14. November 1799 wurde sie von der Kaiserlichen und Königlichen Kriegsmarine beschlagnahmt, und diente danach als Hafenverteidiger sowie als Geleitfahrzeug.  Am 13. Februar 1802 wurde sie als die "S.M.S. Nereide" umbenannt, und hatte dadurch ihren Patennamen mit ihrem Schwesterfahrzeug "S.M.S. Teti" gewechselt.  Sie wurde dann als Transportfahrzeug benutzt, bis sie am 19. Januar 1806 von den italienischen Waffenverbündeten Frankreichs beschlagnahmt wurde.*

4.) "S.M.S. Leggera" had a brief life in the Imperial and Royal Austrian Navy.  Initially, she belonged to the Italian allies of Napoleonic France.  The Austrians obtained her on March 25, 1814 and then sold her to new civilian owners in August 1814.

*Die Segelmartegane "S.M.S. Leggera" wurde am 25. März 1814 von den italienischen Waffenverbündeten Frankreichs beschlagnahmt, und wurde im August 1814 von der Kaiserlichen und Königlichen Kriegsmarine Österreichs als Handelsfahrzeug verkauft.*

## XIII (24) Austro-Venetian Feluccas (for which exact tonnage is not available) / Österreichische Segelfeluken (ohne technische Daten)

A "felucca" (called a "Feluke" in German) was similar to a small wooden sailing galley. It was a smaller and flatter vessel, with 2 masts, a rudder and no upper deck. They were used for guarding and defending lagoons and coastal areas.

*Eine Segelfeluke ("Felucca" auf italienisch) ist einer Segelgaleere ähnlich, ist aber kleiner und flachgehender. Sie ist ein zweimastiges Ruderfahrzeug mit lateinischer Hilfsbesegelung aber ohne Oberdeck. Segelfeluken wurden hauptsächlich im Wachdienst und Stationsdienst in Lagunengebieten und in Küstengewässern eingesetzt.*

1.) "S.M.S. Guardiamarina" was armed with 2 cannon, and was commissioned in Triest in 1753. She was part of the Imperial and Royal Austrian Navy until she was sold to civilian owners in 1773.

*Die Segelfeluke "S.M.S. Guardiamarina" war mit zwei Kanonen bewaffnet, und wurde im Jahre 1753 in Triest getauft. Im Jahre 1773 wurde sie als Handelsfahrzeug verkauft.*

2.) "S.M.S. Fenice" was a former merchant vessel, armed with 4 cannon and built in 1793. The Imperial and Royal Austrian Navy did not keep her long, and she was sold back to civilian owners in early 1798.

*Die Segelfeluke "S.M.S. Fenice" war ein ehemaliges Handelsfahrzeug, und war mit vier Kanonen bewaffnet. Sie wurde im Jahre 1793 gebaut, und wurde im Jahre 1798 wieder als Handelsfahrzeug verkauft.*

3.) "S.M.S. Lepre" was an identical sister ship of "S.M.S. Fenice," and had the same historical dates within the Imperial and Royal Austrian Navy.

*Die Segelfeluke "S.M.S. Lepre" hatte eine Lebensgeschichte die der ihres Schwesternfahrzeuges "S.M.S. Fenice" sehr ähnlich war.*

4.) "S.M.S. Angelica" was armed with 2 cannon and was built in Venice in 1797. She served off the coast of Dalmatia, and was surrendered to Napoleonic France's Italian allies on January 19, 1806.

*Die Segelfeluke "S.M.S. Angelica" war mit zwei Kanonen bewaffnet, und wurde im Jahre 1797 in Venedig gebaut. Sie diente an der Küste von Dalmatien in*

*Kroatien, bis sie am 19. Januar 1806 von den italienischen Waffenverbündeten Frankreichs beschlagnahmt wurde.*

5.) "S.M.S. Bissa" was also armed with 2 cannon, and was built in Venice in 1797. She also served off the coast of Dalmatia (Croatia), and was scrapped by 1805.

*Die Segelfeluke "S.M.S. Bissa" war mit zwei Kanonen bewaffnet, und wurde im Jahre 1797 in Venedig gebaut. Sie diente an der Küste von Dalmatien in Kroatien, bis sie im Jahre 1805 verschrottet wurde.*

6.) "S.M.S. Costanza" was armed with 2 cannon, and was built in Venice in 1797. She served off the coast of Dalmatia, Croatia, and in convoy duties as well. She was surrendered to Napoleonic France's Italian allies on January 19, 1806, and was finally returned to Austria on April 25, 1814. She was scrapped in 1816.

*Die Segelfeluke "S.M.S. Costanza" war mit zwei Kanonen bewaffnet, und wurde im Jahre 1797 in Venedig gebaut. Sie diente als Geleitfahrzeug an der Küste von Dalmatien in Kroatien. Am 19. Januar 1806 wurde sie von den italienischen Waffenverbündeten Frankreichs beschlagnahmt, und wurde erst am 25. April 1814 wieder österreichisch. Im Jahre 1816 wurde sie verschrottet.*

7.) "S.M.S. Deifobe" was armed with 2 cannon, and was built in Venice in 1797. She served off the coast of Dalmatia, Croatia and was scrapped in 1805.

*Die Segelfeluke "S.M.S. Deifobe" hatte eine Lebensgeschichte die der ihres Schwesternfahrzeuges "S.M.S. Bissa" sehr ähnlich war.*

8.) "S.M.S. Diana" was armed with 3 cannon, and was built in Venice in 1797. She also served off the Dalmatian coast, and was surrendered to the Italian allies of Napoleonic France on January 19, 1806.

*Die Segelfeluke "S.M.S. Diana" war mit drei Kanonen bewaffnet, und wurde im Jahre 1797 in Venedig gebaut. Am 19. Januar wurde sie von den italienischen Waffenverbündeten Frankreichs beschlagnahmt.*

9.) "S.M.S Espedita" was armed with 2 cannon, and was built in Venice in 1789. She served off the Dalmatian coast of Croatia (part of the Kingdom of Hungary within the old Habsburg Empire), and was scrapped in 1805.

*Die Segelfeluke "S.M.S. Espedita" war mit zwei Kanonen bewaffnet, und wurde im Jahre 1789 in Venedig gebaut. Sie diente an der Küste von Dalmatien in Kroatien bis sie im Jahre 1805 verschrottet wurde.*

10.) "S.M.S. Forte" was armed with 2 cannon, and was built in Venice in 1797. She also served off the Dalmatian coast of Croatia, and was scrapped by 1805.

*Die Segelfeluke "S.M.S. Forte" war mit zwei Kanonen bewaffnet, und wurde im Jahre 1797 in Venedig gebaut. Sie diente an der Küste von Dalmatien in Kroatien, und wurde im Jahre 1805 verschrottet.*

11.) "S.M.S. Iride" was armed with 2 cannon, and was built in Venice in 1797. She served off the Dalmatian coast of Croatia, and was surrendered to the Italian allies of Napoleonic France on January 19, 1806.

*Die Segelfeluke "S.M.S. Iride" war mit zwei Kanonen bewaffnet, und wurde im Jahre 1797 in Venedig gebaut. Sie diente an der Küste von Dalmatien in Kroatien, und wurde am 19. Januar 1806 von den italienischen Waffenverbündeten Frankreichs beschlagnahmt.*

12.) "S.M.S. Mora" was armed with 3 cannon, and was built in Venice in 1797. She also served off the Dalmatian coast of Hungary, as a station ship and in convoy duties to protect Austrian commercial shipping from enemy attacks. She was sold in 1809.

*Die Segelfeluke "S.M.S. Mora" war mit drei Kanonen bewaffnet, und wurde im Jahre 1797 in Venedig gebaut. Sie diente als Stationsfahrzeug sowie als Geleitfahrzeug an der Küste von Dalmatien in Kroatien, und wurde im Jahre 1809 als Handelsfahrzeug verkauft.*

13.) "S.M.S. Pratica" was armed with 2 cannon, and was built in Venice in 1797. She served off the Dalmatian coast of Croatia, and was surrendered to the Italian allies of Napoleonic France on January 19, 1806. The first so-called "Kingdom of Italy" was merely a puppet state of France, ruled by Napoleon Bonaparte and his relatives.

*Die Segelfeluke "S.M.S. Pratica" war mit zwei Kanonen bewaffnet, und wurde im Jahre 1797 in Venedig gebaut. Sie diente an der Küste von Dalmatien in Kroatien, und wurde am 19. Januar 1806 von den italienischen Waffenverbündeten Frankreichs beschlagnahmt.*

14.). "S.M.S. Prudenza" was armed with 2 cannon, and was built in Venice in 1797. She served off the Dalmatian coast of Croatia, and was surrendered to the Italian allies of Napoleonic France on January 19, 1806.

*Die Segelfeluke "S.M.S. Prudenza" hatte eine Lebensgeschichte die der ihres Schwesternfahrzeuges "S.M.S. Pratica" sehr ähnlich war.*

15.) "S.M.S. Ragno" was armed with 2 cannon, and was built in Venice in 1797. She too served off the Dalmatian coast of Croatia, and was scrapped in 1805.

*Die Segelfeluke "S.M.S. Ragno" war mit zwei Kanonen bewaffnet, und wurde im Jahre 1797 in Venedig gebaut. Sie diente an der Küste von Dalmatien in Kroatien, und wurde im Jahre 1805 verschrottet.*

16.) "S.M.S. Riguardo" was armed with 2 cannon, and was built in Venice in 1797. She served off the Dalmatian coast of Croatia, and was scrapped in 1802.

*Die Segelfeluke "S.M.S. Riguardo" war mit zwei Kanonen bewaffnet, und wurde im Jahre 1797 in Venedig gebaut. Sie diente an der Küste von Dalmatien in Kroatien, und wurde im Jahre 1802 verschrottet.*

17.). "S.M.S. Rondinella" was armed with 2 cannon, and was built in Venice in 1797. She was based in the Dalmatian port of Sebenico (called "Sibenik" in modern Croatia), and was active both as a station ship and in convoy duties to protect Austrian commercial shipping from enemy attacks. She was surrendered to the Italian allies of Napoleonic France on January 19, 1806. The Imperial and Royal Austrian Navy recaptured her on July 21, 1809, and then sold her to France in November 1809. She was lost in a storm off the coast of Fiume ("Sankt Veit am Pflaumb" in German and "Rijeka" in modern Croatia) in 1810.

*Die Segelfeluke "S.M.S. Rondinella" war mit zwei Kanonen bewaffnet, und wurde im Jahre 1797 in Venedig gebaut. Sie war im Hafen von Sibenning ("Sebenico" auf italienisch, und heute "Sibenik" in Kroatien) stationiert, und diente als Stationsfahrzeug sowie als Geleitfahrzeug. Am 19. Januar 1806 wurde sie von den italienischen Waffenverbündeten Frankreichs beschlagnahmt, und wurde am 21. Juli 1809 von der Kaiserlichen und Königlichen Kriegsmarine zurückerobert. Im Jahre 1810 strandete sie in einem Sturm vor Sankt Veit am Pflaumb ("Fiume" auf italienisch und heute "Rijeka" in Kroatien).*

18.) "S.M.S. Tremenda" was armed with 2 cannon, and was built in Venice in 1797. She served off the Dalmatian coast of Croatia, and was scrapped in 1804.

*Die Segelfeluke "S.M.S. Tremenda" war mit zwei Kanonen bewaffnet, und wurde im Jahre 1797 in Venedig gebaut. Sie diente an der Küste von Dalmatien in Kroatien, und wurde im Jahre 1804 verschrottet.*

19.) "S.M.S. Vigilanza" was armed with 2 cannon, and was built in Venice in 1797. She served in convoy and station duties, and was surrendered to the Italian allies of Napoleonic France on January 19, 1806.

*Die Segelfeluke "S.M.S. Vigilanza" war mit zwei Kanonen bewaffnet, und wurde im Jahre 1797 in Venedig gebaut. Sie diente als Geleitfahrzeug sowie als Stationsfahrzeug, und wurde am 19. Januar 1806 von den italienischen Waffenverbündeten Frankreichs beschlagnahmt.*

20.) "S.M.S. Lovis" was armed with 2 cannon, and was a former merchantman. She was armed as a "corsair" in Livorno in July 1799, and partook in a war on commerce in the Ligurian Sea. She was sold back to her civilian owners in November 1799.

*Die Segelfeluke "S.M.S. Lovis" war mit zwei Kanonen bewaffnet, und war ein ehemaliges Handelsfahrzeug. Sie wurde im Juli 1799 in Livorno as Korsar umgebaut, und diente im Handelskrieg im ligurischen Meer bis sie im November 1799 wieder als Handelsfahrzeug verkauft wurde.*

21.) "S.M.S. Langhendone" was armed with 2 cannon, and was also a former merchantman. She was armed as a "corsair" in July 1799, and also partook in a war on commercial shipping in the Ligurian Sea. She was sold back to her civilian owners in November 1799.

*Die Segelfeluke "S.M.S. Langhendone" hatte eine Lebensgeschichte die der ihres Schwesternfahrzeuges "S.M.S. Lovis" sehr ähnlich war.*

22.) "S.M.S. Citta del Gand" was armed with 2 cannon, and was another former merchantman. She was also converted into a "corsair" in July 1799, and partook in the war against commercial shipping in the Ligurian Sea until November 1799 – when she was sold back to her civilian owners. She was named after the city of Ghent in the Flemish Netherlands.

*Die Segelfeluke "S.M.S. Citta del Gand" hatte eine Lebensgeschichte die der ihres Schwesternfahrzeuges "S.M.S. Lovis" sehr ähnlich war.*

23.) "S.M.S. La Peppina" was yet another former merchantman purchased by the Imperial and Royal Austrian Navy. She became part of the Imperial and Royal Flottilla of the (Italian) Riviera on February 3, 1800. She was sold back to her civilian owners in July 1800, after having partook in the war against commercial shipping in the Ligurian Sea.

*Die Segelfeluke "S.M.S. La Peppina" war ein ehemaliges Handelsfahrzeug, das von der Kaiserlichen und Königlichen Kriegsmarine gekauft wurde. Vom 3. Februar 1800 bis Juli 1800 gehörte sie zur Rivierenflottille der K.u.K. Kriegsmarine, wo sie im Handelskrieg im ligurischen Meer teilnahm. Danach wurde sie wieder als Handelsfahrzeug verkauft.*

24.) "S.M.S. Melas" was armed with 6 cannon, and was another former merchantman "purchased" by the Austrian Navy, or better yet, by one of her officers. In April 1800, she was converted into a "corsair" by the Austrian Linienschiffsleutnant Schram (at his own personal expense!). She thus served as the flagship of the "Corsair Flottilla" of the Ligurian Sea. She partook in blockade, convoy and transport duties.

*Die Segelfeluke "S.M.S. Melas" war mit sechs Kanonen bewaffnet, und war auch ein ehemaliges Handelsfahrzeug. Im April 1800 wurde sie von dem Kaiserlichen und Königlichen Linienschiffsleutnant (gleich einem Korvettenkapitän bei der Deutschen Marine) Schram persönlich gekauft, und als Korsar umgebaut. Sie diente als Flaggschiff der K.u.K. Korsarenflottille im ligurischen Meer.*

25.) "S.M.S. Mora" was laid down in Venice in 1811, and launched in 1812. On December 5, 1813 she was captured from the Italian allies of Napoleonic France, and stationed in the Dalmatian port of Zara by the Imperial and Royal Austrian Navy. She was scrapped by 1817.

*Die Segelfeluke "S.M.S. Mora" wurde im Jahre 1811 in Venedig auf Kiel gelegt, und lief im 1812 vom Stapel. Ursprünglich gehörte sie dem italienischen Waffenverbündeten Frankreichs. Am 5. Dezember 1813 wurde sie von der Kaiserlichen und Königlichen Kriegsmarine beschlagnahmt, und wurde im Jahre 1817 verschrottet.*

26.) "S.M.S. Volpe" was armed with 5 cannon, laid down in Venice in 1811 and launched in 1812. On April 25, 1814 the Italian allies of Napoleonic France surrendered her to the Imperial and Royal Austrian Navy. She was scrapped by 1823.

*Die Segelfeluke "S.M.S. Volpe" war mit fünf Kanonen bewaffnet, wurde im Jahre 1811 in Venedig auf Kiel gelegt, und lief im 1812 vom Stapel. Ursprünglich gehörte sie dem italienischen Waffenverbündeten Frankreichs. Am 25. April 1814 wurde sie von der Kaiserlichen und Königlichen Kriegsmarine beschlagnahmt, und wurde im Jahre 1823 verschrottet.*

27.) "S.M.S. Spedita" was a former merchantman, taken as a prize from the Italian allies of Napoleonic France by Austria in 1813. She was stationed on the Dalmatian coast of Croatia.

*Die Segelfeluke "S.M.S. Spedita" war ein ehemaliges Handelsfahrzeug der italienischen Waffenverbündeten Frankreichs, und wurde im Jahre 1813 von der Kaiserlichen und Königlichen Kriegsmarine beschlagnahmt. Danach diente sie an der Küste von Dalmatien in Kroatien.*

28.) "S.M.S. Fortunata" was the final named Imperial and Royal Austrian wooden sailing felucca. She was commissioned at least by 1815 and served until 1841 in the Austrian naval base of Venice (called "Venedig" in German).

*Die "S.M.S. Fortunata" war die letzte genannte Segelfeluke der Kaiserlichen und Königlichen Kriegsmarine. Sie wurde im Jahre 1815 getauft und diente bis 1841 im österreichischen Hafen von Venedig.*

## XIII (25) Austro-Venetian Brazzeras / Österreichische Segelbrazzeren

A "brazzera" (called a "Brazzere" in German) was a small wooden sailing vessel originally intended for use as a fishing boat. They were anywhere from 10 to 100 tons in total displacement, and came from the Island of Brazza (now known by its Croatian name of "Brac" on the Eastern side of the Adriatic Sea). They normally had 2 masts, but those from Istria had just one mast. The Istrian Peninsula is now shared by 3 countries, including Croatia, Slovenia and Italy. In Italy (on the Western side of the Adriatic Sea), they were called "Tartana" vessels. Please see the following section on the "Tartana."

*Eine Segelbrazzere ("Brazzara" auf italienisch) ist ein kleines Segel-Fischerfahrzeug mit einer Einsatzverdrängung zwischen 10 und 100 Tonnen, ein Typ der von der Insel Brazza (in Dalmatien in Kroatien) stammt. Es hat zwei Masten mit Lateinsegeln und Klüver, aber in Istrien ("Küstenland" auf deutsch) hat es nur einen Mast mit Lateinsegel. In Italien wird eine Segelbrazzere eine Segeltartana genannt.*

1.) "S.M.S. Corriere" was a former civilian vessel, purchased by the Imperial and Royal Austrian Navy in Venice in August 1799. She was used for convoy and patrol duties, and was sold back to her civilian owners in 1802. Tonnage unknown.

*Die Segelbrazzere "S.M.S. Corriere" war ein ehemaliges Zivilfischerfahrzeug, das im August 1799 von der Kaiserlichen und Königlichen Kriegsmarine gekauft wurde. Sie wurde als Geleitfahrzeug sowie als Patrouillenfahrzeug benutzt, und sie wurde im Jahre 1802 wieder als Zivilfischerfahrzeug verkauft. Wir wissen leider nicht, wie groß sie war.*

2.) "S.M.S. Lepre" was also a former civilian vessel, purchased by the Imperial and Royal Austrian Navy in January 1800. She was used for convoy duties, until being surrendered to the Italian allies of Napoleonic France on January 19, 1806. She displaced just 15 tons. She was built out of oak, was armed with 2 cannon (both 6-Pounders) and had a crew of just 12 officers and men.

*Die Segelbrazzere "S.M.S. Lepre" war auch ein ehemaliges Zivilfischerfahrzeug, das im Januar 1800 von der Kaiserlichen und Königlichen Kriegsmarine gekauft wurde. Sie wurde als Geleitfahrzeug benutzt, bis sie am 19. Januar 1806 von den italienischen Waffenverbündeten Frankreichs beschlagnahmt wurde. Sie hatte eine Einsatzverdrängung von 15 Tonnen, war aus Eichenholz gebaut, war mit zwei Sechs-Pfunder bewaffnet, und sie hatte eine Besatzung von 12 Offiziere und Matrosen.*

## XIII (26) Austro-Venetian Tartanas (for which exact tonnage is not available) / Österreichische Segeltartanen (ohne technische Daten)

A "tartana" is similar to a "brazzera" fishing boat of the Adriatic Sea. The former was found on the Italian (Western) side, whereas the latter was found on the Dalmatian (Eastern side). Among the Italian boats, the average-sized ones (those from 40 to 70 tons displacement) were called "tartana." The larger ones (those from 70 to 100 tons displacement) were called "tartanone," whereas the smallest ones (those from 10 to 40 tons displacement) were called "tartanella." I am most intrigued by this, because the horse-drawn carts manufactured by my Cebu City, Philippines great-grandfather José Maria Borromeo y Galan (1847-1930) were called "Tartanilla." This is merely the Spanish word for the Italian "Tartanella." The Philippines were of course a Spanish Crown Colony from 1521-1898, after which they were annexed by the United States, which held them from 1898-1946.

**Segeltartana / Sailing Tartana (source: Rallos de Borromeo Family Archives) – mit österreichische Kriegsflagge (shown flying the Austrian Naval ensign)**

*Eine Segeltartana ist einer Segelbrazzere sehr ähnlich. Eine Segeltartana ist eine Segelbrazzere, die aus Italien und Istrien ("Küstenland" auf deutsch) stammt. Sie werden für Fischereizwecken benutzt, zum Segeln und Rudern, und haben eine Einsatzverdrängung von je zwischen 10 und 100 Tonnen. Eine Segeltartana hat einen, zwei oder drei Masten mit Lateinsegel und zwei Klüvern sowie von 16 bis 20 Riemen. Die kleineren Segeltartanen (mit einer Einsatzverdrängung zwischen 10 und 40 Tonnen) werden "Segeltartanellen" genannt, und die größeren Segeltartanen (mit einer Einsatzverdrängung zwischen 70 und 100 Tonnen) werden "Segeltartanonen" genannt. Auf spanisch heißt Segeltartanella "Tartanilla." Die Firma meines Ururgroßvaters aus Cebu City, die Philippinen,*

*José Maria Borromeo y Galan (1847-1930) hat Pferdekarren, die "Tartanillas"
heißen, von 1879 bis 1933 gebaut. Die Philippinen waren zwischen 1521 und
1898 eine Kronkolonie von Spanien, und das Adelhaus Habsburg beherrschte
Spanien bis 1700.*

1.) "S.M.S. Madonna della Grazia" was originally part of the Genoese Navy.
Genoa is a very important seaport on the Ligurian coast. She was purchased by
the Imperial and Royal Austrian Navy in 1719, and partook in the occupation of
Lipari Island, which is just North of Sicily. Her name means "Mother of Grace"
in English.

*Die Segeltartana "S.M.S. Madonna della Grazia" gehörte ursprünglich der
Kriegsmarine von Genua (in Ligurien). Sie wurde im Jahre 1719 von der
Kaiserlichen und Königlichen Kriegsmarine gekauft, und nahm an der Besatzung
von der Insel Lipari (nördlich von Sizilien) teil.*

2.) "S.M.S. Chasteler" was armed with 4 cannon, and was a former civilian
fishing boat. She was purchased by the Imperial and Royal Austrian Navy on
December 25, 1799, and was then fitted out (armed) in the port of La Spezia.
This is yet another important seaport on the Ligurian coast. She became part of
the Austrian "Imperial and Royal Flottilla of the (Italian) Riviera."
Unfortunately, she was sunk by 3 Algerian pirate ships in the Gulf of Taranto on
July 25, 1800. Taranto is another important seaport and naval base located in
extreme Southern Italy. The popular Italian folk melody known as the
"Tarantella" is named for Taranto. It is used throughout the Sicilian and
Neapolitan region.

*Die Segeltartana "S.M.S. Chasteler" war mit vier Kanonen bewaffnet, und war
ein ehemaliges Zivilfischerfahrzeug. Am 25. Dezember 1799 wurde sie von der
Kaiserlichen und Königlichen Kriegsmarine gekauft, und wurde im Hafen von La
Spezia bewaffnet. Sie gehörte zur K.u.K. Rivierenflottille in Ligurien. Am 25. Juli
1800 wurde sie von drei algerischen Piratenschiffe am Golf von Taranto versenkt.*

3.) "S.M.S. Ott" was armed with 6 cannon, and was another former civilian
fishing vessel. She was purchased by the Imperial and Royal Austrian Navy on
December 25, 1799, and was fitted out (armed) in the port of La Spezia on the
Ligurian Sea. She was attached to the "Imperial and Royal Flottilla of the
(Italian) Riviera" after July 1800.

*Die Segeltartana "S.M.S. Ott" war mit sechs Kanonen bewaffnet, und war auch
ein ehemaliges Zivilfischerfahrzeug. Am 25. Dezember 1799 wurde sie von der*

*Kaiserlichen und Königlichen Kriegsmarine gekauft, und wurde im Hafen von La Spezia bewaffnet. Ab Juli 1800 gehörte sie zur K.u.K. Rivierenflottille in Ligurien.*

4.) "S.M.S. Querini" was armed with 6 cannon, and was also a former civilian fishing vessel. She had an identical history to her sister ship "S.M.S. Ott."

*Die Segeltartana "S.M.S. Querini" war mit sechs Kanonen bewaffnet, und hatte eine Lebensgeschichte die der ihres Schwesternfahrzeuges "S.M.S. Ott" sehr ähnlich war.*

5.) "S.M.S. Isabella" was armed with 20 cannon, and was an already armed civilian fishing vessel when she was purchased by the Imperial and Royal Austrian Navy in January 1805. She was fitted out in the Austrian naval base of Triest, and became a convoy lead ship. She was briefly captured as a prize by the enemy from April 13 until April 29, 1809, off the coast of Capodistria (the most important seaport in modern Slovenia, now called "Koper" in Slovene or "Gafers" in German). She was sold back to civilian owners on November 8, 1809.

*Die Segeltartana "S.M.S. Isabella" war ein Zivilfischerfahrzeug mit 20 Kanonen bewaffnet, und wurde im Januar 1805 von der Kaiserlichen und Königlichen Kriegsmarine gekauft. Sie war in Triest stationiert, und diente als Geleitzugflaggschiff. Zwischen den 13. April und den 29. April 1809 wurde sie vor Gafers ("Capodistria" auf italienisch und heute "Koper" in Slowenien) beschlagnahmt. Danach wurde sie von den Österreichern befreit. Am 8. November 1809 wurde sie wieder als Zivilfischerfahrzeug verkauft.*

6.) "S.M.S. Aquila" was armed with 16 cannon, and was yet another already armed civilian fishing vessel. She was purchased by the Imperial and Royal Austrian Navy, and then fitted out in the base of Triest in July 1805. She served as a convoy lead vessel, and was then sold back to civilian owners in February 1806.

*Die Segeltartana "S.M.S. Aquila" war ein Zivilfischerfahrzeug mit 16 Kanonen bewaffnet, und wurde von der Kaiserlichen und Königlichen Kriegsmarine gekauft. Ab Juli 1805 war sie in Triest stationiert, und sie diente auch als Geleitzugflaggschiff. Im Februar 1806 wurde sie wieder als Zivilfischerfahrzeug verkauft.*

7.) "S.M.S. Glorioso" was armed with 10 cannon, and had a very similar history to her sister ship "S.M.S. Aquila."

*Die Segeltartana "S.M.S. Glorioso" war mit zehn Kanonen bewaffnet, und hatte eine Lebensgeschichte die der ihres Schwesternfahrzeuges "S.M.S. Aquila" sehr ähnlich war.*

## XIII (27) Austro-Venetian Paranzas (for which exact tonnage is not available) / Österreichische Segelparanzen (ohne technische Daten)

A "paranza" (called a "Paranze" in German) was a small, flat and sharply designed sailing vessel with one mast and a rudder – usually used as a fishing boat. It also had from 8 to 10 oars and 2 small cannon.

*Eine Segelparanze ("Paranza" auf italienisch) ist ein kleines, flachgehendes, vorn und achtern scharf gebautes Ruder-und Segelfahrzeug für die Fischerei mit einem Mast und einem Lateinsegel an sehr langer Rah und mit acht bis zehn Rudern sowie zwei kleine Geschütze ausgerüstet.*

1.) "S.M.S. Eugene" was armed with 6 cannon, and was a former civilian fishing vessel. She was purchased by the Imperial and Royal Austrian Navy, and armed as a "corsair" to attack enemy merchant shipping in the Ligurian Sea in July 1799. She was sold back to her civilian owners in November 1799.

*Die Segelparanze "S.M.S. Eugene" war mit sechs Kanonen bewaffnet, und war ein ehemaliges Zivilfischerfahrzeug. Zwischen Juli und November 1799 wurde sie von der Kaiserlichen und Königlichen Kriegsmarine als Korsar im Handelskrieg im ligurischen Meer benutzt. Danach wurde sie wieder als Zivilfischerfahrzeug verkauft.*

2.) "S.M.S. Marianna" was armed with 6 cannon, and had an identical history to her sister ship "S.M.S. Eugene."

*Die Segelparanze "S.M.S. Marianna" war mit sechs Kanonen bewaffnet, und hatte eine Lebensgeschichte die der ihres Schwesternfahrzeuges "S.M.S. Eugene" sehr ähnlich war.*

3.) "S.M.S. Klenau" was armed with 3 cannon, and was another former civilian fishing vessel. She was purchased by the Imperial and Royal Austrian Navy on December 25, 1799, and was fitted out in the port of La Spezia. She was attached to the "Imperial and Royal Flottilla of the (Italian) Riviera, and partook in convoy duties after August 1800.

*Die Segelparanze "S.M.S. Klenau" war mit drei Kanonen bewaffnet, und war auch ein ehemaliges Zivilfischerfahrzeug. Am 25. Dezember 1799 wurde sie von der Kaiserlichen und Königlichen Kriegsmarine gekauft, und war im Hafen von La Spezia stationiert. Ab August 1800 gehörte sie zur Rivierenflottille der K.u.K. Kriegsmarine, wo sie als Geleitfahrzeug diente.*

4.) "S.M.S. Vedetta" was captured from the Italian allies of Napoleonic France on October 29, 1813, and was assigned to transport and station duties within the Imperial and Royal Austrian Navy. She was scrapped in 1825.

*Die Segelparanze "S.M.S. Vedetta" gehörte ursprünglich dem italienischen Waffenverbündeten Frankreichs, und wurde am 29. Oktober 1813 von der Kaiserlichen und Königlichen Kriegsmarine beschlagnahmt. Sie wurde als Transportfahrzeug sowie als Stationsfahrzeug benutzt, und wurde im Jahre 1825 verschrottet.*

5.) "S.M.S. Agile" was captured either from the Napoleonic forces of France or Italy in 1814, and was assigned to station duties within the Imperial and Royal Austrian Navy. She was scrapped in 1817.

*Die Segelparanze "S.M.S. Agile" gehörte ursprünglich entweder den Franzosen oder deren italienischen Waffenverbündeten, und wurde im Jahre 1814 von der Kaiserlichen und Königlichen Kriegsmarine beschlagnahmt. Sie wurde im Jahre 1817 verschrottet.*

6.) "S.M.S. Pronta" was captured from the Italian allies of Napoleonic France in 1814, and then briefly assigned to transport duties within the Imperial and Royal Austrian Navy. She was sold to civilian owners in August 1814.

*Die Segelparanze "S.M.S. Pronta" gehörte ursprünglich den italienischen Waffenverbündeten Frankreichs, und wurde im Jahre 1814 beschlagnahmt. Zuerst wurde sie als Transportfahrzeug benutzt, und dann wurde sie im August 1814 als Zivilfischerfahrzeug verkauft.*

7.) "S.M.S. Superiora" was captured from the Italian allies of Napoleonic France in 1809, and then assigned to station duties within the Imperial and Royal Austrian Navy. She was scrapped in 1827.

*Die Segelparanze "S.M.S. Superiora" wurde im Jahre 1809 von den italienischen Waffenverbündeten erobert, und wurde dann als Stationsfahrzeug bei der*

*Kaiserlichen und Königlichen Kriegsmarine benutzt. Sie wurde im Jahre 1827 verschrottet.*

8.) "S.M.S. Teriscore" was captured from the Italian allies of Napoleonic France in 1814, and then assigned to station duties within the Imperial and Royal Austrian Navy. She was scrapped in 1828.

*Die Segelparanze "S.M.S. Teriscore" wurde im Jahre 1814 von den italienischen Waffenverbündeten Frankreichs beschlagnahmt, und wurde dann als Stationsfahrzeug bei der Kaiserlichen und Königlichen Kriegsmarine benutzt. Sie wurde im Jahre 1828 verschrottet.*

9.) "S.M.S. Stella" was captured from the Italian allies of Napoleonic France off the port of Ancona in June 1815, and then assigned to station duties within the Imperial and Royal Austrian Navy. She was scrapped by 1828.

*Die Segelparanze "S.M.S. Stella" wurde im Juni 1815 vor Ancona von den italienischen Waffenverbündeten Frankreichs beschlagnahmt, und wurde dann als Stationsfahrzeug bei der Kaiserlichen und Königlichen Kriegsmarine benutzt. Sie wurde im Jahre 1828 verschrottet.*

## XIII (28) Austro-Venetian Bragozzos (for which exact tonnage is not available) / Österreichische Segelbragozzen (ohne technische Daten)

A "bragozzo" (called a "Bragozze" in German) was a small, flat, sailing vessel intended for use as a fishing boat. They had 2 masts, and came from the region of Chioggia (a coastal suburb of Venice).

*Eine Segelbragozze ("Bragozzo" auf italienisch) ist ein kleines, flachgehendes Segel-Fischerfahrzeug mit zwei Masten, wovon der kürzere Fockmast Fall nach vorn hat, nur als Fischerfahrzeug ohne Klüversegel. Die Segelbragozzen stammen aus Chioggia bei Venedig.*

1.) "S.M.S. Speranza" was a former civilian fishing vessel, captured from the Italian allies of Napoleonic France in November 1805. She was taken into the Imperial and Royal Austrian Navy, armed and then served until being sold to civilian owners in 1809.

*Die Segelbragozze "S.M.S. Speranza" war eine ehemaliges Zivilfischerfahrzeug, das im Jahre 1805 von den italienischen Waffenverbündeten Frankreichs erobert wurde. Sie wurde im Jahre 1809 wieder als Zivilfischerfahrzeug verkauft.*

2.) "S.M.S. Foresto" was a former civilian fishing vessel, purchased from her owners in September 1861. She served very briefly off Miramare Castle in the port of Triest (called "Schloss Miramar" in German), which was owned by the Habsburg Archduke Maximilian. He was a great personal supporter of the Imperial and Austrian Navy, and held the rank of Vice Admiral therein (like a "three star" Admiral in the U.S. Navy). He briefly served as the Emperor of Mexico from 1864-1867 before being murdered by Mexican rebels.

*Die Segelbragozze "S.M.S. Foresto" war ein ehemaliges Zivilfischerfahrzeug, das im September 1861 von der Kaiserlichen und Königlichen Kriegsmarine gekauft wurde. Sie diente vor Schloß Miramar bei Triest. Schloß Miramar ("Castello di Miramare" auf italienisch) liegt auf einer Felsenklippe der Bucht von Grignano an der Adria etwa fünf Kilometer nordwestlich der Hafenstadt Triest. Das Schloß wurde zwischen 1856 und 1860 von Erzherzog Ferdinand Maximilian von Österreich, den jüngeren Bruder Kaiser Franz Josefs I, und seiner Gattin Charlotte von Belgien erbaut. Architekt und Bauleiter war Carl Junker. Das Schloß und seine Inneneinrichtung sowie die umliegende Parkanlage wurden entsprechend den detaillierten Anweisungen und Vorstellungen des Erzherzogs erbaut und spiegeln in vielen Bereichen die große Liebe Maximilians zum Meer wider. Die Innenausstattung wurde erst 1870, nach dem Tod Ferdinand Maximilians, fertig gestellt. Seit 1955 ist das Schloß als Staatliches Museum für Besucher geöffnet.*

## XIII (29) Austro-Venetian Avisos (for which exact tonnage is not available) / Österreichische Segelavisos (ohne technische Daten)

"Aviso" is a Spanish word, meaning "warning." The larger avisos evolved into the future sailing corvettes and small cruisers in use before World War One. The smaller avisos (such as the vessels listed below) evolved into the the future dispatch boats, torpedo ships and torpedo boats in use before the First World War.

*Eine Segelaviso ist ein schnelles, kleines Kriegsschiff für Nachrichtenübermittlung. Neben späteren Depeschenfahrten diente es auch als Vorposten-, Aufklärungs-und Verbindungsboot. Ausserdem fanden Avisos auch als Führungsschiffe und für leichte Kampfaufgaben im späteren Kolonialkrieg Verwendung. Avisos waren normalerweise leicht bewaffnet und ungepanzert.*

1.) "S.M.S. Alessandro" was a former civilian vessel, purchased by the Imperial and Royal Austrian Navy and armed as a "corsair" in July 1799. She briefly partook in a war on enemy commerce in the Ligurian Sea, before being sold back to civilian owners in November 1799.

*Die Segelaviso "S.M.S. Alessandro" war ein ehemaliges Handelsschiff, das im Juli 1799 als bewaffneter Korsar von der Kaiserlichen und Königlichen Kriegsmarine gekauft wurde. Sie nahm am Handelskrieg im ligurischen Meer teil, bevor sie im November 1799 wieder als Handelsschiff verkauft wurde.*

2.) "S.M.S. Principessa di Tourdajo" was armed with 2 cannon, and was another former civilian vessel purchased by the Imperial and Royal Austrian Navy in July 1799. She was fitted out as a "corsair," and then partook in the war on enemy commerce in the Ligurian Sea. She was sold back to civilian owners in November 1799.

*Die Segelaviso "S.M.S. Principessa di Tourdajo" war mit zwei Kanonen bewaffnet, und hatte eine Lebensgeschichte die der ihres Schwesternschiffes "S.M.S. Alessandro" sehr ähnlich war.*

3.) "S.M.S. Costante" was armed with 6 cannon, and was yet another former civilian vessel purchased by the Imperial and Royal Austrian Navy. Her history of service therein was identical to that of "S.M.S. Alessandro" and "S.M.S. Principessa di Tourdajo."

*Die Segelaviso "S.M.S. Costante" war mit sechs Kanonen bewaffnet, und hatte eine Lebensgeschichte die der ihres Schwesternschiffes "S.M.S. Alessandro" sehr ähnlich war.*

4.) "S.M.S. Henriette" was armed with 2 cannon, and was a former civilian vessel purchased by the Imperial and Royal Austrian Navy in July 1799. She was armed as a "corsair" in the port of Livorno and partook in a war on enemy commerce until being sold back to civilian owners in November 1799.

*Die Segelaviso "S.M.S. Henriette" war mit zwei Kanonen bewaffnet, und hatte eine Lebensgeschichte die der ihres Schwesternschiffes "S.M.S. Alessandro" sehr ähnlich war. Sie war im Hafen von Livorno stationiert.*

5.) "S.M.S. Cherteler" was armed with 2 cannon, and had a very similar history to her sister ships listed above. She was also sold back to civilian owners in November 1799, after having partook in the war against enemy shipping in the Ligurian Sea. Her home port while in the Imperial and Austrian Navy was Livorno on the Italian Riviera.

*Die Segelaviso "S.M.S. Cherteler" war mit zwei Kanonen bewaffnet, und hatte eine Lebensgeschichte die der ihres Schwesternschiffes "S.M.S. Alessandro" sehr ähnlich war. Sie war auch im Hafen von Livorno stationiert.*

## XIII (30) Austro-Venetian Piroges (for which exact tonnage is not available) / Österreichische Segelpirogen (ohne technische Daten)

A "piroge" was a light, flat vessel designed for use in lagoons – commonly made out of one log. It was powered by both sails and 8 oars, and had one mast. It was a very common type of small vessel, and was also used on rivers. These boats were usually assigned to station and customs duties within the navy.

*Eine Segelpiroge ist ein leichtes, flaches Lagunenfahrzeug mit Segel-und Riemenantrieb. Es hat einen Mast mit einem Lateinsegel und acht Riemen. Zur Zeit der Kaiserlichen und Königlichen Kriegsmarine Österreichs waren sie sehr zahlreich, und sie wurden immer wieder als Stationsfahrzeuge sowie als Zolldienstfahrzeuge nachgebaut.*

1.) "S.M.S. Bradamante" was laid down in Venice in 1804, launched in 1805 and surrendered to the Italian allies of Napoleonic France on January 19, 1806.

*Die Segelpiroge "S.M.S. Bradamante" wurde im Jahre 1804 in Venedig auf Kiel gelegt, und lief im 1805 vom Stapel. Am 19. Januar 1806 wurde sie von den italienischen Waffenverbündeten Frankreichs beschlagnahmt.*

2.) "S.M.S. Clorinda" was the 2nd member of the "S.M.S. Bradamante" class, with identical historical dates.

*Die Segelpiroge "S.M.S. Clorinda" war das zweite Mitglied der "S.M.S. Bradamante" Klaße, und hatte eine Lebensgeschichte die der ihres Schwesternfahrzeuges sehr ähnlich war.*

3.) "S.M.S. Colomba" was the 3rd member of the "S.M.S. Bradamante" class, with identical historical dates.

*Die Segelpiroge "S.M.S. Colomba" war das dritte Mitglied der "S.M.S. Bradamante" Klaße, und hatte eine Lebensgeschichte die der ihres Schwesternfahrzeuges sehr ähnlich war.*

4.) "S.M.S. Ellena" was the 4th member of the "S.M.S. Bradamante" class, with identical historical dates.

*Die Segelpiroge "S.M.S. Ellena" war das vierte Mitglied der "S.M.S. Bradamante" Klaße, und hatte eine Lebensgeschichte die der ihres Schwesternfahrzeuges sehr ähnlich war.*

5.) "S.M.S. Ellizia" was the 5th member of the "S.M.S. Bradamante" class, with identical historical dates.

*Die Segelpiroge "S.M.S. Ellizia" war das fünfte Mitglied der "S.M.S. Bradamante" Klaße, und hatte eine Lebensgeschichte die der ihres Schwesternfahrzeuges sehr ähnlich war.*

6.) "S.M.S. Felicita" was the 6th member of the "S.M.S. Bradamante" class, with identical historical dates.

*Die Segelpiroge "S.M.S. Felicita" war das sechste Mitglied der "S.M.S. Bradamante" Klaße, und hatte eine Lebensgeschichte die der ihres Schwesternfahrzeuges sehr ähnlich war.*

7.) "S.M.S. Isabella" was the 7th member of the "S.M.S. Bradamante" class, with identical historical dates.

*Die Segelpiroge "S.M.S. Isabella" war das siebte Mitglied der "S.M.S. Bradamante" Klaße, und hatte eine Lebensgeschichte die der ihres Schwesternfahrzeuges sehr ähnlich war.*

8.) "S.M.S. Marfisa" was the 8th member of the "S.M.S. Bradamante" class, with identical historical dates.

*Die Segelpiroge "S.M.S. Marfisa" war das achte Mitglied der "S.M.S. Bradamante" Klaße, und hatte eine Lebensgeschichte die der ihres Schwesternfahrzeuges sehr ähnlich war.*

9.) "S.M.S. Olimpio" was the 9th member of the "S.M.S. Bradamante" class, with indentical historical dates.

*Die Segelpiroge "S.M.S. Olimpio" war das neunte Mitglied der "S.M.S. Bradamante" Klaße, und hatte eine Lebensgeschichte die der ihres Schwesternfahrzeuges sehr ähnlich war.*

10.) "S.M.S. Pronta" was the 10th member of the "S.M.S. Bradamante" class, with identical historical dates.

*Die Segelpiroge "S.M.S. Pronta" war das zehnte Miglied der "S.M.S. Bradamante" Klaße, und hatte eine Lebensgeschichte die der ihres Schwesternfahrzeuges sehr ähnlich war.*

11.) "S.M.S. Psiche" was the 11th member of the "S.M.S. Bradamante" class, with identical historical dates.

*Die Segelpiroge "S.M.S. Psiche" war das elfte und letzte Mitglied der "S.M.S. Bradamante" Klaße, und hatte eine Lebensgeschichte die der ihres Schwesternfahrzeuges sehr ähnlich war.*

## XIII (31) Austro-Venetian Sloops (for which exact tonnage is not available) / Österreichische Segelschaluppen (ohne technische Daten)

A wooden sailing sloop (called a "Schaluppe" in German) was a cannon-armed boat known for its high quality of construction and for its longevity. Sloops were flat and low, and were originally designed by the Spaniards. Sloops had one upper deck, one mast, one fore and one aft rig. The single mast on a sloop was located farther foreward compared to that aboard a cutter.

*Eine Segelschaluppe ist ein kleines, einem Segelkutter ähnelndes Segelboot mit einem Mast und wurde meist als größeres Beiboot verwendet. Der Begriff entstammt aus der französischen Sprache ("Chaloupe" ist eine Bezeichnung für das größte Beiboot eines Schiffes). Früher wurden so die größeren, einfachen Boote der Küstenschiff-Fahrt benannt. Die Bezeichnung stammt höchstwarscheinlich vom flandrischen Ausdruck für ein holländisches Schiff ("Sloep") im Zusammenhang mit "Sluipen," was so viel wie "gleiten," oder auch "schlüpfen," bedeutet.*

1.) "S.M.S. Cisalpine" was armed with one cannon, and was captured from the French Navy. She became part of the Imperial and Royal Austrian Navy in the port of Ancona on November 14, 1799.

*Die Segelschaluppe "S.M.S. Cisalpine" war mit einer Kanone bewaffnet, und wurde von den Franzosen erobert. Ab den 14. November 1799 gehörte sie der Kaiserlichen und Königlichen Kriegsmarine. Sie war im Hafen von Ancona stationiert.*

2.) "S.M.S. Bondi" was captured from the Italian allies of Napoleonic France off the Dalmatian port of Zara on December 5, 1813. She was scrapped in 1817.

*Die Segelschaluppe "S.M.S. Bondi" wurde am 5. Dezember 1813 von den italienischen Waffenverbündeten Frankreichs beschlagnahmt, und im Jahre 1817 verschrottet.*

3.) "S.M.S. Moro" had an identical history to her sister sloop "S.M.S. Bondi."

*Die Segelschaluppe "S.M.S. Moro" hatte eine Lebensgeschichte die der ihres Schwesternbootes "S.M.S. Bondi" sehr ähnlich war.*

4.) "S.M.S. Guardacoste" was commissioned into the Imperial and Royal Austrian Navy in 1813.

*Die Segelschaluppe "S.M.S. Guardacoste" wurde im Jahre 1813 getauft.*

5.) "S.M.S. Vigilante" was laid down in 1813, and commissioned in 1814.

*Die Segelschaluppe "S.M.S. Vigilante" wurde im Jahre 1813 auf Kiel gelegt, und im Jahre 1814 getauft.*

6.) "S.M.S. Aventuriere" was captured from the Italian allies of Napoleonic France in 1814, and had been originally commissioned in 1807. She was scrapped in 1820.

*Die Segelschaluppe "S.M.S. Aventuriere" wurde im Jahre 1807 von den italienischen Waffenverbündeten Frankreichs getauft, und im Jahre 1814 von der Kaiserlichen und Königlichen Kriegsmarine beschlagnahmt. Sie wurde im Jahre 1820 verschrottet.*

7.) "S.M.S. Balena" was commissioned in 1838.

*Die Segelschaluppe "S.M.S. Balena" wurde im Jahre 1838 getauft.*

8.) "S.M.S. Mathilde" was an unarmed former merchantman, purchased by the Imperial and Royal Austrian Navy in 1848.

*Die Segelschaluppe "S.M.S. Mathilde" war ein ehemaliges unbewaffnetes Handelsfahrzeug, das im Jahre 1848 von der Kaiserlichen und Königlichen Kriegsmarine gekauft wurde.*

9.) "S.M.S. Austria" was commissioned at least by 1813, and served in the "Gardaseeflottilla" ("Flottilla of Lake Garda") of the Imperial and Royal Austrian

Navy. Lake Garda is Italy's largest lake, located about halfway between the cities of Venice and Milan in the alpine region of Northern Italy. She was sold to civilian owners in 1838.

*Die Segelschaluppe "S.M.S. Austria" wurde im Jahre 1813 getauft, und diente bei der Gardaseeflottille der Kaiserlichen und Königlichen Kriegsmarine. Der Gardasee (auch "Gartsee" auf deutsch) ist der größte See Italiens. Zwischen den Alpen und der Poebene, etwa 65 Meter über Meereshöhe liegt der Gardasee im Norden der Region Trient-Südtirol, im Westen in der Lombardei, im Osten in Venetien. Die "S.M.S. Austria" wurde im Jahre 1838 als Handelsfahrzeug verkauft.*

10.) "S.M.S. Italia" had the same history of service as did her sister sloop "S.M.S. Austria" on Lake Garda.

*Die Segelschaluppe "S.M.S. Italia" hatte eine Lebensgeschichte die der ihres Schwesternbootes "S.M.S. Austria" sehr ähnlich war.*

11.) "S.M.S. Prepotente" had the same service and historical dates as did her sister sloops "S.M.S. Austria" and "S.M.S. Italia."

*Die Segelschaluppe "S.M.S. Prepotente" hatte eine Lebensgeschichte die der ihres Schwesternbootes "S.M.S. Austria" sehr ähnlich war.*

12.) "S.M.S. La Corriera" was also part of the small "S.M.S. Austria" class of wooden sailing sloops. She was built in Malcesine on Lake Garda, being laid down in 1813 and commissioned in 1814. She was sold to civilian owners in 1838.

*Die Segelschaluppe "S.M.S. La Corriera" hatte eine Lebensgeschichte die der ihres Schwesternbootes "S.M.S. Austria" sehr ähnlich war. Sie wurde im Jahre 1813 im Hafen von Malcesine am Gardasee auf Kiel gelegt, und im Jahre 1814 getauft.*

13.) "S.M.S. Erzherzog Friedrich" was armed with 4 cannon, and was built in Zürich, Switzerland in 1851. She was based in the port of Riva on Lake Garda, and actively served in the Imperial and Royal Austrian Navy at least until 1860.

*Die Segelschaluppe "S.M.S. Erzherzog Friedrich" war mit vier Kanonen bewaffnet, und wurde im Jahre 1851 in Zürich gebaut. Sie war im Hafen von*

*Riva am Gardasee stationiert, und diente mindestens bis 1860 bei der Kaiserlichen und Königlichen Kriegsmarine Österreichs.*

## XIII (32) Austro-Venetian Transport Vessels (for which exact tonnage is not available) / Österreichische Transportfahrzeuge (ohne technische Daten)

One can think of these wooden sailing vessels as a logical continuation of the sloops listed in the section immediately before this.

*Ein Transportsegelschooner ist als Hochsee-Segelbrigg oder Segelbriggschooner getakelt. Sie dienten zur Versorgung der Flottenabteilungen im Ausland, besonders in der Levante, wofür das Segeltrabakel zu klein war. Sie wurden sehr stark und seetüchtig gebaut, und waren deshalb teilweise sehr langlebig. Obwohl sie Transportfahrzeuge waren, wurden sie gegen Piraten immer kriegsmäßig ausgerüstet, mit bis zehn Kanonen. Als "Levante" (italienisch für "Sonnenaufgang," steht allegorisch für den "Osten" und das "Morgenland") bezeichnet man im weiteren Sinne die Länder des östlichen Mittelmeeres, folglich aller Länder, die östlich von Italien liegen, besonders die griechische Halbinsel und die griechischen Inseln, die mediterranen Küstengebiete Kleinasiens, Zypern, den Libanon, Palästina, das historische Syrien und Ägypten.*

1.) "S.M.S. Sankt Anton" was built in Korneuburg (Lower Austria) in 1771, and was in the style of similar ships built on the River Rhine in Western Germany. She served on both the Danube and the Save Rivers. In 1776, she sailed from Laibach (in modern day Slovenia) to Semlin (part of the city of Belgrade).

*Der Transportsegelschooner "S.M.S. Sankt Anton" wurde im Jahre 1771 in Korneuburg in Niederösterreich gebaut, und diente auf der Donau sowie auf der Save (auch "Sawe" oder "Sau" auf deutsch). Im Jahre 1776 reiste sie von Laibach in der Oberkrain bis Semlin in Belgrad (Serbien).*

2.) "S.M.S. Sankt Michael" was built in Karlstadt (now known as "Karlovac" in Croatia) in 1774, and had a history of service just like her sister ship "S.M.S. Sankt Anton."

*Der Transportsegelschooner "S.M.S. Sankt Michael" wurde im Jahre 1774 in Karlstadt (heute "Karlovac" in Kroatien) gebaut, und hatte eine Lebensgeschichte die der ihres Schwesternschiffes "S.M.S. Sankt Anton" sehr ähnlich war.*

3.) "S.M.S. Casale" was built in Zürich, Switzerland in 1849, and was assigned to the port of Riva on Lake Garda in Northern Italy. She was part of the "Gardaseeflottilla" of the Imperial and Royal Austrian Navy at least until 1860.

*Der Transportsegelschooner "S.M.S. Casale" wurde im Jahre 1849 in Zürich gebaut, und war im Hafen von Riva am Gardasee stationiert. Sie gehörte der Gardaseeflottille der Kaiserlichen und Königlichen Kriegsmarine mindestens bis 1860.*

4.) "S.M.S. Novara" was built in Zürich, Switzerland in 1850, and was also part of the "Gardaseeflottilla" in the port of Riva on Lake Garda in Northern Italy.

*Der Transportsegelschooner "S.M.S. Novara" wurde im Jahre 1850 in Zürich gebaut, und hatte eine Lebensgeschichte die der ihres Schwesternschiffes "S.M.S. Casale" sehr ähnlich war.*

5.) "S.M.S. Mortara" had the same historical dates and service as did her sister ship "S.M.S. Casale."

*Der Transportsegelschooner "S.M.S. Mortara" hatte eine Lebensgeschichte die der ihres Schwesternschiffes "S.M.S. Casale" sehr ähnlich war.*

6.) "S.M.S. Mincio" had the same historical dates and service as did her sister ship "S.M.S. Novara."

*Der Transportsegelschooner "S.M.S. Mincio" hatte eine Lebensgeschichte die der ihres Schwesternschiffes "S.M.S. Novara" sehr ähnlich war.*

7.) "S.M.S. Sarca" was built in Zürich, Switzerland in 1851, and was also part of the "Gardaseeflottilla" of the Imperial and Royal Austrian Navy.

*Der Transportsegelschooner "S.M.S. Sarca" wurde im Jahre 1851 in Zürich gebaut, und gehörte auch zur Gardaseeflottille der Kaiserlichen und Königlichen Kriegsmarine.*

### XIII (33) Austro-Venetian Trabaccolos (for which exact tonnage is not available) / Österreichische Segeltrabakel (ohne technische Daten)

A "trabaccolo" (called a "Trabakel" in German) had 2 masts, and was intended for coastal use. They were of robust construction quality, and were used for transport duties. They were the most common type of wooden sailing vessel to be found along the coasts of the Adriatic Sea, and would displace anywhere from 15 to 110 tons. The navy also used them as tenders at home and abroad.

*Ein Segeltrabakel ("Trabaccolo" auf italienisch) ist ein robust gebautes kleineres Segelfahrzeug für Transportzwecke, mit zwei Masten mit Lateinsegeln und zwei Klüvern, für weite Reisen zusätzlich Rahsegel am Fockmast. Die Segeltrabakeln waren die am gebräuchlichsten Segelfahrzeuge der Adria-Küstenfahrt, mit einer Einsatzverdrängung von je zwischen 15 und 110 Tonnen. Sie wurden zur Versorgung der heimischen Küstenstationen und Schiffsabteilungen im Ausland benutzt.*

1.) "S.M.S. Hoche" was captured from the French, and was armed with 6 cannon. She became part of the Imperial and Royal Austrian Navy in the port of Ancona on November 14, 1799.

*Das Segeltrabakel "S.M.S. Hoche" war mit sechs Kanonen bewaffnet, und wurde am 14. November 1799 im Hafen von Ancona von den Franzosen beschlagnahmt.*

2.) "S.M.S. Loupe" was armed with 4 cannon, and was a former merchantman captured from the French. The Imperial and Royal Austrian Navy took her as their prize in Ancona on November 18, 1799.

*Das Segeltrabakel "S.M.S. Loupe" war mit vier Kanonen bewaffnet, und wurde am 18. November 1799 im Hafen von Ancona von den Franzosen beschlagnahmt.*

3.) "S.M.S. Fortune" was armed with 2 cannon, and was captured from the French Navy off Ancona on November 18, 1799.

*Das Segeltrabakel "S.M.S. Fortune" war mit zwei Kanonen bewaffnet, und hatte eine Lebensgeschichte die der ihres Schwesternfahrzeuges "S.M.S. Loupe" sehr ähnlich war.*

4.) "S.M.S. San Antonio di Padova" (1802) was a former merchant vessel purchased by the Imperial and Royal Austrian Navy, and used for transport duties.

*Das Segeltrabakel "S.M.S. San Antonio di Padova" (1802) war ein ehemaliges Handelsfahrzeug, das von der Kaiserlichen und Königlichen Kriegsmarine als Transportfahrzeug gekauft wurde. Antonius von Padua (1195-1231) war ein portugiesisch-italienischer Franziskaner, Theologe und Prediger. Er ist ein Heiliger der Römisch-Katholischen Kirche.*

5.) "S.M.S. Delfino" (1802) was used for tranport duties by the Imperial and Royal Austrian Navy, until she was surrendered to the Italian allies of Napoleonic France on January 19, 1806.

*Das Segeltrabakel "S.M.S. Delfino" (1802) wurde als Transportfahrzeug benutzt, bis sie am 19. Januar 1806 von den italienischen Waffenverbündeten Frankreichs beschlagnahmt wurde.*

6.) "S.M.S. Dario" (1804) was used as a transport vessel by the Austrian Navy.

*Das Segeltrabakel "S.M.S. Dario" (1804) wurde als Transportfahrzeug von der Kaiserlichen und Königlichen Kriegsmarine benutzt.*

7.) "S.M.S. Anima del Purgato" (1805) was a former merchant vessel purchased by the Imperial and Royal Austrian Navy. She was used for station duties.

*Das Segeltrabakel "S.M.S. Anima del Purgato" (1805) war ein ehemaliges Handelsfahrzeug, das als Stationsfahrzeug von der Kaiserlichen und Königlichen Kriegsmarine gekauft wurde.*

8.) "S.M.S. San Antonio" (1805) had a history of service identical to that of her sister ship "S.M.S. Anima del Purgato."

*Das Segeltrabakel "S.M.S. San Antonio" (1805) hatte eine Lebensgeschichte die der ihres Schwesternfahrzeuges "S.M.S. Anima del Purgato" sehr ähnlich war.*

9.) "S.M.S. Madonna Carmelitana" (1806) was a former merchant vessel purchased by the Imperial and Royal Austrian Navy, and assigned to serve off the coast of Dalmatia. She was eventually captured by the French and the Italians, where she was renamed "Fermo" by the Italians.

*Das Segeltrabakel "S.M.S. Madonna Carmelitana" (1806) war ein ehemaliges Handelsfahrzeug, das von der Kaiserlichen und Königlichen Kriegsmarine gekauft wurde. Sie diente an der Küste von Dalmatien in Kroatien, und wurde eventuell von den Franzosen und den Italienern erobert. Die Italienier haben sie als die "Fermo" umbenannt.*

10.) "S.M.S. Madonna del Carmine" (1806) was a former merchant vessel purchased by the Austrian Navy. She was assigned to courier duties off the coast of Southern Dalmatia, which extends to the Montenegrin border.

*Das Segeltrabakel "S.M.S. Madonna del Carmine" (1806) war auch ein ehemaliges Handelsfahrzeug, das von der Kaiserlichen und Königlichen Kriegsmarine gekauft wurde. Sie diente an der Küste von Dalmatien in Kroatien.*

11.) "S.M.S. Fedele" (1813) was a former merchant vessel purchased by the Imperial and Royal Austrian Navy. She was used for transport duties until she was scrapped in 1830.

*Das Segeltrabakel "S.M.S. Fedele" (1813) war ein ehemaliges Handelsfahrzeug, das als Transportfahrzeug von der Kaiserlichen und Königlichen Kriegsmarine gekauft wurde. Sie wurde im Jahre 1830 verschrottet.*

12.) "S.M.S. Fermo" (1814) was laid down in Venice, and was launched on September 16, 1815. She was assigned to transport and station duties within the Austrian Navy, and was scrapped in 1833.

*Das Segeltrabakel "S.M.S. Fermo" (1814) wurde in Venedig auf Kiel gelegt, und lief am 16. September 1815 vom Stapel. Sie diente als Transportfahrzeug sowie als Stationsfahrzeug, und wurde im Jahre 1833 verschrottet.*

13.) "S.M.S. Ecclisso" (1814) was captured from the Italian allies of Napoleonic France, and was assigned to transport duties in the Austrian Navy.

*Das Segeltrabakel "S.M.S. Ecclisso" (1814) wurde von den italienischen Waffenverbündeten Frankreichs beschlagnahmt, und diente danach als Transportfahrzeug bei der Kaiserlichen und Königlichen Kriegsmarine.*

14.) "S.M.S. Intrepido" (1814) was also captured from the Italian allies of Napoleonic France, and was assigned to transport duties in the Austrian Navy. She was scrapped in 1829.

*Das Segeltrabakel "S.M.S. Intrepido" (1814) hatte eine Lebensgeschichte die der ihres Schwesternfahrzeuges "S.M.S. Ecclisso" sehr ähnlich war. Sie wurde im Jahre 1829 verschrottet.*

15.) "S.M.S. Ulisse" (1814) was captured from the Italian allies of Napoleonic France, but not kept for long by the Austrians. She was sold to civilian owners in August 1814.

*Das Segeltrabakel "S.M.S. Ulisse" (1814) wurde auch von den italienischen Waffenverbündeten Frankreichs beschlagnahmt, wurde aber schon von der Kaiserlichen und Königlichen Kriegsmarine Österreichs im August 1814 verkauft.*

16.) "S.M.S. Fortunato" (1814) was also captured from the Italian allies of Napoleonic France, and assigned to transport duties within the Imperial and Austrian Navy. She was scrapped in 1833.

*Das Segeltrabakel "S.M.S. Fortunato" (1814) wurde von den italienischen Waffenverbündeten Frankreichs beschlagnahmt, und wurde dann als Transportfahrzeug von der Kaiserlichen und Königlichen Kriegsmarine benutzt. Sie wurde im Jahre 1833 verschrottet.*

17.) "S.M.S. Camello" (1815) was built in Venice, and was launched on October 30, 1815. She was assigned to transport duties in the Austrian Navy. On February 22, 1833 she was unfortunately stranded in the Cortelazzo Canal. She was salvaged and scrapped after March 6, 1833.

*Das Segeltrabakel "S.M.S. Camello" (1815) wurde in Venedig auf Kiel gelegt, und lief am 30. Oktober 1815 vom Stapel. Sie diente als Transportfahrzeug bis sie am 22. Februar 1833 im Cortelazzo-Kanal strandete. Am 6. März 1833 wurde sie geborgen und danach verschrottet.*

18.) "S.M.S Giusto" (1815) was laid down in Venice, and was launched on January 30, 1816. She was assigned to transport duties in the Austrian Navy. On November 19, 1826 she was unfortunately stranded and then lost in a storm off the coast of Cattalo, Greece.

*Das Segeltrabakel "S.M.S. Giusto" (1815) wurde in Venedig auf Kiel gelegt, und lief am 30. Januar 1816 vom Stapel. Sie diente als Transportfahrzeug bis sie am 19. November 1826 in einem Sturm vor Cattalo (Griechenland) strandete.*

19.) "S.M.S Bravo" (1815) was armed with 4 cannon, and was built in Venice. She was launched on February 4, 1816, and was assigned to transport duties in the Imperial and Royal Austrian Navy. She was scrapped in 1833.

*Das Segeltrabakel "S.M.S. Bravo" (1815) war mit vier Kanonen bewaffnet, und wurde in Venedig gebaut. Sie lief am 4. Februar 1816 vom Stapel, und diente als Transportfahrzeug bis sie im Jahre 1833 verschrottet wurde.*

20.) "S.M.S Primogenito" (1815) was assigned to transport duties in the Austrian Navy, and was temporarily stranded in a storm off the coast of Venice (near Lido) in December 1815. She was salvaged on December 30, 1815, repaired and served until being scrapped in 1824.

*Das Segeltrabakel "S.M.S. Primogenito" (1815) diente als Transportfahrzeug. Im Dezember 1815 strandete sie in einem Sturm vor Lido in der Nähe von Venedig. Am 30. Dezember wurde sie geborgen und dann repariert. Sie wurde erst im Jahre 1824 verschrottet.*

21.) "S.M.S. Prudente" (1816) was assigned to transport duties in the Austrian Navy, but was unfortunately stranded and lost in a storm off Malamocco, Venice on October 12, 1818.

*Das Segeltrabakel "S.M.S. Prudente" (1816) diente auch als Transportfahrzeug. Am 12. Oktober 1818 strandete sie in einem Sturm vor Malamocco in der Nähe von Venedig.*

22.) "S.M.S. Madonna della Salute" (1840) was a former merchant vessel purchased by the Imperial and Royal Austrian Navy. She was assigned to transport munitions for the Austrian "Levanteskadre," stationed off the Eastern coast of the Mediterranean (the Sinai, the Holy Land and Lebanon). An "Eskadre" was a squadron of ships within the Austrian Navy. The comparable German term is "Geschwader."

*Das Segeltrabakel "S.M.S. Madonna della Salute" (1840) war ein ehemaliges Handelsfahrzeug, das von der Kaiserlichen und Königlichen Kriegsmarine gekauft wurde. Sie diente als Transportfahrzeug bei der Levanteskadre der K.u.K. Kriegsmarine.*

23.) "S.M.S. Pescatore" (1848) was captured from Italian nationalist rebels, and was assigned to station duties in the Austrian Navy. She was scrapped after 1852.

*Das Segeltrabakel "S.M.S. Pescatore" (1848) wurde von den feindlichen italienischen Nationalisten erobert, und diente als Stationsfahrzeug bei der Kaiserlichen und Königlichen Kriegsmarine. Sie wurde im Jahre 1852 verschrottet.*

24.) "S.M.S. Leonidas" (1848) was a former merchant vessel purchased by the Imperial and Royal Austrian Navy. She was initially assigned to transport duties, and was used as a coal tender after 1862.

*Das Segeltrabakel "S.M.S. Leonidas" (1848) war ein ehemaliges Handelsfahrzeug, das von der Kaiserlichen und Königlichen Kriegsmarine gekauft wurde. Zuerst wurde sie als Transportfahrzeug benutzt, und im Jahre 1862 wurde sie als Kohlenversorger umgebaut.*

25.) "S.M.S. Arturo" (1849) was a former merchant vessel purchased by the Austrian Navy. No further details are known about her service within the navy.

*Das Segeltrabakel "S.M.S. Arturo" (1849) war ein ehemaliges Handelsfahrzeug, das von der Kaiserlichen und Königlichen Kriegsmarine gekauft wurde. Weiteres ist uns leider nicht bekannt.*

## XIII (34) Austro-Venetian Prams (for which exact tonnage is not available) / Österreichische Segelprahms (ohne technische Daten)

A "pram" (called a "Prahm" in German) was a shallow-draught flat-bottomed boat used to approach the shore. They were known to be of very sturdy construction, using oars for propulsion and being armed as floating batteries.

*Ein Segelprahm ("Prame" auf italienisch) ist ein schwer gebautes, flachgehendes Lastboot mit einem flachen Boden und mit Riemenantrieb, etwa wie eine Schwimmende Segelbatterie.*

1.) "S.M.S. Ponton" was built in Venice in 1848, and was briefly captured by Italian nationalist rebels from March 1848 to August 1849, before being returned to the Imperial and Royal Austrian Navy.

*Der Segelprahm "S.M.S. Ponton" wurde im Jahre 1848 in Venedig gebaut, und war zwischen März 1848 und August 1849 unter feindlicher italienischer Beschlagnahme der Nationalisten.*

### Chapter 16 (Kapitel 16): XIII (35) Old Armored Sailing Ships of the North German "Bundesmarine" of 1867-1871 / Panzerschiffe der Norddeutschen Bundesmarine (1867-1871)

The short-lived North German "Bundesmarine" of 1867-1871 was in truth merely the Royal Prussian Navy under a new name, and with a brand new flag. This proud flag would include the colors of black, white and red – black & white from the Kingdom of Prussia, and white & red from the Hanseatic League Cities of Northern Germany. It featured Germany's famous black "Balkan Cross," which became known to the world during both World Wars One and Two. In the middle of the Balkan Cross was the Hohenzollern Eagle of the Royal House of Brandenburg-Prussia. In the upper left was the black, white and red tricolor, which was to become Germany's national flag from 1871 until 1918. In the middle of this Jack was the famous German "Maltese Cross," which has been used for military decorations (such as the "Maria-Theresia Order" of Austria-Hungary, the "Pour le Merite" or "Blue Max" of Brandenburg-Prussia and Imperial Germany and the "Iron Cross" of 1813, 1914 and 1939). The Maltese Cross is still used to this very day by both the modern Federal German Army (the "Bundesheer") and the German Air Force (the "Luftwaffe").

*Die Marine des Norddeutschen Bundes (auch die "Norddeutsche Bundesmarine" oder die "Norddeutsche Bundesflotte" genannt) entstand im Jahre 1867 nach dem gesamtdeutschen Sieg über Dänemark im Jahre 1864 (die Abtretung Schleswig-Holsteins) und dem darauf folgenden Krieg zwischen Österreich und Preußen. Das Königreich Preußen brachte seine Marine in den neu entstandenen Norddeutschen Bund ein. Die neue "schwarz-weiß-rote" Flagge kombinierte sich aus den Farben Preußens (schwarz-weiß), welches den Oberbefehl innehatte, und aus den Farben der Hansestädte (weiß-rot). Der Flottengründungsplan von 1867 sah folgende größeren Schiffe vor: sechs Panzerschiffe, neun Segelkorvetten und acht Segelavisos. Die Aufgaben der Flotte wurden mit dem Schutz des Seehandels, der Verteidigung der norddeutschen Küsten und einer zu entwickelnden Fähigkeit zur Störung feindlichen Handels und zum Angriff auf feindliche Kriegsflotten, Küsten und Häfen beschrieben. Leiter des Marineministeriums war General von Roon, den Oberbefehl der Bundesmarine hatte Prinz Adalbert von Preußen. Im Jahre 1869 wurde Wilhelmshaven als neuer Kriegshafen eingeweiht, weiterer Bundeskriegshafen wurde Kiel. Nach nur geringer Beteiligung am Deutsch-Französischen Krieg (von 1870 bis 1871) wurde aus der Marine des Norddeutschen Bundes im Jahre 1871 die neue "Kaiserliche Marine" des preußisch-deutschen Reiches (1871-1921) gegründet.*

Prussia, Italy and a number of North German States had defeated Austria, Bavaria, Württemberg, Baden, Saxony, Hanover, Nassau and a number of smaller German States in the Austro-Prussian War of 1866. The result of this tragic German Civil War ("Brüderkrieg" or "War of Brothers" in German) was to topple the old order which had endured through the Kingdom of Franconia (482-800), the Holy Roman Empire of the German Nation (800-1806), the Confederation of the Rhine (1806-1815) and the Germanic Confederation (1815-1866). The Hohenzollern Dynasty of Brandenburg-Prussia thus replaced the Habsburg-Lothringen Dynasty of Austria as the most powerful force within the Greater German Empire.

1.) "S.M.S. Friedrich Carl" (1867) was an armored sailing frigate, having been built by Compagnie de Forges et Chantiers in Toulon, France. She was 94 meters long, displaced up to 5,971 tons full load, had a single expansion engine and was rigged as a barque with 2,010 square meters of sail area. She could make up to 13 knots, and her crew consisted of 33 commissioned officers and 500 enlisted men. She was sold for scrapping in the Netherlands in 1906.

*Die Panzerfregatte "S.M.S. Friedrich Carl" (1867) wurde von der Compagnie de Forges et Chantiers in Toulon, Frankreich gebaut. Sie war 94 Meter lang, hatte eine Einsatzverdrängung von 5,971 Tonnen, war als eine Segelbark getakelt und hatte ein Segelbereich von 2,010 Quadratmeter. Ihre Höchstgeschwindigkeit war 13 Knoten, und sie hatte eine Besatzung von 33 Offiziere und 500 Matrosen. Sie wurde im Jahre 1906 in Holland verschrottet, nach einer Dienstzeit von 39 Jahren.*

2.) "S.M.S. Kronprinz" (1867) was an armored sailing frigate, built by Samuda Brothers of London, England and launched on May 6, 1867. She was 90 meters long, displaced up to 5,767 tons full load, had a single expansion engine and was rigged as a barque with 1,980 square meters of sail area. Her crew also consisted of 33 commissioned officers and 500 enlisted men, and her armament was an identical 32 72-pounders. She was scrapped in Rendsburg, Kiel in 1901.

*Die Panzerfregatte "S.M.S. Kronprinz" (1867) wurde von den Gebrüdern Samuda in London, England gebaut, und lief am 6. Mai 1867 vom Stapel. Sie war 90 Meter lang, hatte eine Einsatzverdrängung von 5,767 Tonnen, war als eine Segelbark getakelt und hatte ein Segelbereich von 1,980 Quadratmeter. Sie hatte eine Besatzung von 33 Offiziere und 500 Matrosen, und war mit 32 72-Pfundern bewaffnet. Sie wurde im Jahre 1901 in Rendsburg (Kiel) verschrottet, nach einer Dienstzeit von 34 Jahren.*

3.) "S.M.S. König Wilhelm" (1868) was a very large and powerful armored sailing frigate built by Thames Iron Works in Blackwall (England), displacing a maximum of 10,591 tons.  She was protected by belt armor, was 112,2 meters long, had beam of 18,3 meters and a draught of 8,2 meters.  Her propulsion system was comprised of one 2-cylinder single-acting expansion engine, which produced 8,000 horsepower and gave her a top speed of 15 knots.  The thickness of her armor both on the waterline and in her battery was up to 203 mm.  She was armed with 18-24 cm guns in her battery deck and 5-21 cm guns (4 in bay-window type gun mounts and one on the upper deck).  Her sail area was 2,600 square meters.  After a major refit in 1897, she was reclassed as a large or armored cruiser.  In 1904, she was converted yet again, and this time into a living and training quarters.  She was finally scrapped in 1921, after 53 years of useful service.

**Panzerfregatte "S.M.S. König Wilhelm (1868) als Panzerkreuzer im Jahre 1897 / Armored Frigate "S.M.S. König Wilhelm" (1868) after her rebuild as an Armored Cruiser in 1897 – courtesy of Captain (CA) George J. Albert, Jr., Army Field Historian of the California Center for Military History**

*Die Segelfregatte "S.M.S. König Wilhelm" (1868) wurde von den Thames Eisenwerken in Blackwall (England) gebaut, und hatte eine Einsatzverdrängung von 10,591 Tonnen.  Sie war 112,2 Meter lang, hatte eine Breite von 18,3 Meter und einen Tiefgang von 8,2 Meter. Ihre Höchstgeschwindigkeit war 15 Knoten, und ihre Panzerung an der Gürtellinie sowie am Batteriedeck war bis 203 mm stark. Sie war mit 18 24-cm sowie mit fünf 21-cm Schnellfeuerkanonen bewaffnet, und sie hatte ein Segelbereich von 2,600 Quadratmeter. Im Jahre 1897 wurde sie als Panzerkreuzer umgebaut, und im Jahre 1904 wurde sie wieder als Wohnschiff sowie als Schulschiff umgebaut. Im Jahre 1921 wurde sie endlich verschrottet, nach einer langen und guten Dienstzeit von 53 Jahren.*

4-5.) The sister gunboats "S.M.S. Albatross" (1870) and "S.M.S. Nautilus" (1870) each displaced 413 tons and were 57 meters long. They had 2 single expansion engines, were rigged as barques and had sail areas of 710 square meters. They could make up to 11 knots, and served as survey ships in foreign waters until 1888.

*Die Schwesterkanonenboote "S.M.S. Albatroß" (1870) und "S.M.S. Nautilus" (1870) hatten eine Einsatzverdrängung von je 413 Tonnen und waren je 57 Meter lang. Wie die Segelpanzerfregatten hatten die Kanonenboote auch Dampfantrieb und waren als Segelbarks getakelt. Sie hatten ein Segelbereich von je 710 Quadratmeter, und eine Höchstgeschwindigkeit von 11 Knoten. Sie dienten im Ausland bis 1888.*

### Chapter 17 (Kapitel 17): XIII (36) Old Wooden Sailing Ships of the German "Reichsmarine" of 1848-1852 / Segelschiffe der Deutschen Reichsmarine (1848-1852)

In 1848, Germany (like much of Europe) experienced a failed liberal democratic revolution. The would-be liberal revolutionaries (who would be viewed as "conservatives" in North American political jargon) sought a large, inclusive "Greater German Empire" to include the successor states of the Holy Roman Empire of the German Nation (800-1806), the Confederation of the Rhine (1806-1815) and the Germanic Confederation (which lasted from 1806-1866). This included the Germans, the Austrians, the Bavarians, the Saxons, the Prussians, the Sorbs, the Wends, the Silesians, the Masurians, the Frisians, the Hessians, the Czechs, the Slovaks, the Magyars, the Slovenes, the Tyrolians, the Galician Poles, the Ruthenians, the Slavonians, the Dalmatians and the Croats. The Imperial German armed forces had been known as the "Reichswehr" from 800 until 1806. The German Navy had existed as the Navy of Austria, the Navy of Brandenburg-Prussia and of the Cities of the Hanseatic League. The revolutionaries of 1848 established a national "Reichsmarine" which lasted until 1852.

*Die erste sogenannte "gesamtdeutsche Marine" der deutschen Marinegeschichte wurde während der bürgerlich-demokratischen Revolution von 1848 bis 1849 am 14. Juni 1848 von der Nationalversammlung in Frankfurt am Main gegründet. Sie wurde die deutsche "Reichsflotte" sowie die "Reichsmarine" genannt. Das Großdeutsche Reich, organisiert als Staatenbund, hatte sich nach dem Wiener Kongreß von 1815 eine föderale Verteidigungsstruktur geschaffen. Die Mitgliedstaaten stellten die Streitkräfte des Deutschen Bundes (1815-1866). Bei den Streitkräften verließ man sich auf einige Bundesfürsten, die als Monarchen von Staaten außerhalb des Deutschen Bundes große Kriegsflotten besaßen. Der König von Hannover war (bis 1837) zugleich König von Großbrittanien und Irland, der Großherzog von Luxemburg war König der Vereinigten Niederlande (Holland und Belgien) und der Herzog von Holstein war der König von Dänemark. Das Königreich Preußen besaß als kontinental orientierte Landmacht eine kleine eigene Kriegsmarine im Ostseehafen Danzig, und das Kaiserreich Österreich hatte ihre "Kaiserliche und Königliche Kriegsmarine" im Adria-Hafen Triest stationiert. Während des Schleswig-Holsteinischen Krieges (1848 bis 1852) zeigte sich das Scheitern dieses Seeverteidigungskonzeptes, weil die deutschen Könige von Großbrittanien und dem Niederlande inzwischen nicht mehr deutsche Bundesfürsten waren und Dänemark zum Kriegsgegner wurde. Innerhalb weniger Tage im April 1848 brachte die Blockade der dänischen Kriegsmarine den deutschen Seehandel in Nord-und Ostsee zum Stillstand.*

*Nachdem der Bundestag des Deutschen Bundes den Erfolg der Revolution anerkannt und sein Haushaltsrecht am 12. Juni 1848 an die seit dem 18. Mai 1848 in der Frankfurter Paulskirche tagenden Nationalversammlung abgetreten hatte, beschloß diese angesichts der Situation schon zwei Tage später am 14. Juni 1848 in einer ihrer ersten Entscheidungen, eine gesamtdeutsche Kriegsflotte aufzustellen und dafür sechs Millionen Reichsthaler bereitzustellen.*

1.) "S.M.S. Deutschland" (1818) was a wooden sailing frigate, and the very first German warship to carry this great name, having been named after Germany itself. She had 3 masts, displaced up to 853 tons, was 38,5 meters long, was armed with 36 cannon and was manned by a crew of 230 commissioned officers and enlisted sailors. She was purchased by the new "Reichsmarine" in 1848, but was again sold for 9,200 Thalers in 1852. The firm of Roessingh & Mummy purchased her to carry coal from England to China. The old currency name "Thaler" came from the German word "Tal," which means "valley" in English. The German word "Thaler" is in turn the root of the word for "Dollar," the name of the currency for modern countries such as the United States, Canada, Australia, New Zealand, Taiwan, Singapore, Hong Kong and Rhodesia-Zimbabwe.

*Die Segelfregatte "S.M.S. Deutschland" (1818) war die erste "Deutschland" der deutschen Marine. Sie hatte drei Masten, eine Einsatzverdrängung von 853 Tonnen, war 38,5 Meter lang, hatte eine Bewaffnung von 36 Kanonen und eine Besatzung von 230 Offiziere und Matrosen. Sie wurde im Jahre 1848 von der neuen Reichsmarine gekauft, wurde aber im Jahre 1852 für 9,200 Reichsthaler wieder als Handelsschiff verkauft. Auf englisch heißt Thaler "Dollar." Der Dollar wird heute in den USA, in Kanada, Australien, Neuseeland, Taiwan, Singapur, Hongkong und Simbabwe (vormals Rhodesien) benutzt. Es gibt etwa 63,5 Millionen Deutschstämmige in Amerika, 2,8 Millionen in Kanada, 2 Millionen in Australien und 200,000 in Neuseeland.*

2.) "S.M.S. Hamburg" (1841) was a wooden paddle steamer, carvel-built out of oak and rigged as a schooner-brig. She displaced 435 tons, was built by the Bernhard Wencke Shipyard in Bremen, was 53 meters long and had beam of 12 meters. She was purchased by the "Reichsmarine" on December 15, 1848 and was later sold to the General Steam Navigation Company of London, England in 1852. The English renamed her "S/S Denmark."

*Der Segelbriggschooner "S.M.S. Hamburg" (1841) hatte eine Einsatzverdrängung von 435 Tonnen, war 53 Meter lang, hatte eine Breite von 12 Meter und wurde von der Bernhard Wencke Schiffswerft in Bremen gebaut. Sie wurde am 15. Dezember 1848 von der neuen Reichsmarine gekauft, und wurde im*

*1852 als Handelsschiff an die General Steam Navigation Company von London, England verkauft. Die Engländer hatten sie als die "S/S Denmark" umbenannt.*

3.) "S.M.S. Bremen" (1842) was also a wooden paddle steamer, carvel-built out of oak and rigged as a schooner-brig. She displaced 450 tons, and was launched by the Johann Marbs Shipyard in Altona (Hamburg) on June 22, 1842. She was 56 meters long, had a beam of 12,7 meters and was purchased by the "Reichsmarine" on December 15, 1848. She was also later sold to the General Steam Navigation Company of London, England in 1852, which renamed her "S/S Hanover."

*Der Segelbriggschooner "S.M.S. Bremen" (1842) hatte eine Einsatzverdrängung von 450 Tonnen, war 56 Meter lang, hatte eine Breite von 12,7 Meter und lief am 22. Juni 1842 bei der Johann Marbs Schiffswerft in Altona bei Hamburg vom Stapel. Sie wurde auch am 15. Dezember 1848 von der neuen Reichsmarine gekauft, und wurde im 1852 an die General Steam Navigation Company von London, England verkauft. Die Engländer hatten sie als die "S/S Hanover" ("Hannover" auf deutsch) umbenannt.*

4.) "S.M.S. Lübeck" (1844) was another wooden paddle steamer, carvel-built out of oak and rigged as a schooner-brig. She was built by the firm of S.H. Morton and Company in Leith (the United Kingdom), displaced 435 tons, was 50 meters long and had a beam of 12,6 meters. She, "S.M.S. Hamburg" and "S.M.S. Bremen" had 2 paddle wheels 6 meters in diameter, each with 12 paddles and 2 horizontal 1-cylinder expansion engines. She was also purchased by the German "Reichsmarine" on December 15, 1848 and was sold to the General Steam Navigation Company of London, England in 1852, where she was renamed "S/S Newcastle."

*Der Segelbriggschooner "S.M.S. Lübeck" (1844) hatte eine Einsatzverdrängung von 435 Tonnen, war 50 Meter lang, hatte eine Breite von 12,7 Meter wurde von der S.H. Morton and Company Schiffswerft in Leith, England gebaut. Sie wurde auch am 15. Dezember 1848 von der neuen Reichsmarine gekauft, und wurde im 1852 an die General Steam Navigation Company von London, England verkauft. Die Engländer hatten sie als die "S/S Newcastle" umbenannt.*

5.) "S.M.S. Hansa" (1847) was a paddle-wheeled wooden sailing frigate, and had been built by the Black Ball Shipping Line of the USA. At 1,800 tons total displacement, she was the largest ship in the old "Reichsmarine" of her day. She was purchased by the Imperial German Navy in August 1849, and then sold to the Bremen shipping firm of W.A. Fritze and Company in March 1853. She was chartered to carry British troops during the Crimean War of 1854, and then was used for the Bremerhaven-New York run from 1855 until 1857. Thereafter she was chartered by the British to sail to India, and was then sold to the English Galway Shipping Line – for which she sailed between England and India from 1858 until 1862. They renamed her "S/S Indian Empire," and she served until being gutted by fire in Deptford, England in July 1862.

*Die Segelfregatte "S.M.S. Hansa" (1847) war das größte Kriegsschiff der neuen Reichsmarine, und wurde von der Black Ball Shipping Line Schiffswerft in Amerika gebaut. Sie hatte eine Einsatzverdrängung von 1,800 Tonnen. Sie wurde im August 1849 von der Reichsmarine gekauft, und wurde im März 1853 an der Reederei W.A. Fritze in Bremen verkauft. Zur Zeit des Krimkrieges im Jahre 1854 hatte sie britische Soldaten nach der Ukraine transportiert. Zwischen 1855 und 1857 diente sie auf der Seelinie zwischen Bremerhaven und Neu York. Danach wurde sie an der Galway Shipping Line aus England verkauft, und diente zwischen 1858 und 1862 auf der Seelinie zwischen England und Indien. Sie wurde von den Engländern als die "S/S Indian Empire" (das "Kaiserreich Indien" auf deutsch) umbenannt. Im Juli 1862 verbrannte sie in Deptford, England.*

## Chapter 18 (Kapitel 18): XIII (37) Old Wooden Sailing Ships of Brandenburg-Prussia / Segelschiffe von Brandenburg-Preußen

After Austria, Brandenburg-Prussia was the strongest naval power within the old Holy Roman Empire of the German Nation (800-1806). In 1415, the Hohenzollern Monarchy (their ancestral lands are located in modern-day Baden-Württemberg) was granted the Electorate of Brandenburg, of which the city of Berlin was the capital. In 1618, they also inherited the Duchy of Prussia, which eventually came to be known as East Prussia (of which the city of Königsberg was the capital). After the 30 Years' War of 1618-1648 in which they betrayed the Habsburg Emperor ("Kaiser") of Germany, they were also awarded the region of Further (i.e., Eastern) Pomerania – the capital of which was the city of Stettin. Prussia became a Kingdom in 1701.

*Die "Königlich Preußische Marine" war die Seestreitkraft des Königreiches Preußen. Sie entstand im Jahre 1701 bei der Erhebung des Kurfürstentums Brandenburg zum Königreich Preußen aus der vormaligen Kurbrandenburgischen Marine und bestand mit längerer Unterbrechung bis zur Gründung des Norddeutschen Bundes im Jahre 1867, anläßlich derer die Königlich Preußische Marine in der Marine des Norddeutschen Bundes aufging. Das Kurfürstentum Brandenburg als Vorgänger des Königreichs Preußen besaß seit dem 17. Jahrhundert eigene Seestreitkräfte, die unter dem Großen Kurfürsten Friedrich Wilhelm, ab 1657 zu einer schlagkräftigen Kriegsflotte ausgebaut wurde. Offizielles Gründungsdatum der Kurfürstlichen Brandenburg-Preußischen Marine ist der 1. Oktober 1684. Der Kurfürst bezeichnete Schiff-Fahrt und Außenhandel als die vornehmsten Aufgaben eines Staates und betrieb energisch den Erwerb von Kolonien in Übersee – wie "Großfriedrichsburg" in Westafrika (heute Ghana).*

During the War of the Austrian Succession from 1740-1748, Brandenburg-Prussia betrayed the Holy Roman Empire of the German Nation yet again – after which she was awarded the Province of Silesia (the capital of which was the city of Breslau). In 1772, Brandenburg-Prussia took the so-called "Polish Corridor" from Poland, which became the province of West Prussia (the capital of which was the city of Danzig). In 1793, Brandenburg-Prussia took the province of South Prussia from Poland, the capital of which was the city of Posen. In 1795, Brandenburg-Prussia took the province of "New East Prussia" ("Masovia" in Polish) during the 3rd and final partition of the once great United Kingdom of Poland and Lithuania.

1-2.) In 1683, the Brandenburg-Prussian wooden sailing frigates "S.M.S. Churprinz" and "S.M.S. Mohrian" went to the coast of West Africa to establish the German colony of "Grossfriedrichsburg" ("Great Fredericksburg" in English), which is today the modern nation of Ghana. These great ships had 2 battery decks and 3 masts.

*Im Jahre 1683 haben die zwei brandenburgisch-preußischen Schwester-Segelfregatten "S.M.S. Churprinz" und "S.M.S. Mohrian" Großfriedrichsburg in Westafrika (heute Ghana) gegründet. Die zwei Kriegsschiffe hatten je zwei Batteriedecks und drei Masten.*

3.) "S.M.S. Fridericus Rex" (1710) was a great armed "State Yacht" or galley. She was 26 meters long, had a maximum beam of 7 meters, and was armed with 22 heavy bronze cannon.

*Die Segelgaleere (oder Staatsyacht) "S.M.S. Fridericux Rex" (1710) war 26 Meter lang, und hatte eine Breite von 7 Meter. Sie war mit 22 schweren Bronzkanonen bewaffnet.*

4.) "S.M.S. Amazone" (1843) was a wooden sailing corvette, having been launched in Grabow (near the port of Stettin in Pomerania) on June 24, 1843. She was carvel-built out of oak, was 34 meters long, and had a beam of 9 meters. She had 3 masts, and with full rigging her sails covered an area of 876 square meters. She could make up to 11 knots, and was armed with 12 Swedish-made 18-pounders. Her crew numbered 6 commissioned officers and 139 enlisted men. In 1844, she took her first overseas voyage, and all the way to the Black Sea. In 1845, she sailed via Portuguese Madeira to Genoa in Italy. In 1847, she visited New York City in the USA, and from 1852 to 1853 she undertook a voyage to South America. She was tragically lost along with 107 of her crew members in a violent storm in the Southern part of the North Sea in 1861. She is fondly and proudly remembered as the "Grandmother" of the modern "Deutsche Marine" of the Federal Republic of Germany.

*Die Segelkorvette "S.M.S. Amazone" (1843) lief am 24. Juni 1843 in Grabow (bei Stettin in Hinterpommern) vom Stapel. Sie war aus Eichenholz gebaut, war 34 Meter lang und hatte eine Breite von 9 Meter. Sie hatte drei Masten und ein Segelbereich von 876 Quadratmeter. Ihre Höchstgeschwindigkeit war 9 Knoten, und sie war mit 12 schwedischen 18-Pfundern bewaffnet. Sie hatte eine Besatzung von sechs Offiziere und 139 Matrosen. Im Jahre 1844 reiste sie von Stettin nach dem Schwarzen Meer und zurück. Im Jahre 1845 reiste sie von Stettin nach Madeira und Genua und zurück. Im Jahre 1847 besuchte sie Neu*

*York, und zwischen 1852 und 1853 reiste sie von Stettin nach Südamerika und zurück. Im Jahre 1861 ging sie in einem Sturm in der Nordsee verloren – 107 von den Besatzungsmitgliedern kamen dabei ums Leben. Sie wird heute mit Stolz als die "Großmutter" der heutigen "Deutschen Marine" der Bundesrepublik Deutschland angesehen.*

5.) "S.M.S. Mercur" (1847) was a flush-decked wooden sailing corvette, having been launched by the firm of J. Klawitter in Danzig, West Prussia. Initially, she served as an East India Man of the Prussian Sea Trading Company. In March 1850, she was purchased by the Royal Prussian Navy. She was also carvel-built out of oak, and when fully rigged had a sail area of 805 square meters. She was 43 meters long, and had a beam of 8 meters. She had 3 masts, and displaced up to 650 tons full load, which made her the largest Brandenburg-Prussian ship up to that time. She could make up to 9 knots, and was armed with 6 26-pounders. Like "S.M.S. Amazone," she was used to "show the flag" and to train officer cadets of the Royal Prussian Navy. In November 1850 she left for her first foreign voyage to Rio de Janeiro in Brazil. She was scrapped in the port of Danzig in 1861.

*Die Segelkorvette "S.M.S. Mercur" (1847) lief bei der J. Klawitter Schiffswerft in Danzig vom Stapel, und wurde im März 1850 von der Königlich Preußischen Marine gekauft. Sie war aus Eichenholz gebaut, und sie hatte ein Segelbereich von 805 Quadratmeter. Sie war 43 Meter lang, hatte eine Breite von 8 Meter, drei Masten, und eine Einsatzverdrängung von 650 Tonnen. Ihre Höchstgeschwindigkeit war 9 Knoten, und sie hatte eine Bewaffnung von sechs 26-Pfundern. Sie wurde als Schulschiff benutzt, und reiste im Jahre 1850 von Danzig nach Rio de Janeiro in Brasilien und zurück. Sie wurde im Jahre 1861 in Danzig verschrottet.*

6.) "S.M.S. Nix" (1850) was a swift paddle-driven dispatch boat. She was designed by Prinz Adalbert of Prussia, displaced 530 tons full load, and was built by Robinson and Russell of London, England. She could make up to 13 knots.

*Die Radaviso "S.M.S. Nix" (1850) hatte eine Einsatzverdrängung von 530 Tonnen, und wurde von der Robinson and Russell Schiffswerft in London, England gebaut. Sie hatte eine Höchstgeschwindigkeit von 13 Knoten.*

7.) "S.M.S. Salamander" (1850) was identical to her sister ship "S.M.S. Nix," and had an identical history of service in the Royal Prussian Navy.

*Die Radaviso "S.M.S. Salamander" (1850) hatte eine Lebensgesichte die der ihres Schwesternschiffes "S.M.S. Nix" sehr ähnlich war.*

8.) "S.M.S. Danzig" (1851) was a wooden sailing paddle-corvette, launched by the Royal Shipyards in Danzig, West Prussia in November 1851. She was carvel-built out of oak, and displaced up to 1,200 tons full load. She was overlaid with copper, was 76 meters long and could make up to 11 knots. She was armed with 12 68-pounders, and became the fleet flagship. In 1863, she was sold to the English, who in turn sold her to the Japanese. She was burnt out due to an accident in Japan in 1869.

*Die Segelkorvette "S.M.S. Danzig" (1851) lief im November 1851 von der Königlichen Schiffswerft in Danzig vom Stapel, und war aus Eichenholz gebaut. Sie hatte eine Einsatzverdrängung von 1,200 Tonnen, war 76 Meter lang und ihre Höchstgeschwindigkeit war 11 Knoten. Sie war mit 12-68 Pfundern bewaffnet, und diente als Flottenflaggschiff. Im Jahre 1863 wurde sie an England verkauft, und die Engländer haben das Schiff sofort an Japan verkauft. Im Jahre 1869 verbrannte sie in Japan.*

9-13.) The 5 wooden sailing frigates of the "S.M.S. Arcona" (1858) class each displaced up to 1,527 tons, were 72 meters long and had a beam of 13 meters. They could make up to 12 knots, and were armed with 6 68-pounders plus 20 36-pounders. They were used largely for "showing the flag," and for training officer cadets of the Royal Prussian Navy and thus made numerous overseas voyages. "S.M.S. Arcona" took part in the opening of the Suez Canal in 1869, with the Prussian Crown Prince Friedrich III on board. She was abroad in the Portuguese Azores when war with France broke out in 1870. She avoided capture by a numerically superior French naval force by making her way to the neutral port of Lisbon, where she remained until the end of hostilities in 1871. She was broken up in the German port of Kiel in 1877. The other members of this class were "S.M.S. Gazelle" (1859), "S.M.S. Vineta" (1863), "S.M.S. Hertha" (1864) and "S.M.S. Elisabeth" (1868).

*Die fünf Segelfregatten der "S.M.S. Arcona" (1858) Klaße hatten eine Einsatzverdrängung von je 1,527 Tonnen, waren je 72 Meter lang und hatten eine Breite von je 13 Meter. Die Höchstgeschwindigkeit eines Schiffes dieser Klaße lag bei 12 Knoten, und die Bewaffnung war sechs 68-Pfunder und 20-36 Pfunder. Diese Kriegsschiffe wurden als Schulschiffe benutzt, und sie hatten viele Auslandsreisen gemacht. Die "S.M.S. Arcona" nahm bei der Eröffnung des Suez-Kanals teil, als Kronprinz Friedrich von Preußen auch dabei war. Zur Zeit des Deutsch-Französischen Krieges (1870 bis 1871) war sie in den Azoren sowie in*

*Lissabon, Portugal. Sie wurde im Jahre 1877 in Kiel verschrottet. Die anderen Mitglieder dieser Klaße waren die "S.M.S. Gazelle" (1859), die "S.M.S. Vineta" (1863), die "S.M.S. Hertha" (1864) und die "S.M.S. Elisabeth" (1868).*

14.) "S.M.S. Frauenlob" (1849) was laid down by the Lübke Shipyard in Wolgast on the Baltic Sea in 1849, and finally launched in 1856. She was built due to financial contributions from women all over Germany – hence her name "Frauenlob" ("for the praise of women" in German). She was wooden sailing schooner with 2 masts, carvel-built of oak. She displaced just 94 tons, was 32 meters long and could make up to 13 knots. Her crew consisted of 5 commissioned officers and 42 enlisted men, all of whom sadly went down with her when she fell victim to a typhoon in Japanese waters on September 2, 1860.

*Der Segelschooner "S.M.S. Frauenlob" (1849) wurde bei der Lübke Schiffswerft in Wolgast auf Kiel gelegt, und lief im Jahre 1856 vom Stapel. Sie hatte zwei Masten, war aus Eichenholz gebaut, hatte eine Einsatzverdrängung von nur 94 Tonnen, war 32 Meter lang und ihre Höchstgeschwindigkeit lag bei 13 Knoten. Die Besatzung des Schiffes bestand aus 5 Offiziere und 42 Matrosen. Am 2. September 1860 ging sie in einem Taifun in japanischen Gewässern verloren, wobei alle Besatzungsmitglieder ums Leben kamen.*

15.) "S.M.S. Grille" (1857) was a wooden sailing dispatch boat with 3 masts. She was built by the Norman Shipyard in Le Havre, France and launched in September of 1857. She served as the Prussian Royal Yacht, and during the Franco-Prussian War of 1870-1871 she withstood an attack by French naval forces upon the Baltic Sea German island of Rügen. After 1892, she served as a training ship. She was scrapped in Hamburg in 1920, after 63 years of faithful service. She was carvel-built out of mahogany, and displaced 326 tons. In addition to her sails, she also had an English-built single expansion engine.

*Die Segelaviso "S.M.S. Grille" (1857) wurde bei der Norman Schiffswerft in Le Havre, Frankreich gebaut, und lief im September 1857 vom Stapel. Sie diente als Königliche Yacht des Adelhauses Hohenzollern. Zur Zeit des Deutsch-Französischen Krieges verteidigte sie erfolgreich die Insel Rügen. Ab 1892 diente sie als Schulschiff. Sie wurde im Jahre 1920 in Hamburg verschrottet – nach einer langen und erfolgreichen Dienstzeit von 63 Jahren. Sie hatte eine Einsatzverdrängung von 326 Tonnen, drei Masten, Dampfantrieb und war aus Eichenholz gebaut.*

16.) "S.M.S. Niobe" (1849) was a wooden training frigate with 3 masts, built by the Royal Dockyard in Portsmouth, England. She displaced 854 tons, could make up to 14 knots and had a sail area of 1,650 square meters. She was armed with 16 68-pounders and 4 30-pounders. Her crew consisted of 35 commissioned officers and 320 enlisted men. She was scrapped in Kiel in 1891, after 42 years of service.

*Die Segelfregatte "S.M.S. Niobe" (1849) wurde von der Royal Dockyard Schiffswerft in Portsmouth, England gebaut. Sie hatte eine Einsatzverdrängung von 854 Tonnen, drei Masten, ein Segelbereich von 1,650 Quadratmeter und ihre Höchstgeschwindigkeit lag bei 14 Knoten. Sie war mit 16-68 Pfundern und vier 30-Pfundern bewaffnet, und sie hatte eine Besatzung von 35 Offiziere und 320 Matrosen. Sie wurde im Jahre 1891 in Kiel verschrottet, nach einer langen und erfolgreichen Dienstzeit von 42 Jahren.*

17.) "S.M.S. Thetis" (1846) was another 3-masted wooden training frigate, with a sail area of 2,370 square meters and a top speed of up to 15 knots. She served as a cadet training ship, and later as a gunnery training ship. Her displacement was 1,082 tons full load. She was also manned by 35 commissioned officers and 320 enlisted sailors. She was scrapped in Kiel in 1895, after 49 years of service.

*Die Segelfregatte "S.M.S. Thetis" (1846) hatte eine Einsatzverdrängung von 1,082 Tonnen, drei Masten, ein Segelbereich von 2,370 Quadratmeter, und ihre Höchstgeschwindigkeit lag bei 15 Knoten. Sie diente als Schulschiff, und hatte eine Besatzung von 35 Offiziere und 320 Matrosen. Sie wurde im Jahre 1895 in Kiel verschrottet, nach einer langen und erfolgreichen Dientszeit von 49 Jahren.*

18.) "S.M.S. Loreley" (1859) was a paddle-wheeled dispatch boat, having been built by the Royal Shipyards in Danzig, West Prussia. She displaced 290 tons, and was 47 meters long. She served largely on overseas voyages.

*Die Segelaviso "S.M.S. Loreley" (1859) wurde von der Königlichen Schiffswerft in Danzig gebaut. Sie hatte eine Einsatzverdrängung von 290 Tonnen, und war 47 Meter lang. Sie hatte hauptsächlich Auslandsreisen gemacht.*

19-20.) The sister ships "S.M.S. Nymphe" (1863) and "S.M.S. Medusa" (1864) were flush-decked wooden sailing corvettes which also served on numerous overseas voyages. Each ship displaced up to 728 tons full load, had a sail area of 1,500 square meters and was 65 meters long. They were equipped with single expansion engines built by J. Penn and Sons of Greenwich, England, and were armed with 10 36-pounders plus 6 12-pounders. "S.M.S. Nymphe" was launched in Danzig on April 15, 1863 and sailed often in foreign waters. During the Franco-Prussian War of 1870-1871, she partook in the Battle of Jasmund in 1870 and successfully prevented a French seaborne invasion of the city of Danzig in West Prussia. She was finally scrapped in Kiel in 1891. "S.M.S. Medusa" also made many overseas trips. During the Franco-Prussian War, she took refuge in the harbor of Yokohama, Japan – thus evading superior French naval forces. She was scrapped in Danzig in 1891.

*Die zwei Schwestersegelkorvetten "S.M.S. Nymphe" (1863) und "S.M.S. Medusa" (1864) hatten eine Einsatzverdrängung von je 728 Tonnen, waren je 65 Meter lang, und hatten ein Segelbereich von je 1,500 Quadratmeter sowie Dampfantrieb. Sie hatten viele Auslandsreisen gemacht. Die Bewaffnung eines Kriegsschiffes dieser Klaße lag bei zehn 36-Pfundern und sechs 12-Pfundern. Die "S.M.S. Nymphe" lief am 15. April 1863 in Danzig vom Stapel. Zur Zeit des Deutsch-Französischen Krieges (1870 bis 1871) nahm sie an der Seeschlacht von Jasmund (1870) teil, und verteidigte auch Danzig erfolgreich gegen einen französischen Landungsangriff. Zur Zeit des Krieges war die "S.M.S. Medusa" in Yokohama, Japan. Sie wurde im Jahre 1891 in Danzig verschrottet.*

21-22.) The sister ships "S.M.S. Augusta" (1863) and "S.M.S. Viktoria" (1863) were also 3-masted flush-decked wooden sailing corvettes, equipped with auxiliary screw propulsion. They were built by L'Arman Freres of Bordeaux, France, and purchased by the Royal Prussian Navy for commissioning on July 3, 1864. They were carvel-built of oak, had a sail area of 1,600 square meters, and were armed with 8 24-pounders plus 6 long 12-pounders. Each vessel was 81,5 meters long, had a beam of 11,1 meters and a draught of 5,03 meters. They were equipped with 2-cylinder expansion engines built by the firm of Mazeline in Le Havre, France and could make up to 13,5 knots. They were manned by crews of 15 commissioned officers and 215 enlisted sailors. "S.M.S. Augusta" was named after the Queen of Prussia, who was the wife of King Wilhelm I "the Great," who reigned from 1861 until his death in 1888. After 1871, he also reigned as German Emperor, or "Kaiser." During the Franco-Prussian War of 1870-1871, "S.M.S. Augusta" took 3 French ships as prizes, and then took refuge in the Spanish port of Vigo until the end of the war. Sadly, she was lost with all her crew in a hurricane off the Gulf of Aden on June 2, 1885. She had been en route from Germany to Australia.

*Die Schwestersegelkorvetten "S.M.S. Augusta" (1863) und "S.M.S. Viktoria" (1863) wurden von der L'Arman Freres Schiffswerft in Bordeaux, Frankreich gebaut, und wurden am 3. Juli 1864 getauft. Sie waren aus Eichenholz gebaut, hatten je drei Masten, Dampfantrieb, ein Segelbereich von je 1,600 Quadratmeter, waren je 81,5 Meter lang, hatten eine Breite von je 11,1 Meter und einen Tiefgang von je 5,03 Meter. Die Bewaffnung eines Kriegsschiffes dieser*

*Klaße lag bei acht 24-Pfundern und sechs langen 12-Pfundern. Die Höchstgeschwindigkeit lag bei 13,5 Knoten, und die Besatzung dieser Schiffe lag bei 15 Offiziere und 215 Matrosen. Die "S.M.S. Augusta" wurde nach Königin Augusta von Preußen genannt. Zur Zeit des Deutsch-Französischen Krieges (von 1870 bis 1871) hatte sie drei französische Schiffe erobert und reiste dann nach Vigo in Spanien. Am 2. Juni 1885 ging sie in einem Sturm am Golf von Aden verloren, wo alle Besatzungsmitglieder ums Leben kamen. Sie hatte es geplant von Deutschland nach Australien zu reisen.*

### Chapter 19 (Kapitel 19): XIII (38) Old Wooden Sailing Ships of the Hanseatic League / Segelschiffe der Deutschen Hanse: Hamburg – Lübeck - Wismar

The League of (Germanic) Hanseatic League cities were also part of the Holy Roman Empire of the German Nation (800-1806), of which the Habsburg-Lothringen Archduke of Austria was Emperor (or "Kaiser" in German). These cities (of which Hamburg, Bremen, Lübeck and Rostock are the largest), formed the 3rd greatest naval power within the old Holy Roman Empire of the German Nation, or First German Empire ("Erstes Reich" in German). To this day, they still provide Germany with a large supply of able and experienced commercial seafaring personnel. The first Hanseatic League Navies were established by the cities of Hamburg and Lübeck in 1267.

*Die Hanse (auf althochdeutsch "Gruppe," "Gefolge" oder "Schar"), auch "Deutsche Hanse," "Dudesche Hanse" oder "Hansa Teutonica" auf lateinisch genannt, ist die Bezeichnung für die zwischen der Mitte des 12. Jahrhunderts und der Mitte des 17. Jahrhunderts bestehenden Vereinigungen niederdeutscher Kaufleute, deren Ziel die Sicherheit der Überfahrt und die Vertretung gemeinsamer wirtschaftlicher Intereßen besonders im Ausland war. Eine Entwicklung von der "Kaufmannshanse" zu einer "Städtehanse" lässt sich spätestens Mitte des 14. Jahrhunderts mit erstmaligen nahezu gesamthansischen Tagfahrten (Hansetagen) festmachen, in denen sich die Hansestädte zusammenschlossen und die Interessen der niederdeutschen Kaufleute vertraten. Die Farben der Hanse (weiß und rot) finden sich auch heute noch in den Stadtwappen vieler Hansestädte. In den Zeiten ihrer größten Ausdehnung waren beinahe 300 See-und Binnenstädte des nördlichen Europas in der Städtehanse zusammengeschlossen. Eine wichtige Grundlage dieser Verbindungen war die Entwicklung des Transportwesens, insbesondere zur See, weshalb die Segelkoggen zum Symbol der Hanse wurde. Die Hanse war nicht nur auf wirtschaftlichem, sondern auch auf politischem und kulturellem Gebiet ein wichtiger Faktor. "Hanse" nannten sich auch andere Kaufmannsverbünde bis nach Österreich, unabhängig von der großen norddeutschen Hanse.*

1.) "S.M.S. Wissemara" (1354): this single-masted wooden sailing cog is the oldest restored vessel existing in Germany today, available for public viewing. Her name is Latin for the Hanseatic City of Wismar, located on Germany's Baltic Sea coast.

*Die Segelkogge "S.M.S. Wissemara" (1354) ist vielleicht das älteste völlig restaurierte Schiff in Deutschland. Sie hat einen Mast, und man kann das alte Schiff heute in der Hansestadt Wismar besuchen.*

2.) "S.M.S. Bunte Kuh" (1401): this was the fleet flagship of the Free and Hanseatic City of Hamburg, which gained great fame for defeating the pirate ship of Claus Störtebeker in a battle off the island of Helgoland in the German Bay of the North Sea. Her name means "colorful cow" in English.

**Flottenflaggschiff "S.M.S. Bunte Kuh" (1401) / Fleet Flagship "S.M.S. Bunte Kuh" (1401) seen battling the pirate Claus Störtebeker near the Island of Helgoland – painting by Naval artist Günther Todt (1928-2009)**

*Das Segelflottenflaggschiff "S.M.S. Bunte Kuh" (1401) gehörte zur Freien und Hansestadt Hamburg. Die "S.M.S. Bunte Kuh" ist berühmt weil sie das Piratenschiff des Claus Störtebeker vor Helgoland besiegte.*

3.) "S.M.S. Grosser Adler von Lübeck" (1566): her keel was laid down by the Wallhalbinsel Shipyard of Lübeck in 1565. She was launched in March of 1566, and was commissioned in 1567. She displaced up to 3,000 tons full load, which made her the largest ship in the entire world at the time – yet another testimony to the very high level of Germany's naval and nautical technology. She was 78,3 meters long, had a beam of 14,5 meters and a draught of 5,3 meters. Her sail area was 1,794 square meters, and her crew consisted of 1,000 commissioned officers and enlisted men (350 crew for the ship and 650 marine soldiers). She was armed with 138 cannon (52 bronze guns and 86 iron guns). Among these guns were 8-48 pounders, 6-24 pounders, 26-10 pounders, 10-6 pounders, 4-5 pounders, 8-3 pounders, 40-1,5 pounders and 36 miscellaneous guns. The height from her waterline to the top of her main mast was 62,5 meters. She was a Galleon (or Frigate) of the Hanseatic City of Lübeck, located on Germany's Baltic Sea coast. She was the Admiral's fleet flagship from 1566 until 1581. She was scrapped in 1588.

**Segelfregatte "S.M.S. Großer Adler von Lübeck (1566) / Sailing Frigate "S.M.S. Grosser Adler von Lübeck" (1566), fleet flagship of the Hanseatic City of Lübeck from 1566 until 1581 – painting by Naval artist Günther Todt (1928-2009)**

*Die Segelfregatte "S.M.S. Großer Adler von Lübeck" (1566) wurde bei der Wallhalbinsel Schiffswerft in Lübeck auf Kiel gelegt, lief im März 1566 vom*

*Stapel und wurde im Jahre 1567 getauft. Sie hatte eine Einsatzverdrängung von 3,000 Tonnen, und war zur Zeit das größte Schiff der Welt. Sie war 78,3 Meter lang, sie hatte eine Breite von 14,5 Meter und einen Tiefgang von 5,3 Meter. Ihr Segelbereich lag bei 1,794 Quadratmeter, und sie hatte eine Besatzung von 1,000 Offiziere und Matrosen (350 Besatzungsmitglieder des Kriegsschiffes und 650 Marineinfanteristen). Sie war mit 138 Kanonen bewaffnet (52 Bronzkanonen und 86 Eisenkanonen): darin waren acht 48-Pfunder, sechs 24-Pfunder, 26-10 Pfunder, zehn Sechs-Pfunder, vier Fünf-Pfunder, acht Drei-Pfunder, 40-1,5 Pfunder und 36 andere Kanonen. Von der Wasserlinie bis zur Höhe des Masts war sie 62,5 Meter hoch. Von 1566 bis 1581 diente sie als Flottenflaggschiff des Admirals, und sie wurde im Jahre 1588 verschrottet.*

4.) "S.M.S. Wappen von Hamburg" (1669): this was a Heavy Frigate, which served as the first convoy vessel of the Free and Hanseatic City of Hamburg. She served under the command of Admiral Bernd Jacobsen Karpfanger, in the duty of escorting German commerce ships and protecting them from hostile forces, be they pirates or of other nations.

**Schwere Fregatte "S.M.S. Wappen von Hamburg" (1669) / Heavy Frigate "S.M.S. Wappen von Hamburg" (1669) – painting by Naval artist Günther Todt (1928-2009)**

*Die Schwere Segelfregatte "S.M.S. Wappen von Hamburg" (1669) diente als Geleitschiff der Freien und Hansestadt Hamburg unter Admiral Bernd Jacobsen Karpfanger.*

5.) The Elbe Frigate "S.M.S. Stormarn" (1703) had two main and third half (stern) battery decks.  She was based at Neumühlen in Hamburg.

*Die Elbe-Fregatte "S.M.S. Stormarn" (1703) hatte zwei Hauptdecks und ein Halbachterndeck.  Sie war bei Neumühlen in Hamburg stationiert.*

### Chapter 20 (Kapitel 20) PLANNED AIRCRAFT CARRIERS / Geplante Flugzeugträger der Kaiserlichen Marine und der Kriegsmarine

### XIV. "Flugzeugträger" (Aircraft Carriers)

### XIVa. "Graf Zeppelin" Class (1938) / "Graf Zeppelin" Klasse

Germany even had aircraft carriers planned before and during World War Two. The 34,000-ton "Graf Zeppelin" (launched in 1938) was 85% complete but never commissioned. She was capable of an extremely impressive 38,8 knots and was to have been armed with more than 40 aircraft, including the Messerschmitt Bf-109 fighter and the Junkers Ju-87 dive bomber. Steaming radius was 8,000 miles. She was scuttled by the Soviets in the Baltic Sea in 1947, where she remains to this very day. Her sister ship "Peter Strasser" (named for the commanding officer of Germany's Zeppelin airship fleet during World War One) was laid down in 1939 but scrapped due to the outbreak of the war. They were to have been followed by six further sister carriers. Germany had a total of 131 lighter-than-air dirigible Zeppelin airships until the 1930s, most of them built during World War One. They were designed by Count Ferdinand von Zeppelin (1838-1917), who built them in the city of Friedrichshafen on the shore of Lake Constance (the "Bodensee" in German) in Southern Germany. They are still being built today, albeit with much more improved technology that makes them a great deal safer than before.

*Der Flugzeugträger "Graf Zeppelin" (1938) war ein Schiff der deutschen Kriegsmarine, das bedauerlicherweise nicht fertiggestellt wurde. Namensgeber war der Luftschiffpionier Ferdinand Graf von Zeppelin (1838-1917). Der Bauauftrag für den "Flugzeugträger A," die spätere "Graf Zeppelin," wurde am 16. November 1935 an den Werftbetrieb Deutsche Werke AG in Kiel vergeben. Der Bauauftrag für das Schwesterschiff, den Flugzeugträger B ("Peter Straßer"), wurde gleichzeitig an die Friedrich Krupp Germaniawerft AG, ebenfalls in Kiel ansäßig, erteilt. Peter Straßer war der Kommandeur von Deutschlands Zeppelinflotte während des Ersten Weltkrieges. Bis Anfang des Zweiten Weltkrieges wurden 131 Zeppelin-Luftschiffe gebaut. Der Stapellauf des ersten, und bis heute einzigen, deutschen Flugzeugträgers fand am 8. Dezember 1938 statt. Getauft wurde das Schiff von Hella von Zeppelin, der Tochter des Grafen Zeppelin. Der weitere Ausbau des Schiffes wurde im Oktober 1939 zunächst gestoppt. Ende 1942 wurden jedoch noch Veränderungen am Rumpf vorgenommen und man bereitete die Turbinenanlage für ein teilweise Inbetriebnahme vor. Am 2. Februar 1943 wurde jedoch der entgültige Baustopp verfügt. Am 21. April 1943 wurde der unfertige Flugzeugträger nach Stettin in Hinterpommern geschleppt. Hier wurde er, bereits zu 85 Prozent fertiggestellt, am 25. April 1945 von Sprengkommandos versenkt, um zu verhindern, daß er in feindliche rußische Hände geriet. Im März 1947 wurde die Schleppverbindung zur "Graf Zeppelin" kurz vor einem Sturm gelöst, um ein Reißen der Schleppleinen zuvorzukommen. Das Schiff wurde anschließend mit zwei Torpedos 30 Seemeilen vor Großendorf in der Danziger Bucht versenkt, wo es heute noch liegt. Die geplante Einsatzverdrängung der "Graf Zeppelin" war 34,000 Tonnen, und die geplante Höchstgeschwindigkeit war eine sehr gute 38,8 Knoten – schnell auch für heutige Begriffe. Die geplante Bewaffnung des Schiffes war 40 Flugzeuge (das Messerschmitt Bf-109 Jagdflugzeug sowie das Junkers Ju-87 Sturzkampfbombenflugzeug), und die geplante Reichweite des Flugzeugträgers lag bei 8,000 Seemeilen. Die geplante Besatzung des Schiffes war 1,760 Offiziere und Matrosen und dazu 306 Fliegerpersonal. Zwischen 1937 und 1943 wurden mindestens 170 Flugzeuge für Deutschlands geplante Flugzeugträger gebaut. Die Kriegsmarine hatte es vor, eventuell acht Mitglieder der "Graf Zeppelin" Klaße zu bauen. Am 4. September 2004 haben zwei Deutsche (Richard Wagner und Manfred Wilske) ein 1:100 Maßtab Modell der "Graf Zeppelin" hergestellt. Die Vorbereitung, die Planung und die Konstruktion dafür dauerten fast zwei Jahrzehnte.*

In between 1937 and 1943, no fewer than 170 fixed-wing aircraft were manufactured and tested for the purpose of use aboard aircraft carriers in Germany. When one includes such aircraft completed and sold to both Italy and Japan, as well as prototype helicopters, the number of aircraft exceeds 250. These included biplanes such as the Heinkel 50, the Heinkel 66, the Arado 195, the Arado 197 and the Fieseler 167. It also includes more modern monoplanes such as the Messerschmitt 109, the Messerschmitt 155, the Junkers 87, the Arado 96 and the Heinkel 118. Helicopters include the Flettner 265 and the Flettner 282. Two Germans named Richard Wagner and Manfred Wilske recently built a very large and highly detailed 1:100 scale model of the aircraft carrier "Graf Zeppelin," which was "commissioned" on September 4, 2004. The two men put a tremendous amount of research and labor into the project, which took the better part of two decades.

### XIVb. "Hilfsflugzeugträger" (Auxiliary Aircraft Carriers)

Planned civilian conversions into auxiliary aircraft carriers included the passenger liners "Europa" (56,500 tons and with 42 aircraft), the "Potsdam" (23,500 tons and with 24 aircraft) and the "Gneisenau" (18,160 tons and with 23 aircraft). This ship is not to be confused with the entirely different battlecruiser "Gneisenau" of

38,900 tons. "Europa" was commissioned as a passenger liner in 1929, survived World War Two, and was finally scrapped in 1962. "Potsdam" was commissioned as a passenger liner in 1936, also survived the Second World War, and was scrapped in 1976. "Gneisenau" was commissioned as a passenger liner in 1936, but did not survive World War Two. She was sunk by an American submarine in the Pacific Ocean in November 1944.

*Die deutsche Kriegsmarine hatte es auch vor, sogenannte "Hilfsflugzeugträger" umzubauen. Die geplanten Schiffe waren das Passagierschiff "Europa" (eine Einsaztverdrängung von 56,500 Tonnen und 42 Flugzeuge), das Passagierschiff "Potsdam" (eine Einsatzverdrängung von 23,500 Tonnen und 24 Flugzeuge), das Passagierschiff "Gneisenau" (eine Einsatzverdrängung von 18,160 Tonnen und 23 Flugzeuge), der geplante Schwere Kreuzer "Seydlitz" (eine Einsatzverdrängung von 18,000 Tonnen und 18 Flugzeuge) und zuletzt der beschlagnahmte französische geplante Leichte Kreuzer "De Grasse" (eine Einsatzverdrängung von 11,400 Tonnen und 23 Flugzeuge). Nichts geschah, weil die Kriegsmarine für den Zweiten Weltkrieg zu klein war und auch total unvorbereitet war. Flugzeugträger sind doch sehr wichtig, aber Deutschlands Hochseeflotte war einfach zu klein und Deutschland brauchte immer mehr Unterseeboote um einen Handelskrieg gegen Großbrittanien und Amerika zu führen. Das Passagierschiff "Europa" wurde im Jahre 1962 verschrottet, und das Passagierschiff "Potsdam" wurde im Jahre 1976 verschrottet. Das Passagierschiff "Gneisenau" wurde von einem amerikanischen Unterseeboot im November 1944 torpediert. Der geplante Schwere Kreuzer "Seydlitz" wurde im Jahre 1958 verschrottet, und der Leichte Kreuzer "De Grasse" wurde im Jahre 1956 von den Franzosen getauft und im Jahre 1976 endlich verschrottet.*

Other ships to be converted into carriers included the former Heavy Cruiser "Seydlitz" (18,000 tons and with 18 aircraft). This "Seydlitz" was originally to have been a heavy cruiser of the "Admiral Hipper" class. She survived World War Two and was finally scrapped in 1958. The other planned auxiliary aircraft carrier was the captured French light cruiser "De Grasse" (11,400 tons and with 23 aircraft). She was returned to France after World War Two, commissioned into the French Navy as a light cruiser in 1956 and finally scrapped in 1976. One passenger ship to aircraft carrier conversion was even planned during World War One – the "S.M.S. Ausonia" (12,585 tons and with 29 aircraft). This conversion was not completed either, and the ship was finally scrapped in 1922.

*Im Ersten Weltkrieg hatte es die Kaiserliche Marine Deutschlands vor, das Paßagierschiff "Ausonia" auch als Flugzeugträger umzubauen. Die geplante Einsatzverdrängung lag bei 12,585 Tonnen und die geplante Bewaffnung des*

*Schiffes lag bei 29 Flugzeugen. Nichts geschah, und die "Ausonia" wurde im Jahre 1922 endlich verschrottet.*

In today's world, aircraft carriers are the largest active duty ships in any navy. The era of battleships is gone, likely never to return.

## XIVc. "Großflugzeugkreuzer" (Large Aircraft Cruisers)

Perhaps among the most valuable German capital ship design studies which never came to fruition were for future aircraft carriers. In 1942, a number of so-called "Grossflugzeugkreuzer" (literally "large aircraft cruisers" in English) were designed. The two larger ones were to have displaced 70,000 tons each. These were hybrid ships, part battleship in the forward half and part aircraft carrier in the rear or aft half. Primary forward armament would have consisted of either 4-11 inch guns in dual turrets or 6-11 inch guns also in dual turrets. Each ship would have had 32 aircraft as well. Maximum steaming radius would have been a most impressive 20,000 miles and top speed would have been an equally impressive 34 knots.

*Als Flugdeckkreuzer wird ein Typ von Kriegsschiffen bezeichnet, der zwar primär dem Einsatz von Flugzeugen und Hubschraubern dient, aber kein durchgehendes Flugdeck hat. Im Jahre 1942 gab es einige Studien für geplante deutsche Flugdeckkreuzer. Die zwei größten "Großflugzeugkreuzer" hatten je eine Einsatzverdrängung von 70,000 Tonnen und 32 Flugzeuge. Vorne waren sie wie Schlachtschiffe (mit großen Schnellfeuerkanonen) und achtern wie Flugzeugträger. Die geplante Bewaffnung war entweder vier 28-cm Schnellfeuerkanonen oder sechs 28-cm Schnellfeuerkanonen. Die geplante Reichweite war gute 20,000 Seemeilen und die geplante Höchstgeschwindigkeit auch gute 34 Knoten. Die zwei nächsten "Großflugzeugkreuzer" hatten je eine geplante Einsatzverdrängung von 40,000 Tonnen und 23 oder 24 Flugzeuge. Die geplante Bewaffnung (vorne) war entweder sechs 28-cm Schnellfeuerkanonen oder vier 20,3-cm Schnellfeuerkanonen. Die geplante Reichweite eines Schiffes war 18,000 Seemeilen und die geplante Höchstgeschwindigkeit lag bei 34 Knoten. Die drei ehemaligen sowjetrußischen Flugdeckkreuzer der "Kiew" Klaße der 1970er Jahre waren ähnlich, mit einer Einsatzverdrängung von je 43,000 Tonnen und 35 Flugzeuge / Hubschrauber pro Schiff. Es gab auch zwei Vorschläge für kleinere Flugdeckkreuzer. Der erste Vorschlag hatte eine geplante Einsatzverdrängung von 19,150 Tonnen, und eine geplante Bewaffnung von 18 Flugzeuge und acht 15-cm Schnellfeuerkanonen. Die geplante Höchstgeschwindigkeit lag bei 35,5 Knoten. Der zweite Vorschlag hatte eine geplante Einsatzverdrängung von 12,750 Tonnen, und eine geplante Bewaffnung von zehn Flugzeuge und vier 15-cm Schnellfeuerkanonen. Die geplante Höchstgeschwindigkeit lag bei 34 Knoten. Sowjetrußland hatte zwei ehemalige Flugdeckkreuzer der "Moskwa" Klaße der 1960er Jahre, mit einer Einsatzverdrängung von je 19,200 Tonnen und einer Bewaffnung von 18 Hubschrauber. Man kann den Einfluß der geplanten deutschen Flugdeckkreuzer darin sehen.*

There were also two design studies for 40,000 ton "Grossflugzeugkreuzer." Primary foreward armament would have been either 6-11 inch guns in dual turrets or 4-8 inch guns in a single turret. Maximum steaming radius would have been 18,000 miles and top speed an impressive 34 knots. Each vessel would have carried 23 and 24 aircraft, respectively. The post-World War Two Soviet Navy actually did commission similar ships, but armed with missiles instead of cannon. The former "Kiev" class of 3 ships displaced 43,000 tons each and were armed with 35 helicopters and V/STOL (Vertical / Short takeoff and landing) aircraft. The smaller "Moskva" class of 2 ships displaced 19,200 tons each and were armed with 18 ASW (anti-submarine warfare) helicopters. The World War Two "Kriegsmarine" of Germany also designed a 19,150 "Flugdeckkreuzer" (literally "air deck cruiser" in English) armed with 8-6 inch guns plus 18 aircraft. Top speed would have been a very impressive 35,5 knots. I have to believe the Russians were influenced by these old German plans, because both the Western Allies and the Russians raided Germany's superior technology after the war. They took plans for diesel-electric submarines, jet aircraft, rocket engines, ballistic missiles and very large battle tanks. The smallest planned "Flugdeckkreuzer" would have displaced just 12,750 tons and was to have been armed with 4-6 inch guns plus 10 aircraft. Top speed would have been 34 knots. Germany's smallest aircraft carrier plan was for a 6,000 ton ship. This light carrier would have been armed with 8-4 inch guns and up to 15 aircraft. The Western Allies used such ships to escort their merchant convoys, especially in between North America and the British Isles in the North Atlantic Ocean. Such small escort carriers were the single most important factor in defeating the German submarine arm during World War Two, and contributed more than any other weapon to the so-called "Black May" of 1943, when the tide in the Battle of the Atlantic turned against Germany.

*Der kleinste geplante Flugzeugträger der deutschen Kriegsmarine hatte eine geplante Einsatzverdrängung von nur 6,000 Tonnen und eine geplante Bewaffnung von 15 Flugzeuge und acht 10,5 cm Schnellfeuerkanonen. Besonders die Amerikaner haben fiele von solchen "Geleitflugzeugträger" zur Zeit des Zweiten Weltkrieges gebaut, aber die amerikanische Kriegsmarine war jedoch viel größer. Geleitflugzeugträger verteidigten den Seehandel, aber zur Zeit des*

*Zweiten Weltkrieges war Deutschlands Seehandel bedauerlicherweise schon zu gering. Heutzutage ist Deutschlands Seehandel doch sehr groß und auch wichtiger geworden. Flugzeugträger sind heute immer noch sehr wichtige Kriegsschiffe, besonders bei den größeren Seemächten wie Amerika, Großbrittanien, Rußland, Frankreich, Italien, Spanien, Brasilien, Indien und Thailand. Hoffentlich gibt es auch in Deutschlands Zukunft wieder Flugzeugträger.*

In sum, an amazing 9 planned German aircraft carriers already had proposed names – 7 of which were already launched. Germany's political leadership in World Wars One and Two failed to recognize their true value. Germany's senior naval leaders also failed to recognize the true potential of this new weapon. The fact that 9 ships were named and that 7 were actually launched is a testament to the foresight of more middle and junior-level German naval officers.

**Chapter 21 (Kapitel 21): Vessels of the modern German Navy (since 1990), the former West German "Bundesmarine" (1956-1990) and the former East German "Volksmarine" (1956-1990) / die heutige Deutsche Marine (seit 1990), die Bundesmarine (1956-1990) und die Volksmarine der ehemaligen DDR (1956-1990)**

**The "Berlin" and the "Spessart" Class Naval Tenders / die Versorger der Klassen "Berlin" und "Spessart"**

**1. "Berlin" Class (2001) / "Berlin" Klasse (2001)**

The largest vessels in the modern German Navy are the two sister tenders "Berlin" (commissioned in 2001) and "Frankfurt am Main" (commissioned in 2002) of 20,400 tons each. They are each armed with 4-1 inch guns, 2 Surface-to-Air Missiles (SAM) and 2 helicopters on an aft flight deck. They can make up to 20 knots with their diesel engines. They support German combat vessels when deployed far from home, but are not considered to be combat vessels. The most recent Commander of the "Frankfurt am Main" is Fregattenkapitän Stefan Berger, whom I had the opportunity to meet in both 1988 and 1990. He now works as the media spokesman for the German Ministry of Defense in Berlin, serving under Minister of Defense Karl-Theodor zu Guttenberg of Bavaria. A third unit is planned in the "Berlin" class which will be commissioned with the name "Bonn." Bonn served as the capital city of the former West Germany from 1949 until peaceful German reunification in 1990.

*Die größten Schiffe der modernen "Deutschen Marine" sind die zwei Schwester-Einsatzgruppenversorger "Berlin" (2001) und "Frankfurt am Main" (2002). Sie haben je eine Einsatzverdrängung von 20,400 Tonnen, und je eine Bewaffnung von zwei Hubschrauber, zwei Flugzeugabwehrraketen (SAMs) und einer Schnellfeuerkanone. Die Höchstgeschwindigkeit liegt bei 20 Knoten. Einsatzgruppenversorger (EGV) sind Versorgungsschiffe der Deutschen Marine, die der logistischen und sanitätsdienstlichen Unterstützung gemischter Einsatzgruppen dienen. Sie versorgen Kriegsschiffe mit Betriebsstoffen, Verbrauchsgüter, Proviant und Munition und sind so ausgerüstet, daß sie diese Güter während der Fahrt von Schiff zu Schiff übergeben können. Die Hubschrauber dienen dem Transport von Personen und Material. Zur sanitätsdienstlichen Unterstützung führen die EGV ein Marineeinsatzrettungszentrum (MERZ) mit, dessen notfallmedizinische Kapazität etwa der eines Krankenhauses entspricht. In der Bettenstation gibt es 45 Krankenbetten, davon vier Intensivbetten. Das MERZ-System besteht aus einem Verbund von Containern, die nach Bedarf auf dem EGV aufgebaut werden. Beide*

*Schiffe dieser Klaße wurden auf der Werft der Flensburger Schiffbau-Gesellschaft gebaut. Die Beschaffung eines dritten Schiffes wurde am 17. Dezember 2008 bewilligt. Es soll im Jahre 2012 in Dienst gestellt werden und den Namen "Bonn" tragen.*

### 2. "Spessart" Class (1977) / "Spessart" Klasse (1977)

The tankers "Spessart" (commissioned 1977) and "Rhön" (commissioned 1977) of 14,260 tons each do likewise. These tanker ships make merely 16 knots with their diesel engines. The first two tenders are named for large German cities, whereas the latter two tankers are named for famous German rivers. These ships are considered to be large auxiliary vessels of the navy – built to support warships, but not designed for combat themselves. These 2 ships were built by the Kröger Shipyard of Rendsburg, and are 130,2 meters long, have beams of 19,3 meters and draughts of 8,7 meters. Each vessel is powered by a MAK 12-cylinder diesel engine, which drives a single screw and produces up to 8,000 horsepower. Crews consist of just 42 commissioned officers and enlisted men each.

*Die zwei Schwester-Betriebsstofftransporter "Spessart" (1977) und "Rhön" (1977) sind die zweitgrößten Schiffe der modernen "Deutschen Marine." Sie haben eine Einsatzverdrängung von je 14,260 Tonnen, und eine Höchstgeschwindigkeit von 16 Knoten. Sie wurden bei der Kröger Schiffswerft in Rendsburg gebaut, und sind je 130,2 Meter lang, mit einer Breite von 19,3 Meter und einen Tiefgang von 8,7 Meter. Sie sind nicht bewaffnet. Die Besatzung eines Schiffes besteht aus 42 Offiziere und Matrosen.*

## MODERN CAPITAL SHIPS OF THE GERMAN NAVY TODAY / Schiffe der heutigen Deutschen Marine (seit 1990) und der nachkriegs Bundesmarine (1956-1990)

### XV. "Fregatten und Zerstörer" (Frigates and Destroyers)

In modern navies, the largest capital surface warships are now aircraft carriers. The USA has by far largest number, with 12 carriers still on active duty. This is extremely expensive to do, and with the American economy in rapid decline it seems unlikely to continue at this level. The UK is second with merely two carriers, and a number of countries maintain single carriers (such as Russia, France, Italy, Spain, Brazil and Thailand). The only country with battlecuisers is Russia with one active ship (now armed with missiles instead of guns, since missiles replaced guns as the most important primary ship armament after World War Two). A few countries maintain light cruisers, including the USA, Russia,

France and Peru. Most modern navies only build surface combat vessels up to destroyer size, and Germany is among these.

*Die größten Kampfschiffe der modernen "Deutschen Marine" sind die Fregatten. Deutschlands moderne Fregatten sind die größten und auch die besten Fregatten der Welt, so groß und so gut wie die Zerstörer anderer Kriegsmarinen. Deutschland hat leider keine modernen Flugzeugträger oder Kreuzer. Nur Amerika, Rußland, Frankreich und Peru haben noch Kreuzer, die größer als Fregatten oder Zerstörer sind.*

### XVa. "Baden-Württemberg" Class (2009) / "Baden-Württemberg" Klasse (2009)

The modern air-defense frigates of the "Baden-Württemberg" class (6,800 tons each) will be the largest combat vessels to be commissioned into the German Navy since World War Two. In other navies, these would be called destroyers, but the German Navy has chosen a different nomenclature for political reasons (they feel "frigate" sounds less threatening than "destroyer"). The first member of this class is scheduled to join the fleet in 2014. Each of the four planned new ships will be armed with 8 Surface-to-Surface Missiles (SSM) and two anti-submarine helicopters (the flight deck and hangar / elevator are located aft). They will be able to make up to 28 knots with their diesel engines and turbines. "Baden-Württemberg" is the name of the modern German State of Baden-Wuerttemberg, located in Southwestern Germany. 4 units of this class are currently planned, but 38 "call" or "pennant" numbers are available in between this class and the "Braunschweig" class of modern corvettes. Thus far, two names have been chosen for this new class of ships: for the "Baden-Württemberg" herself (pennant number F223) and for her first sister ship the "Nordrhein-Westfalen" (pennant number F224). North Rhine-Westphalia is a large and populous state in Northwestern Germany.

*Die "Baden-Württemberg" (2009) Klaße (auch Klaße 125 oder Fregatte 125 genannt) ist eine neue Klaße von Fregatten der Deutschen Marine, von denen derzeit die erste Einheit gebaut wird. Hersteller der Fregatten ist die ARGE F125 (Arbeitsgemeinschaft Fregatte 125), bestehend aus der ThyssenKrupp Marine Systeme AG (aus Hamburg) und der Friedrich Lürssen Werft GmbH & Company KG (aus Bremen). Die Kriegsschiffe dieser Klaße (die größten Fregatten der Welt) werden eine Einsatzverdrängung von je 6,800 Tonnen haben. Sie werden 145,6 Meter lang sein, mit einer Breite von 18,4 Meter und einen Tiefgang von 5 Meter. Die Höchstgeschwindigkeit wird bei 28 Knoten liegen, und die Reichweite bei 4,000 Seemeilen. Die geplante Bewaffnung pro Schiff liegt bei acht*

*Schiffabwehrraketen (SSM), 42 Flugzeugabwehrraketen (RAM), zehn
Schnellfeuerkanonen und zwei Bordhubschrauber. Die geplante Besatzung ist
170 Offiziere und Matrosen pro Einheit. Das zweite Mitglied dieser Klaße wird
"Nordrhein-Westfalen" (F224) heißen.*

## XVb. "Sachsen" Class (2003) / "Sachsen" Klasse (2003)

The largest air-defense frigates now in active German naval service are the trio of
the "Sachsen" (2003), the "Hamburg" (2004) and the "Hessen" (2006), which are
of 5,960 tons maximum displacement each. They are the largest frigates in the
world, comparable to destroyers of other navies and comparable to the light
cruisers of World War Two. All four ships are named for German states.
"Sachsen" is German for "Saxony," Hamburg is one of modern Germany's City-
States and a Hanseatic City as well and "Hessen" is German for "Hesse" or
"Hessia." Each ship of this class is armed with 8 Surface-to-Surface Missiles
(SSM) and one anti-submarine helicopter (the flight deck and hangar / elevator
are located aft). They can make up to 28 knots with their diesel engines and
turbines.

*"F124" ist die marineinterne Bezeichnung für die Fregatten der zweiten
"Sachsen" (2003) Klaße der Deutschen Marine. Typschiff ist die Fregatte
"Sachsen" (F219), die nach intensiver Erprobung Anfang November 2004 in
Dienst gestellt wurde. Die Klaße umfaßt noch die beiden Schwesterschiffe
"Hamburg" (Indienstellung am 13. Dezember 2004) und "Hessen"
(Indienstellung am 21. April 2006). Die "Sachsen" Klaße ersetzt die drei
Zerstörer der Klaße 103B (die nachfolgende "Lütjens" Klaße von 1969), die bis
2003 außer Dienst gestellt wurden. Die drei modernen Fregatten der "Sachsen"
Klaße sind als Mehrzweckfregatten konzipiert, die zum Geleitschutz und zur
Gebietssicherung eingesetzt werden können sowie sehr effektiv feindliche
Flugzeuge und andere Flugkörper abwehren können. Die Sensoren und
Effektoren dieser Kriegssschiffe sind auf Verbandsführung und
Verbandsflugzeugabwehr optimiert, welches die Hauptaufgaben dieses
Fregattentyps darstellen. Die drei Einheiten der "Sachsen" Klaße haben eine
Einsatzverdrängung von je 5,960 Tonnen, und sind mit acht Schiffabwehrraketen
(SSM) und einen Bordhubschrauber ausgerüstet. Die Höchstgeschwindigkeit
liegt bei 28 Knoten.*

## XVc. "Lütjens" Class (1969) / "Lütjens" Klasse (1969)

After the large modern frigates come the three destroyers of the "Lütjens" (1969)
class (4,720 tons each), based upon the "U.S.S. Charles F. Adams" class. The

"Lütjens" (named for Admiral Günter Lütjens who went down with the battleship "Bismarck" in May 1941) is now in reserve, while the "Mölders" (commissioned in 1969 and named for the great fighter ace Werner Mölders of the German Air Force or "Luftwaffe" in World War Two) is a museum ship in Germany's main North Sea base of Wilhelmshaven. The "Rommel" (commissioned in 1970 and named for Field Marshall Erwin Rommel who commanded Germany's "Afrika Korps" in North Africa during World War Two) was recently scrapped. Each ship is armed with 40 Surface-to-Surface Missiles (SSM), 2 Surface-to-Air Missles (SAM) and 8 Anti-Submarine Rockets (ASROC). Top speed is an impressive 36 knots with diesel engines and turbines. These vessels were built by the Bath Iron Works of Bath, Maine (USA). They are 134,4 meters long, have a beam of 14,38 meters and a draught of 6,4 meters. They are equipped with both radar and sonar, are powered by 4 boilers which drive 2 screws, and can produce up to 70,000 horsepower. They can carry up to 900 tons of fuel oil, and have a range of operations of up to 6,000 nautical miles. Their crews consist of 39 commissioned officers and 319 enlisted men each.

*Die "Lütjens" (1969) der Deutschen Marine war ein Zerstörer und Typschiff der Klaße 103B (die "Lütjens" Klaße), einer Modifikation der amerikanischen "Charles F. Adams" Klaße. Das Kriegsschiff wurde nach dem deutschen Admiral Günther Lütjens benannt, der im Zweiten Weltkrieg mit dem Schlachtschiff "Bismarck" im Mai 1941 unterging. Es wurde am 18. Dezember 2003 außer Dienst gestellt. Der Zerstörer war mehr als 30 Jahre in Diensten der Deutschen Marine und nahm an zahlreichen Übungen im Rahmen der NATO teil. Das Schiff legte in 35 Jahren über 800,000 Seemeilen zurück. Heimathafen war Kiel. Seit 2006 befand sich das Schiff mit Hilfe von Schleppern im Marinestützpunkt Wilhelmshaven bei der Wehrtechnischen Dienststelle 71 für Sprengversuche. Dort soll das Schiff zum Verkauf über die bundeseigene Verwertungsgesellschaft "VEBEG" vorbereitet werden. Die zwei Schwesterschiffe der "Lütjens" (D185) sind die "Mölders" (D186) und die "Rommel" (D187). Der Zerstörer "Mölders" ist seit den 28. Mai 2003 außer Dienst gestellt und ist nun als Museum in Wilhelmshaven zu sehen. Werner Mölders (1913 bis 1941) war ein deutscher Luftwaffenoffizier und Fliegerass im Zweiten Weltkrieg. Er war einer der beliebtesten Jagdflieger im Deutschland und einer der höchstdekorierten Helden der Luftwaffe. Der Zestörer "Rommel" wurde im Jahre 1998 ausser Dienst gestellt und dann im Jahre 2004 abgewrackt. Johannes Erwin Eugen Rommel (1891 bis 1944) war deutscher Heeresoffizier, seit 1942 Generalfeldmarschall. Er ist Vater des langjährigen Stuttgarter Oberbürgermeisters Manfred Rommel (CDU). Die drei Einheiten dieser Klaße wurden bei Bath Iron Works in Maine (USA) gebaut. Sie haben eine Einsatzverdrängung von je 4,720 Tonnen, sind je 134,4 Meter lang, haben eine*

*Breite von je 14,38 Meter und einen Tiefgang von je 6,4 Meter. Die Höchstgeschwindigkeit liegt bei 36 Knoten und die Reichweite bei 6,000 Seemeilen. Die Besatzung dieser Schiffe bestand aus je 39 Offiziere und 319 Matrosen. Die Bewaffnung einer Einheit bestand aus 40 Schiffabwehrraketen, (SSM), zwei Flugzeugabwehrraketen (RAM) und acht Unterseebootabwehrraketen (ASROC).*

### XVd. "Hamburg" Class (1959) / "Hamburg" Klasse (1959)

The "Hamburg" (1959) class of postwar destroyers also included the "Schleswig-Holstein" (1959), the "Bayern" (1960) and the "Hessen" (1961). They were all named after states of the Federal Republic of Germany, and displaced up to 4,700 tons full load. They were built by the H.C. Stückeln Shipyard in Hamburg (Germany's largest seaport), and could make up to 35 knots. Each ship was 133,7 meters long, had a beam of 13,4 meters and a draught of 5,2 meters. Armament consisted of 4 "Exocet" Surface-to-Surface Missiles (SSM), 3 100-mm and 8 40-mm anti-aircraft guns. They were also equipped with 4 533-mm torpedo tubes and 2 375-mm "Bofors" Anti-Submarine Warfare Rocket Launchers (ASWRL) plus up to 80 mines. They also had radar, sonar and Electronic Countermeasures (ECM). They were powered by 4 boilers which drove 2 screws, and which produced up to 68,000 horsepower. Range of operations was up to 6,000 nautical miles, and total crew consisted of 280 commissioned officers and enlisted men. The ships had been decommissioned by 1984, and were scrapped shortly thereafter. My cousin Gerd Nonnenkamp served aboard the "Hamburg" for a good number of years.

**Shanty Choir Marinekameradschaft Barsinghausen (a Naval Veterans Organization), led by my cousin Gerd Nonnenkamp (Shanty Choirs are popular in Germany, Austria, Switzerland and Scandinavia (Denmark, Iceland, Norway, Sweden and Finland) – photo courtesy of Gerd Nonnenkamp**

*Die "Hamburg" (1959) Klaße (auch Klaße 101, nach Umbau Klaße 101A) war eine Klaße von Zerstörern der Bundesmarine, die Ende der 1950er Jahre und Anfang der 1960er Jahre gebaut wurde. Die vier Einheiten der "Hamburg" Klaße waren bis Mitte der 1990er Jahre im Dienst und gehörten mit einer Verdrängung von je 4,700 Tonnen zu den größten Schiffen der damaligen Bundesmarine. Sie wurden bei der H.C. Stückeln Schiffswerft in Hamburg gebaut. Die drei anderen Mitglieder der "Hamburg" Klaße hießen "Schleswig-Holstein" (1959), "Bayern" (1960) und "Hessen" (1961). Sie waren je 133,7*

*Meter lang, hatten eine Breite von je 13,4 Meter, einen Tiefgang von 5,2 Meter und die Höchstgeschwindigkeit lag bei 35 Knoten. Die Bewaffnung eines Schiffes war vier "Exocet" Schiffabwehrraketen (SSM), drei 100-mm und acht 40-mm Flugzeugabwehrkanonen (FLAK), vier 533-mm Torpedorohre, zwei 375-mm "Bofors" Unterseebootabwehrraketen (ASWRL) sowie 80 Minen. Die Reichweite eines Schiffes war 6,000 Seemeilen, und die Besatzung bestand aus 280 Offiziere und Matrosen. Im Jahre 1984 wurden die vier Einheiten dieser Klaße außer Dienst gestellt, und die Abwrackung folgte kurz danach. Mein Vetter Gerd Nonnenkamp aus Barsinghausen in Niedersachsen diente auf dem Zerstörer "Hamburg," und leitet heute das Shantykorps der Marinekameradschaft Barsinghausen.*

### XVe. "Bremen" Class (1982) / "Bremen" Klasse (1982)

The backbone of the modern German fleet are the eight smaller guided missile frigates of the "Bremen" class (3,800 tons each). They are very similar to the Dutch "Kortenaer" class frigates. They include the "Bremen" (1982), the "Niedersachsen" (1982), the "Rheinland-Pflalz" (1983), the "Emden" (1983), the "Köln" (1984), the "Karlsruhe" (1984), the "Augsburg" (1989) and the "Lübeck" (1990). Each ship is armed with 8 Surface-to-Surface Missiles (SSM), 24 Surface-to-Air Missiles (SAM) and one 76 mm anti-aircraft gun. They can make up to 30 knots and are powered with a combination of diesel engines and turbines. Each ship is 130 meters long, has a beam of 14,4 meters and a draught of 4,26 meters. They are equipped with radar, sonar and Electronic Countermeasures (ECM). They are powered by 2 General Electric turbines, plus 2 MTU diesel engines, which drive 2 5-bladed screws and which can produce up to 60,400 horsepower. Range of operations is up to 4,000 nautical miles, and crews consist of 21 commissioned officers and 160 enlisted men (plus 6 commissioned officers and 12 enlisted men for the air crew). The air crew operate 2 Lynx Mark 88 Anti-Submarine Warfare (ASW) helicopters.

*"F122" ist die marineinterne Bezeichnung für die acht Fregatten der "Bremen" (1982) Klaße der Deutschen Marine. Typschiff ist die Fregatte "Bremen," die am 9. Juli 1979 auf Kiel gelegt und am 7. Mai 1982 als erstes von acht Kriegsschiffen in Dienst gestellt wurde. Der Schiffsentwurf leitet sich von der niederländischen "Kortenaer" Klaße ab. Die Schiffe der "Bremen" Klaße sind heute in Wilhelmshaven stationiert und bilden das 4. Fregattengeschwader der Deutschen Marine. Die sieben anderen Mitglieder dieser Klaße sind die "Niedersachsen" (1982), die "Rheinland-Pfalz" (1983), die "Emden" (1983), die "Köln" (1984), die "Karlsruhe" (1984), die "Augsburg" (1989) und die "Lübeck" (1990). Sie haben eine Einsatzverdrängung von je 3,800 Tonnen. Die Bewaffnung dieser*

*Schiffe besteht aus je acht Schiffabwehrraketen (SSM), 24
Flugzeugabwehrraketen (SAM), einer Flugzeugabwehrkanone (FLAK) und zwei
Unterseebootabwehr-Bordhubschrauber Typ "Lynx Mark 88." Die
Höchstgeschwindigkeit liegt bei 30 Knoten und die Reichweite bei 4,000
Seemeilen. Sie sind je 130 Meter lang, haben eine Breite von je 14,4 Meter und
einen Tiefgang von je 4,26 Meter. Die Besatzung eines Schiffes besteht aus 21
Offiziere und 160 Matrosen (und sechs Offiziere und 12 Matrosen
Marinefliegerpersonal).*

Bremen is a coastal city-state in Northern Germany and one of Germany's
Hanseatic cities. Niedersachsen ("Lower Saxony" in English) is also one of
modern Germany's states, located in Northern Germany. Lower Saxony is mostly
Evangelical-Lutheran, like much of Northern Germany. It was formed out of the
former Kingdom of Hanover, the Grand Duchy of Oldenburg and the Duchy of
Brunswick. Rheinland-Pfalz ("Rhineland-Palatinate" in English) is a mostly
Roman Catholic State in Southern Germany, and the home of former Chancellor
Helmut Kohl, who held office from 1982 until 1998. "Emden" is a coastal port
city on the North Sea, and part of East Frisia in Lower Saxony, a very
Evangelical-Lutheran region. Köln ("Cologne" in French and English) is a very
large mostly Roman Catholic city along the Rhine River, and the home of the late
Chancellor Konrad Adenauer, who held national office from 1949 until 1963.
Karlsruhe was the capital city of the old Grand Duchy of Baden, now part of the
German State of Baden-Württemberg in mostly Roman Catholic Southern
Germany. Augsburg is a city in the South German Free State of Bavaria, which is
Germany's largest Roman Catholic State. Lübeck is one of Germany's coastal
Hanseatic cities, located on the Baltic Sea in the mostly Evangelical-Lutheran
State of Schleswig-Holstein. In German-speaking Europe, the Western and
Southern regions are mostly Roman Catholic, whereas the Eastern and Northern
areas are mostly Evangelical-Lutheran. This division has held since the turbulent
time of the Protestant Reformation in 1517, and the Roman Catholic regions are
also those which were ruled by the old Roman Empire in antiquity.

### XVf. "Köln" Class (1958) / "Köln" Klasse (1958)

The "Köln" (1958) class of 6 postwar German frigates also included the
"Karlsruhe" (1958), the "Emden" (1958), the "Augsburg" (1958), the "Lübeck"
(1959) and the "Braunschweig" (1960). They were built by the H.C. Stückeln
Shipyard of Hamburg, and each displaced up to 2,970 tons full load. They could
make up to 30 knots, were 109,83 meters long, had a beam of 10,5 meters and a
draught of 4,61 meters. Armament consisted of 2 100-mm and 6 40-mm guns,
plus 2 375-mm "Bofors" Anti-Submarine Warfare Rocket Launchers (ASWRL).

Each ship also had 4 533-mm torpedo tubes and 82 mines, plus radar and sonar. They were powered by 4 M.A.N. V-16 cylinder diesel engines, plus 2 Brown-Boveri gas turbines, which produced a total of 36,000 horsepower for 2 screws. Each ship carried up to 333 tons of fuel oil, and range of operations was up to 2,700 nautical miles. Crews consisted of 17 commissioned officers and 193 enlisted men each. One of these ships is still in the German Navy today, with the remainder having been scrapped or sold to the Turkish Navy.

*"F120" bezeichnet eine ehemalige Fregattenklaße der Bundesmarine, auch benannt nach ihrem Typschiff "Köln" (1958) Klaße. Sechs dieser Schiffe wurden zwischen 1961 und 1964 in Dienst gestellt. Zusammen mit den Zerstörern der "Hamburg" (1959) Klaße waren sie die ersten Neubauten für die nachkriegs Bundesmarine. Entwickelt wurden sie bei H.C. Stückeln & Sohn in Hamburg. Als Aufgaben waren Geleitaufgaben, aber vorwiegend Unterseebootjagd vorgesehen. Die Schiffe wurden zunächst als "Geleitboot 55" bezeichnet und dem 2. Geleitgeschwader in Cuxhaven zugeordnet. Am 3. April 1968 wurde das 2. Geleitgeschwader von Cuxhaven nach Wilhelmshaven verlegt. Die "Emden" (1958) und die "Karlsruhe" (1958) schieden aus dem Geschwader aus und traten vorübergehend dem Flottendienstgeschwader in Flensburg bei, von dem die "Karlsruhe" am 1. Oktober 1973, und die "Emden" am 1. April 1974 wieder zum 2. Geleitgeschwader zurückkehrten. Zwischen 1982 und 1989 wurden die Fregatten der "Köln" Klaße außer Dienst gestellt. Die "Augsburg" (1958) wurde verschrottet, die "Köln" in der Lehrgruppe Schiffssicherung Neustadt als Übungsprojekt verwendet, die Fregatten "Emden" (1958), "Karlsruhe" (1958), "Lübeck" (1959) und "Braunschweig" (1960) wurden an die türkische Kriegsmarine verkauft. Die Kriegsschiffe dieser Klaße haben eine Einsatzverdrängung von je 2,970 Tonnen. Die Höchstgeschwindigkeit liegt bei 30 Knoten und die Reichweite bei 2,700 Seemeilen. Sie sind je 109,83 Meter lang, haben eine Breite von je 10,5 Meter und einen Tiefgang von 4,61 Meter. Die Bewaffnung dieser Schiffe besteht aus je zwei 100-mm Schnellfeuerkanonen in Einzellafetten, sechs 40-mm Flugzeugabwehrkanonen (FLAK) in Doppellafetten, zwei 375-mm "Bofors" Unterseebootabwehrraketen (ASWRL), vier 533-mm Torpedorohre und 82 Minen. Eine Besatzung besteht aus 17 Offiziere und 193 Matrosen.*

### XVg. "Rostock" Class (1978) / "Rostock" Klasse (1978)

The former East Germany (the so-called "German Democratic Republic" which was actually Communist) had three guided missile frigates of the "Rostock" class which displaced 1,900 tons each. The ships were based upon the Russian "Koni" class frigates, and were named "Rostock" (1978), "Halle" (1979) and "Berlin

Haupstadt der DDR" (commissioned in 1979 and named "Berlin, capital city of the German Democratic Republic" in English). Each vessel was armed with 20 Surface-to-Surface Missiles (SSM), 2 depth charge-launchers plus 4-76 mm and 4-30 mm anti-aircraft guns. They could make up to 30 knots with their diesel engines. Rostock is a Hanseatic city on the Baltic Sea, Halle is an inland city and Berlin is of course the current capital of the Federal Republic of Germany ("Bundesrepublik Deutschland") which the Western Allies established out of the American, British and French zones of occupation in 1949. The former East Germany reunified peacefully with Western Germany in 1990.

*Es gab drei ehemalige Fregatten der sowjetrußischen "Koni" Klaße unter der Flagge der ehemaligen Deutschen Demokratischen Republik (DDR). Sie hießen "Rostock" (1978), "Halle" (1979) und "Berlin Hauptstadt der DDR" (1979), und hatten eine Einsatzverdrängung von je 1,900 Tonnen. Mit der Wiedervereinigung des Deutschen Vaterlandes wurden die Schiffe mit NATO-Kennung zunächst von der Bundesmarine übernommen, wenig später jedoch außer Dienst gestellt und im Marinehafen von Peenemünde aufgelegt. Die Bewaffnung dieser Schiffe bestand aus je 20 Schiffabwehrraketen (SSM), zwei Wasserbomben-Werfer, vier 76-mm sowie vier 30-mm Flugzeugabwehrkanonen (FLAK). Die Höchstgeschwindigkeit lag bei 30 Knoten.*

## XVh. "Gneisenau" Class (1958) / "Gneisenau" Klasse (1958)

The postwar Navy of the former Western Germany (the "Bundesmarine") had seven training frigates of the "Gneisenau" (1958) class, each of which displaced 1,350 tons and was armed with 6-4 inch guns and 4-1,5 inch guns. They could only make up to 27,5 knots with their diesel engines, which explains why they were only used for training. The other ships of this class were the "Scharnhorst" (1959), the "Admiral Hipper" (1959), the "Graf Spee" (1959), the "Scheer" (1959), the "Raule" (1959) and the "Brommy" (1959). The first five ships were obviously named after famous namesakes of World Wars One and Two. "Raule" was named after Benjamin Raule (1634-1707), general director of the Brandenburg Navy from 1676-1698. "Brommy" was named after German Rear Admiral Karl Rudolf Brommy (1804-1860). Brommy served in the Chilean Navy from 1822-1825, in the Brazilian Navy from 1825-1827, in the Greek Navy from 1827-1849, in the Prussian Navy from 1849-1853 and in the Austrian Navy until his death in 1860. Back then, it was not uncommon for both officers and enlisted men to serve for pay in foreign militaries as so-called "mercenaries."

*Während ihrer Aufbauphase hatte die damalige deutsche Bundesmarine ab 1958 insgesamt sieben Fregatten in Betrieb, die unter dem Oberbegriff "Schulfregatte*

*Klaße 138" bezeichnet wurden. Sie wurden gebraucht vom England erworben (sie gehörten zur britischen "Hunt" Klaße von 1939). Benannt wurden sie in der damaligen Tradition nach ehemaligen Militärs vorgehender Armeen beziehungsweise Kriegsmarine Brandenburg-Preußens sowie Deutschlands. Die sieben Einheiten gehörten zu zwei Klaßen beziehungsweise drei Unterklaßen. Sie hießen "Gneisenau" (F212), "Scharnhorst" (F213), "Hipper" (F214), "Graf Spee" (F215), "Scheer" (F216), "Raule" (F217) und "Brommy" (F218), und wurden im Jahre 1968 außer Dienst gestellt. Sie hatten eine Einsatzverdrängung von je 1,350 Tonnen, und waren mit je sechs 10,5-cm Schnellfeuerkanonen, vier 4-cm Schnellfeuerkanonen, zwei 20-mm Flugzeugabwehrkanonen (FLAK) sowie mit 40 Wasserbomben ausgerüstet. Die Höchstgeschwindigkeit lag bei 27,5 Knoten, und die Reichweite bei 3,500 Seemeilen. Sie waren je 85 Meter lang, hatten eine Breite von je 8,8 Meter und einen Tiefgang von 3,27 Meter. Die Besatzung dieser Schiffe bestand aus 146 Offiziere und Matrosen. Benjamin Raule (1634-1707) war ein niederländischer Reeder und kurbrandenburgischer Generalmarinedirektor. Er entstammte einer hugenottischen Familie aus dem Teil Flanderns, der heute zu Frankreich gehört. Seine Familie hatte sich von Dünkirchen und dann von Zeeland aus als Freibeuter ein einträgliches Leben erwirtschaftet. Raule wandte sich 1675 nach Brandenburg, das sich zwischen 1674 und 1678 im Krieg mit Schweden befand, und bot Kurfürst Friedrich Wilhelm, dem Großen Kurfürsten, die Dienste seiner Korsaren an. Er erhielt von Friedrich Wilhelm einen Kaperbrief, der ihm die Wegnahme schwedischer und niederländischer Schiffe, die Schweden versorgten, erlaubte. Brandenburg war auf derartige Hilfe gegen die Seemacht Schweden angewiesen, da es kaum über eigene Seestreitkräfte verfügte. Nach einigen Erfolgen und Rückschlägen wurde Raule im Jahre 1676 mit dem Aufbau der kurbrandenburgischen Kriegsmarine beauftragt. Er ließ den Kaperkrieg fortsetzen und erzielte einige spektakuläre Erfolge im Kaperkrieg gegen Spanien. Zugleich engagierte er sich für den Aufbau von Handelsbeziehungen nach Übersee und gründete im Jahre 1682 die "Brandenburgisch-Afrikanische Compagnie," die im Jahre 1684 ihren Hauptsitz mit insgesamt 30 Handels-und 10 Kriegsschiffen von Königsberg in Ostpreußen nach Emden in Ostfriesland verlegte und als Schiffe-und Geldgeber die kolonialen Bestrebungen des Großen Kurfürsten unterstützte. An der guineischen Goldküste im heutigen Ghana errichtete Otto Friedrich von der Groeben eine Kolonie und hißte dort am 1. Januar 1683 die brandenburgischen Flagge. Er gründete im gleichen Jahre "Großfriedrichsburg" beim Cape Three Points (Ghana) als Hauptniederlassung. Weitere Stützpunkte befanden sich auf den Arguin-Inseln im heutigen Mauretanien (Nordafrika) und auf der Insel Sankt Thomas, heute zu den U.S.-Jungferninseln gehörig. Karl Rudolf Brommy (1804 in Anger bei Leipzig als "Karl Rudolf Bromme" geboren und 1860 in Sankt Magnus gestorben) war ein*

*Marineoffizier und deutscher Admiral. Er war Befehlshaber der ersten gesamtdeutschen Reichsflotte (1848-1852).*

This "Gneisenau" class was based upon the British "Hunt" class destroyer of 1939. Each ship was 85 meters long, had a beam of 8,8 meters and a draught of 3,27 meters. They were powered by 2 diesel boilers which drove 2 shafts, producing up to 19,000 horsepower. Range was up to 3,500 nautical miles, and crews consisted of 146 commissioned officers and enlisted men. Each vessel was armed with 4 4-inch guns, 4 2-pounder guns, 2 20-mm Oerlikon anti-aircraft guns and 40 anti-submarine depth charges.

## XVI. "Korvetten" (Corvettes)

The smallest major surface units of the modern German Navy are the five brand new corvettes of the "Braunschweig" (2006) class (1,840 tons each and incorporating modern stealth technology much like the "Sachsen" and "Baden-Württemberg" class frigates). The four other ships of this class include the "Magdeburg" (2008), the "Erfurt" (2008), the "Oldenburg" (2008) and the "Ludwigshafen am Rhein" (2008). Each ship is armed with 4 Surface-to-Surface Missiles (SSM) and one anti-submarine helicopter (flight deck and hangar / elevator are located aft). They can make up to 26 knots with their diesel engines and turbines. All are named after large German cities, and many have namesakes from the past. Corvettes are smaller than destroyers or frigates, but larger than fast attack craft or patrol craft.

*Die fünf Korvetten der zweiten "Braunschweig" (2006) Klaße (auch "Klaße 130" genannt) sind als Ergänzung für die Schnellboote der Deutschen Marine in der Beschaffung. Sie stellen eine neue Klaße zwischen großen Schnellbooten und kleinen Fregatten dar, verfügen über eine Reihe technischer Innovationen und sind somit ein für die Marine neues Waffensystem, was auch in der Klaßifizierung als Korvette zum Ausdruck kommt. Wichtigste Aufgaben werden die Seeraumüberwachung, Aufklärung und Bekämpfung von See-und Landzielen sein. Unterseebootjagt ist nicht vorgesehen, weshalb die Korvette K130 nicht mit Sonar zur Jagd von Unterseebooten ausgestattet ist. Die vier anderen Mitglieder dieser Klaße heißen "Magdeburg" (2008), "Erfurt" (2008), "Oldenburg" (2008) und "Ludwigshafen am Rhein" (2008). Sie haben eine Einsatzverdrängung von je 1,840 Tonnen, und sind mit je vier Schiffabwehrraketen (SSM) ausgerüstet. Die Höchstgeschwindigkeit liegt bei 26 Knoten.*

## XVIa. "Hans Bürkner" Class / "Hans Bürkner" Klasse

The "Hans Bürkner" displaced 1,348 tons and was armed with anti-submarine warfare rocket launchers (ASWRL) plus one 37,5 mm anti-aircraft gun. Her top speed was just 24 knots, which illustrates her prototype nature. She was the sole ship of her class and has since been scrapped.

*Die ehemalige Fregatte "Hans Bürkner" wurde als Einzelschiff und Prototyp der Bundesmarine gebaut. Sie hatte eine Einsatzverdrängung von 1,348 Tonnen und ihre Höchstgeschwindigkeit lag bei 24 Knoten. Ihre Bewaffnung bestand aus einer 37,5-mm Flugzeugabwehrkanone (FLAK) und einige Unterseebootabwehrraketen (ASWRL oder "Anti-Submarine Warfare Rocket Launchers" auf englisch).*

## XVIb. "Parchim" Class (1981) / "Parchim" Klasse (1981)

The former navy of Eastern Germany had sixteen corvettes of the "Parchim" class commissioned from 1981 to 1984, each of which displaced 1,200 tons and was armed with 2-57 mm guns plus 2-30 mm guns. These vessels could make up to 25 knots with their diesel engines. These ships have since been sold to the Indonesian Navy and still serve there today. All ships were named for cities in the former East Germany, and were built by the Peenewerft Shipyard of Wolgast on the Baltic Sea coast. They include the "Gadebusch," the "Grevesmühlen," the "Bergen," the "Angermünde," the "Lübz," the "Bad Doberan," the "Güstrow," the "Waren," the "Prenzlau," the "Ludwigslust," the "Ribnitz-Damgarten," the "Teterow," the "Wismar," the "Perleberg" and the "Bützow." The new Federal German states in the former East Germany are now named Mecklenburg-Vorpommern ("Mecklenburg-Near Pomerania" in English), Sachsen-Anhalt ("Saxony-Anhalt" in English), Sacshen ("Saxony" in English), Thüringen ("Thuringia" in English), Brandenburg and of course the reunited German capital city of Berlin. The "Wismar" was named after a cog of the Middle Ages, commissioned in 1354 and recently raised and restored. The original ship is on public display in the coastal city of Wismar, located on the Baltic Sea. Her name was "S.M.S. Wissemara," which is the Latin name for Wismar.

*Die "Parchim" (1981) Klaße ist eine Unterseebootjagdschiff-Klaße in Korvettengröße, die ab 1981 von der Volksmarine der ehemaligen Deutschen Demokratischen Republik ("Ostdeutschland") und der ehemaligen sowjetrußischen Kriegsmarine in Gebrauch war. Die 16 Schiffe der ehemaligen DDR wurden im Jahre 1993 an Indonesien verkauft. Die "Parchim" Klaße* wurde in den 1970er Jahren auf der Peenewerft Wolgast als "Projekt 133.1" geplant und bis 1985 gebaut. Diese Kriegsschiffe sollten die veralteten Schiffe der "Hai" Klaße ersetzen. Die Planungen des ehemaligen Warschauer Pakts für einen Ernstfall im Kalten Krieg sahen für die Volksmarine der DDR ausgedehnte Anti-Unterseeboot Operationen in Küstengewässer vor. Aus diesem Grund wurden in den 1970er Jahren diese modernen Kriegsschiffe für küstennahe Einsätze gebaut. Die Schiffe dieser Klaße haben eine Einsatzverdrängung von je 1,200 Tonnen und sind mit zwei 57-mm sowie mit zwei 30 mm Schnellfeuerkanonen bewaffnet. Die Höchstgeschwindigkeit liegt bei 25 Knoten. Die 15 anderen Mitglieder dieser Klaße hießen zur Zeit der Volksmarine "Gadebusch," "Grevesmühlen," "Bergen," "Angermünde," "Lübz," "Bad Doberan," "Güstrow," "Waren," "Prenzlau," "Ludwigslust," "Ribnitz-Damgarten," "Teterow," "Wismar," "Perleberg" und "Bützow."

## XVIc. "Thetis" Class (1961) / "Thetis" Klasse (1961)

The five corvettes of the "Thetis" (1961) class displaced 658 tons each and were armed with 2-40 mm guns and one 37,5 mm anti-submarine warfare rocket launcher (ASWRL). They could make up to 23,5 knots with their diesel engines, and have since been sold to the Greek Navy. The other ships in the class were the "Hermes" (1961), the "Najade" (1962), the "Triton" (1962) and the "Theseus" (1963). Their names were taken from classical mythology. These ships were all built by the Roland Werft Shipyard, which is located in Bremen-Hemelingen. They were 69,78 meters long, had a beam of 8,2 meters and a draught of 2,65 meters. They were equipped with both radar and sonar, and were powered by 2 M.A.N. diesel engines which drove 2 screws and generated up to 6,800 horsepower. Range of operations was up to 2,760 nautical miles, and crews consisted of 5 commissioned officers and 43 enlisted men each.

Die fünf Korvetten der "Thetis" (1961) Klaße haben eine Einsatzverdrängung von je 658 Tonnen, und sind mit zwei 40-mm Schnellfeuerkanonen sowie mit einer 37,5-mm Unterseebootabwehrrakete (ASWRL) bewaffnet. Die Höchstgeschwindigkeit liegt bei 23,5 Knoten und die Reichweite bei 2,760 Seemeilen. Ab 1992 wurden die fünf Einheiten an Griechenland verkauft. Die vier anderen Mitglieder dieser Klaße hießen bei der Deutschen Marine "Hermes" (1961), "Najade" (1962), "Triton" (1962) und "Theseus" (1963). Sie wurden bei der Rolandwerft in Bremen-Hemelingen gebaut. Sie sind je 69,78 Meter lang, haben eine Breite von je 8,2 Meter und einen Tiefgang von 2,65 Meter. Eine Besatzung besteht aus 5 Offiziere und 43 Matrosen.

## XVId. "Sassnitz" Class (1990) / "Saßnitz" Klasse (1990)

The old East German Navy (the "Volksmarine" or "Peoples' Navy") planned three corvettes of the "Sassnitz" (1990) class, each of which displaced 540 tons and was armed with eight Surface-to-Air Missiles (SAM), 1-76 mm gun and 1-30 mm gun. They can make an impressive 38 knots with their diesel engines. The other ships in this class include the "Neustrelitz" (1993) and the "Bad Düben" (1996). They are named for German cities, and were eventually completed for the Federal German Coast Guard where they still serve today.

*Die drei Kriegsboote der "Saßnitz" (1990) Klaße wurden in der Deutschen Demokratischen Republik (DDR) als "Balcom-10-Klaße (Projekt 151)" entwickelt. Sie waren die ersten Verdränger-Schnellboote (oder kleine Korvetten), die nach eigenem Entwurf von der Peenewerft in Wolgast gebaut wurden. Die Volksmarine der ehemaligen DDR bezeichnete sie als "Kleine Raketenschiffe." Sie sollten die Boote der "Osa" Klaße ablösen, und waren auch für den Export in die damalige UdSSR und andere Bündnispartner des ehemaligen Warschauer Pakts gedacht. Von diesem Korvettenboottyp wurden vier Stück von der NVA ("Nationale Volksarmee") in Auftrag gegeben. Drei davon wurden in Dienst gestellt, das vierte befand sich noch im Bau als die DDR aufgelöst wurde. Formell gingen die Boote damit in den Bestand der Deutschen Marine über, die sie aber nicht einsetzte. Zwei Boote wurden im Jahre 1993 nach Umbau vom Bundesgrenzschutz (BSG) übernommen. Drei weitere Einheiten wurden nach der deutschen Wiedervereinigung für die polnische Marine gebaut und dort als "Orkan" Klaße in Dienst gestellt. Die zwei anderen Einheiten der BSG heißen "Neustrelitz" (1993) und "Bad Düben" (1996). Sie haben eine Einsatzverdrängung von je 540 Tonnen, und sind mit acht Flugzeugabwehrraketen (SAM oder "Surface to Air Missile" auf englisch) sowie mit einer 76-mm und einer 30-mm Schellfeuerkanone bewaffnet. Die Höchstgeschwindigkeit liegt bei 38 Knoten und die Reichweite bei 2,200 Seemeilen. Die Besatzung dieser Klaße besteht aus 34 Offiziere und Matrosen.*

## XVIe. "Gadebusch" Class (1962) / "Gadebusch" Klasse (1962)

The smallest modern German corvettes belonged to the "Gadebusch" (1962) class of the "Volksmarine" of the former East Germany. Each vessel displaced just 400 tons, and was armed with 4-30 mm guns plus 4 anti-submarine warfare rocket launchers (ASWRL). They could make up to 25 knots with their diesel engines, and were built by the Peenewerft Shipyard on the Baltic Sea. All of the vessels were named after cities and towns in the former East Germany. The other members of this class were named "Grevesmühler.," "Dirna," "Ribnitz-Damgarten," "Bad Doberan," "Wismar," "Teterow," "Sternberg," "Ludwigslust," "Bützow," "Perleberg" and "Lübz."

*Die kleinsten Korvetten der ehemaligen Volksmarine der DDR waren die 12 Einheiten der "Gadebusch" (1962) Klaße. Sie hatten eine Einsatzverdrängung von je 400 Tonnen, und waren mit vier 30-mm Schnellfeuerkanonen sowie mit vier Unterseebootabwehrraketen (ASWRL) bewaffnet. Die Höchstgeschwindigkeit lag bei 25 Knoten, und sie wurden bei der Peenewerft in Wolgast gebaut. Die 11 anderen Mitglieder dieser Klaße hießen "Grevesmühlen," "Dirna," "Ribnitz-Darmgarten," "Bad Doberan," "Wismar," "Teterow," "Sternberg," "Ludwigslust," "Bützow," "Perleberg" und "Lübz."*

## MODERN COMBAT BOATS OF THE GERMAN NAVY TODAY / Kampfboote der Deutschen Marine / Bundesmarine / Volksmarine

### XVII. "Schnellboote" (Fast Attack Craft)

Protecting the German coast are the Fast Attack Craft (large patrol craft) of the "Albatros" (1976) class (ten boats at 393 tons each). They are each armed with 4 Surface-to-Surface Missiles (SSM), 1-76 mm anti-aircraft gun and two torpedo tubes. They can make an impressive 38 knots with their diesel engines. The other boats of this class include the "Falke" (1976), the "Geier" (1976), the "Bussard" (1976), the "Sperber" (1976), the "Greif" (1976), the "Kondor" (1976), the "Seeadler" (1977), the "Habicht" (1977) and the "Kormoran" (1977). They are all named after different types of birds, and have since either been sold to the Turkish Navy or in some cases transferred to the Federal German Coast Guard. "Falke" is German for "falcon" and "Seeadler" is German for "sea eagle." "Habicht" is German for "hawk" and from this comes the original name of the Habsburg Dynasty of the Holy Roman Empire of the German Nation (First Reich) and Austria-Hungary. "Habichtsburg" means "hawks' castle" and this castle is located in the Canton of Aargau in modern Switzerland, where the Habsburg family used to have its ancestral home. Their surname was eventually changed to "Habsburg."

*Die "Albatros" (1976) Klaße (auch "Klaße 143" genannt) war eine Klaße von zehn Flugkörper-Schnellbooten der Deutschen Marine. Mit der folgenden "Gepard" (1982) Klaße stellten sie den Endpunkt der Entwicklung im deutschen Schnellbootbau dar. Wie ihre Vorgänger bei der Bundesmarine waren sie als hochseetaugliche Verdrängerboote mit vier leistungsstarken Dieselmotoren ausgerüstet. Am 13. Dezember 2005 wurden die letzten beiden Boote dieser*

*Klaße außer Dienst gestellt. Sechs Boote wurden an Tunesien verkauft, vier dienen als Ersatzteilträger für die noch im Dienst befindlichen Boote der "Gepard" Klaße. Die neun anderen Mitglieder dieser Klaße heißen "Falke" (1976), "Geier" (1976), "Bussard" (1976), "Sperber" (1976), "Greif" (1976), "Kondor" (1976), "Seeadler" (1977), "Habicht" (1977) und "Kormoran" (1977). Sie haben eine Einsatzverdrängung von je 393 Tonnen, und sind mit vier Schiffabwehrraketen (SSM oder "Surface to Surface Missile" auf englisch), einer 76-mm Schnellfeuerkanone und zwei Torpedorohre bewaffnet. Die Höchstgeschwindigkeit liegt bei 38 Knoten.*

## XVIIa. "Gepard" Class (1982) / "Gepard" Klasse (1982)

The "Gepard" (1982) class of ten boats at 391 tons each are armed with 4 Surface-to-Surface Missiles (SSM), 21 Surface-to-Air Missiles (SAM) and one 76 mm anti-aircraft gun. They can make a good 32 knots with their diesel engines. The other boats of this modern class include the "Puma" (1982), the "Hermelin" (1983), the "Nerz" (1983), the "Zobel" (1983), the "Fretchen" (1983), the "Dachs" (1984), the "Ozelot" (1984), the "Wiesel" (1984) and the "Hyäne" (1984). They are all named after various animals and actively serve in the German Navy today.

*Die zehn modernen Schnellboote der "Gepard" (1982) Klaße haben eine Einsatzverdrängung von je 391 Tonnen, und sind mit vier Schiffabwehrraketen (SSM), 21 Flugzeugabwehrraketen (SAM) und einer 76-mm Flugzeugabwehrkanone (FLAK) ausgerüstet. Die Höchstgeschwindigkeit liegt bei 32 Knoten. Die neun anderen Mitglieder dieser Klaße heißen "Puma" (1982), "Hermelin" (1983), "Nerz" (1983), "Zobel" (1983), "Fretchen" (1983), "Dachs" (1984), "Ozelot" (1984), "Wiesel" (1984) und "Hyäne" (1984).*

## XVIIb. "Tiger" Class (1972) / "Tiger" Klasse (1972)

The "Tiger" (1972) class of twenty boats at 264 tons each are armed with 4 Surface-to-Surface Missiles (SSM), 1-76 mm gun and 1-40 mm gun. They can make an impressive 36 knots with their diesel engines. These boats have since been sold to other navies, including those of Greece and Turkey. The remaining boats in this class include the "Iltis" (1973), the "Luchs" (1973), the "Marder" (1973), the "Leopard" (1973), the "Fuchs" (1973), the "Jaguar" (1973), the "Löwe" (1974), the "Wolf" (1974), the "Panther" (1974), the "Häher" (1974), the "Storch" (1974), the "Pelikan" (1974), the "Elster" (1974), the "Alk" (1975), the "Dommel" (1975), the "Weihe" (1975), the "Pinguin" (1975), the "Reiher" (1975) and the "Kranich" (1975). The names are of various birds and mammals.

For instance, "Fuchs" is German for "fox," "Löwe" is German for "lion" and "Storch" is German for "stork.

*Die zwanzig Schnellboote der "Tiger" (1972) Klaße wurden an Griechenland und die Türkei verkauft. Sie haben eine Einsatzverdrängung von je 264 Tonnen, und sind mit vier Schiffabwehrraketen (SSM), einer 76-mm Schnellfeuerkanone und einer 40-mm Flugzeugabwehrkanone (FLAK) bewaffnet. Die Höchstgeschwindigkeit liegt bei 36 Knoten. Die 19 anderen Mitglieder dieser Klaße heißen "Iltis" (1973), "Luchs" (1973), "Marder" (1973), "Leopard" (1973), "Fuchs" (1973), "Jaguar" (1973), "Löwe" (1974), "Wolf" (1974), "Panther" (1974), "Häher" (1974), "Storch" (1974), "Pelikan" (1974), "Elster" (1974), "Alk" (1975), "Dommel" (1975), "Weihe" (1975), "Pinguin" (1975), "Reiher" (1975) und "Kranich" (1975).*

## XVIIc. Post-World War One German Fast Attack Craft (1930-1945) / Schnellboote der Reichsmarine und der Kriegsmarine (1930-1945)

The German naval differentiation between "Torpedoboote" (torpedo boats, which were basically small destroyers) and "Schnellboote" (fast attack craft, which are basically large patrol craft) began in 1930. The first new "Schnellboote" were of 52 tons displacement, could make 34 knots with their diesel engines and were armed with one 20 mm anti-aircraft gun plus two torpedo tubes. They had a crew of 18 men. They were built in large numbers (up to S.800 which stood for "Schnellboot 800") until 1945. The last boats had a displacement of 112 tons each. There were 100 of these boats built in 1944 and 1945. They could make a very impressive 42 knots with their diesel engines, and were armed with 6-20 mm anti-aircraft guns plus 4 torpedo tubes. Their crews consisted of 23 men each. Some boats were sold to Spain, and some were sold to Germany's World War Two allies in Bulgaria and Romania. After the war, many of the boats were taken as war booty by the British, the Americans, the Russians and the French. Some found their way into the new navy of Western Germany, and many were simply scrapped. The Western Allies referred to them as "E-Boats."

*Die ersten deutschen "Schnellboote" wurden ab 1930 gebaut, vorher wurden sie "Torpedoboote" genannt. Die ersten Schnellboote der ehemaligen Reichsmarine (1922-1935) hatten eine Einsatzverdrängung von je 52 Tonnen und eine Höchstgeschwindigkeit von 34 Knoten. Sie waren mit je einer 20-mm Flugzeugabwehrkanone (FLAK) und zwei Torpedorohre bewaffnet. Die Besatzung lag bei 18 Offiziere und Matrosen. Bis Mai 1945 wurden insgesamt 800 deutsche Schnellboote geplant, gebaut oder in Dienst gestellt. Die größten und die modernsten Schnellboote in 1944 und 1945 hatten eine*

*Einsatzverdängung von je 112 Tonnen, eine Höchstgeschwindigkeit von 42 Knoten, und waren mit je sechs 20-mm Flugzeugabwehrkanonen (FLAK) und vier Torpedorohre ausgerüstet. Die Besatzung dieser 100 Kriegsboote waren je 23 Offiziere und Matrosen. Einige Schnellboote der ehemaligen Kriegsmarine (1935-1945) wurden an Spanien, Bulgarien und auch Rumänien verkauft. Nach dem Zweiten Weltkrieg wurden viele deutsche Schnellboote von den Briten, den Amerikanern, den Russen und auch den Franzosen beschlagnahmt. Einige Schnellboote der ehemaligen Kriegsmarine dienten eventuell auch bei der nachkriegs deutschen Bundesmarine (1956-1990).*

## XVIId. Former Enemy Fast Attack Craft (1939-1945) / Beuteschnellboote von 1939-1945

The 4 former Bulgarian boats of the "Velebit" (1939) class were taken over by the German Navy after Bulgaria switched sides to join the Soviet Union in 1944. The other boats in this class were also renamed after former Austro-Hungarian Navy vessels. They included the "Dinara" (1939), the "Triglav" (1939) and the "Rudnik" (1939). Each boat displaced up to 57 tons full load, and was armed with 1-40 mm gun, 1-15 mm gun plus 2-21 inch (53,3 cm) torpodo tubes. Top speed was an impressive 35,5 knots with diesel turbines. Range of action was up to 350 nautical miles, and the crews consisted of 14 officers and enlisted men.

*Vier ehemalige bulgarische Schnellboote der "Velebit" (1939) Klaße wurden im Jahre 1944 von der deutschen Kriegsmarine beschlagnahmt. Die vier anderen Schnellboote hießen "Dinara" (1939), "Triglav" (1939) und "Rudnik" (1939). Sie hatten eine Einsatzverdrängung von je 57 Tonnen, waren mit je einer 40-mm Schnellfeuerkanone, einer 15-mm Schnellfeuerkanone und zwei 53,3-cm Torpedorohre ausgerüstet. Die Höchstgeschwindigkeit war gute 35,5 Knoten und die Reichweite lag bei 350 Seemeilen. Die Besatzung dieser Klaße war je 14 Offiziere und Matrosen.*

## Chapter 22 (Kapitel 22): THE GERMAN SUBMARINE FORCE / die Deutsche Unterseebootwaffe

### XVIII. "Unterseeboote" (Submarines)

Both world wars gave rise and fame to the submarine arm of the German Navy, during which time German and Austrian submarines sank 9,536 Allied vessels. The Germans did not invent submersible boats, but they made much more efficient use of them during time of war compared to any other combatant nation on earth until the end of hostilities in May 1945. One reason was that the Germans decided to spend more time developing ocean-going boats as opposed to merely coastal boats even before the outbreak of World War One in July 1914. The next reason, and far more significant, is that Germany and her allies were hopelessly outnumbered during both world wars. Germany could never hope to defeat the enemy fleets in open battle, because the enemy had such a profound numerical advantage in capital warships. Capital warships would have included battleships, battlecruisers and all other cruisers, both large and small. German foreign policy leading up to both 1914 and 1939 was a failure of massive proportions, and the German people would pay the horrible price for this failure. German colonies and/or German trade would virtually cease to exist by the end of both world wars. Submarines proved to the "poor man's" weapon, whereby an "underdog" could hope to compete. In any event, the submarine and the torpedo were to revolutionize naval warfare. The effects of this can still be seen today, where large battle fleets have all but disappeared in the face of the submarine menace. Virtually all navies today have proven the old German and Austrian admiralties correct merely by the strategies they employ – limited surface fleets with smaller warships and greater numbers of attack submarines. Any naval wars of the future will be wars against commerce – exactly what Germany and Austria did from 1914 until 1945. With 90 percent of all physical goods being transported by water, one can see just how vital this is.

*In zwei Weltkriegen hatte Deutschlands Unterseebootwaffe 9,536 feindliche Schiffe versenkt. Deutschland hatte weniger Unterseeboote als die Gegner des Vaterlandes, aber mehr und auch bessere Hochseeunterseeboote. Die Kaiserliche Marine (1871-1921) und besonders auch die Kriegsmarine (1935-1945) waren viel kleiner als die Seestreitkräfte des Feindes. Zur Zeit des Zweiten Weltkrieges dienten 40,000 deutsche Unterseebootmänner – 30,000 davon sind für das beliebte großdeutsche Vaterland gefallen. Die 40,000 deutsche Helden haben gegen 2 Millionen Marineleute des Feindes (hauptsächlich Amerikaner und Engländer) tapfer gekämpft. Mehr als 1,100 deutsche Unterseeboote wurden in Dienst gestellt, aber 780 davon kehrten nie zurück. Das zahlreichste Unterseeboot der Kriegsmarine war der Typ VII – wie das restaurierte Unterseeboot 995 in Laboe bei Kiel. Die besten Unterseeboote des Zweiten Weltkrieges waren natürlich auch deutsch – wie der Typ XXI (wie die restaurierte "Wilhelm Bauer" in Bremerhaven). Der Bayer Wilhelm Bauer hatte Deutschlands erstes Unterseeboot (die "Seetaucher") im Jahre 1850 gebaut. Das erste Unterseeboot der Kaiserlichen Marine (1871-1921) wurde im Jahre 1905 getauft. Die restaurierte "S.M.U.1" kann man heute in München bei dem Deutschen Museum besuchen. Die Kaiserliche und Königliche Kriegsmarine Österreich-Ungarns (1369-1918) hatte ihr erstes "S.M.U.1" ("Seine Majestät Unterseeboot") im Jahre 1909 getauft.*

During World War Two, German submariners still accomplished heroic feats in the face of being outnumbered by an astounding 50 to 1. Of 40,000 German submariners who served during World War Two, 30,000 never returned home to Germany. Over 1,100 German submarines were commissioned between 1935-1945, of which more than 780 were sunk or destroyed. The most common type of German submarine during World War Two was the Type VII, which one can see in the movie "Das Boot" and in the German Navy Memorial at Laboe near Kiel (U-995 has been restored there and is of course available for public viewing). The most modern German submarine during World War Two was the Type XXI, which was first "true" submarine in the entire world by being able to spend much more time under water and in having a much greater submerged speed. One can see such a restored boat in the German port of Bremerhaven (U-2540 christened "Wilhelm Bauer," and thereby named after the Bavarian man who built the very first German prototype submarine in 1850 – the "Seetaucher" or "sea diver" in English). Both Germany and Austria used submarines during World War One. The first U-1 was commissioned in Germany in 1905, and today she can be viewed restored at the "Deutsches Museum" in Munich, Bavaria. The Austrian U-1 was commissioned into the Imperial and Royal Austro-Hungarian Navy in 1909.

## XVIIIa. German Submarines from 1905 – 1918 (the Period of World War One) / Deutsche Unterseeboote von 1905 bis 1918

During World War One (which lasted from the Austro-Hungarian declaration of war against Serbia on July 28, 1914 until the surrender of German troops in East Africa on November 23, 1918), German submarines sank 5,861 Allied ships for a grand total of more than 12,851,000 gross tons of shipping. Germany commissioned 376 submarines during the First World War, of which 178 were lost in action and 198 returned safely home to ports in Germany, Austria-Hungary and occupied Belgium. 5,132 German submariners gave their lives for the Fatherland during those four terrible years. These submarines ranged in size from 238 tons all the way up to 2,483 tons each. The total number of German submarines ordered by the Imperial Navy during World War One was 533, but those units beyond the 376 commissioned boats were never completed due to the end of the war. These were either scrapped incomplete after the war, or were merely on the drawing boards.

*Zur Zeit des Ersten Weltkrieges (Juli 1914 bis November 1918) hatte die Unterseebootwaffe der Kaiserlichen Marine (1871-1921) 5,861 feindliche Schiffe (oder 12,851 Millionen Tonnen) versenkt. Die Kaiserliche Marine des Deutschen Reiches hatte 533 Unterseeboote in Auftrag genommen, aber nur 376 in Dienst gestellt. 178 davon gingen verloren und 198 hatten den Krieg überstanden. Die Unterseeboote der Kaiserlichen Marine hatten je eine Einsatzverdrängung zwischen 238 und 2,483 Tonnen. 5,132 Unterseebootmänner starben für Deutschland. Die Unterseebootklaße "UA" genannten Flotten-Unterseeboote der Kaiserlich Deutschen Marine setzten sich aus vielen verschiedenen Unterseebootklaßen und Einzelbooten zusammen. Diese 108 Hochsee-Zweihüllenboote wurden von 1905 bis 1918 gebaut. Unter den Petroleumbooten (kurz "Petrolboote" genannt) werden die Unterseeboote S.M.U.1 bis S.M.U.18 zusammengefasst. Es waren Zweihüllenboote mit Petroleummotoren als Hauptantrieb. Für die Unterwasserfahrt dienten Elektromotoren als Antriebsaggregat. Alle weiteren Unterseeboote der Kaiserlichen Marine (ab S.M.U.19) wurden dieselelektrisch angetrieben. Bei Überwasserfahrt wurde das Unterseeboot von Dieselmotoren angetrieben; bei Unterwasserfahrt von Elektromotoren. Die Elektromotoren dienten auch als Generator zum Wiederaufladen der Akkumulatoren. Hierbei trieben die Dieselmotoren die Elektromotoren an, die dann elektrischen Strom erzeugten. Die Unterseebootklaße "UB" wurden für die Kaiserliche Marine zwischen 1914 und 1918 gebaut. Bei den "UB-I-Booten" handelte es sich um sehr kleine Einhüllen-Unterseeboote für den küstennahen Einsatz. Bei den "UB-II-Booten" handelte es sich ebenfalls um kleine Einhüllen-Unterseeboote für den küstennahen Einsatz. Diese Boote wurden jedoch im Vergleich zu den "UB-I-Booten" stark verbessert. Der "UB-III-Typ" war ein Zweihüllen-Hochsee-Typ, der für Handelskriegsoperationen um Großbrittanien und im Mittelmeer entwickelt wurde. Der Entwurf dieses Typs leitete sich von der Unterseebootklaße "UC-II" ab. Allerdings sollte er keine Seeminen (die "UC-Booten"), sondern Torpedos aufnehmen und größere Reichweite und höhere Geschwindigkeit besitzen. Dadurch vergrößerte sich das Boot auf rund 600 Tonnen. Um eine höhere Geschwindigkeit zu erreichen, mußten stärkere Dieselmotoren eingebaut werden. Insgesamt wurden 136 "UB-Boote" und 95 "UC-Boote" in Dienst gestellt. Bei der "Unterseebootklaße UD" handelte es sich um fünf Unterseeboote, die ursprünglich für Österreich-Ungarn gebaut wurden. Nach Ausbruch des Ersten Weltkrieges im Juli 1914 wurden die Boote nach Verhandlungen mit Österreich von der deutschen Marine übernommen und fertiggestellt. Sie wurden zwischen Juli und September 1915 als S.M.U.66 bis S.M.U.70 in Dienst gestellt. Die "Unterseebootklaße UE" bestand aus den Minen-Unterseeboot-Typen "UE-I" und "UE-II" der Kaiserlichen Marine. Der "Typ UE-I" war der erste deutsche Unterseeboot-Typ mit Trockenlagerung für Minen. Die "Unterseebootklaße UE-II" war ein Minen-Unterseeboot-Typ der Kaiserlichen Marine. Er wird oft auch als "Großes Minen-Unterseeboot" statt Typ UE-II bezeichnet. Insgesamt wurden 19 "UE-Boote" in Dienst gestellt.Es gab auch vier große "Unterseebootkreuzer" (S.M.U.139 bis S.M.U.142), die in Dienst gestellt wurden. "S.M.U. Kapitänleutnant Schweiger" (S.M.U.139) hatte eine Einsatzverdrängung von 2,483 Tonnen, eine Überwassergeschwindigkeit von 15,8 Knoten, eine Unterwassergeschwindigkeit von 7,6 Knoten, sechs Torpedorohre (vier vorne und zwei achtern), zwei 15-cm Schnellfeuerkanonen und zwei 10,5-cm Schnellfeuerkanonen. Sie wurde nach Kapitänleutnant Walther Schweiger (1885-1917) genannt. Er hatte 49 feindliche Schiffe, oder 183,883 Tonnen, versenkt.*

In between 1905 and 1918, German submarine classes were denoted by capital letters ranging from A up to E. There could also be numerous boats of different displacements within a particular class. "UA" denoted fleet submarines which were intended for deployment on the high seas. 108 of the UA boats were commissioned. "UB" denoted coastal boats which were smaller in size compared to the fleet submarines. 136 of the UB boats were commissioned. "UC" denoted coastal minelaying submarines as opposed to coastal submarines which had torpedos as their primary offensive armament. 95 of the UC boats were commissioned into active duty service. "UD" denoted a small number of fleet submarines originally intended for the Imperial and Royal Austro-Hungarian Navy which Germany unfortunately decided to keep for its own use. 5 of the UD boats were commissioned. "UE" denoted large minelaying submarines, of which 19 were commissioned. Beyond those classes denoted by capital letters were the much larger "Unterseebootkreuzer" ("submarine cruisers" in English) of the U.139 class (3 boats) and of the U.142 class (one boat). U.139 was one of the few German submarines ever to be named – as "S.M.U. Kapitänleutnant Schweiger," after one of the great submarine captains of World War One. She displaced 2,483 tons full load, could make up to 15,8 knots on the surface and up to 7,6 knots submerged. She was armed with 6-19,7 inch torpedo tubes (four bow and two stern), 2-6 inch plus 2-4 inch deck guns. "S.M.U" stands for "Seine Majestät Unterseeboot," or "His Majesty's Submarine." The German naval rank of "Kapitänleutnant" is equivalent to a Lieutenant in the U.S. Navy. Walther

Schweiger (1885-1917) was the 6th highest scoring German submarine commander during World War One, with 49 Allied ships, or 183,883 tons of shipping to his credit. The final class of World War One German submarine was the "Deutschland" class of large commercial submarines. 7 of these boats were commissioned. They were designed to circumvent the terribly effective Allied naval blockade of Germany and her Central Powers allies, which virtually starved much of central Europe by November 1918. It was for this sad reason that so many "Ersatz" ("substitute" in English) products were designed in Germany. Many people were sadly reduced into eating food products with sawdust.

*Zur Zeit des Ersten Weltkrieges hatte Deutschland sieben Handelsunterseeboote wie die "S.M.U. Deutschland" und die "S.M.U. Bremen." Als Handelsunterseeboote werden nicht-militärische Unterseeboote bezeichnet, mit deren Hilfe Güter oder Rohstoffe trotz der feindlichen Seeblockade gegen Deutschland und den Mittelmächten (Österreich-Ungarn, Bulgarien und die Osmanische Türkei) gehandelt werden können. S.M.U. ("Seine Majestät Unterseeboote") war auch die allgemein gebräuchliche Bezeichnung für das Unterseebootswesen in der Kaiserlichen und Königlichen Kriegsmarine Österreich-Ungarns. 120 Unterseeboote wurden in Auftrag genommen, aber nur 27 wurden in Dienst gestellt. Die feindliche Seeblockade bedeutete, daß die Mittelmächte nicht genug Rohstoffe hatten. Im Jahre 1909 lief das erste Unterseeboot der k.u.k. Kriegsmarine, S.M. Unterseeboot 1, vom Stapel. Zuvor wurden zwischen 1907 und 1910 drei Probeboote der Typen Simon Lake, Germania (aus Deutschland) und John Philip Holland (aus Amerika) gebaut. Aus diesen wurde nach gründlicher Erprobung jener Typ ausgewählt, der sich am besten bewährt hatte. Alle Boote waren als Küstenboote für den Adriaraum gedacht. Die Unterseebootstation in Polei ("Pola" auf italienisch und heute "Pula" in Kroatien) mit dem Mutterschiff "S.M.S. Pelikan" unterstand dem Hafenadmiral. Zur Zeit des Ersten Weltkrieges hatten die 27 Unterseeboote Österreich-Ungarns 132 feindliche Schiffe (oder 237.000 Tonnen) versenkt. Die erfolgreichsten Unterseebootkommandeure der k.u.k. Kriegsmarine waren Zdenko Hudecek und Georg Ritter von Trapp.*

The Imperial and Royal Austro-Hungarian submarine force was born in 1909, just three years after the Imperial German submarine force. They deployed merely 27 coastal submarines, but managed to sink 132 Allied ships in the Adriatic and Eastern Mediterranean Sea for a total of 237,000 gross registered tons. 9 of the boats were lost in action and the remainder made it safely home to Austria's Adriatic ports. Up to 120 boats were ordered by the Imperial and Royal Navy, but the rest beyond the 27 competed boats were never finished due to the lack of supplies and due to the end of the war. Many Austro-Hungarian submarines were purchased from Germany, but 18 of their boats were locally designed and manufactured coastal units. The most famous Austrian submarine commander of World War One was Korvettenkapitän Georg Ritter von Trapp, who became immortalized in Rodger and Hammerstein's movie titled "The Sound of Music." Von Trapp was Austria's second highest scoring U-Boat Ace in World War One after Zdenko Hudecek.

## XVIIIb. German Submarines from 1935 – 1945 (Period of World War Two) / Deutsche Unterseeboote der Kriegsmarine (1935-1945)

During World War Two in Europe (September 1, 1939 until May 7, 1945), the German submarine force sank 3,675 Allied ships for a grand total 14,5 million tons of shipping. Germany lost 783 submarines to enemy action, and just 372 boats made it back home safely to Germany and to German-occupied bases in France, Belgium, the Netherlands, Denmark, Norway, Italy, Yugoslavia and Greece. The 1,155 commissioned submarines tended to range in size from 258 tons to 2,177 tons in size. Up to 7,569 submarines were ordered by the navy during World War Two, but most were obviously never completed due to lack of supplies, due to heavy Allied air raids and due to the end of the war. This fantastically high number includes one and two man "midget" submarines, but most of them were to have been full-sized boats.

*Zur Zeit des Zweiten Weltkrieges in Europa (September 1939 bis Mai 1945) hatte die Unterseebootwaffe der deutschen Kriegsmarine 3,675 feindliche Schiffe (oder 14,5 Millionen Tonnen) versenkt. 7,569 Unterseeboote wurden in Auftrag genommen, aber nur 1,155 wurden in Dienst gestellt. 783 davon (mit 30,000 deutschen Unterseeboothelden) gingen verloren, und 372 hatten den Krieg überstanden. Die 1,155 getauften Unterseeboote hatten je eine Einsatzverdrängung zwischen 258 und 2,177 Tonnen.*

In between 1935 and 1945, German submarine classes were denoted by Roman numerals as opposed to the class system of capital letters in use from 1905 to 1918. Just 2 examples of the Type I were commissioned, an ocean-going boat of 983 tons total displacement and 43 crew members. These boats had a top surface speed of 17,75 knots and a submerged speed of up to 8,25 knots. They were armed with 2 deck cannons and 14 torpedos, and had a range of 6,700 miles on the surface and 78 miles submerged.

*Von der Unterseebootklaße I, offiziell "Typ I" genannt, wurden in den Jahren 1935 bis 1936 zwei Boote bei Deschimag AG Weser in Bremen gebaut. U.25 und U.26 waren im Prinzip Versuchsboote, die aus dem für die türkische*

*Kriegsmarine von deutschen Technikern in Spanien gebauten Unterseeboot "Gür" weiterentwickelt wurden. Diese zwei Boote hatten eine Einsatzverdrängung von je 983 Tonnen, 43 Besatzungsmitglieder, eine Überwassergeschwindigkeit von 17,75 Knoten, eine Unterwassergeschwindigkeit von 8,25 Knoten, zwei Schnellfeuerkanonen, 14 Torpedos, eine Überwasserreichweite von 6,700 Seemeilen und eine Unterwasserreichweite von 78 Seemeilen.*

The Type II was Germany's first post-World War One coastal submarine class, of which 50 units were commissioned from 1935 until 1941. The variants within the German submarine classes built from 1935 until 1945 were denoted by capital letters after the Roman numeral. For instance, The Type II class had the Type IIA, the Type IIB, the Type IIC and finally the Type IID. The Type II boats ranged in size from 303 tons up to 364 tons each, with 25 crew members. They had a top surface speed of up to 13 knots and a maximum submerged speed of 7,25 knots. They were armed with one anti-aircraft deck gun and either 6 torpedos or 8 mines. Their maximum range was 3,500 miles on the surface and up to 56 miles submerged.

*Die Unterseebootklaße II, offiziell "Typ II" genannt, war eine Klaße relativ kleiner Unterseeboote der deutschen Kriegsmarine, die hauptsächlich zur Küstenpatrouille benutzt wurden. Der Typ II wurde in den 1920er Jahren vom in Den Haag (Niederlande) ansäßigen "Ingenieuskaantor voor Scheepsbouw" (IvS) entwickelt. Zwischen 1935 und 1941 wurden insgesamt 50 Boote in Dienst gestellt. Sie hatten je eine Einsatzverdrängung zwischen 303 und 364 Tonnen, und 25 Besatzungsmitglieder. Die Überseegeschwindigkeit lag bei 13 Knoten, und die Unterseegeschwindigkeit bei 7,25 Knoten. Die Bewaffnung dieser Klaße bestand aus einer Flugzeugabwehrkanone (FLAK) und entweder sechs Torpedos oder acht Minen. Die Überseereichweite war 3,500 Seemeilen und die Unterseereichweite 56 Seemeilen.*

The designs for Types III through VI were never built.

*Die Unterseebootklaßen "Typ III" bis "Typ VI" sowie "Typ VIII" wurden nie gebaut.*

The Type VII was Germany's main weapon at sea from 1939 until 1945. This class was actually based upon the coastal UBIII of World War One, but enlarged by an initial 25 percent in size. 703 boats were actually completed and commissioned out of 1,452 ordered from 1935 until 1944, which also makes this the most common submarine class in the history of the entire world (and by a huge margin, too). These boats ranged in size from 745 tons (the Type VIIA) all the way up to 1,181 tons (the Type VIIF). The most common sub-type was the Type VIIC at 871 tons. Crew size ranged from 44 to more than 50 officers and men. Surface speed was a maximum 17,25 knots and submerged speed was up to 8 knots. They were armed with up to 6 deck guns (all except one were anti-aircraft guns) and either 14 torpedos or 39 mines. Maximum range was 10,000 miles on the surface and 90 miles submerged. One must always keep in mind that only diesels were used on the surface and only batteries while submerged. One had to come up for air for the human crew and to recharge the batteries. The German invention of the "Schnorchel" ("snorkel" in English) in 1943 permitted the boats to recharge their air supply and their batteries without fully surfacing, which thus increased their chance of survival somewhat. Nowadays, modern snorkels have very long "stacks" which allow boats to recharge both air supply and batteries from up to 250 feet below the surface – greatly increasing their chances for survival. Torpedos were much more expensive compared to ammunition for deck guns (deck guns are no longer used today), but firing on the surface eventually became far too dangerous for the submarines to even attempt. Deck guns were never very accurate, so the firing range had to be short. Furthermore, if the intended "target" ever hit a submarine with its own gun, the submarine was usually finished. Submarine hulls could not be armored, and once the hull was pierced the submarine was helpless. The interior pressure hull of a Type VIIB submarine was 20 mm thick, and would allow the boat to dive to a maximum 250 meters, or 812 feet. The standard German torpedoes in early World War Two were 7 meters long, 53 cm in diameter, carried a 300 kilogram (662 lbs.) explosive warhead, had electric motors, propellers, a range of 14 kilometers (8,7 miles), a top speed of at least 30 knots and displaced up to 1,5 tons each. Allied depth charges would explode at least down to 120 meters (390 feet below the surface), and would descend at the rate of 4 meters (or 13 feet) per second.

**Atlantik-Unterseeboot Typ VIIC (1939) / "Atlantic" Submarine Type VIIC (1939) – painting by Naval artist Günther Todt (1928-2009)**

*Die Unterseebootklaße Typ VII, offiziell "Typ VII" genannt, war eine Bauserie von Tauchbooten der deutschen Kriegsmarine im Zweiten Weltkrieg. Sie war die am häufigsten produzierte Unterseebootklaße aller Zeiten, mit ihr wurde auch mehr Schifftonnage versenkt als mit jedem anderen Typ. Zwischen 1935 und 1944 wurden 1,452 Boote in Auftrag genommen, aber nur 703 wurden in Dienst gestellt. Charakteristisch für Typ VII Boote sind die aussenliegenden Brennstoffbunker, die sogenannten Satteltanks in den seitlichen Rumpfausbuchtungen. Im Gegensatz zu den Hochseebooten des Typ IX und den Küsten Unterseebooten des Typ II wurden sie "Atlantikboote" genannt. Sie erreichten von allen im Zweiten Weltkrieg gebauten Booten die größte Tauchtiefe, diese ging in Praxis deutlich über die Werftgarantie hinaus. Die höchstentwickelte Baureihe des Typ VII Modell C/42 hatte eine Werftgarantie von 200 Meter, die Maximaltauchtiefe ohne Schäden am Druckkörper war mit 400 Meter angegeben. Die Mitlglieder dieser am zahlreichsten Klaße hatten eine Einsatzverdrängung von je 745 Tonnen (Typ VIIA) bis 1,181 Tonnen (Typ VIIF). Der berühmte Typ VIIC hatte eine Einsatzverdrängung von 871 Tonnen. Die Besatzung des Typs VII bestand von je zwischen 44 und 50 Offiziere und*

*Matrosen. Die Überwassergeschwindigkeit lag bei 17,25 Knoten und die Unterwassergeschwindigkeit bei 8 Knoten. Die Bewaffnung dieser Boote bestand aus je sechs Kanonen (davon fünf Flugzeugabwehrkanonen und einer Schnellfeuerkanone) und entweder 14 Torpedos oder 39 Seeminen. Die Überwasserreichweite lag bei 10,000 Seemeilen und die Unterwasserreichweite bei 90 Seemeilen. Die Reichweite eines deutschen Torpedos lag bei 14 Kilometer (mit einer Höchstgeschwindigkeit von 30 Knoten und einer Einsatzverdrängung von 1,5 Tonnen).*

The Type VIII was never built, so the next class was Type IX, of which 193 boats were actually completed and commissioned out of 360 ordered from 1936 until 1944. This was a larger boat, based upon the "Unterseebootkreuzer" (submarine cruisers) of World War One. They ranged in size from 1,153 tons (the Type IXA) all the way up to 1,804 tons (the Type IXD2). They could make up to 19,25 knots on the surface and up to 7,75 knots submerged. They were armed with up to 5 deck guns (mostly anti-aircraft, of course), 22 torpedos and 42 mines – a tremendous arsenal for the time. The crew ranged in size from 48 up to 57 officers and men. Maximum range of operations was an amazing 23,700 miles on the surface and 65 miles submerged. This is the reason such boats served all over the world – even in the Indian and Pacific Oceans far from Germany. The German Navy used bases in Japan, the Dutch East Indies (modern Indonesia), Malaya and Borneo (modern Malaysia).

*Die Unterseebootklaße IX, offiziell "Typ IX" genannt, war eine Klaße hochseetauglicher Unterseeboote der deutschen Kriegsmarine. Die Entwicklung begann im Jahre 1935, und die ersten Boote wurden im Jahre 1938 in Dienst gestellt. In den folgenden Jahren wurden fünf verbesserte Versionen dieser Klaße entwickelt und gebaut. 360 Boote wurden in Auftrag genommen, aber nur 193 davon wurden in Dienst gestellt. Neben der Unterseebootklaße VII war der Typ IX der am meisten gebaute und erfolgreichste Typ im Zweiten Weltkrieg. Diese Boote hatten eine Einsatzverdrängung von je zwischen 1,153 Tonnen (Typ IXA) und 1,804 Tonnen (Typ IXD2). Die Überwassergeschwindigkeit lag bei 19,25 Knoten und die Unterwassergeschwindigkeit bei 7,75 Knoten. Die Bewaffnung dieser Klaße bestand aus fünf Kanonen (davon vier Flugzeugabwehrkanonen und einer Schnellfeuerkanone), und entweder 22 Torpedoes oder 42 Seeminen. Die Besatzung eines Bootes bestand aus zwischen 48 und 57 Offiziere und Matrosen. Die Überwasserreichweite lag bei gute 23,700 Seemeilen und die Unterwasserreichweite bei 65 Seemeilen. Diese Unterseeboote dienten rund um den Erdball – einige davon waren in Japan, Indonesien, Malaya und Borneo stationiert.*

The Type X was Germany's first purpose-built minelayer after World War One, but merely 8 boats were actually commissioned into active duty service from 1939 until 1944. This class displaced up to 2,177 tons, could make up to 16,5 knots on the surface and up to 7 knots submerged. Radius was an impressive 14,550 miles on the surface and up to 93 miles submerged. Armament included 3 deck guns (2 of which were anti-aircraft), 15 torpedos and 66 mines – an impressive arsenal for a larger boat.

*Die Unterseeboote der Klaße X, offiziell "Typ X" genannt, waren die größten Unterseeboote der deutschen Kriegsmarine. Es war eine Entwicklung des Unterseeminenkreuzer-Projektes 45 des Ersten Weltkrieges. Sie wurden als Minenleger-Unterseeboote konstruiert. Die Bewaffnung dieser Unterseeboote bestand aus Minenschächten (jeweils zwei Gruppen zu sechs Schächten an Back- und Steuerbord, und eine Gruppe mit sechs Schächten im Vorschiff). Darin konnten 66 Minen aufgenommen werden. Neben zwei Torpedorohren mit maximal 15 Torpedowaffen waren noch ein 10,5-cm Seezielgeschütz, ein 2-cm und ein 3,7-cm Flugabwehrgeschütz (FLAK) eingebaut. Später wurden die beiden gegen einen 2-cm Flakvierling ausgetauscht. Zwischen 1939 und 1944 wurden nur acht Boote in Dienst gestellt. Sie hatten eine Einsatzverdrängung von je 2,177 Tonnen, eine Überwassergeschwindigkeit von 16,5 Knoten, eine Unterwassergeschwindigkeit von 7 Knoten, eine Überwasserreichweite von 14,550 Seemeilen und eine Unterwasserreichweite von 93 Seemeilen.*

The Type XI was never built, but this would have been Germany's largest submarine class ever had it been built – up to this very day. Specifications called for a displacement of 3,630 tons, a top suface speed of 23 knots and up to 7 knots submerged. This would have been very fast on the surface for a submarine. Armament was to have included 8 deck guns (half of them anti-aircraft), 12 torpedos and 1 aircraft. These specifications show that the class was obviously designed more for surface operations, and the navy wisely chose to shelve the project. This would have been alright during World War One, but suicidal for World War Two. There was simply too much danger from enemy aircraft. The project was cancelled in 1938, at which time 3 boats were projected but never built.

*Die Unterseebootklaße "Typ XI" wurde nie gebaut, aber die geplante Einsatzverdrängung war 3,630 Tonnen (Deutschlands größter Unterseebootplan). Die geplante Überwassergeschwindigkeit war gute 23 Knoten und die Unterwassergeschwindigkeit acht Knoten. Die geplante Bewaffnung dieser Boote bestand aus acht Schnellfeuerkanonen (davon vier Flugzeugabwehrkanonen), 12*

*Torpedos und ein Seeflugzeug. Drei Boote wurden in Auftrag genommen, aber nie auf Kiel gelegt. Die Unterseeboottypen XII und XIII wurden auch nie gebaut.*

The plan for the Type XII submarine was similar to the Type IX and the Type XIII was a coastal plan somewhat larger than the Type II. Both projects were cancelled before any such boats were ever built. The Type XIV was Germany's first purpose-built submarine tanker, meant to refuel other submarines at sea. 10 boats were completed and commissioned out of 14 ordered from 1939 until 1943. This class displaced up to 1,932 tons, could make 14,5 knots on the surface and 6,25 knots submerged. Radius was 9,300 miles on the surface and up to 53 miles submerged. Armament included 3 anti-aircraft guns on the deck and 4 torpedos as cargo.

*Die Unterseebootklaße XIV, offiziell "Typ XIV" genannt, war eine Modifikation des Typs IXD und wurde entworfen, um andere deutsche Unterseeboote während des Zweiten Weltkrieges mit Treibstoff, Lebensmitteln und Munition (mit je 4 Torpedos eines Typs XIV) zu versorgen. Der Spitzname dieser Klaße war "Milchkuh." Zwischen 1939 und 1943 wurden 14 Boote in Auftrag genommen, aber nur 10 in Dienst gestellt. Sie hatten eine Einsatzverdrängung von je 1,932 Tonnen, eine Überwassergeschwindigkeit von 14,5 Knoten, eine Unterwassergeschwindigkeit von 6,25 Knoten, eine Überwasserreichweite von 9,300 Seemeilen und eine Unterwasserreichweite von 53 Seemeilen. Diese Unterseeboote hatten selbst keine Offensiv-Waffen, nur drei Flugabwehrgeschütze (FLAK) zur Verteidigung gegen Luftangriffe. In der Mitte des Zweiten Weltkrieges (im Jahre 1942) spielten sie eine wichtige Rolle bei der Unterstützung kleinerer Unterseeboote vom Typ VIIC beim Angriff auf die amerikanische Küste (Unternehmen "Paukenschlag").*

The next German submarine plans of true importance involved those for "Walter" boats, so-named after their designer, Professor Hellmuth Walter (1900-1980). Up to this time in history, all submarines around the world were actually "submersibles" which spent far more time above water than below the surface. The main problem was propulsion. In the very beginning, the early boats of World War One actually used kerosene. This was not good, because kerosene left a very visible wake in the form of pollution. Diesel solved the problem of a visible wake, but the diesel engines still required a lot of air. The Walter was a "closed cycle" engine in terms of exhaust, which addressed the problem of air. The problem with the Walter system was the nature of the fuel – it was rather unstable and prone to be explosive. Early jet and rocket engines for aircraft had a similar problem.

*Eine technische Revolution stellte der "Walter-Antrieb" des Professors Hellmuth Walter (1900-1980) dar, der in Form von Wasserstoffperoxyd eine Sauerstoffquelle mitführte und hohe Geschwindigkeiten auch unter Wasser erreichte, um feindlichen Unterseebootjägern zu entkommen. Einzelne Elemente des Walter-Versuchsbootes (Basis für die späteren "Elekroboot" Typen XXI und XXIII) wie zum Beispiel der Schnorchel wurden auch in konventionelle Unterseeboote übernommen. Zudem gab es die Entwicklung zielsuchender Torpedos, zum Beispiel der "Zaunkönig." Zwischen 1942 und 1944 wurden 236 Unterseeboote des Typs "XVII" in Auftrag genommen, aber nur vier gebaut. Sie hatten eine Einsatzverdrängung von je 368 Tonnen, eine Unterwassergeschwindigkeit von 26 Knoten (immer noch gut für heute), eine Überwassergeschwindigkeit von 9 Knoten, eine Unterwasserreichweite von 224 Seemeilen und eine Überwasserreichweite von 6,000 Seemeilen. Die Bewaffnung eines Bootes bestand aus vier Torpedos und die Besatzung aus 19 Offiziere und Matrosen.*

4 of the Type XVII Walter submarines were completed and commissioned in between 1942 and 1944, largely for experimental purposes. This was out of 236 boats originally ordered; the remainder were merely scrapped incomplete or just cancelled. They were coastal units, and displaced up to 368 tons each. They could make up to 26 knots submerged (very fast for a submarine even today) and up to 9 knots on the surface. Due to high fuel consumption, the boats had a maximum surface range of just 6,000 miles on the surface and 224 miles submerged. The explosive fuel was known as aurol and perhydrol. Armament was just 4 torpedos per boat and the crew size was 19 commissioned officers and enlisted men.The Type XX was a design for a "freighter submarine," intended to break the Allied naval blockade between Germany and Japan. This was a large design, which would have displaced up to 2,962 tons each. Planned speed was 12,5 knots surfaced and up to 5,75 knots submerged. Radius of operations was to have been 13,000 miles on the surface or up to 49 miles submerged. Armament was to have been 5 anti-aircraft guns and crew was planned at 58 commissioned officers and enlisted men. 200 boats were ordered, but never completed.

*Das geplante Unterseeboot "Typ XX" war ein "Frachterunterseeboot," das nie gebaut wurde. Der Plan war für Unterseeboothandel zwischen Deutschland und Japan. Die geplante Einsatzverdrängung war je 2,962 Tonnen, eine Überwassergeschwindigkeit von 12,5 Knoten, eine Unterwassergeschwindigkeit von 5,75 Knoten, eine Überwasserreichweite von 13,000 Seemeilen und eine Unterwasserreichweite von 49 Seemeilen. Die geplante Besatzung eines Bootes lag bei 58 Offiziere und Matrosen. 200 Boote wurden in Auftrag genommen, aber nie auf Kiel gelegt.*

The next important design was the famous Type XXI submarine, the basic blueprint for all post-World War Two diesel submarines in the world. 1,500 of these impressive boats were ordered by the German Navy, but just 123 were commissioned by the end of the war. And most of these were still training their crews in the Baltic Sea – very few saw active duty against Germany's enemies. The Type XXI displaced 2,100 tons, had a top surface speed of 15,5 knots but a top submerged speed of 17,25 knots, which was very significant. This clearly demonstrates that the Type XXI was meant to operate more often submerged than surfaced. Armament was comprised of 4 anti-aircraft guns on the deck and 20 torpedos & 18 small mines or 14 torpedos & 12 large mines. Even their torpedos were more advanced compared to before – they were guided torpedos which could be fired while deeply submerged and without ever having seen the enemy through a periscope. They would have revolutionized the Battle of the Atlantic, and turned the tide for Germany after the "Black May" of 1943, when the war at sea turned in favor of Britain and America. The Type XXI crew consisted of 58 officers and men, range was 11,850 miles on the surface and up to 285 miles submerged. Due to a much increased battery capacity, the Type XXI was often called an electric boat. They still had diesel engines of course, but were now able to spend much more time below the surface compared to their predecessors. These boats also had refrigerators for foodstuffs and more lavatory facilites for the crew, including a shower.

*Die Unterseebootklaße XXI, offiziell "Typ XXI" genannt, ist eine deutsche Unterseebootklaße, die zwischen 1943 bis 1945 gebaut wurde. Diese Boote waren die weltweit modernsten ihrer Zeit und wurden wegen ihrer großen Akkumulatoranlage, mit der sie viel länger als andere zeigenössische Typen tauchen konnten, sowie den Elektromotoren, die mehr Leistung als die Dieselmotoren aufwiesen, als "Elektro-Unterseeboote" oder "Elektroboote" bezeichnet. Sie waren mit Schnorcheln ausgerüstet und dafür ausgelegt, fast ständig unter Wasser zu fahren. Dadurch waren sie die ersten echten Unterseeboote, anders als alle bisherigen, die im Grunde nur "tauchfähige" Überwassereinheiten darstellten. Sie wurden am Ende des Zweiten Weltkrieges in Sektionsbauweise am "Fliessband" gebaut. Trotzdem kamen sie bedauerlicherweise nicht mehr zum Fronteinsatz. Wegen seiner revolutionären Eigenschaften leitete gerade der Typ XXI einen Paradigmenwechsel der Unterseeboot-Waffen aller nachkriegs Seemächten ein. 1,500 Einheiten wurden in Auftrag genommen, aber nur 123 davon wurden in (Lehr)-Dienst gestellt – sie kamen für Deutschland leider zu spät. Die Einsatzverdrängung eines Bootes lag bei 2,100 Tonnen. Die Überwassergeschwindigkeit lag bei 15,5 Knoten, die Unterwassergeschwindigkeit bei 17,25 Knoten, die Überwasserreichweite bei 11,850 Seemeilen und die Unterwasserreichweite bei 285 Seemeilen. Eine*

*Besatzung bestand aus 58 Offiziere und Matrosen. Die Bewaffnung eines Bootes bestand aus vier Flugzeugabwehrkanonen (FLAK), und entweder 20 Torpedos und 18 kleine Seeminen oder 14 Torpedos und 12 große Seeminen.*

One must understand that all previous submarines around the world had no means of freezing food and no shower facility within the boat! One would eat fresh food at the start of a cruise, but was reduced to canned food for the rest of the trip. Restroom facilities were limited – two toilets and sinks for more than 50 men. Not only this, but the sinks often used sea water. When one washes with sea water, it leaves a sticky feeling on the skin unlike fresh water. Men were unable to shave and unable to shower in a submerged boat before advent of the Type XXI submarine – one can just imagine how the boats smelled after patrols lasting for months. And the men came back home to port with full beards after these long patrols, some of which lasted for the better part of a year on the larger boats. During World War One (before the advent of enemy aircraft), submarine crews could shower on the deck with a portable shower and sea water – better than nothing but still not ideal by any means. The Type XXI had a coastal counterpart known as the Type XXIII submarine. The German Navy ordered 480 of these boats, but only 62 were commissioned by the end of World War Two. The situation was pretty much the same as with the Type XXI – most of these were still training their crews in the Baltic Sea by May 1945. Displacement was 258 tons, top speed was 9,75 knots surfaced and 12,5 knots submerged. Range was 1,350 miles on the surface and up to 175 miles submerged. The small crew consisted of just 14 officers and men. Armament was a mere 2 torpedos per boat. The Type XXI, Type XXIII and the Walter boats all shared "teardrop" submarine hulls. The earliest boats before World War One had such hulls, and they only came back into use some time after World War Two for the Allied countries. A teardrop hull meant a greater submerged speed due to more aerodynamic styling.

*Die Unterseebootklaße XXIII, offiziell "Typ XXIII" genannt, war ein deutscher Unterseeboot Typ gegen Ende des Zweiten Weltkrieges; sie wurde als Küsten-Unterseeboot eingestuft, da das Boot sehr klein war. Nach dem Krieg wurden zwei Boote vom Typ XXIII von der Bundesmarine vom Meeresboden geborgen und als "Unterseeboot Klaße 240" wieder in Dienst gestellt. Genau wie die größere Unterseebootklaße XXI war dieser Typ ein "Elektro-Unterseeboot" und auf große Unterwasserfahrleistung ausgelegt. Im Gegensatz zum Typ XXI war die Klaße XXIII ein Boot mit nur einer Hülle. Durch die geringe Größe konnte dieses Unterseeboot zwar nur zwei Torpedos mitführen, war aber einfacher zu produzieren und gelangte noch vor Kriegsende zum Einsatz. Die Einsatzverdrängung eines Bootes lag bei 258 Tonnen, die Überwassergeschwindigkeit bei 9,75 Knoten, die Unterwassergeschwindigkeit bei*

*12,5 Knoten, die Überwasserreichweite bei 1,350 Seemeilen und die Unterwasserreichweite bei 175 Seemeilen. Eine Besatzung bestand aus 14 Offiziere und Matrosen. 480 Einheiten wurden in Auftrag genommen, aber nur 62 wurden in Dienst gestellt. Sechs davon gingen noch auf Feindfahrt und versenkten insgesamt fünf feindliche Schiffe. Sieben Boote des Typs XXIII gingen im Krieg verloren, jedoch alle davon auf Ausbildungsfahrten oder im Hafen. Der letzte Versenkungserfolg der deutschen Unterseebootflotte wurde am 7. Mai 1945 von einem Boot dieses Typs erzielt, als die U.2336 unter Kapitänleutnant Emil Klusmeier zwei feindliche Schiffe mit je einem Torpedo zerstörte.*

In addition to this, the German Navy also ordered more than 2,350 "midget" submarines during World War Two, meant for one or two man crews. 1,200 of these midget submarines were actually completed, with the remainder scrapped incomplete or never even started building. Some nations, including both Italy and Croatia, still use some midget submarines. German examples can be seen in a number of German museums today. The largest "Seehund" class ("seal" in English) displaced 15 tons and had a maximum speed of 7,75 knots surfaced or 6 knots submerged. Range was 500 miles on the surface and up to 63 miles submerged. Armament consisted of just 2 torpedos and the boat was operated by 2 men. One can just imagine what these were like in heavier seas – no fun at all. The sea could be more than rough enough in conventional submarines and most surface vessels, with smaller boats being tossed around like toys in heavy seas.

*Weitergehend wurde die Entwicklung von Kleinst-Unterseebooten vorangetrieben. Zunächst besaßen diese die Form zweier übereinander angeordneter Torpedos, wobei der untere die Waffe selbst war und der obere dem Unterseebootfahrer Platz bot (Typ "Marder" und "Neger"). Diese Modelle wurden kontinuierlich weiterentwickelt, doch erst die Modelle "Hecht" und besonders "Seehund" (Typ XXVIIA und Typ XXVIIB) konnten als echte Unterseeboote bezeichnet werden. 2,350 Kleinst-Unterseeboote wurden in Auftrag genommen, aber nur 1,200 in Dienst gestellt. Einige Nationen (wie zum Beispiel Italien und Kroatien) haben immer noch Kleinst-Unterseeboote. Der Typ "Seehund / XXVIIB" hatte eine Einsatzverdrängung von 15 Tonnen, eine Überwassergeschwindigkeit von 7,75 Knoten, eine Unterwassergeschwindigkeit von 6 Knoten, eine Überwasserreichweite von 500 Seemeilen und eine Unterwasserreichweite von 63 Seemeilen. Eine Besatzung bestand aus nur zwei Leute.*

Submarines of World War One and World War Two could not go anywhere as deep as modern boats. Germany developed some boats before 1945 which could reach 1,000 feet – but this was extremely rare. Most could go down only a few hundred feet below the surface. In World War One, you would be lucky to get down 200 feet below the surface. The pressure of water increases with depth, and boats and humans will literally be crushed if they go too far down. Of course, one often wants to go deep down to avoid bad weather, rough seas and above all hostile enemy destroyers with depth charges and enemy aircraft with bombs and torpedos. Another big issue was ASDIC and early sonar, which would try to locate submarines under water. Even more important was Germany's World War Two "enigma" code (named "Ultra" by the Allies). The British scored one of the war's greatest intelligence coups when they broke the German code. This was all the more critical considering it was used by all German military branches and by Germany's World War Two allies including Imperial Japan. Many Allied military victories have since been attributed to the enigma code – including the Battle of Britain, the Battle of the Atlantic, the Battle of Midway, the Battle of the Coral Sea and the Battle of Normandy. In addition to the very large number of German-built submarines, the World War Two German Navy took a number of classes of captured foreign submarines into German service. These included submarines from the Allied nations of Turkey (1), the United Kingdom (1), Norway (2), the Netherlands (5), France (3) and Italy after she switched sides in 1943 (25).

*Zur Zeit des Zweiten Weltkrieges hatte Deutschland 36 feindliche Unterseeboote entweder beschlagnahmt oder gekapert (eins aus der Türkei, eins aus England, zwei aus Norwegen, fünf aus Holland, drei aus Frankreich und endlich ab 1943 25 aus Italien).*

1.) The former Italian submarines "Bario" and "Litio" were the largest of these captured submarines, at 2,600 tons each. "Bario" was returned to Italy after World War Two, whereas "Litio" was scuttled by the Germans on May 1, 1945.

*Die ehemaligen italienischen Unterseeboote "Bario" und "Litio" hatte eine Einsatzverdrängung von je 2,600 Tonnen. Die "Litio" wurde am 1. Mai 1945 von den Deutschen selbst versenkt, aber die "Bario" wurde an Italien zurückgegeben.*

2.) The former British submarine "H.M.S. Seal" (1938) displaced up to 2,157 tons full load. She was armed with 6-21 inch torpedo tubes, 1-4 inch deck gun and 50 mines. She could make up to 15 knots with her diesel engines. The Germans scuttled her in Kiel on May 3, 1945.

*Das ehemalige britische Unterseeboot "H.M.S. Seal" (1938) hatte eine Einsatzverdrängung von 2,157 Tonnen, und war mit sechs 533-mm Torpedorohre, einer 10-cm Schnellfeuerkanone und 50 Seeminen ausgerüstet. Die*

*Überwassergeschwindigkeit lag bei 15 Knoten. Am 3. Mai 1945 wurde sie von den Deutschen bei Kiel selbst versenkt.*

3.) The former Italian submarine "Giuseppe Finzi" (1935) displaced up to 2,060 tons full load. She was armed with 8-21 inch torpedo tubes, 2-4,7 inch deck guns plus 4-13 mm anti-aircraft guns. She could make up to 17 knots with her diesel engines. Her German crew scuttled her in the French port of Bordeaux on August 25, 1944.

*Das ehemalige italienische Unterseeboot "Giuseppe Finzi" (1935) hatte eine Einsatzverdrängung von 2,060 Tonnen, und war mit acht 533-mm Torpedorohre, zwei 12-cm Schnellfeuerkanonen (SFK) und vier 13-mm Flugzeugabwehrkanonen (FLAK) bewaffnet. Ihre Überwassergeschwindigkeit lag bei 17 Knoten. Sie wurde am 25. August 1944 im Hafen von Bordeaux selbst versenkt.*

4.) The two formerly Italian submarines "Alpino Bagnolini" (1939) and "Reginaldo Giuliani" (1939) each displaced up to 1,484 tons full load. They were armed with 1-4 inch deck gun, 4-13 mm anti-aircraft guns and 8-21 inch torpedo tubes. Top speed was up to 18 knots with diesel engines. The first boat was sunk by South African aircraft off the Cape of Good Hope on March 11, 1944 and the second boat was torpedoed by a British submarine in the Straits of Malacca on February 14, 1944. As one can see, the Germans deployed these larger boats far from Europe.

*Die zwei ehemaligen italienischen Unterseeboote "Alpino Bagnolini" (1939) und "Reginaldo Giuliani" (1939) hatten eine Einsatzverdrängung von je 1,484 Tonnen, und waren mit je einer 10-cm Schnellfeuerkanone (SFK), vier 13-mm Flugzeugabwehrkanonen (FLAK) und acht 533-mm Torpedorohre bewaffnet. Die Überwassergeschwindigkeit lag bei 18 Knoten. Die "Alpino Bagnolini" wurde am 11. März 1944 am Kap der Guten Hoffnung (Südafrika) durch Fliegerbomben versenkt. Die "Reginaldo Giuliani" wurde am 14. Februar 1944 an der Straße von Malakka (Malaysia) von einem englischen Unterseeboot torpediert. Man kann sehen, daß die deutsche Kriegsmarine diese beschlagnahmten Boote wirklich benutzte.*

5.) The ex-Turkish submarine "Batiray" (1938) was actually built in Germany. She displaced up to 1,357 tons full load, and was armed with 1-4 inch deck gun, 1-20 mm anti-aircraft gun plus 6-21 inch torpedo tubes. She could make up to 20 knots with her diesel engines – a very good speed for a submarine. She survived World War Two, and was scuttled by the Germans on May 3, 1945 to prevent her from falling into enemy hands.

*Das ehemalige türkische Unterseeboot "Batiray" (1938) wurde in Deutschland gebaut. Sie hatte eine Einsatzverdrängung von 1,357 Tonnen, und war mit einer 10-cm Schnellfeuerkanone (SFK), einer 20-mm Flugzeugabwehrkanone (FLAK) und sechs 533-mm Torpedorohre bewaffnet. Die Überwassergeschwindigkeit lag bei 20 Knoten. Sie wurde am 3. Mai 1945 selbst versenkt.*

6.) The former Italian submarine "Comandante Cappellini" (1939) displaced up to 1,313 tons full load, and was armed with 2-4 inch deck guns, 4-13 mm anti-aircraft guns plus 8-21 inch torpedo tubes. She could make up to 17,5 knots with her diesel engines. She served with a German crew in the Pacific Ocean from 1943 to 1945, and was turned over to Japan when Germany surrendered to the Allies in May 1945. The Japanese in turn surrendered her to the Americans on September 2, 1945. The Americans scuttled her on April 15, 1946.

*Das ehemalige italienische Unterseeboot "Comandante Cappellini" (1939) hatte eine Einsatzverdrängung von 1,313 Tonnen, und war mit zwei 10-cm Schnellfeuerkanonen (SFK), vier 13-mm Flugzeugabwehrkanonen (FLAK) und acht 533-mm Torpedorohre bewaffnet. Die Überwassergeschwindigkeit lag bei 17,5 Knoten. Ab 1943 war sie in Japan stationiert. Im Mai 1945 (der Waffenstillstand in Europa) hatte ihre deutsche Mannschaft die "Comandante Cappellini" an die japanische Kriegsmarine übergeben. Am 2. September 1945 haben die Japaner das Boot den Amerikanern übergeben. Am 15. April 1946 haben die Amerikaner das Boot selbst versenkt.*

7.) The 3 former French submarines "L'Africaine" (1945), "L'Favorite" (1940) and "L'Astree" (1940) each displaced up to 1,180 tons full load. They were armed with 1-3,5 inch deck gun, 4-20 mm anti-aircraft guns plus 10-21 inch torpedo tubes. They could make up to 17,3 knots with their diesel engines. The Germans scuttled "L'Favorite" in the West Prussian port of Gdynia ("Gdingen" or "Gotenhafen" in German) in May 1945. The other two boats were returned to France after World War Two, surviving and serving into the 1960s.

*Die drei ehemaligen französischen Unterseeboote "L'Africaine" (1945), "L'Favorite" (1940) und "L'Astree" (1940) hatten je eine Einsatzverdrängung von 1,180 Tonnen. Die Bewaffnung dieser Boote bestand aus je einer 9-cm Schnellfeuerkanone (SFK), vier 20-mm Flugzeugabwehrkanonen (FLAK) und zehn 533-mm Torpedorohre. Die "L'Favorite" wurde im Mai 1945 in Gotenhafen (Westpreußen) selbst versenkt. Die zwei anderen Boote wurden an Frankreich zurückgegeben, und dienten bis in den 1960er Jahren bei der französischen Marine.*

434

8.) The 6 formerly Italian submarines "Sodio" (1944), "Potassio" (1943), "Rame" (1943), "Ferro" (1943), "Piombo" (1943) and "Zinco" (1943) were all named after various types of minerals, including sodium, potassium and zinc. Each boat displaced up to 1,180 tons full load, and was armed with 1-4 inch deck gun, 4-20 mm anti-aircraft guns plus 6-21 inch torpedo tubes. They could make up to 16 knots with their diesel engines. The Germans took these boats in 1943, but none of them were ever completed. They were all scrapped shortly after the end of World War Two.

*Die sechs ehemaligen italienischen Unterseeboote "Sodio" (1944), "Potassio" (1943), "Rame" (1943), "Ferro" (1943), "Piombo" (1943) und "Zinco" (1943) hatten eine Einsatzverdrängung von je 1,180 Tonnen, und waren mit je einer 10-cm Schnellfeuerkanone (SFK), vier 20-mm Flugzeugabwehrkanonen (FLAK) und sechs 533-mm Torpedorohre bewaffnet. Die Überwassergeschwindigkeit lag bei 16 Knoten. Im Jahre 1943 hatte die deutsche Kriegsmarine diese sechs neuen Boote im unvollendeten Bauzustand gekapert, sie aber nie in Dienst gestellt. Sie wurden nach dem Krieg verschrottet.*

9.) The 4 ex-Italian submarines "Sparide" (1943), "Murena" (1943), "Nautilo" (1943) and "Grongo" (1943) each displaced up to 1,070 tons full load. They were armed with 1-4 inch deck gun, 4-13 mm anti-aircraft guns and 6-21 inch torpedo tubes. They could make up to 16 knots with their diesel engines. "Sparide," "Murena" and "Grongo" were all bombed and sunk by British aircraft in the Italian port of Genoa on September 4, 1944. "Nautilo" survived World War Two, and was handed over to Yugoslavia as reparations in 1949.

*Die vier ehemaligen italienischen Unterseeboote "Sparide" (1943), "Murena" (1943), "Nautilo" (1943) und "Grongo" (1943) hatten eine Einsatzverdrängung von je 1,070 Tonnen, und waren mit je einer 10-cm Schnellfeuerkanone (SFK), vier 13-mm Flugzeugabwehrkanonen (FLAK) und sechs 533-mm Torpedorohre bewaffnet. Am 4. September 1944 wurden die "Sparide," die "Murena" und die "Grongo" im Hafen von Genua von englischen Fliegerbombern versenkt. Die "Nautilo" überstand den Krieg, und wurde im Jahre 1949 an Jugoslawien übergeben.*

**XVIIIc. Post World War Two German Submarines (since 1951) / Deutsche Unterseeboote seit 1951**

1960 marked the official beginning of Germany's national postwar submarine arm. To date, 36 "Unterseeboote" (German for "submarines") have been built for the German Navy. The 6 newest units of the Type 212 Class are the most modern non-nuclear submarines in the world, being powered by hydrogen fuel cells. Their diving depth is an impressive 2,275 (official) feet – true diving ability is always much more and classified for reasons of national security.  They displace 1,830 tons submerged and have an official top speed of at least 20 knots under water.  Since 1951, German submarine yards have manufactured at least 199 boats, most of them being successfully exported to places such as Latin America, Asia, Africa and the Middle East.  Germany's submarine customers since 1951 include Argentina, Colombia, Denmark, Ecuador, France, Greece, Indonesia, Iran, Israel, Italy, Norway, Peru, South Korea, Turkey, Uruguay and Venezuela.  One note: the 6 French "Narval" class boats built from 1951 until 1958 were virtual copies of the World War Two Type XXI from Germany, built before "official" post-World War Two German submarine construction commenced in earnest in 1960.  The "Narval" class displaced up to 1,910 tons and was armed with 20 torpedos.  Top speed was 15 knots on the surface and up to 18 knots submerged. Range was an impressive 15,000 miles on the surface and the crew consisted of 63 commissioned officers and enlisted men (7 plus 56, respectively).

*Seit 1960 wurden 36 neue nachkriegs Unterseeboote in Deutschland in Dienst gestellt.  Seit 1951 wurden mindestens 199 neue Unterseeboote in Deutschland entwickelt und gebaut – 36 für die Deutsche Marine und 163 als Export-Unterseeboote.  Drei ehemalige Kriegs-Unterseeboote wurden auch geborgen, repariert und dann wieder neu in Dienst gestellt.  Die "Hecht" und die "Hai" gehörten zur Typ XXIII-Klaße, und die "Wilhelm Bauer" gehörte zur Typ XXI-Klaße (alle "Elektroboote").  Die "Wilhelm Bauer" ist heute als Museum in Bremerhaven zu sehen.*

Also, three (3) World War Two boats were raised and restored to serve the new "Bundesmarine" as early as 1958.  One of these boats was a Type XXI (the "Wilhelm Bauer" mentioned earlier) and 2 were Type XXIII coastal boats, named "Hecht" and "Hai," respectively.  "Hecht" is German for "pike," and "Haifisch" is German for "shark."Post-World War Two German submarine classes begin with the number 201, in order to distinguish them from the boats built in between 1935 and 1945.  In the beginning, the Western European Union (WEU) military alliance placed restrictions upon German submarine construction, specifying that only coastal units were allowed and that no unconventional (i.e., nuclear) powerplants were permitted. Germany's modern submarines are all manufactured by Howaldtswerke of Kiel in Schleswig-Holstein.  Three Type 201 submarines were commissioned from 1960 until 1962.  This class displaced up to 450 tons, was armed with 8 torpedos, could make 10 knots on the surface, up to 17 knots submerged and was manned by a crew of 21 commissioned officers and enlisted men.  The Type 202 (2 boats commissioned from 1960 to 1962) and Type 205 (14 more boats commissioned from 1960 until 1969) were virtually identical to the Type 201. Range was up to 4,200 miles on the surface and up to 228 miles submerged. All of these submarines have since been decommissioned and scrapped, with the exception of three boats preserved as museums available for public viewing in Germany. U.9 is in the city of Speyer in the state of the Rhineland-Palatinate, U.10 is at the German Naval Museum in Wilhelmshaven in Lower Saxony and U.11 is in the coastal city of Fehmarn in Schleswig-Holstein. Every single U.9 since World War one has been decorated with the Iron Cross of Kapitänleutnant (equivalent to a Lieutenant in the American Navy) Otto Eduard Weddigen, the famous submarine commander who sank three British cruisers early in the war with Germany's very first U.9. His boat went down due to enemy action in March of 1915 off the coast of Scotland. Two more Type 205 submarines have been built for Denmark, which are essentially very similar to the Type 201.

*Die Unterseeboote der "Klaße 201' waren die ersten deutschen Unterseeboote, die nach dem Zweiten Weltkrieg gebaut wurden. Ihre Aufgabe war primär der Küstenschutz in der Ostsee. Drei Unterseeboote der Klaße 201 wurden am 16. März 1959 bei den Kieler Howaldtswerken in Auftrag gegeben. Für Konstruktion und Entwicklung war das "Ingenieurkontor Lübeck" unter Ulrich Gabler verantwortlich. "U.1" wurde von der Ehefrau des berühmten Unterseeboot-Kommandanten Otto Kretschmer getauft. Das Boot ging im Jahre 1963 wieder außer Dienst. "U.2" wurde am 3. Mai 1962 von der Ehefrau des ehemaligen "U.98" Kommandanten Wilhelm Schulze getauft und erhielt auch den schwarzen Kater von "U.98" als Wappen. "U.3" wurde am 10. Juli 1962 getauft und erhielt Sankt Georgen im Schwarzwald als Patenstadt sowie das Wappen der Stadt. Ab August 1963 wurden die drei Boote abgebrochen, "U.1" und "U.2" wurden durch gleichnamige Boote der Klaße 205 ersetzt. Das bereits stillgelegte "U.4" wurde wieder abgebrochen und ebenfalls als Klaße 205 neugebaut. Die Boote wurden aus antimagnetischem Stahl gefertigt, damit magnetischen Seeminen nicht durch die Boote ausgelöst werden konnten. Doch bereits im Juli und August 1963 wurden die Boote außer Dienst gestellt, da sich Mikrofrakturen im Stahlmantel der Boote zeigten. Die drei Boote der Klaße 201 hatten je eine Einsatzverdrängung von 450 Tonnen, und waren mit je entweder acht Torpedos oder 16 Seeminen ausgerüstet. Die Überwassergeschwindigkeit lag bei 10 Knoten, die Unterwassergeschwindigkeit bei 17 Knoten, die Überwasserreichweite bei 4,200 Seemeilen und die Unterwasserreichweite bei 228 Seemeilen. Eine Besatzung bestand aus 21 Offiziere und Matrosen. Die Unterseeboote der Klaße 205 waren die ersten erfolgreichen Serien-Unterseeboote der Deutschen Marine nach dem Zweiten Weltkrieg. Sie dienten der Bekämpfung von gegnerischen Kriegsschiffen in der Ostsee. Im Kriegsfall war ihnen eine wichtige Rolle bei der Abwehr von Angriffen mit Landungsschiffen gegen das NATO-Gebiet im Bereich der Ostseezugänge (Norddeutschland, Dänemark und Norwegen) zugedacht. 11 Boote wurden für Deutschland und zwei für Dänemark gebaut, keines ist noch in Dienst. Die Boote der Klaße 205 sind die Boote der Klaße 201 sehr ähnlich, aber sie wurden ohne dem problematischen antimagnetischen Stahl gebaut. Die "U.9" ist jetzt im Technikmuseum Speyer zu sehen, und die "U.10" im Deutschen Marinemuseum Wilhelmshaven.*

The Type 206 coastal submarine was built from 1973 until 1975, with 18 boats having been commissioned. Of these, 7 are still in active duty service with the German Navy and 2 have been sold to Indonesia. Displacement is 498 tons and armament consists of 8 torpedos plus 24 mines. The crew consists of 23 officers and men. Top speed is also 10 knots on the surface and up to 17 knots submerged. Range is 4,500 miles on the surface and up to 228 miles submerged. In addition to the German Type 206 boats, Israel has 3 such vessels in service.

*Die Unterseeboote der Klaße 206 sind eine deutsche Unterseeboot-Klaße die für die Bundesmarine gebaut wurden. Die Boote wurden alle in den 1970er Jahren in Dienst gestellt und wurden seit 1998 außer Dienst gestellt. Ein Teil von ihnen wird durch die neue Unterseeboot-Klaße 212A abgelöst. Das letzte Boot soll im Jahre 2012 außer Dienst gestellt werden. Die Entwicklung der Klaße begann bereits im Jahre 1962. Die Boote sind in erster Linie für die Verwendung im küstennahen Raum gebaut worden und sollten Überwasserschiffe, Unterseeboote und den Nachschubverkehr bekämpfen. Zum Schutz vor Minen und Entdeckung durch MAD-Sensoren wurden die Boote aus nicht magnetischem Stahl gefertigt. 18 Boote wurden für Deutschland gebaut, und sieben davon sind immer noch im Dienst. Zwei davon wurden an Indonesien verkauft, und drei neue Boote wurden für Israel gebaut. Die Boote dieser Klaße haben eine Einsatzverdrängung von je 498 Tonnen, und sind mit je acht Torpedos und 24 Seeminen bewaffnet. Die Besatzung eines Bootes besteht aus 23 Offiziere und Matrosen. Die Überwassergeschwindigkeit liegt bei 10 Knoten, die Unterwassergeschwindigkeit bei 17 Knoten, die Überwasserreichweite bei 4,500 Seemeilen und die Unterwasserreichweite bei 228 Seemeilen.*

The Type 207 coastal submarine was designed specifically for Norway. 15 boats were commissioned from 1962 until 1967. Displacement is a maximum 435 tons per boat. Armament consists of 8 torpedos, top speed is 10 knots on the surface and up to 17 knots submerged. The crew consists of 18 commissioned officers and enlisted men (5 plus 13, respectively).

*Die Klaße 207 ist eine Klaße von diesel-elektrischen Unterseebooten, die in der norwegischen Marine unter dem Namen "K.N.M. Kobben-Klaße" gedient haben und in Deutschland bei den Nordseewerken in Emden gebaut wurden. Sie ist eine speziell auf die Anforderungen der norwegischen Marine abgestimmte Weiterentwicklung der deutschen Unterseeboot-Klaße 205. Der Typ 207 war der erste große nachkriegs Exportentwurf deutscher Werften, die Kiellegung der ersten Boote begann im Jahre 1961. Zu dieser Zeit gab es für die deutschen Werften noch Beschränkungen in der Verteidigung durch die WEU, weshalb deutsche Unterseeboote vergleichsweise klein, jedoch trotzdem auf dem neusten Stand der Technik, waren. Insgesamt wurden 15 Einheiten des Typs 207 gebaut, die zwischen 1962 und 1967 in Dienst gestellt wurden. Die Einsatzverdrängung dieser Klaße waren je 435 Tonnen. Sie waren mit je acht Torpedos bewaffnet, die Überwassergeschwindigkeit lag bei 10 Knoten und die Unterwassergeschwindigkeit bei 17 Knoten. Eine Besatzung bestand aus 5 Offiziere und 13 Matrosen. Fünf Boote wurden an Polen verkauft, wo sie noch im Dienst sind. Ein Boot ist jetzt als Museumsschiff in Horten (Norwegen) zu sehen, und die neun anderen Boote existieren nicht mehr.*

The Type 209 ocean-going submarine was designed specifically for the export market, and therefore none of these fine boats are in German service. 80 boats have been sold and commissioned in the navies of numerous foreign countries, and construction continues to this day. Argentina owns 4 such boats. They displace 1,230 tons each, are armed with 16 torpedos, have a top surface speed of 10 knots and can make a good 22 knots submerged. The crew consists of 32 officers and men. Colombia owns 2 Type 209 submarines. Their boats displace up to 1,290 tons. Ecuador owns 2 Type 209 submarines as well, and its boats displace up to 1,356 tons each. Greece has purchased 12 Type 209 submarines from Germany, and their boats are like those owned by Colombia. The Indonesian Navy has 2 Type 209 boats. Iran purchased 6 Type 209 boats prior to the fall of the Shah. The Peruvian Navy has 6 Type 209 boats which are identical to those owned by Columbia and Greece. Turkey owns 13 Type 209 submarines identical to those of Columbia, Greece and Peru. The Uruguayan Navy has 2 Type 209 submarines, and Venezuela has 4 boats which displace 1,350 tons each. 6 similar Type 210 submarines have been built and sold for the export market as well.

*Die Unterseeboote der Klaße 209 werden seit 1960 in Deutschland gefertigt und wurden ausschliesslich exportiert. In den vergangenen 49 Jahren wurden sie immer wieder dem Stand der Technik angepasst, so daß die Unterseeboote, die sich derzeitig im Bau befinden, zu den modernsten Booten gezählt werden können. Insgesamt wurden von dieser Klaße mindestens 80 Boote für mehrere Länder gebaut. Sie dienen heute in Argentinien (vier Boote), in Kolumbien (zwei Boote), in Ekuador (zwei Boote), in Griechenland (12 Boote), in Indonesien (zwei Boote), in Iran (sechs Boote), in Peru (sechs Boote), in der Türkei (13 Boote), in Uruguay (zwei Boote), in Venezuela (vier Boote), in Brasilien (sechs Boote), in Chile (zwei Boote), in Indien (vier Boote), in Portugal (zwei Boote), in Südafrika (drei Boote) und in Südkorea (zehn Boote). Es gibt auch sechs Boote des Typs 210, die dem Typ 209 ähnlich sind, die für Norwegen gebaut wurden. Die Boote dieser Klaßen (209/210) haben eine Einstazverdrängung von je 1,356 Tonnen. Die Überwassergeschwindigkeit liegt bei 10 Knoten, die Unterwassergeschwindigkeit bei 22 Knoten, die Überwasserreichweite bei 11,000 Seemeilen und die Unterwasserreichweite bei 400 Seemeilen. Die Bewaffnung dieser Klaßen besteht aus je 16 Torpedos, und eine Besatzung besteht aus 32 Offiziere und Matrosen.*

The Type 211 was a planned 940 ton ocean-going submarine which never went into production. Instead, the German Navy waited for the far superior Type 212 submarine. This class has a maximum displacement of 1,830 tons, a top speed of 12 knots on the surface and up to 20 knots submerged. Range is 8,000 miles on the surface and up to 420 miles submerged. The Type 212 can remain submerged for up to 3 weeks without using a snorkel to replenish its supply of oxygen. Maximum diving depth is an amazing 2,275 feet below the surface and the powerplant is a hydrogen fuel cell plant. The crew consists of 27 commissioned officers and enlisted men. Armament consists of either 24 21-inch torpedos or 24 mines. The German Navy has ordered 6 Type 212 submarines thus far (U.31 through U.36), 4 of which are already commissioned. On top of this, the Italian Navy also has two such boats. Israel owns 5 such boats under the so-called "Dolphin" class which can be armed with nuclear missiles. The South Korean Navy has yet 7 more of these boats under the designation "Type 214" class, which is essentially similar to the Type 212 and Dolphin. Other nations ordering the Type 214 submarines include Greece (4 boats), Turkey (6 boats) and Portugal (2 boats).

*Es gibt auch sechs deutschgebaute (Nordseewerke in Emden) Unterseeboote des Typs "TR 1700," die in Argentinien dienen. Sie wurden seit 1984 ausgeliefert, und haben eine Einsatzverdrängung von je 2,265 Tonnen. Die 32 Unterseeboote der Klaße "Dolphin-212A-214" sind die modernsten und auch die besten nachkriegs deutschentwickelten und deutschgebauten Unterseeboote. Sie werden für Deutschland (sechs Boote), für Italien (zwei Boote), für Südkorea (sieben Boote), für Griechenland (vier Boote), für die Türkei (sechs Boote), für Portugal (zwei Boote) und auch für Israel (fünf Boote) gebaut. Die neuen Boote dieser Klaße (Dolphin/212A/214) haben eine Einsatzverdrängung von je 1,900 Tonnen. Die Überwassergeschwindigkeit liegt bei 12 Knoten, und die*

*Unterwassergeschwindigkeit bei 20 Knoten. Sie sind mit je entweder 24 533-mm Torpedos oder 24 Seeminen bewaffnet. Eine Besatzung besteht aus 27 Offiziere und Matrosen. Die Tauchtiefe ist eine sehr gute 400 Meter, und die Zerstörungstauchtiefe ist mindestens 700 Meter – noch viel besser als die Atomunterseeboote aus den USA, Rußland, China, Großbrittanien oder Frankreich. Die Unterseeboote dieser deutschen Klaße sind auch weltweit die ersten, deren außenluftunabhängiger Antrieb auf Bennstoffzellen basiert sind.*

In spite of all the many advances in submarine technology (and there have been very many), serving aboard a submarine is still not as comfortable compared to serving aboard most surface vessels. Even today aboard the nuclear submarines of such countries as the USA, Russia, the United Kingdom, France and China quarters are still cramped. Enlisted men and non-commissioned officers share bunks. In other words, when one half of the crew is on duty, the other half is asleep. One still gets to know one's comrade by his "stink" – something submariners have known for over a century. At the very start of World War One, small coastal submarines did not even provide bunks for their crews – the former Austrian submarine commander Georg von Trapp talks about this fact in his memoirs. But as Grand Admiral Karl Dönitz once said, every submariner believes himself to be the member of an elite group, and he would never trade places with anyone else in the navy. Submariners help to make submarines the lethal weapons they are – perhaps even more lethal than aircraft carriers or any other combat surface ships in our day and age, especially considering the ballistic missile submarines of countries such as the United States of America, Russia, France, the United Kingdom, Mainland China and Israel. The Israeli boats are German-built boats of the Type 212 or 214 class.

**End of Volume One (Ende von Band Nummer Eins)**

Printed in Great Britain
by Amazon.co.uk, Ltd.,
Marston Gate.